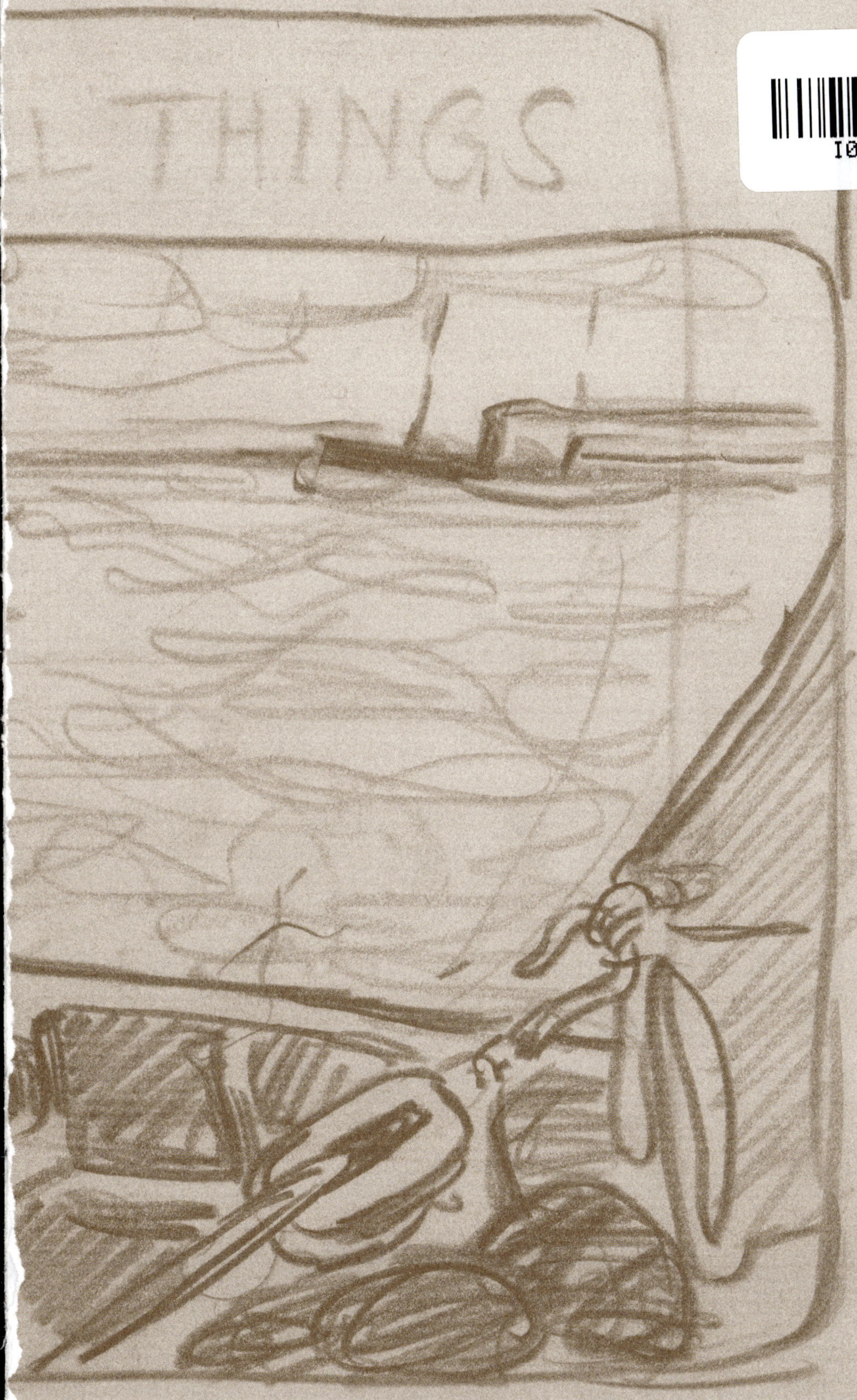
L THINGS

STAITHES

Life, Light and Landscape

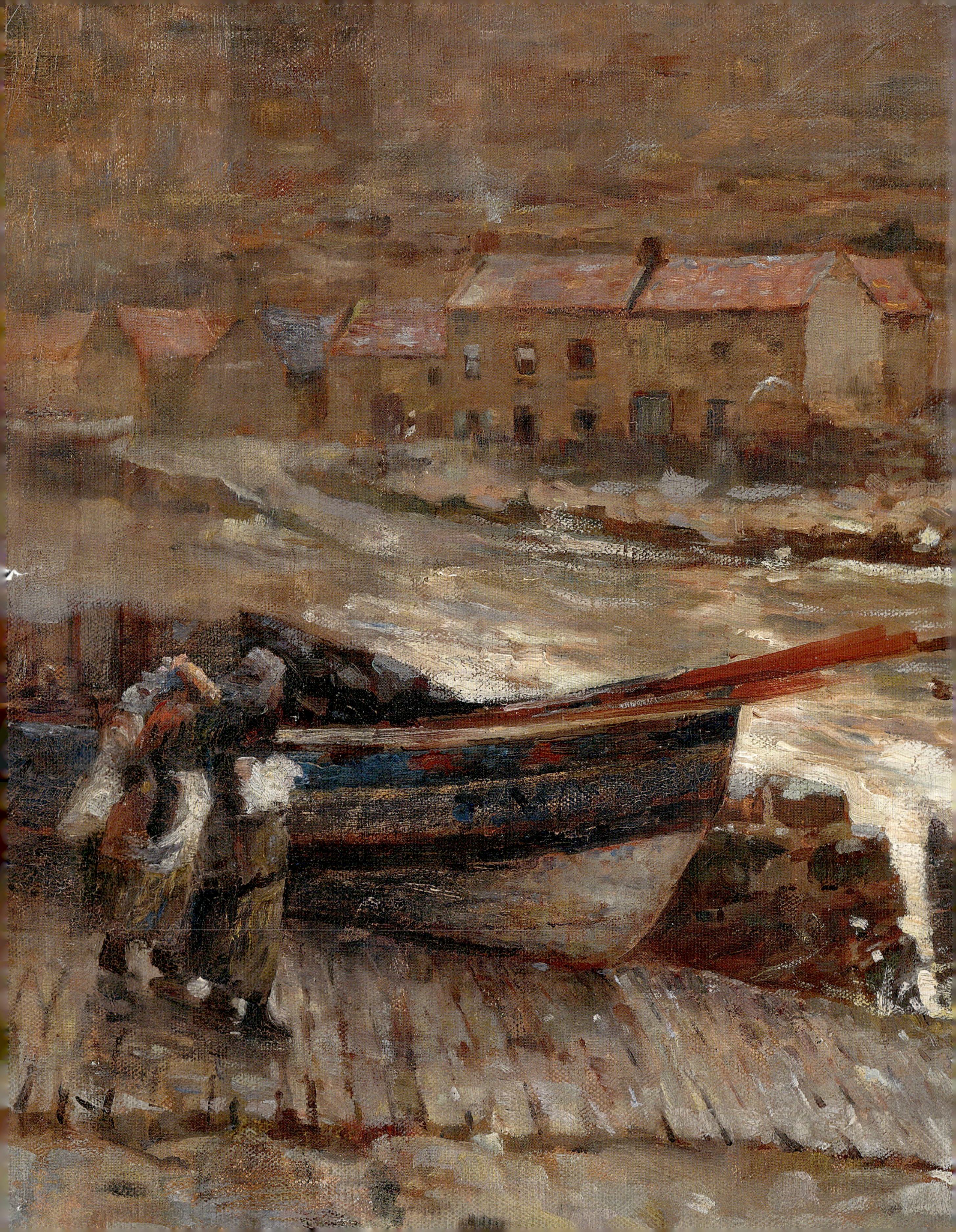

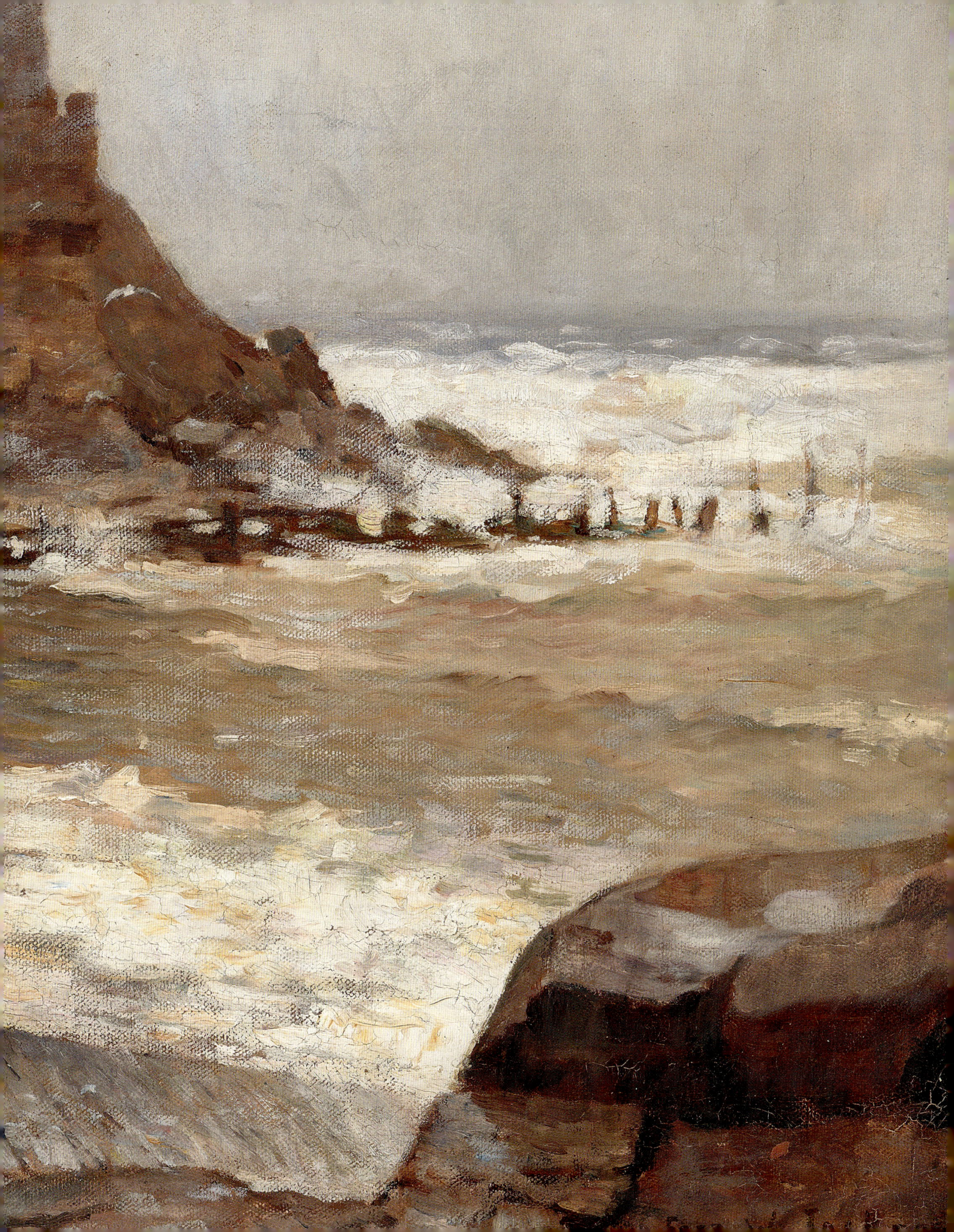

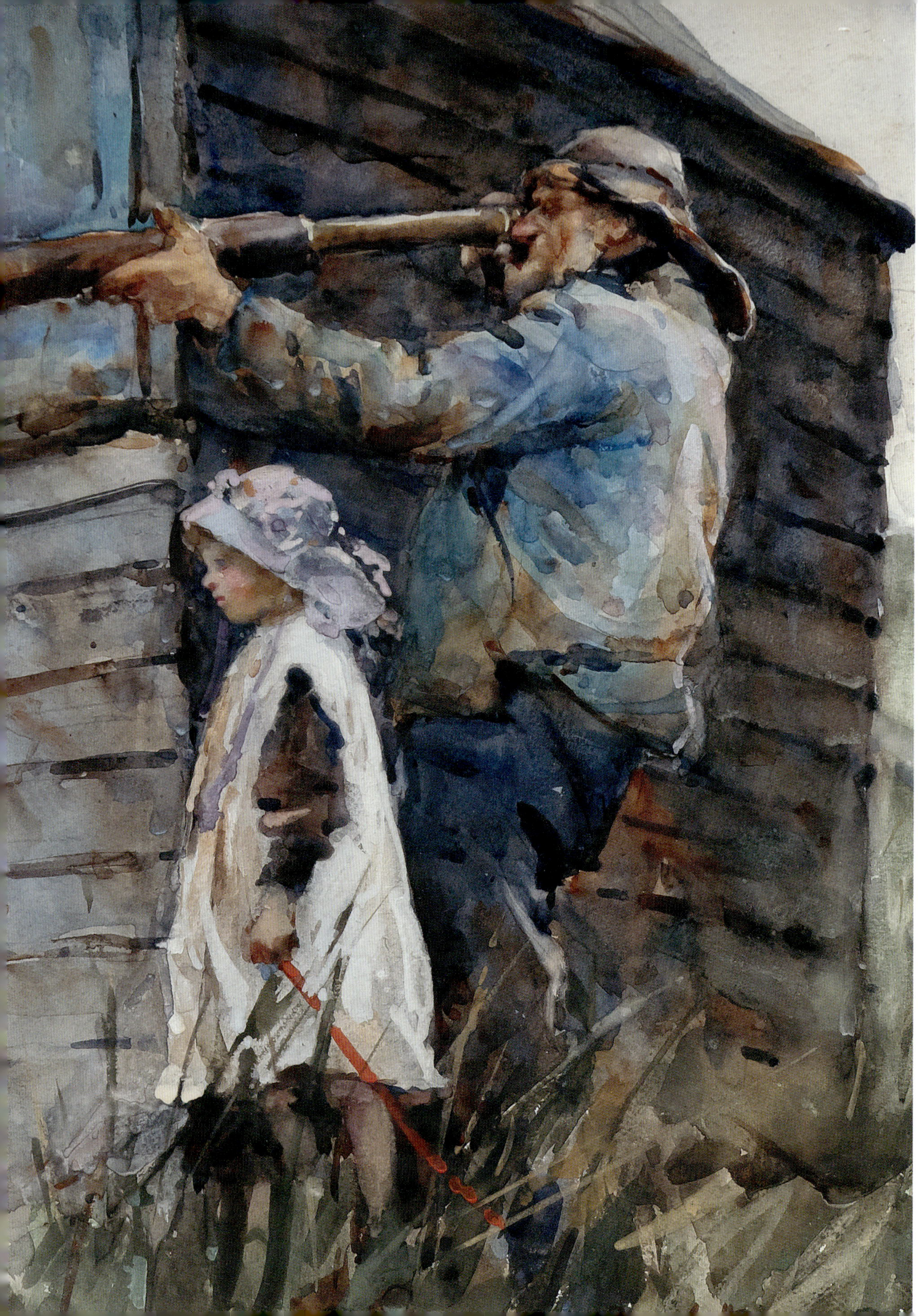

STAITHES

Life, Light and Landscape

Adam Chadwick

Kulturalis

A&A ARTS

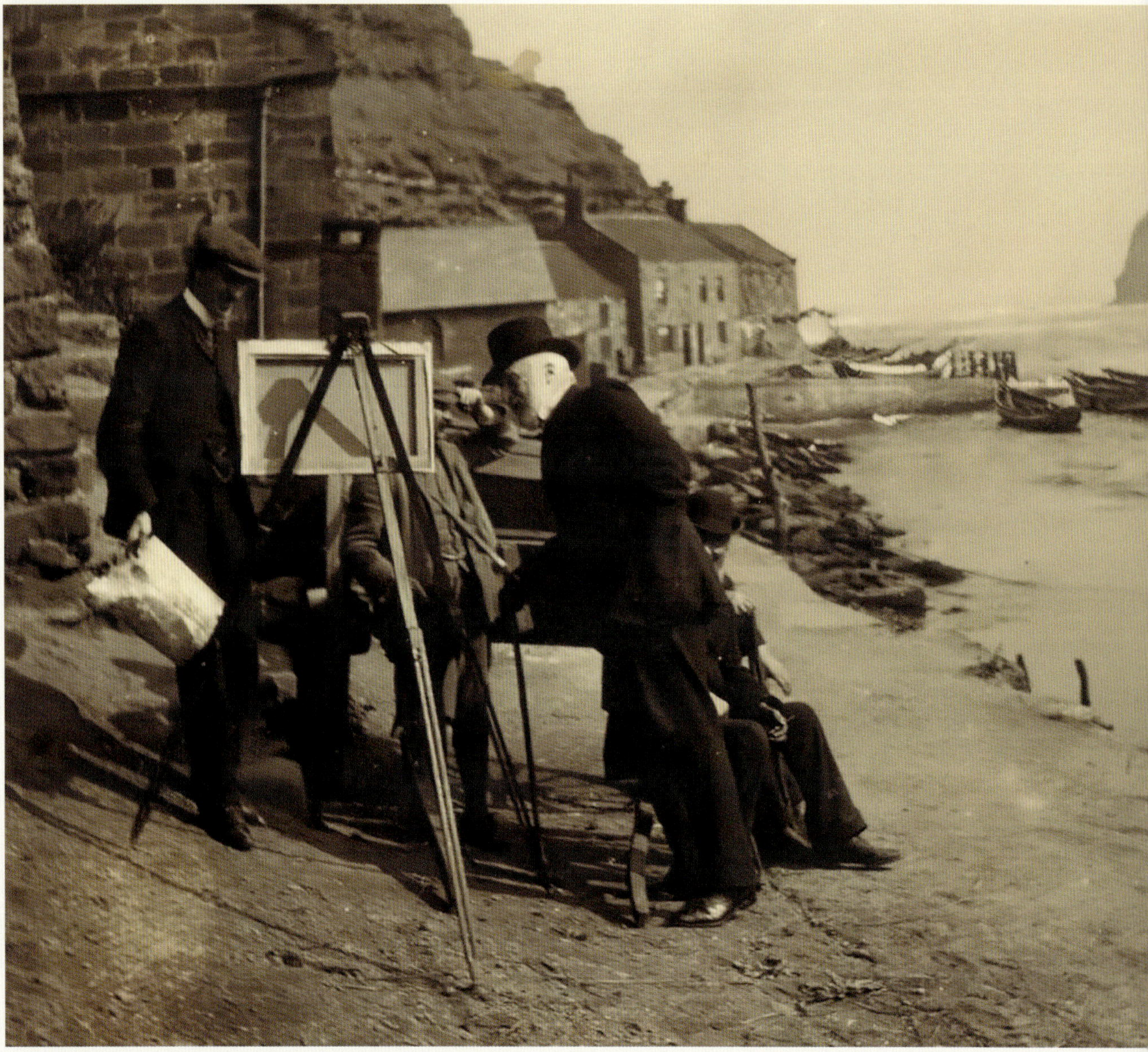

3. This recently discovered photograph pictures a crucial figure in the Art Club's history. Sir Charles Palmer provided patronage and a connection not only to important local but also national figures. Here he is pictured with artists, possibly Charles Mackie and Arthur Friedenson.

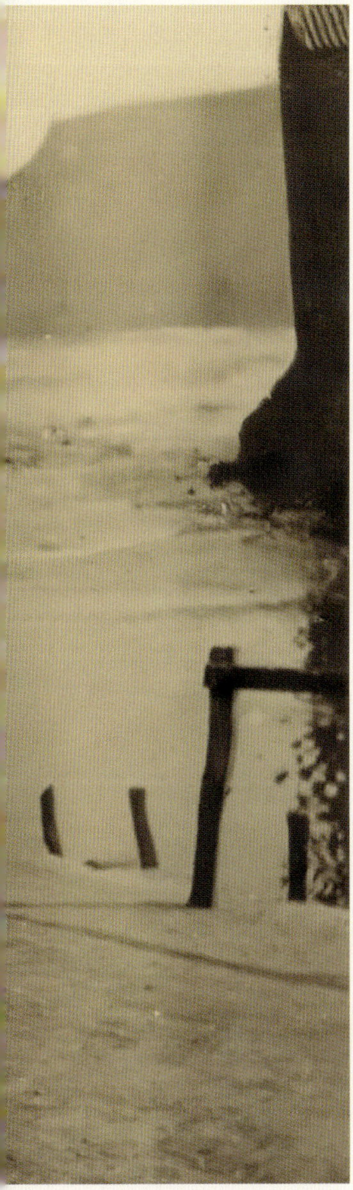

Contents

AUTHOR'S ACKNOWLEDGEMENTS

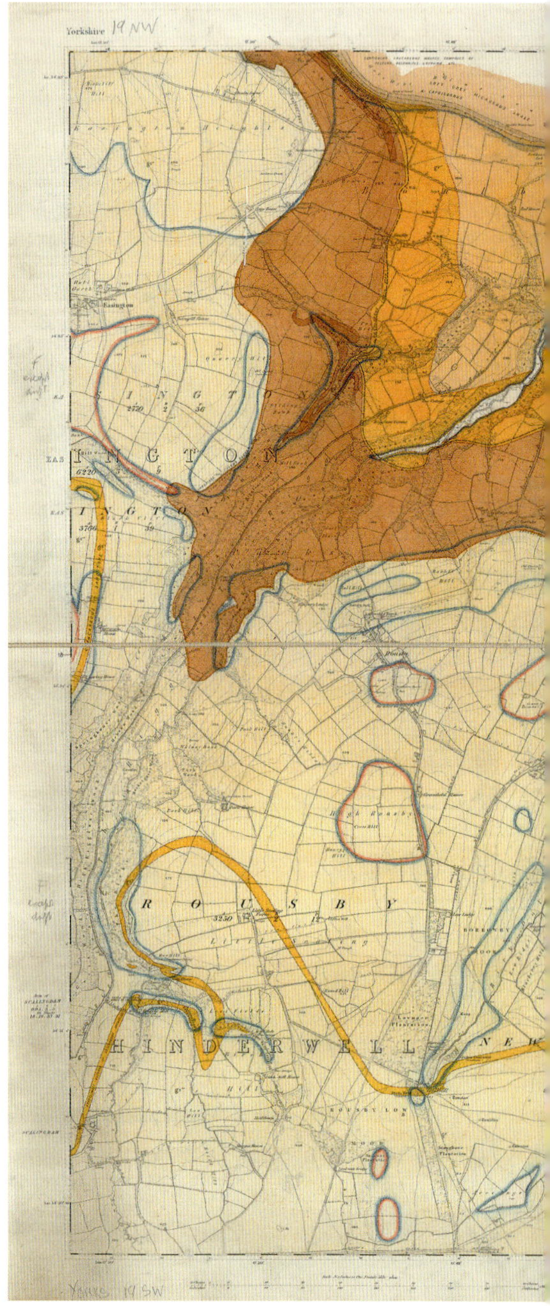

The enthusiasm for this book was first sparked on visits to Harrogate in the early 2000s, shortly before my parents retired to East Anglia.

Although not collectors to that point, they admired the work of the artists who became members of the Staithes Art Club and, perhaps in part because they were retiring farther away from Yorkshire, their enthusiasm blossomed. The firm friendship and unstinting encouragement of those who helped to develop my parents' collection have been warmly extended by all those who responded to my enquiries and pleas for assistance.

Accompanying them to viewings, my enthusiasm for the area was rekindled by childhood memories of holidays in Flamborough, Ravenscar, Whitby and to the north along the Northumbrian coast. It was furthered by research into our family history undertaken by my father and daughter which revealed more of our paternal roots in the shipbuilding and fishing industries of the northeast. Revisiting Staithes, Runswick Bay

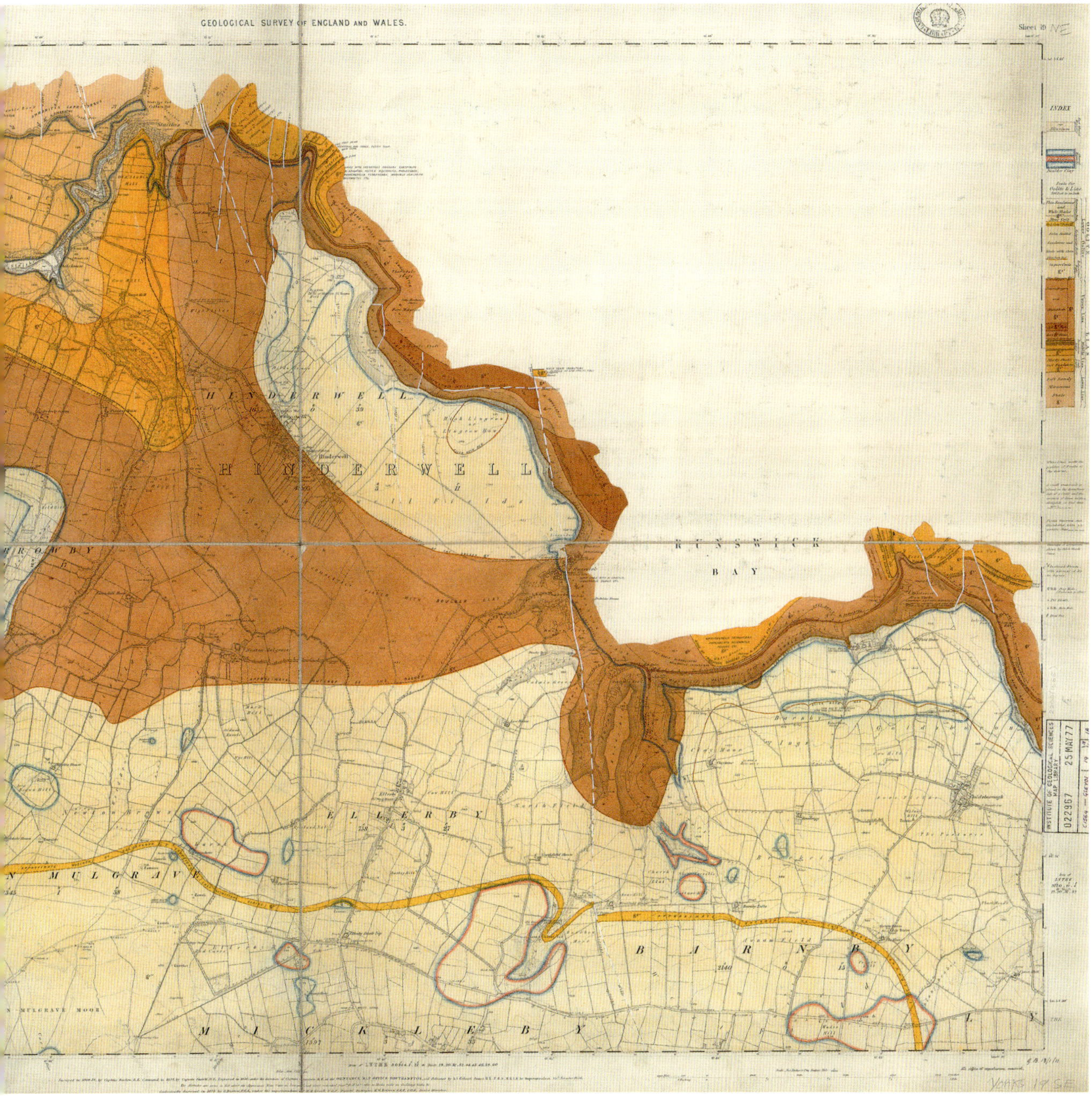

4. From the mid-eighteenth century this area of the north-east coast yielded rich mineral deposits of alum, ironstone and jet, as illustrated in this geological map of Yorkshire from the 1890s. Alongside fishing and whaling, they produced a prosperity that was never recaptured after the First World War.

and surroundings in the course of writing has allowed me to discover the area anew. I am grateful to all those who have contributed their knowledge so willingly and are lucky enough to live there, such as Sandra Barwick and Rod Jewell, or who have enjoyed long associations with the area, such as Simon Wood. I also acknowledge my debt to the historians such as John Howard, Peter Frank and Robert Slater whose research, published works and inherited knowledge of the area have enriched these pages.

The purpose of this book – cognisant of its relatively tight timelines – could not have been to provide a comprehensive catalogue of painters who worked in the area; the Staithes Art Club (1901–1907) alone had a diverse and significant list of members. Its focus is therefore on those acknowledged members of this core group, with the inclusion of works and mention made of artists who influenced, accompanied or in certain cases studied with their guidance.

This wider group is open to constant amendment and oftentimes subjective. It is reassuring to know that other researchers undertaking studies of specific artists or parallel groups continue to add new detail. Potted biographies for all artists can be found elsewhere, but should be read with the understanding that many have been derived from the same sources, often over 30 years old.

In this re-introduction to the Art Club, there was no expectation of unearthing new original material – although, pleasingly, some fresh research does appear. Had significant troves remained, perhaps this publication would have been pre-empted by some years.

The one source that seemed to be taking shape over the past decade was that being prepared by Rosamund Jordan. She, together with her husband Tom, had been harbouring an ambition to produce a more complete work than their regular sale and exhibition catalogues had allowed. Very sadly no sign of her research has to this point transpired since their untimely deaths through illness in 2022–3.

MEMBERS OF THE STAITHES ART CLUB

1901 Henry Silkstone Hopwood 1860–1914 *(Chairman)*
Joseph Richard Bagshawe 1870–1909 (*Secretary*)
Thomas Barrett 1845–1924 (*Treasurer*)
Arthur Friedenson 1872–1955 (*Hanging Committee*)
Robert Jobling 1841–1923 (*Hanging Committee*)
Harold Knight 1874–1961 *(Hanging Committee)*

Harold Edward Conway 1872 fl.1900–1923
Rowland Henry Hill 1873–1952
Hannah Hoyland (*Mayor from 1902*) 1871–1947
Laura Johnson (*Knight from 1903*) 1877–1970
Charles Hodge Mackie 1862–1920
William Frederick Mayor 1866–1916
Frederick Stuart Richardson 1855–1934

Isa Thompson (*Jobling from 1893*) 1851–1926 (*exhibitor but non-member*)
James William Booth 1867–1953 (*exhibitor but non-member*)
Hirst Walker 1868–1957 (*exhibitor but non-member; Treasurer from 1905*)

1902 John Bowman 1872–1915
Ernest Dade 1864–1935
Frederick William Jackson 1859–1918 *(Secretary from 1905)*
John Spence Ingall 1850–1936
Frank Henry Mason 1876–1965
Ernest Higgins Rigg 1868–1947
Mark Senior 1862–1927
Albert George Stevens 1863–1925

1903 Sidney V. Gardner *c.* 1870–1957
James Watson 1851–1936

1904 Edward Enoch Anderson **1878–1961**
Owen Bowen 1873–1967
Lionel Townsend Crawshaw 1864–1949
Percy Morton Teasdale 1870–1961
John Wright 1857–1933

1905 Paul Paul 1865–1937

1906 John Atkinson 1863–1924
Charles Cutts Elmhirst 1897–1937
Leandro Ramon Garrido 1868–1909
Joseph Alfred Terry 1872–1939

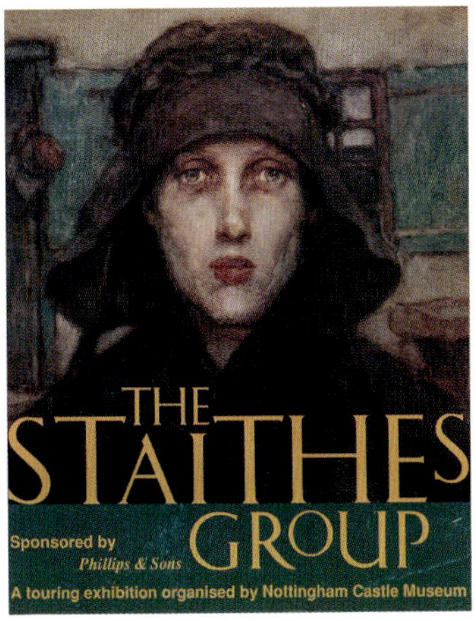

5. The Staithes Group 1993 exhibition poster featured *Grief* by Harold Knight, the most unflinching of all his works. His wife Laura recounted in her memoir: 'One large watercolour I cannot forget… The still and subtle beauty of his rendering … tells of her widowhood, a loss to which she was never reconciled'.

Their Centenary catalogue of the Staithes Art Club (2004), produced with Simon Wood, and the parenthetical exhibitions around that time (2002 and 2005), instigated by Peter Haworth in conjunction with the Fine Art Society, are the most thorough recent attempts to represent the works of the group as a whole.[1]

Dr Peter Phillips's catalogue of 1993, published to accompany a touring exhibition at Nottingham, York, Sunderland and Kirkleatham, is universally recognised as the most significant milestone in research around these artists. It represents the apogee of his efforts over at least 20 years, from the mid-1970s to the end of the 1990s, to resurrect the group from obscurity.

While acknowledging Neil Walker's contribution to this achievement, and Nottingham Museums' commitment to the story of Laura (and Harold) Knight more generally, there is surprisingly little equivalent trace in regional museums of paintings or archive records on other artists from the group. This is notwithstanding their local roots, and the fact that their work often formed part of the museums' initial acquisitions.

Notable exceptions are the admirable displays at the Laing and Shipley Art Galleries and, of course, the 'Staithes' room at The Pannett Gallery. This last was inspired and opened by Dr Phillips and has been consistently supported, most notably by George Bednar.

There also seems little space for 'Staithes artists' amidst the continuous stream of temporary exhibitions, given perhaps the fashion for shows of contemporary art. The exception to this may be Frank Mason, about whom exhibitions have been staged since 2015 in Hartlepool, Greenock, Scarborough and, most recently in 2019, Beverley. In other cases, such as that of Robert and Isa Jobling, one has to go back to 1992, and for Ralph Hedley to 1990 (both in Tyne & Wear Museums); to 1983 for an exhibition on Mark Senior in Wakefield and even further, to 1978, for a major exhibition on Fred Jackson in Rochdale.[2] All (with the exception of Hedley) were prominent members of the club.

At the time of writing, while acknowledging budgetary and resource pressures, it seems that museums can also find little time for researchers seeking to consult their records or to view the objects themselves in storage. Some are under development, still years away from allowing access either to works or archive. Others profess an inability to assist, adopting the reasons given above. One council wished to charge a three-figure sum for time spent assisting me, another a similar amount for the use of a single image.

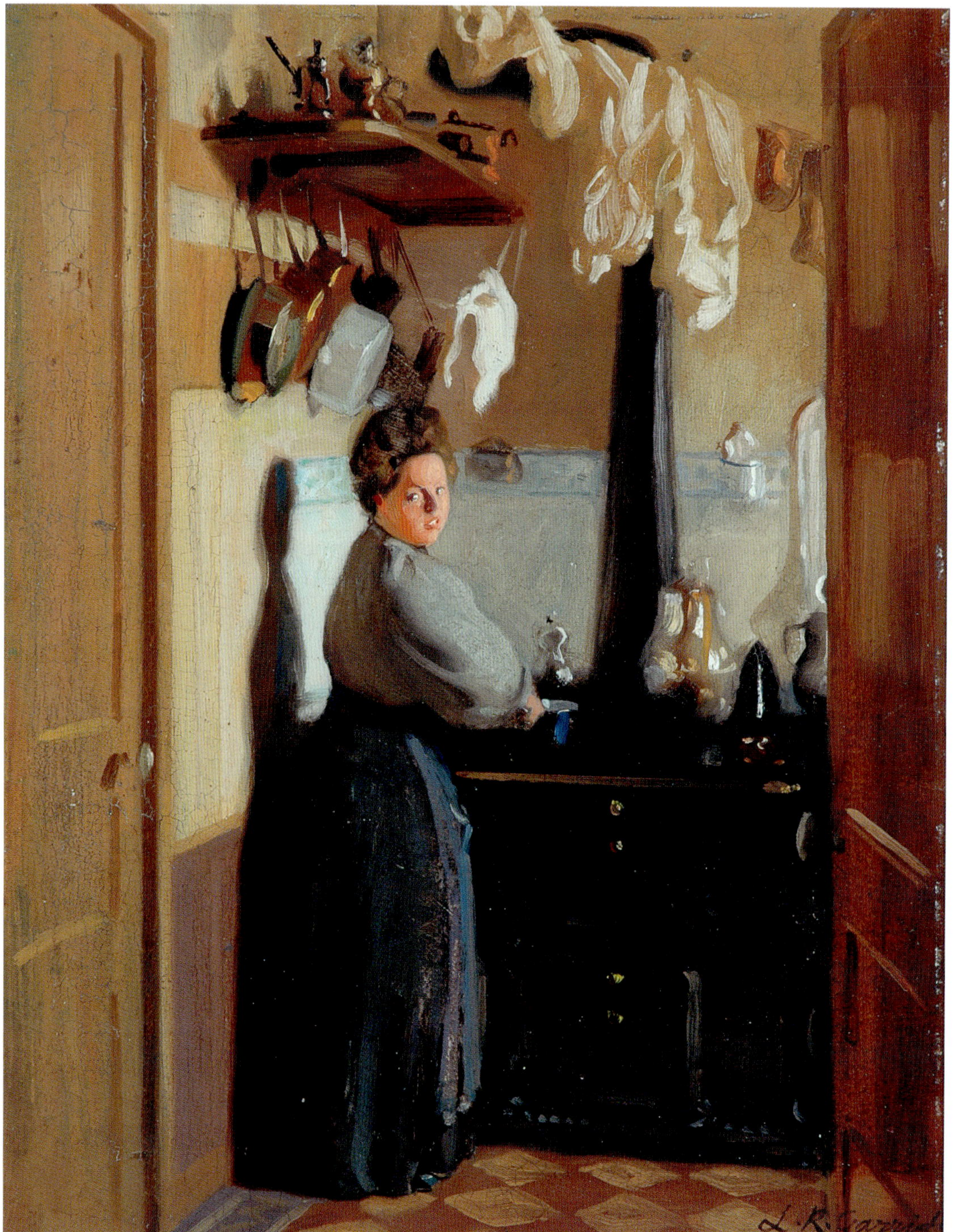
L. R. Garrido

Opposite: 6. Leandro Garrido's portrait was one of a number of gifts from dedicated supporter George Bednar to the local council's art gallery in Whitby. *Woman in a Kitchen* (c. 1905) stands testament not only to the range of artists active in the area, but also to the particular brilliance of still-life elements in his pictures.

The exceptions to this are listed here. I thank them sincerely, not only for their enthusiasm and willingness to make their collections available, but also for their efforts to follow up with further information:

Helen Berry and Effie Burns at The Pannett Art Gallery and Emma Gates at the Museum in Whitby; Rosie Barnes at Staithes Museum; Neil McGregor at Danum Gallery, Doncaster; Anna Bates Patel at Touchstones, Rochdale; Caitlin Doley at York City Art Gallery; Louisa Krzyz at Oldham Art Gallery; Farah Dallami at the Hepworth, Wakefield; Louise Dunning at Nottingham Museums and Anne Adams at Nottingham Trent University; Melanie Williamson and Kate Jesson at Manchester Art Gallery; Peter Davis, archivist of the Manchester Academy of Fine Art; Angela Thomas at Hartlepool Borough Council; Daniel Sudron at the North Yorkshire County Record Office; Cameron Fragoso and her assistant Freddie at the University of Salford.

Other public libraries and galleries further afield provided access to valuable resources and information not available to me without their help:

Librarian teams at both Tate Britain and the National Art Library in London; Ruth Hallinan, Rónán Ó Raghallaigh and Clare Lymer at the National Irish Visual Arts Library (NIVAL) at the National College of Art and Design (NCAD); Tim Jones at the Christchurch Art Gallery, Roger Smith at the Te Papa Museum, Wellington and Petrena Fishburn and Izzy Hillmann at the Aigantighe Art Gallery, Timaru in New Zealand; Glenda Veitch and Ciara Derkenne at the Art Gallery of New South Wales in Sydney and Hayley Da Quinta at the National Library of Australia in Canberra.

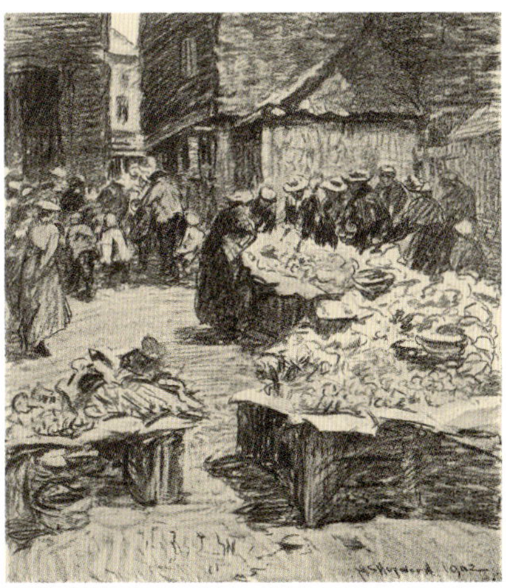

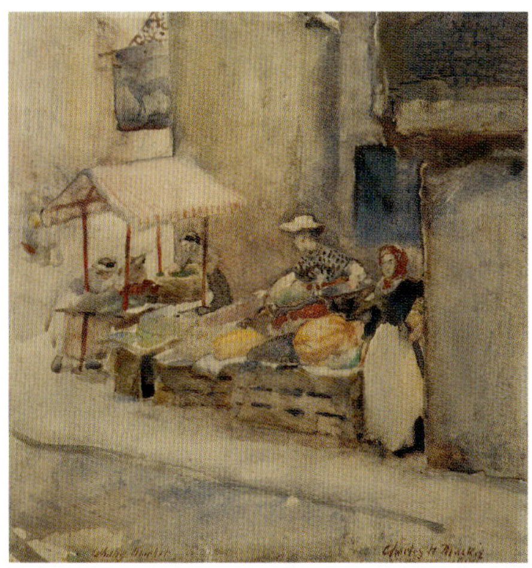

Right: 7. Whitby's marketplace was a centre of activity for townspeople, fisherfolk and artists. Henry Hopwood, for whom such places held great fascination, whether in Africa, Europe or Yorkshire, here presents a vigorous charcoal study exhibited at the Fine Art Society in London in 1902. *Whitby Market Place* was reproduced in *The Studio* magazine of 1910.

Far right: 8. Rather than the bustle of the central market, Charles Mackie's 1900 watercolour *Whitby Market Place* matches his archetypal subdued colour tone. It was Mackie to whom Laura Johnson credits both the practical organisation of her palette and advancement in the use of colour.

As a result, I hope this book will be a timely reminder of the collective talents of these artists, their works intermingled in an effort to focus on themes and relationships rather than just on individual chronologies and exhibiting records. The photographs of the artists' contemporary, Frank Meadow Sutcliffe, have been included to the same end, for their artistic as much as their illustrative qualities, emblematic of a time when heated public debate took place over the nature of photography as art.

Much effort has been lent to presenting top-quality colour illustrations. Our thanks must go in this respect to the expertise, care, patience and good humour of photographers Steve Ward and

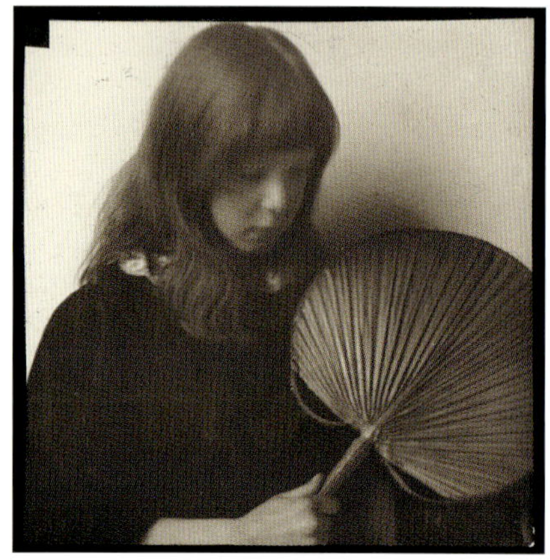

Above right: 9. This untitled image of a girl with a fan forms part of a recently discovered group of magic lantern slides that focus on W. G. Foster, his friends and family. They considerably strengthen the connection between art and photography in relation to the artists' life at the coast (see **113** and **114**).

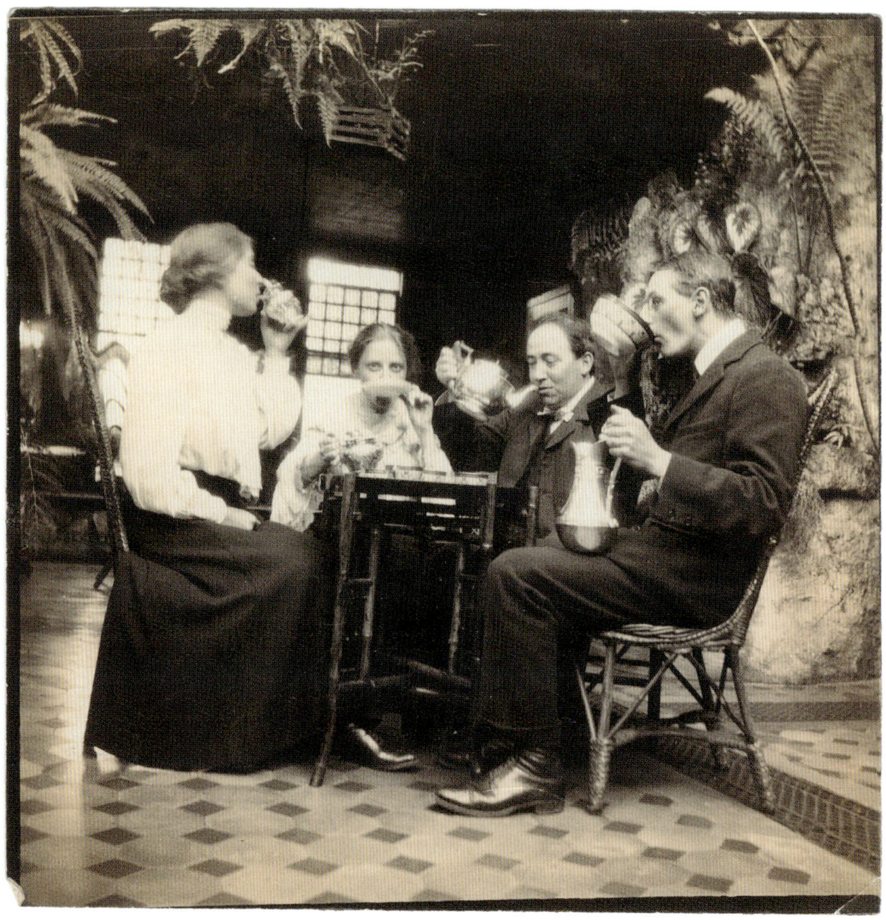

Right: 10. This uncredited photograph of Laura Johnson and Harold Knight (foreground), Rosie Good and Oliver Sheppard was probably taken at Rosie's family home in Nottingham and is dated in the Knight family album to 1899. It nicely captures a flavour of the bohemian spirit too little credited to artists in Staithes and Runswick.

latterly Tom Morrison, with smaller but important contributions from James Stoker and Giulio Sheaves. Such quality has not been a consistent feature of either the aforementioned exhibition catalogues (still in an age of black and white transparencies) or more recent publications, often limited by prohibitive expense.[3] Such images are crucial to enabling a thorough appreciation of the range of technique and styles, from sketch to exhibition piece, in the absence of seeing the works themselves. I am delighted too to have worked with old friends, at new publisher Kulturalis, to present the whole.

The Art UK website has proved invaluable in being able to track down many works in public collections and it is pleasing to be able to include such a geographically diverse range of institutions in the credits. However, digital imagery is only as good as a face-to-face viewing allows, and in this respect my thanks must go overwhelmingly to the many individuals, artists' family members and dealers who have made works available to me. In the case of the artists' families, much has been related and written about the efforts of Mark Senior's granddaughter, the late Mary Oddie, to bring attention to his work. It is my misfortune not to have been able to meet her, but the ongoing enthusiasm of her various relations has been a significant recompense. Likewise, members of the Bagshawe family allowed me to consult their family papers and were unfailingly generous with their time. The descendants of Enid Pease Robinson gave their blessing for reproduction of material from her diary, the discovery of which at last presents a first-hand glimpse of the elusive inaugural Staithes Art Club exhibition. Credit for this is entirely due to James Hart, who has also unselfishly shared his further knowledge. Likewise John Croft, the grandson of Laura Knight's sister, has lent significant support, though his catalogue raisonné of Laura and Harold's works is a huge

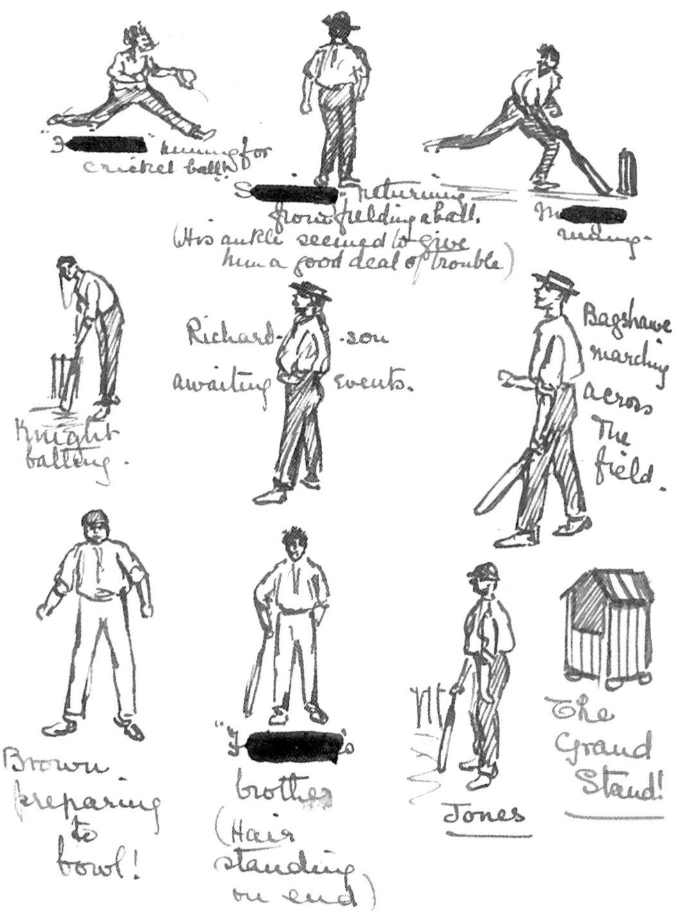

11. An illustrated diary by Enid Pease Robinson provides the only extant eyewitness account of the Staithes Art Club's initial exhibition of 1901. Alongside a number of other female sources, it provides invaluable first-hand testimony to the artists' characters and social life, here exemplified in caricatures of them playing cricket (see also 27).

undertaking which must absorb all of his efforts. Other families too have provided copyright to works or sources for which I am indebted.

Given that commercial galleries were coming into their own at the time the artists in question were also establishing careers, it is fitting that dealers' contributions are also properly recognised. To their names I have added other specialists who have been particularly helpful. I would like to express my sincere thanks to the following:

Simon Wood at Brockfield Hall, Ian Walker at Walker Galleries, Charlotte Conboy and Alan Darwell, Dominic Cox at David Duggleby's, David Messum and Patrick Duffy at Messum's, Chris Beetles and Pascale Oakley-Birch at Chris Beetles Gallery, Camilla Riva at The Fine Art Society, Peter Howarth, Paul McTague, Christine Pybus and Rod Jewell.

And finally to those who assisted in concluding what proved a testing but ultimately rewarding search for images: John Croft (again) and the trustees of the Estate of Dame Laura Knight, without whose kind agreement this book would have been much the poorer; Sian Phillips at Bridgeman Art Library, Marie-Claude Saia at the Musée des Beaux-Arts de Montréal, Emily Putnam at the National Gallery of Art in Ottawa, Rosie Keane and Sarah Corcoran at the National Gallery of Ireland, Stephen Weir at National Museums Northern Ireland, Erica Martin at The Imperial War Museum, Lucia Rinolfi at the British Museum, Cristina D'Alessandro at Scala Archives, Kate Hudson at Tennant's, Thomas Seaman and Hannele Hellerstedt at Bonhams, Emma Gordon at Sotheby's, Dominic Cox and Ella Shaw at David Duggleby's, Philip Maggs (then) at John Nicholson's, Wendy Jemison at Elstob, Emma Saber at Charles Miller, Emma Pawsey at Adam Partridge, Clare Durham at Woolley & Wallis and Freddy Lines at Bishop and Miller.

Opposite: 12. Written in response to a BBC TV interview in 1967, Mrs Longster's letter to Dame Laura Knight prompted fond recollections, included in her reply, of her Staithes experience. It reinforces comments in her memoir concerning her gratitude to its inhabitants at what was a formative time for her, both as person and artist.

ENDNOTES

1 *Painting at the Edge*, an exhibition and book edited by Laura Newton, took place in Penzance and Newport in 2005. It featured five members of the Staithes Art Club: Laura and Harold Knight, Charles Mackie, Mark Senior and Isa Jobling. Colin Bullamore's self-published *The Staithes Group of Artists* (2014) should also be noted.

2 Touchstones Rochdale did produce a gallery exhibition on Jackson from July to November 2002.

3 Those by Peter Haworth, published by the Fine Art Society, must be excepted, but no transparencies remain.

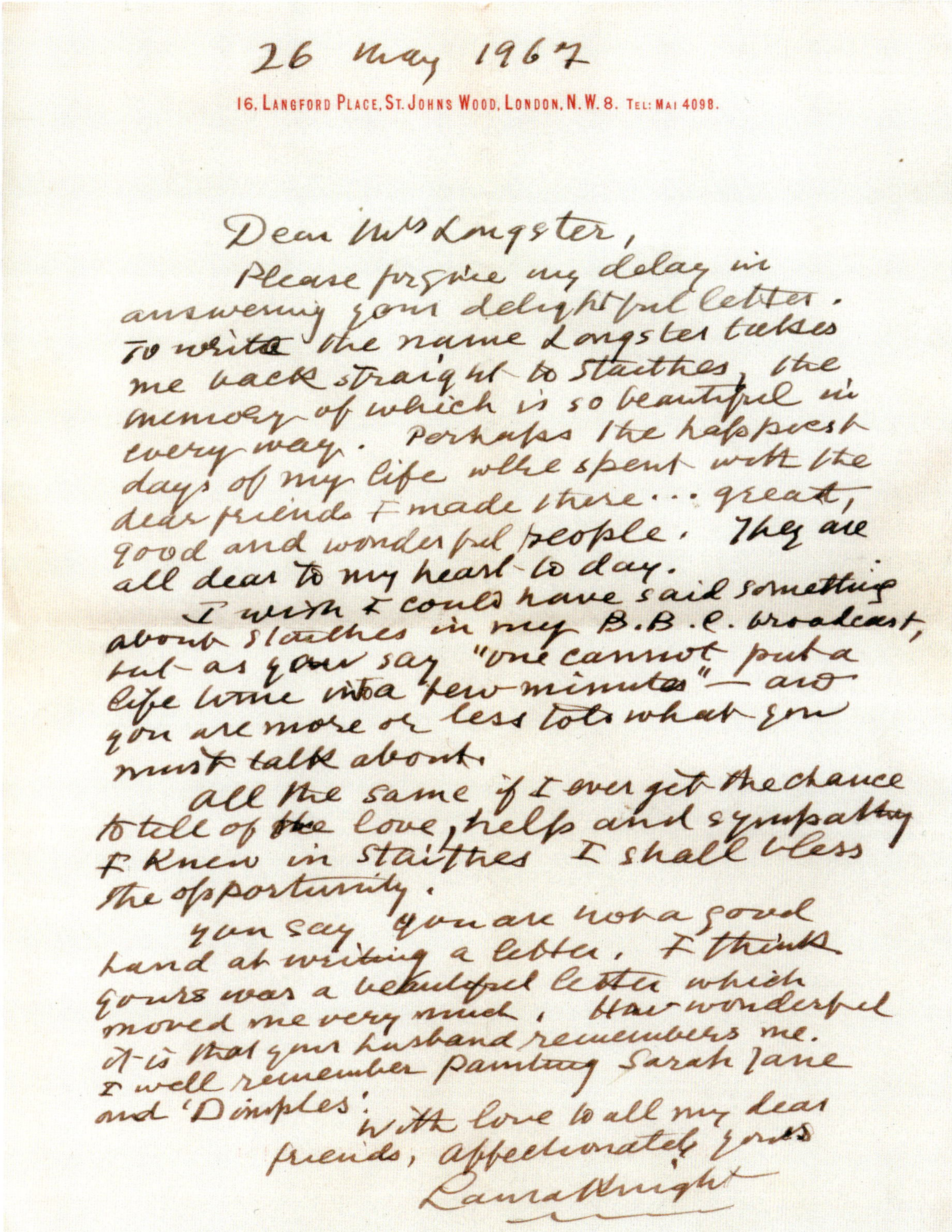
26 May 1967

16, Langford Place, St. Johns Wood, London, N.W. 8. Tel: Mai 4098.

Dear Mrs Longster,

Please forgive my delay in answering your delightful letter. To write the name Longster takes me back straight to Staithes, the memory of which is so beautiful in every way. Perhaps the happiest days of my life were spent with the dear friends I made there... great, good and wonderful people. They are all dear to my heart to day.

I wish I could have said something about Staithes in my B.B.C. broadcast, but as you say "one cannot put a life time into a few minutes" – and you are more or less told what you must talk about.

All the same if I ever get the chance to tell of the love, help and sympathy I knew in Staithes I shall bless the opportunity.

You say you are not a good hand at writing a letter. I think yours was a beautiful letter which moved me very much. How wonderful it is that your husband remembers me. I well remember painting Sarah Jane and 'Dimples'.

With love to all my dear friends, Affectionately yours

Laura Knight

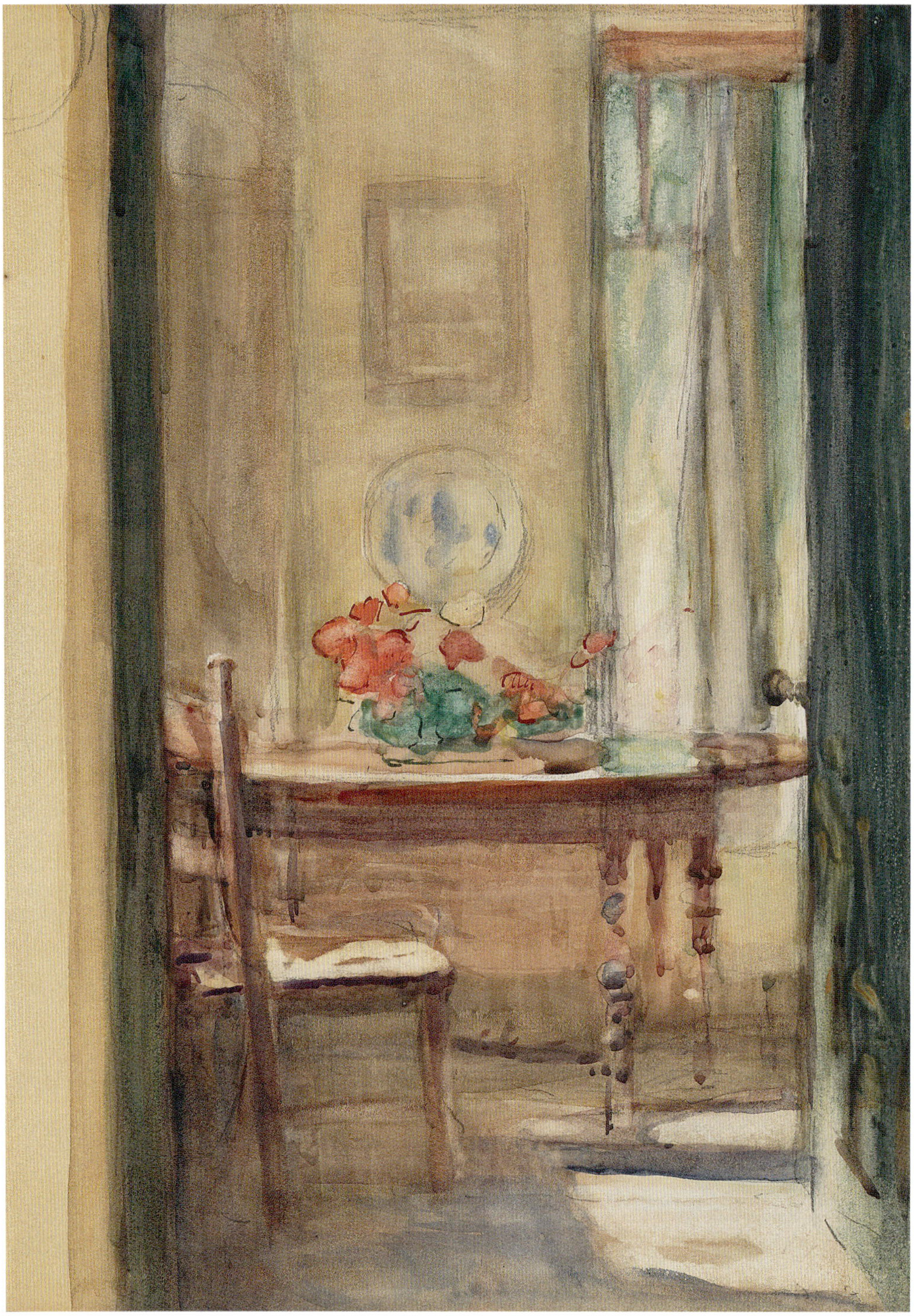

Opposite: 13. Mark Senior's connection with Runswick Bay lasted for almost 50 years; his family's association continues to this day. In 1919 he bought land from a pupil, Gertrude Hudson, and built a new house. His *Interior of Hillside*, dating from c. 1920, pictures it soon after the house was completed.

AUTHOR'S NOTE

The title of this book was inspired by the 1906 and 1907 shows of Laura and Harold Knight's work at the Leicester Galleries and they are the two most prominent artists featured.

Their time in Staithes was a formative period both in artistic and personal terms and, as with three other artist couples, their marriage took place during this period. Wishing to acknowledge both their individuality as artists and to assist in dating works, maiden and married names have been used interchangeably. So for works before 1903 Laura Johnson has been preferred to Knight, though every effort has been made to point equivalence. The case is similar for Isa Thompson, who became Jobling in 1893, Rosie Good, who took Oliver Sheppard's name in 1901, and Hannah Hoyland, who married Fred Mayor in 1902.

The Knights were present in Staithes for roughly a decade from 1897–1907. Their work at this time is due to be included as part of the larger catalogue raisonné by John Croft, who has generously shared his attempts to track down accurate titles and dates. Anomalies remain, however, not least because so few of their early works are precisely dated.

An appreciation of this should be extended to many of the Staithes painters, whose works have yet to be researched and matched to exhibit records. Where possible, details have been added from physical examination of the works and archival records, in some cases suggested by circumstantial evidence. Elsewhere, works have been left undated and titles provided from the earliest known source, though they may not be original.

Artists and subject matter all inspire fierce loyalties and sharp discussion; any errors are, of course, the author's own.

A&A Arts is the partnership in which the author works and is responsible for arranging the photography of many of the paintings in this book. The partnership logo was an original commission from Kate Baylay.

Overleaf: 14. Henry Hopwood travelled to Australia and back at the end of the 1880s. He produced several paintings of life on board ship, including this notably large watercolour, *Messmates*, dated 1892. Hopwood's works were exhibited in both Sydney and Manchester after each voyage.

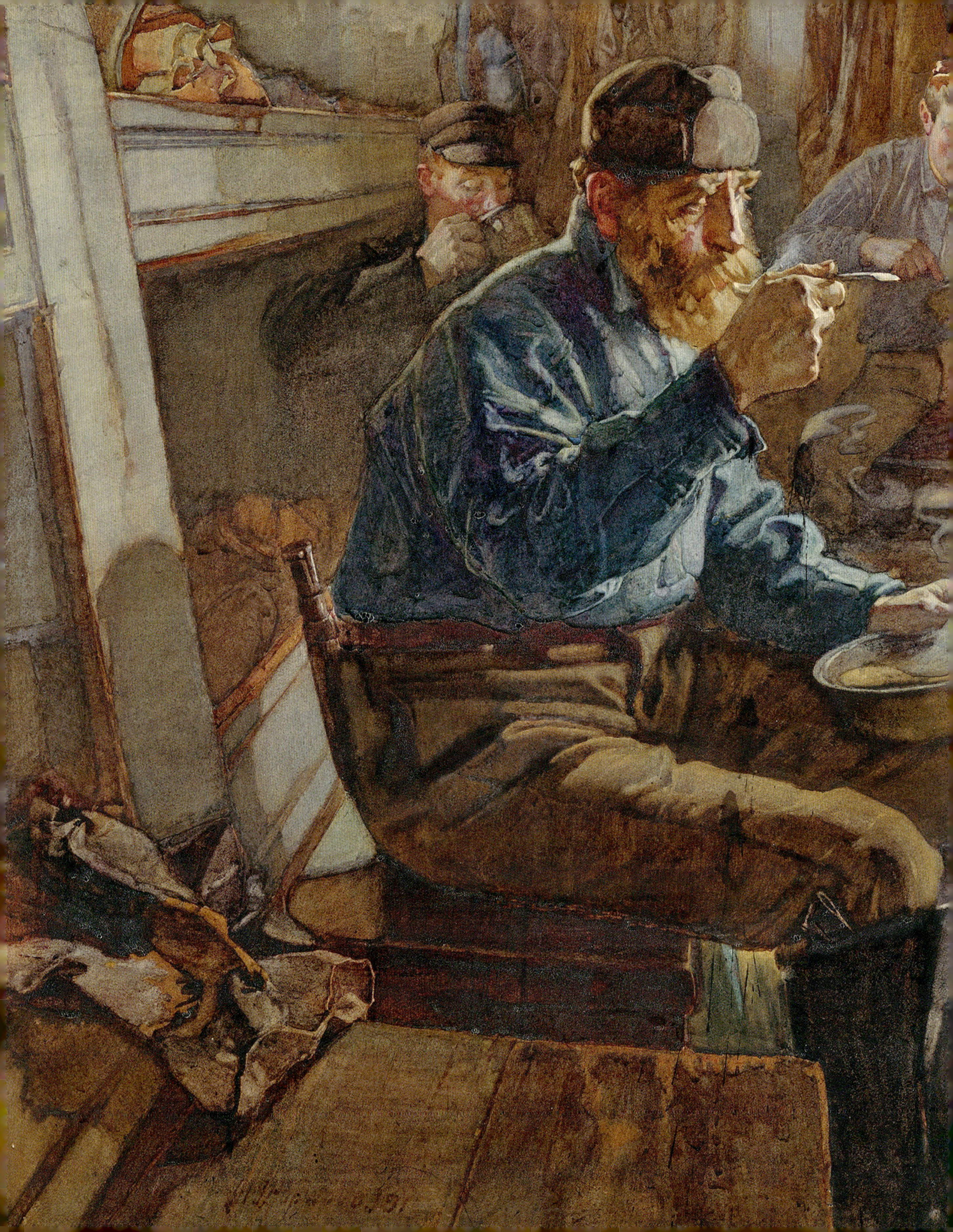

INTRODUCTION

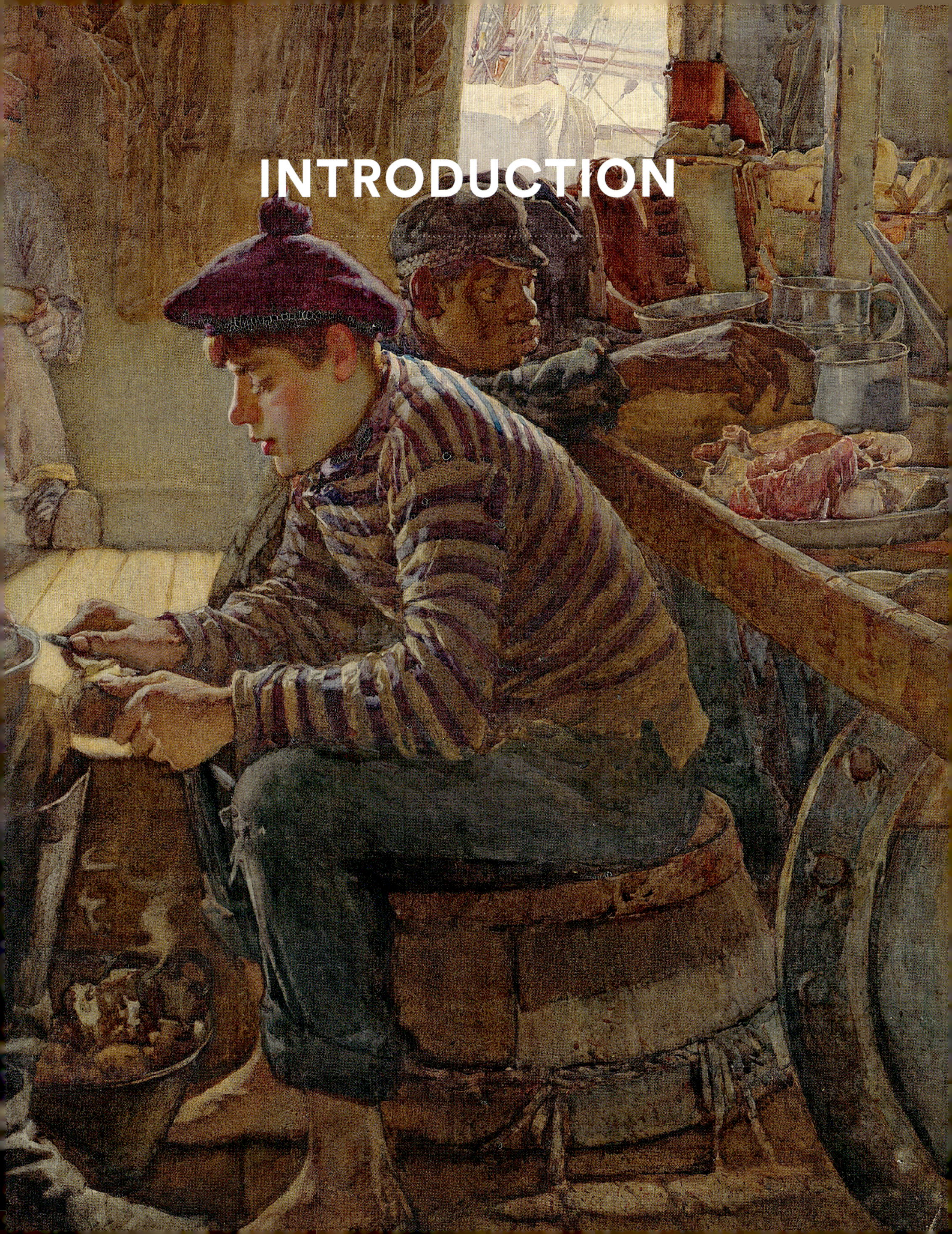

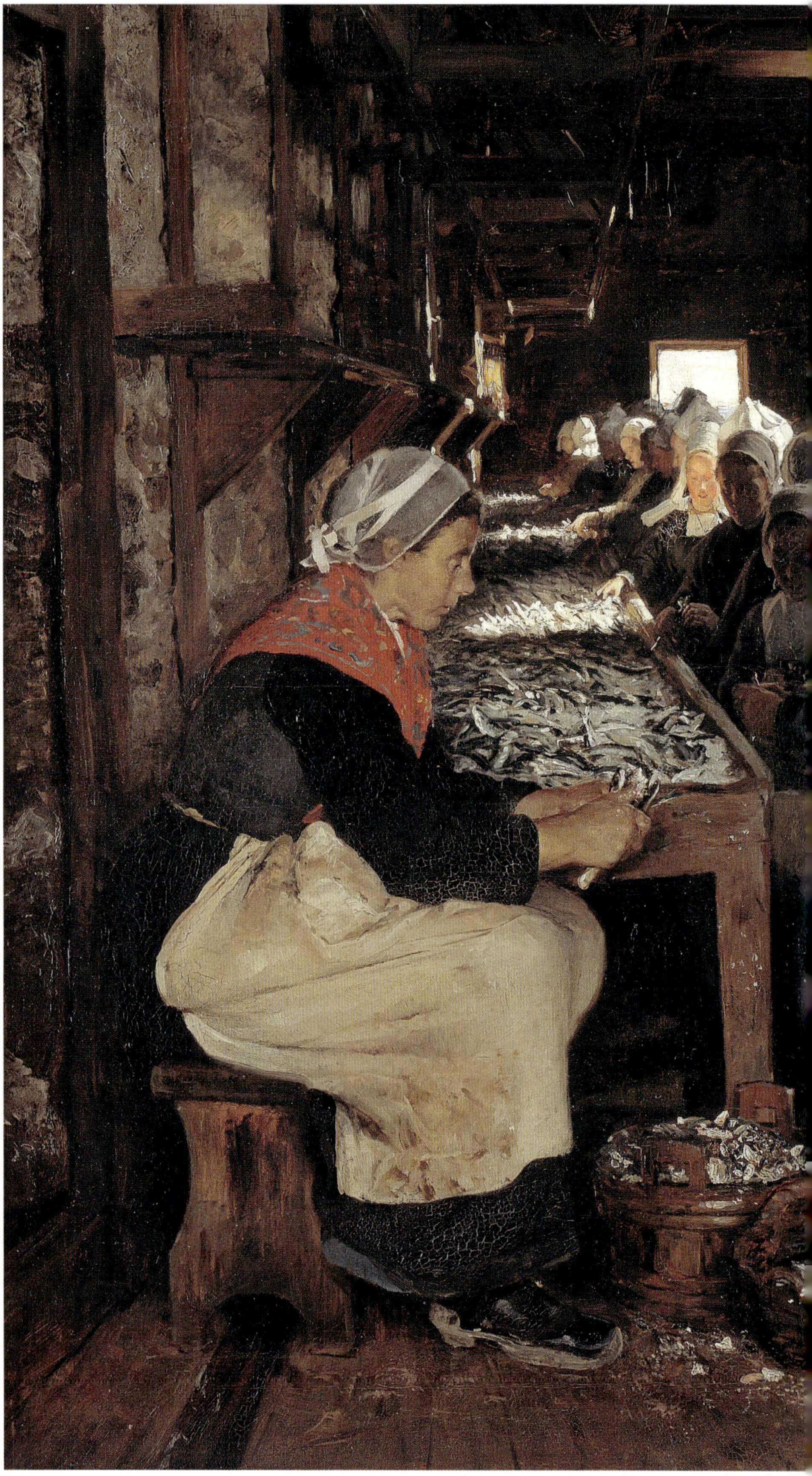

15. The Danish artists' colony at Skagen was headed by artists Michael Ancher and Peder Severin Kroyer. The latter took advantage not only of his established reputation, but also of his precocious talent to depict the life of the artists there. *A Sardinery in Concarneau* (1879) exemplifies these skills from Kroyer's time at the French artists' colony.

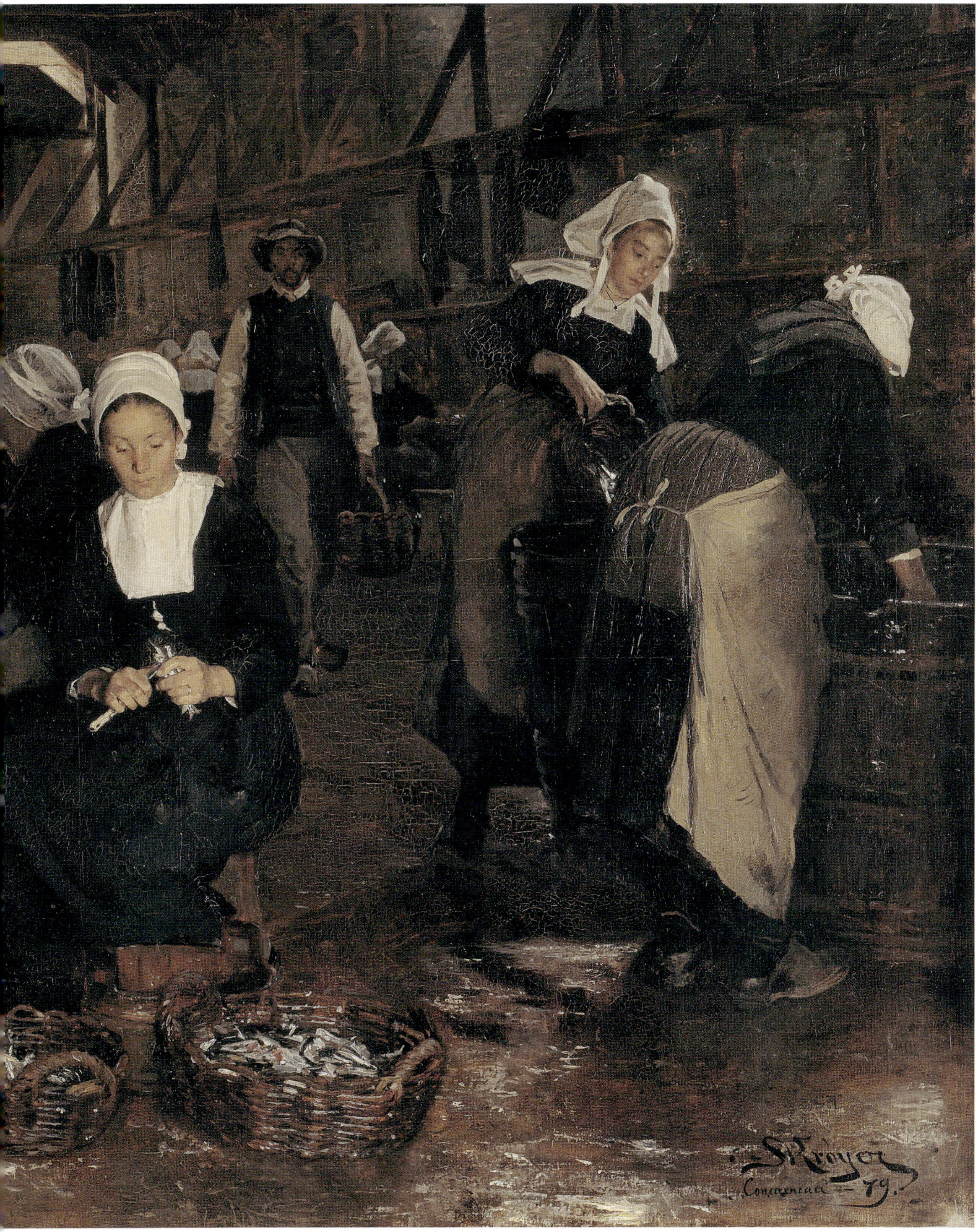
SKrøyer
Concarneau – 79.

INTRODUCTION

The opening of the inaugural Staithes Art Club exhibition was scheduled to take place on 26 August 1901. The weather was not auspicious: a violent storm had been brewing for days previous, high winds blew visitors almost off their feet and the opening was in question until the very afternoon itself.

It may therefore be no surprise that we lack definitive detail of the paintings on display and must resort to subsequent exhibition notices to deduce what was contributed and by whom.

Those same notices (see Appendix) detail a club which had an annually expanding number of members, a mixture of established exhibitors and relative newcomers, but which endured regular changes of premises and had a lifespan of only six years before several of the main protagonists dispersed or pledged their loyalties elsewhere. Posterity has also complicated matters by assigning links to a further range of painters who did not exhibit with the Club, and by varying descriptions of the whole from a group to a school to a colony.

The initial exhibition's entrance fee was charged to benefit the Fishermen's Institute (**33**) that acted as its backdrop and part of the time as a studio for the artists.[4] The Institute also provided a focal point for the village, Staithes, a traditional community of fisherfolk on the north-east Yorkshire coast (**4**). The village was considered 'otherworldly' to the local area, let alone the mainstream of either contemporary commerce or art, and while Staithes had once hosted a significant fishing fleet and population of almost 1,000, the geographic advantages of larger neighbouring ports for industry and shipping had left it a place increasingly out of time.

This suggests an inauspicious context for what has been claimed as bold contemporary artistic expression. Yet, in adopting membership of the club, the artists emphasised their commitment to the prevailing artistic current of the day and laid claims to a similar legacy as other established and formative gatherings of artists across Europe. In exploring the life, light and landscape of the coast, they also bore witness to the ebb tide of the local traditions that had persisted for hundreds of years. In combining both these aspects they created a kaleidoscope of work which may be viewed as a touchstone to our own times.

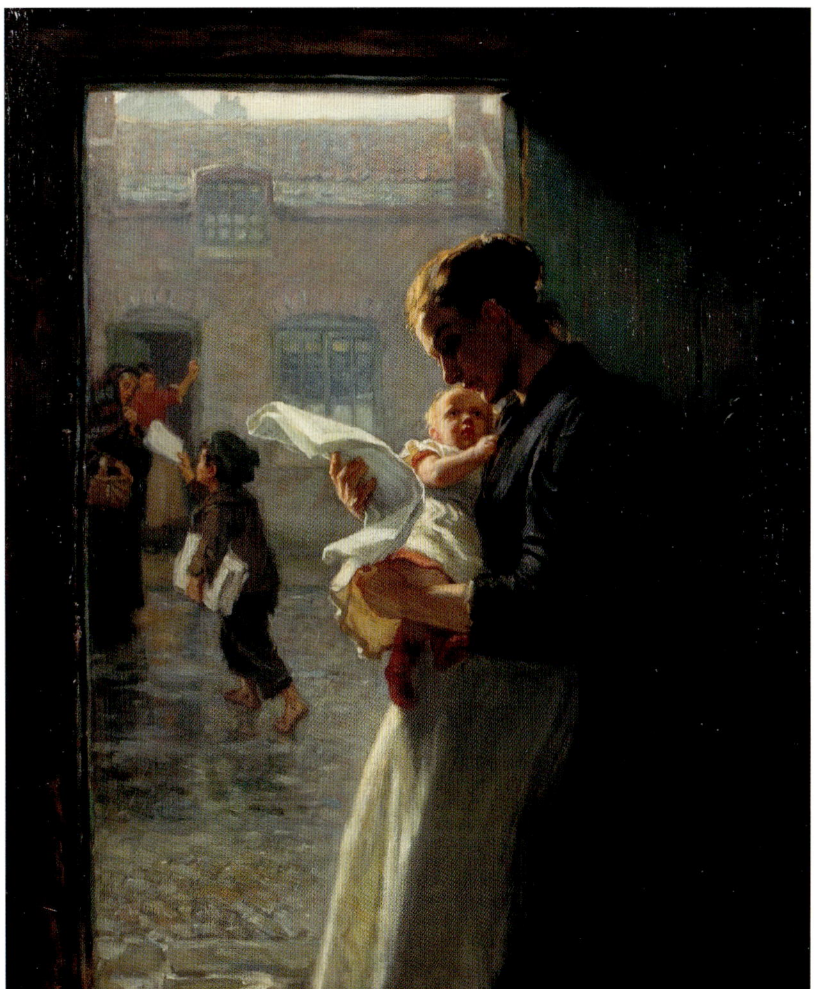

16. *The Reservist's Wife* hung at the Royal Academy in 1900 as one of a pair. Its pendant pictures the safe return of the solider from Africa. Ralph Hedley rarely referred to contemporary news, but he did paint two further scenes on this specific theme, *Ladysmith Day* and *Fighting His Battles Over Again*.

EMPIRE AND PATRIOTISM

For the second half of the nineteenth century the British were almost constantly facing conflict in one corner of the Empire or another. Perhaps nowhere were they more consistently opposed than in South Africa, where mineral deposits caused constant friction between competing international interests. The initial 'Boer War' started and ended as the first of the Club's artists arrived to paint at Staithes and its neighbour Runswick Bay; in the lead-up to the formation of the Staithes Art Club, it erupted again and occupied the national news.[5] Even men from this seemingly inaccessible spot went off to fight; Edward, the brother of Joseph Bagshawe (first Secretary of the Club), served with the Princess of Wales's own Yorkshire regiment and E. W. Beckett, one of the Club's early patrons and MP for Whitby, acted as Adjutant General from 1900 to 1902.[6] All survived, and the return of the Staithes men was reported in the *Whitby Gazette*. They were treated as heroes in the village, with celebrations led by Captain Pinder, known as the 'King of Steers' ('Staithes' in the local dialect).[7] He turned out proudly displaying the blue and yellow beribboned medals of his service in the Crimean War of the 1850s:

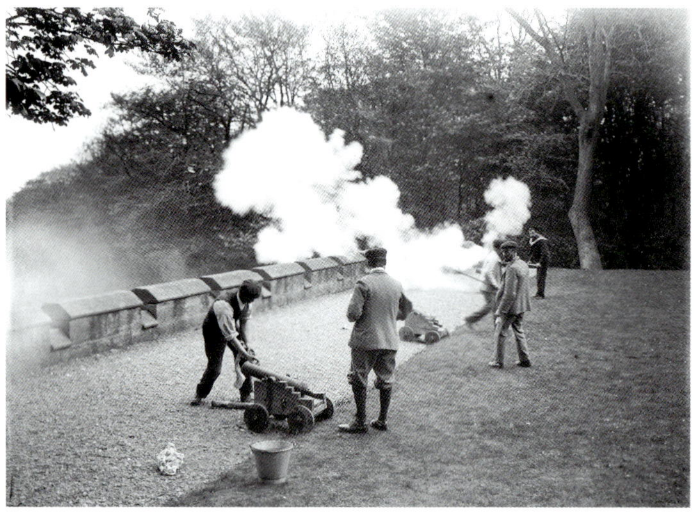

> It was feared that Captain Pinder might lose his reason, he got so worked up if things went wrong for England, or news of our victories came. When Mafeking and Ladysmith were in turn relieved ... [he] organised celebrations and became king indeed; he was crowned publicly and set on a throne lashed on to a lorry. Round him were his courtiers, dressed in a medley of colours ... bunting filled the street. The lorry was garlanded with paper flowers. Captain Pinder waved a Union Jack instead of a sceptre.... The cortege drove round the countryside, stopping at every public house.[8]

17. Tom Watson, who began his working life in the Normanby estate's joiner's shop, was commissioned by the Marquis to take a series of photographs of life in the house and grounds. In *Mafeking Salute* he framed the jubilation on the 'quarterdeck' at Mulgrave Castle, on receiving the news that the British garrison at Mafeking had been relieved.

Pictures of Queen Victoria hung in many Staithes' parlours and 'there was a genuine sense of grief' when, during the second conflict, she died. It must

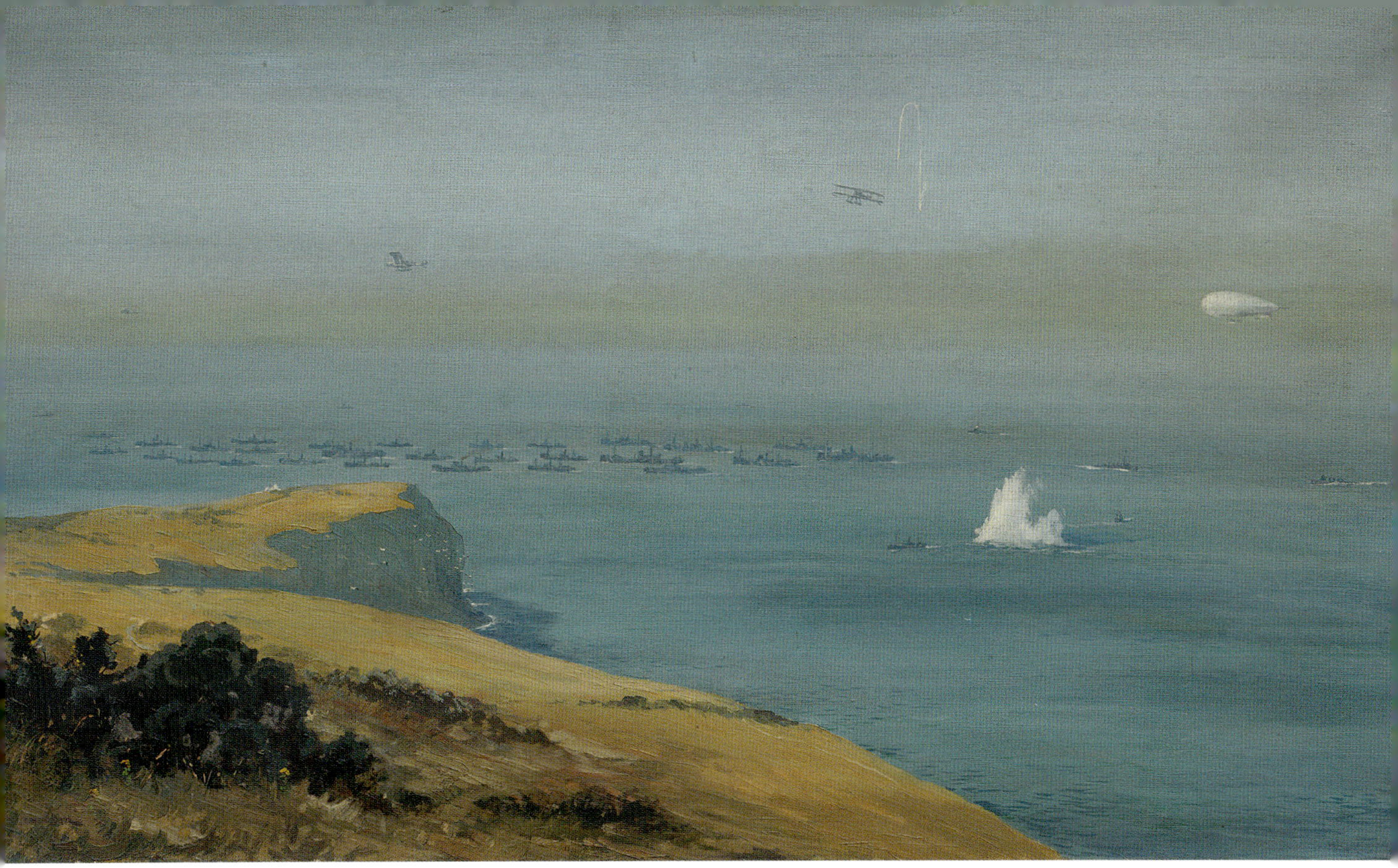

18. Ernest Dade's image of 1919, *A Convoy passing Whitby High Lights*, depicts activity typical up and down the East Coast during the First World War. For artists wartime brought significant challenges; John Howey was reported to the police for sketching, while Frank Sutcliffe had to mask the German makers' mark on his cameras.

have seemed fitting to many in the village that part of her funeral cortege was by boat (from the Isle of Wight). The German Kaiser attended Victoria's funeral in Westminster Abbey – emblematic of a time before the First World War when Staithes' fishermen sailed the German Ocean, not the North Sea, and trade with the markets of Eastern Europe and the Baltic was at its strongest.

However, just as had been the case in previous centuries when establishing Britain's share of the whaling industry, the sailors of the north-east coast suffered in an atmosphere of increasing international hostility. In 1904 the Russian navy, en route to fight the Japanese, attacked a fleet of trawlers in error, resulting in fatalities and a relief fund to which Edward VII donated over 200 guineas.[9] Then, following the onset of the First World War and open hostility, Scarborough was shelled by German battleships. Artists such as Robert and Isa Jobling, who had remained regular visitors after the Club dissolved, became wary of sketching:

> I am not pushing myself very much with work here. Indeed, from all that I hear I am fortunate in being allowed to paint at all in this neighbourhood so near the coast. Indeed, I cannot say I have any express permission to do so.[10]

INDEPENDENCE AND FEALTY

The nationalism engendered by the various British conflicts was somewhat at odds with the long-harboured individualism of the fishing communities. Traditional geographic rivalries, even between neighbouring villages such as Staithes and Runswick Bay, were evidenced in everything from pronunciation and dialect to marriage and religion. The inclination towards nonconformity with the established Church, for example, was nowhere so magnified as within the community of Staithes itself, as Laura Knight relates when settling in the village.

With several Methodist chapels to choose from, loyalties were split and independence of political outlook – typically a 'liberal' concern for material wellbeing and individual self-respect – exacerbated.[11] Even as political Liberalism collapsed and a more collectivist ethic espoused by the socialism of the Labour movement arose, there seems to have persisted a tension along the coast on account of the inherently competitive, free-enterprise nature of the fishermen. This left many fishing communities slow to disavow their liberal roots, a situation encouraged by the ineffective communication and faltering practical assistance provided by the seamen's and sailors' unions beyond urban centres such as Sunderland and Hull.

From the Tees to the Esk (Middlesbrough to Whitby), liberalism was retrenched through the local aristocrats, industrialists and politicians (Whitby MPs) who, named by turns as patrons of the Art Club, displayed liberal loyalties. Charles Palmer, MP for first North Durham and then Jarrow, bought the manor of Seaton in 1868 from the Marquis of Normanby (himself a Liberal peer); it included lands from Staithes to Runswick Bay as well as inland to Dale House and Easington. An industrialist and shipbuilder, Palmer became so well-connected that William Gladstone came to visit him. The Prime Minister inspected Port Mulgrave[12] and, as noted in his diary, also visited Staithes, an event commemorated by two of the fleet's cobles (small fishing boats) being named *William Ewart Gladstone* and *The Grand Old Man* in his honour.[13]

Throughout this period Gladstone, both in and out of government, wrestled with the question of Home Rule for Ireland. The unrest generated by this issue was still at a pitch as the Staithes Art Club formed, evidenced by a demonstration that disrupted the chamber of the House of Commons. Laura Johnson's great friend Rosie Good married Harold Knight's fellow artist and teaching colleague Oliver Sheppard who, at the behest of none other than

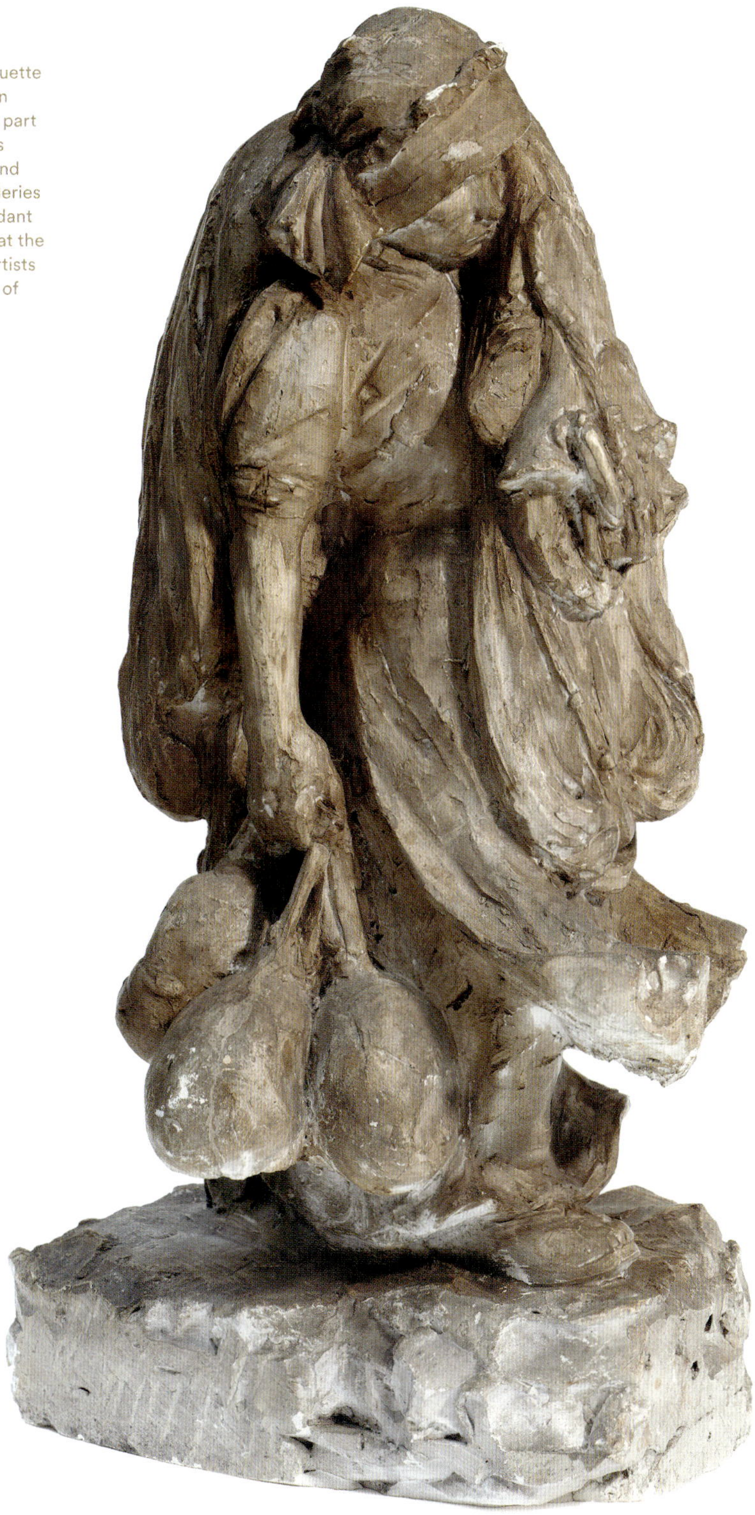

19. Oliver Sheppard's statuette of a Staithes Fisherwoman was surely mislabelled as part of his daughter Cathleen's bequest to the National and Hugh Lane Memorial Galleries in Dublin. A possible pendant – a *Fisherman*, exhibited at the Nottingham Society of Artists in 1900 – suggests a date of 1899 for both works.

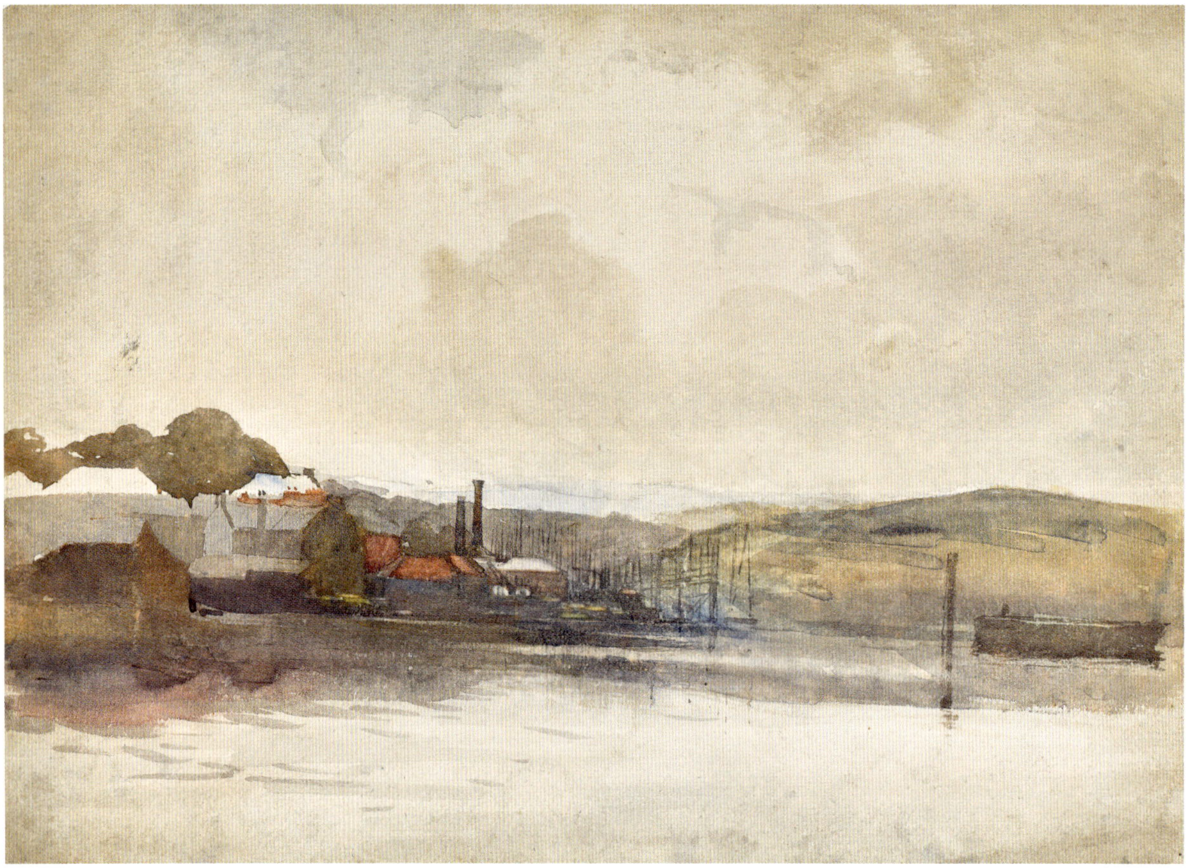

20. Edward Anderson was the only locally born artist associated with the Staithes Art Club. His family's art galleries were in the town, and in *Turnbull Shipyard, Whitby* (*c.* 1900) he pictures the business of another local family visited by William Gladstone during his 1871 visit to Whitby. The Turnbulls' father and brother were both patrons of the Art Club, while daughter and sister Mildred married its Secretary, Joseph Bagshawe.

W. B. Yeats, was persuaded home to Ireland to work as part of the Nationalist resurgence in the arts.

It is notable too that Joseph Bagshawe, married weeks after the Sheppards in 1901, provided illustrations to a story written by Kathleen Tynan, another of Yeats's associates.[14] Having spent his honeymoon in Ireland, Bagshawe maintained support for the cause of the Irish Catholics – to the extent that his biographer claims his early death (1909) relieved him of the momentous decision over Irish independence faced by others, such as the activist and author Erskine Childers.[15]

RESOURCES ON LAND AND SEA

Much as the late nineteenth-century conflicts in southern Africa centred on the economic advantages of mineral deposits, so too the history of ports and villages on the north-east coast revolved around resources discovered both onshore and off. Fishing, though remaining a staple element of livelihoods throughout the eighteenth and nineteenth centuries, was variously sidelined by industries that waxed and waned in response to the demand of their markets.

The rise of whaling at Whitby responded to the multifarious uses of whale oil and was also boosted, at times, by government subsidies in an early desire to establish a sound naval reserve. Traditions and memories of whaling ventures were alive in the local communities of the 1880s and 90s. Charles Palmer, mentioned above, was the son of a whaling captain and Joseph Bagshawe, whose wife's family was a cornerstone of local shipbuilding, became an active advocate for the use of fisherman as a modern naval reserve.

The identification of alum in the shale rock of the coasts north of Scarborough proved a resource of equal if not greater value. Given the enormous demands of the associated activities needed to mine, smelt and refine this mineral, the requirement for the building and provision of cargo shipping surged in parallel with that of whaling. In times of conflict – the American War of Independence or the Napoleonic Wars – demand only increased, cementing Whitby's place among the leading ports of England. It then supplied the market for vessels that travelled from the Caribbean islands to the Baltic states.

This only made the subsequent economic downturn hit the port harder. A dip in whale populations caused by an industry at its peak forced alternative light and heat resources to be identified, just as alum was replaced as the fixative in the cloth industry.

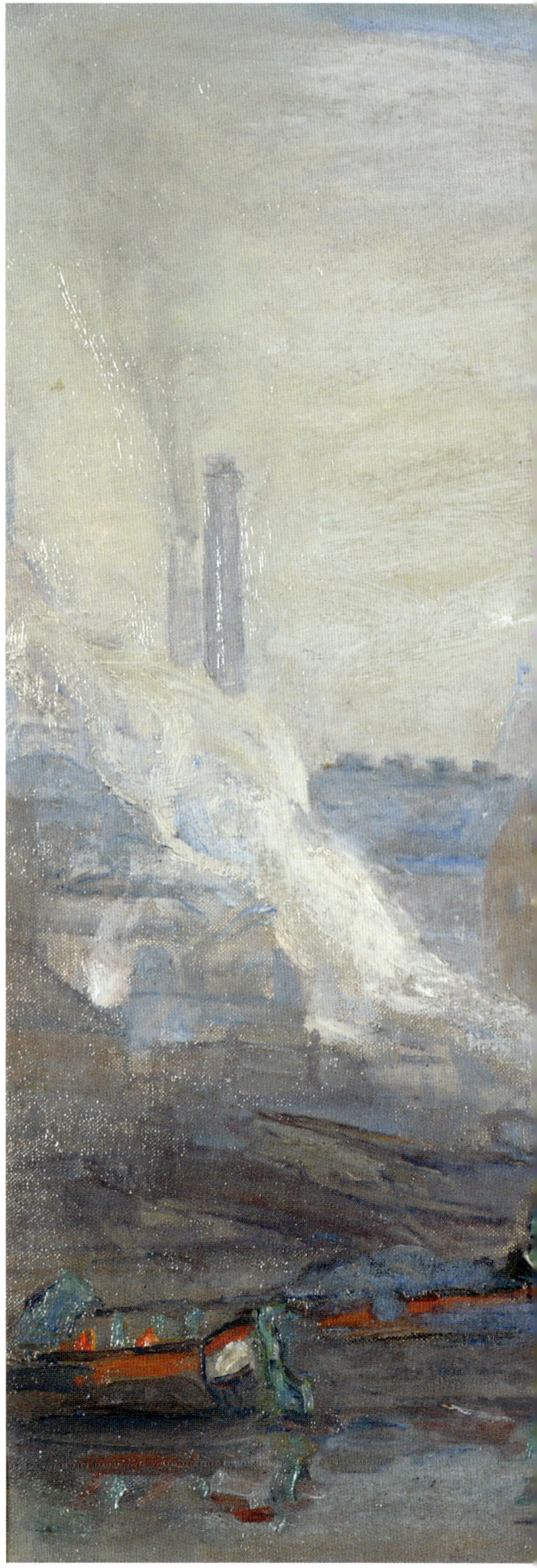

21. Florence Hess was introduced to Runswick Bay by her teacher Mark Senior, as earlier Staithes artists had been by their respective teachers: William Gilbert Foster, Thomas Barrett and Ralph Hedley. Most came from the urban centres of the northeast, Yorkshire and Lancashire – here captured in her undated picture *Leeds Wharf.*

The end of conflict did not cushion this blow for the town. However, just as fishing had supplied a stable economy before both shipbuilding and shipping took off, so it took up the slack again in this faltering economy. It did need a catalyst, though, which arrived in the form of the railways and was supplemented by the discovery of yet another resource: ironstone. Whitby's early connection to the mainline at York was consequently coordinated with the formation of two companies, Whitby Herring and Stone, to facilitate the supply of both to the growing markets of the UK. Its development persisted, with further deposits being identified and transported from the Grinkle Mines in the Boulby Hills further north to a newly created harbour at Port Mulgrave.[16] They were shipped via a dedicated stretch of rail down past Hinderwell, at the behest of the owner, Sir Charles Palmer.

Whitby jet was a further success story of the 1850s and 1860s. The naturally occurring black mineraloid, found in its finest form in and around the sedimentary cliffs of the Yorkshire coast, was

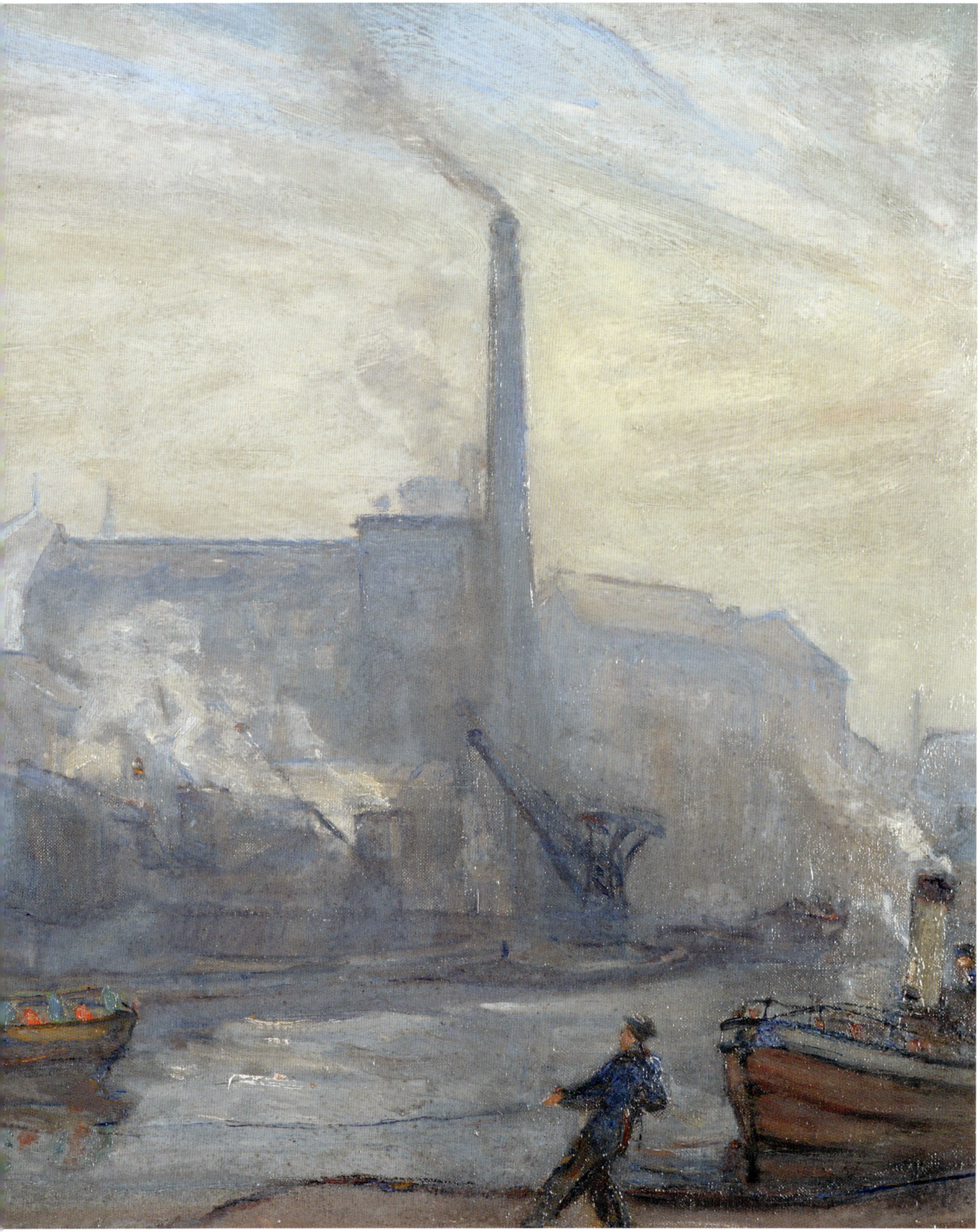

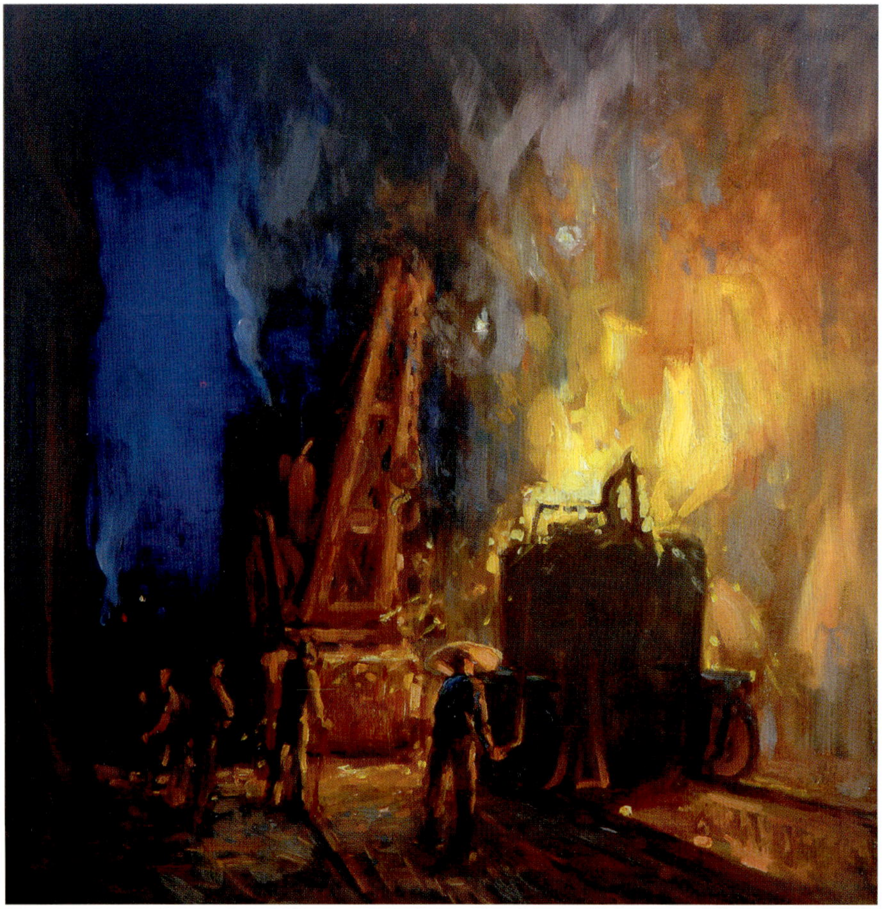

Left: 22. John William Howey never became a professional artist. Instead, he painted alongside his career in industry in West Hartlepool, here illustrated by *Tapping the Furnace*, c. 1924. Howey nevertheless became firm friends with Mark Senior and Rowland Hill, visiting them in Runswick Bay to paint in the area.

Opposite: 23. Albert George Stevens painted several highly praised figure studies of jet workers still employed in the industry after its peak in 1880; this work is dated to around 1900. The sort of workshops pictured here were later occupied by businesses such as Anderson's picture galleries and Frank Sutcliffe's initial photography studio.

used as mourning jewellery and became the height of fashion at the time of Prince Albert's death. This somewhat more than temporary spike in the industry boosted the number of those involved in its manufacture to almost 1,500.

Yet as quickly as prosperity had come, it faded again. The last shipment of alum left Sandsend, between Whitby and Runswick Bay, in 1867. Around the same time iron ore was found closer to the industrial heartland of Middlesbrough, rendering shipment from the Grosmont quarries through Whitby redundant. The fashion for jet also passed within ten years of its peak in the mid-1870s. Gradually its workshops gave way to businesses such as the photographic studio of Frank Sutcliffe and the art galleries of the Anderson family.

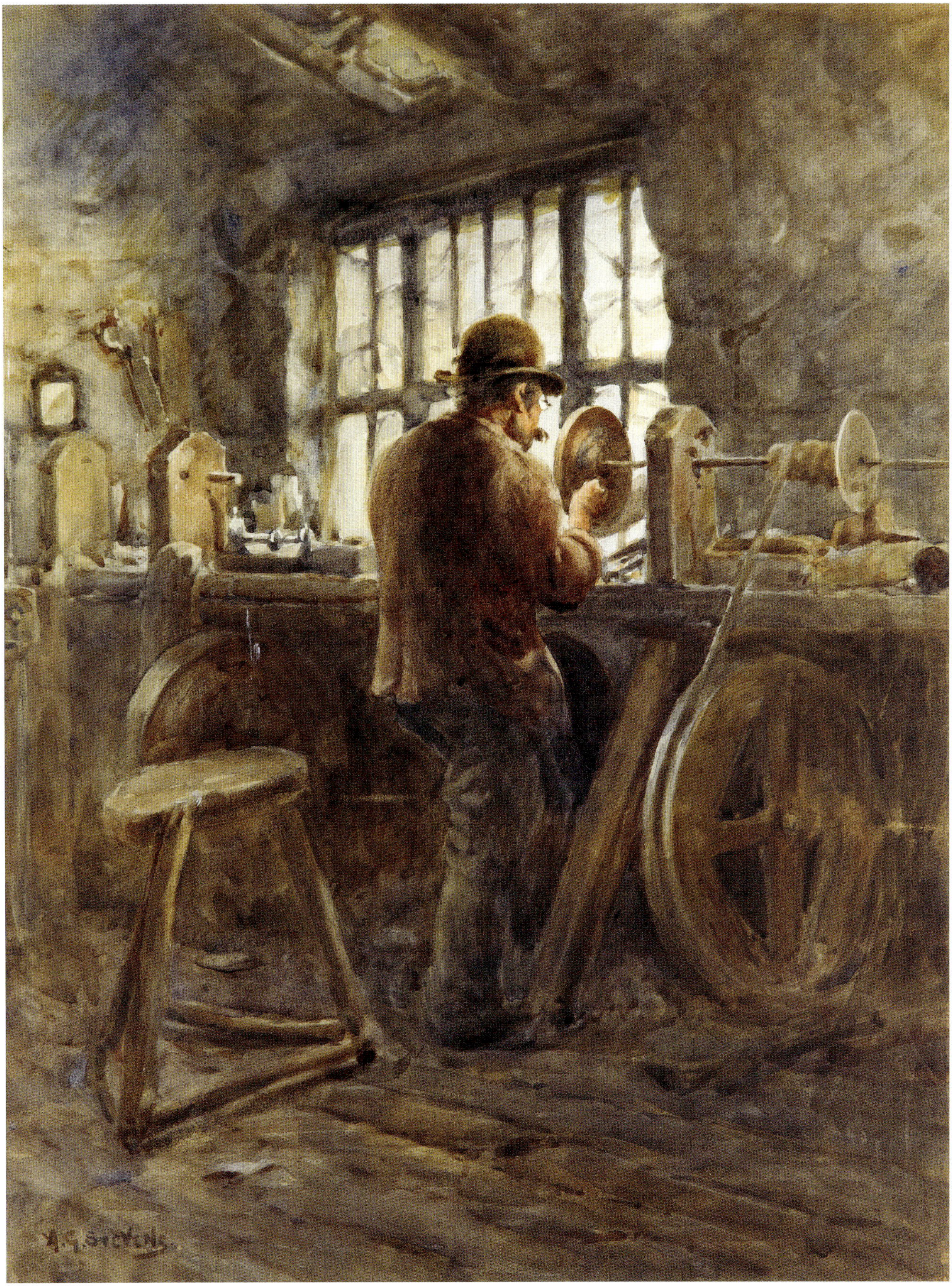
A.G. STEVENS

BUST AND BOOM

Throughout this period, the need for dynamic expansion created pressures on the mixed economy of Whitby.[17] As the mouth of the River Esk, the harbour suffered regular problems with silt, but the competing interests of the town found it surprisingly difficult to ensure the costs of regular dredging were resolved. Nor was its physical geography advantageous to associated industrialisation. Despite Whitby being the point of access for the only river to join the coast between The Humber (at Hull) and Tyne (at Newcastle), enhanced mechanisation was increasingly handled by ports further up and down the coast.

In the 1880s, following a sustained series of bad harvests, a depression occurred in the onshore economy. No ships were built in the town after 1902, with consequences for the surrounding communities.[18] These were resilient and had weathered lean times before, when industrial pollution had affected salmon stocks or the vicissitudes of the market had resulted in gluts and resulting drops in fish prices. However, the continuously bad harvests in the 1880s were accompanied by prolonged storms that destroyed craft and affected the coastline. Unable to sustain a living on sea or land, villagers increasingly turned to the mines or merchant navy for more regular income.[19] This disavowal of their heritage was encouraged by factors within their

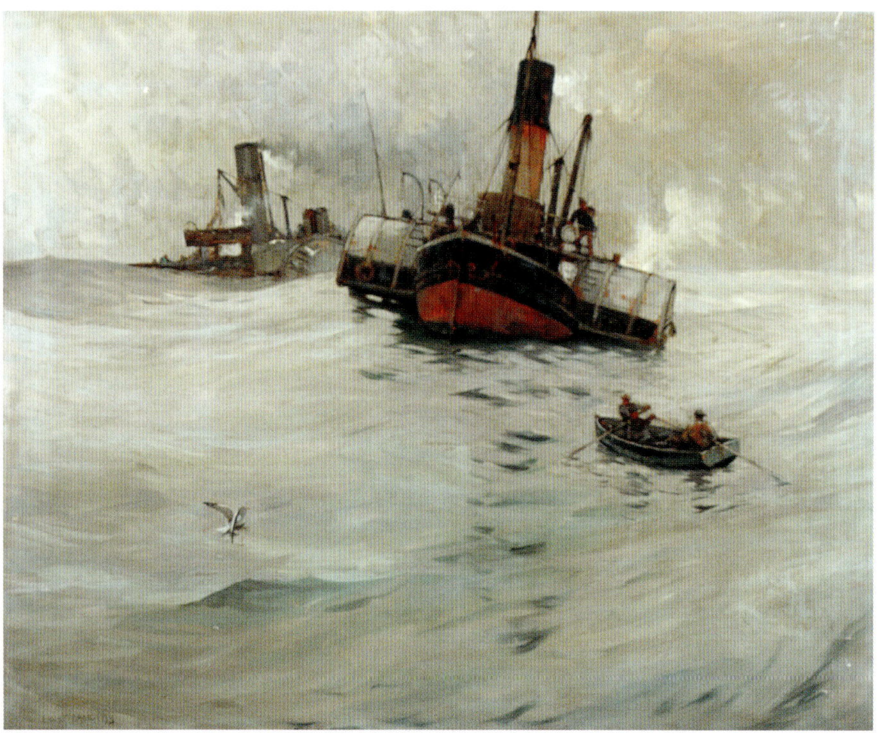

24. Ernest Dade's relish for the sea prompted his detailed portrayal of huge changes affecting the fishing industry. Staithes in-shore fishermen were outspoken witnesses to the damage ships such as those shown in *Trawlers Waiting for their Crews* (1893) caused to their livelihoods. However, they could not stem their steam power or larger catches.

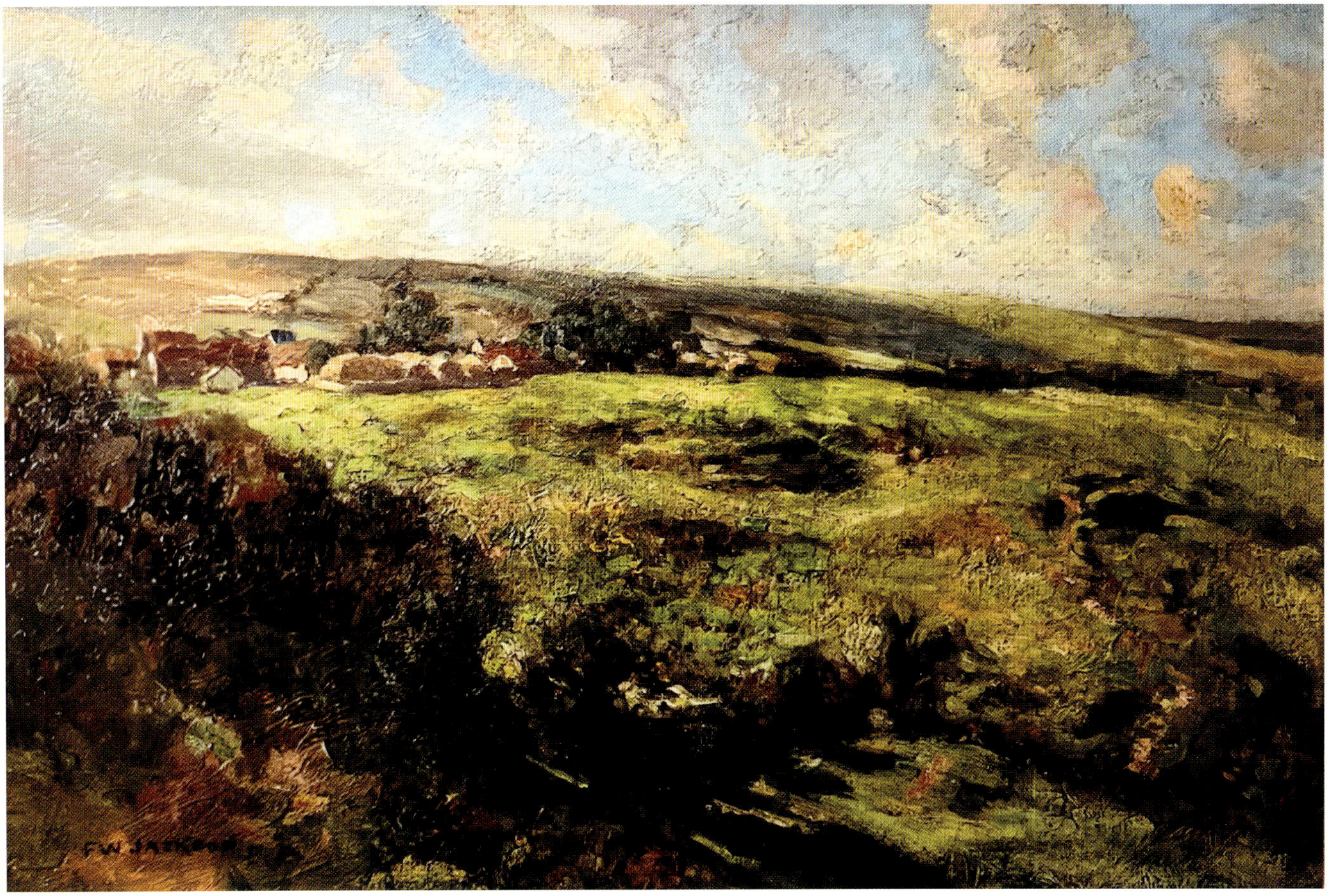

25. Fred Jackson arrived in Staithes in 1884, a year after the railway. His *Railway Sorting Office, Hinderwell* omits any sense of the concomitant modernisation it brought both for industry and tourism. In doing so Jackson anticipated the predilection of the other artists for avoiding this in all but their depictions of harbour life.

livelihood too. The technology that enabled mechanisation and the growth of industry in the area forced sail gradually to give way, first to steam and then to oil. Enhancements in materials, telegraphic communication, sonar and a range of fishing techniques – brought to the industry by greater national and international demand and competition – resulted in much larger scales of economy. New technology increasingly rendered the catching of fish feasible only to those with enhanced capital, refrigeration and transport capability.

This rapid sea change resulted, once again, in overfishing. This time many spawning grounds were also destroyed as well as fish stocks depleted, notwithstanding discoveries of areas such as the Silver Pits which intermittently provided harvests on a previously unheard-of scale. Royal Commissions were set up to address the issues, but, despite emphatic remonstrances from the inshore fishermen, little was done to prevent the trawlermen and larger companies from continuing to catch indiscriminate cargos of fish and to disturb the sea bed. Ironically, when fish stocks did finally realise the opportunity to rebound, during the wartime years from 1914, the major markets for salted fish in Europe and the

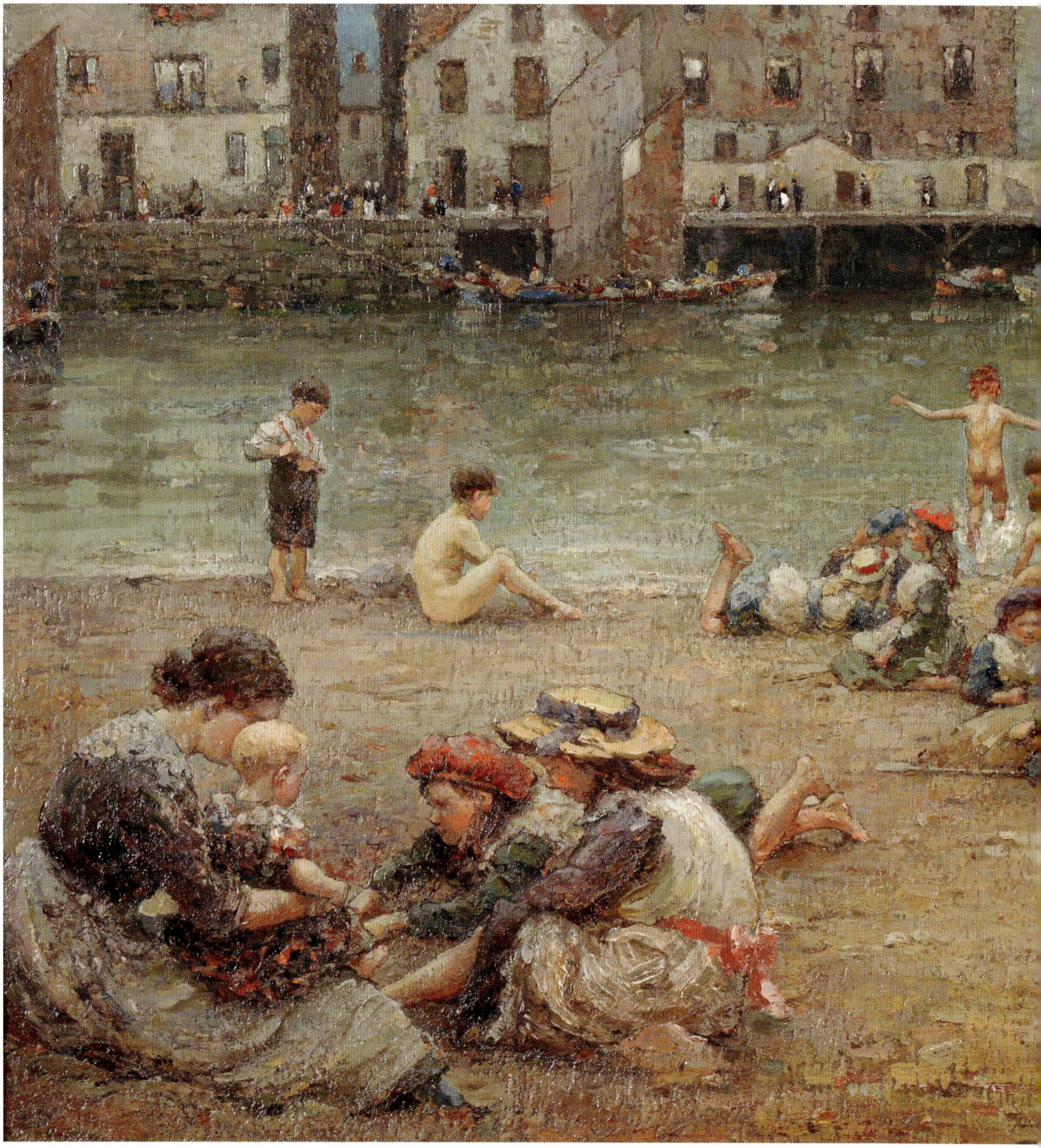

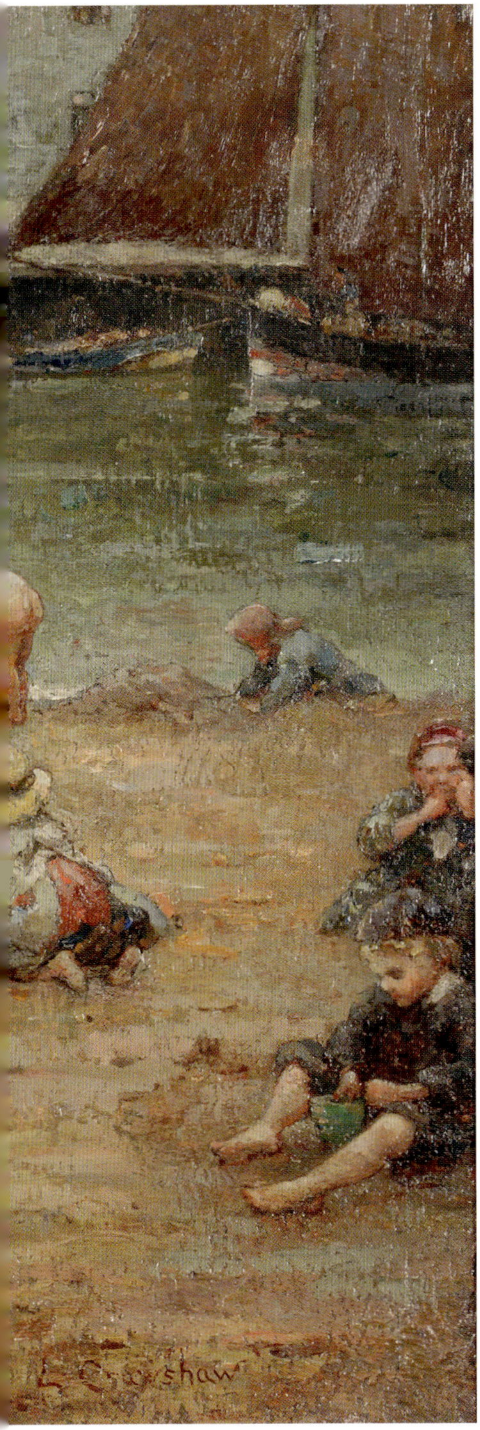

Baltic had collapsed, with ongoing turmoil from the Russian Revolution on the one hand and the failure of the German economy on the other.

Railways, initially introduced to ferry resources away from the ports and mines of the area, were to provide a partial reprieve. In an initially unintended consequence for their entrepreneurs, they generated a significant amount of paying customers who signed up to travel out to the coast. The numbers were remarkable: over 6,000 people travelled on the Whitby to Grosmont railway in its first three months.

As the requirement for natural resources shipped through the ports decreased, the human cargos from the large industrial centres of Lancashire and the West Riding of Yorkshire only increased. In the 30 years between 1840 and 1870 railway passenger numbers rose 20 times. Such growth was reflected from Tynemouth to the north, acting as a small-scale version of Brighton for the people of Newcastle, to Scarborough and Filey to the south, drawing upon their earlier reputations as spa towns and resorts.

The burgeoning tourist and holiday market, abetted by the growing efficiency and economy of transport, translated the middle-class market of the 1870s to the mass market of working-class day trippers towards the turn of the century. The development of infrastructure to serve it consequently became a priority, in the same way that it had for traditional industries. Responsibility for this moved from the landed gentry to either municipal councils or private enterprise, often in the form of Land companies, such as that formed by the Pease family of ironmasters at Saltburn.[20]

26. Lionel Crawshaw maintained a studio in Whitby for over 40 years, although he remained living in Doncaster. As with several fellow artists, he was drawn to paint attractive beach scenes such as *Whitby Holiday*, c. 1925, reflecting the increasing waves of tourists up and down the coast.

After improvements in sanitation and accommodation, a wide variety of entertainments were generated as part of the resorts' allure. Initial attractions such as museums and industrial sites 'as things of wonder' gave way to winter gardens, promenades, theatres, aquaria and piers, such as that at Saltburn, which was enabled by the technology employed in the construction of the railways.

Associated services expanded to cater to the visitors too. Among them was photography, with Frank Meadow Sutcliffe being one of at least a dozen in Whitby. Even Staithes boasted its own, H.C. Morley, while Brighton, the leading English resort, had almost 79 firms.

Towns that had established industries, such as Whitby, struggled to balance their requirements (often in decline) with the demands of the new tourism. However, Scarborough, with its two bays and spa history, was well placed to handle its domestic activity alongside the competing markets. Other smaller, more traditional communities, such as Staithes, Runswick and Robin Hood's Bay, could not take advantage; natural inlets with restricted cliff-top development and limited provision of water and sewerage, they remained relatively 'unspoiled' in comparison. Increasingly they featured as desirable destinations to middle-class visitors seeking to get off the beaten track and appreciate the 'quaint' local dress and customs, thus recalling the original eighteenth-century purposes for visiting the coast.

THE AUDIENCE AND MARKET FOR ART

Many of the artists of the Staithes Art Club, and those who became associated with them, formed part of this seasonal exodus to the coast. Most came from industrial towns such as Oldham – a pioneer in tourism terms – as well as Nottingham, Wakefield, Leeds and Bradford. The artists came from a range of social backgrounds. Some maintained a family tradition in the arts, from painting and photography to framing, teaching and industrial design, while others had switched from the professions – law, the military, medicine and the Church.

Though there were Yorkshiremen and women among them, it is hard to say – much as at other early colonies – that there were 'local' artists.[21] In addition, though there does not appear to have been a significant international component, there was certainly an international presence both within and without the Club. Whitby's tradition of hosting literary tourists, such as Henry James and James Russell Lowell, served to attract pre-eminent artists such as John Singer Sargent and other 'colonists', for instance Walter Langley, one of the founders of the Newlyn 'school'. The American artist Winslow Homer spent 18

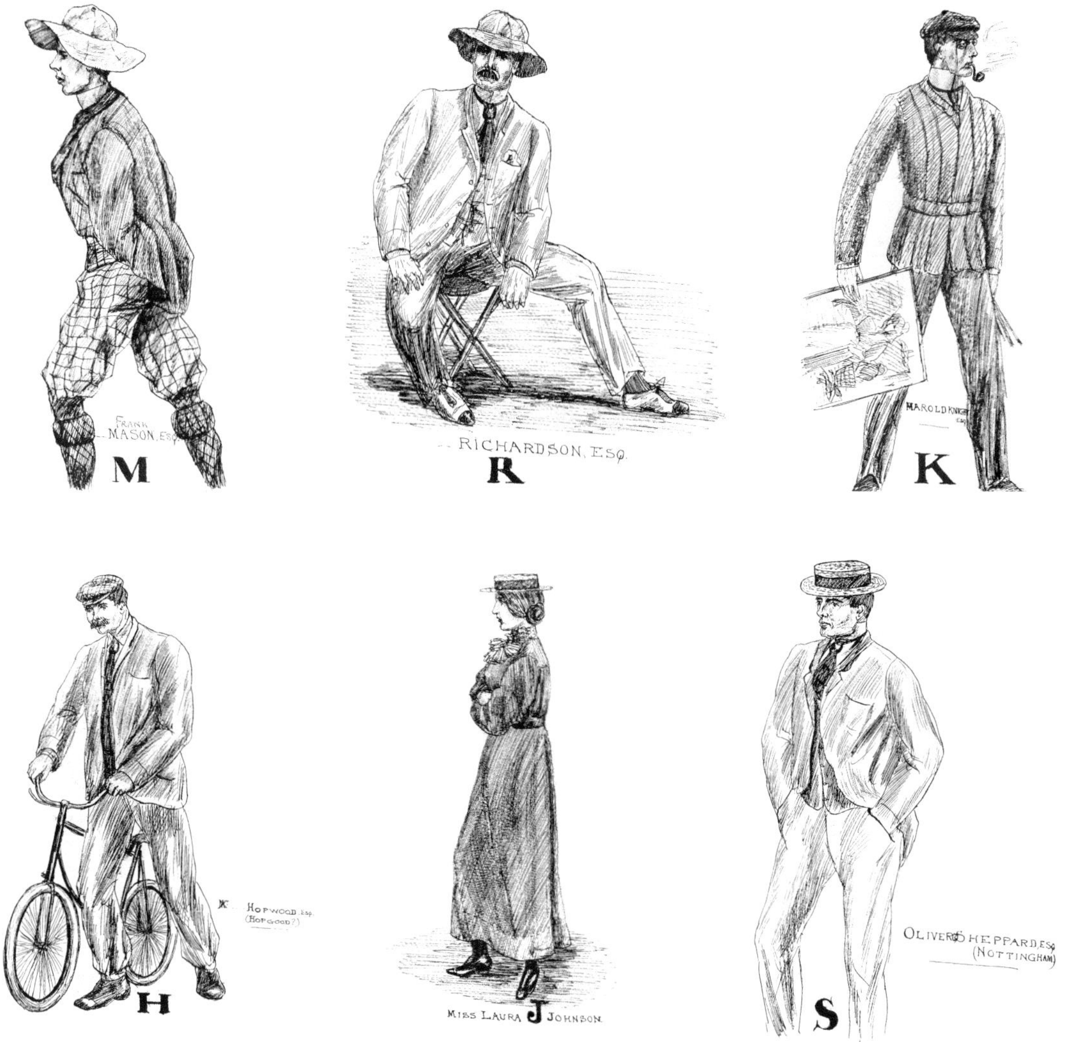

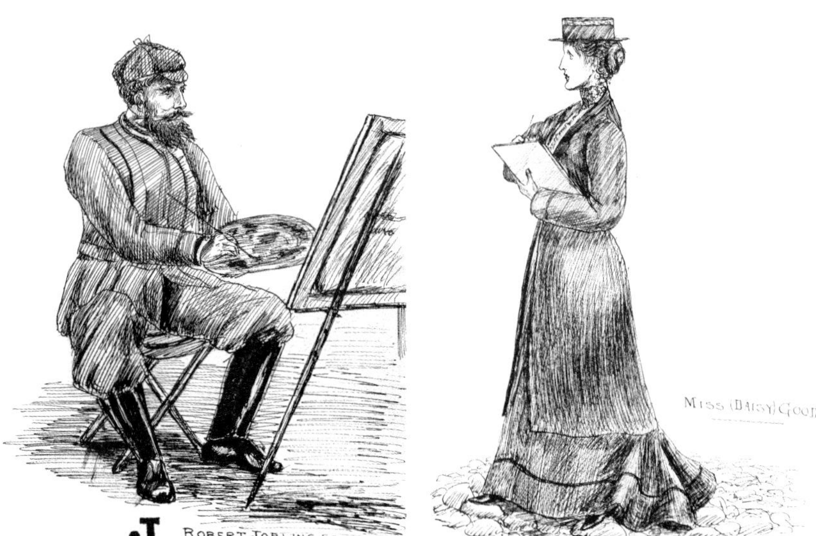

27. In her diary of 1901, Enid Pease Robinson recalls Laura Johnson's request to share her caricatures of Staithes Club Artists. These sketches, many of which are published for the first time,explain why Enid demurred, appended as they are with personal notes that flattered or criticised her subjects.

months at Cullercoats (just north of Newcastle), but he also painted up and down the coast as far south as Flamborough Head. Meanwhile William Brymner from Canada, Arthur Burgess from Australia, Sydney Lough Thompson from New Zealand and the group's own Leandro Garrido and Paul Politachi all painted at Runswick Bay and Staithes.

Reacting to an unprecedented public interest in art, both in terms of exhibition viewing and in the celebrity status increasingly awarded to the top London artists, many aspiring students and amateurs identified a true professional career path. Nevertheless several struggled to obtain family approval for a role that still hovered on the fringes of acceptability. Henry Hopwood, Harold Knight and Rowland Hill were prime examples of this, while artists such as John Bowman, John Spence Ingall and Robert Jobling had to work alongside their studies. Others, including Ernest Dade, Frank Mason, Frederick Richardson and Lionel Crawshaw, embarked on other careers or, in the case of Charles Mackie and Albert Stevens, enrolled in other studies before they could realise their desire to focus on painting.

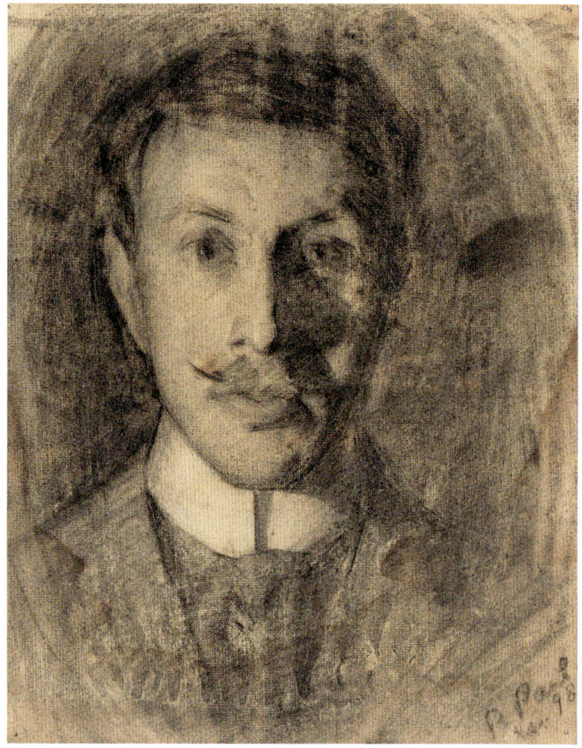

28. Like Rowland Henry Hill, Paul Paul attended Herkomer's Academy in Hertfordshire. The son of Greek immigrants from Constantinople, he attempted a variety of careers before settling on that of an artist. With provenance from the artist's family, this is thought to be a self-portrait, dating from 1898.

Though examples of success presented themselves, and promising opportunities did arise, many quickly became dissatisfied with what they perceived as an overbearing establishment. Secession, or the threat of secession, from the mainstream of English art education and exhibitions proved an insistent trend. The Staithes artist Fred Jackson was a founder member of the New English Art Club; Charles Mackie was instrumental in securing success for the new Society of Scottish Artists, despite opposition from the established Royal Scottish Academy. The progressive Frank Meadow Sutcliffe also signed up to the commitments of the 'Linked Ring' in opposition to the photographic establishment.[22]

Such moves incorporated a rejection of the established Victorian notion of painting as narrative and part of a 'social mission'. Study abroad, either in Paris or in similar academies on the continent, resulted in a shift in techniques to complement this new outlook. This development was practically furthered and developed by extended 'sketching' tours, which allowed painters to establish themselves out of doors in remote locations. There they might take full advantage of the availability of a new range of colours and the innovation of ready-mixed paint in tubes.

This disconnection from the 'ideals' of society, however, resulted in a rapid contraction of the art public over the latter part of the century. The revolving cycle of fashionable taste moved the market away from its traditional ornate, mid-Victorian template towards a sparer aesthetic, with increasing emphasis on the combination of fine and decorative arts.

Even the highest profile of established artists changed their practice, with those of the status of Holl, Fildes and Sargent working at frantic rates to answer their new market for portraits.[23] Others, such as their fellow Royal Academician Hubert Herkomer, answered the call of teaching and the growth in demand for art schools from amateur artists; he established an academy which several of the Art Club members attended.[24] In the regions many of the members were themselves attached to the local municipal schools or even, as with Owen Bowen, set up their own.

Brought up with the idea of a strong and vital market, artists now increasingly faced the reverse. Henry Hopwood who, like Owen Bowen and others, had found work as lithographer and engraver was sufficiently discouraged by a slump in the market and lack of sales for his exhibited work to travel abroad. In Australia he sought fresh audiences and improved commercial markets.

Those who stayed found themselves seeking new patrons as buyers for a new wave of painting, to which they were committed by the new techniques and training they had followed. Some were helped in this by dealerships in London that opened to promote artists with shows, following the anti-Academy examples of the Grosvenor and its successor, the New Gallery. Others made the most of regional audiences, exploiting family connections or the social networks provided by clubs or local exhibiting organisations.

Regional patrons certainly did exist, buoyed up by wealth created by waves of industrialisation. Through their acts of philanthropy new museums began to be established – prestigious adornments to the various towns and cities that formed their manufacturing base. The process of creating and then handing over their personal collections was encouraged by the example of the Chantrey Bequest, established to secure works of art for a national collection.

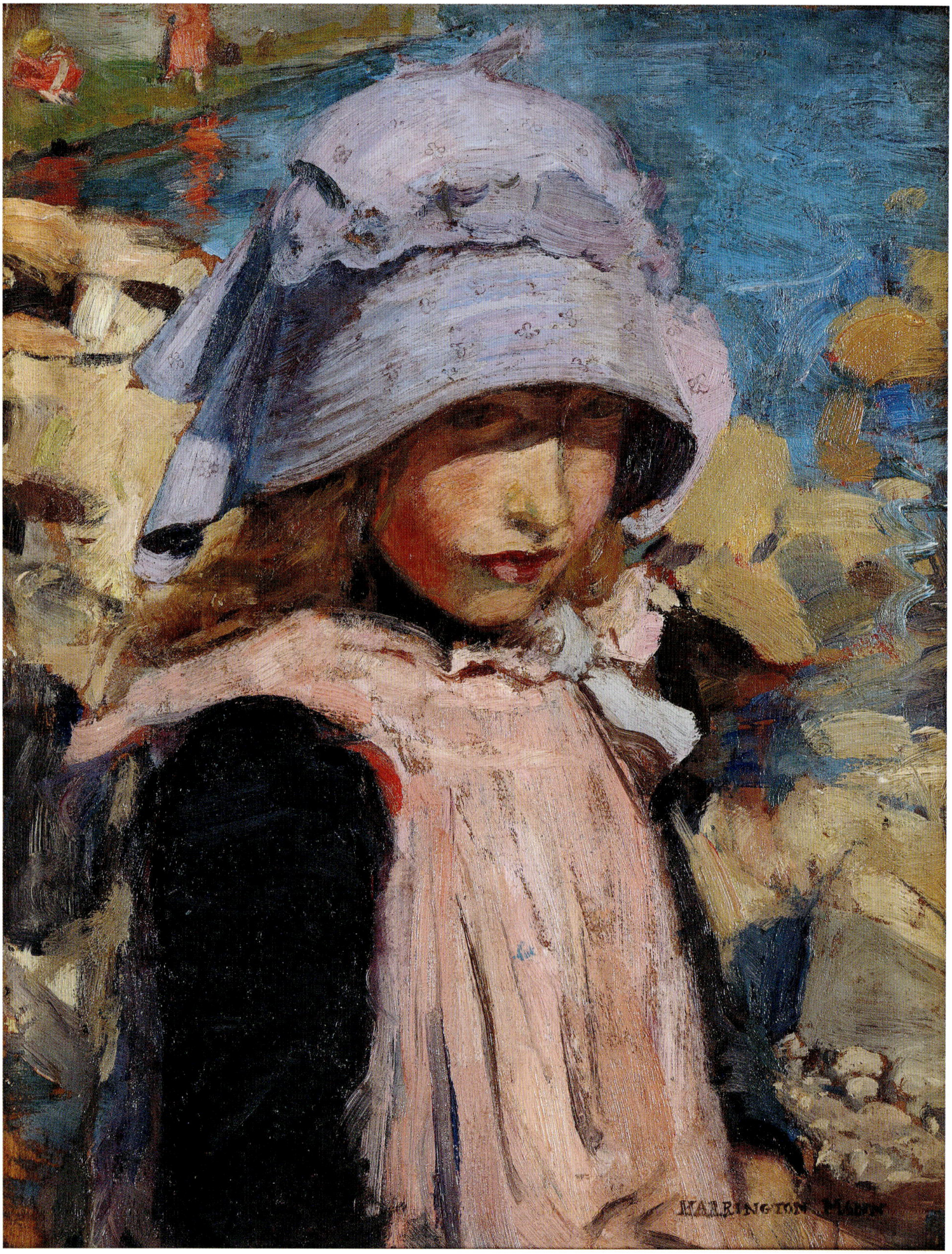
HARRINGTON MANN

29. Never an Art Club member, nor properly a Glasgow 'Boy', Harrington Mann nevertheless maintained a consistent presence in Staithes from the 1880s to 1900. His ongoing connection with the progressive elements of Scottish art are evidenced by this stylish portrait, thought to be titled *A Fishergirl*, from 1899.

To this collection, and to others across the regions, paintings by Staithes' artists were added, recognising their contribution to the contemporary art of the day. Members of the Club such as Mark Senior even became involved alongside artists and agents, such as Sir George Clausen, in their organisation and display.

Yet as their progress was affirmed and the Staithes Art Club formed, the first major exhibitions of Van Gogh and Picasso were being held. Exhibitions in London, increasingly dominated by the post-impressionists, served to draw the art world's eye away to the urban avant-garde, where it has for a large part remained.

A sustained reappraisal of the work of artists' colonies in general has been slow to gather momentum. Not until the latter part of the twentieth century have the Newlyn school artists, or those who painted at Walberswick or on the Scottish coasts, gained critical acclaim. It has continued to prove the case for those who painted on the north-east coast, but this book is yet another step forward, it is hoped, in acknowledgement and support of their aims and efforts.

ENDNOTES

4 Knight, L., *Oil Paint and Grease Paint*, 1936, 92. In his interview with the *Yorkshire Evening Post* in 1939, Rowland Hill also reminisces that the Institute built in Runswick Bay, with help from the artists, was used as a concert hall and studio.

5 Knight, L., *Oil Paint and Grease Paint,* 1936, 92.

6 Dr Peter Phillips records that James Booth was congratulated by Winston Churchill on his first Royal Academy exhibit as the latter was 'en route to the Boer War' in 1896. Phillips, *The Staithes Group*, 1993, 33.

7 *Whitby Gazette*, 1 March 1901. In Howard, J., *Staithes: Chapters from the History of a Seafaring Town*, 2000, 246.

8 Knight, L., *Oil Paint and Grease Paint*, 1936.

9 Freethy, Ron, *Memories of the Yorkshire Fishing Industry*, 2012, 111.

10 Letter from Robert Jobling to son Joseph Jobling, 13 June 1915. In Millard, John, *A Romance with the Northeast – Robert & Isa Jobling*, 1992, 52.

11 See *The Magazine of Art* for an example of liberalism personified in fishing community.

12 Port Mulgrave was situated just south of Staithes on Sir Charles Palmer's lands.

13 Matthew, H. (ed.), *The Gladstone Diaries*, vol. VIII, 1982, 29.

14 'The Hand of the Crusader' was published in 1899 in *St Peter's,* a Catholic sixpenny magazine.

15 Author of *The Riddle of the Sands,* published in 1903, Erskine Childers became a fervent supporter for Irish Home Rule. He was executed in 1922 for his activities in this regard.

16 Slater, Robert, 'Artists' Colonies in Staithes and Runswick Bay', 2010, unpublished PhD thesis, University of Leicester, 99.

17 As the main town of the region, with connections to the Staithes and Runswick Bay communities, economic issues affected the two villages as a matter of course.

18 *Whitehall Shipyard: Thomas Turnbull and Sons*. In *Graces Guide to British Industrial History*, 2025. www.gracesguide.co.uk.

19 Howard, John, *Staithes: Chapters from the history of a seafaring town*, 2000, 79.

20 Enid Pease Robinson, the diarist who witnessed the first of the Staithes Art Club's exhibitions (see Chapter 1), seems likely to have been a member of this extended family.

21 E. E. Anderson was born in Whitby to a family in the art business.

22 Harker, Margaret, *The Linked Ring: The Secession Movement in Photography in Britain 1892–1910*, 1979.

23 Sir Frank Holl, Sir Luke Fildes and John Singer Sargent were three of the pre-eminent portraitists of their day.

24 Rowland Henry Hill and Paul Paul, members of the Staithes Art Club, both attended Herkomer's Academy in Bushey, Hertfordshire.

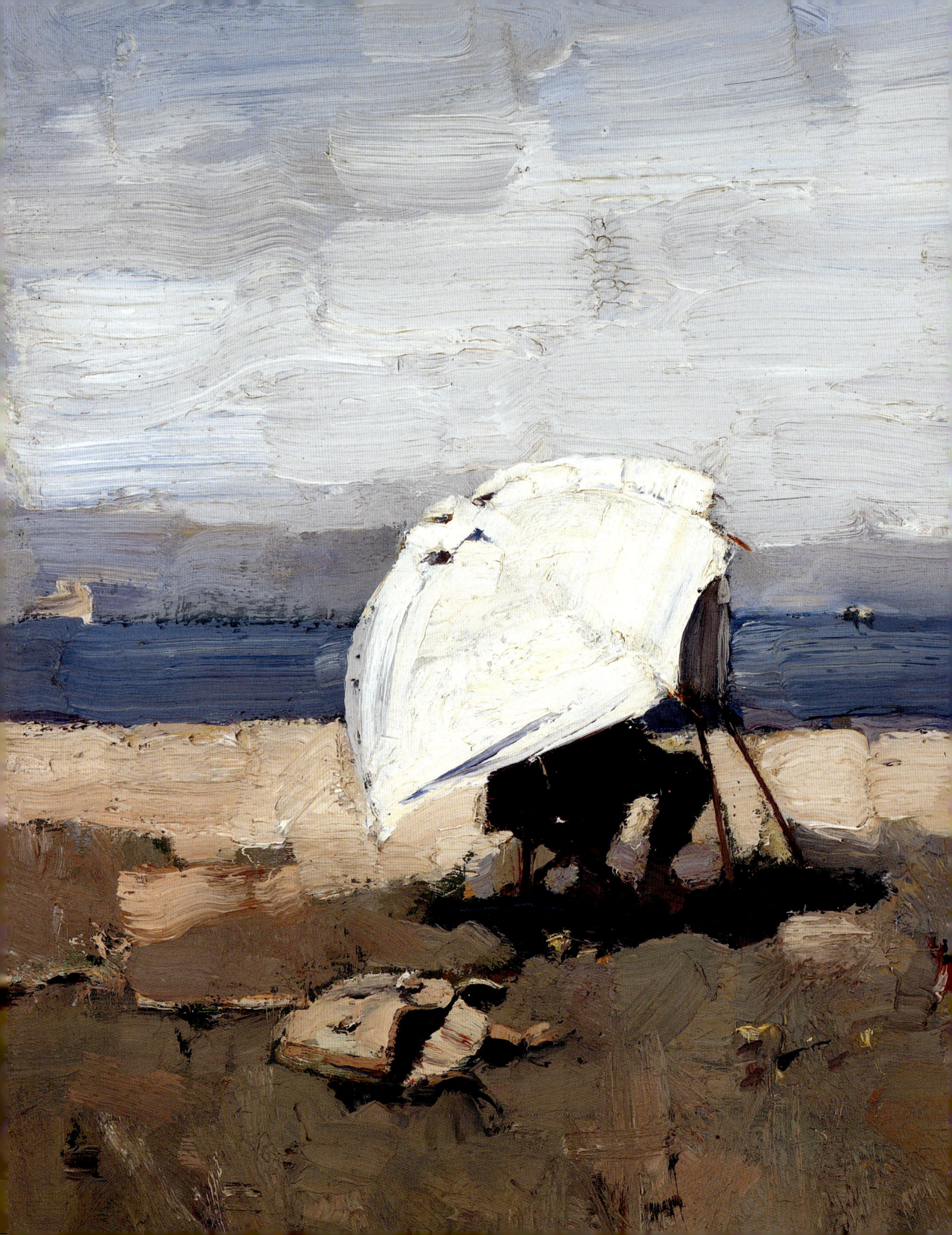

CHAPTER 1

THE STAITHES ART CLUB

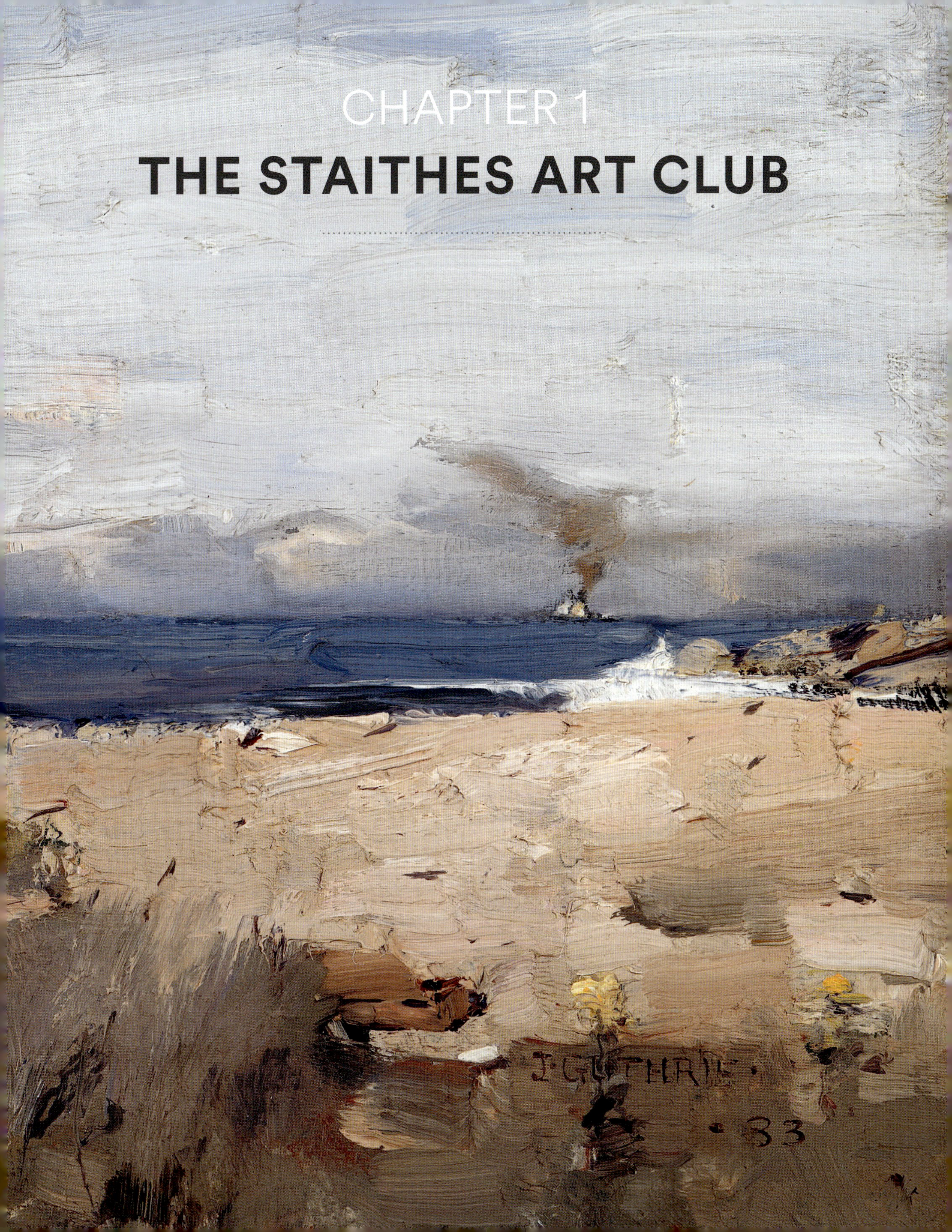

Previous spread: 30. James Guthrie left Glasgow to become the mainstay of the colony at Cockburnspath, staying year-round in the bleak village on Scottish east coast. *Hard At It*, a work of 1883, encapsulates the contemporary artists' situation in terms of experience, subject matter and technique.

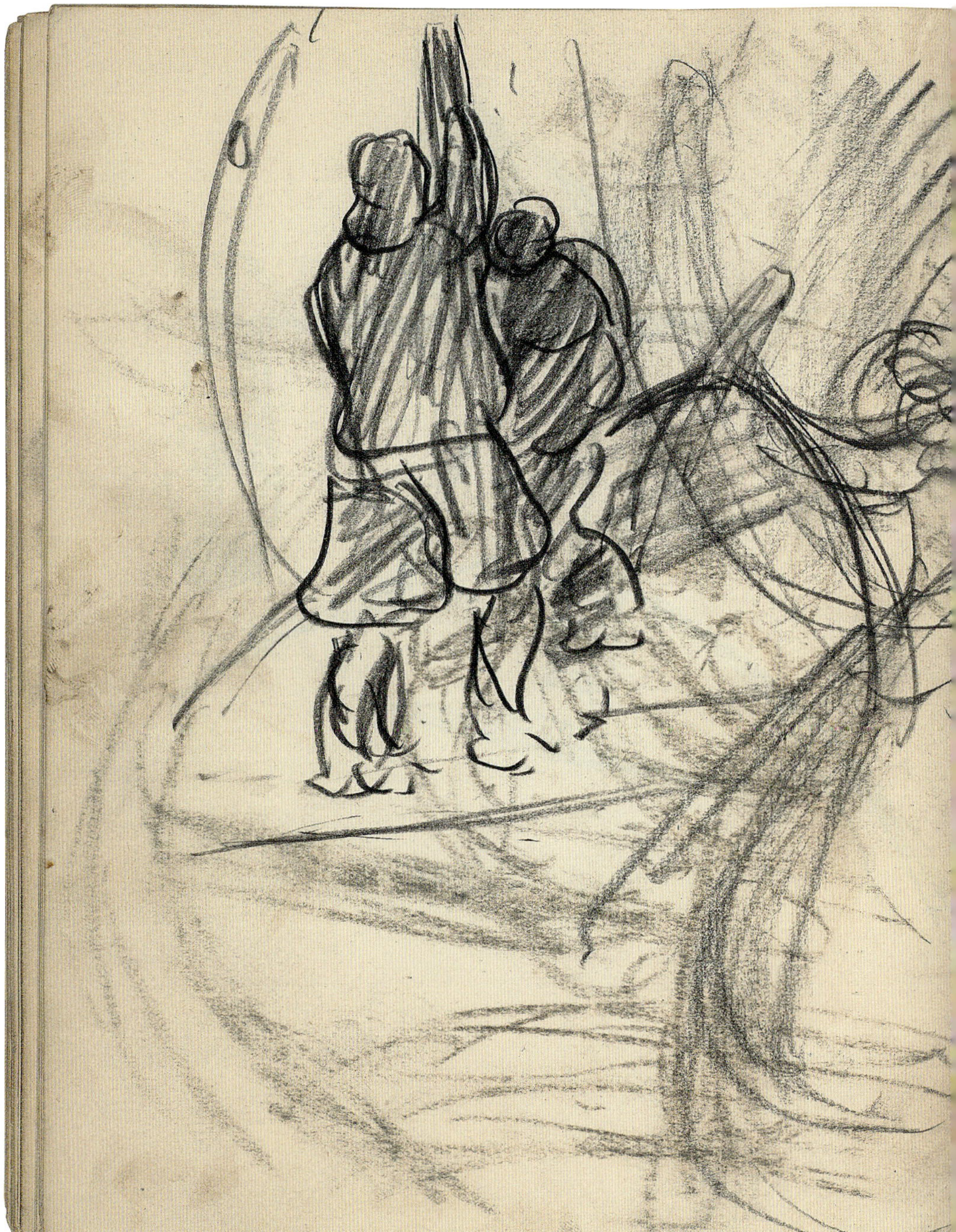

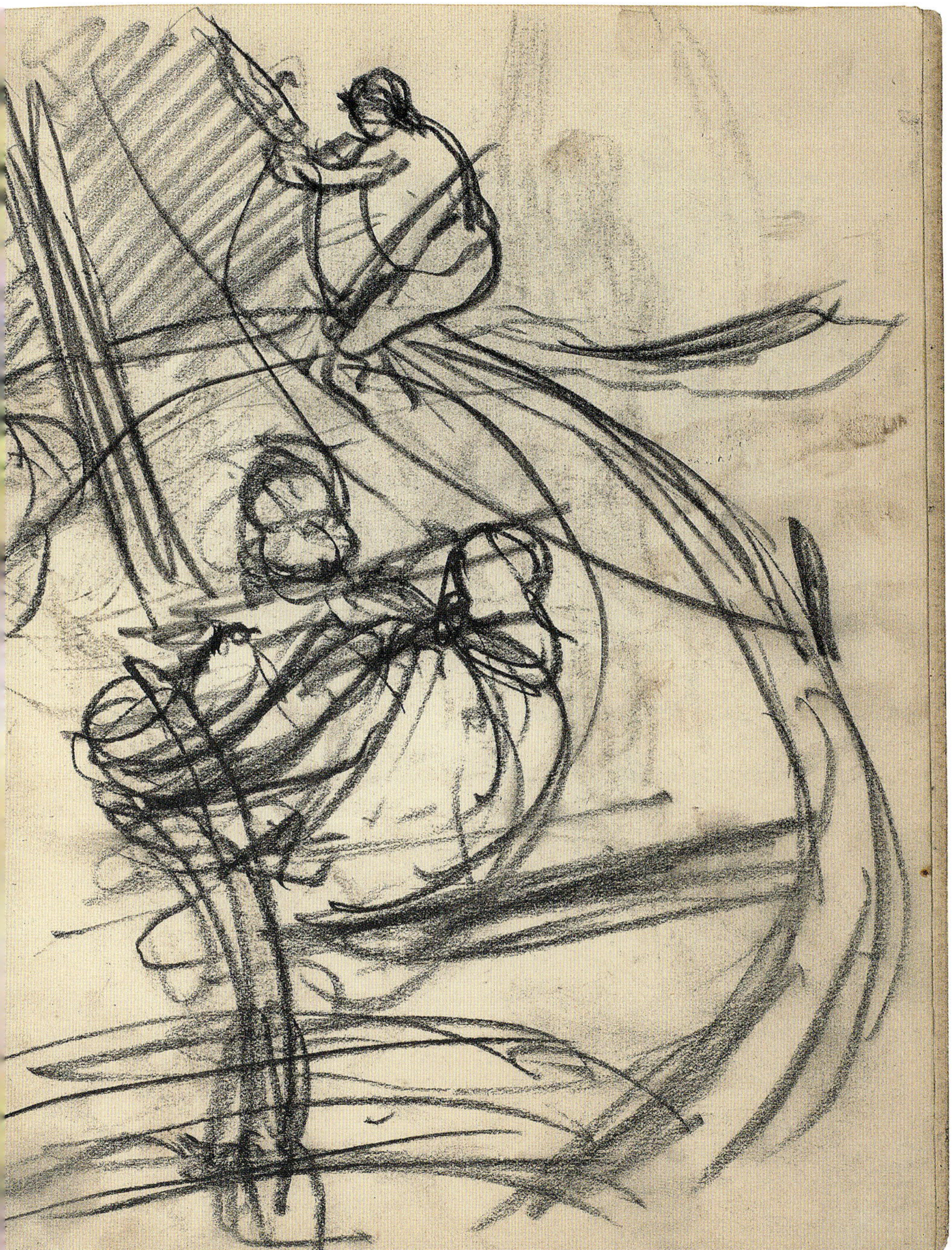

31. Grandson of the famed marine artist William Clarkson Stansfield, Joseph Bagshawe was as happy on board ship as on land. Images such as this undated sketch were produced from his own yacht and fisherman's cobles, as well as the larger yawls and cargo boats in which he sailed around Britain and across the Baltic.

CHAPTER 1

THE STAITHES ART CLUB

> A cold, dull, cheerless morning which ripened into a violent northern gale in the afternoon and evening. The first Exhibition of the Staithes Art Club was to have opened in the afternoon, at about half-past two or a quarter to three, but there wasn't any definite opening on account of the storm.[25]

> I used the big room above in the Institute building for a time until it was turned into a pictures exhibition, to which we all sent our sketches. A handsome poster was hung at the street door and nearly all the visitors who passed paid their threepence to come in and sometimes even bought a picture.[26]

So read the only two direct reports of the exhibition at the Staithes Fisherman's Institute in 1901, the first of three that were staged in the village from which the Club took its name.

The former quotation, a contemporary diary excerpt, goes on to detail a number of those who attended and confirms the supposition that Joseph Bagshawe's fiancée Mildred Turnbull was intended to open the show. She was the daughter of Thomas Turnbull, a Club vice-president and a prominent local shipbuilder.[27]

The diary's author, Enid Pease Robinson, describes borrowing the entrance fee from her mother and seeing 'a whole troupe of men' at the exhibition. They included Bagshawe himself, Fred Mayor and a [Mr] Brown, as well as Ernest and Alfred Rigg; three of them founding Club members. The diary also describes how, three days earlier, other likely exhibitors

32. Enid Pease Robinson studied art in Scarborough and seems to have been a regular visitor to the area. Her romantic musings about the two Ernests, Rigg and Dade, form the backdrop in her diary of 1901 to her descriptions and caricatures of the artists and their life in Staithes.

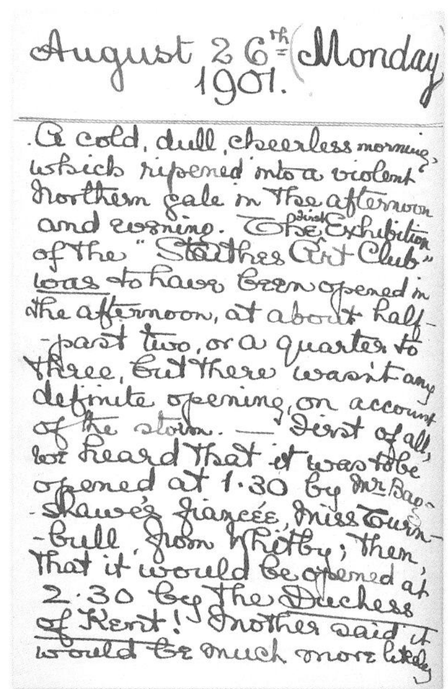
August 26th (Monday) 1901.
A cold, dull, cheerless morning, which ripened into a violent northern gale in the afternoon and evening. The first Exhibition of the "Staithes Art Club" was to have been opened in the afternoon, at about half-past two, or a quarter to three, but there wasn't any definite opening, on account of the storm. — First of all, we heard that it was to be opened at 1.30 by Mr Bagshawe's fiancée, Miss Turnbull, from Whitby; then that it would be opened at 2.30 by the Duchess of Kent! Mother said it would be much more likely

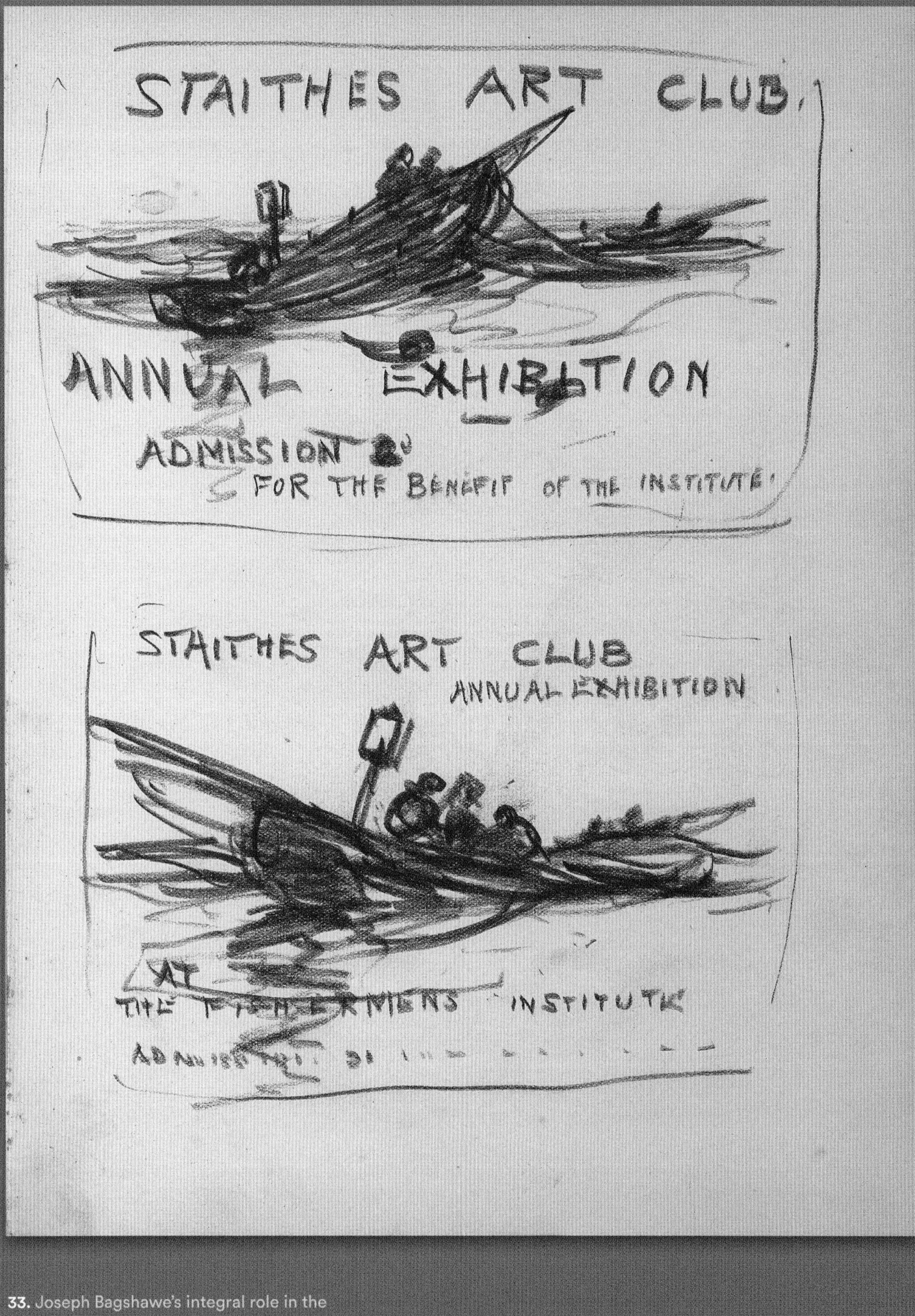

33. Joseph Bagshawe's integral role in the establishment of the Art Club – including these poster designs, dating from c. 1901 – kept pace with plans for his wedding into the Turnbull family. His social connections encouraged wealthy local figures to act as Club patrons and several artists to attend his celebrations.

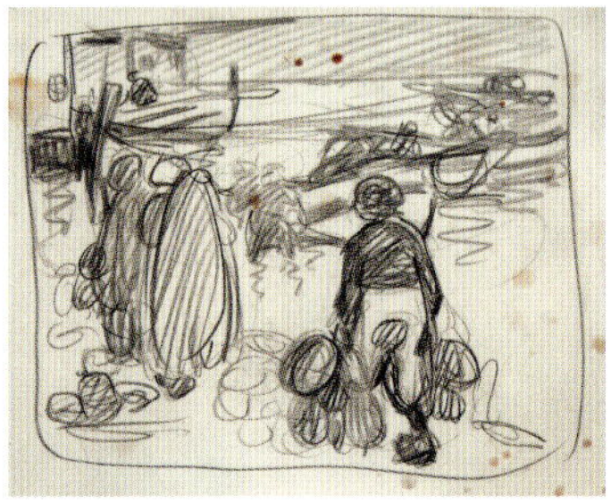
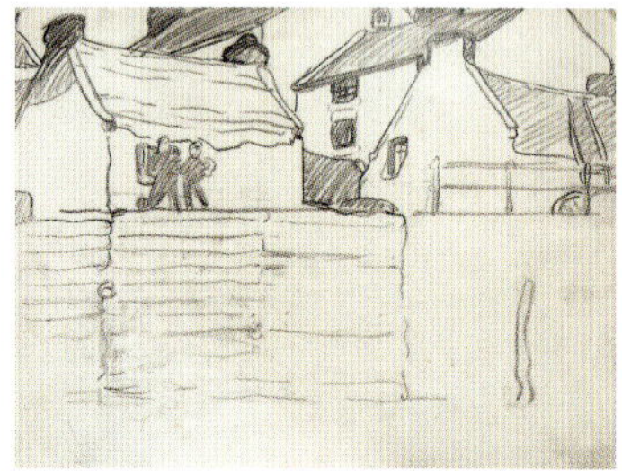
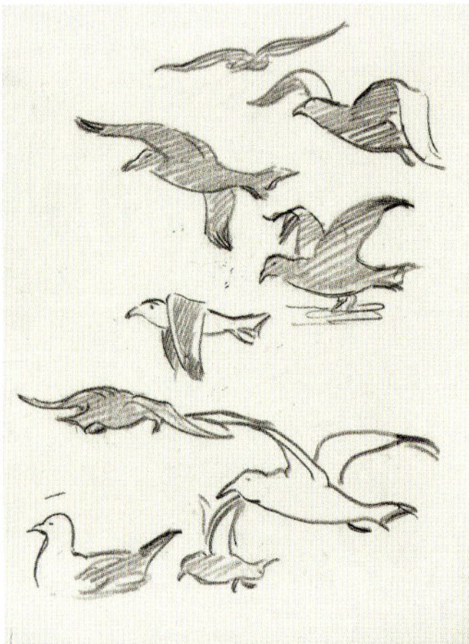
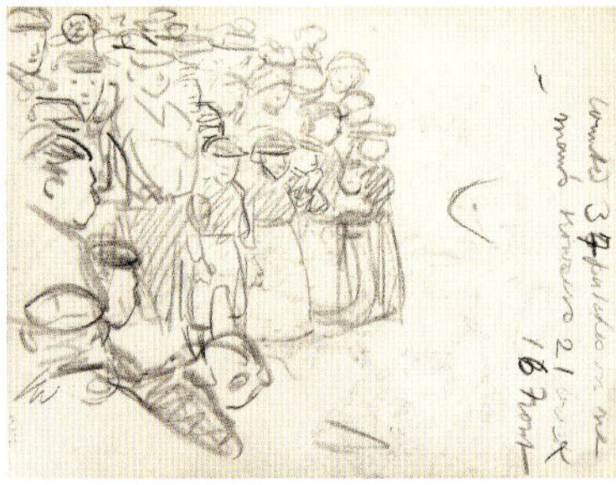
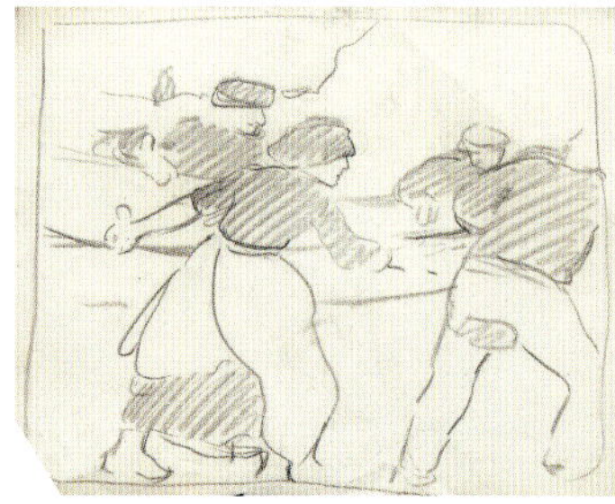
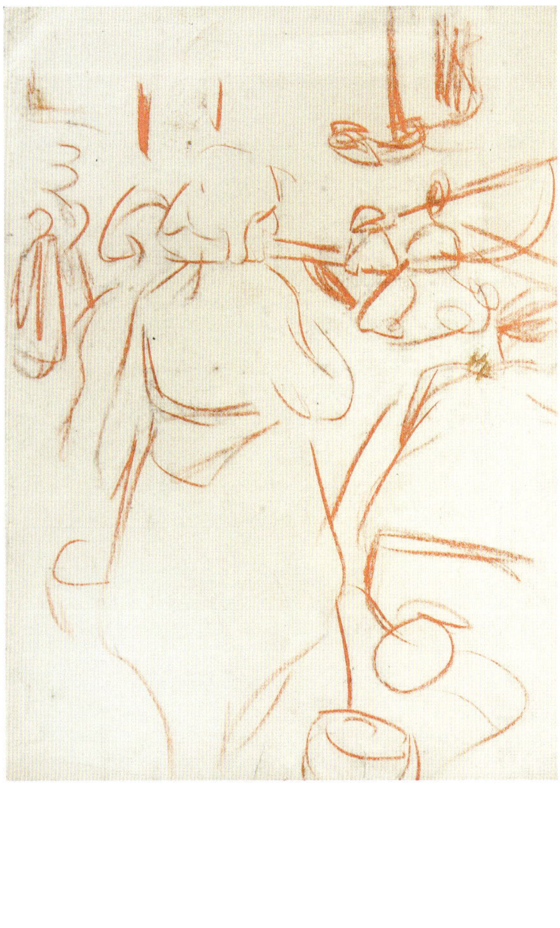
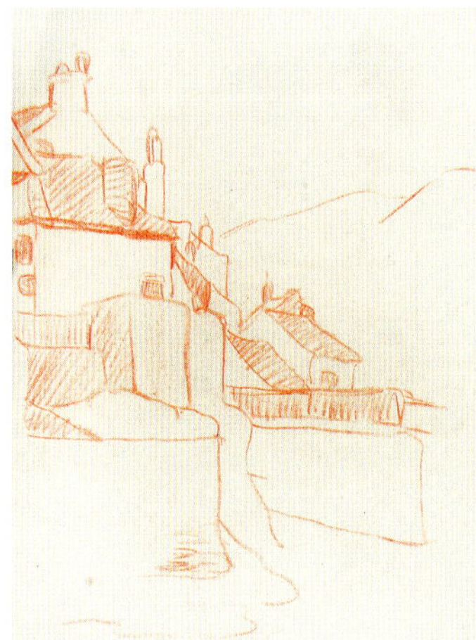

34. Laura Knight recalled in her 1930s memoir that only one sketchbook survived from her time at Staithes, though she drew constantly and always had one about her. In these untitled leaves (c. 1898 to 1903) she captured diverse aspects of village life and sometimes noted specific details: ['Counted 37 patches on a man's trousers this morning'].

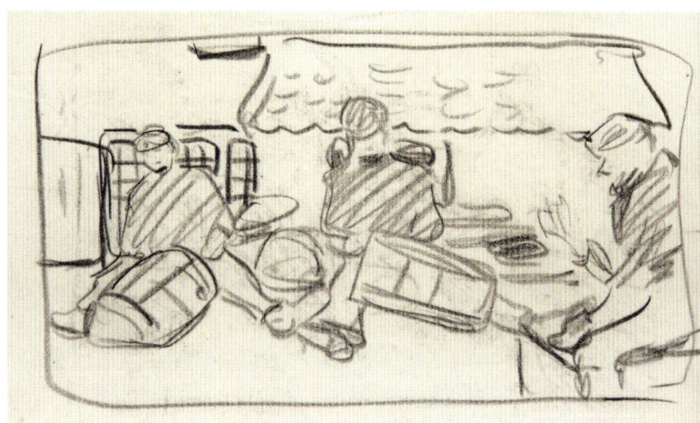

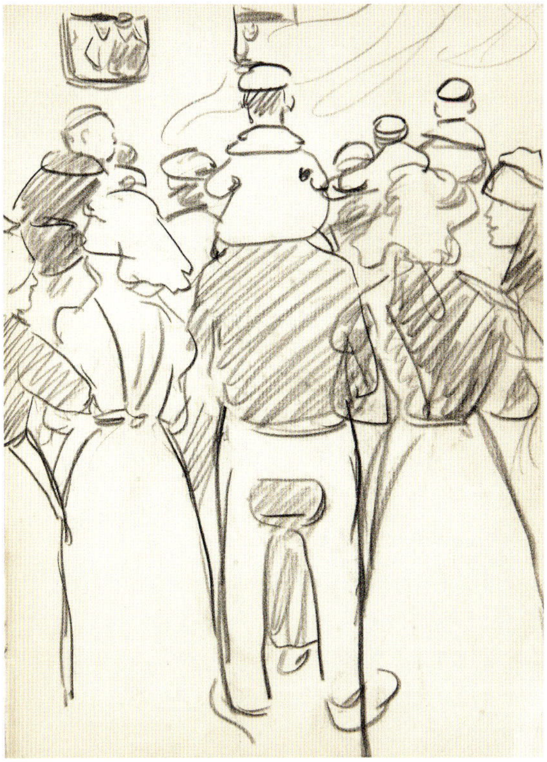
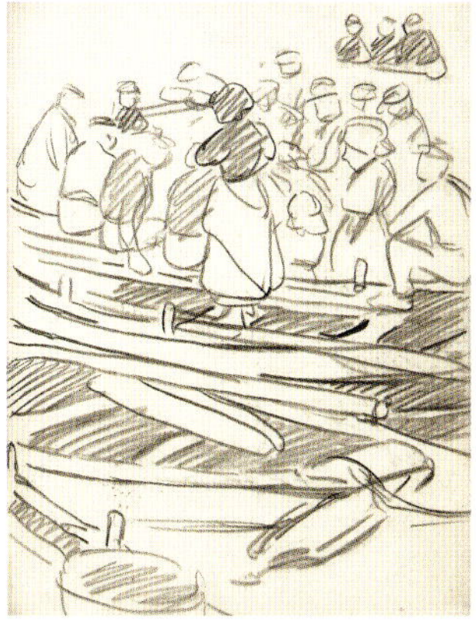
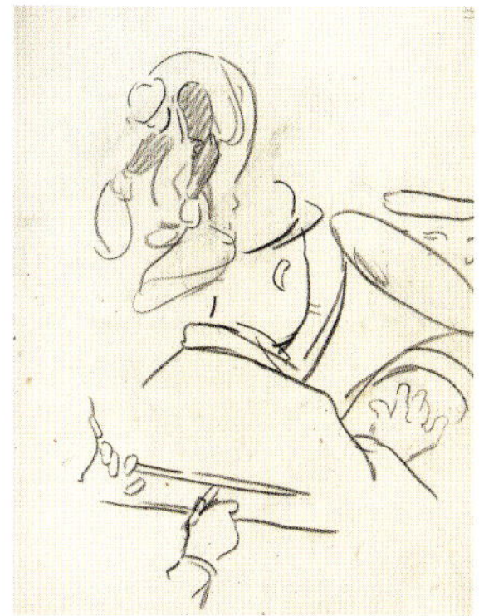
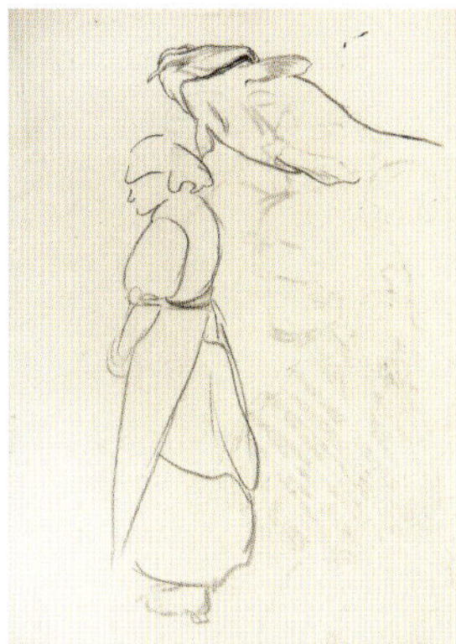
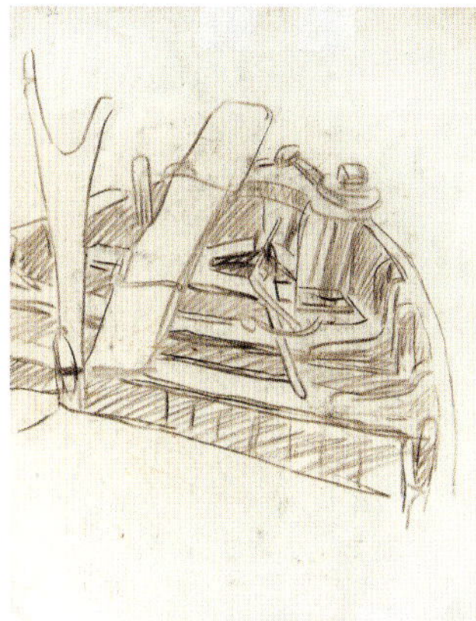
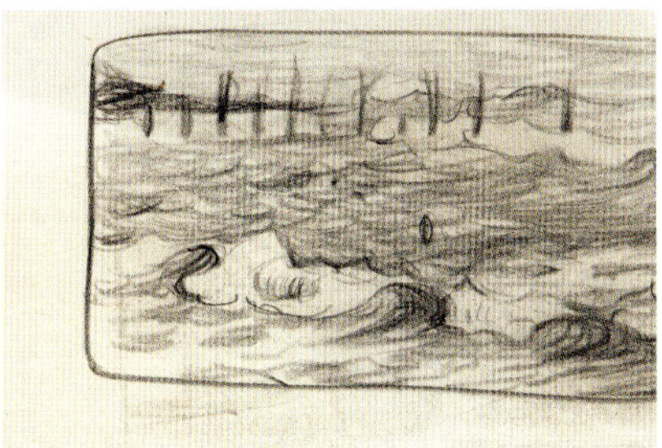
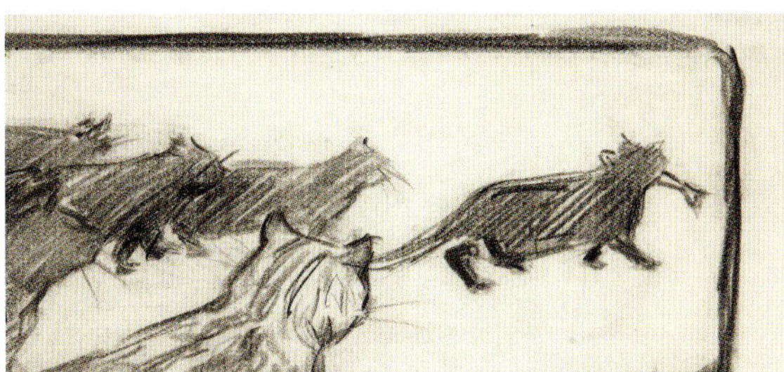
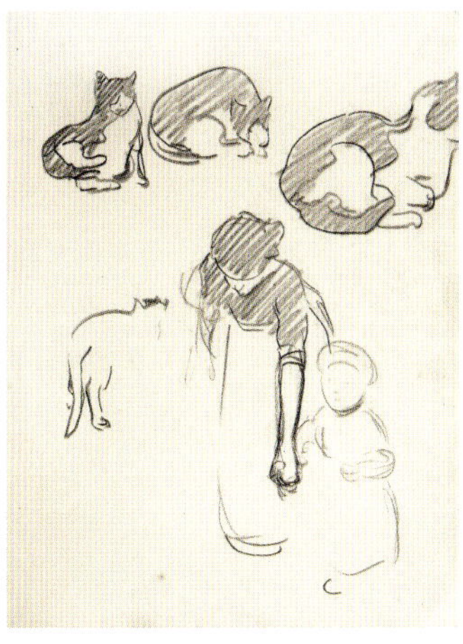
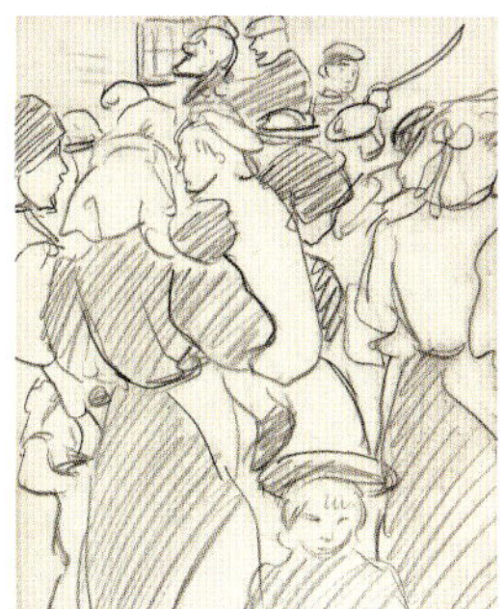

were in the village. A game of cricket had been arranged between the 'Whitby Visitors' and a side of artists captained by Mayor. Playing for the artists' team were Arthur Friedenson and his brother, Harold Knight, Frederick Richardson, George Swinstead, Bagshawe and Brown again, as well as another 'new artist whose name I do not know'.[28]

Robinson had been invited to the match by Laura Johnson, whose studio she had visited that morning; it abutted the house where she was staying on Church Street and there she had met both Johnson's sister Cissie (Sissy) and Ettie Knight.

Opening on Monday 26 August 1901, the exhibition was staged in the latter half of the holiday season. This was a busy time for the coastal resorts and a moment when most artists of the time would have been on their summer sketching trips. There seems to be no clear evidence of these artists showing at alternative venues in the immediate area, with the exception of one brief notice – eliciting no press review – four years later. This appeared in the *Whitby Gazette* of 1904, which advertised:

> A Small Exhibition of Sketches and Drawings in Holland by Mr. H. S. Hopwood and Mr. and Mrs. Harold Knight is now on view and will remain open until 22nd. September at "The Studio", adjoining Mr. Hopwood's house at Hinderwell, near the station.[29]

The second excerpt is taken from Laura Knight's memoir of 1936. Although written over 30 years later, she accurately records details at the time – as will be shown elsewhere – and goes on to confirm not only her ambitions for the exhibit but also her own lack of success in submissions to the Royal Academy to that point.

THE YORKSHIRE SCENE

Some Art Club exhibitors, however, had already shown successfully in London, as well as at other regional venues. Three years after the opening exhibition, all the pictures from the 1904 Art Club exhibition were sent *en masse* to form part of the Yorkshire Union of Artists autumn displays, staged in Hull. The Union, arguably the largest such regional organisation in the country, had been established for around 13 years, its shows well-represented with work by future Club members.

Opposite: 35. A native of Bradford, Ernest Rigg is perhaps better known for his later landscape oil sketches and scenes. However, his earlier work contains fine portraiture, here displayed in *A Fireside Read* (c. 1895), which showcases an additional finesse with lighting and drapery.

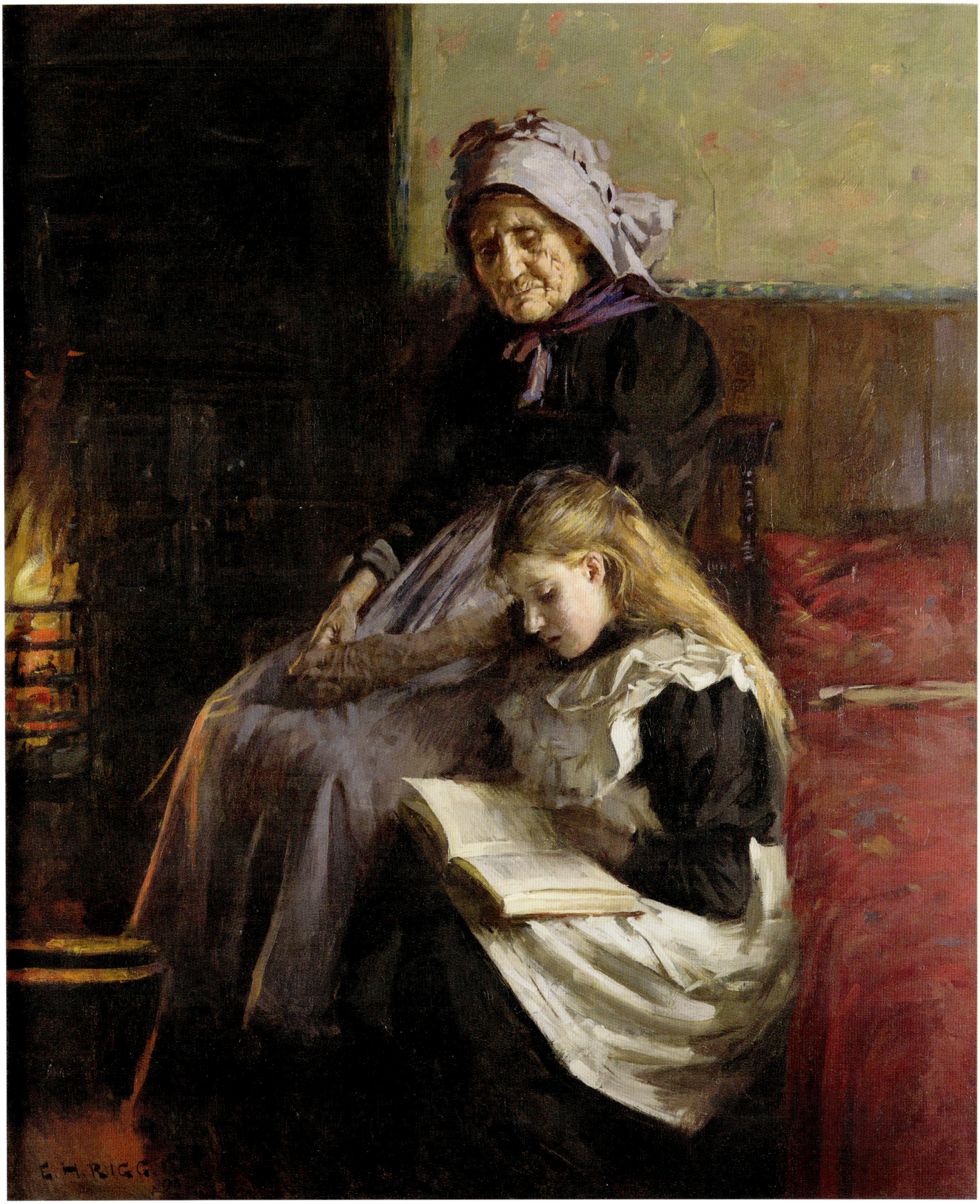
E. H. RIGG

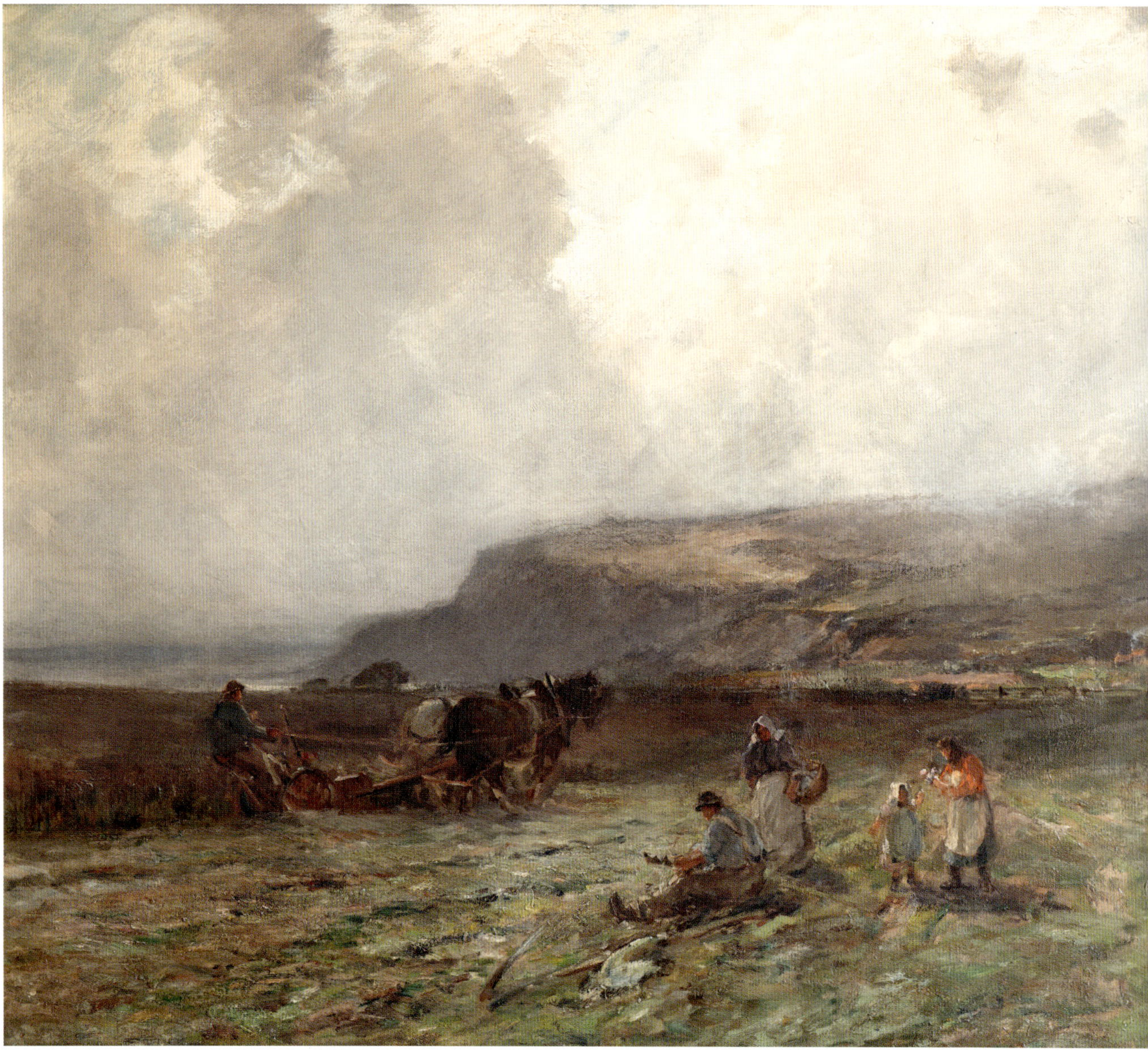

36. Initially taught by W. G. Foster, Owen Bowen set up on his own in Leeds and rented a cottage at Robin Hood's Bay from 1898. A mobile studio, complete with stove, enabled him to cope with the variable weather, here depicted in *Showery Haytime at Robin Hood's Bay*. Dating from 1903, this is one of Bowen's largest paintings from one of his finest periods.

Starting in Bradford, with Ernest and Alfred Rigg in attendance, the annual display featured in cities and towns across Yorkshire.[30] Owen Bowen was aged only 14 when he first showed but was not to commit for long; a disagreement with the secretary resulted in his expulsion from the Union three years later. Others displayed greater longevity; Lionel Crawshaw, Charles Elmhirst, Arthur Friedenson, John Spence Ingall and Joseph Terry all sent works consistently, while William Gilbert Foster, Percy Teasdale and Fred Jackson were all members of the Union's council or elected vice-presidents during the 1890s.[31]

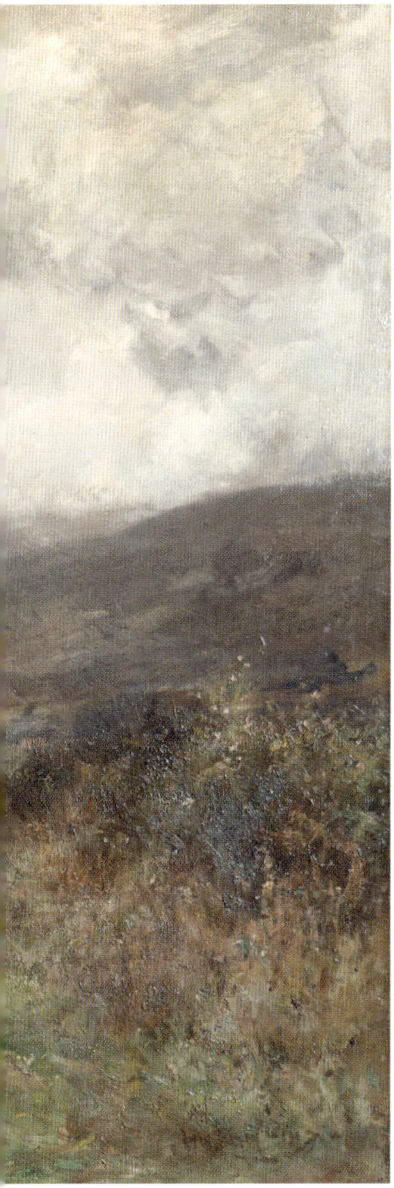

Harrogate, York and Leeds also acted as venues before the Union settled on the coast in Whitby for a period of four years (1894–8). This seems to have coincided with what is acknowledged as the beginning of the most intense period of activity in Staithes and the surrounding area. After the show moved on from Whitby, albeit with a brief return to the area at Scarborough in 1900, artists who either lived or regularly worked in the area might well have felt the absence of a local focus for their combined work. As a result, the Art Club members seem then to have focused their attention away from the Union. However, the two came together in 1905 with, as has been noted, exhibited works making their way from one to the other in Hull in 1904.

In line with other so-called artists' 'colonies', there seem to have been almost no local artists who were members of the Club. Edward Anderson should probably be considered the exception to the rule. He was born in Whitby to a family whose jet business turned into a fine art business, and in whose family's gallery the 4th Staithes Club Art Exhibition was held. The Andersons opened further premises, *The Rembrandt*, in 1905 and not only represented Staithes Club members, but also regularly displayed works by a range of local painters.

Among these artists were Frank Rousse, Frank Wasley and various Weatherills, then the most prominent artistic family of the area. Their central figure, George, born in Staithes, was still alive when the first members of the Club began painting there and worked and exhibited almost exclusively within a short distance of Whitby. He taught his four children – Mary, Sarah, Elizabeth and Richard – to paint, and all in turn worked and showed locally up until the First World War. Their subjects, however, ranged further afield – as far as Scandinavia.

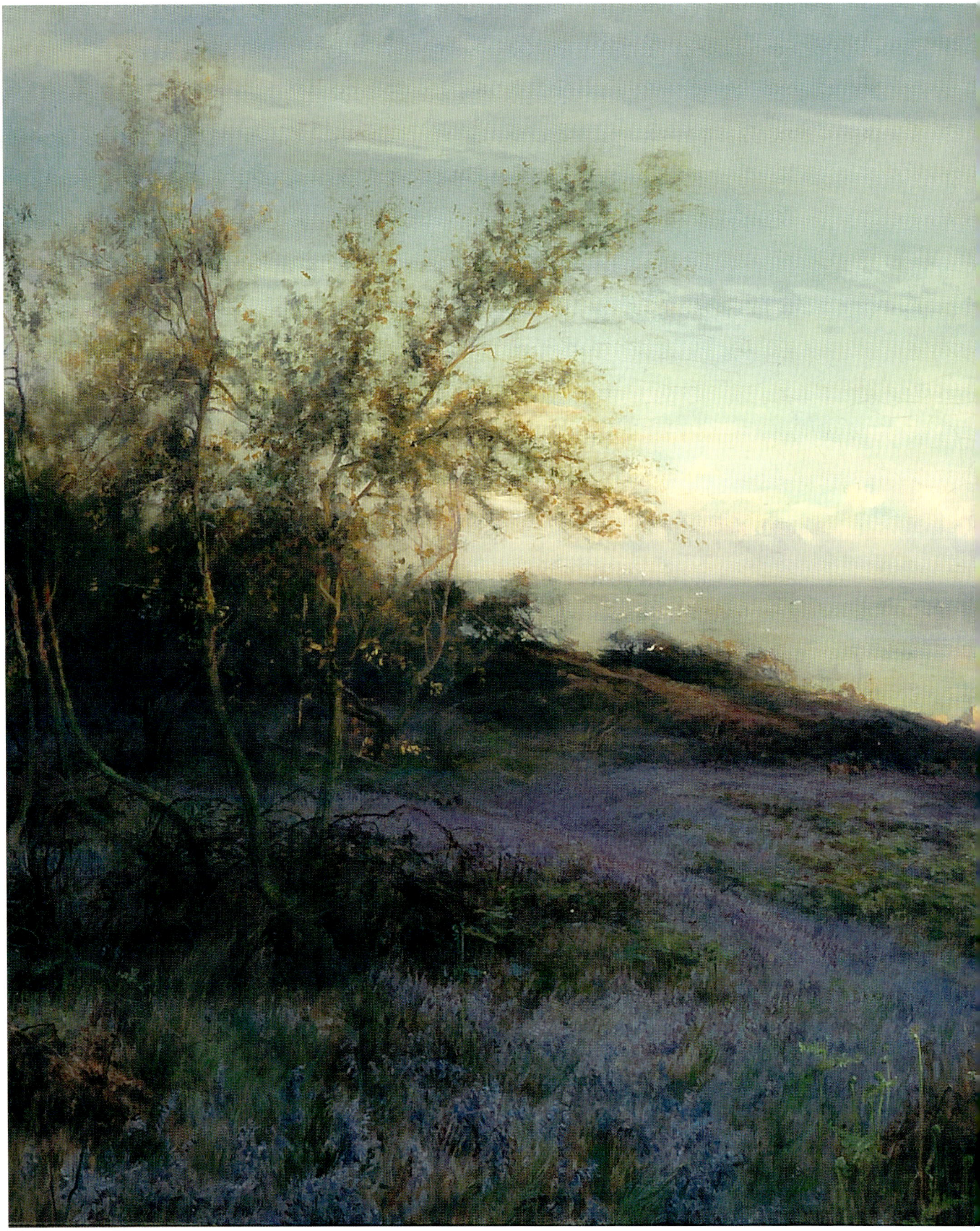

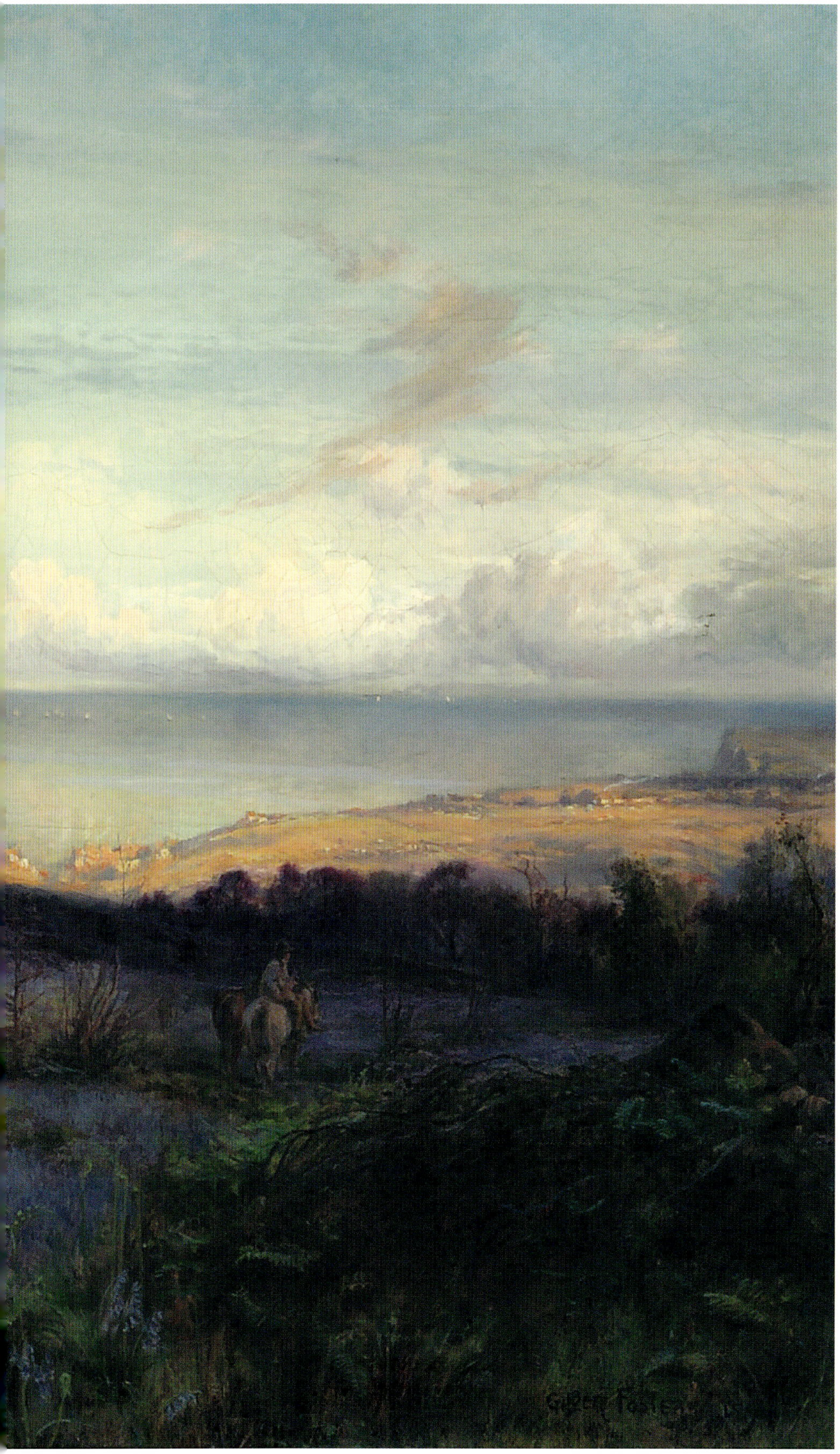

37. William Gilbert Foster's speciality was reported in 1904 to be 'the combination of floral effects with landscapes, woodscapes ... banks and ditch-sides of meadow-sweet and wild thyme, blue wood jacinths [*sic*] and nodding yellow daffodils, thistledown, and mist'. Here in *The Azure Mead* he applies his skills to the approach to Staithes in 1894.

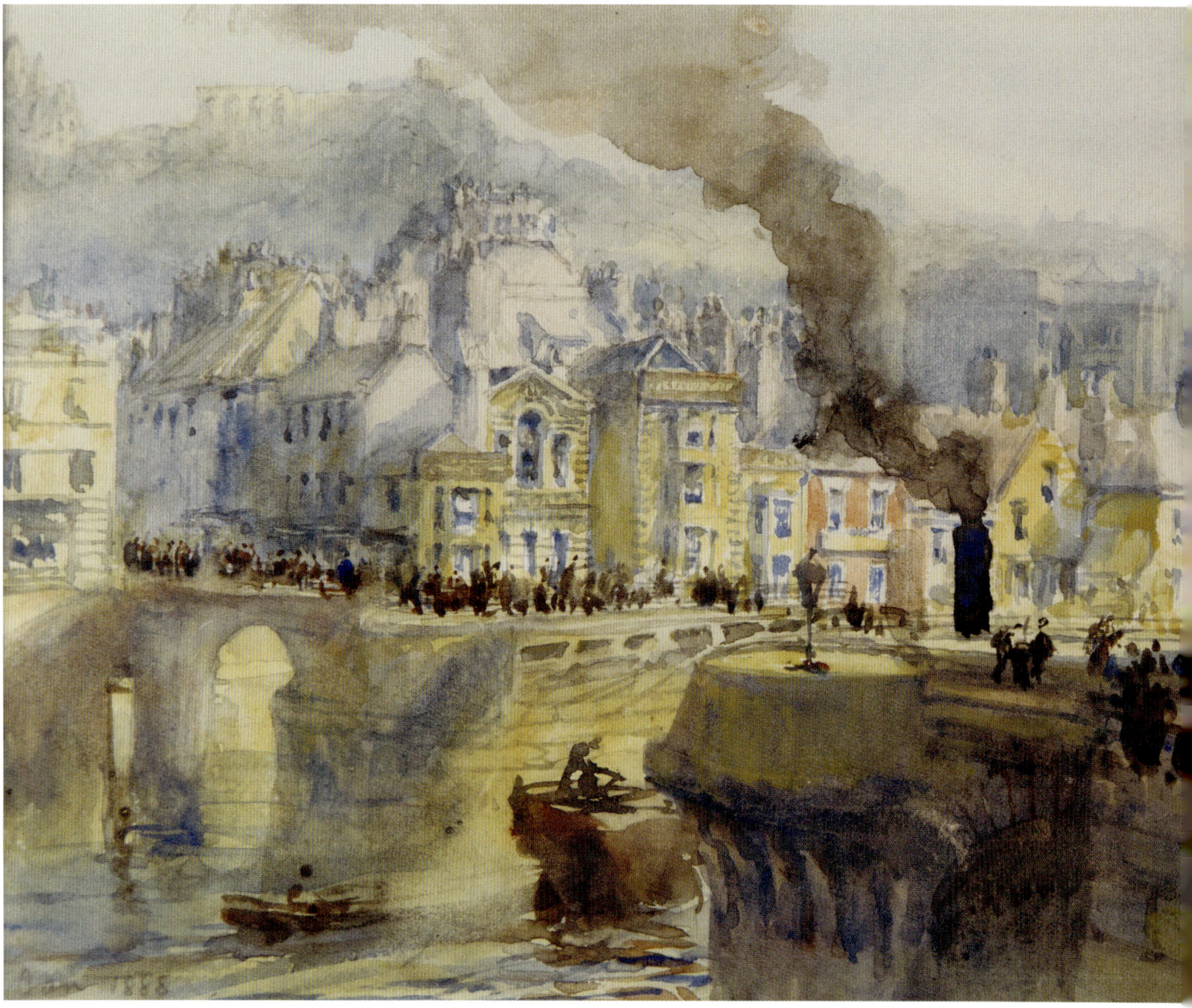

Today many Weatherill paintings hang alongside those of the Staithes Art Club in the Pannett Gallery in Whitby, established as a gift to the town by the industrialist after whom it was named. The Whitby Museum, which shares the same building, also now holds significant photographic collections, notably those of Tom Watson and Frank Meadow Sutcliffe. Both men lived almost their entire lives in the district, the latter retiring to act as the first curator of the gallery. They were two of around twelve photographers in the area at the turn of the century, aiming to satisfy the demands of the burgeoning tourist industry and their activities were often grouped together with those of the artists by the local press.

38. Born in Staithes and father to the best-known artistic family in Whitby, George Weatherill focused on local scenes, sketching almost exclusively in watercolour. In *Steam Tug, Whitby Bridge* he depicts the obvious change from sail to steam in Whitby's harbour scene, just two years before his death in 1890.

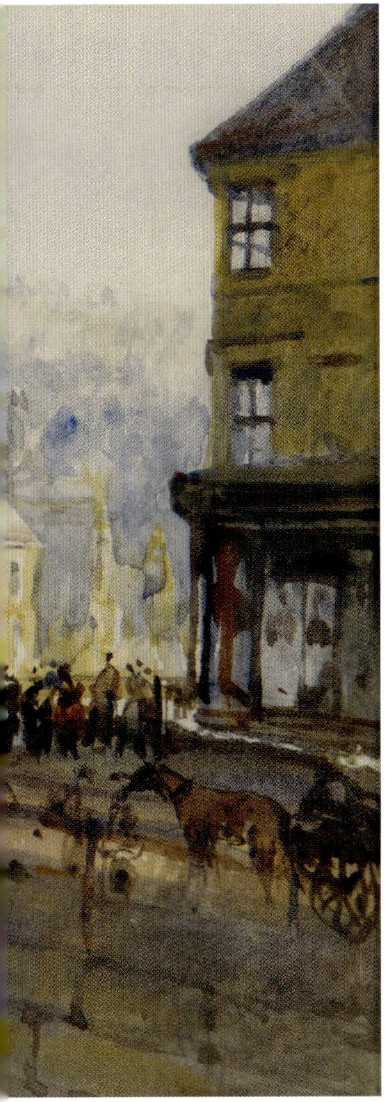

> If Runswick has no great sights to offer the visitor, it has at least that of which he is perhaps most in need – it has restfulness... The only sounds that he will hear as he reclines on the cliff tops will be the cries of the sea birds, the hum of the voices of the children in the bay, and the feeble lullaby of the distant sea. ... Runswick Bay has long been a resort for the knights of the easel and camera.[32]

Dade and Jackson, two of the Art Club's earliest arrivals in the area, were both sons of photographers. The latter's father, David Jackson, was reputedly one of the first professionals in Lancashire. A chemist and 'druggist', he incorporated photography into his business, with his card offering 'portraits, landscapes and machinery'. His son Charles (Chas) took over the business, although he is more often mentioned as a Manchester fine art dealer and framer and long-term supporter of Fred.

Sutcliffe's alignment with the artists was justified as he proved a not insignificant national figure in the emerging art of photography. He became a fixture in the town and surrounding area over a period of around 60 years from the mid-1870s. Having initially used an old jet workshop as his studio, he graduated to bigger premises with a retail window on Skinner Street. Though

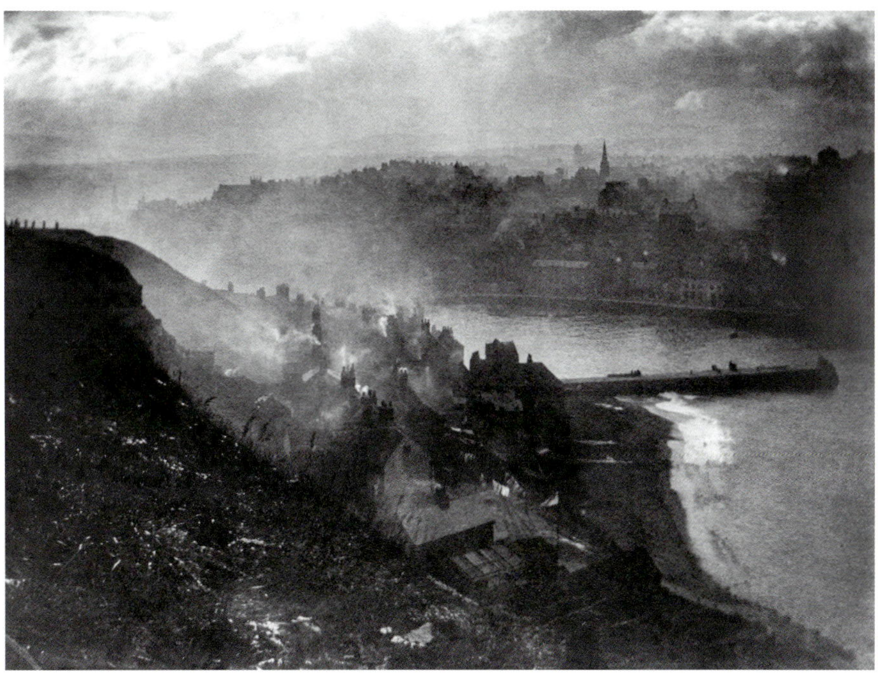

39. Frank Meadow Sutcliffe was a photographer of Whitby and surrounding area for over 60 years (c. 1870–1930). As committed as Art Club members to working *en plein air*, he much preferred the use of natural effects such as mist or chimney smoke to artificial cleverness within the photographic process.

his stock trade was to serve the tourist business, Sutcliffe was progressive; he exploited his new space to full advantage, focusing on the manipulation of light effects to enhance his portraits. The improved windows allowed for the display of some of his more experimental works, and he joked that the Whitby clerics had excommunicated him when he displayed his most renowned image, *The Water Rats*, in 1886 (p. 146).

Though no written evidence currently supports direct connection between local photographers and Staithes artists, Sutcliffe faced many of the same issues. He worked and lived in the same places, establishing premises on the street that was home to the Westcliff Gallery, owned by the Andersons, and sold art supplies. He was also only too aware of artists' techniques and clear in his belief that artists had used his photographs.[33] The visual parallels that John Atkinson Grimshaw's scenes of Whitby harbour by moonlight bear to those of Sutcliffe, for instance, are only part of extensive circumstantial evidence.

40. Born into a noble Suffolk family, the Hon. Duff Tollemache stayed alongside artists such as Jackson, Brymner and Brown at the Sheffield Hotel, Runswick. He had also studied in Paris and Brussels and painted in Brittany. He exhibited *After the Catch* in 1885, the year after his stay in Yorkshire.

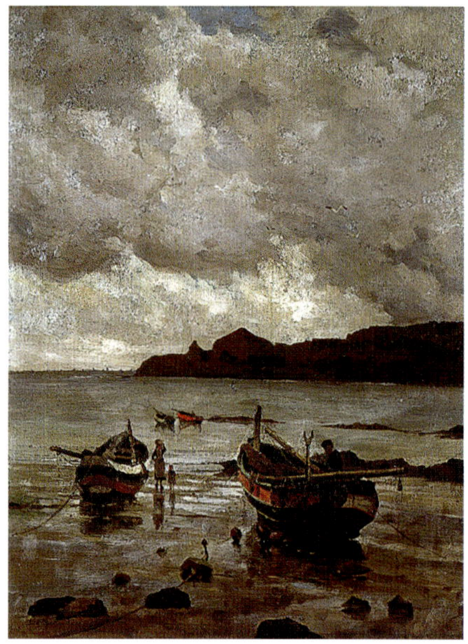

EARLY VISITORS

From the 1880s onwards, thanks in no small part to the extension of the railway north from Whitby through Sandsend to Saltburn, there was a gradual increase in the seasonal influx of artists to Staithes and Runswick Bay. James Aumonier, who had visited as early as 1874, was still visiting when Jackson started to frequent Runswick Bay. So was John Buxton Knight, and all three were early exhibitors at the New English Art Club. Fred Brown, The Hon. Duff Tollemache, William Brymner and Jackson all stayed together at the Sheffield Hotel in 1884, the year in which Mark Senior seems to have started working in the area for the first time and Thomas Hemy (one of three Newcastle-based brothers) was in both Runswick and Staithes.

Hemy and Terrick Williams, who visited two years later, had trained in Antwerp as well as Paris, anticipating the route by which many Art Club members would arrive. Williams later came to be particularly associated with Cornwall, along with other visitors such as William Blandford Fletcher (Newlyn), William

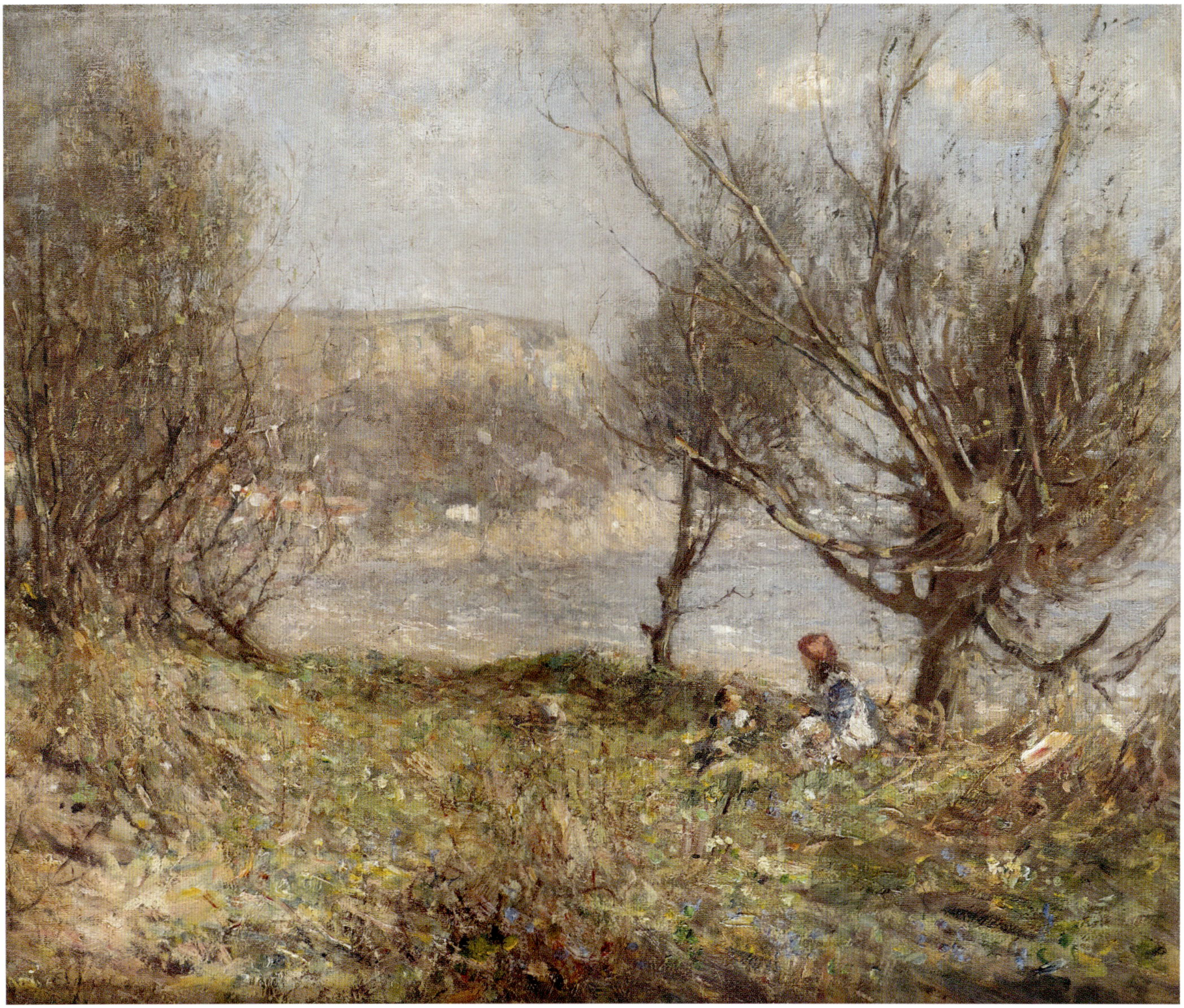

41. Fred W. Jackson was the first Art Club painter to visit Staithes, Runswick Bay and the surrounding area. He arrived from Paris, along with Canadian travelling companions and fellow students William Brymner and James Kerr-Lawson. This archetypal view of Runswick shows him at the height of his powers and likely dates from the period of the Art Club (1901–1907).

Manning (St Ives) and John Robertson Reid (Polperro). Fletcher, Brown and Aumonier can also be linked to Walberswick in Suffolk, a village to which Vincent Yglesias and George Swinstead, fellow Runswick tourists, made regular visits from London. Like Yglesias, Nelly Erichsen was English-born (Newcastle) but with European parentage, in her case Danish. She attended the Academy schools and worked from the same address in Chelsea as Frank Brangwyn, Fred Mayor and Ernest Dade, visiting Staithes and writing of her experiences in 1885–6.

After Hemy, Ralph Hedley and William Charlton shared the role of trailblazing the route from Newcastle, taken in turn by John Hodgson

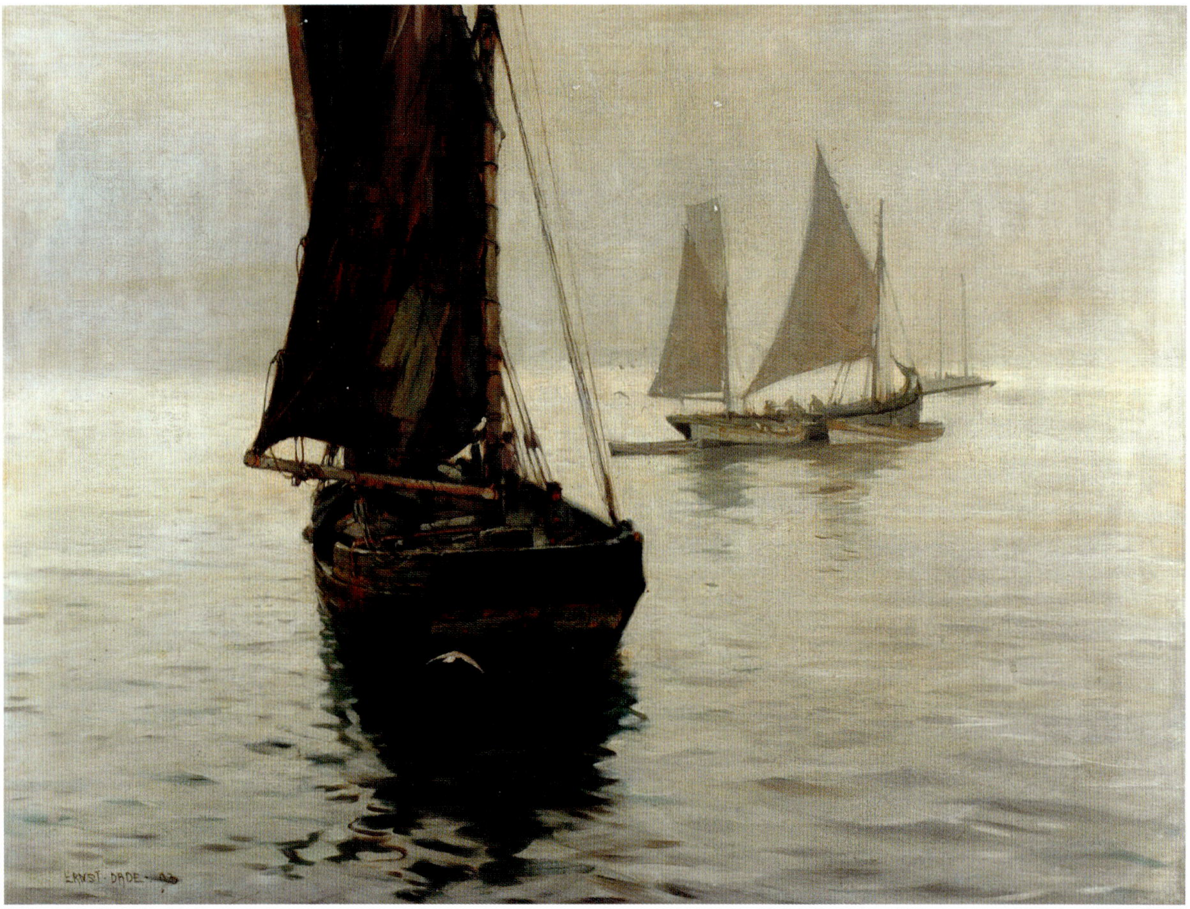

Campbell, Robert Jobling and Isa(bella) Thompson. William Llewellyn, Edward R. Taylor, Edward S. Harper and James Jelley all visited from the West Country, where they were involved in the Birmingham Schools of Art, Arts and Crafts and Society of Artists.

Painters from Scotland toured throughout the period too. Charles Mackie was a significant central figure for the Art Club, but Harrington Mann's consistent presence in Staithes, recalled several times in Laura Knight's memoir, was also notable. In 1906 he was joined by the prominent artist and designer E. A. Taylor, who in turn became a regular visitor. Club member Owen Bowen, whose regular coastal haunt was Robin Hood's Bay, also maintained a long-term friendship with Edward Hornel from Glasgow. Charles Oppenheimer's first experience of colony life was at Runswick Bay, probably

42. The son of a 'photographic artist', Ernest Dade trained in Paris, the South of France and London. His experience as a deckhand on a racing yacht and enthusiasm as a modelmaker enabled him to create particularly sensitive and accurate marine depictions, such as *The Amity Going to Sea* in 1893.

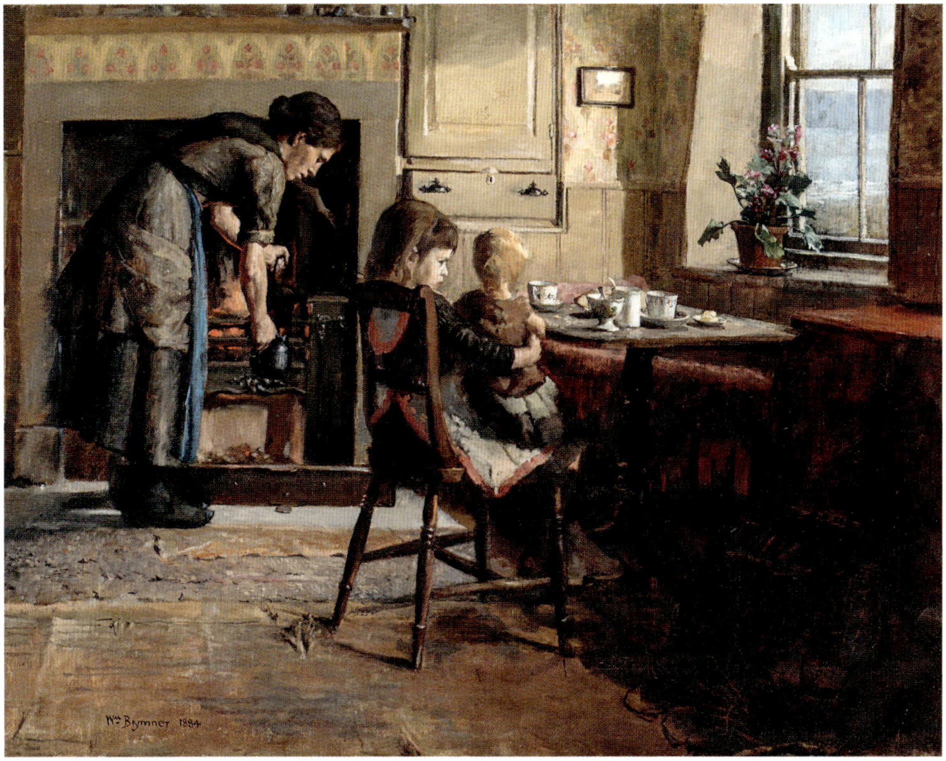

43. William Brymner visited Yorkshire in 1884 at the invitation of Fred Jackson. He had painted with Fred Brown in Burgundy, and the two artists then stayed with Jackson in Runswick, producing pictures such as *The Lonely Orphans Taken to Her Heart.* Brymner exhibited in Manchester and Liverpool before returning to a first success at the Paris salon in the spring of 1885.

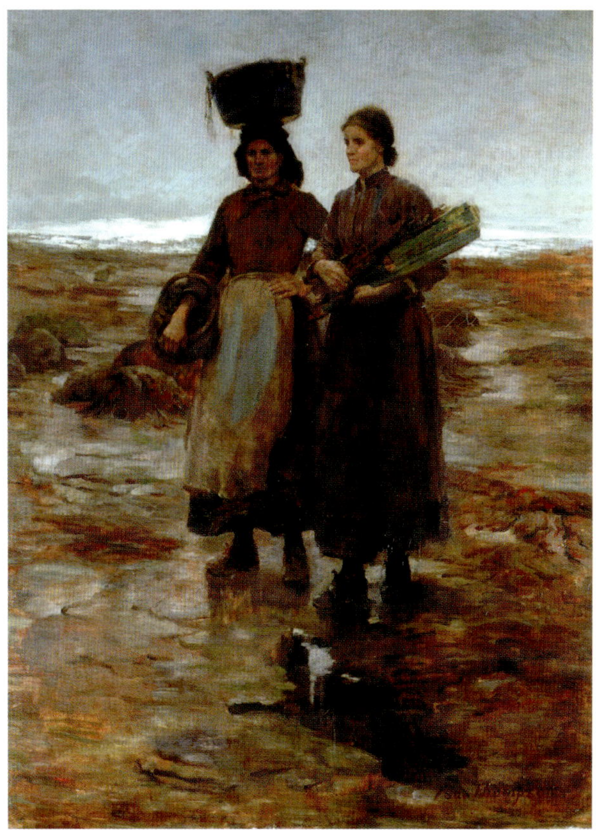

44. A Royal Academy exhibit in 1893, *Fisherfolk* was only the second showing by Isabella Jobling (née Thompson), despite her having exhibited in the northeast for a decade. The work displays the palette from her time at the colony in Cullercoats, as well as a growing individuality that was baulked by her marriage of the same year.

influenced through his Manchester hometown by Jackson. He, Taylor and Hornel provide a connection to the Kirkcudbright colony on the west coast and Cockburnspath on the east, later visited by Henry Hopwood who had worked at Staithes since 1892.

Other consistent early visitors include W. G. Foster (who bought a cottage not long after) and future members of the Club Thomas Barrett and Dade in 1886, followed by Spence Ingall in 1889. These artists' continued presence was bolstered in the 1890s by Thompson, first on her own and then, from 1893, accompanied by her husband Robert Jobling, Johnson, Knight, Friedenson and Mayor in Staithes and Booth, Hoyland and Hill in or near Runswick.

By the late 1890s, therefore, almost all of those who exhibited with the Staithes Art Club had visited the area periodically, along with a slew of peregrinating artists who had connections all across Britain. Many of them, though not all, had also been exhibiting with the Yorkshire Union of Artists.

45. Harrington Mann exhibited work from Staithes from as early as 1886. Although these pictures caught the attention of critics, he increasingly showed only portraits at his major exhibitions. He continued to visit, however, and his 'bravura and dash' are evident in *Low Tide on the Beck* of 1898.

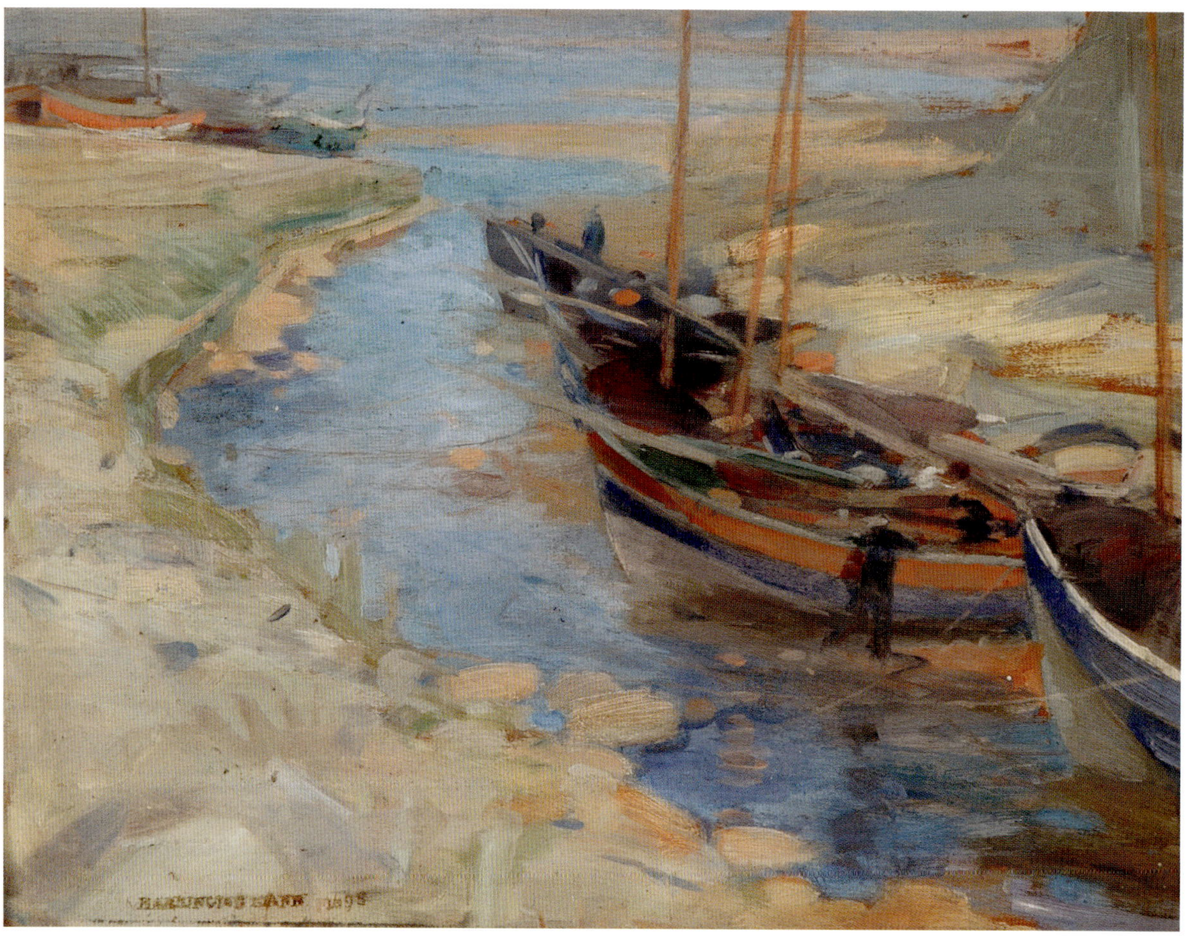

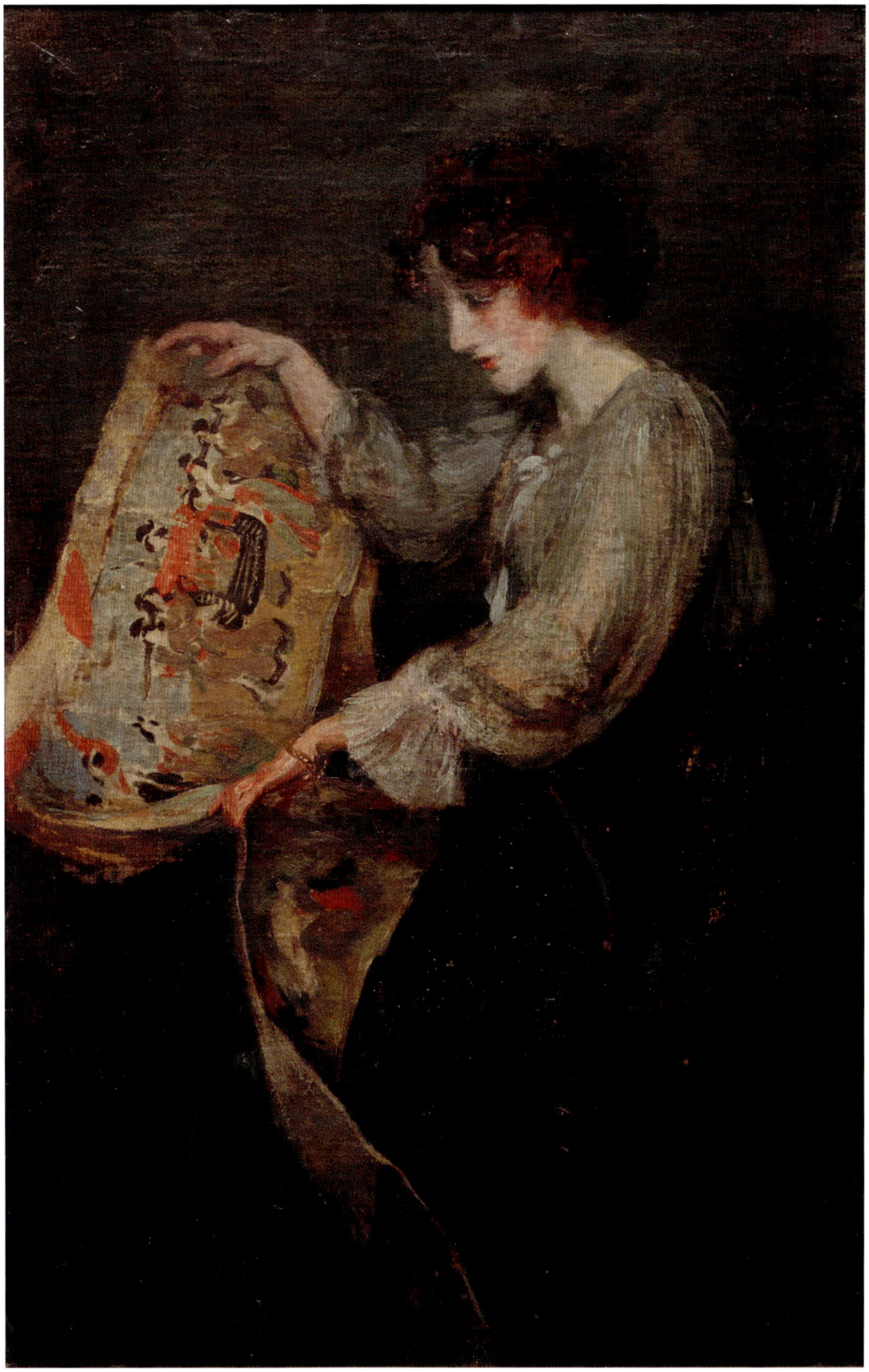

46. The Director of the Art Gallery of New South Wales visited the 1912 exhibition in Wellington organised by the dealer John Baillie. There he purchased a group of works including *The Jap Album* by Charles Mackie, which had first been exhibited at the Royal Scottish Academy and the Staithes Art Club exhibitions of 1904.

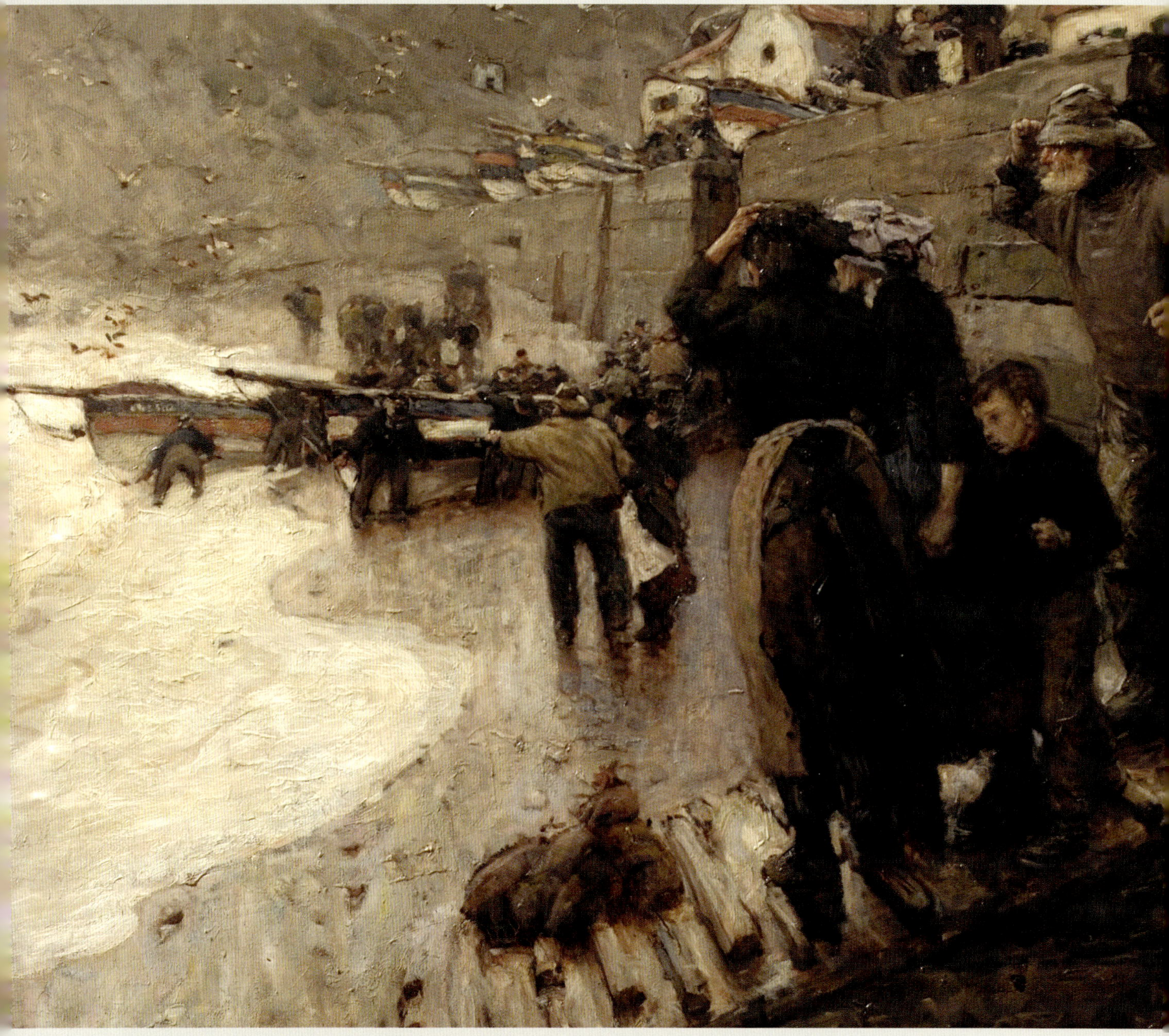

47. Although the first Art Club exhibition yielded nothing worthy of the Royal Academy, Harold Knight's *The Last Coble* had been exhibited in 1900 and was purchased two years later. Works by Knight and Fred Mayor from 1898–9, when they lodged together with Arthur Friedenson, bear close comparison for style and subject.

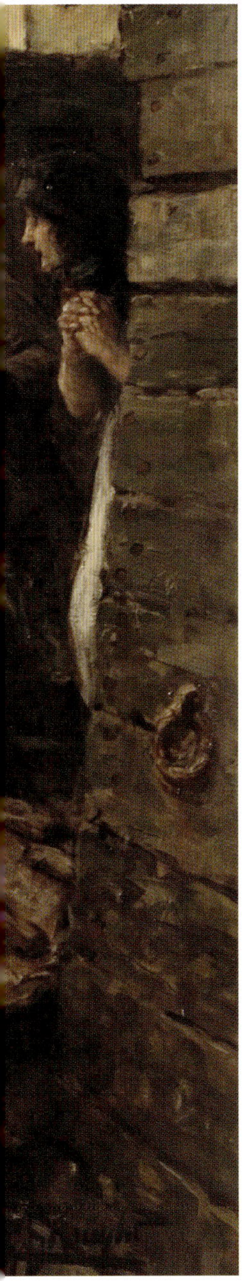

CLUB AND ACADEMY

As mentioned, Laura Knight's memoir observes the initial exhibitions at the Fishermen's Institute did not produce any pictures meriting a hang at Burlington House. Her contemporary writings, however, make it clear this was not for want of trying, despite the unrest in artistic circles that resulted in the establishment not only of independent galleries such as the Grosvenor and New but also the New English Art Club. The Royal Academy Summer Shows were still considered by most of the Staithes artists to be the route to success. Paintings were submitted, repainted and resubmitted, sometimes with title changes to reflect current events in the hope of added appeal to the jury. Laura Knight describes the trials of the process:

> Harold has had an awful business with his big picture; he thought it was pretty nearly finished a month ago, but he got dissatisfied with it and has almost completely repainted the whole of it and has improved it immensely; everyone here thinks it a great success.[34]

The importance of success at the Royal Academy is implicit too in the foreword to the 1905 Staithes Art Club exhibition. In it Jackson, who had just taken over as Secretary of the Club, seems to suggest both the somewhat low-key nature of the initial displays and the importance of their collective ambition:

> The Staithes Art Club was originally formed in 1901 by a number of painters working in the district, with the idea of holding an annual exhibition of sketches. Lately, it has been the desire of the members to give the exhibitions a more serious character, and, while still including sketches, to endeavour to show works which, whether slight or elaborate, represent their honest interpretation of nature. Many of the members have already attained some position in their profession.[35]

Without knowing the precise details of the first exhibition, we can say that the contributing artists of the following two exhibitions were almost identical – with the exception of Mackie and Robert Jobling, who did not show in 1903.[36] Handwritten minutes of a meeting from July 1902 confirm a core group of Hopwood, Barrett, Bagshawe, Jobling, Knight and Friedenson in attendance who are subsequently listed as the hanging committee for the show to be held in August. Their names are repeated alongside those of Mayor, Richardson, Conway, Hoyland, Johnson, Mackie and Hill next to details of 'Sending in day on July 28th'. There is a further group of Jackson, Rigg, Stephens [*sic*], Ingall, Dade, Mason, Senior and Bowman who are 'proposed as members'.

A natural differentiator between the lists, such as that of location, is not obvious. Of those included, nine did not exhibit in 1902, while Booth, Walker and Isa Jobling all did.[37] Each subsequent time members were added they appear to have exhibited in their year of election such as Gardner and Watson in 1903. Hill's record is chronicled with subtle difference by writers; his name is included in the minutes for sending in works in 1902, but he only started exhibiting in 1903, which he followed up consistently in each subsequent year.[38]

There was a folio of unframed, unlisted work, as part of the shows, and it is possible that some artists contributed only to this, but it is highly unlikely that any further artists submitted work in this way. Prices at these initial shows were not high, ranging, with the odd exception, between £2-2 and £25. The only exception to this was Walker, whose work is listed without prices and whose picture *Autumn Sunset* is described in the following review as appearing:

> with great credit amongst the other exhibits ... though from the hand of an unattached member, and a non-professional.[39]

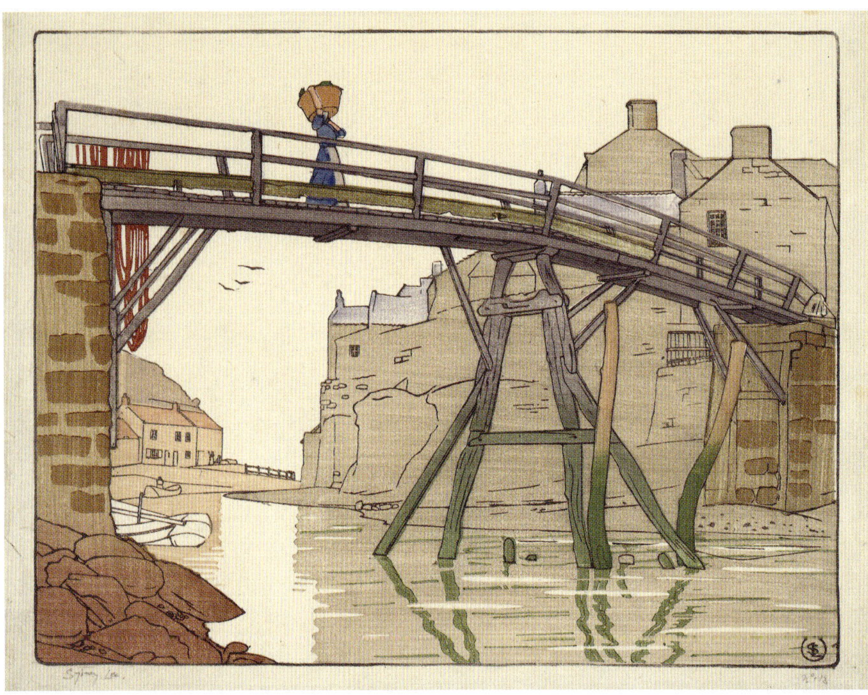

48. Sydney Lee's woodcut was mentioned in Laura Knight's memoir and set a precedent for printmakers such as Frank Short and William Manning. *The Bridge, Staithes* (1904) was produced in five colour schemes, reworked as a wood engraving in 1911 and exhibited as a painted, nocturnal version in 1930.

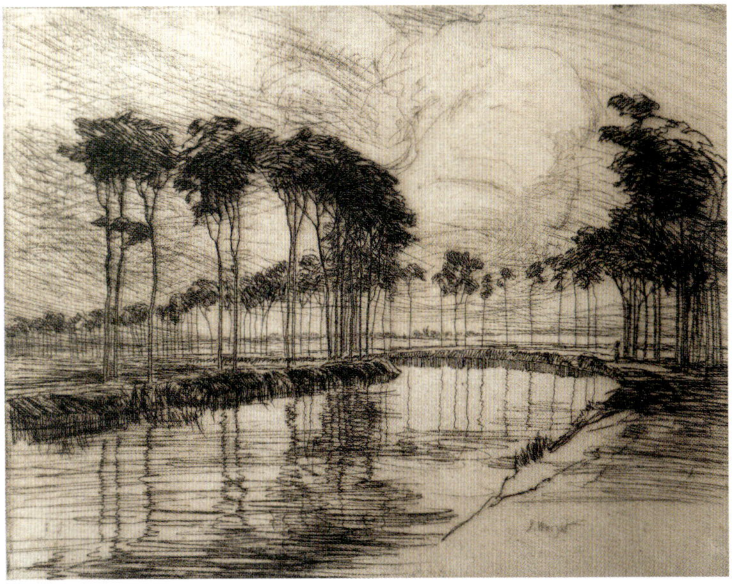

49. John Wright became a member of the Art Club in 1904. He exhibited six prints at the Whitby show, including this picture, *Canal at Sluys* [*sic*]. Although at the time he was already an Associate of the Royal Society of Engravers, his work has seldom featured in subsequent exhibitions on the work of the Club.

The Club's accounts produced by Barrett, at whose house (Kirkhill) the members met at the beginning of July 1902, showed cash in hand of 15 shillings and 2 pence. This does not record sales from the initial exhibition, simply cash received of 3 pounds and 5 shillings with monies paid out of 2 pounds 9 shillings and 10 pence.[40]

Reports of the second show indicated that the sale of works went well, with 31 works sold out of a possible 41. However, neither the published press critique nor the artists' own retrospective comments seem to evidence the commerciality of the venture:

> Many of the cleverest of nature's artists have found inspiration hereabouts … There can be but one opinion among the fraternity of the brush as to the value of an exhibition of this kind, for compassion and criticism are the very soul of improvement, and are valuable guides to a complete success.[41]

WHITBY AND LONDON

No record of the finances for the third show seems to be extant, but it is clear that the 1904 move to Anderson's West Cliff Gallery in Whitby was a step change in the exhibiting habits of the Club and pre-empts the comments of Jackson for the 1905 show. The larger, more commercial premises allowed for more contributors and a larger number of works submitted by an individual. Whereas size and number of works (four) were previously restricted, from 1904 10 of the now 21 artists submitted between five and 10 works to the display. Prices too were significantly higher, though the minimum value was still the same. Jackson, for example, submitted five works with a minimum value of £15 and a maximum of £200; around 10 per cent of exhibits were of a value greater than any of the pictures in previous shows. The only notable figure who failed to exhibit was Hopwood, explained by the exhibition of works he hosted from his aforementioned trip to Holland with the Knights in June.[42]

Interestingly, the *Whitby Gazette* suggests studies by Harold Knight (only) from this show were added to the Art Club displays after opening, but did not feature in the catalogue.[43]

The move to Whitby while anticipating bigger audiences also situated the painters in the midst of competitors. The latter were not only exhibiting within walking distance, but even in the sister gallery, The Rembrandt, to that in which the Staithes Art Club showed in 1904. A further move within Whitby in 1905, possibly for this reason, left the Club with less exhibiting space, even though the exhibition was enhanced by a printed catalogue. Despite eliciting critical praise, this and subsequent shows do not seem to have brought increased sales and perhaps justified certain Club members (Mason and Anderson, to name two) in showing work simultaneously at the other galleries.

Letters that have recently come to light document the concerns of the Club's second Treasurer, Walker, in this regard. In the Statement of Accounts for

50. Hirst Walker became Treasurer of the Club in 1905 in succession to Thomas Barrett, whose house had hosted early meetings of the Club. Walker was close to the Secretary Joseph Bagshawe and, as an amateur, found this the most acceptable route to membership. These letters to Robert and Isa Jobling of 1907 are a recent discovery.

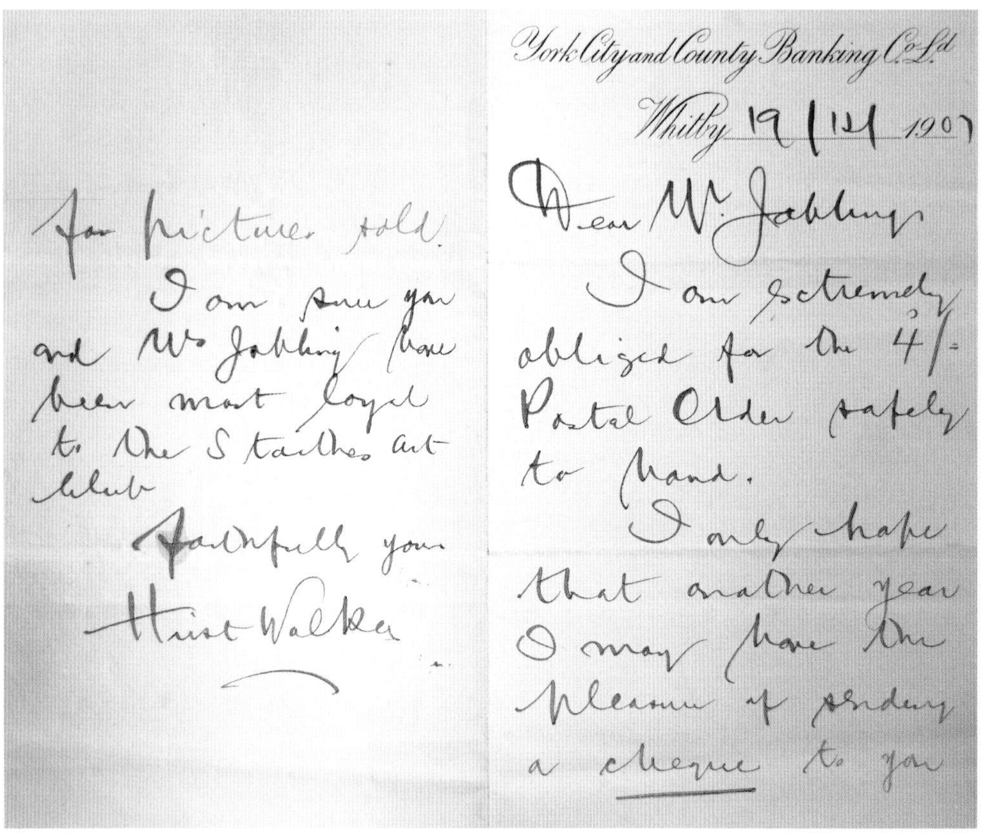
York City and County Banking Co. Ltd
Whitby 19/12/1907
Dear Mr Jobling
I am extremely obliged for the 4/- Postal Order safely to hand.
I only hope that another year I may have the pleasure of sending a cheque to you
for pictures sold.
I am sure you and Mrs Jobling have been most loyal to the Staithes Art Club
Faithfully yours
Hirst Walker

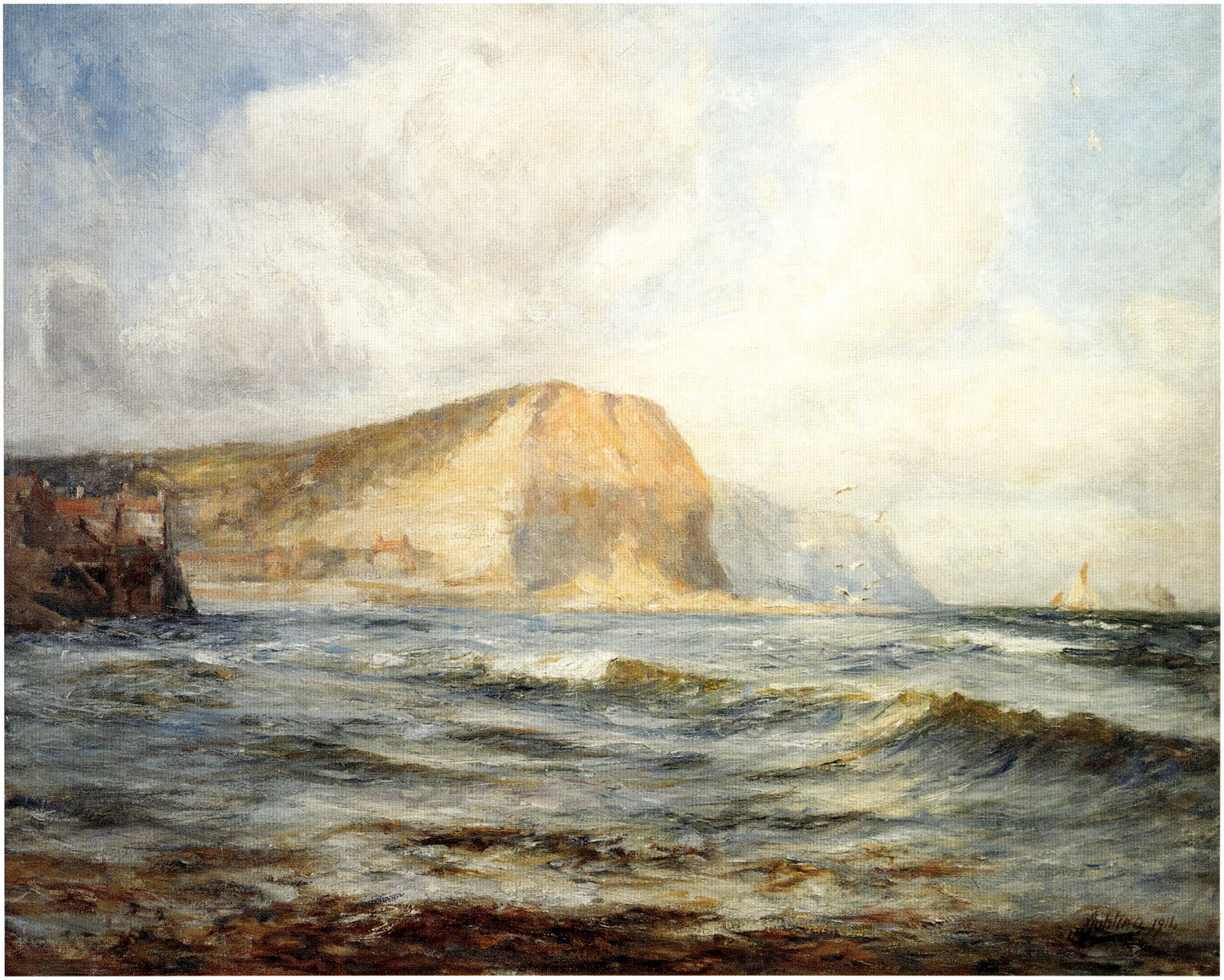

51. Robert Jobling's reputation was forged at the artists' colony in Cullercoats before he came south to paint in Staithes. Following a well-trodden path, he subsequently helped to mentor strong exhibiting links for Art Club members in Newcastle. He stayed on when many Club members dispersed and continued to paint images such as *Cowbar Nab, Staithes* of 1914.

1907, he makes plain that the commission rate on sales previously established to cover costs has not been sufficient, given the number of pictures sold. Therefore, as previously agreed, a higher commission rate has retrospectively been instituted, as well as the request for an additional levy to pay off the Club's deficit. Walker wrote to the Joblings in November 1907:

> I feel I hardly like to call on you and Mrs. Jobling for the call up of 2–0 (shillings) each now due from members of the Club. However, as you both paid your subscription – (tho' showing no work), I feel you wish to be treated as are our other members. We have had a very bad year. I hope that some entirely fresh arrangements may be made for a future show, and that you and Mrs. Jobling will contribute a full number of pictures.

Having received the subscriptions sent at the end of December, he goes on to reply:

> I am extremely obliged for the 4–0 Postal Order safely to hand. I only hope that another year I may have the pleasure of sending a cheque to you for pictures sold. I am sure you and Mrs. Jobling have been most loyal to the Staithes Art Club.

52. An early arrival to Runswick Bay in the mid-1880s, Mark Senior remained painting in the village until the late 1920s. He only exhibited sporadically, but successfully submitted *Eventide* to the Royal Academy in 1892. This picture was accurately described but titled *A Fisherman's Home* in the *Leeds Mercury*, 24 December 1904.

This deference reflects Walker's awareness that the Joblings were among those artists to whom Jackson had referred as 'hav[ing] already attained some position in their profession'. They were of the initial generation of artists to join the Club who had been exhibiting for almost 20 years, including regular contributions to the Royal Academy.[44] The couple had attained significant standing in their home region of Newcastle, both in establishing the reputation

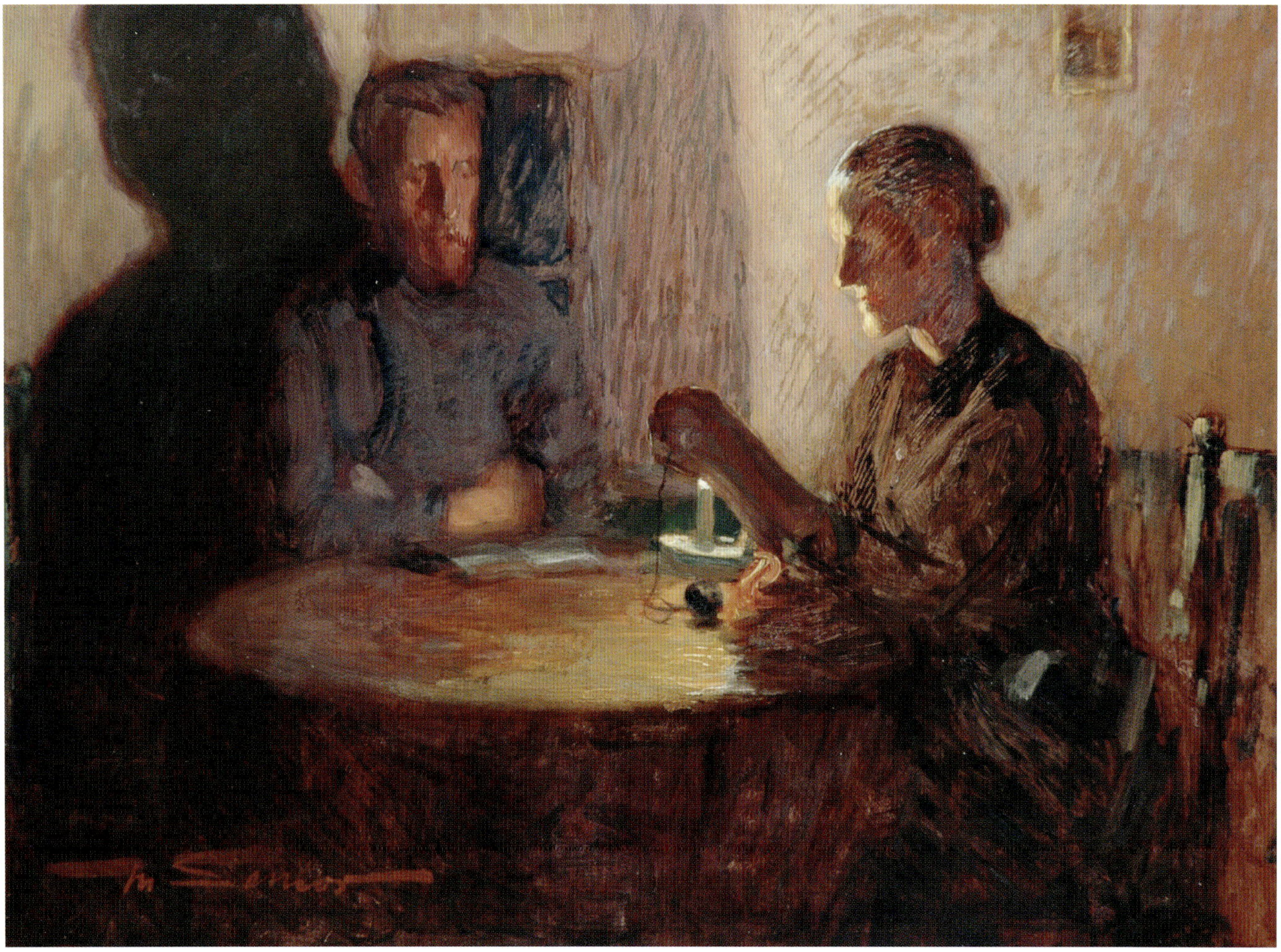

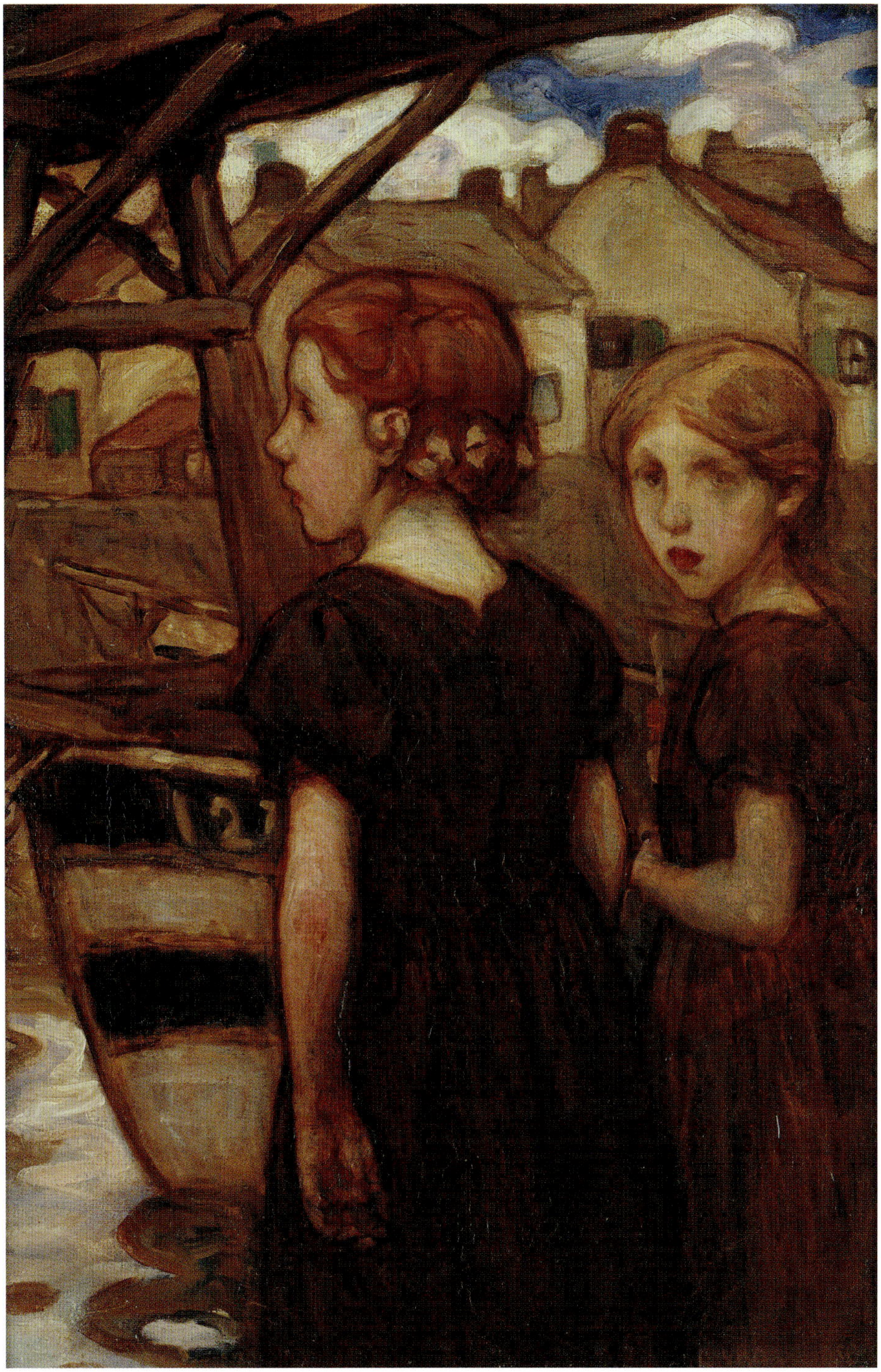

53. Laura Johnson's *Under the Bridge, Staithes* was exhibited at the Royal Society of Oil Painters in 1901. It pre-empted her first successful entry to the Royal Academy, which was shown in 1903, the year she married Harold Knight, and bought by fellow artist Edward Stott.

of the colony at Cullercoats and supporting and sustaining the Bewick Club. This latter had shouldered the responsibility as the exhibiting society of the north-east from 1884, in the face of a distinct lack of support from the council and a large swathe of public disinterest. Their contributions to the activities of Staithes Art Club were consequently part of a strong call on their works and had apparently been sparked by Isa's commitment to Staithes, though possibly facilitated by Robert's alienation from the Bewick.

Their failure to exhibit with the Club did not at this point suggest a weakening of ties, but rather mirrored a pause in their wider exhibiting pattern; Robert was apparently away in Holland again, this time with John Hodgson Campbell.[45] However, the lack of sales cannot have been encouraging and their own example of consistent submissions to the Royal Academy and other London institutions such as the Royal Society of British Artists had provided a template for others. Future members of the Art Club began contributing in waves throughout the 1890s and 1900s. Among these artists were Mason, Walker, Paul Paul, Joseph Terry and Jackson, though the last sent significant pictures to Manchester and Liverpool as well. There were those such as Rigg and Senior who seem to have limited their exhibiting. During the same period, they sent only sporadically to regional centres or to the Royal Academy, but the list of submissions inexorably expanded.

In the following decades several artists managed to secure one-off shows or to nurture working relationships with different private galleries in London. Dade, for example, exhibited with the Dowdeswell Gallery in 1888 (where Jackson showed in 1913), while Crawshaw showed consistently with Walker's Galleries, both on New Bond Street. Johnson and Knight visited Ernest Brown and Phillips at Leicester Galleries (on Leicester Square) in

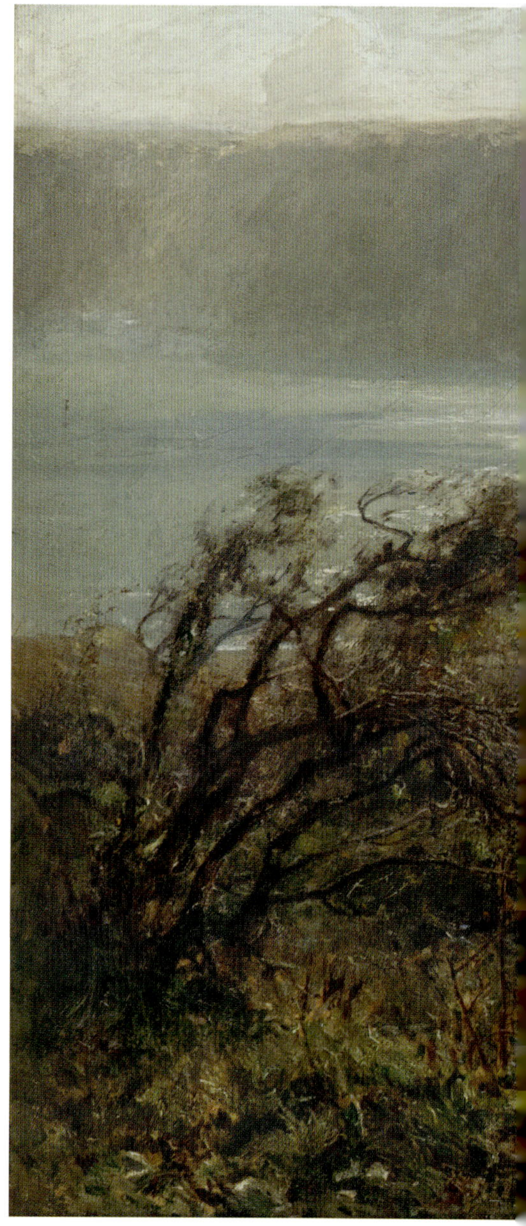

54. Arthur Friedensen painted a series of cliff-top images of Runswick Bay bathed in morning light. One was bought via the Trustees of the Chantrey Bequest for the National Collection (Tate) and others were acquired by Leeds and Aberdeen museums. This version of *Runswick Bay* was exhibited at the Franco-British Exhibition in London in 1908.

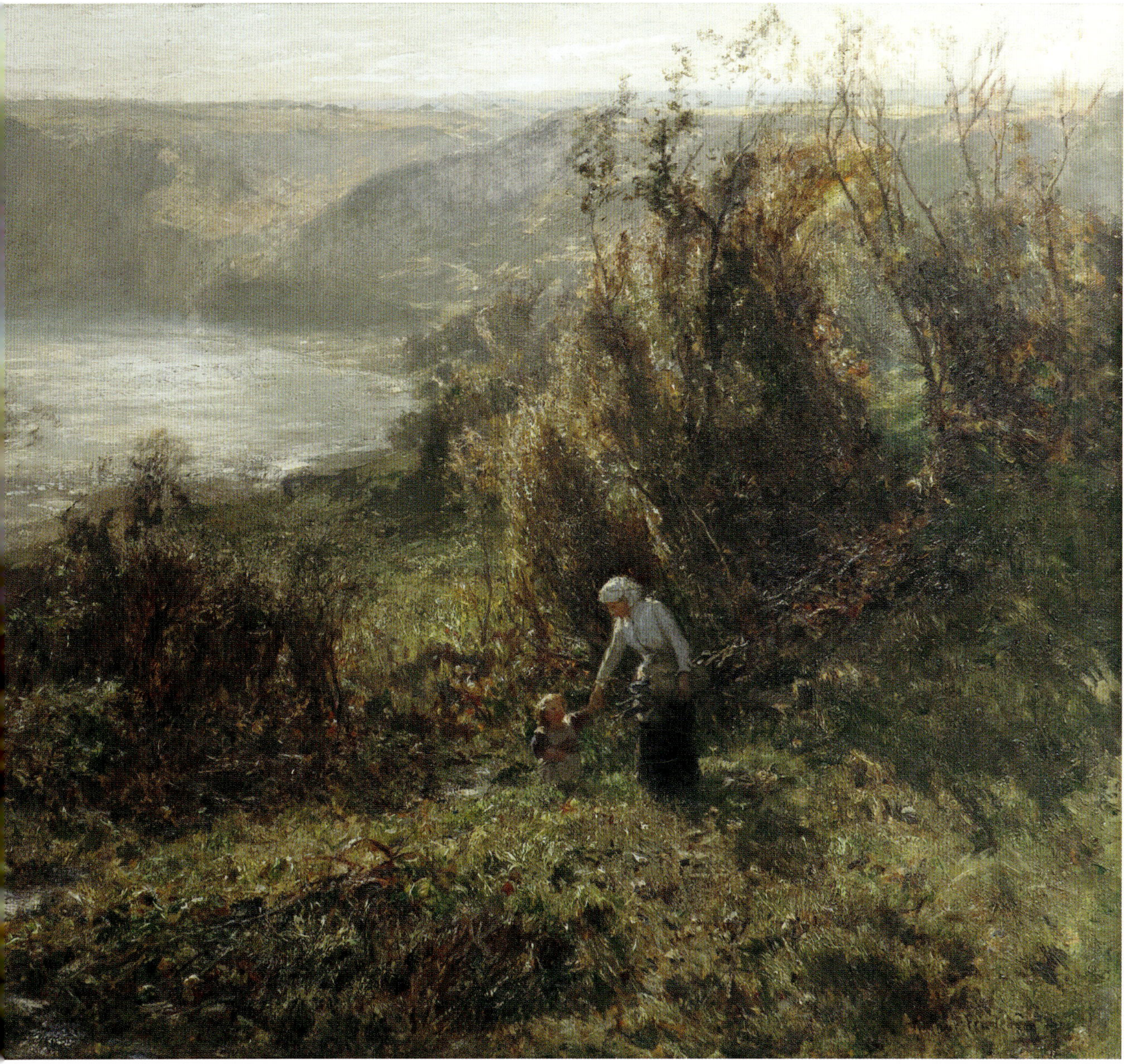

1903, subsequently holding three shows there in 1906, 1907 and 1912. Mayor had already exhibited with the newly opened gallery in 1902. He went on to exhibit at The Paterson Gallery (Old Bond Street) in 1908 and the Goupil Gallery on Regent Street in 1913, at which Friedenson exhibited in 1911. The Fine Art Society (New Bond Street) also showed displays by Friedenson and Hopwood, who had three solo shows in 1897, 1902 and 1913; the latter also exhibited at what had been the Dutch Gallery on Grafton Street in 1907.[46]

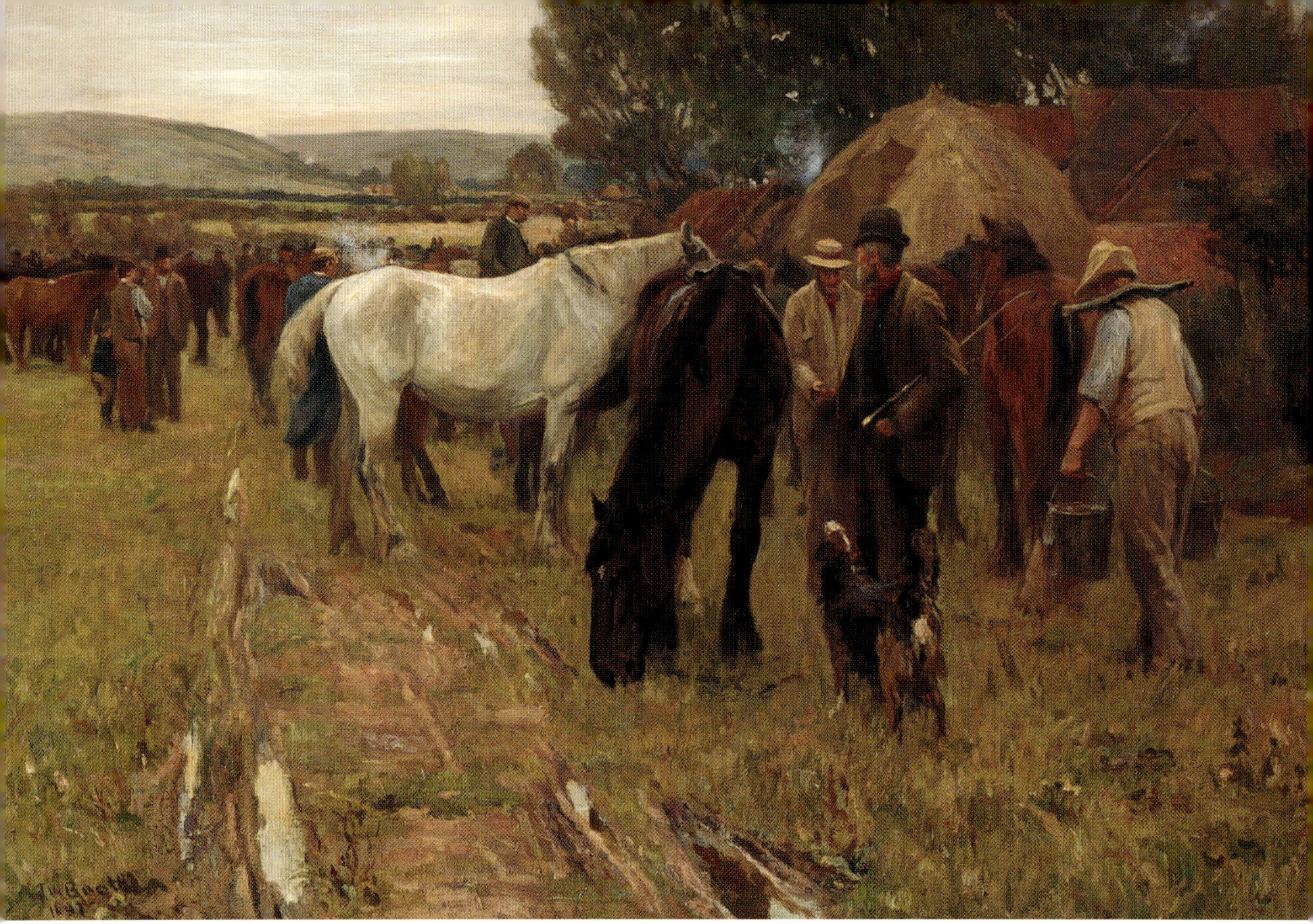

Hopwood had exhibited in Manchester early in his career. However, lacking commercial success, he looked rather towards London and, in addition to his solo shows, exhibited regularly with the Royal Society of Painters in Watercolours, of which he became an associate in 1908. Other watercolourists in the Club acted similarly, with Mackie, Crawshaw and Richardson all showing extensively with the Royal Scottish Society of Painters in Watercolour. Mackie and Crawshaw also exhibited at the Royal Scottish Academy and Glasgow Institute (as did Walker), while Richardson also settled on the Royal Institute of Painters in Watercolour (where Mason exhibited).

Finally, a small contingent of artists committed to showing at the Royal Cambrian exhibitions. This included Percy Teasdale, James Booth and, by far the largest contributor, Owen Bowen. Over the course of an admittedly long career, Bowen sent almost 200 works, as well as making significant showings at the Walker Art Gallery in Liverpool (to which Hill also contributed), the Royal Academy and Royal Institute of Oil Painters.

55. James Booth's favourite subjects such as this exhibition piece of 1897, *A Country Horse Fair at Hinderwell*, centred on the rural life of the inland villages and towns of the local districts. Inevitably he painted the horse in all its settings, from fairs to farms, quarries and gypsy encampments.

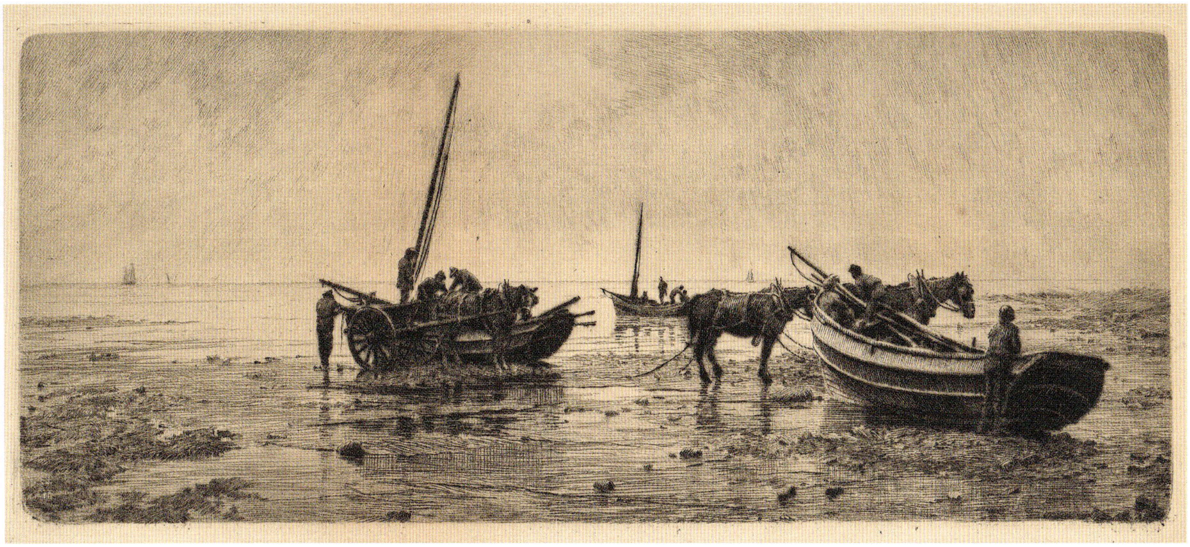

56. Like W. G. Foster, Thomas Barrett was an established art schoolteacher and noted for his printmaking, such as this etching *Pilchard Boats* (c. 1890). He was probably responsible for the introduction of artists to both Staithes and Runswick Bay; one-third of the early Art Club exhibitors came from his home town of Nottingham.

Continual or even annual presence at the exhibitions of all these societies usually resulted in associate membership, with full membership the ultimate target. Either attainment enabled artists to charge higher prices. Through the initial Art Club lists one can identify that the associate membership initials listed by Mackie, Hopwood and Barrett were later supplemented by equivalent memberships for Bagshawe, Bowen, Richardson, Anderson and John Wright.

REGIONAL TIES

Alternative or atypical exhibition venues, sales and commissions also look to have been influenced by Art Club connections. The Doncaster-based Crawshaw started to exhibit regularly in Scotland, having travelled with Mackie to Europe; the Knights showed in Ireland after their friends, the Sheppards, moved to Dublin; and several Staithes artists sent regularly to Newcastle after contact with the Joblings, Ralph Hedley and John Atkinson.[47]

Dade, Mason and Bagshawe all produced illustrations and articles for magazines based on their particular marine interests. Several of the Staithes artists were commissioned to provide scenes for postcard publication by firms such as Raphael Tuck and J. W. Ruddock. In addition to the three mentioned above, they included Albert (George) Stevens and Valentine Sidney Gardner. Both men proved quick to take the opportunity of generating income from a market that by the turn of the century was at its zenith.

Postcard publishers could be found in villages as well as towns. Watson, the photographer from Lythe, made a habit of questioning shopkeepers on his rounds to find out which cards were selling best. In contrast to the painterly images of the artists, he (and others such as Ross and Morley) increasingly adapted his technique to match the publishers' specific requirements for photographs. They highlighted a preferred area of each negative sent for publication, and sent only pin-sharp images, rather than those with the type of effects favoured by Sutcliffe.[48]

Just as pupil–teacher relationships were thought to be responsible for regional groups and individual student artists arriving at Staithes and Runswick, so the roles taken up by Club members established strong reciprocal links and regional reputations. Atkinson and Watson worked as teachers in art schools in Newcastle, County Durham and Northumberland; Anderson taught in Yorkshire, Berkshire and Hampshire. Foster's father had run a portrait studio in Leeds and though never a paid-up member of the Art Club (he died in 1906), W. G. taught Owen Bowen, who in turn started his own art school. He was also at the Leeds School of Art when it is suggested Mark Senior was a part-time teacher and Percy Teasdale a student. His local reputation culminated in his sitting on the Yorkshire Union of Artists Council and acting as a vice-president in 1898–9.

These connections extended between many other councils, clubs and societies of the towns and cities of Yorkshire – Barnsley, Bradford, Doncaster, Halifax, Scarborough, Wakefield and York – and beyond to Lancashire and Nottingham.[49] The Nottingham connection proved particularly strong and is mostly credited to Thomas Barrett, the Club's first Treasurer; he spent his whole career in the city, retiring from the Art School there.

Gardner, about whom little is known other than his postcard images and who exhibited only two pictures in Staithes in 1903, was one of the early Nottingham recruits. He was joined by contemporaries Bowman, Johnson and Knight, all of whom contributed several works to the first exhibitions at the Fishermen's Institute. In her memoir Knight (née Johnson) famously credits Barrett with the suggestion of heading to Staithes. Like Foster, he had visited the village regularly, taking student groups.

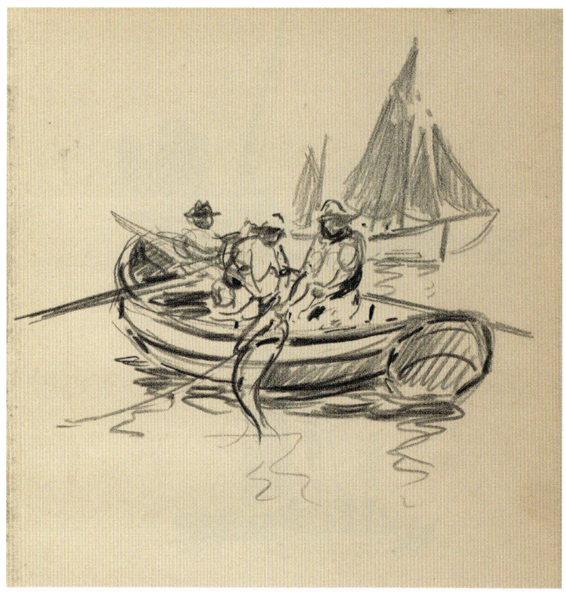

57. This sketch was reproduced on the cover of a series of articles by Joseph Bagshawe, published posthumously by his son Wilfrid as *The Wooden Ships of Whitby*. It depicts the yawl *True Love*, in which Bagshawe spent a week on the Dogger Bank, off the Yorkshire coast, in 1909.

THE INFLUENCERS

The context for the Art Club shows thus suggests that the artists involved included those with strong representation or reputation in their home regions and a consistent connection to London. The quality of artists exhibiting indicates that Staithes was well known to those working at all of the British colonies, and to many who had experience of the continent. It may be no exaggeration that Laura Knight recalls:

> We sent out invitations to the whole country to come to a really grand private view. We had a large reception and gave tea in the gallery.[50]

Yet did all of the contributing artists have realistic commercial expectations? Should the foundation of the Club perhaps rather be seen as part of an attempt to enhance relationships with each other and an effort to sustain an artistic reputation in the area and its communities? Hill suggests this might have been the case, recalling the example of their contribution to the building of the Runswick Institute, which seems to have benefited both the village and accommodated their artistic needs.[51]

Exploring the motivations and backgrounds of those who acted as 'officers' of the Club and who were its early patrons may assist in answering these questions. Barrett, the Treasurer, has been mentioned as a long-term visitor and the probable catalyst for contributions from Nottingham artists, who comprised one-third of the early exhibitors. Perhaps the most important member of the Club, however, at least in its initial stages, was Joseph Bagshawe, designated Secretary for the second exhibition in 1902.

Although the impetus for his family's initial visit from London to the north-east coast in 1896 is unclear, Bagshawe rapidly established a firm connection. At first he stayed at the end of Skinner Street in Whitby, on which both Anderson's Westcliff Gallery and Sutcliffe's photography studio stood. His friendship with other artists is borne out by the presence of Johnson, Knight and the Hopwoods as guests at his wedding in 1901, as well as gifts from others such as Richardson and Friedenson. Laura Knight's memoir recalls him helping to haul cobles with Harold during a storm in Staithes in 1899, on the eve of the terrible loss of the Unthank family.[52] Mildred Turnbull, Bagshawe's bride-to-be, and Laura both knew the Brotchie family in Hinderwell. Her journal of the time describes how the Brotchies not only shared cycling trips,

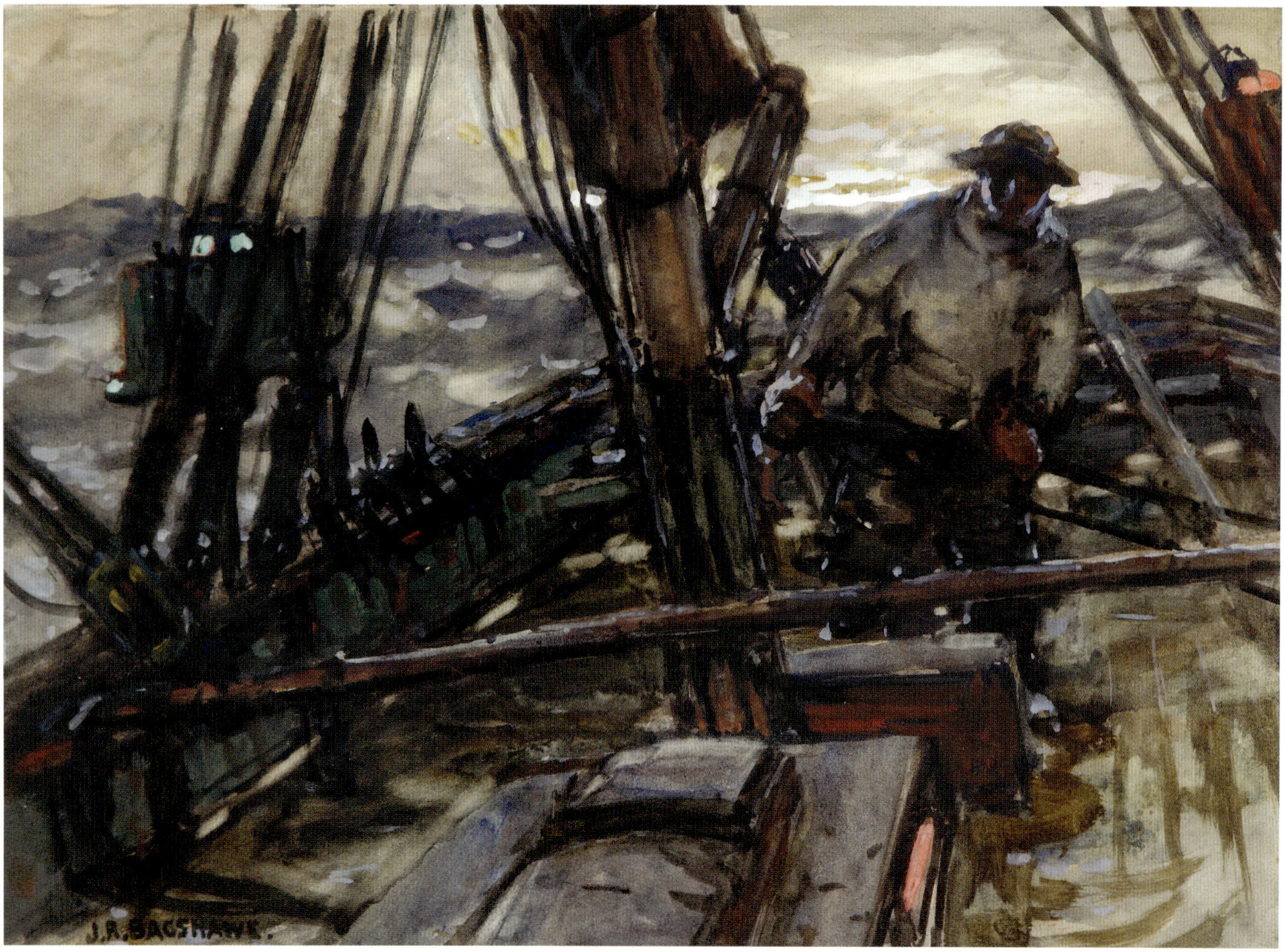

58. The sketch for this watercolour was entitled *The Old Skipper in a Squall* when it illustrated an article on the yawl *True Love*. In it Joseph Bagshawe enhances the drama of the scenes with glimmers of light on the horizon, the glow from the bogie fire and below-decks, and the counterpoise of helmsman and boat in the swell.

but also hosted refreshments for them after arranging a local hockey match.[53]

As noted, Mildred was the daughter of wealthy local shipyard owner Thomas Turnbull. Her marriage to Bagshawe attracted four columns of print in the *Whitby Gazette* in 1901. The arrangements bear significant resemblance to those of Joseph's sister Teresa in London in February of the same year, reported in the *Tablet*.[54]

With two large family celebrations, plus preparing and submitting *In Peril* and *The Ebb Tide* to the Royal Academy that year (and responding to their subsequent success), one might conjecture Bagshawe was fully occupied, as did Enid Pease Robinson:

> The sky was lovely – a delicate pale silver grey, with a darker line for the sea, on the horizon, and beautiful gleaming light on the softly rippling water far below. Mr. Bagshawe evidently thought it was lovely too, for he was gazing out to sea and up at the gathering masses of fleecy grey clouds with a very solemn expression, quite unlike his usual merry, mischievous self. He has changed much during the past year; it must be his impending marriage.[55]

However, it appears that his new family connections proved useful, as both Mildred's brother and father acted as vice-presidents to the Art Club; his sister's new husband, the Marchese Mattei of Capua Palace, Malta, is additionally listed alongside them in the *Gazette* of 1902.

Bagshawe also had to secure suitable accommodation for the couple. After casting around in Staithes for unfurnished lodgings, he settled on a house called Moss Brow close to Sandsend, as Pease Robinson's diary observes. It was rented to him by G. H. Pyman, a member of the Pyman shipping family and owner of a Whitby building firm. Whether a consequence or reason for his choice or not, his new landlord was another of the Club's 'non-executives'. The association seems to have continued beyond the life of the Club as a 'J. Pyman' drove Joseph home after a shooting party at Grinkle Park in the week of his premature death in 1909.

Grinkle Park, an estate owned by Sir Charles and Lady Palmer, had been recently developed along the lines of Waddesdon Manor, using a gardener lured from Castle Howard and a land agent, George Brotchie. Sir Charles acted as both patron and president of the Art Club. He also collected works by Bagshawe which hung in the house, redesigned by the renowned architect Alfred Waterhouse. Mentioned in the Introduction as a nationally significant industrialist (p. 28), his interest in the development of Port Mulgrave, which supplied his own shipyard in Jarrow, was also tied to the Art Club; its resident manager, Mr J. Bruce, was also recruited to 'the board'.

With such connections, it is no surprise that the local MPs for Whitby also joined the patrons. Ernest Beckett (later Lord Grimthorpe), Noel Buxton and Gervase Beckett successively served in this role.[56] The Becketts, who came from a banking family in Leeds, were educated at Eton and Cambridge.[57] Ernest's commitment to the arts is notable for commissioning Auguste Rodin in 1901 to model a bust of Eve Fairfax, then his fiancée.[58]

Two other names are listed as serving in this capacity during the life of the Club. The first is a C. H. Hoyland, whom it is tempting to associate with the artist Hannah (Miss C. H. Hoyland), though there is at present no hard evidence for this. The family of wealthy manufacturers from Sheffield were regular seasonal visitors to the area and their background would certainly have provided the right profile for the role; in 1908 Hoyland is listed as a patron of Jackson's work, for example.[59]

The other name is that of a Mr John (G.) Lyon, who hailed from Pontefract. His business was concerned with the refining of tar into pitch, but it had also diversified into lighterage, using barges for transport to the ports supplying the export market. Lyon was a committed art collector. Initially a patron of Hopwood, he had been introduced by him to Johnson and Knight in particular, who credited the meeting as leading to 'much happiness and enlargement of our social life'.[60]

Notwithstanding the contributions of others, it seems clear that Bagshawe's connections made him the logical choice as Secretary. From his own point of view, endeavours in this regard would clearly have served to raise his own profile both with fellow artists and his future family. The reviewer of the 4th Art Club exhibition, for one, clearly admired his industry:

> It seems mainly owing to Mr. J. R. Bagshawe's enterprise that the exhibition has, this year, enlarged its borders, by adding to the size and importance of the works shown: and we congratulate that energetic and able artist on the measure of success he has attained for the club's efforts.[61]

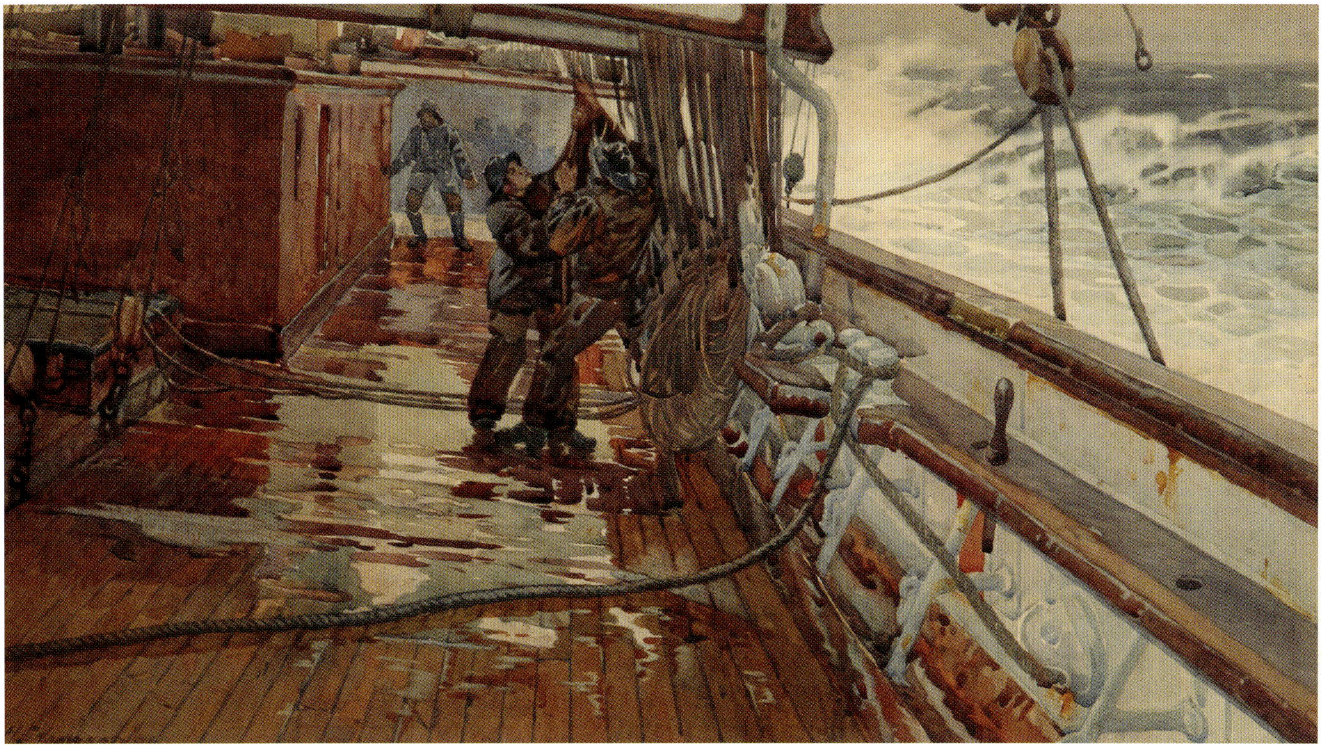

59. Henry Hopwood, *Hauling the Sheets*. Hopwood's experience on his voyages to and from Australia aligned him with several of the other Staithes artists who had not only travelled abroad but had first-hand experience of crewing or sailing vessels, from racing yachts to fishing boats.

Much as Bagshawe may have seemed the obvious choice for Secretary, Henry Hopwood may have appeared a natural fit as Chair of the Club. It seems there was no central senior 'leader', either stylistically or by dint of character, as has been credited to certain other artists' colonies. Other experienced artists who might have taken the role included Mackie, Jackson, Senior and Foster, though the last was to die just a few years later. Mackie had assumed a leading role in the establishment of the Society of Scottish Artists; he had consequently plenty of recent experience in staging shows and good contacts with the contemporary art world. Jackson and Senior both brought links to established patrons in Lancashire and Yorkshire; Jackson was working to an annual stipend from Samuel Barlow and Senior had a close, ongoing association with Sam Wilson, notable for his later donations to Leeds Art Gallery.

Both were also clearly attached to the area. Senior rented, bought and was to build property in Runswick Bay while Jackson married and settled in Hinderwell from 1907. However, at the time of the Art Club's formation neither was to make the commitment – and indeed architectural statement – that Hopwood ventured in 1901–2. He engaged Edgar Wood, friend and sketching companion of Jackson, to design and convert a Hinderwell house known as the Croft.[62] Wood was a successful, avant-garde designer based in Manchester and his Arts and Crafts style made the most of local materials and vernacular forms.

Hopwood also brought the aforementioned patron, J. G. Lyon, who acted as a vice-president to the Club. Whether or not he had an ongoing relationship with Sir Charles Palmer, it is interesting to note that one of the few portraits that Hopwood exhibited was that of Palmer's daughter Hilda in 1893.[63] Alongside this apparent affluence and his connections sat an artistic reputation, established in 1894 by the purchase of one of his first Royal Academy exhibits, via the Chantrey Bequest, for the national collection.

Yet this was not the first such purchase of his work. Discouraged by his lack of commercial success both in painting and lithography, Hopwood had left for Australia around 1888. Exhibiting his on-board pictures upon arrival, one had been purchased for the Art Gallery of New South Wales. Assimilating quickly into the art scene in and around Sydney, he exhibited to some acclaim, garnering comparison with the work of Arthur Streeton when they showed together and painting at the artists' colony at Balmoral with Julian Ashton, among others.[64] After his return, Hopwood remained in touch with the Art Society there, having been charged with finding a premises in London suited to the staging of an exhibition of Australian Art.[65]

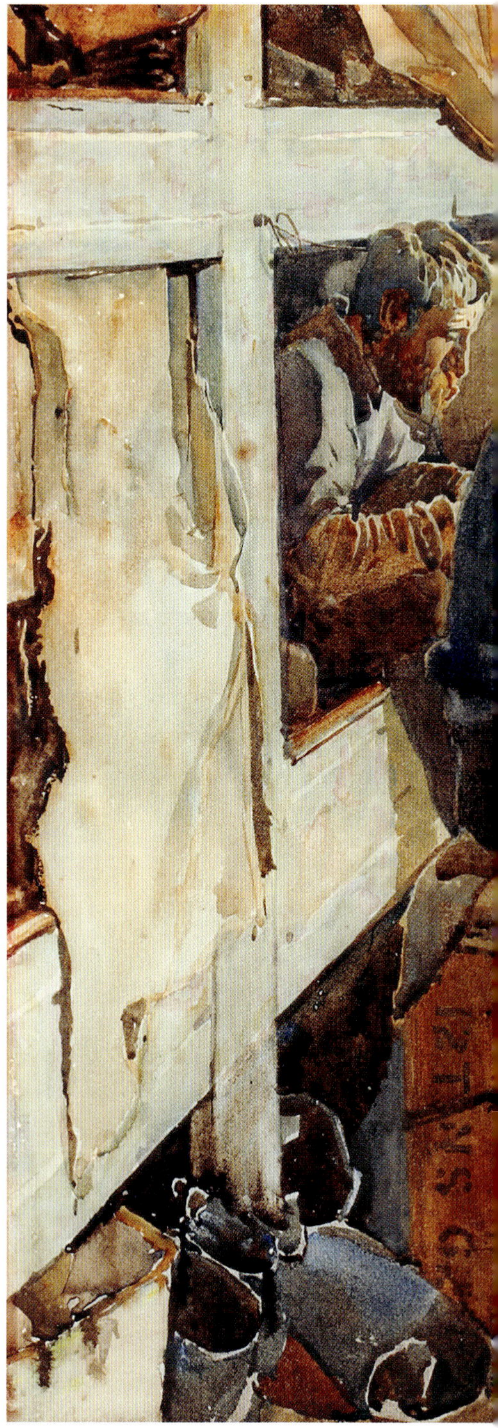

60. Henry Hopwood's departure for Australia kick-started his career as an artist. Arriving in Sydney in 1888, he showed at the New South Wales Art Society and sold this work of 1889, *Dinner in the Foc'sle*, to the Art Gallery. He painted in similar fashion on the return journey and exhibited a selection from both voyages at the Manchester Academy and the Walker Art Gallery, Liverpool in 1891–2 (**14** and **59**).

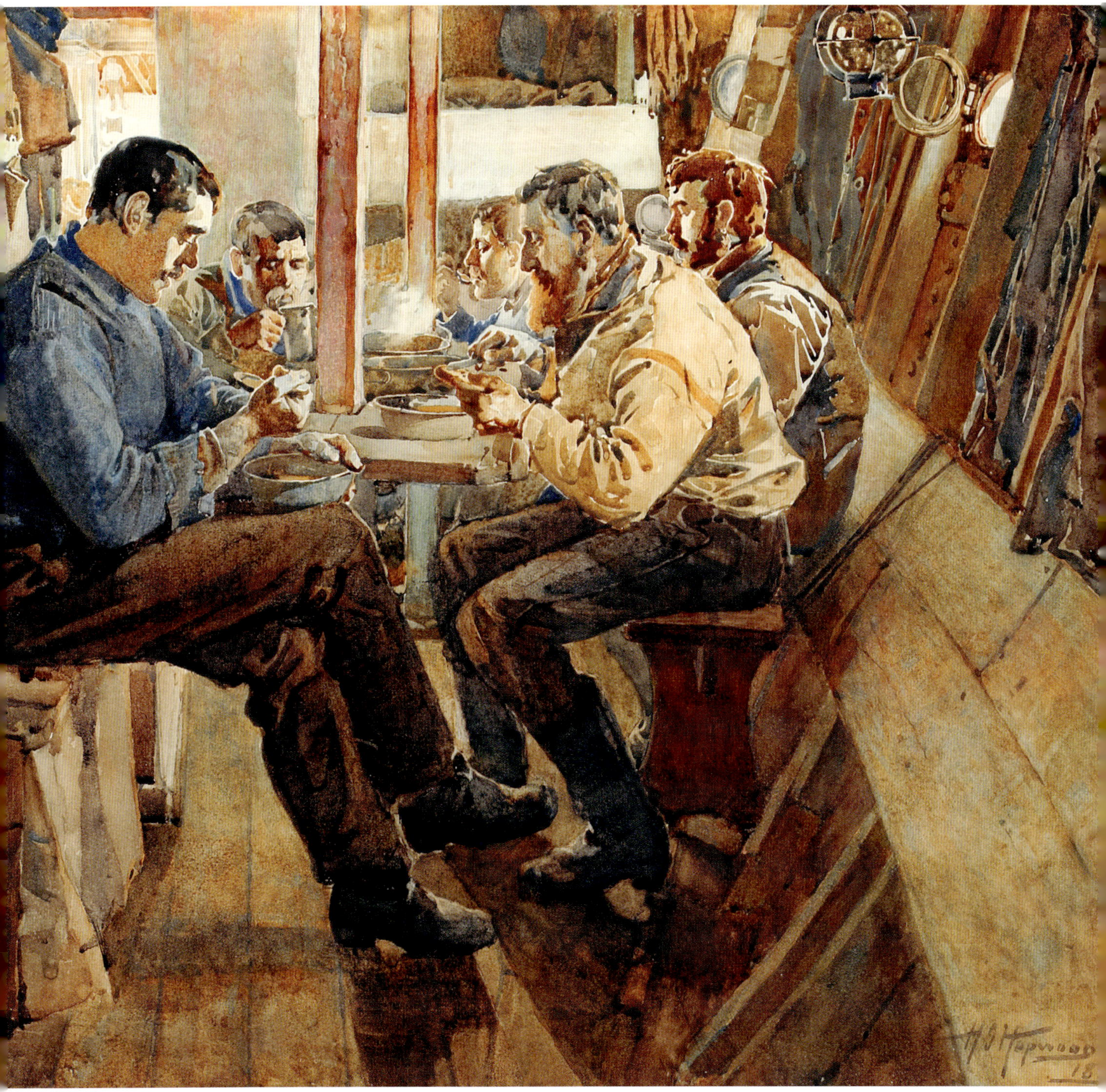

CONTINENTAL CONNECTIONS

Hopwood's artwork on the journeys to and from Australia aligned his interests with those among the Staithes artists such as Dade, Bagshawe, Mason and Mayor whose maritime interest was a vital element of their work. Furthermore, this period of travel and relative success in Australia seems to have spurred him to further improvement, with time in the years immediately afterwards spent at academies in both France and Belgium.

As a result, Hopwood shared a common continental experience with at least 17 other members of the group.[66] Throughout the 1880s Richardson, Rigg, Dade, Jackson, Mayor and Ingall were all in Paris. Following in their footsteps in the 1890s were Crawshaw, Terry, Teasdale, Conway, Knight and Friedenson. The last spent time there with Hopwood which the pair extended, travelling together to Antwerp, just before Bagshawe in his turn left London for Belgium to study for two years in Bruges.

The Royal Academy in Antwerp did not have the status of its equivalent in Paris. However, by this time it had acquired an established tradition of English students including another Staithes member, Albert Stevens. The British intake had increased as the result of a favourable reception for the head of the National Art Training School (South Kensington) in 1877.

John Sparkes's report on his visit to review their facilities and training methods was highly complimentary. He stressed the benefits of a more testing series of timed exercises and competitions, including more challenging compositions. Practice laid emphasis on boldness of handling and colour in life classes, as well as more options for genre and landscape painting and a strong bias towards realism. In addition, under the directorship of Charles Verlat, British students through the 1870s and 1880s found particular favour. The smaller and more intimate environment of masterclasses – originally a German discipline, which Crawshaw may well have experienced in his time in Dusseldorf and Karlsruhe – was opened to them, having been previously reserved for Dutch and Belgians, and introductions to influential figures were proffered.

This may have been where Hopwood initially picked up an inclination to visit Holland, which he was to do in the company of the Knights. His Belgian experience was shared by Senior and Hill, both of whom painted in Bruges at later points in their career. Although studying in England, Hill's first pictures for the Staithes Art Club detail scenes in Bavaria, attributed by previous writers to his travelling with the head of the school, Hubert Herkomer, to the latter's native region.[67]

Opposite: 61. Dermod O'Brien followed the same path to France and Belgium as many Staithes artists, eschewing study in Britain. He spent four years at the Fine Art Academy, Antwerp, the title of this work from 1890, and a further two in Paris as a contemporary of Friedenson, Hopwood and Mayor, before heading home to Ireland.

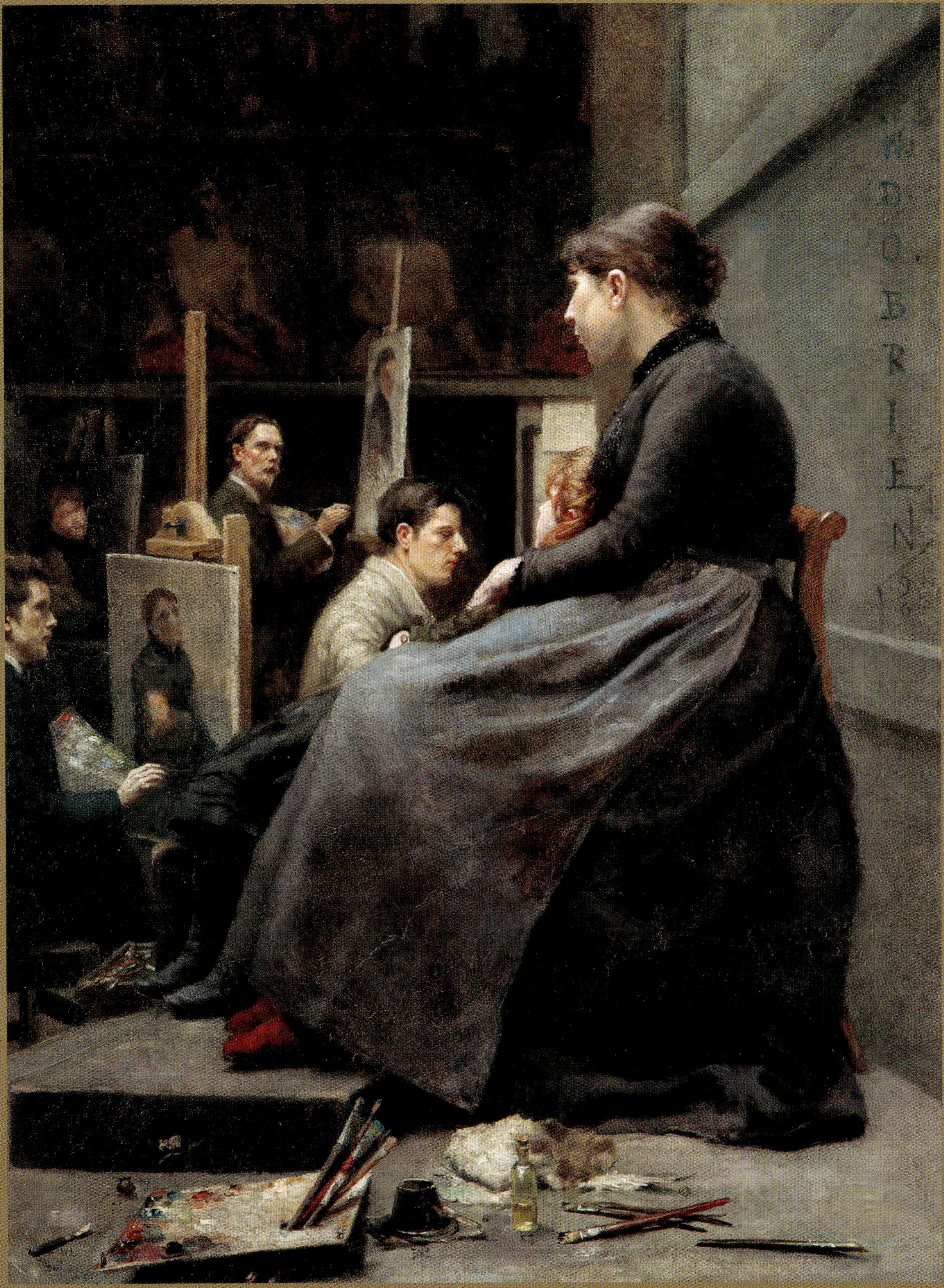

The Knights cited both Dutch influence and that of the Newlyn school from their formative exhibition-going. Indeed 'Newlyners' often referred to the Belgian Academy as 'Verlat's', so strong was its influence over many of the British artists who painted there. Stanhope Forbes noted the connection in 1885:

> What lodestone of artistic metal the place contains I know not, but its effects were strongly felt, in the studios of Paris and Antwerp particularly, by a number of young English painters studying there, who just about then, by some common impulse, seemed drawn towards this corner of their native land.[68]

Notwithstanding this, the majority of the artists who painted at Staithes attended various studios and academies in Paris. The Ecole des Beaux Arts, though the pinnacle of the art school system in France, presented challenges for foreign students. As travel to Paris became increasingly popular, it gradually closed its doors to those from abroad. Private academies such as the Colarossi, where Crawshaw and Garrido met, capitalised, with that run by Rodolphe Julian proving particularly popular. It proposed a Parisian training for all, including women, and Staithes artists attended the classes there both full and part time. They often supplemented this experience with further learning in individual studios, such as that of Bonnat or Carolus-Duran.

Confirmation of their attendance can be gleaned from registers and exhibiting records. It is harder to judge what effect the teaching had on the artists' techniques, given that so few pieces remain from their student days; difficult too to judge what individual mark may have been left by the experience, though the wider contemporary journal accounts and range of other artist memoirs are numerous.

Likely of most importance was the cosmopolitan and communal nature of the establishments and the discipline shown by the hours many kept. Henry Herbert La Thangue, who was there at the same time as Jackson, appreciated the discipline of working to a demanding schedule, though by his own admission he did not take full advantage of Paris as a whole.[69]

Jackson was registered at the Académie Julian in 1885, following in the footsteps of his fellow Lancastrians; Edward Stott had left for Paris in 1879 and studied under Gerome and Carolus-Duran; William Stott, his schoolfriend, was there in 1880–1 with John Lavery,[70] who returned in 1884.[71] Correspondence from Jackson's Runswick Bay travelling companion suggests that he too was

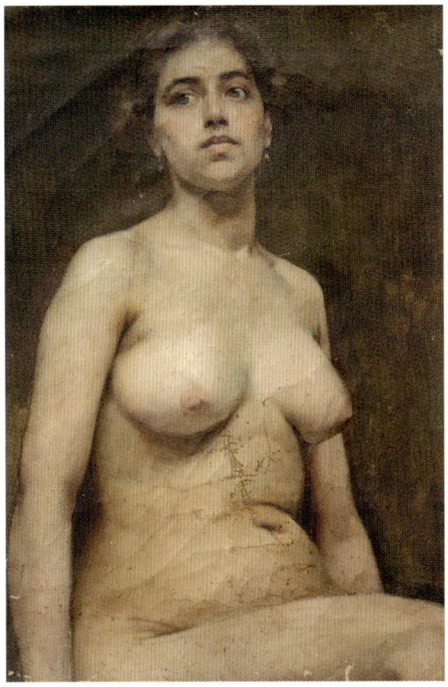
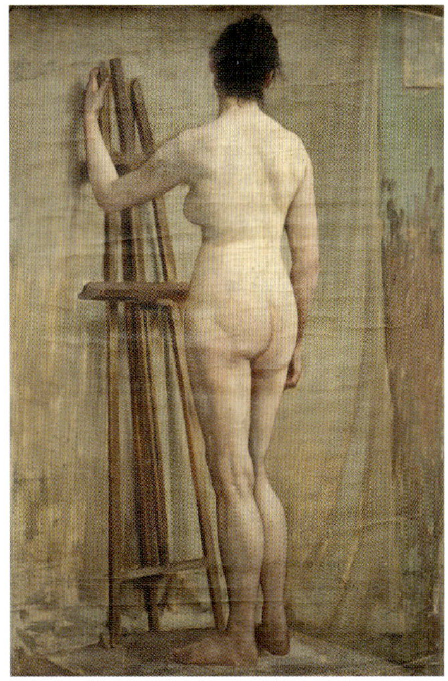

62a and 62b. Ernest Rigg studied at the Académie Julian in Paris in the 1890s, as did over 15 of the artists connected to the Club. They took full advantage of the opportunity presented to paint the nude from life. Rigg's untitled extant canvases are the only examples of his work from this period presently known to the author.

present in Paris that year, as was Ernest Dade. It proved a momentous year in artistic terms, as the first *Salon des Indépendants* was held in December 1884.[72]

A decade after the Impressionists' first exhibition, this featured works by Cézanne, Signac, van Gogh and Gauguin. Although many students admitted retrospectively to such exhibitions bypassing them, Charles Mackie, though not studying in Paris, was there in the early 1890s viewing a Manet show at Paul Durand-Ruel's gallery; he then went on to visit both Vuillard and Gauguin.[73]

Many students (particularly Scots) returned year on year – for example, Lavery was back in Paris with James Guthrie at the same time as Mackie. They took advantage of the breaks in the concentrated work at academies either to return to Britain or else go on sketching trips. It is clear from correspondence and resulting works that Jackson did both. He painted in Brittany at Concarneau,[74] having already travelled with Mackie through Italy in 1882.

Interestingly even the photographer Tom Watson, whose professional portfolio rarely pictures scenes beyond cycling distance of Lythe, travelled at regular intervals across Europe. He visited the USA at the time of Chicago's World Fair in 1893 and Paris for the Exposition Universelle in 1900. Between 1899 and 1902 Watson visited Norway and went to Switzerland at least five times (**17**).

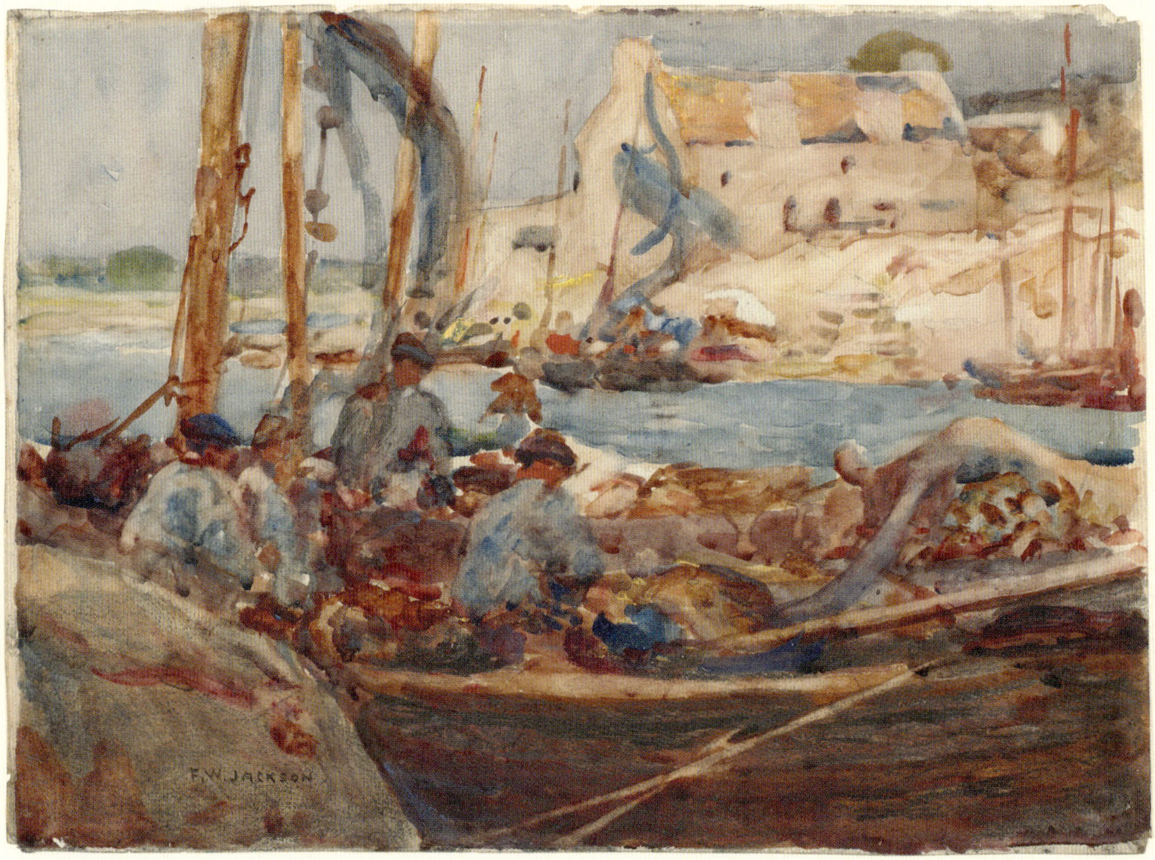

63. Fred Jackson followed fellow Lancastrians William and Edward Stott to Paris to study at the Académie Julian in the 1880s. Though he did not visit the famed colony at Grez-sur-Loing, where William Stott made his name, it seems from this picture, *Sardine Boats at Concarneau*, that Jackson did travel to Brittany at that time.

Hopwood too, after his studies on the continent, presented works in a solo show in 1897 as the culmination of an extended stay, encompassing both Brittany and Normandy. Yet probably the most obvious example is Fred Mayor, who seems to have regularly been in Paris between 1886 and 1892, and about whose subsequent French connections more is written in Chapter 4. He alternated his studies in Paris with time at a studio in London, staying at the same address as Frank Brangwyn, as well as more travel abroad. Mayor had studied at the South Kensington schools, as had Oliver Sheppard, a future art master at Nottingham and friend of Knight and Johnson. Further study in Paris was seen as a natural next step by both Mayor and Sheppard, despite the London option of the Slade, where Mark Senior is said to have learned about the latest French techniques from the professor Alphonse Legros.[75]

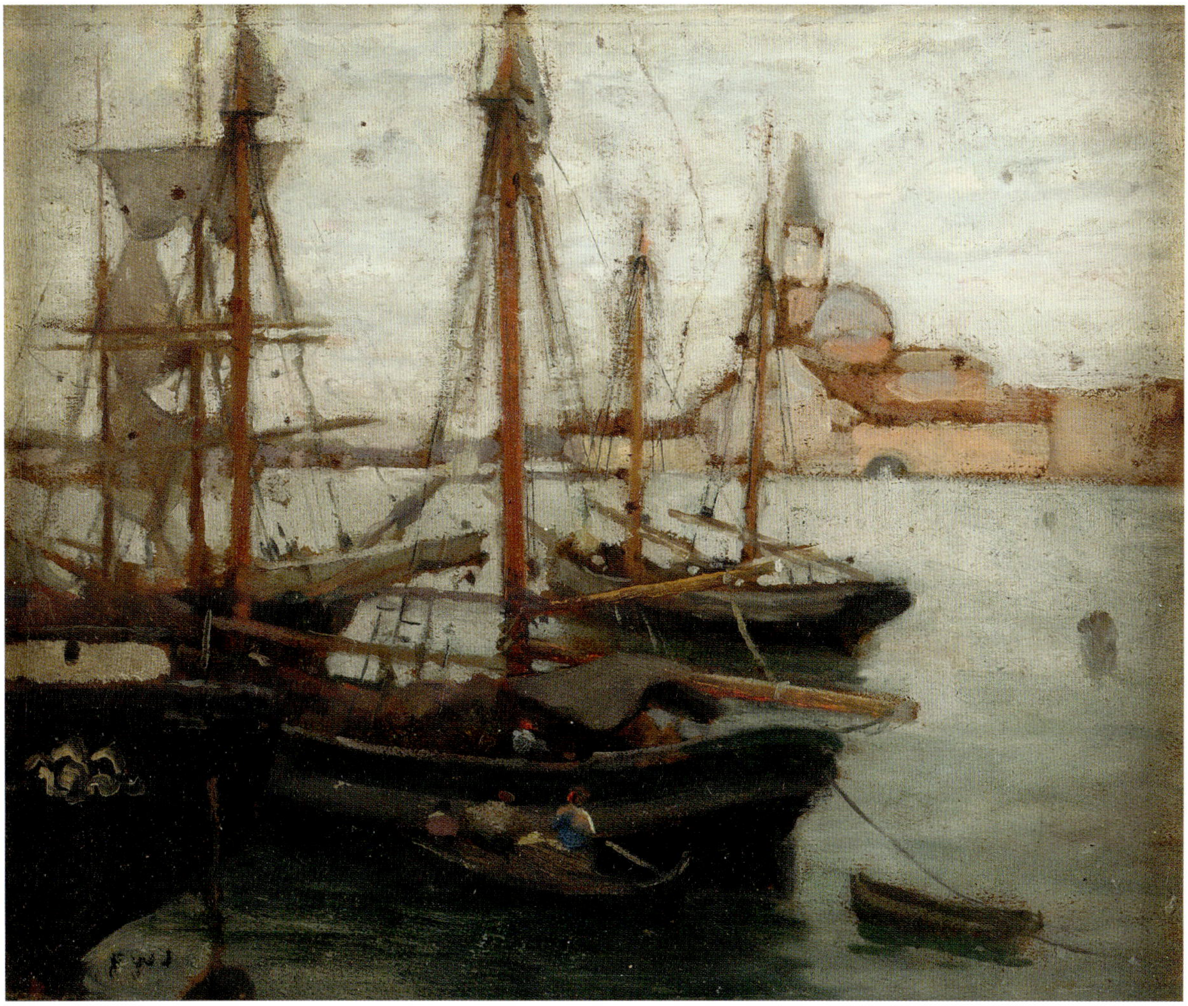

64. Before studying in Paris Jackson had travelled with Charles Mackie to Italy; he subsequently painted in Spain and North Africa too. This painting, *Venice* (c. 1890), was donated to York Art Gallery in memory of Walter Butterworth, his companion on a final trip to Russia shortly before the First World War.

This pattern was still the case in 1901 as Sydney Lough Thompson, arriving from New Zealand and quickly tiring of his experience at Heatherley's art school in London, travelled to Staithes for the summer and then to Paris, heading for the Académie Julian.[76]

By 1884 the South Kensington schools were at the apex of a network of 180 state associated schools across Britain and Ireland. Although clearly failing the students (in the eyes of 'modernists') in a strong tradition of life painting and modelling, the schools ran competitions to which artists from across the regions submitted work. Of the Staithes artists, Knight seems to have been the most regular contributor, winning several prizes. Works by others also bear the competition stamp, including Johnson and Hannah Hoyland, who attended the Royal Female and the Westminster Schools of Art.

As with those abroad, many travelled while not attending the colleges. Anecdotal evidence places Senior in Walberswick in Suffolk, Friedenson in Scotland and Jackson, arguably the most peripatetic, in Wales at Conwy, painting early in his training days with the so-called Manchester school of artists. However, no other location exerted the attraction that prompted their regular visits to the north-east coast. It is thus time to turn to Staithes, Runswick Bay and the surrounding area which became a centre of their artistic activity and, for many, developed as an increasingly important part of their lives.

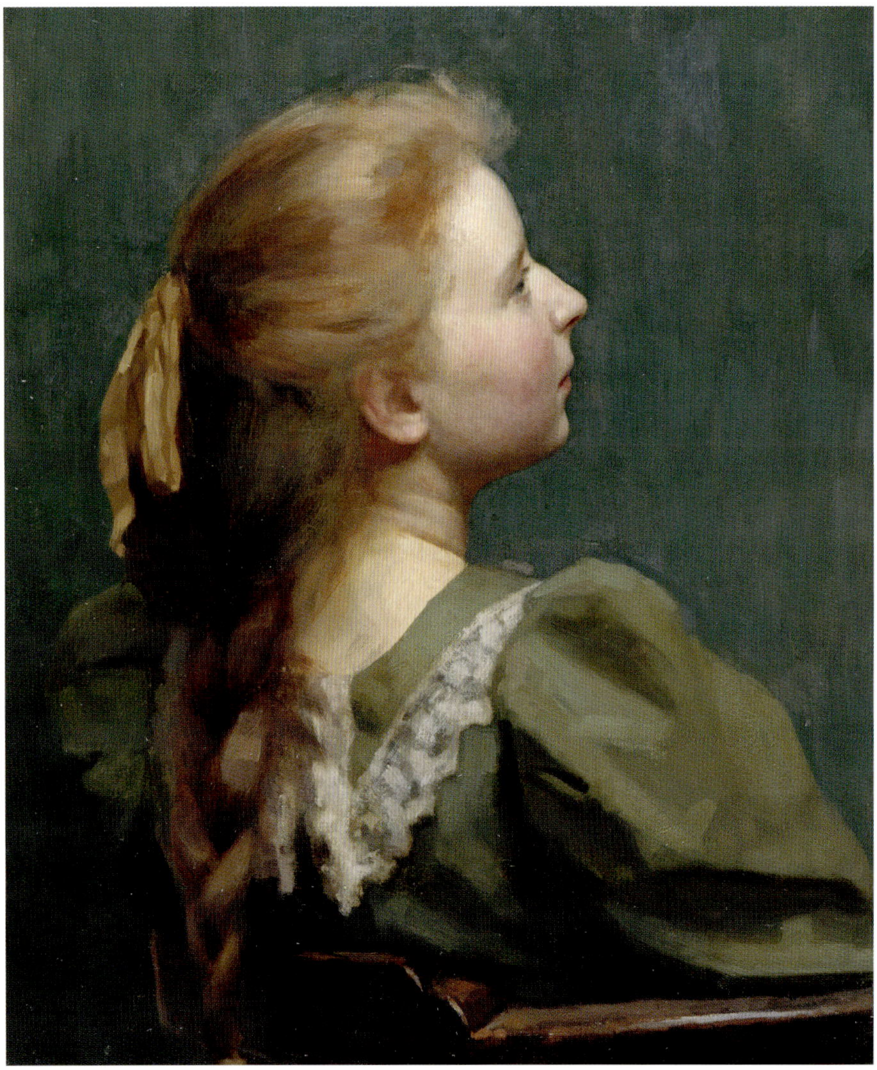

65. Harold Knight was the outstanding student at Nottingham School of Art, and his submissions to the National Schools competitions at South Kensington garnered multiple awards. This *Portrait of Laura Johnson*, dated c. 1900, was kept by his fellow student (and future wife) Laura Johnson until her death in 1970. She bequeathed it to the Royal Academy.

66. Very few recognised pieces by Hannah Hoyland remain to define her style. This untitled still life bears the stamp of the South Kensington schools, attesting to its submission to one of their competitions and a date of around 1890. At this time Hannah attended both the Royal Female and the Westminster Schools of Art in London.

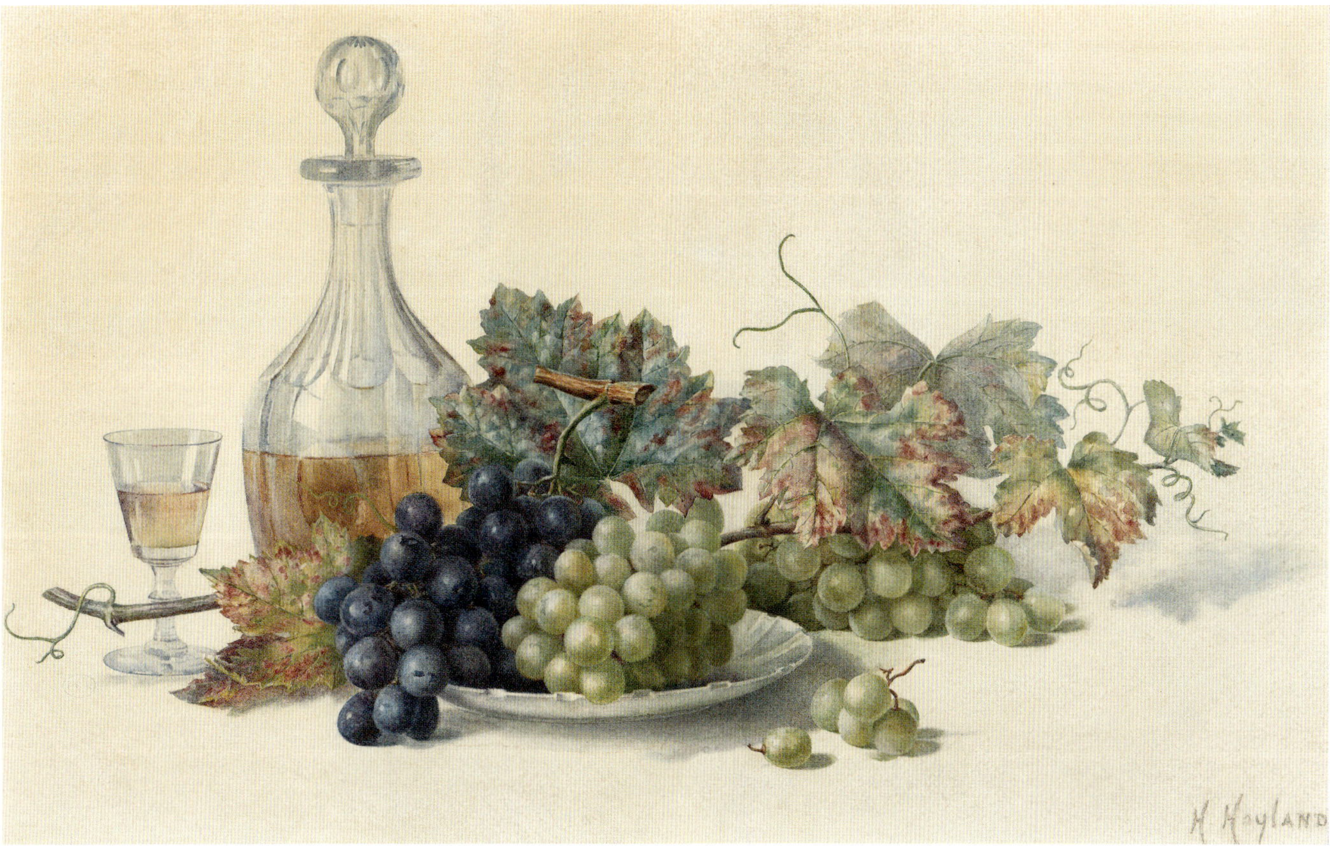

ENDNOTES

25 Hart, J. (ed.), *The Secret Staithes Diary of Enid Lucy Pease Robinson*, 2010, 75.

26 Knight, Laura, *Oil Paint and Grease Paint*, 1936, 91–2.

27 Newton, Laura, *Painting at the Edge: British Coastal Art Colonies 1880–1930*, 2005, 111.

28 George Swinstead was not a member of the Art Club, but was a regular visitor to Walberswick in Suffolk from his home in London. It is fascinating to conjecture who the 'new artist' might have been; Sydney Lough Thompson, a New Zealander, was also painting in Staithes at this time.

29 *Whitby Gazette*, 26 August 1904, 1. Included in Slater, R., *Artists Colonies in Staithes & Runswick Bay*, unpublished PhD thesis, 2010, 203; Bullamore, C., *The Staithes Group of Artists*, 2014, 29. Fred Jackson, James Booth and Mark Senior are others known to have built studios adjoining their properties. Although informal gatherings are evidenced as taking place, no notices are thought to have been issued.

30 They represented the local art society, as well as a club known as the Arcadians.

31 William Gilbert Foster did not sign up to the Staithes Art Club himself. However, he is credited as a crucial figure in introducing several of the members to the area.

32 *The Newcastle Weekly Chronicle*, 23 June 1900. In Slater, R., *Artists' Colonies in Staithes and Runswick Bay*, unpublished PhD thesis, 2010.

33 Hiley, Michael, *Frank Sutcliffe – Photographer of Whitby*, 1974, 79.

34 National Visual Arts Library of Ireland (NIVAL), Special Collections: The Oliver Sheppard Papers. Letter dated November 1903 from Laura Johnson (Knight) to Rosie Good (Sheppard); Knight, L., *Oil Paint and Grease Paint*, 1936, 107–8. An example

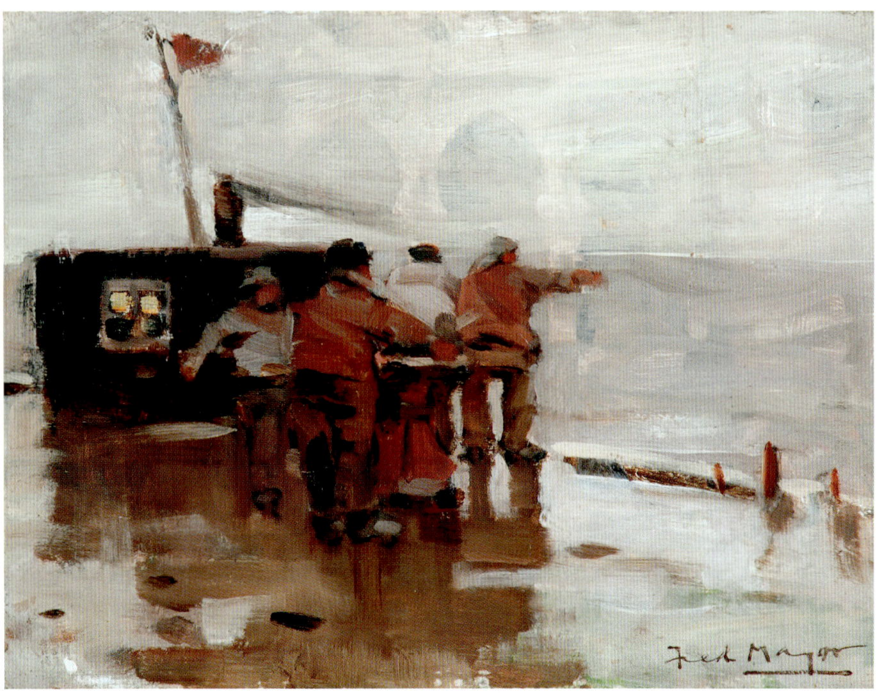

67. William Fred Mayor spent several years in Paris and is known to have travelled widely. His work, such as this small undated oil *Fishermen*, is compared to that of Edward Stott and Frank Brangwyn. Mayor is reputed to have lived and worked near to both artists during his early years in London and Sussex.

of a retitled painting, though from the Newlyn group, is an 1897 view of St Ives by William Titcomb (Oldham Art Gallery Collection). Originally titled *Jubilee*, it was not hung at the Royal Academy, but was accepted when resubmitted bearing the name *Good news from the Front*.

35 Staithes Art Club 1905 Exhibition list, Bagshawe Family Archive.

36 Clark, Pat, *People, Places, Piazzas: The Life of Charles Hodge Mackie*, 2017, 91. It seems likely that Mackie was abroad in Spain with Lionel Crawshaw; work from their Spanish travels was shown the following year.
The titles of two of Jobling's 1904 exhibits support his travelling to Holland in 1903 (see Appendix).

37 Isa Jobling was the only married woman who was a female member and perhaps therefore not listed, being 'represented' by her husband.

38 Jordan, Rosamund, *Staithes Group Centenary Exhibition*, York, 2003, 48: Hill is credited as being a founding member;
Phillips, Peter, *The Staithes Group*, 1993, 49: Hill is credited as being an 'early member';
Haworth, *Staithes Group*, 5: Hill is not listed as a member; 8: Hill is listed as being present at a meeting to elect a committee for 1902 exhibition.

39 *Whitby Gazette*, 8 August 1902.

40 Phillips, *The Staithes Group*, 1993, 15.

41 *Whitby Gazette*, 8 August 1902.

42 Harold and Laura Knight contributed seven works to the 1904 show, which Hopwood is reported as hosting at his home in Hinderwell from 26 August to 22 September.

43 Phillips, *The Staithes Group*, 1993, 23.

44 Isa Jobling's exhibition history is explored in Chapter 3.

45 Newton, L., 2005, *Painting at the Edge: British Coastal Art Colonies 1880–1930*, 125.
Millard, J., *Romance with the Northeast*, 41.

46 The Dutch Gallery changed its name to E. J. van Wisselingh in 1906.

47 Newton, L., 2005, *Painting at the Edge*, 124.

48 Richardson, G., *T. Watson, Photographer of Lythe, Near Whitby*, 1992, 15.

49 Mark Senior was a member of the Savage Club in Leeds, Ernest Rigg The Arcadians in Bradford and Robert Jobling the Bewick, then the Pen and Palette in Newcastle.

50 Knight, L., *Oil Paint and Grease Paint*, 1936, 92.

51 *Yorkshire Evening Post*, 30 August 1939, Rowland Hill, 'A Seaside Colony of Artists'. This would prove a direct parallel to the building of glass studios in Newlyn organised by the artists there, or the arrangements in Skagen with Brondum's Inn, in which artists' work was displayed.

52 The Unthanks' coble was lost at sea the night before the wedding of their son and adopted daughter. Harold Knight's portrait *Grief* has been linked to this tragedy, which affected the whole village. Knight, L., *Oil Paint and Grease Paint*, 1936, 109.

53 Frank, *Sea Painter: The Life and Work of J. R. Bagshawe*, 2010, 37. Mildred went on a cycling excursion with a party including the Brotchies.
Knight, L., *Oil Paint and Grease Paint*, 1936, 87. Laura played hockey and took tea at the Brotchies' house in Hinderwell; George Brotchie was Sir Charles Palmer's land agent.

54 *The Tablet: The International Catholic News Weekly*, 23 February 1901.

55 Hart, J. (ed.), *The Secret Staithes Diary of Enid Lucy Pease Robinson*, 2010, 20.

56 The *Whitby Gazette*, 19 September 1902, reports a visit by E. Beckett and Sir Charles Palmer to the Staithes Art Club.

57 It appears that Noel Buxton, as well as the Becketts, was educated at Trinity College, Cambridge.

58 The bust is now in the collection of the Victoria & Albert Museum, London.

59 Manchester City Art Gallery, exh. cat., 1908. 110: *Ploughing the Headland*; 135: *Discussing the Night's Catch.*

60 Knight, L., *Oil Paint and Grease Paint*, 1936, 139.

61 *Whitby Gazette*, 19 August 1904.

62 Now titled Silkstone Hall, it still stands on the edge of Hinderwell today. It was Grade II listed in 2015.

63 *Old Watercolour Society's Club*, vol. II, 1925, 59.

64 *The Centennial Magazine*, vol. 3, no. 2 (September 1890), 99.

65 This exhibition eventually took place in 1898 at the Grafton Galleries, under the direction of the Trustees of the Art Gallery of New South Wales, at the urging of Julian Ashton. It featured over 400 works and was critically acclaimed.

66 Of these 17, Laura Johnson, through her family connections, spent a brief period learning art in Saint Quentin while Isa Thompson, it is said, 'was sent to complete her studies in Paris'. Phillips, *The Staithes Group*, 1993, 28.

67 Phillips, *The Staithes Group*, 1993, 48; Jordan, *Staithes Group Centenary Exhibition*, 2003, 27.

68 Stanhope Forbes: 'A Newlyn Retrospect', 81. In Slater. R.,unpublished PhD thesis, 2010, 95.

69 The letters and memoirs of artists from Runswick and Staithes contain frequent references to how hard they were working in spite of the weather, temperatures, studio conditions and similar issues.

70 Campbell, Julian, *Irish Impressionists in France and Belgium 1850–1914*, 1984, 65. They are known to have frequented the same café on the rue Luxembourg.

71 Lavery, John, *The Life of a Painter*, 1940, 41–56.

72 Jackson and the Canadian William Brymner travelled from Paris to Runswick Bay in June 1884 (see Chapter 2). This is confirmed in correspondence from Brymner to his family. It therefore appears that Jackson must have already been in Paris in 1883–4.

73 Mackie honeymooned in France in 1892 and travelled both to Normandy and Brittany via Paris.

74 One of the pictures that he exhibited at the 2nd Staithes Art Club Exhibition was of Concarneau (see Appendix).

75 This is anecdotal evidence from Mary Oddie, the artist's granddaughter.

76 King, Julie, *At Home and Abroad: Sydney Lough Thompson*, 1990, exh. cat., 24.

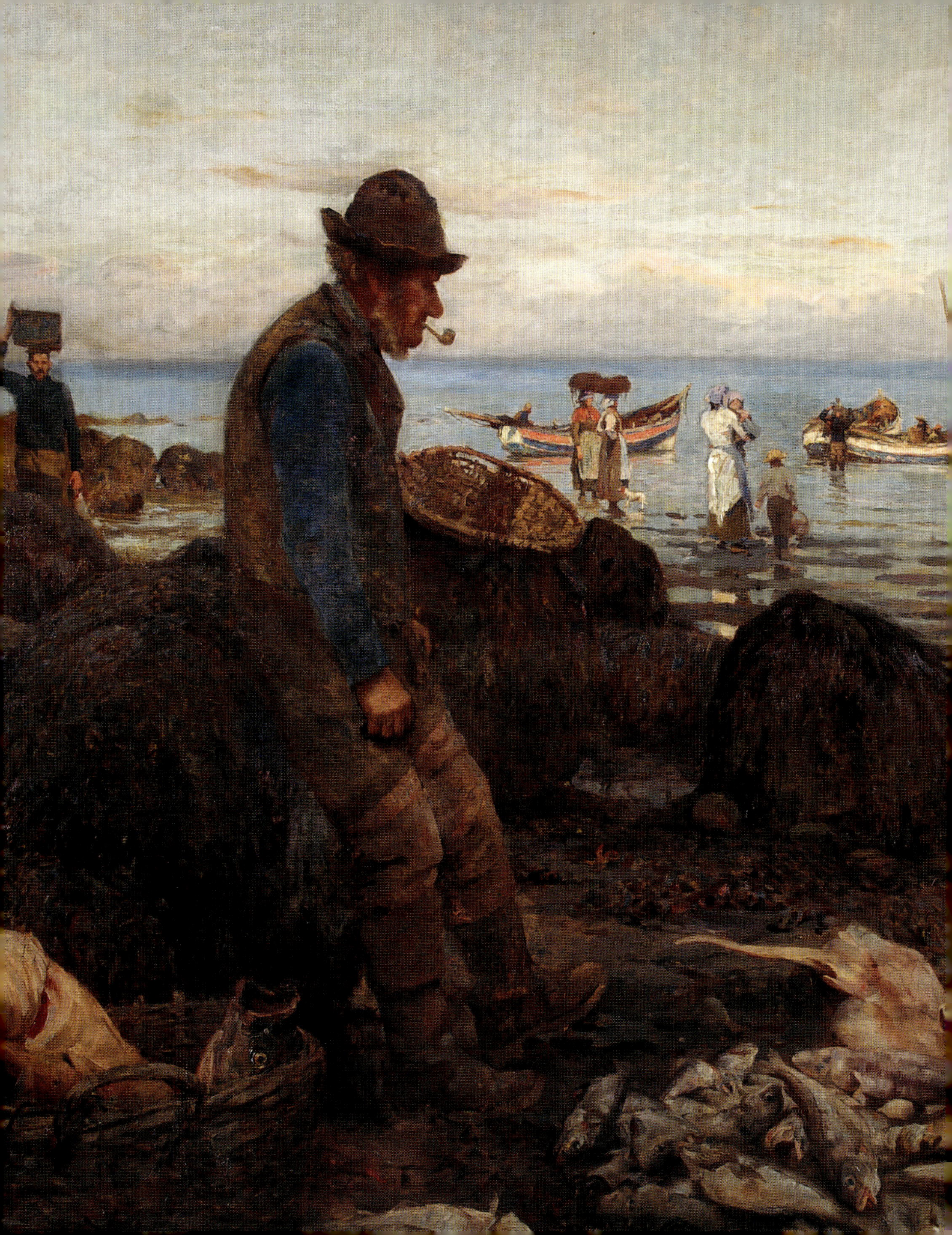

CHAPTER 2

LIFE

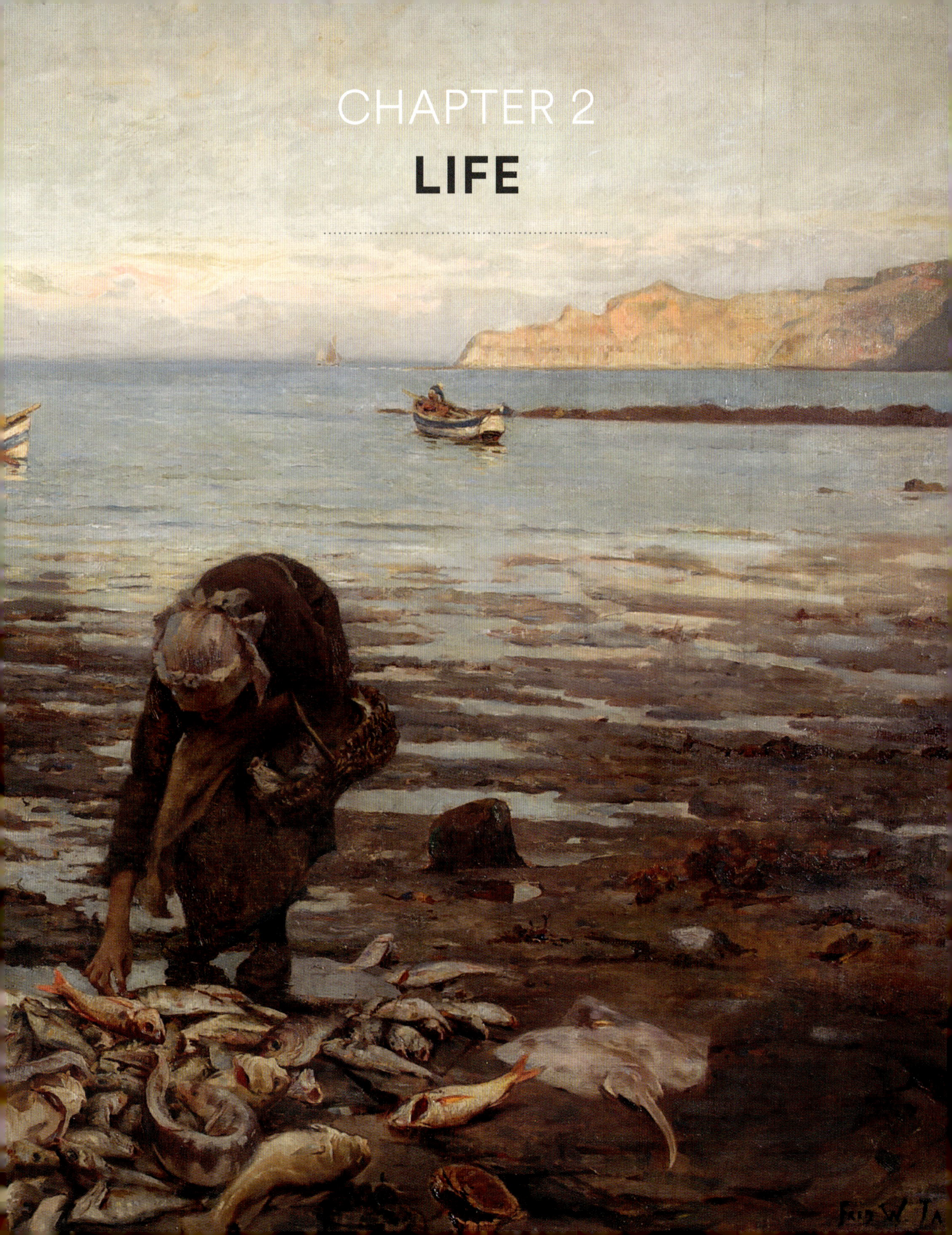

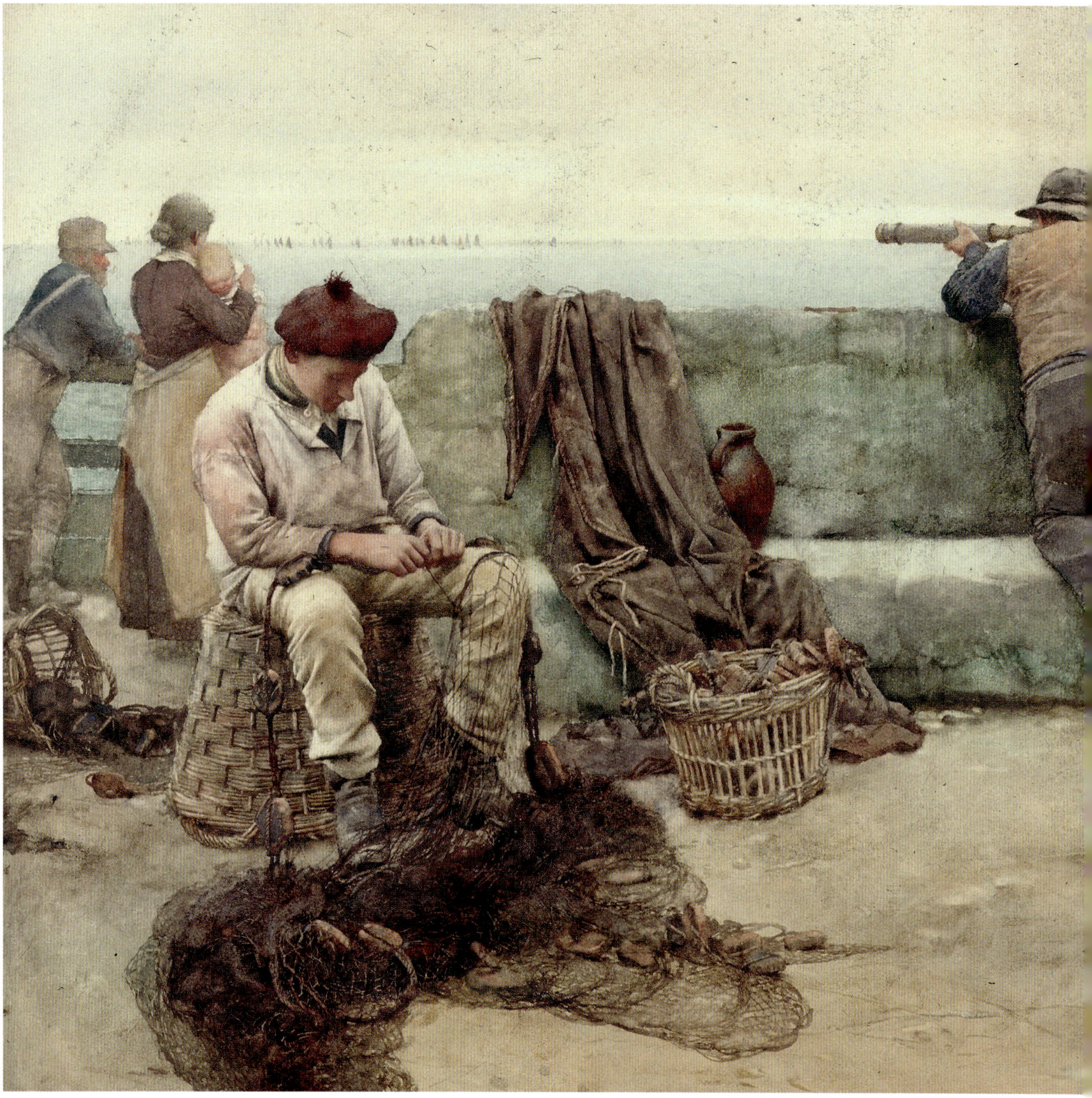

Previous spread: 68. The mid-1880s was an important time for Fred Jackson. He started painting in Runswick Bay and also enjoyed success in Paris, where he had just studied. He exhibited at the Salon in both 1884 and 1885 with coastal and landscape scenes, such as this work, entitled *The Harvest of the Sea* and dated 1885.

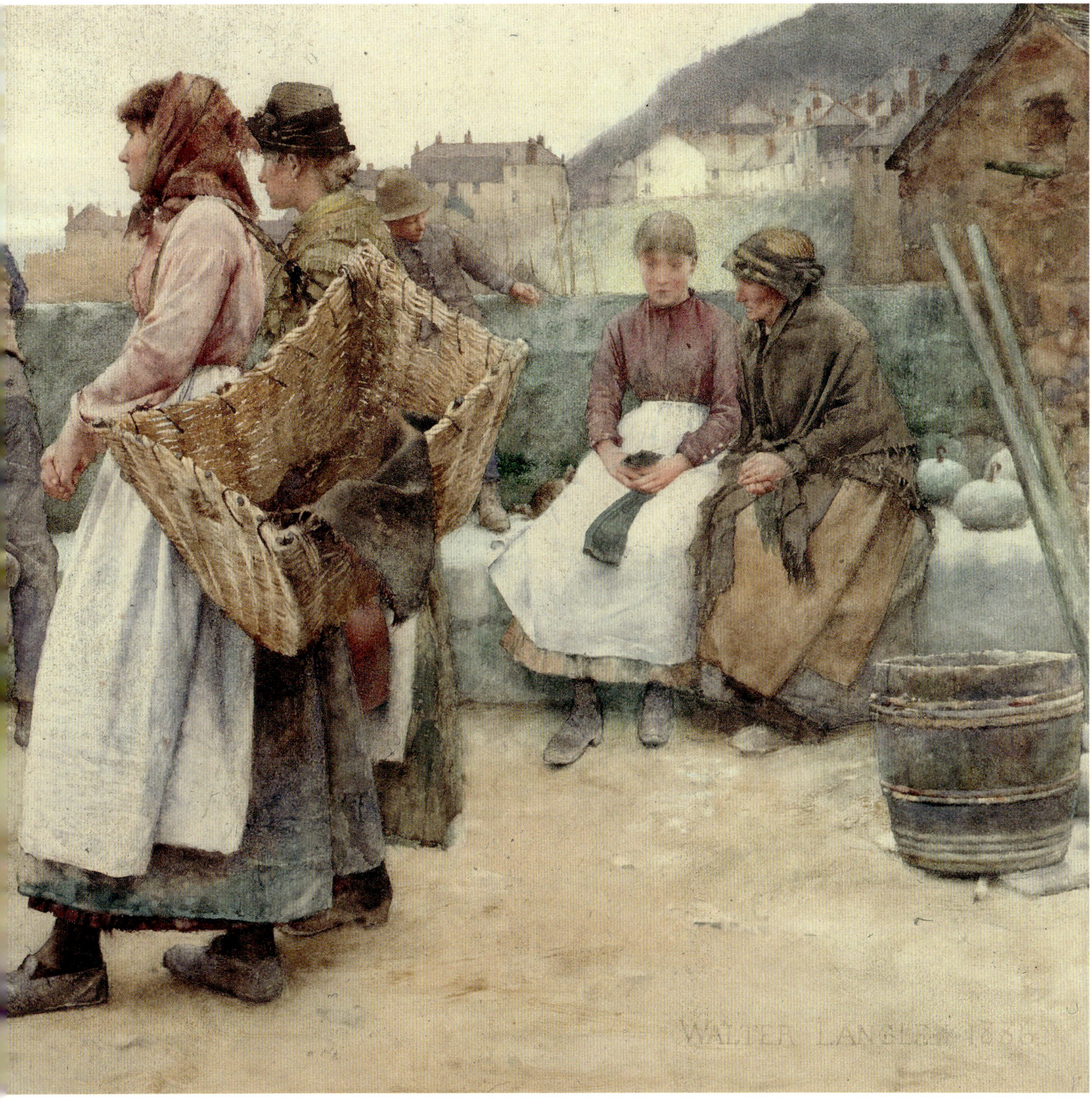

69. Walter Langley, pioneer of the Newlyn school, began his career as a lithographer like several of the Staithes artists; he also came from a similarly poor background. *In a Cornish Fishing Village – Departure of the Fleet for the North*, a large watercolour of 1886, he shows the fishing fleet leaving for Yorkshire. Boats from the Cornish fleet were a feature on the east coast, following the herring there from June to September.

CHAPTER 2
LIFE

> On both sides of us is a precipitous line of coast, with bristling cliffs, washed by a boiling surf in some places, and in others fringed with a narrow beach, on which gigantic moss-strewn bowlders [*sic*] are piled. The sea itself melts in the extreme horizon ... the wind strikes with unrestrained violence ... [it is a] high white coast ... with the German Ocean chafing against it.[77]

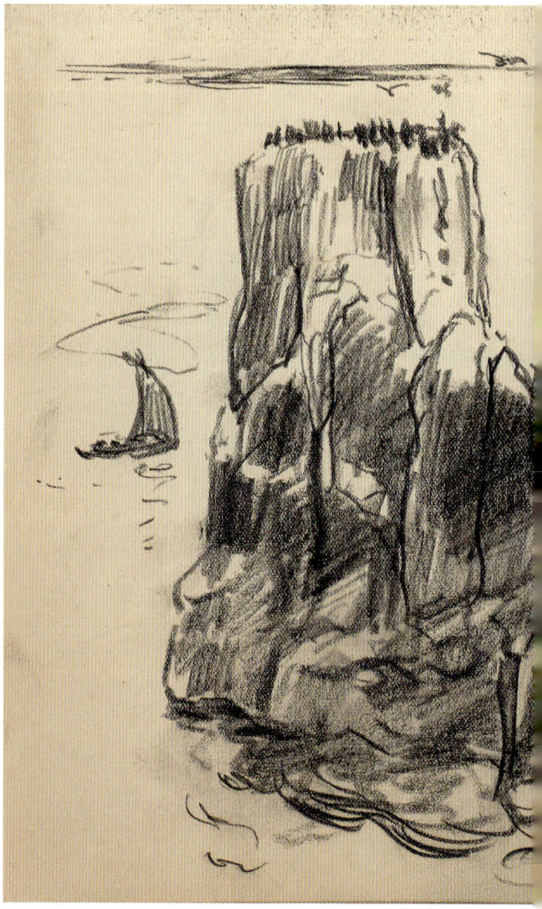

So reads a description of the north-east coast in *Harper's Magazine* of 1884 as Fred Jackson and fellow artists arrived in Runswick Bay.

It goes on to detail, in slightly less daunting but no less pictorial fashion, the quaintness and historic nature of the towns, the 'paintable' aspect of the villages and the intriguing fact that there were those among the 'dales of the north-east coast' who 'cling to the belief in witchcraft even yet'.

These qualities were seemingly the object of popular artistic endeavour as, during the second half of the nineteenth century, knots of artists established themselves in rural communities – first across France and then through the rest of Europe. Training in the art schools of Paris, in particular, they fanned out during their vacations to identify places and subjects worthy of their new ambitions. These ambitions consisted of a desire to be true to nature, which consequently led to painting *en plein air* in a range of locations. In doing so the students followed the example of early pioneers such as Jean-François Millet and his Barbizon school in the forests at Fontainebleau.

Increasingly these young artists sought out the hinterland of Brittany, famous for its wildness, as well as the region's coasts and villages. Here they sought to test themselves against the challenges of nature, with Brittany's rock-bound coast in particular offering 'endless variety of colour and form to the tourist, painter or zoologist'.

Yet it was not just the rugged beauty of the landscape that caught the artists' attention but also the way of life of its inhabitants, conspicuous for a picturesque religiosity. *The Magazine of Art*, citing an earlier text, describes how:

> The love of certain customs and habits has been transmitted in great fidelity, owing to the isolated position and the strong clannishness of the race. At times we wonder whether we are in France, on hearing the native *patois*, partly Welsh, partly Cornish, both in sound and accent. The old Arthurian legends still haunt the land, the rites and ceremonies inherited from early times still exist... Over all the country is thrown a strange romance, in which religion, history, and superstition have played a prominent part.[78]

70. Joseph Bagshawe's sketchbooks (1890–1909) are full of coastal features – not only from Yorkshire, but also Ireland, France, Holland and even the Channel Islands. It is tempting to place this untitled drawing at the famous cliffs and seabird colonies around Flamborough Head.

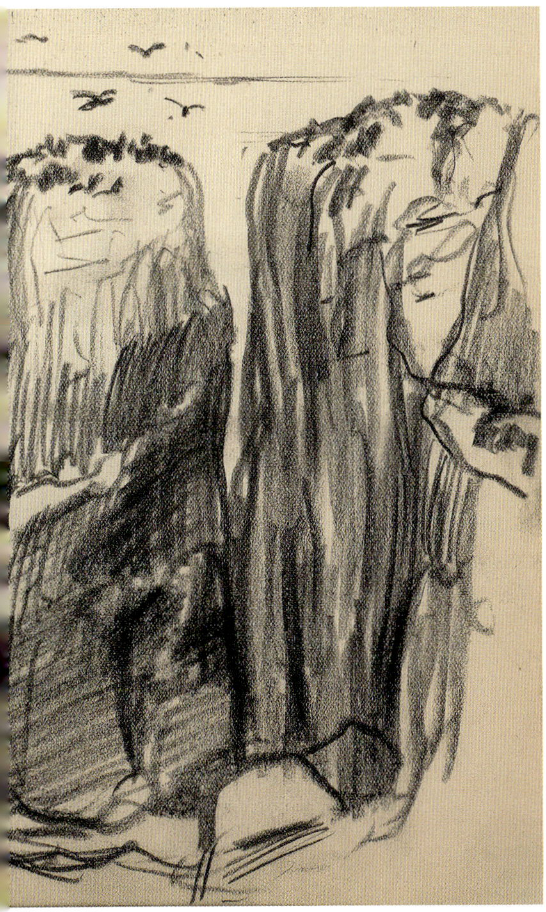

The writer goes on to acknowledge that Britain's closest geographic counterpart was Cornwall. He notes both the 'affinity in nomenclature' between the two regions and their enduring cultural links: 'the same customs and idiosyncrasies make a comparison very interesting'.[79]

Cornwall had certainly established itself as a popular location for artists. Many of those attracted to it during this period had already spent time in France and/or trained in Antwerp (pp. 88–90). They arrived there in much the same way as in Staithes and Runswick; initially as seasonal visitors, with few settling, but later committing to living there through the year, often starting families and gradually coalescing as a group. Even their central

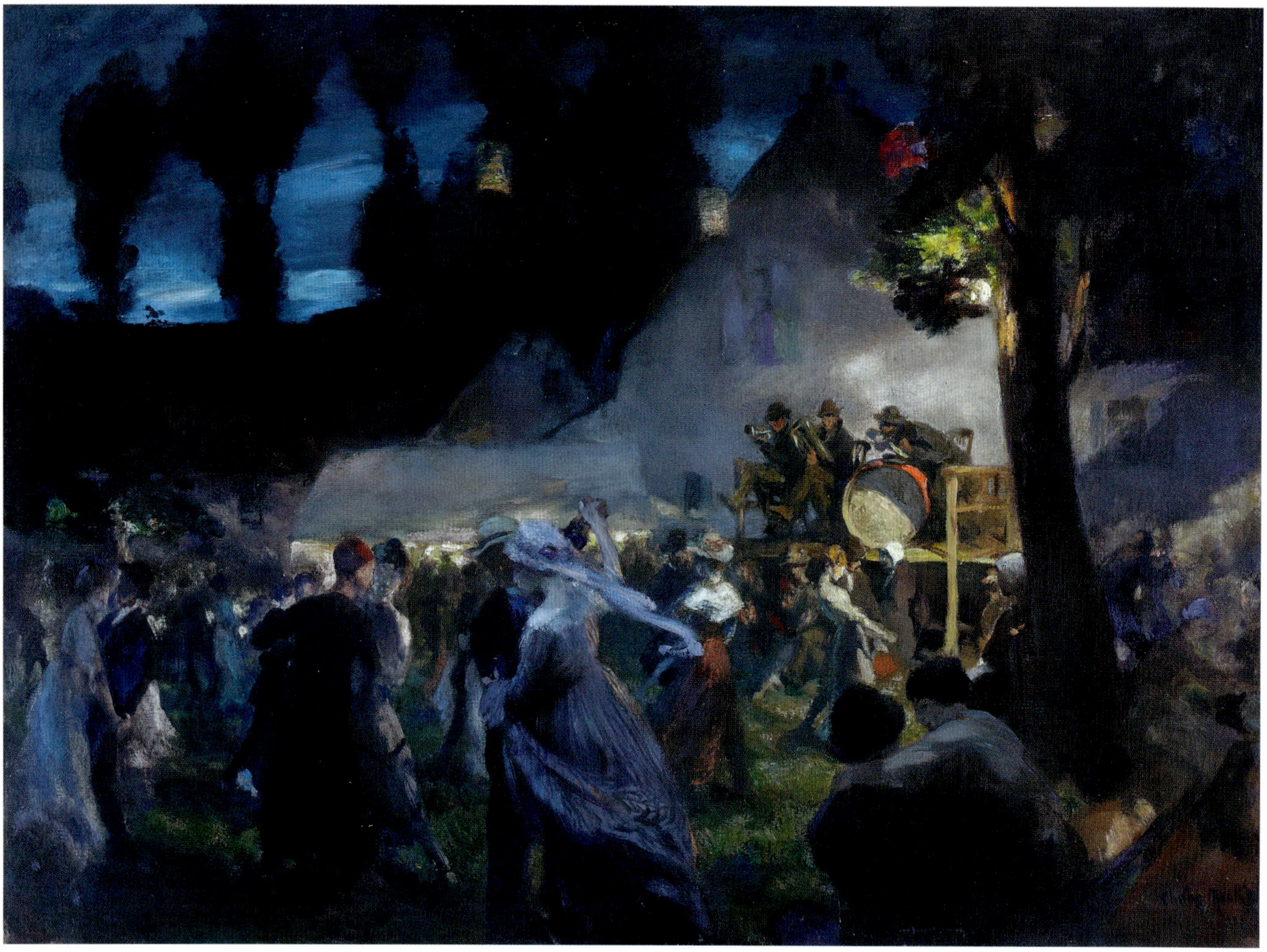

figure Stanhope Forbes (1857–1947) was somewhat mystified as to why Newlyn specifically had proved such a draw. Norman Garstin wrote retrospectively:

> Friendship and camaraderie of the ateliers of Paris and Antwerp, a sympathy with each other's intentions, a mild climate for out of door work, a gray [*sic*] roofed village overhanging a lovely bay – these were the determining causes that led to the young artists setting up their easels hard by the Cornish sea.[80]

71. Charles Mackie painted this picture, *La Danse du Village*, while or soon after renting a studio at Étaples in France (*c.* 1908). His widow Anne, in her memoir of 1921, referred to the painting as '*La Ducasse*' – the expression for a popular 'fête' held in many regions of France, with origins in centuries-old religious festival.

A ROMANTIC REALISM

The paths of Fred Jackson and his Canadian travelling companion William Brymner, travelling from Paris, mirrored that of the 'Newlyners'. They aimed to test their new-found technical confidence and ambitions on subject matter that encompassed the customs and costume of the local fishing population.

In the case of Staithes and Runswick, these in part derived, like the language, from the boatbuilding tradition and associated trading in materials such as tar and timber with Baltic and Scandinavian countries. Traces of the Vikings are embedded in the names of the region – the name of Staithes itself, the dialect that persisted in the village, geographical terms such as *wyke* and the particular terms of the fishermen and their gear – kess bowls, gog sticks, haaf pieces and smouts.

In setting themselves this target, they sought to capture nature in balance with its inhabitants at a time when they perceived it to be overrun in an urban setting. Artistic commentators recognised this too. They spelled it out in literary terms, hymning praise for the magnificent physical features of locations such as Clovelly to which many, Thomas Barrett and Joseph Bagshawe included, had been attracted:

> The glorious rugged picturesqueness of the cliffs amidst which it nestles is eternal, and defies alike the ruthless hand of time and the demon of modern improvement.[81]

Indeed, the writers of these descriptions, often artists themselves, increasingly went on to give vent to their fears of the encroachment of modern society even here. The spectacular Normandy coastline of Étretat, captured so beautifully by Monet and which artists from Staithes were to visit, inspired regretful observations from one correspondent:

> On this last drive we passed the one costume we saw all those weeks, and sighed to think how all the world is dressed in the same gowns... If [they] had but worn ... their costumes, and the washerwomen and the Spaniards and the Dutch maids theirs, what a scene Étretat would have been.[82]

The patterns of the fishermen's lives were also threatened with change. This same writer noted how whining capstans were still used to haul boats back up the beach. The sight was attractive, despite the effort for those involved, but its days were almost certainly numbered:

> It must be very hard work and some enlightened destroyer of the picturesque will, no doubt, soon teach them better ways.[83]

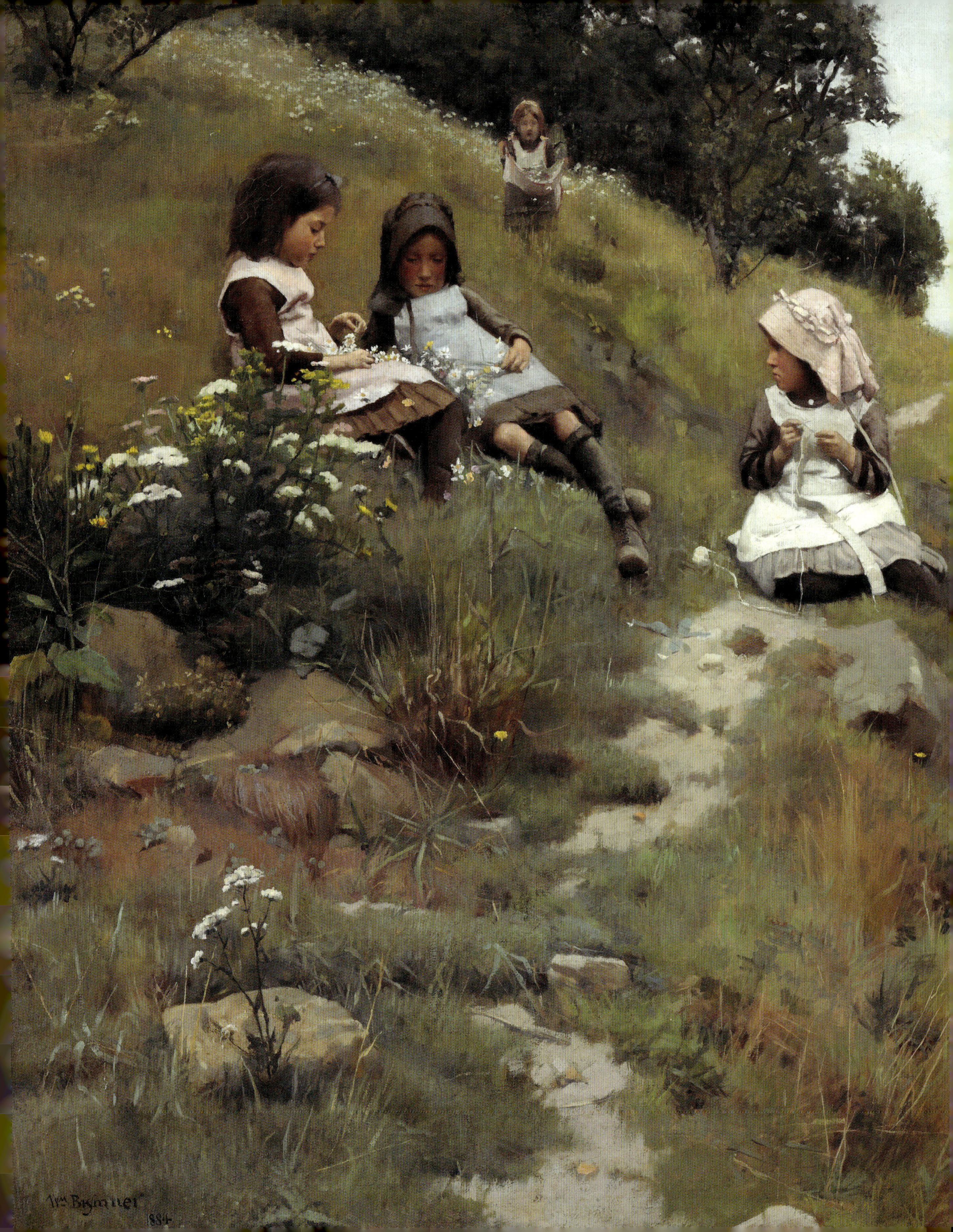
Wm Brymner
1884

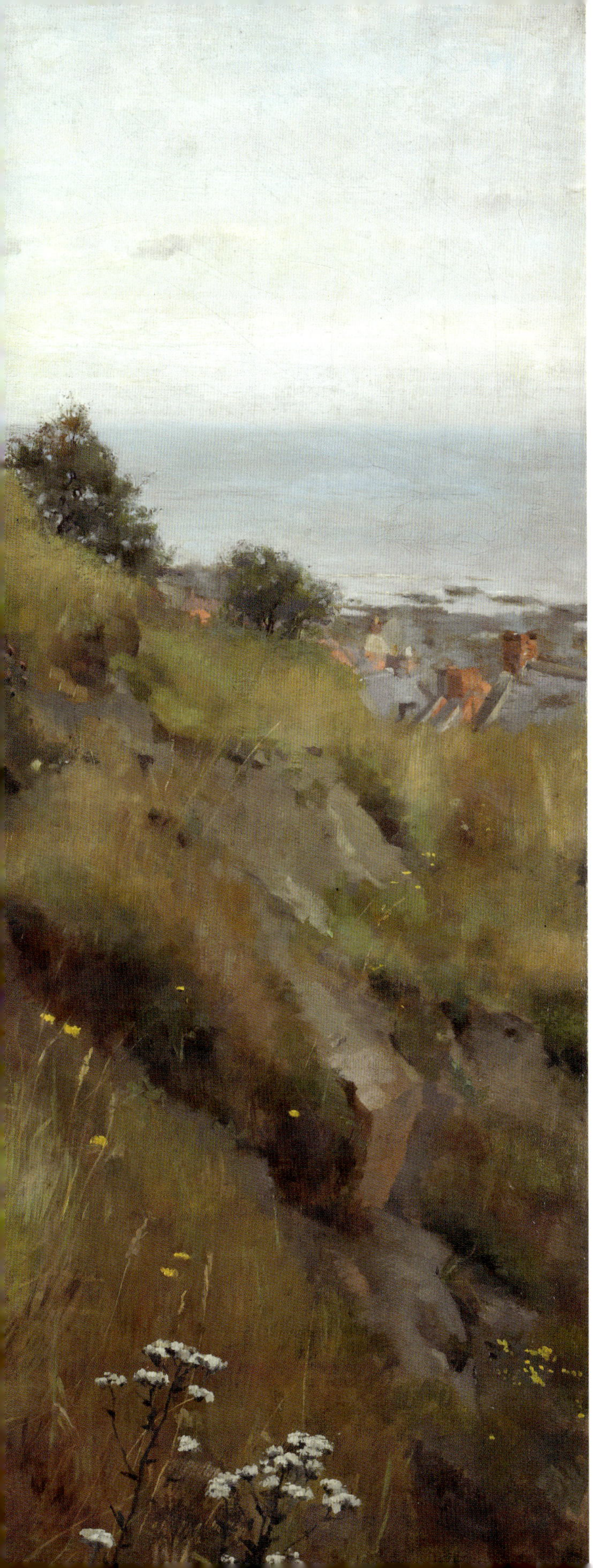

72. William Brymner wrote letters to his Canadian family throughout his time in Runswick Bay (March to November 1884). *A Wreath of Flowers*, his diploma submission to the Royal Canadian Academy of Arts, shows modelling typical of his French training and revels in the landscape and costume of the local children.

Though advanced here in terms of the picturesque, the Staithes artists couched it rather in terms of following their guiding principles and painting an 'honest interpretation of nature'.[84] This was the realism of their work as opposed to the modernity demanded by retrospective criticism but, as is so often the case, boundaries were never definitive. Rarely does an artist insert herself or himself into their surroundings, though modern shipping is increasingly a part of scenes at the larger ports.[85]

What is clear is the popularity and size of the international art movement of which they formed a part, and that guidebooks written over 40 years later were still expressing wonderment at villages such as Runswick Bay managing to retain their authenticity in the face of the annual tide of tourism and the rapacious demands of industrial cities.[86]

The traditional threat facing the inhabitants of that stretch of coast, hemmed in by the large expanse of North Yorkshire moorland,[87] had, of course, been

73. In the early 1880s Winslow Homer travelled from the USA to the colony of Cullercoats near Newcastle. This watercolour, *Tynemouth*, painted in 1881, combines several elements unusual in his work at the time; out on the water, it uses a particularly low viewpoint and pictures men and women together fishing. However, it sets them against a backdrop of the ruined Abbey, harmonising the group with its ancient landscape.

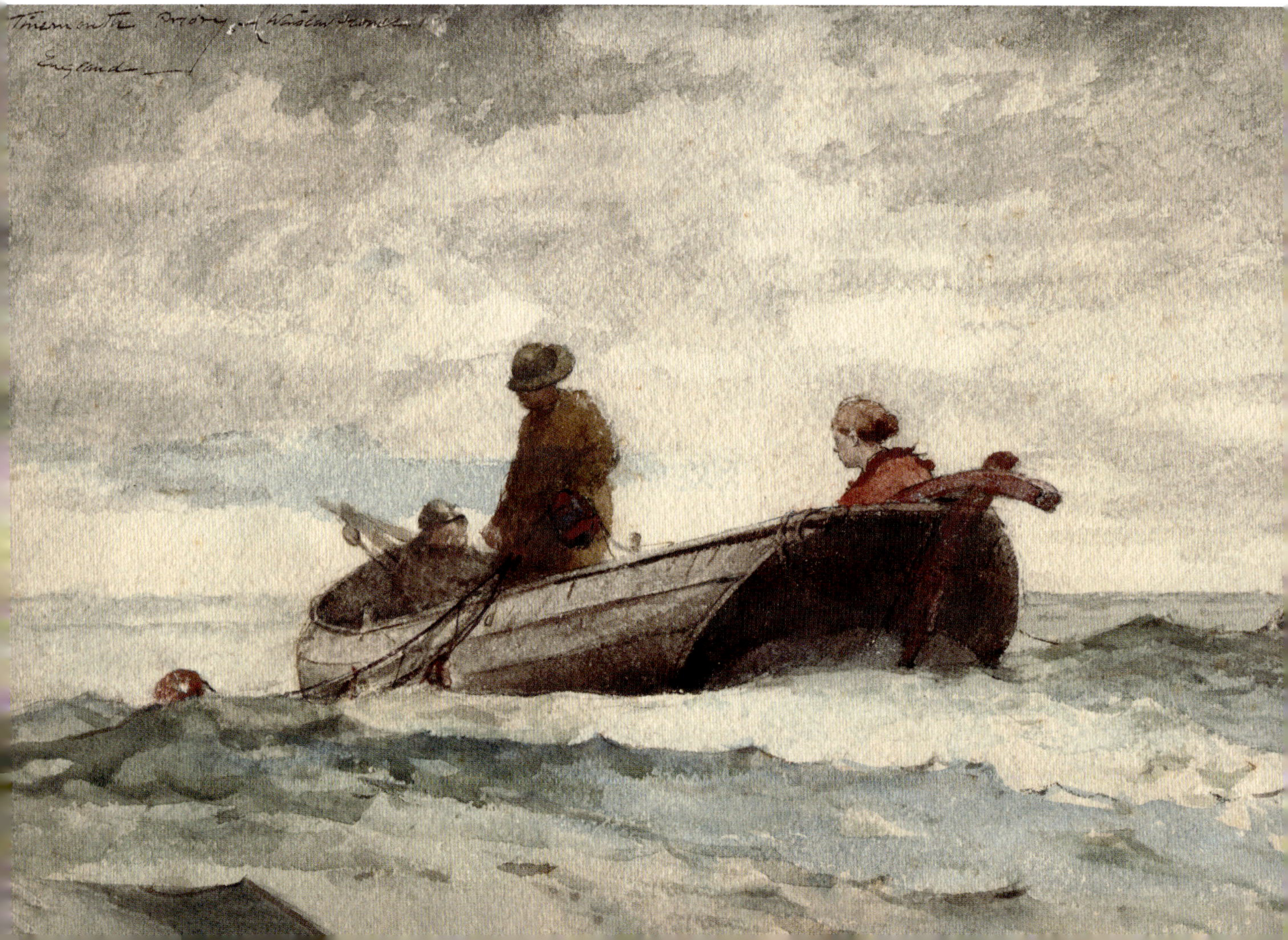

eastwards from the ocean. Their means of access and communication had been the fishing, trade and shipping routes rather than the railways. Ancient ruins on top of headlands reaching from Scarborough to Tynemouth and Lindisfarne still bore witness to past riches and disasters.[88]

With unpainted stone cottages naturally camouflaged within the landscape, villages themselves had often been oriented away from the sea; this was supposed to give them greater protection from storms that always threatened and often overwhelmed their lower reaches. In the case of Staithes, powerful encroaching breakers might come running up the streets, entering the lower floors and sometimes pouring down the chimneys, even tearing down whole buildings.

The formidable coastline of cliffs mentioned in *Harper's Magazine*, of which those close by at Boulby and Flamborough were the most notable, acted as effective ramparts. They ensured a degree of insularity, allowing small, close-

Below right: 74. Joseph Terry's landscapes usually combine various elements and locations and feature small figure groups as part of the vista. Here, in contrast, he focuses purely on the drama of the rugged *Yorkshire Cliffs at Sunset*. Terry himself donated the picture to York Art Gallery in 1924.

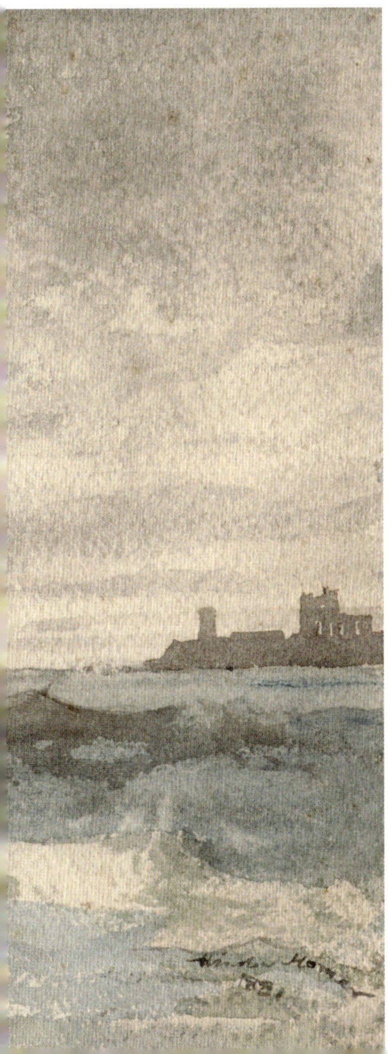

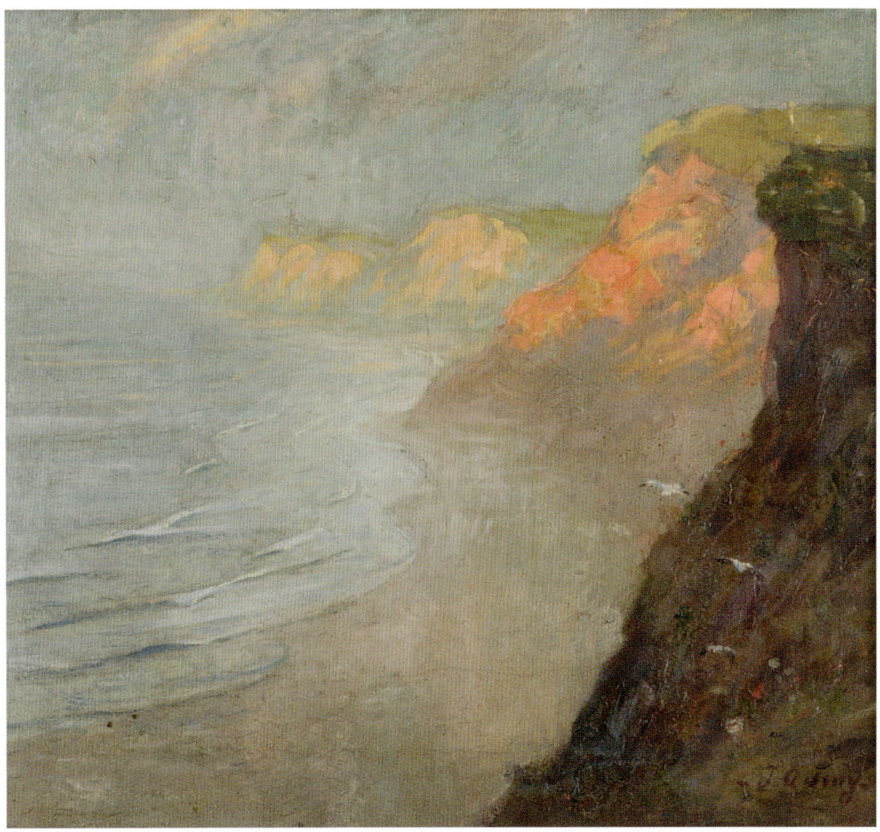

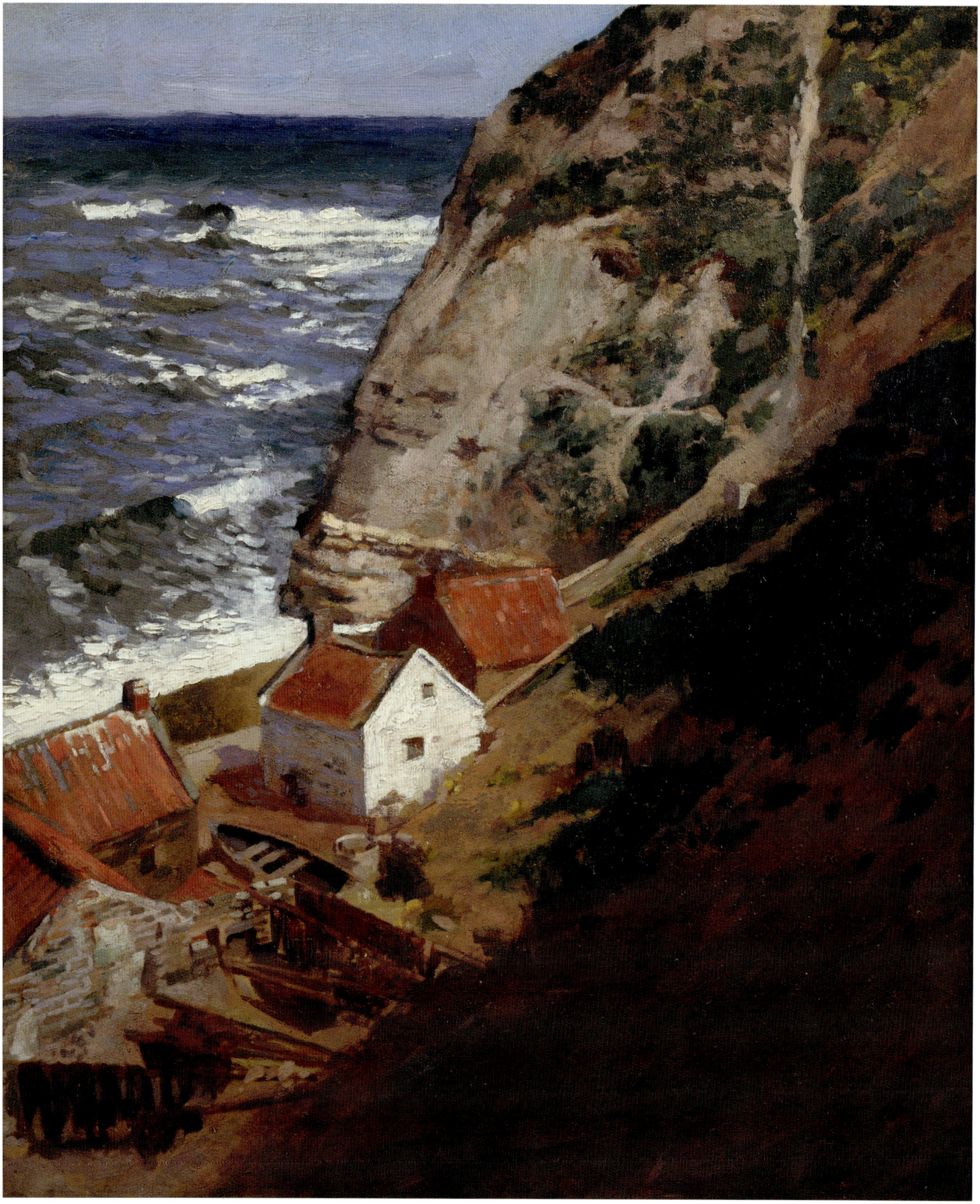

Opposite: 75. As with the previous image by Terry, Laura Johnson's landscape, devoid of figures, is unusual for the artist. Entitled simply *Staithes*, it pictures the sharp descent into the village and Jackdaw's Well, located at the foot of Penny Nab. Laura Johnson's signature dates the picture to the period around 1900.

knit groups to establish themselves in the lee of the available spits or 'Nabs'. These scraps of land were unreliable, however, given the constant erosion from the prevailing winds and currents, and, although some were sited at the junction of river or beck and sea, most had little natural fresh water to support large populations.[89]

The wildness, danger and beauty of their rugged rock formations, as at Étretat in Normandy, prompted both the wonder of tourists and the superstitions of locals; Robin Lyth's hole, The King and Queen at Flamborough Head and the Hob Holes at Runswick Bay, to the last of which was ascribed luck in childbirth, were but three. Laura Knight, nonplussed by the aesthetic possibilities around her, exalted in their sheer vitality, scrambling up and down the cliffs until made fearful by rockfalls.[90]

These havens were purely natural at first – Cowbar Nab at Staithes, Filey Brigg – and though breakwaters, piers or harbour walls were added, danger remained on the approach. Wreckage was common within sight of safety, regardless of whether tugboats, an increasingly common feature at the time, were employed. Mark Senior's granddaughter remembered as a child racing round the cliffs to Kettleness point to watch when the ships went aground, while Rowland Hill's son recalled the effect that the wrecking of a hospital ship had on his father in October 1914.[91]

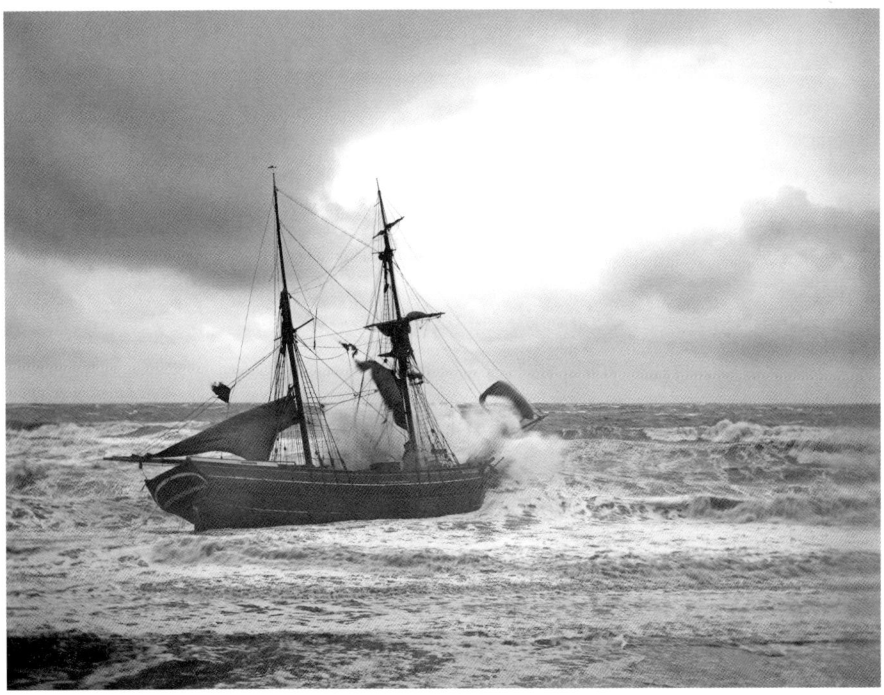

76. Frank Meadow Sutcliffe took this photograph, which he entitled *The Flag of Distress*, in October 1885 when the *Mary & Agnes* ran aground between Sandsend and Whitby. He later described the terrible conditions and the near impossibility of capturing the scene (p. 222).

These challenges to the sailors staged ongoing spectacles for visitors, photographers and artists alike, and many spent lengthy periods in the vantage points of the bigger ports. The interest of Ernest Dade, Joseph Bagshawe and Frank Mason, in particular, encompassed all aspects of 'marine' painting, in the best traditions of artists at the coast; they worked thoroughly through the themes and activities of Yorkshire's largest herring fishery (Scarborough) and the boatbuilding activities of the old whaling town (Whitby). Their example was followed by others such as Richardson, Elmhirst, Jackson, Crawshaw and Jobling, who all went on to exhibit Whitby pictures, with Anderson showing four, each featuring a different tidal aspect, at the Club exhibition of 1904 alone.

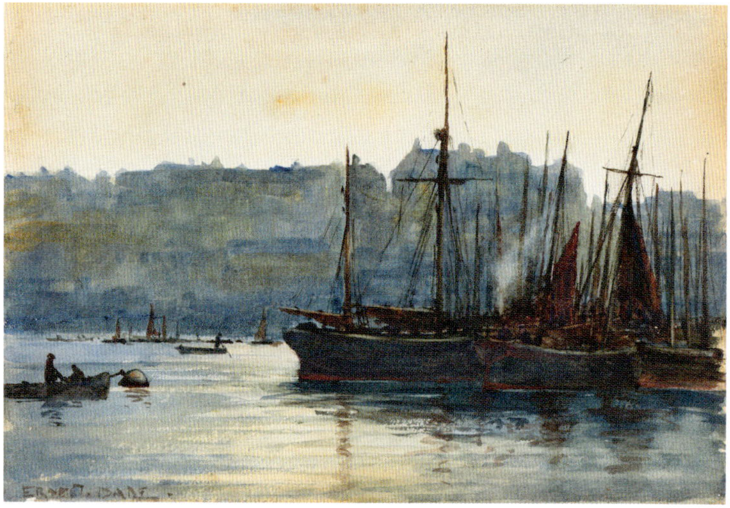

77. Ernest Dade was resident in Scarborough, the capital of Yorkshire's herring industry, from 1889 until 1917. Here he captures the silhouette of the town's southern bay, with its harbour and large cliff-top hotels, at dusk. The work, entitled *Scarborough Harbour at Sunset*, is undated.

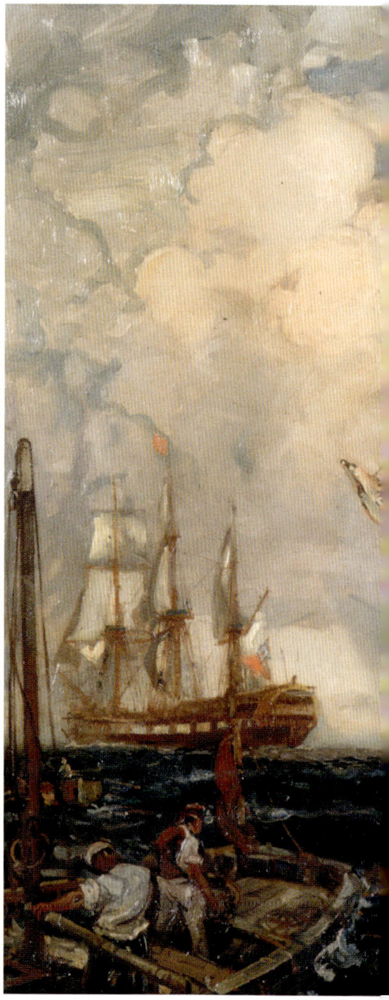

THE SPECTACLE OF THE SEA

With its lower and upper harbours, Whitby overwintered the larger, off-shore boats of the Staithes fishermen, its reputation burnished by its most famous apprentice James Cook.[92] Much as Newlyn artists such as Frank Bourdillon had pictured Elizabethan scenes in their Cornish beach settings, so Mason and others used this tradition to picture historic sailing vessels as well as contemporary subjects. Lionel Crawshaw's most popular picture proved an imaginary scene of the sailing ship *Endeavour* leaving harbour to head off on Cook's first voyage.[93]

Several of the artists spent time on the water. In answering the lure or challenge of painting at sea, Bagshawe was indulged by the wedding present of a yacht, *Beatrice*, from his father-in-law;[94] Dade in turn became part-owner of a fishing boat, the *North Star*, which he rigged as a yacht and floating studio.[95] Mason, schooled on HMS *Conway* and trained as a marine engineer, had ample opportunity in the Navy; he studied art in Scarborough after leaving and shared an interest in yacht design with Albert Strange, the school principal and founder of Scarborough Sailing Club. Mason's studio on Marine Parade was the meeting place for the club of which Dade was the first captain in 1895.[96]

For artists with the level of sailing experience boasted by Dade, Mason and also Mayor,[97] the period in which they painted saw significant technical change. The transition from sail to steam presented not only new types of iron and steel ships, but also the adaptation of sailing craft in vain response to this challenge. The consequent pictorial alterations are evident in their depiction of not only tugs and steamers, but also of the town's architectural profile.[98]

The artists' personal feelings about this change are not seemingly recorded. However, the photographer Frank Sutcliffe, a long-term resident of Whitby, made his thoughts clear both in interview and his own writing.[99]

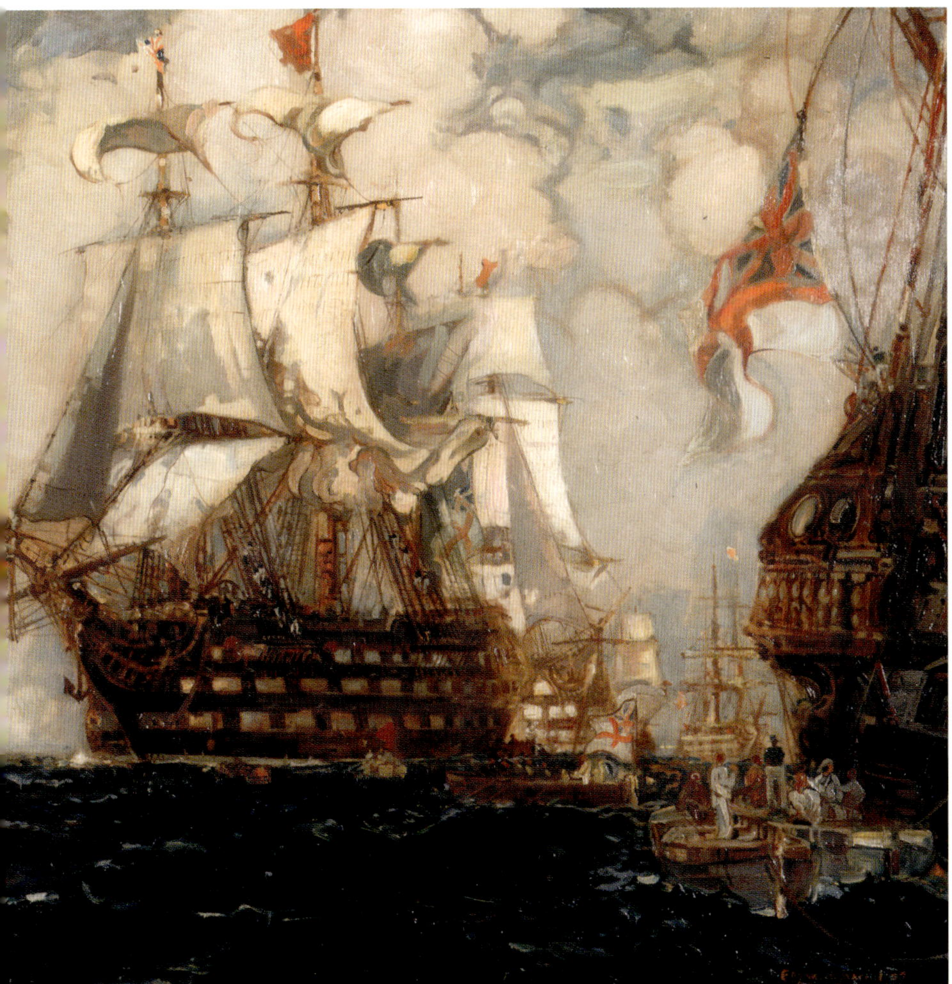

78. *After Trafalgar*, an imagined historic scene, was exhibited at the Royal Academy in 1908 – almost a decade after Frank Mason first showed there. In 1912 the artist was commissioned in similar vein by the Royal Hotel Whitby; he produced scenes of sailing ships in the Esk, fishing craft and 'old world' whalers in the inner and outer harbours.

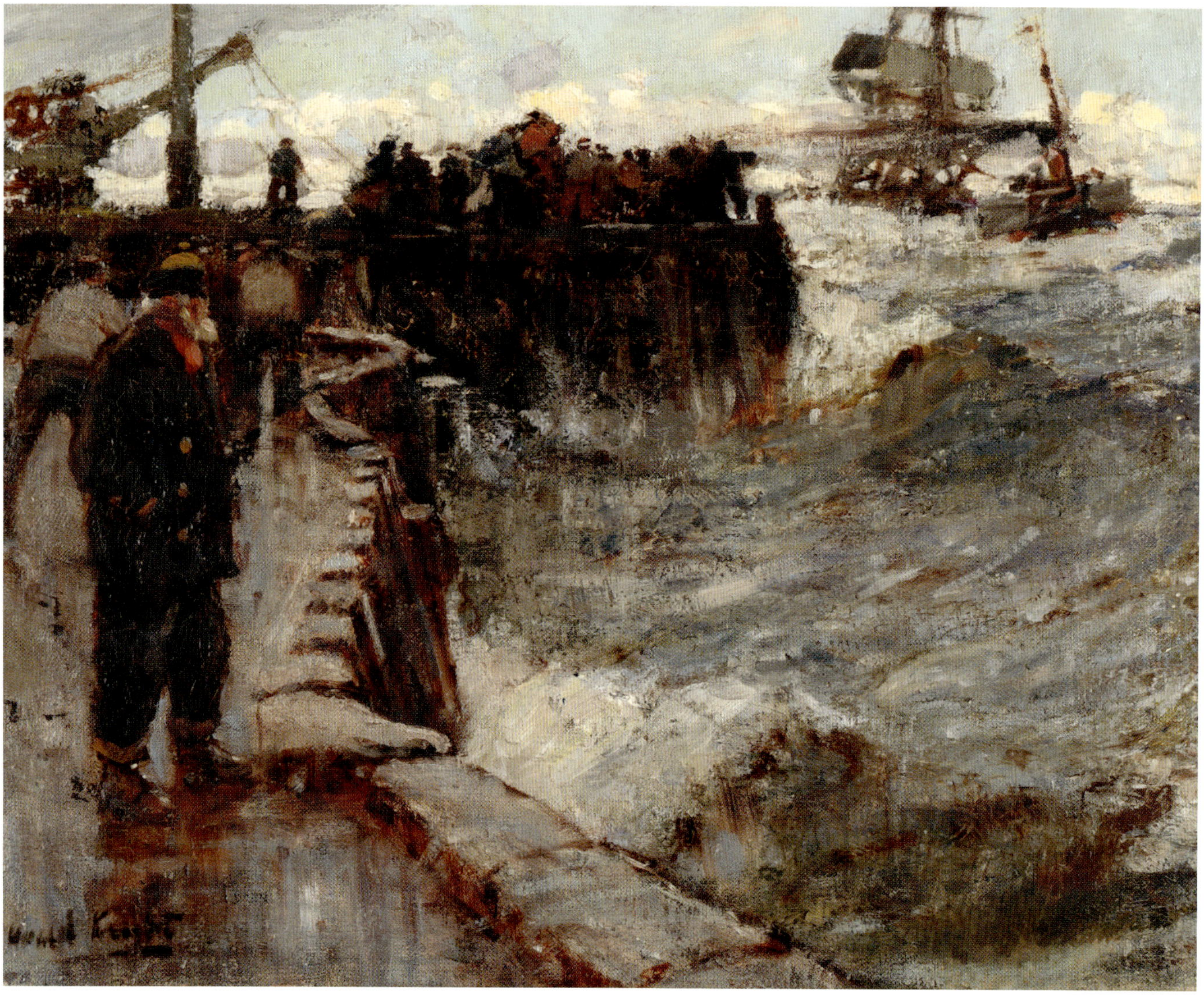

> The tide was unusually high, the air as calm as it often is on a frosty December morning, and there was one solitary Scotch boat riding grandly on the lake-like water in Whitby Upper Harbour ... behind, in grey pearly mist, was the old town crowned by the Abbey and Church. The sea was perfect, but for one little cockle shell of a boat ... which I gave a man tuppence to move away ... when suddenly, from behind an ugly gin-palace, appeared a paddle-wheeled tugboat, churning up the lovely reflections and belching out dirty smoke. This beast of a boat was made fast to the quay between my camera and the Scotchman.[100]

79. In *Rough Sea at Whitby*, painted around 1900, Harold Knight provides another example of the Staithes artists' willingness to include modern facets of the town's life. Here he pictures a trawler-tug towing a sailing vessel into port; an attendant crowd watch from the pier.

For the majority of the artists, though, the attraction continued to be the lives of the fisherfolk, who remained distinct communities even within the larger towns.

FOLLOWING THE FLEETS

> I wish to carry the reader away to the North. First of all, to quiet seaside hamlets, where the small, quaint cottages of the fisher-folk cling like limpets to the grey-green cliffs; then to the mouth of a great river, where commerce unfolds a thousand sails, and the morning sun welcomes into the harbour fleet after fleet of fishing-boats, laden with the spoils of the sea; and then, far out over the German Ocean, into night and silence and the light of stars. It is the herring season, and all along the north-east coast the sea-line is dotted over with brown sails.[101]

This poetic contemporary description transported the reader to the lives of the fishermen out at sea, where they would work for long stretches of time depending on the season. Beyond the reach even of photographers such as Sutcliffe, several of the artists nonetheless made outings with them, sketching and exhibiting scenes onboard despite the obvious challenges. Bagshawe's interest in and commitment to this ultimate environment of vibrant, rapid

80. Frank Mason's depictions of sailing vessels included a panoply from around the British coastline. The Cornish craft shown in *St Ives Lugger Coming to Shore in a Storm*, painted in 1900, is heading for a Yorkshire harbour. Boats from other coastal communities were an increasing feature of life in the northeast up until the end of the nineteenth century.

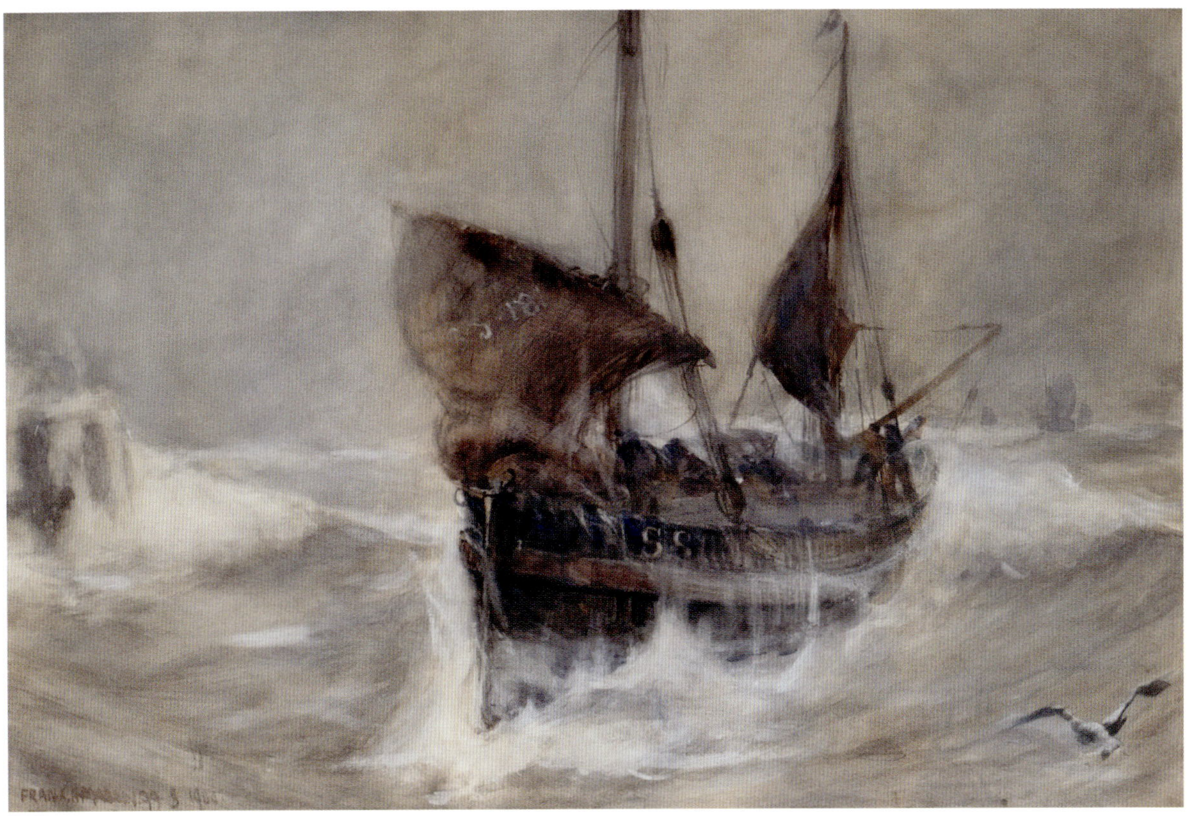

activity, accompanied by a soundscape of almost impenetrable dialect and specific terminology, endeared him to the fishermen. His sketchbooks reveal a ferocious energy (**31**, **89** and **91**) in attempting to capture onboard activity despite the minimal scope for modelling or questioning. Bagshawe capitalised on these trips by publishing a series of articles that reflected his persistent eagerness for the sea.[102]

Ernest Dade's work is different, though just as exacting. In it he depicts the departure or arrival of the herring fleets as a whole, or captures the atmospheric passage of individual boats to land in all weathers, picking out details down to their registration numbers. Instituted in 1869, these numbers recorded the fact that from the 1870s the herring season was marked by the arrival of an increasing tally of Scottish boats in the wake of the first shoals;[103] their crews not only sailed different boats, but also used different nets and methods of offloading their catch. They were also accompanied by a vibrant convoy of fishing girls, who would light up the quayside with their costume and colloquialisms as they packed the herring on landing.

These arrivals attracted other artists from the group, as the disembarcation resulted in more than just traditional maritime scenes. Harold Knight rarely painted onboard, but sketched and painted harbour scenes. Laura Johnson worked on quayside watercolours and figure groups in the market place in Whitby, as did Charles Mackie and Henry Hopwood. Though they moored and lived off the coast, the passing crews of fishermen came ashore to restock on supplies. The local market was renowned for the Cornish fishermen satisfying their predilection for cabbage among the fresh vegetables.[104]

'Luggers' from Cornwall could also reach Yorkshire in only three days, and Walter Langley depicts the Cornish fleet leaving for the north in one of his earliest Newlyn pictures (**69**). French boats made the trip from the coasts of Brittany and Normandy, as did the Dutch coasters from Holland and boats from Belgium and Denmark. The Suffolk port of Lowestoft boasted much admired smacks that were regular visitors too. It is thus surprising that the departure of the Knights from Staithes in 1907 has been linked to their 'discovery' of Cornwall; it seems more likely that their awareness had been growing throughout their time in Yorkshire.

Much has been made of the couple's early friendship with James 'Jimmy' James, a local fish auctioneer who hailed from Newlyn.[105] However, Laura writes of her later visit to the family in St Ives who had made a yawl, named

True Love. This sailing boat was Whitby-owned and sailed by a Staithes family, a fact of which she was clearly cognisant. Many of her fellow artists such as Bagshawe and Richardson had also painted in Cornwall, while her friend Rosie Good holidayed there with her sister Catherine in May 1901. The two women had travelled throughout the county, spending time in both Newlyn and Penzance.[106]

It is clear from other works by Staithes artists that they actively followed the herring fleet's route as part of their artistic peregrinations. North Shields, Hartlepool, Bridlington, Filey and Hull are all pictured in works by those such as Atkinson, Dade and Booth.[107] Friedenson went further north and painted scenes at St Monan's in Fifeshire. Owen Bowen and Florence Hess both painted in Norfolk, picturing Blakeney, Kelling, Cromer and Yarmouth – the end point of the herring fleet's eastern arc (**84** and **203**).

81. Lionel Crawshaw's 1920s picture *Dancing on the Pier at Whitby* echoes Charles Mackie's *La Ducasse* (**71**). This scene too is redolent of literary descriptions of the ancient fairs held in Staithes in particular. However, the artist brings the picture up to date with a full variety of costume, from townspeople to fisherfolk.

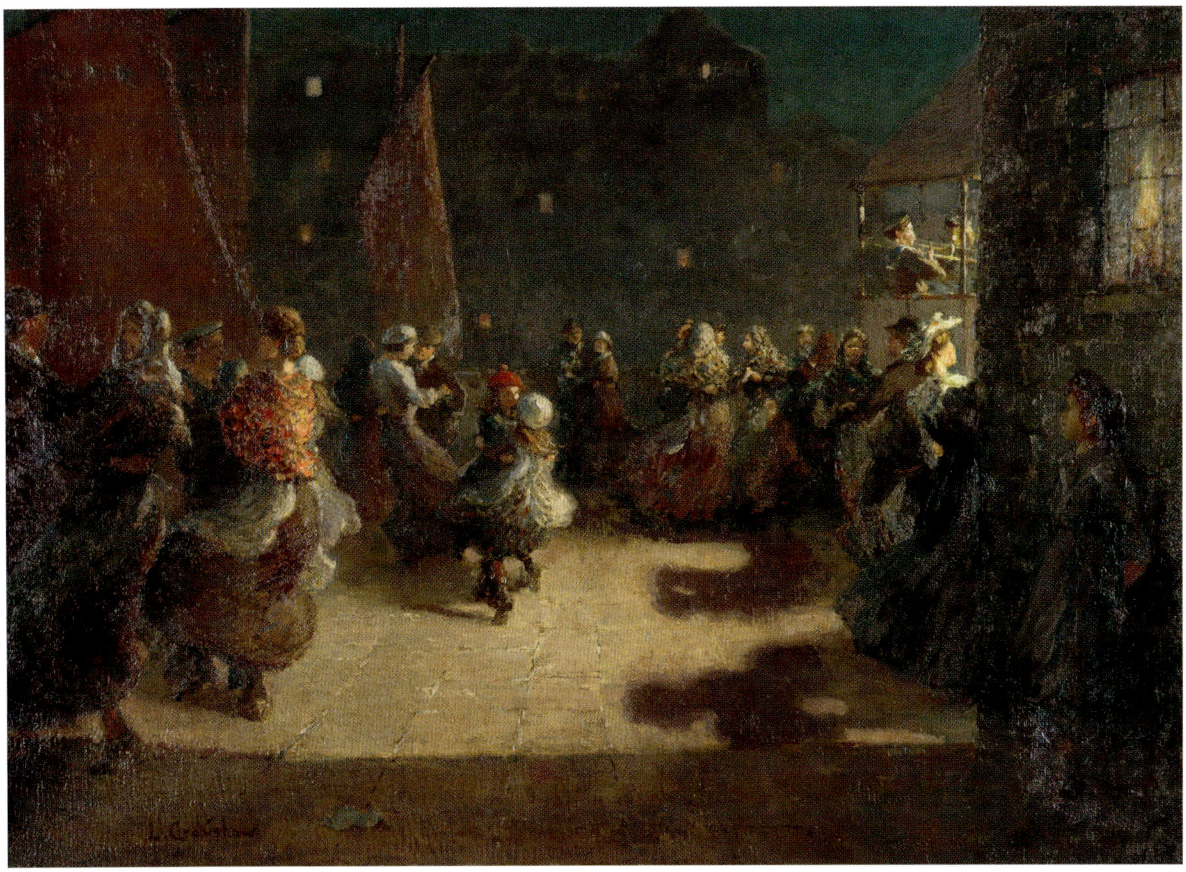

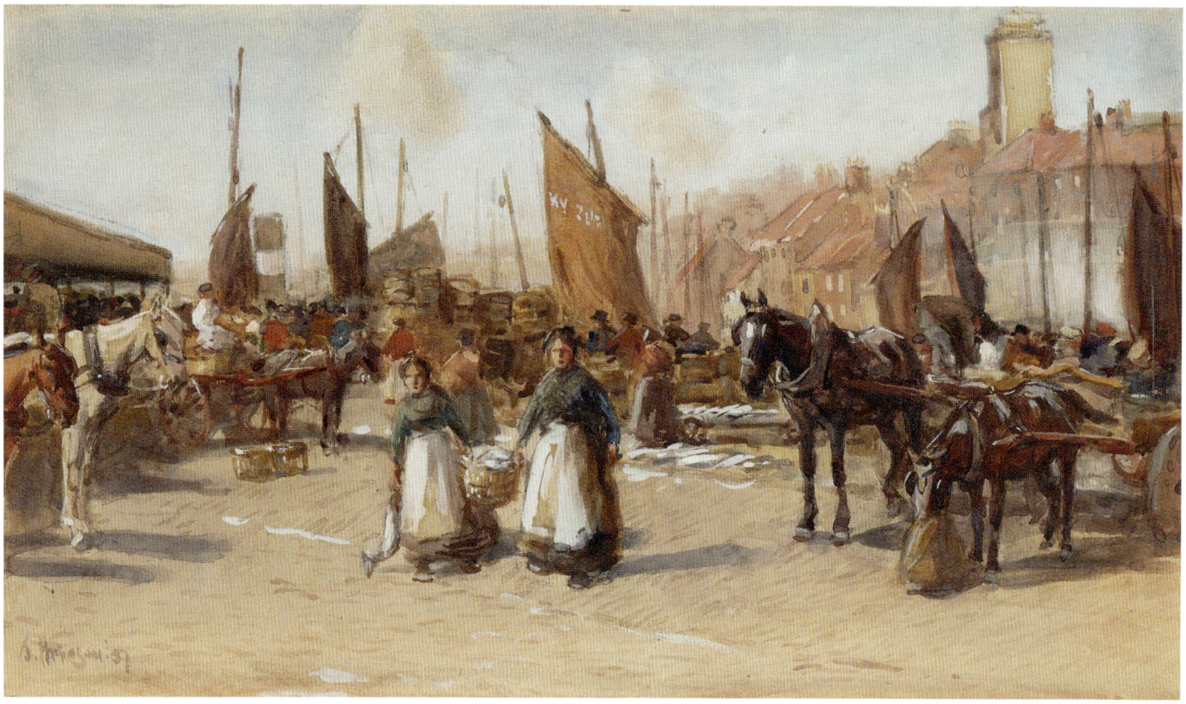

82. John Atkinson, a native of Newcastle, moved to Yorkshire around 1900, where he painted almost exclusively in countryside villages. Here, however, Atkinson depicts *The Fish Quay, North Shields* where he painted often, perhaps reflecting his early days in a shipyard's drawing office.

It was usually during the fleet's time off Yorkshire that those artists not resident in the area migrated to the Yorkshire coast. The *Whitby Gazette* announced the arrival of these seasonal visitors to the boarding houses and hotels of the towns and villages. Individuals, friends and families stayed for sometimes a week, sometimes a couple of months or more; Robert Jobling vividly recalled an early visit to Staithes in which:

> He once lived in a little house close to the quay where every thud of the sea shook the beds and the splash of water became a familiar sound.[108]

Some of the artists stayed consistently with a particular host or family, others lodged with a variety year on year. This might result in quite different experiences given strong family ties within the villages. In her memoir, Laura Knight recounts that her initial choice of Staithes lodging resulted in her pledging loyalty to the particular Methodist chapel of the family with whom she stayed.[109]

In neither Runswick Bay or Staithes was there one main hostelry, as was the case with some other colonies, where it provided a focus for the artists' socialising. In some locations such as Newlyn, where Stanhope Forbes recalls the village inhabitants eschewing drink and frowning on the artists' activities, friction occurred between the religion of the chapels and the various public houses. In Cornwall the artists consequently formed a club in which to congregate or travelled to Penzance for their increasingly large theatricals. In Skagen in Denmark the colonists stayed or ate at Brondum's Inn (later a hotel), decorating the dining room with their work,[110] while in Pont Aven in Brittany the Pension Gloanec specifically catered to the artists' community.

In Staithes the Cod and Lobster had a prominent position to one end of the staith and is pictured in many paintings.[111] There were also around half a dozen public houses centrally positioned, such as the Shoulder of Mutton on the High Street, close to the original Fishermen's Institute, and Robert Atkinson's White Horse between Gun Gutter and Church Street. The last, perpendicular to the sea front, was opposite several houses popular with lodging artists. These were owned by families such as the Verrills, Porritts and Crooks who jostled for trade with those on the High Street, such as the Lavericks and Browns. In a letter to her fiancé Oliver Sheppard, Rosie Good asked him to be careful when discussing prices:

83. Arthur Friedenson exhibited works with Scottish titles at the Art Club show of 1906 and there exist similar dated works from Fifeshire in 1907, the year in which he was married in Edinburgh. In this work, *Harbourside, St. Monan's*, he pictures two 'Fifies', the Scottish equivalent of cobles, with the town's distinctive church on the horizon.

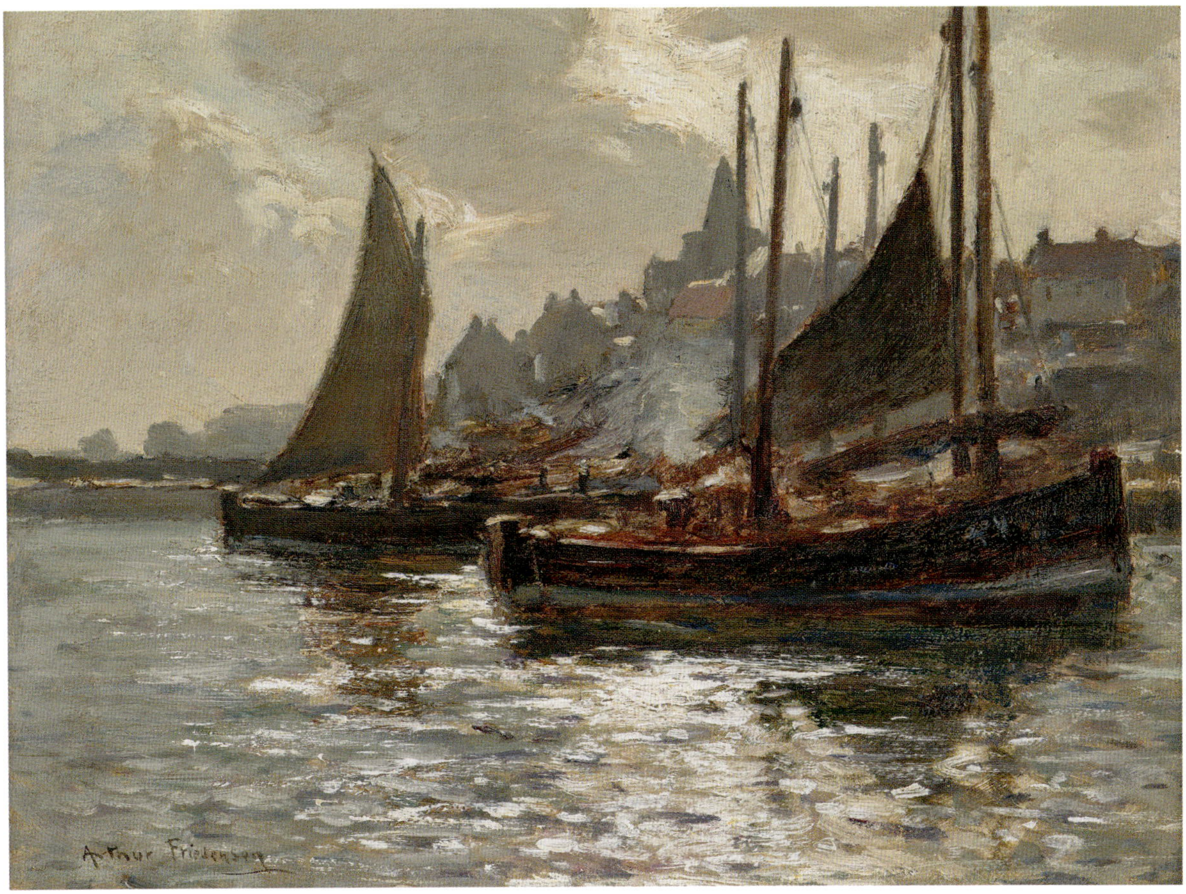

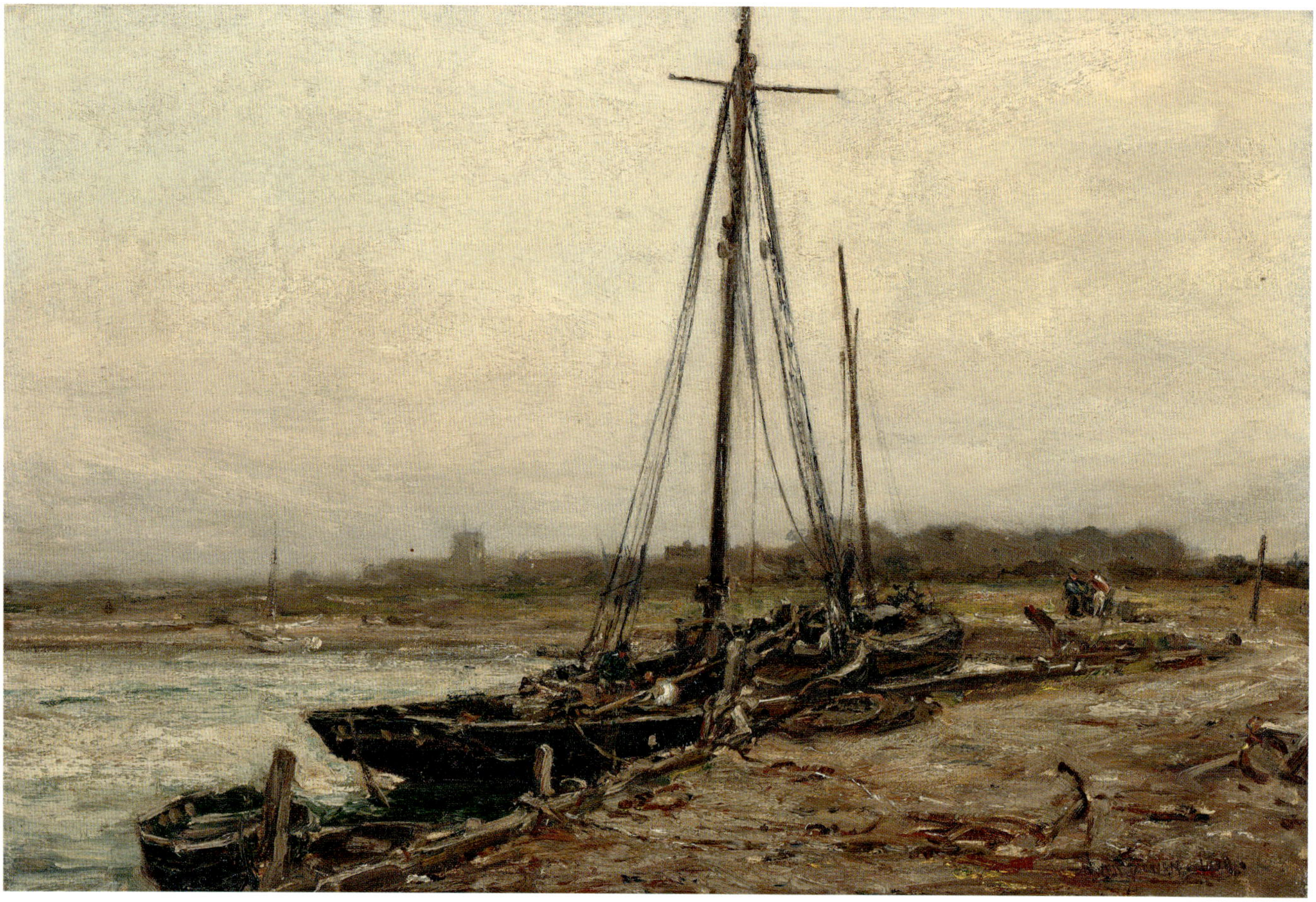

I think I told you he is not going to stay at Mrs Crooks. Did Mrs Porritt say anything about charging more for that bedroom because I hope you did not say you would pay more for it? We told Mrs Crooks she charged too much for visitors. You must talk it over with her and make some arrangement when you come back.[112]

As fishermen's cottages, the lodging houses lacked space; children were often forced to make way for guests, or surplus accommodation might be provided by relatives a few doors away. Artists also had to rent separate studios, often simply empty stables or derelict buildings, which were to be found variously throughout both Staithes and Runswick. Hess lodged with the Patton family but took a studio space adjoining that of Senior. He

Above: 84. Owen Bowen travelled widely both in Britain and on the continent. He visited East Anglia and Holland in 1909–10 and here portrays the boats on what is thought to be a tidal creek on the North Norfolk coast.

Opposite: 85. Percy Teasdale's large canvas *His First Ship* describes Friendship Cottage on Gun Gutter in Staithes around 1904. Its position, close to the seafront, necessitated steps up to the entrance, as stormy seas often overran the street. Several artists painted members of the Verrill family (pictured) or lodged on this street.

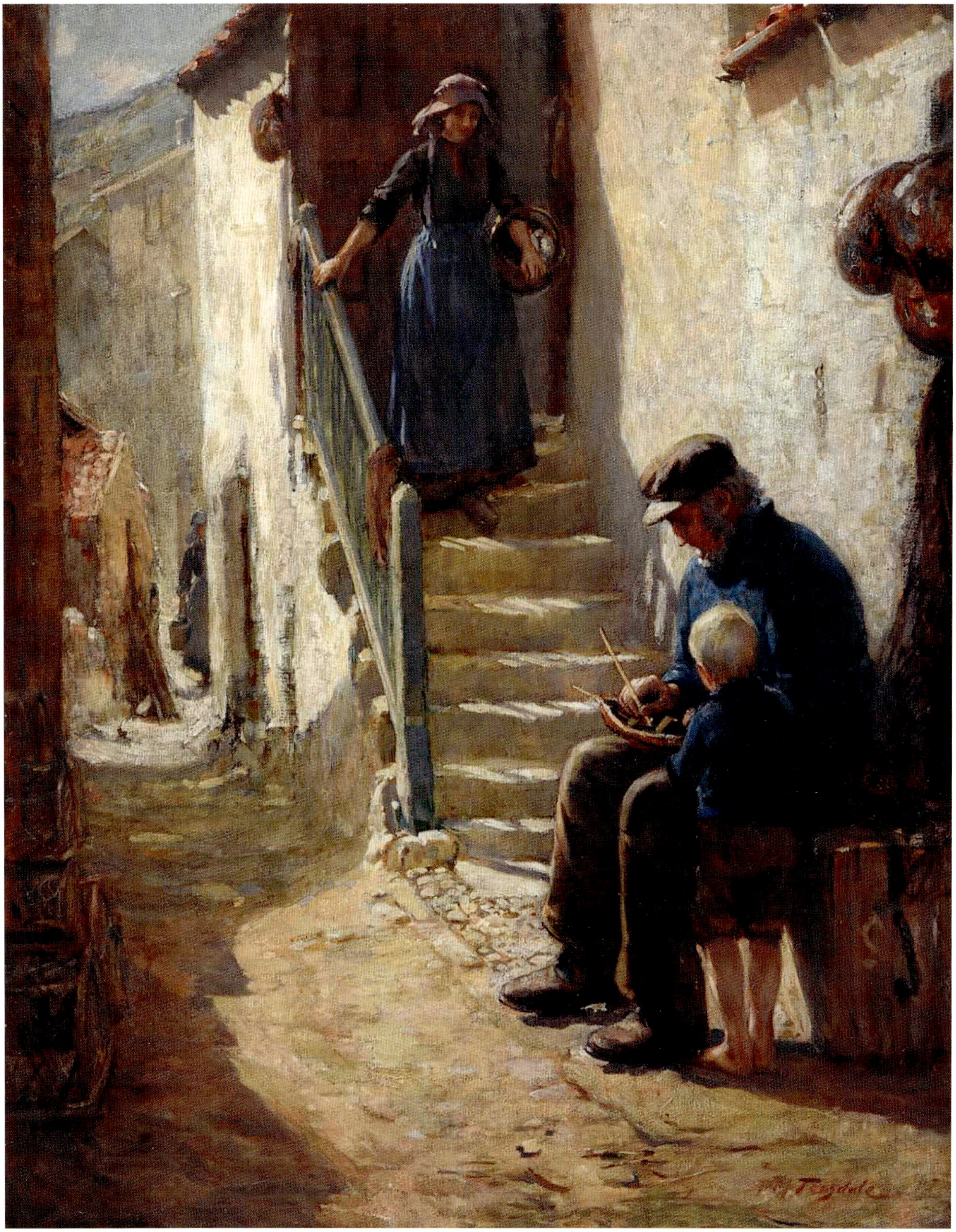

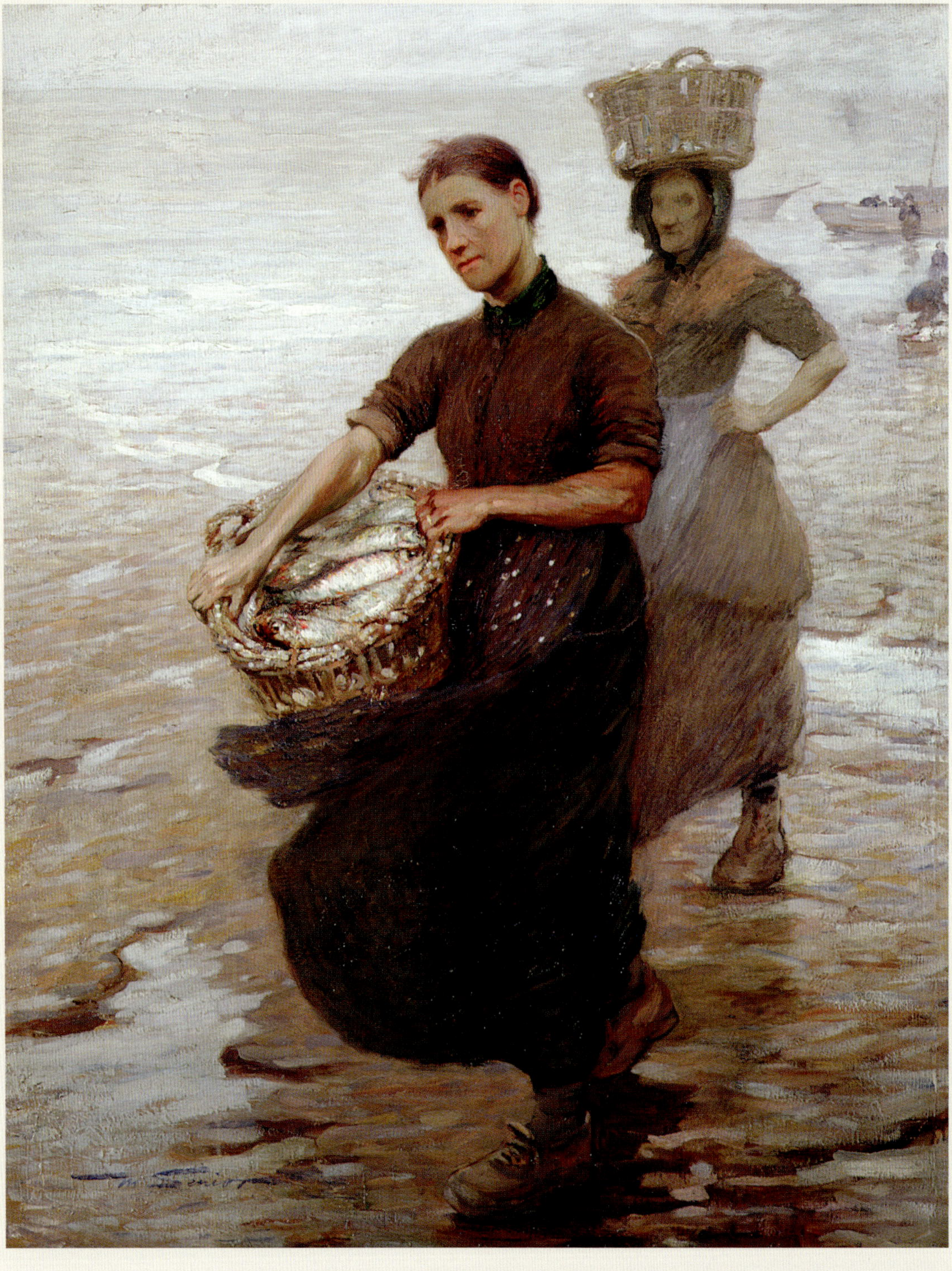

Opposite: 86. Although the focus of Mark Senior's painting of 1900, *Toil*, is the fisherwomen and their labour, his painterly description of the 'scaurs' of rock is a distinctive feature. Often the women would collect driftwood or limpets for baiting lines, walking for miles along these plateaux at low tide.

in turn had distanced his studio from his lodging to divide family and working time more effectively. Rigg hired a wooden studio in a field belonging to the Runswick Bay Hotel. Johnson and Good occupied a space overlooking the beck mouth, during a period when Laura and her sister rented a cottage and took paying guests and pupils themselves. On returning from time away once married, the Knights took lodgings in a space above the post office that they had previously rented as a studio.

Cottages in the inland villages or farms were often welcome alternatives to the closeness of the villages. Spence Ingall, Hill and others took houses on Banktop just above Runswick. The Joblings installed their family of three daughters at Dale House, up the beck from Staithes, and the Mackies and Knights lodged variously at moorland farms near Roxby.[113] Friedenson rented accommodation at Ellerby and Jackson, Hopwood and Rigg all stayed in Hinderwell.

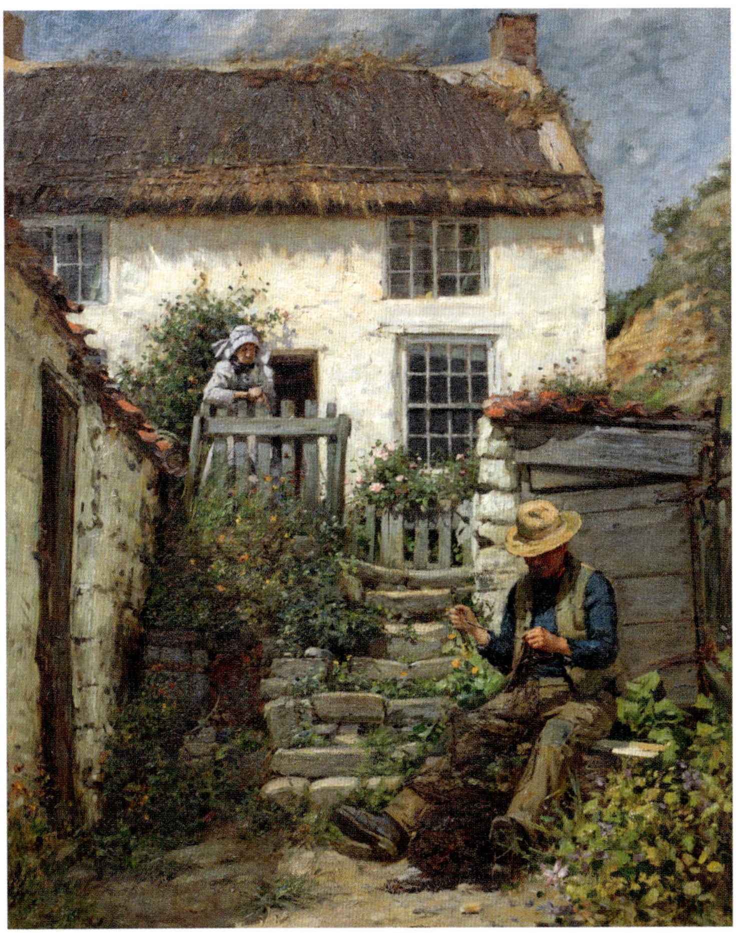

Below: 87. Fettling t'nets was one of the few tasks that enabled fishermen to work and pose simultaneously; the slow, rhythmic action involved created minimal movement, allowing the sitter to take advantage of days when the wind refused to blow. In *Mending Nets, Runswick Bay*, Ernest Rigg's picture uses Craig Lea Cottage at Runswick as its backdrop.

Some eventually put down roots by buying property. Foster and Senior had cottages in Runswick Bay; the latter eventually bought land from Gertrude Hudson, one of his pupils, to build a house, 'Hillside', in 1919 (**13**). Hopwood took a house in Hinderwell, as noted above, which he then converted to include a studio; Jackson, who married the daughter of a local farmer, did the same. Bowen rented a house at Robin Hood's Bay and Booth moved to a house called Haswell in Scalby, also adding a studio; he lived there for over 30 years. Terry married and lived at 'The Firs' in Sleights and Atkinson spent almost a decade at Broad Carr in Glaisdale.

THE SAUCY COBLE

Although Runswick and Robin Hood's Bay differed from Staithes in having large open bays, all three villages shared the underwater geography of the region: the 'scaurs', or flat, smooth plateaux, and the 'steels' – long fingers of rock stretching out into the sea. Navigation over and between these was a hazardous business; routes to safety often had to be marked with piles driven into the sea bed. The scaurs and steels were nevertheless responsible for many wrecks, as they rendered deep-waisted vessels and keels impractical close to shore. They also resulted in the coble, 'a thing of saucy shape, graceful lines and gay colours', the design of which seems to have been unique to this coast. It was apparently a hybrid of Scandinavian techniques and the empirical practice of local boatbuilders.[114]

A signature of coastal life, its plunging bow, flat bottom and canted stern was as suited to small harbours, such as Staithes, as it was to the wide, sandy beaches of, say, Filey. The coble thus became a natural feature of almost all the artists' work. Originally black, colour schemes had been introduced in the 1830s and were tailored to individual craft. Each was also named, even after registration numbers were added, connecting it to a family, cottage or event.[115]

The complex line of the coble shows particularly well in the work of Joseph Bagshawe. His time at the coast was spent initially at Staithes, where in 1901 he stayed with a family at Bluejacket house (their yawl was named *Bluejacket* after it). Of the smaller villages and towns, Staithes maintained a predominant share of both cobles and yawls, dating from the earliest period of the nineteenth century. However, its beach did provide specific challenges for the fishermen who launched from it.[116]

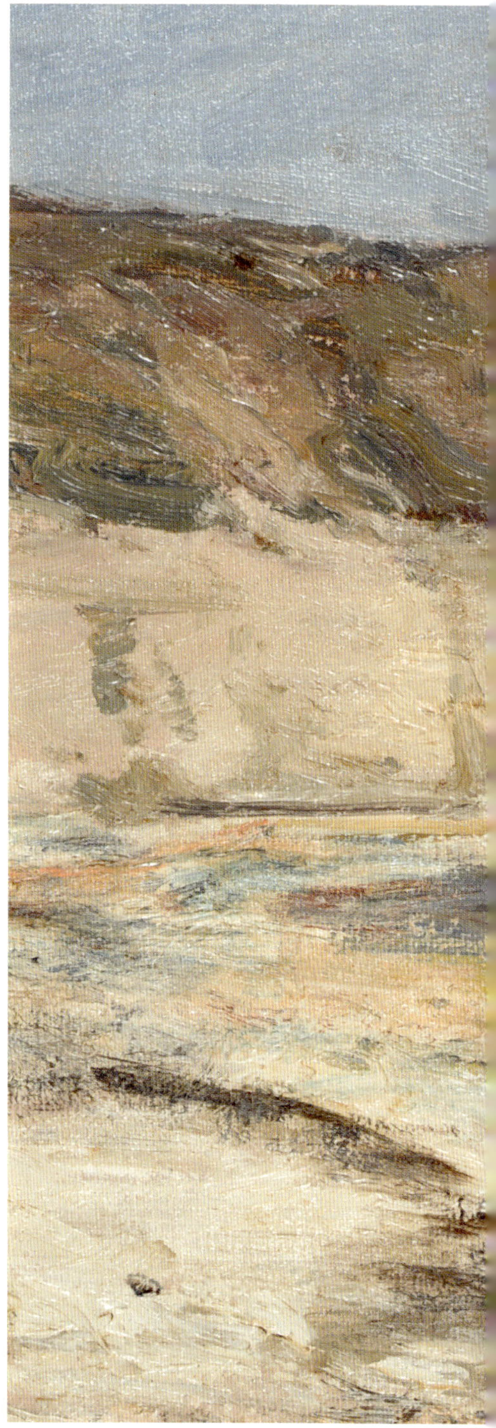

88. Owen Bowen's image of a *Beached Fishing Coble, South Landing, Flamborough* pays tribute to the individuality of the coble, both in terms of its line and decoration. Painted in 1906, it was completed at arguably Bowen's finest artistic period.

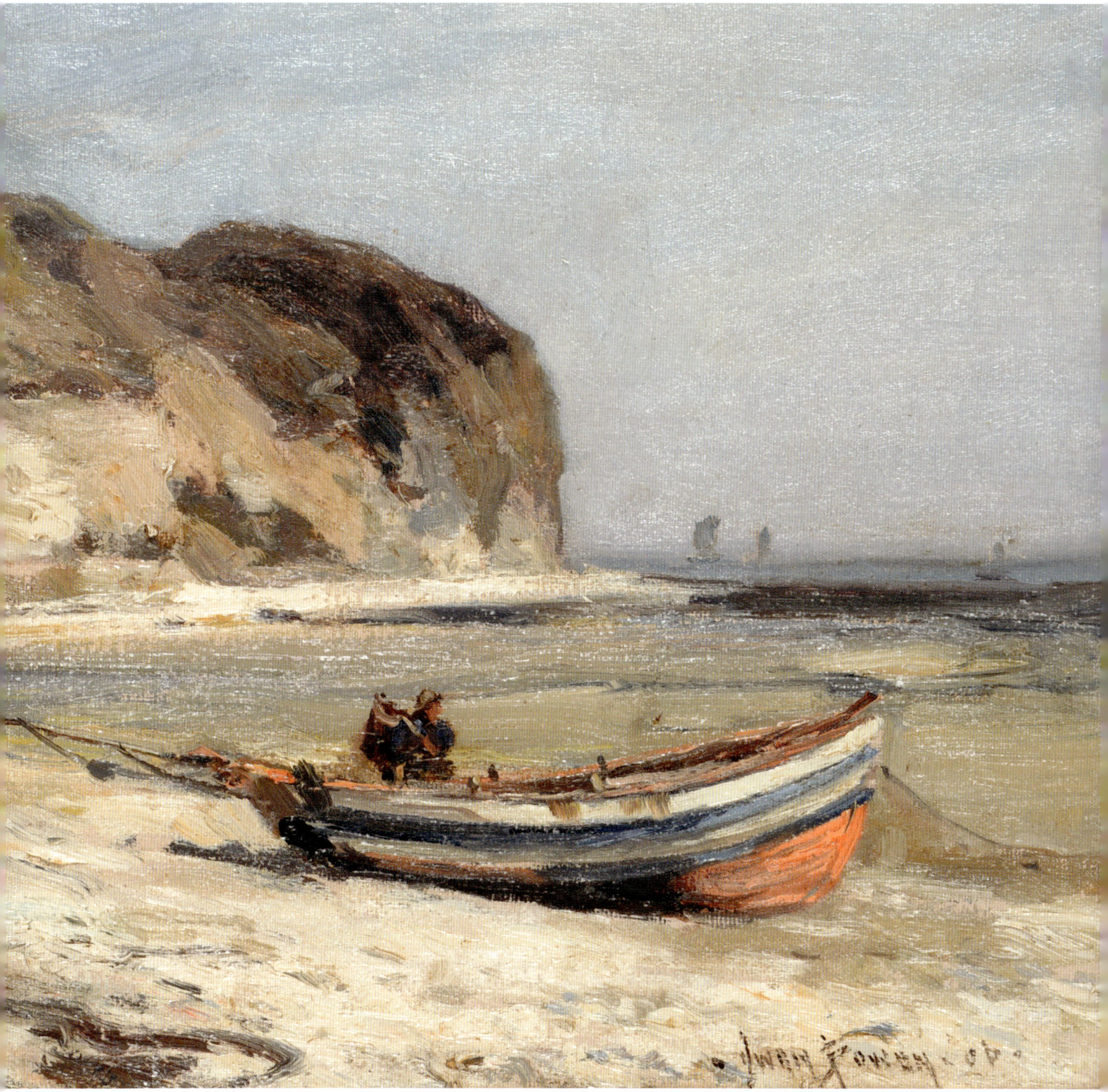

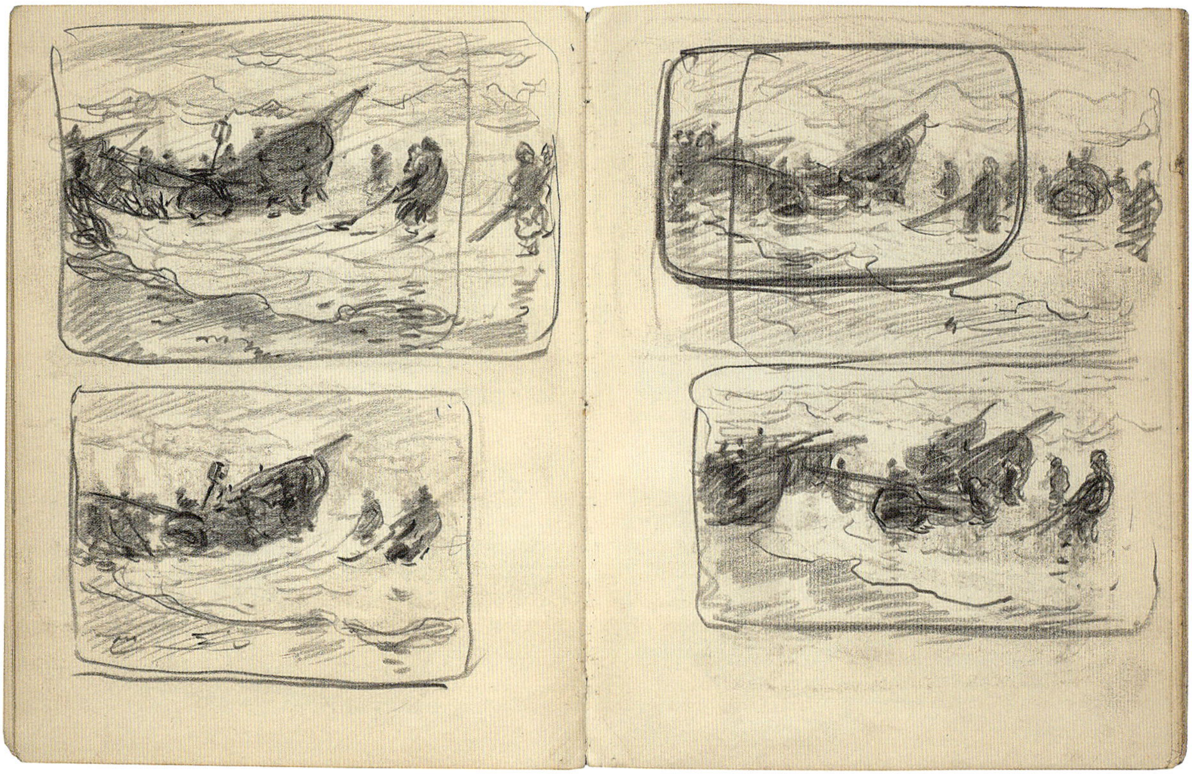

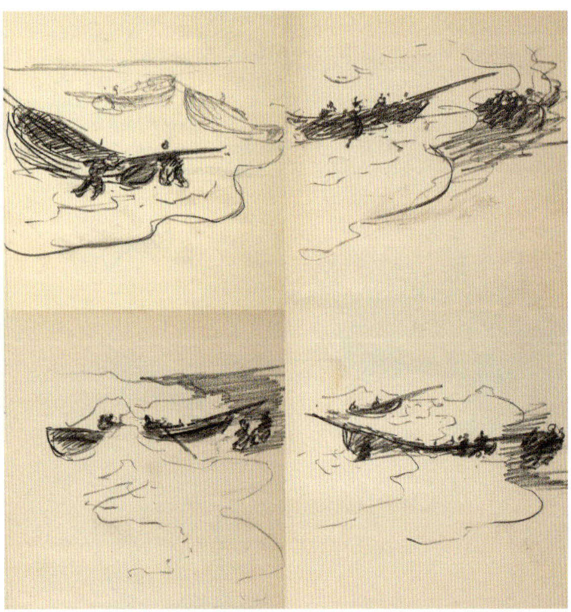

89. Bagshawe spent a sustained period during the years 1898–1901 visiting Staithes, according to the journal of Mildred Turnbull, his fiancée. Two of his sketchbooks support this view. They are filled with scenes from the clearly identifiable Staithes beach, featuring all kinds of weather and a variety of different craft.

Opposite: 90. Laura Johnson's one extant sketchbook shows continuous attempts to explore the line and features of the coble. Her oil painting *Cobles at Runswick*, set somewhat unusually in Runswick Bay around 1900, while illustrating all a fisherman's gear, seems rather to be an exercise in colour harmony; the artist's experiments at this time are well documented in her memoir.

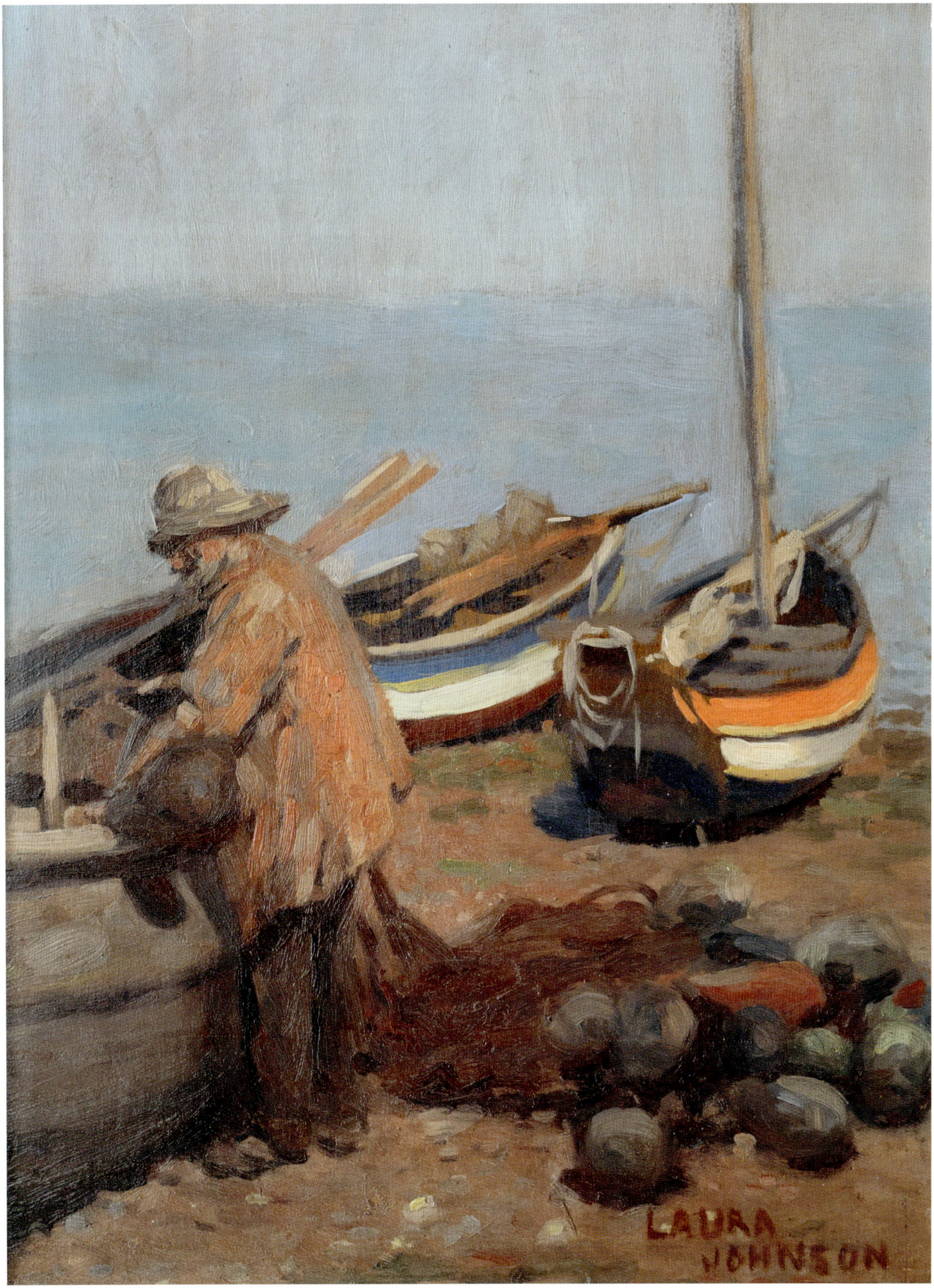
LAURA
JOHNSON

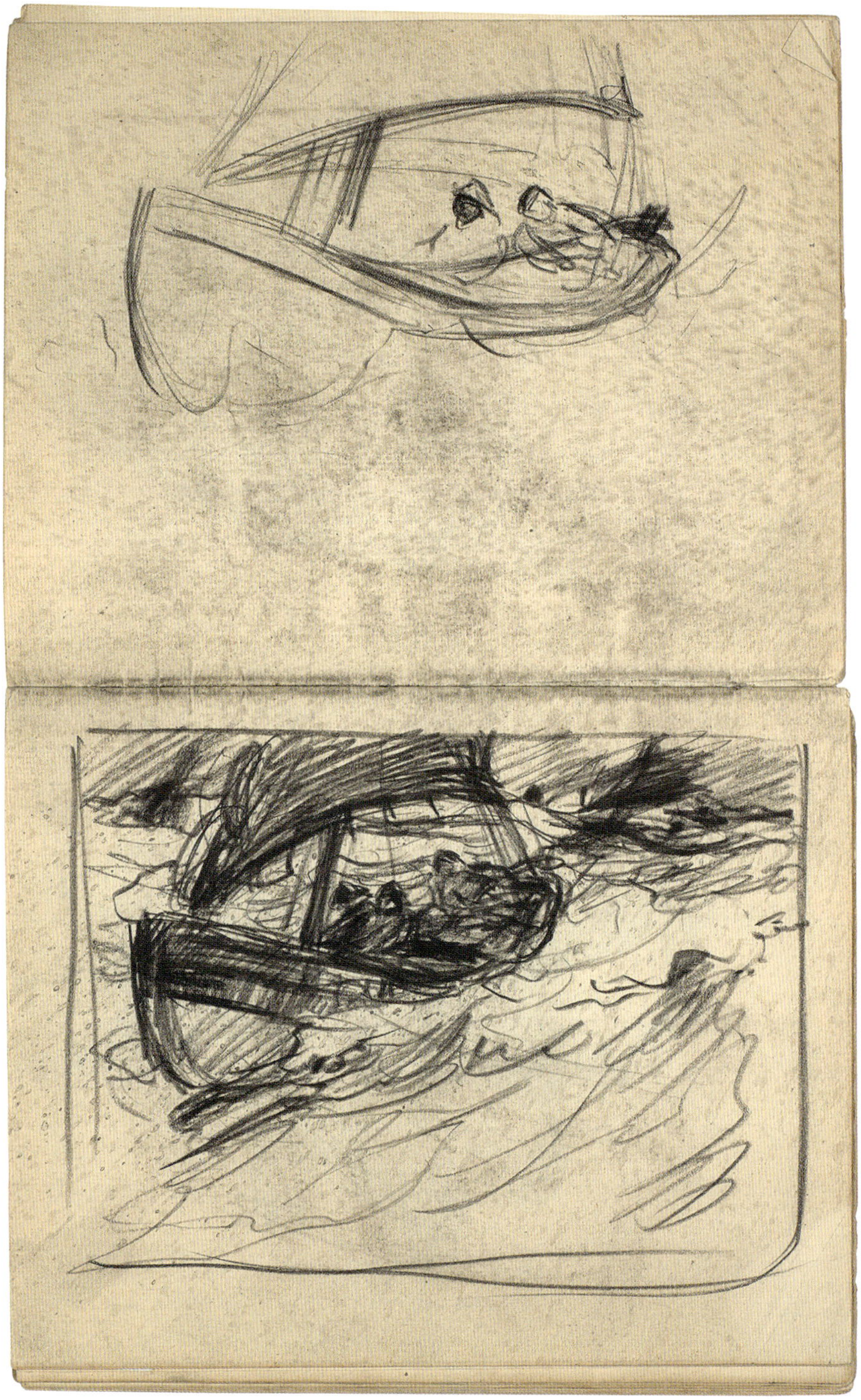

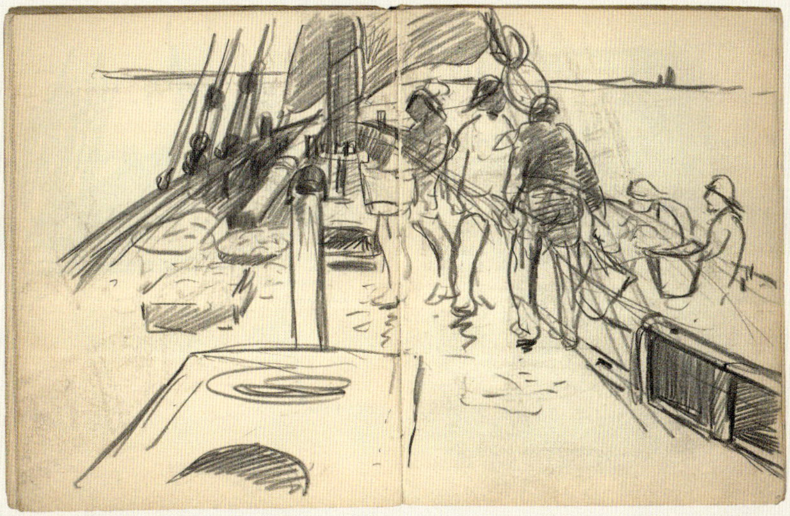

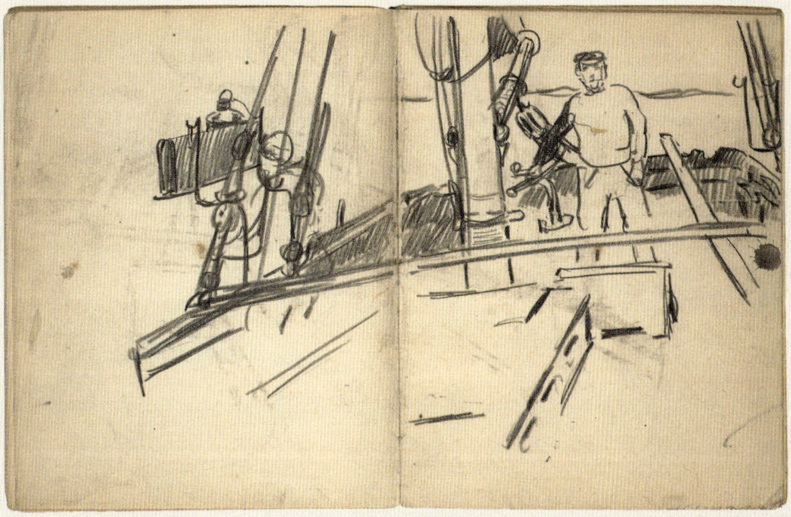

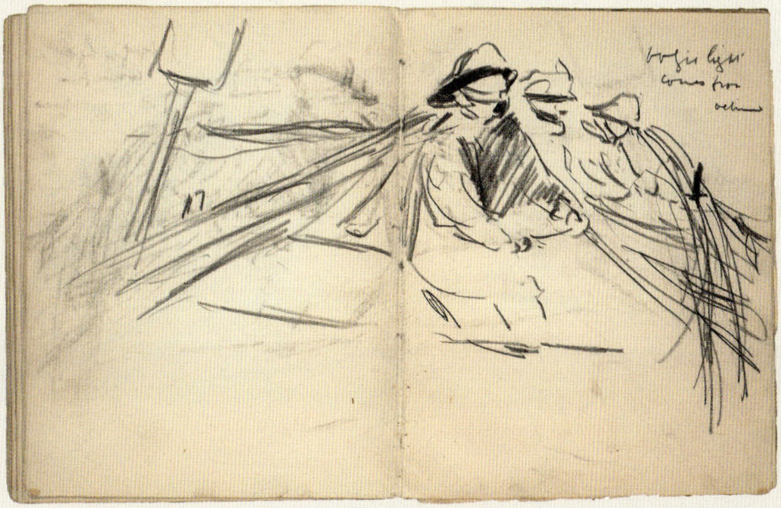

91. Bagshawe's accumulated knowledge of the variety of craft in the North Sea was condensed into a series of articles for a variety of publications shortly before he died in 1909. These were illustrated with line drawings worked up from his sketchbooks (**58**).

Whereas in Robin Hood's Bay or Runswick cobles were pulled down to the water by horses on boat carriages, at Staithes they were hauled by hand directly to and from the sea using the oars – designed specifically for the double purpose – as rollers. Bagshawe's sketches in particular capture the crucial moments as the crews took off for the open sea or returned amidst the breakers, making their finely-judged efforts to land stern first.[117]

Individual families, and often the entire village, were involved in the casting off and hauling of the boats up and down the sloping beach, unprotected at that time from the prevailing wind and weather. Rosie Good mentions how she and Laura Johnson spent an afternoon helping to drag boats and carry up lines. Harold Knight, along with Bagshawe, is described by Laura as helping the villagers to bring in cobles on a stormy night.[118]

The obligation on all is clear. Knight's first Royal Academy piece, entitled *The Last Coble* (**47**), describes just such a gathering, with an entire family group, positioned close to the picture plane, drawing the viewer into the drama of the beach. Similarly, Jackson depicts the launching of a lifeboat, directing the gaze from a group of all ages in the foreground to the diminutive figures in the distance manhandling their craft into the breaking surf.[119]

SENSE OF COMMUNITY

Quite apart from the physical challenges presented by bad weather (see Chapter 4), occasions such as these may have presented a social challenge to the artists, especially as they became increasingly assimilated to their communities. Tradition had it, for example, that painting on the Sabbath might result in altercations with the fisherfolk, so to observe a rescue launch or hurried, storm-tossed beaching and not participate might well have been difficult to brook. A fuller analysis of such scenes – and indeed the relative paucity of other larger village gatherings, such as church services, funerals and even weddings – might prove informative.[120]

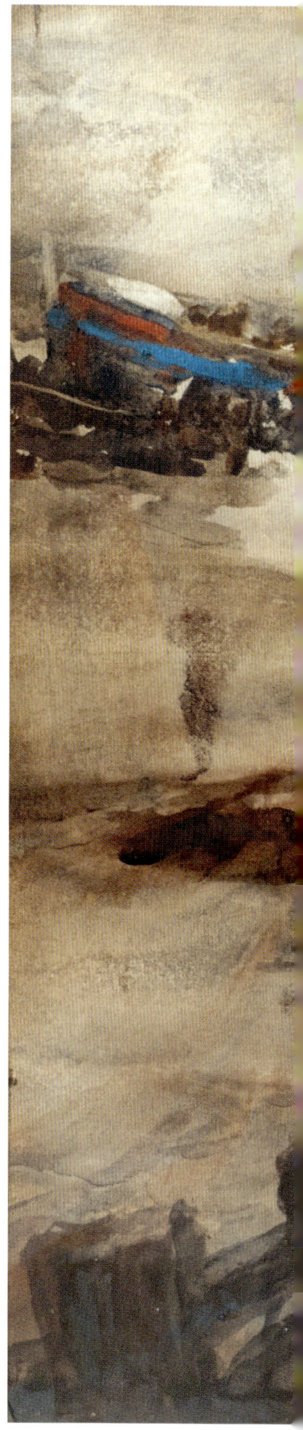

92. Scenes of shipwreck and rescue by lifeboat caught the public's imagination in the late nineteenth century. Fred Jackson's 1903 Art Club exhibit *Off to the Rescue* sold immediately. In this watercolour, *Fisherfolk Watching the Lifeboat Rescue*, he echoes the format of Harold Knight's RA success, *The Last Coble.*

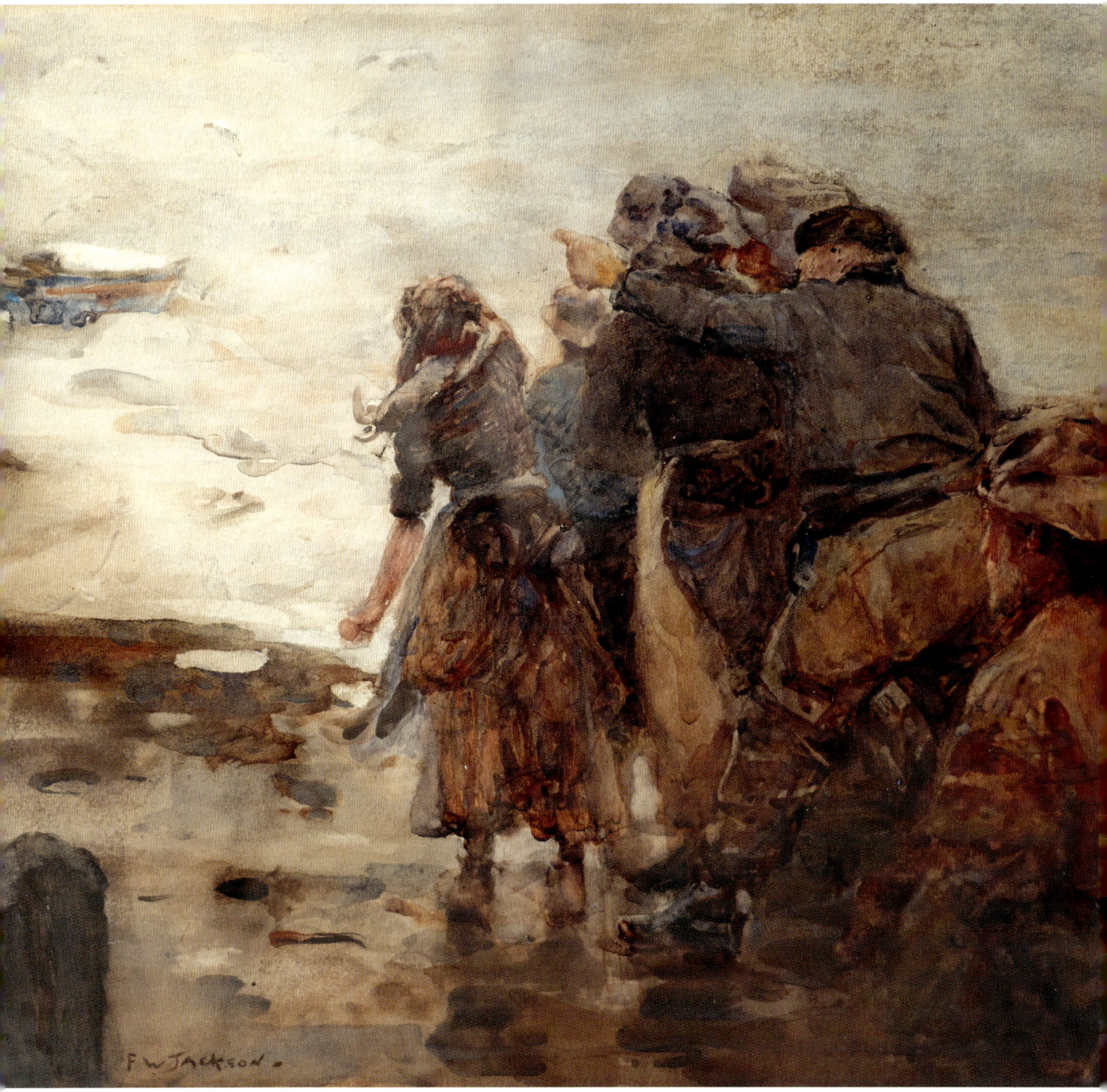
F W JACKSON

In reflecting years later on his time there, Rowland Hill observed:

> Whenever there was a storm or shipwreck we were always ready to give a hand launching the lifeboat, and we often gave shelter to fishermen from cobles who had been forced to run for a strange harbour. I think it was a feeling of mutual help and camaraderie...[121]

Exhibition lists do reveal works with titles such as *Wives and Mithers Maist Desparin'* and *Women Must Weep* by Johnson and *A Fisherman's Funeral*, attributed to Harold Knight. However, with no physical pictures to corroborate, association with Staithes gatherings cannot be confirmed. The latter's watercolour *Grief* (**5**) is a most unusual work. Intrusive in its proximity and unflinching in aspect, it sets itself apart from any of his other early pictures or those of Johnson, despite the couple's seemingly close relationship to the community.

Laura first came to Staithes as an unmarried woman, accompanied by female relations. Her continuing presence in the village was marked by an assimilation – if the evidence of memoir and letters is to be believed – that surely owed something to the impecunious lifestyle and to the poverty she had experienced. Yet Johnson's works display none of the larger, community gatherings of her literary descriptions, rarely even in her sketches. Seeking comparisons with other colonies, one can find only the example of the artist Anna Ancher at Skagen. As daughter of the innkeeper, she was the only figure of their artists' group (which included her husband Michael) to picture scenes of funerals and death.

On their travels, Staithes artists appeared to have no inhibitions about painting religious ceremonies and feast days. Jackson had painted such scenes in France, and exhibited them at the second Art Club exhibition; in his 1897 exhibition Hopwood titled pictures *Ready for the first communion – Brittany*, *Breton wedding dance* and *Church interior*, and depicted A *Cottage Service in the Hebrides* twice, but no equivalents with Staithes or Runswick subjects. Scenes by Senior in Bruges and Mackie in Brittany only amplify the case.

Perhaps even more strangely, the same may be said about occasions such as the annual fair, although Laura Knight recalls sketching at the time and cursory drawings do exist of the June Fair band (**34**). There is an exhibit listed *Staithes Fair* in 1906 by Booth and artists did depict fairs elsewhere, for example Middleton Wakes by Jackson and Woodhouse in Leeds by Hess. In the surrounding countryside Booth and Atkinson painted scenes of horse fairs at Egton and Hinderwell.

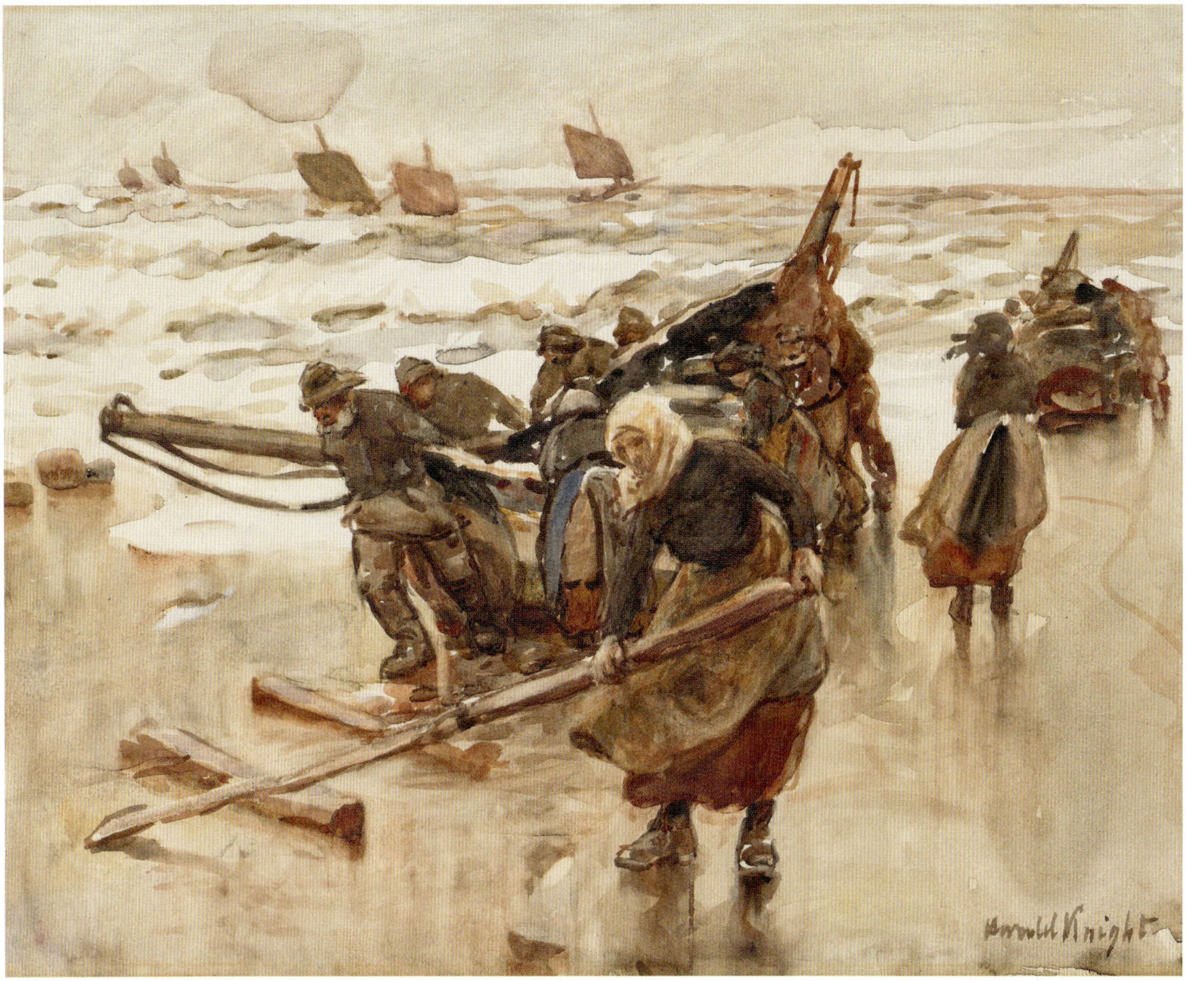

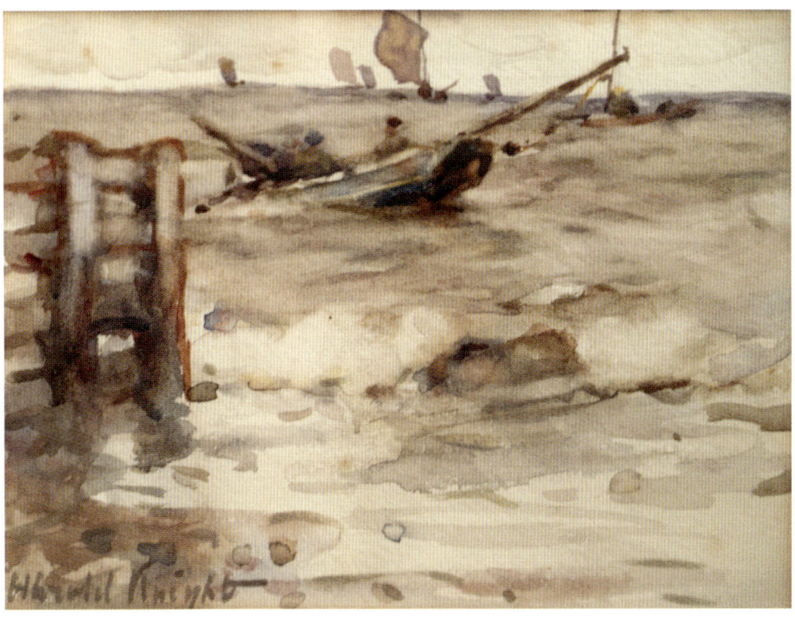

93 and 94. Both these watercolours by Harold Knight, *Hauling Cobles* and its small untitled counterpart, date from around 1900. Their sombre tones and suppressed colours suggest the boats running for the shore, to be beached and dragged to safety either in a storm or harsh winter weather. Using oars to provide rollers, the cobles were hauled well up the beach and, in the worst weather, even onto the staith.

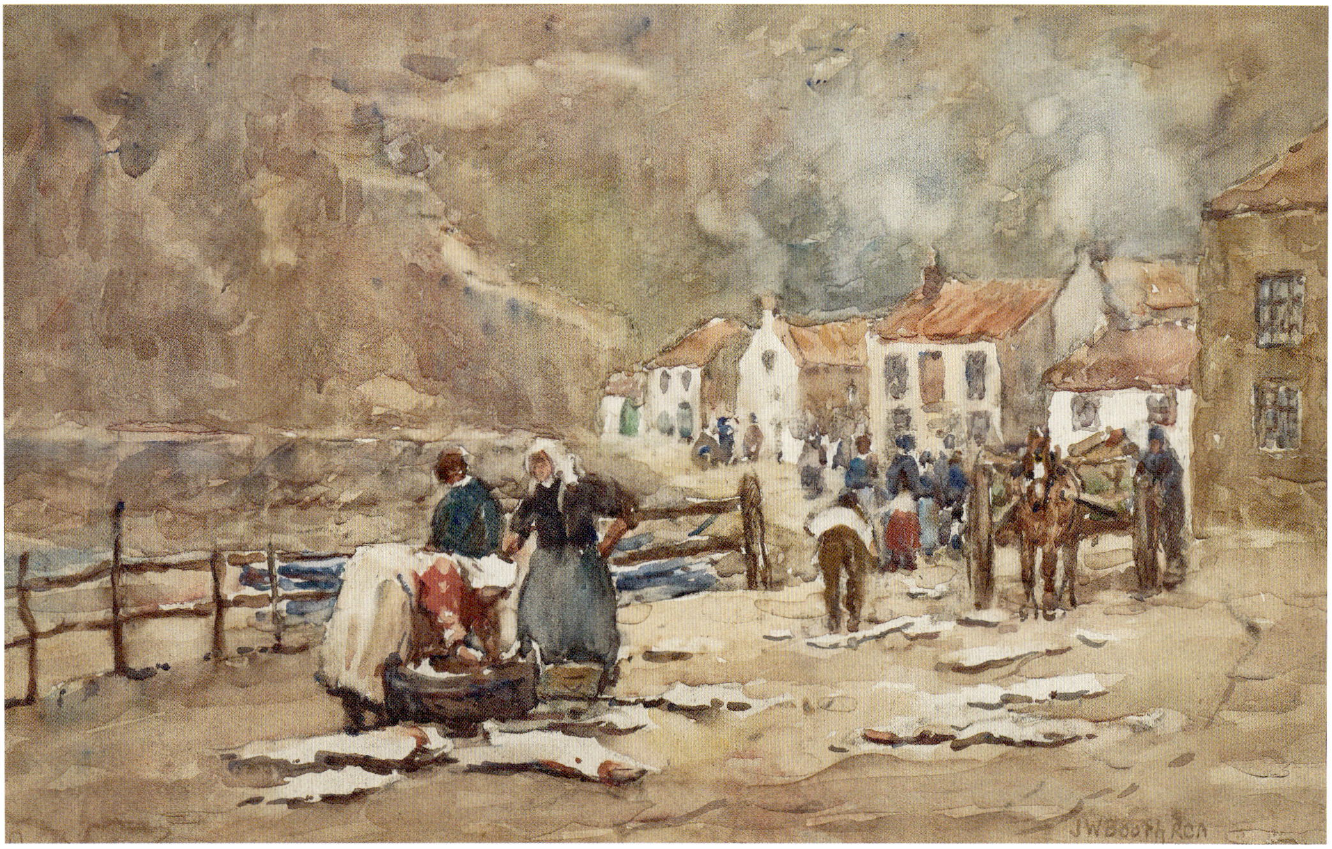

95. James Booth's work usually focuses on the agricultural communities inland from the coast. However, he did paint *Fishmarket on the Staith*, an archetypal Staithes scene, several times in both oil and watercolour. Ling, cod, rock salmon (dogfish), catfish, conger-eel and skate were staple features of the fish on sale, along with crabs and lobsters.

STAITHES

The staith, one of two features particular to Staithes, was an area of flat common ground fronting the sea that had traditionally hosted the fair days. It remained a centre of village activity, including the landing and selling of fish.[122] Johnson, Knight, Mayor, Friedenson, Booth and Dade all pictured lively scenes there; other artists such as Jackson took advantage of its relative openness to describe the view all along the seafront from Jackdaw's Well (**75**).[123]

The other particular feature is the beck (stream) which separates the main village from the cottages (once the alum warehouses) on Cowbar Nab, the protective headland to the north of Staithes. It was crossed by a picturesque wooden bridge, possibly the leitmotif of Staithes art, which provided a popular subject for one-time visitors as well those

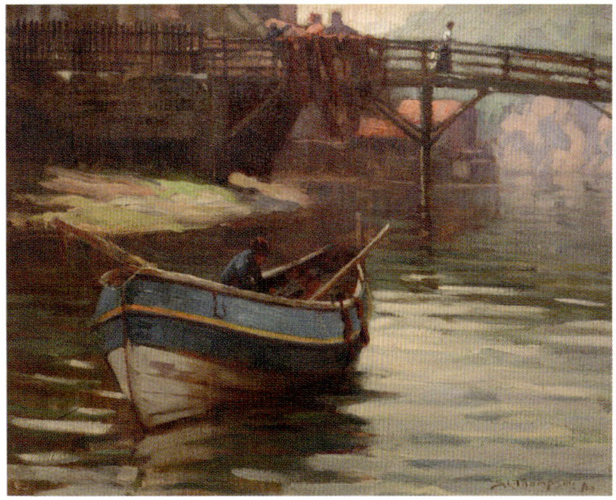

96 and 97. Sidney Thompson's 1901 visit to Staithes is vividly recalled in Enid Pease Robinson's diary. He shared an old, dilapidated cottage close to the beck and bridge shown here in his paintings *Coble on the Beck* and *Entrance to o'er t'Beck*. Thompson and his companion Charlie Sanderson hung a sign with the Māori term *Wharepuni* ('resting house') over the door. They slept in hammocks, eschewed formal clothes and were universally known by their first names.

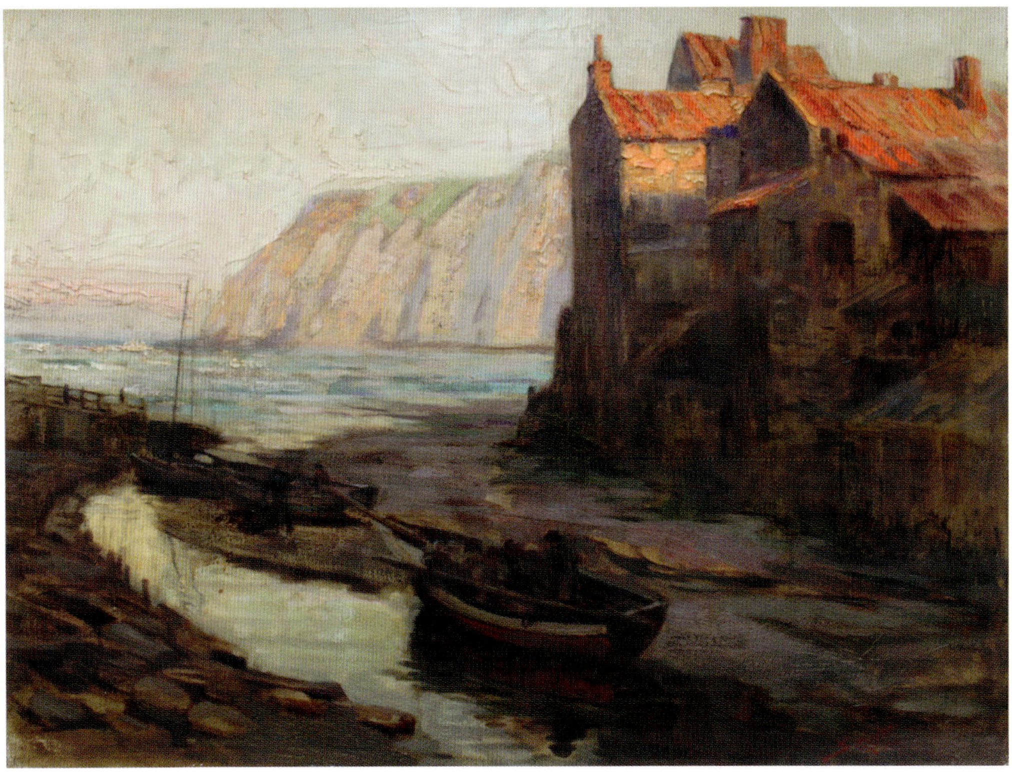

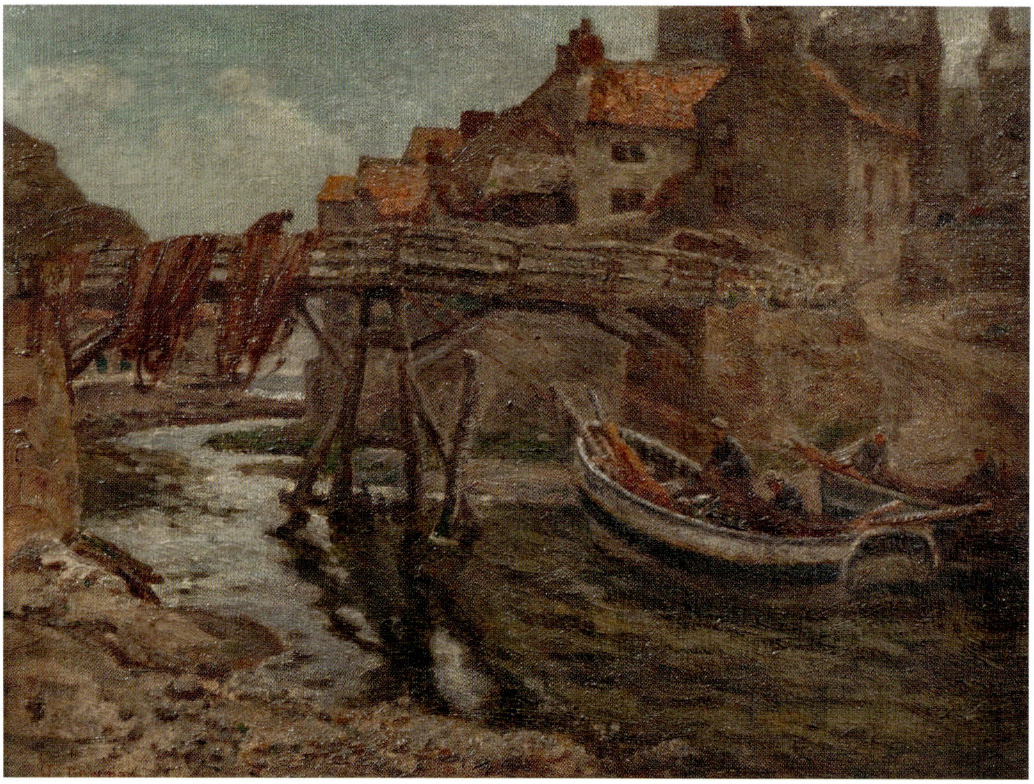

98. Little is known of John Bowman, a contemporary of Laura Johnson and Harold Knight at Nottingham School of Art where he studied part-time. He was among the original Art Club members and eventually settled in Sandsend. *The Bridge at Staithes*, painted in oil and undated, is one of only a few extant works.

from the Art Club. Sydney Lough Thompson, for example, who visited briefly in 1901, included it in his work and it was the subject for the prize-winning watercolour of the South Kensington Sketch Club Holiday Competition for 1900, judged by Sir George Clausen RA.[124]

In stormy weather cobles were often crowded into the beck and moored three or four deep, tethered to the bridge supports.[125] Knight and Robert Jobling picture just such scenes, but their focus in this instance tends to be on the boats rather than their crews – even if, as Laura Knight later remembered, the men can be identified from the details of the cobles. Single boats or part-groups were painted by Bowman, Hill and Mann (**45**); Johnson and Bagshawe also sketched the cobles tying up. Richardson's wintry scene (**170**) show women hurrying to cross to Cowbar Nab. Jobling's figures are paused half-way, while Frank Sutcliffe photographed fisherfolk at the Cowbar end.

Though the artists themselves arrived on the railway, whose viaduct arched over the beck further up the hill, they rarely pictured it. Nor, with the exception of Robert Jobling, did any paint the modern iteration after the old bridge collapsed around 1905 – to be replaced, in the words of Laura Knight, by a 'hideous thing of iron girders'.[126]

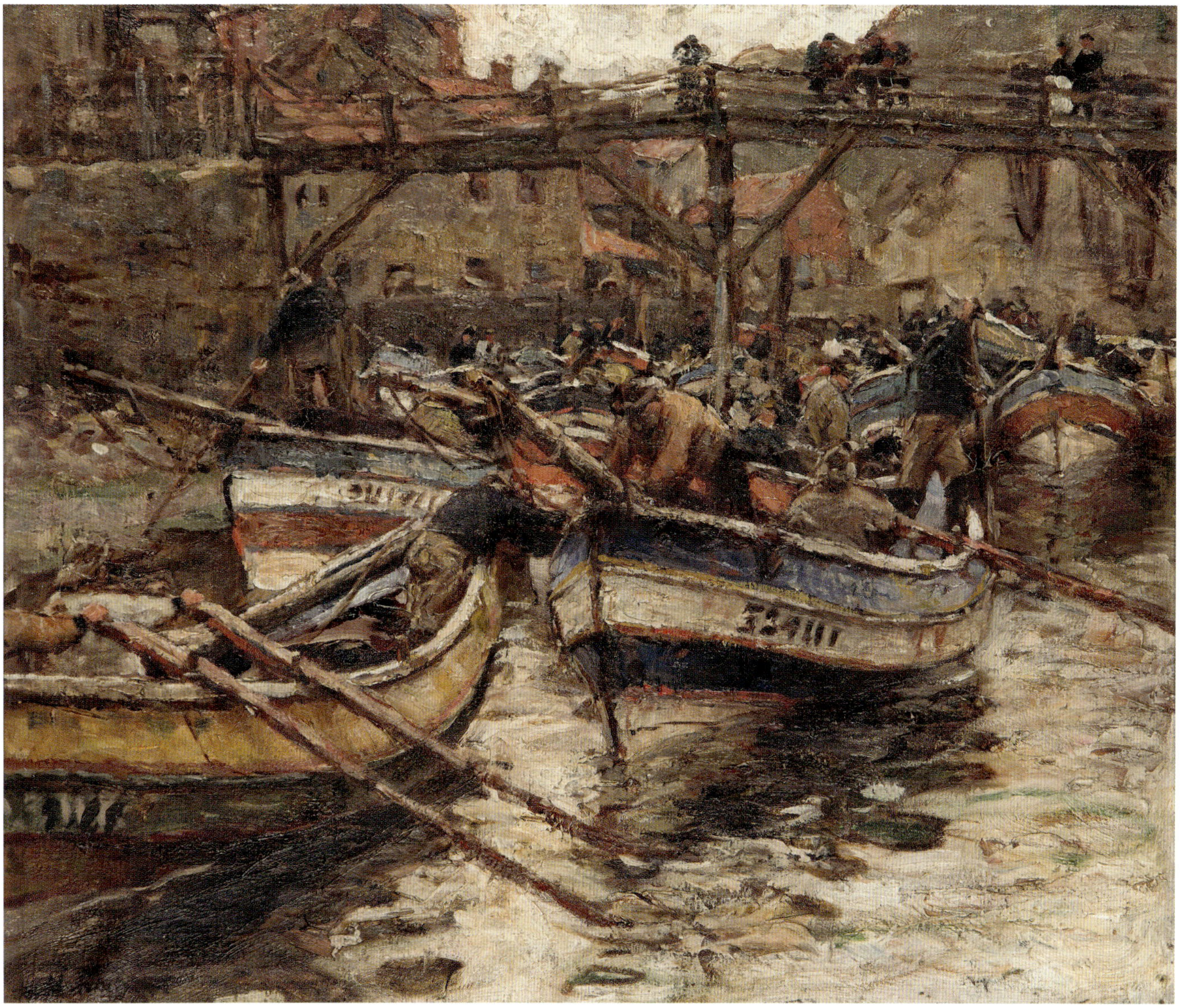

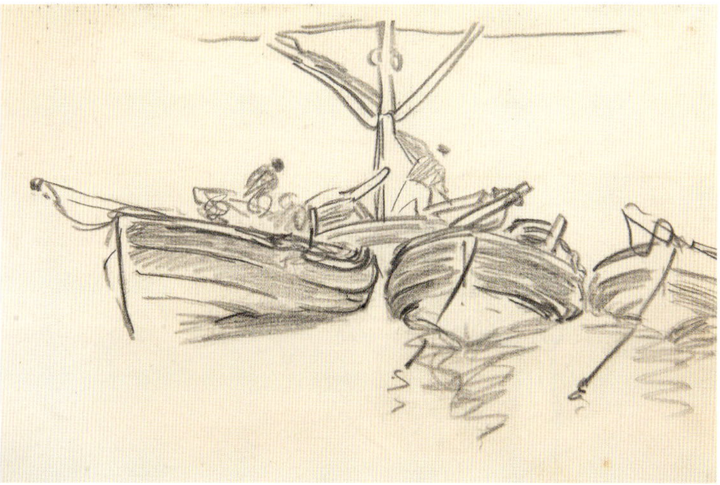

Above: 99. Harold Knight's image *Herring Boats* appears to have been one of two which illustrated opposing viewpoints up and down the beck around 1900. Laura Knight clearly remembered in her writing 'the men and nets a'sparkle with fish scales, the auld'oaken bridge and the rocky grip of Cawbor Nab [*sic*]'.

Left: 100. Both Laura Johnson and Joseph Bagshawe were attracted to the subject of fishermen mooring their cobles to the bridge in anticipation of bad weather; their untitled works are thought to date from around 1898. Her surviving sketchbook also contains several detailed studies of the coble *Star of Hope*, registered to the Verrill family with whom she lodged.

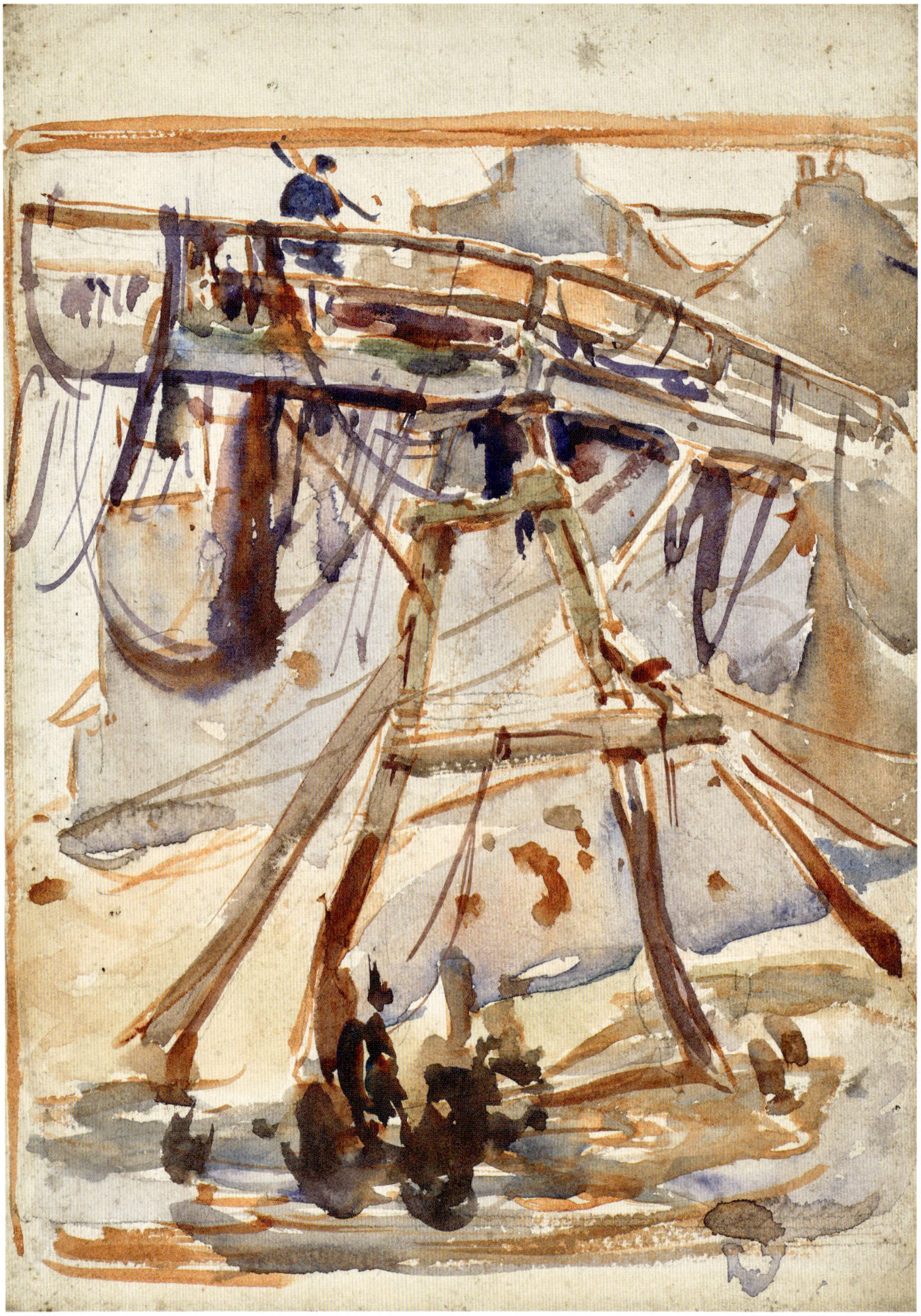

101. Fred Mayor's skills as a watercolourist are clearly evident in this untitled sketch of Staithes Bridge, dating from 1898–9. What might have been considered a static and leisurely scene is in fact full of dynamism, prompted by the use of a strong diagonal axis and flourishing brushwork.

102. Using the same palette as Mayor, Robert Jobling's *Girl on the Bridge* is contemplative rather than dynamic. He employs an unusual, foreshortened viewpoint, along with a 'blanket' of nets to simplify the complex structure of wooden beams; the figure pairings serve to hold one another in check.

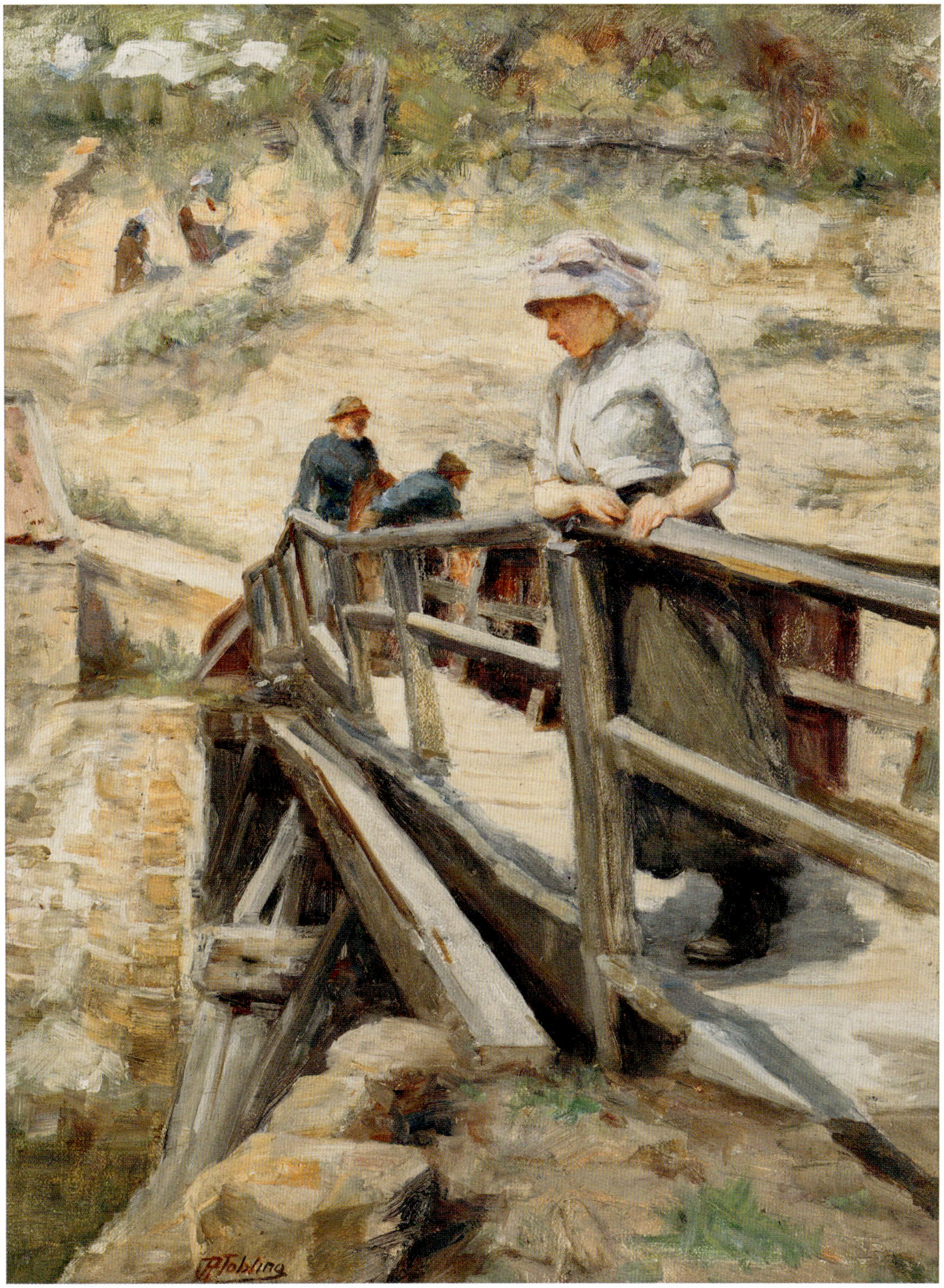

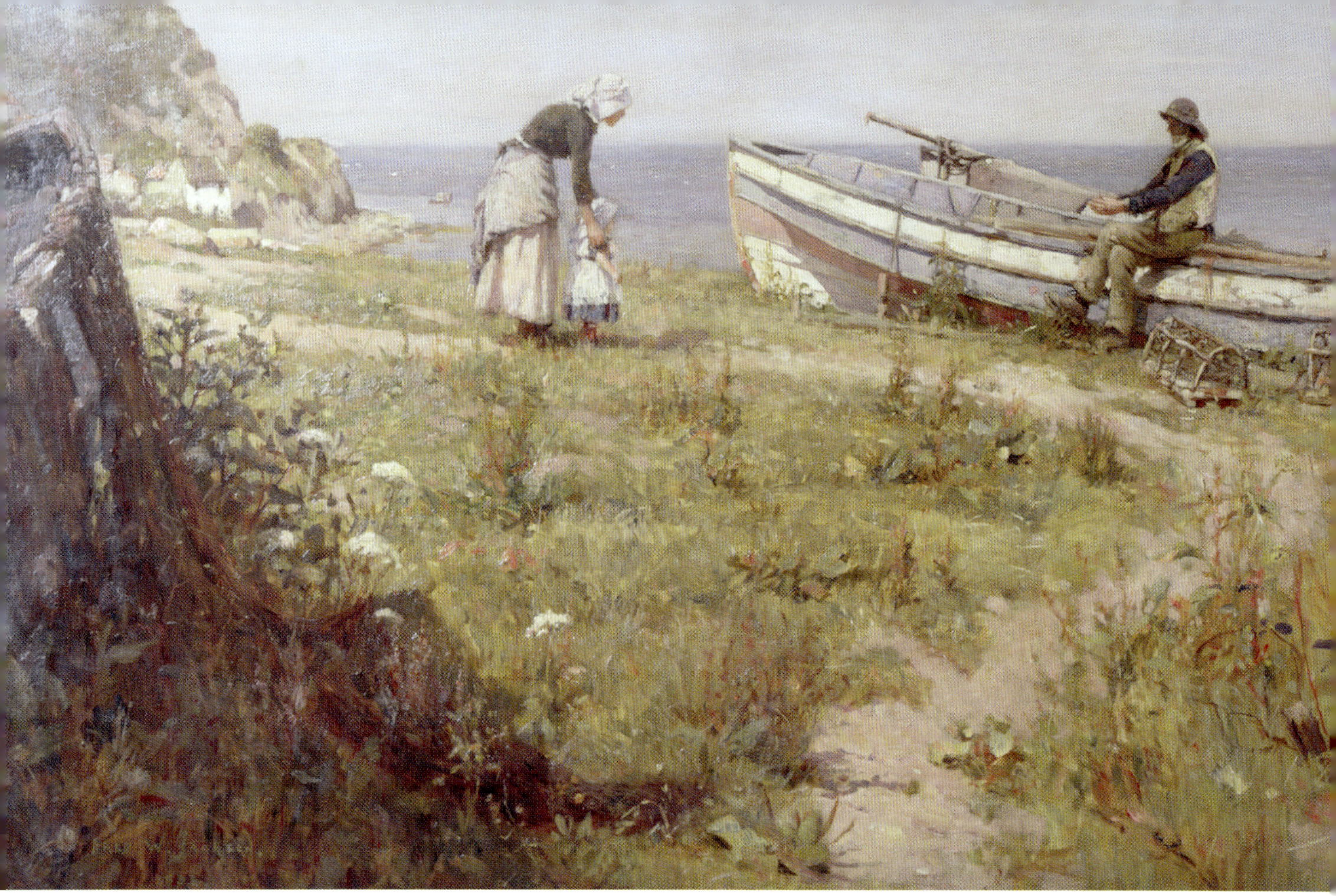

Above: 103. *A Welcome Visitor* of 1893 by Fred Jackson is one of a number of large canvases he painted of the Runswick Bay shoreline. In this work he uses the village and Lady Palmer's cottage in particular as the backdrop, subtly locating an essentially generic scene of fisherfolk with their coble.

RUNSWICK

The equivalent landmark in Runswick Bay is the building now known as Lady Palmer's cottage. As with views along the staith, the sea front of the village when looked at from the land recedes, to the point where the cottage's whitewash and thatched roof act as a visual punctuation mark against the sandy stone and red-tiled roofs of the other houses. Like the staith and bridge, the building was used as a leitmotif and often as the focus of work in paintings such as those by Senior, Hill and Paul. It also featured, more subtly, as part of the landscape element of figural compositions in paintings such as Jackson's *A Welcome Visitor*, Lionel Crawshaw's *Hauling Cobles* and Foster's photograph (**114**).[127]

Though not a single location or one specific feature, the gardens of Runswick offer the other defining element of paintings here at this time. On the south face of the headland, enjoying a slightly gentler gradient than the corresponding slope of Cowbar Nab at Staithes, the village provided – and still provides – enough space for a picturesque tangle of trees, shrubs

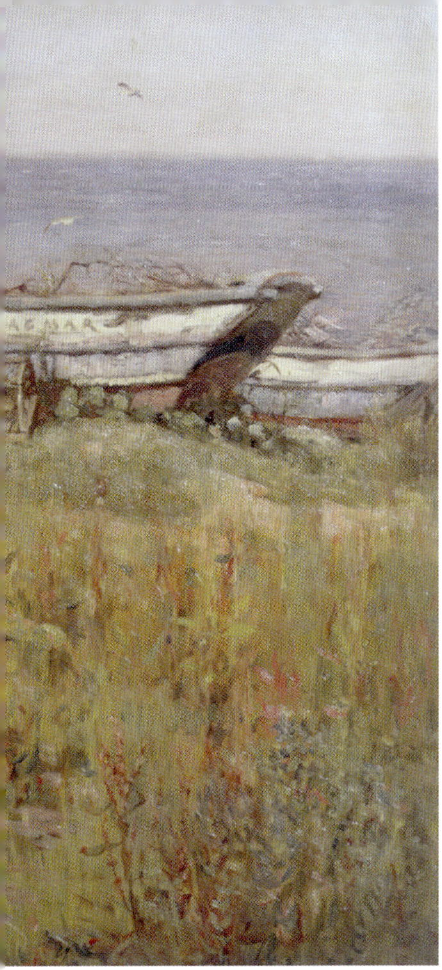

and flowers. Protected from the worst of the gales and frost-free in their proximity to the sea, they are able to benefit from long, sunny summer days.

The artists were quick to take advantage of the shows of spring blossom and summer blooms, set off as they were against the geometry of the buildings and the increasing fashion for whitewashed walls and green-painted woodwork. Pictures by Isa Jobling, Jackson, Senior, Hill, Foster, Friedenson, Hopwood and

Below: 104. Lionel Crawshaw painted two versions of this picture, *Hauling Cobles, Runswick Bay*, one much smaller than the other, around 1930. Distinctive differences in the two compositions include the elements of the figure group and, as here, the inclusion of Lady Palmer's cottage – the most distinctive house of the Runswick landscape.

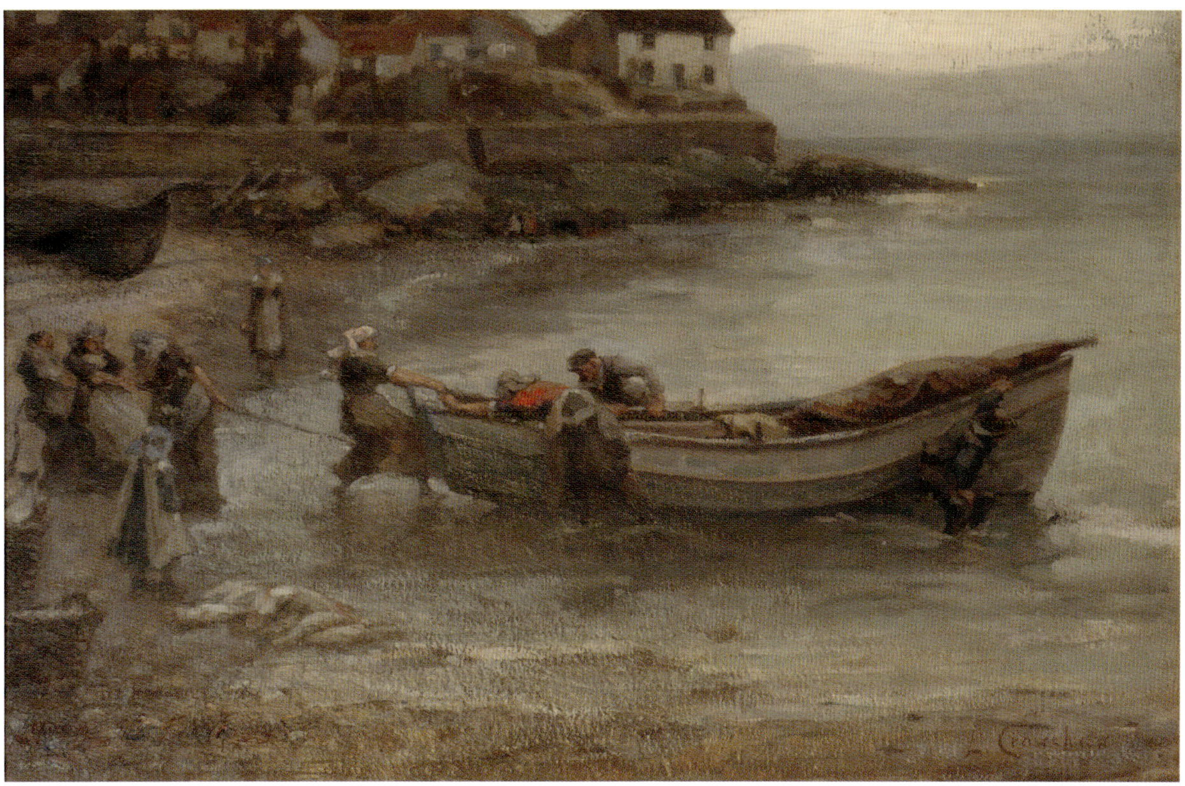

Watson all illustrate this, and indeed the vegetable plots at the top of the bank; others ranged still further afield seeking the wild flowers, as seen in Jackson's *Faraway Thoughts* (**111**) and Foster's *Azure Mead* (**37**). Of course, it was natural for these to be included in their many still lives, and it is particularly noticeable, after staying in Runswick, how great a proportion of the Knights' exhibited pictures that October were of flowers and gardens.[128]

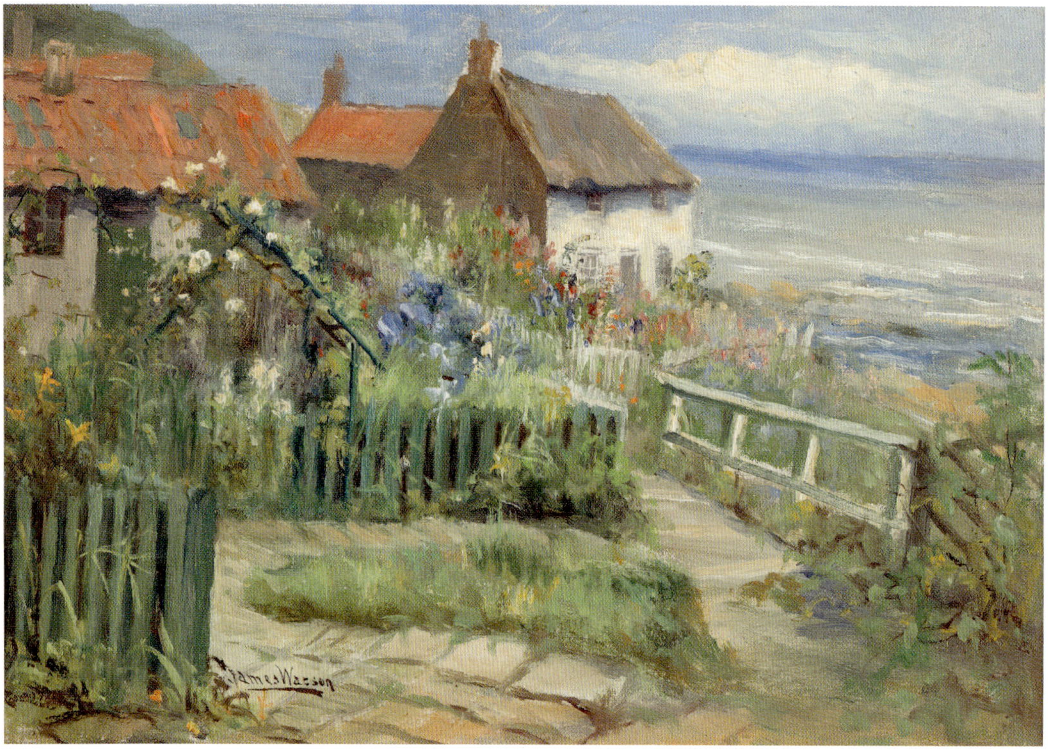

105. James Watson, the long-time art master at Newcastle Grammar School, rented a cottage in Runswick at the turn of the century – possibly the one pictured in this work, *A Runswick Garden*. The gardens shown here are a feature of the property, as they were of the village as a whole.

Opposite: 106. Gilbert Foster owned a 'charming big cottage' in Runswick Bay decorated with pictures, gessowork and a wood mantel carved by one of his daughters. He painted multiple images of the village gardens, vegetable patches and wildflowers. These latter are a crucial element of this impressive view, *The Village Fleet*, of 1892.

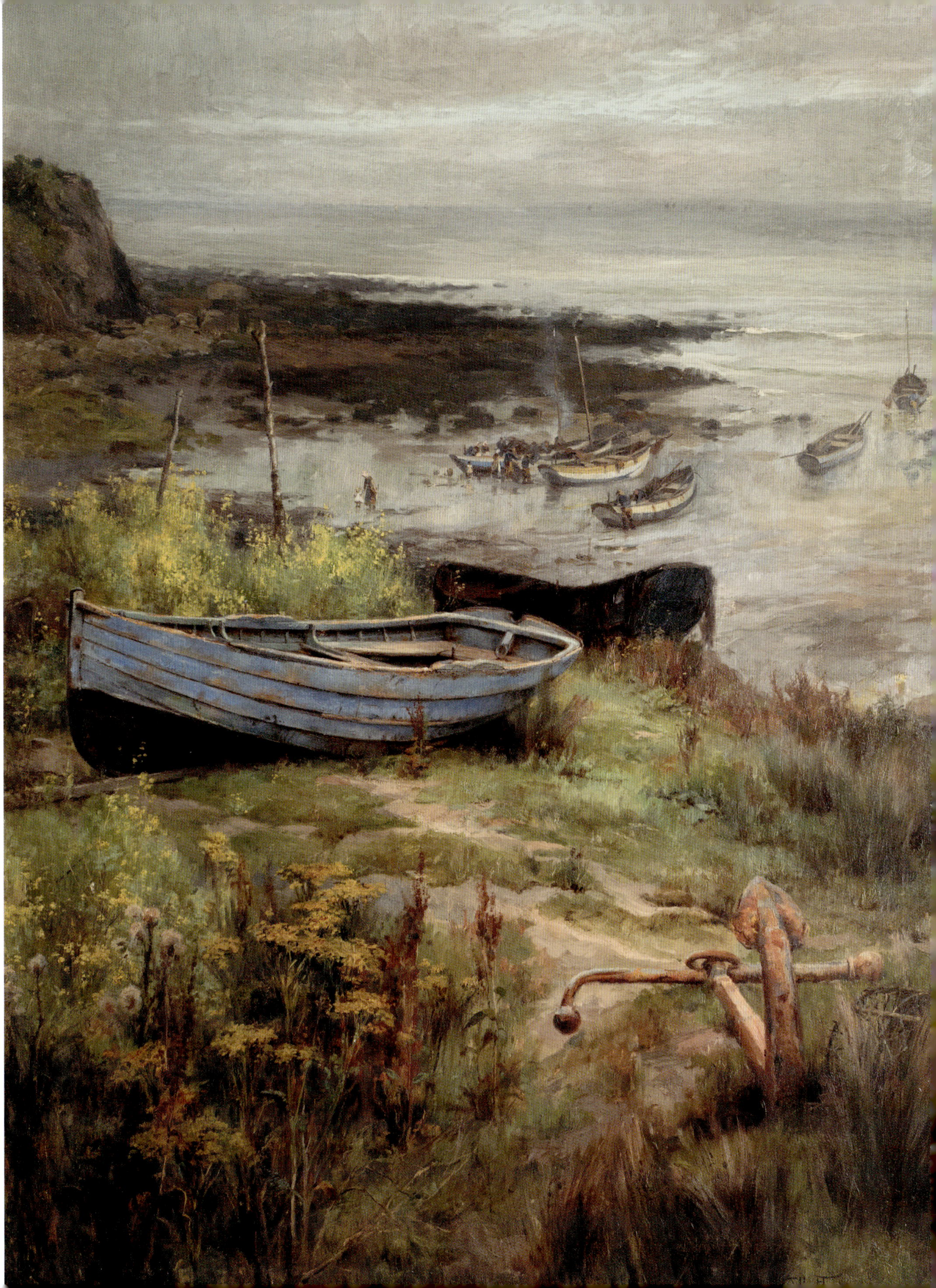

LIFE MODELS

While it is clear that fishermen followed a seasonal rhythm, spending many weeks away at sea at particular times, they might equally be kept to land by summer storms, inshore calm or even the consequences of successful fishing trips.[129] A glut of fish, resulting in low prices for those selling it, might necessitate further income. Modelling for an artist was one of the more convenient, if not lucrative, options available for supplementing it. Heading to the mines or docks meant travelling much farther afield with no certainty of satisfactory income, as Knight's bitter description of the mining family whom she hired in 1905 makes clear.[130]

Tasks such as 'fettling t'nets' and mending pots might be done at the same time as sitting for a picture, with minimal though regular movement, and such tasks proved rewarding subjects for the artists. Women were rarely at leisure, but similarly chores such as baiting and gutting, or knitting and crochet, enabled them to pose simultaneously.[131]

At busy times for the villages, this income might be earned from older men, women and children, able to commit to regular sittings. Mark Senior used a specific and recognisable model in Runswick Bay; she had begun as a girl and in her later years was used by Senior's pupil, Florence Hess. She even returned to the Hess family home in Leeds to sit during the winter.[132]

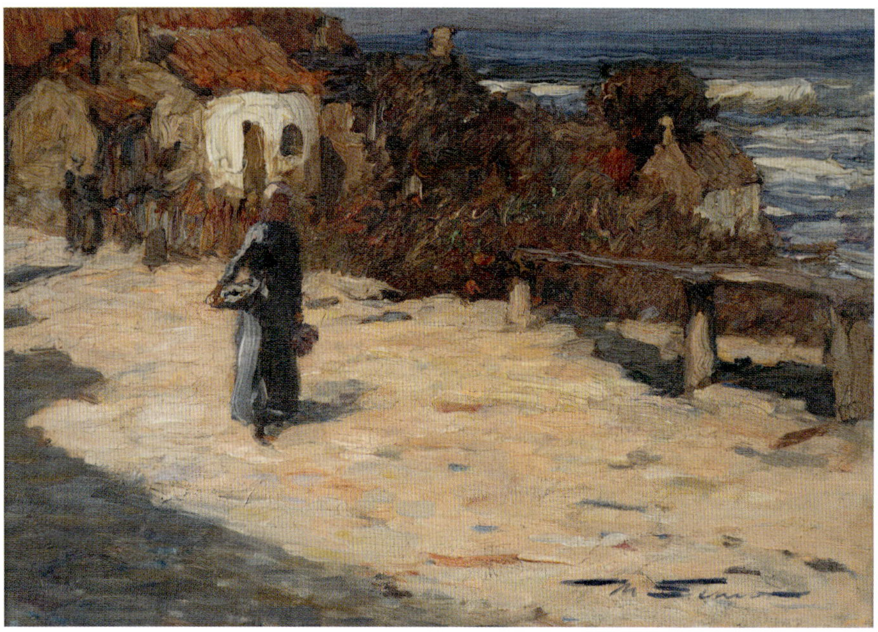

107. Mark Senior's undated work *The Cockpit* depicts the area of the village still named for its ancient location of traditional entertainments. The model, Margaret Calvert, was among several who sat consistently for the artist; others included William Tose, William Beswick and the Patton family.

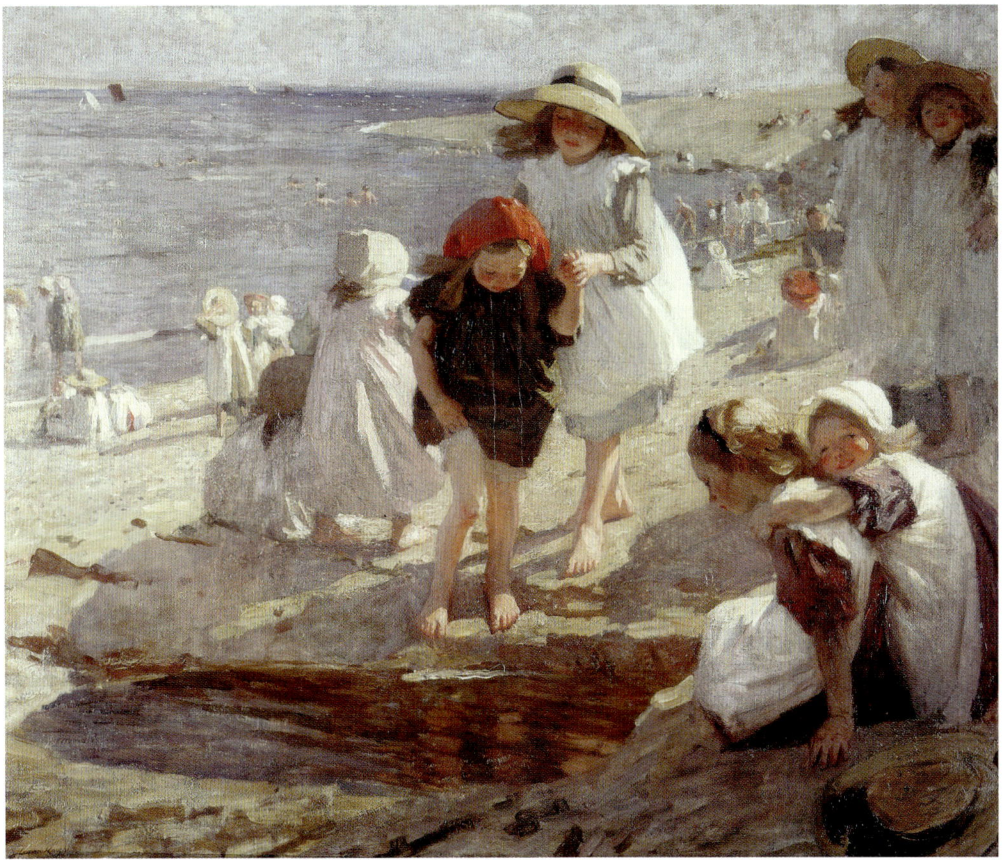

108. *On the Beach* by Laura Knight, painted in 1909, was described by the artist as a 'large picture that took its inspiration from Staithes, although it was actually produced in Newlyn'. In Laura Knight's memoir it is identified as one of a series in which she 'endeavoured to make use of my study and experience at Staithes', clearly an important influence on her later work.

'Old Peg' (Margaret Calvert), as this model was known, is pictured in a series of images, ranging from quite detailed portraits to figure studies metaphorically woven into the Runswick landscape. There was no specific male equivalent, but Senior often used members of the Tose or Patton families. His exhibition piece *Toil* (**86**) featured Lizzie Tose, also thought to be the model for *Girl Knitting outside a cottage*, while Willy Tose was his hard-pressed model for *In the Orchard*.[133]

Children's availability was far greater, though one can imagine that they presented their own challenges to an artist. Laura Knight recalls a selection of sessions with her various sitters, explaining that:

> I had no money to pay for proper models. I remember paying one penny for a year-old child, and his elder sister coming to fetch him home for his dinner.[134]

Nevertheless, she sketched endlessly, and in parallel with Harold Knight painted a series of watercolours on the beach at Staithes, taking full advantage of low tide and good weather. She was also unabashed about crediting her work in Staithes for the success of her early Cornish pictures of children such as *On the Beach*.[135]

A further series of sketches, attributed to Harold, includes portraits of the Verrill family as well as Hannah Ward, a model who also features in Laura's work. Oliver Sheppard, in one industrious summer, worked on a number of young female portraits (**129**), using a variety of children. The experience of sitting for Arthur Friedenson was remembered years later by his young model, the granddaughter of the Runswick Hotel owner, and Rowland Hill's son Peter recalled posing for his father.[136] Hill often painted children (one small exquisite sketch in a private collection comes to mind) and liked to picture them gathering spring flowers. Foster's equivalent depictions scatter children amidst the streets and houses of Runswick.

As indirectly confirmed by conversations recorded in Enid Pease Robinson's diary, naked boys and babies were a common sight in Staithes.[137] She describes how the artists used them as models, for example Fred Mayor:

> painting poor little Anthony Marshall stark naked all the morning under the blazing sun (M took great care to have an artist's umbrella) – for which he gave him only 4d.

Fred Jackson and Lionel Crawshaw, as their work shows, also sketched groups of nude boys in oils. They were clearly intent on exploring the theme as a part of the 'real' life of the coast, as had other colonists such as Tuke at Falmouth and Steer at Walberswick.

One of the most famous photographic images of the time, taken in Whitby harbour in 1886 by Frank Sutcliffe, was known as *The Water Rats*. The image was much copied by other photographers, who even claimed originality for the composition. Consequently Sutcliffe felt the need not only to confirm the relative spontaneity of the picture but also to give the reason for the boys' nudity, which they used to spare themselves the potential interruption of the truant officer.

In Percy Teasdale's *His First Ship* (**85**), research by the owner of Friendship Cottage suggests that the sitters were Patience, Johnny and his grandfather, Isaac 'Argy' Verrill. Pictured only shortly before his death, Enid Pease Robinson brings Isaac to life in her diary, not only recounting meetings and incidents but also noting conversations, mimicking his dialect and illustrating his sense

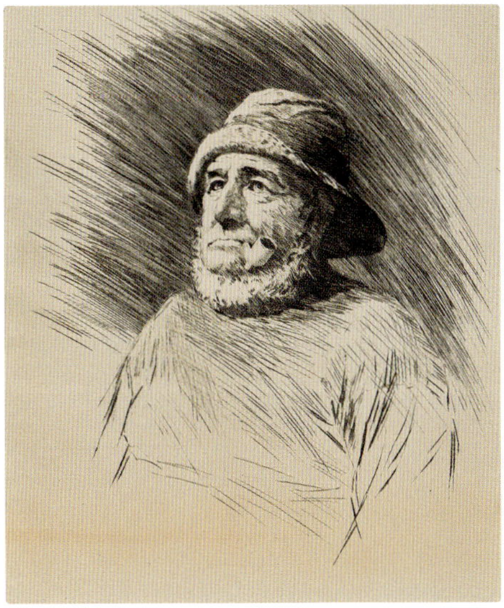

109. This famous postcard image of Joseph Verrill by Staithes photographer H. C. Morley is here etched by Mabel Annie Levy, a pupil of Thomas Barrett. Verrill was the first coxswain of the Staithes lifeboat (1875–86), as noted in the etching's title. Artists Ernest Rigg and John Spence Ingall took responsibility for a concert to raise funds for Verrill's care on retirement from working at sea, 13 May 1898.

of humour. Isaac also features throughout Laura Knight's memoir and in letters between Rosie Good and her future husband. He was a well-known sitter for Frank Sutcliffe, as well as other artists such as Joseph Bagshawe. The latter not only painted a vivid watercolour of Isaac, but also included him in a sketchbook, labelling him, exceptionally, as Verrill.

Working men are understandably rarer to find in the work of the artists, though both Hopwood and Jackson painted a series of watercolours of men in cottage interiors. Hopwood, in contrast to his pictures of women and children, painted fishermen at rest, often smoking, while Jackson tended to depict them working at tasks such as basket-making or pot-mending. Frank Sutcliffe, though requiring much less time for photography and with a long-established local reputation for his work, still met with resistance in the case of one potential model. The man refused his requests to sit until the other fishermen, believing him to be unreasonable, forced him into a session. After that, Sutcliffe remarked, he had no further problems; it helped that the man admired the resulting image.

ARTISTIC IDENTITY

This anecdotal, undated story hints not only at the difficulties still to be encountered by artists and photographers, but also at the mutual respect given by one group to the other, as described by Rowland Hill.[138] If one looks to other colonies, it is not unreasonable to suggest that, notwithstanding a level of familiarity, there remained something of a distance between the two groups. One has only to think of Newlyn's central figure Stanhope Forbes. Comments made in his early letters home disparaged not only local villagers, but also fellow artists such as Walter Langley, who came from a different social class.[139]

At Skagen, this distance seems to have been cultivated as part of a conscious effort on the part of their leading figures to create a distinct image of the artists' lives. There seem to have been no local exhibitions there, prior to the later attempts to establish a museum of the colony's achievements, and there are certainly no images depicting artists and fishermen together. There is much less evidence with the Art Club members of the 'myth-making' carried out in Denmark, although the establishment and exhibitions of the Staithes Art Club reveal the artists' intentions to create a more coherent representation of their work.[140] However, this did not seem to extend to self-representation, either with other artists or the fishing community.[141]

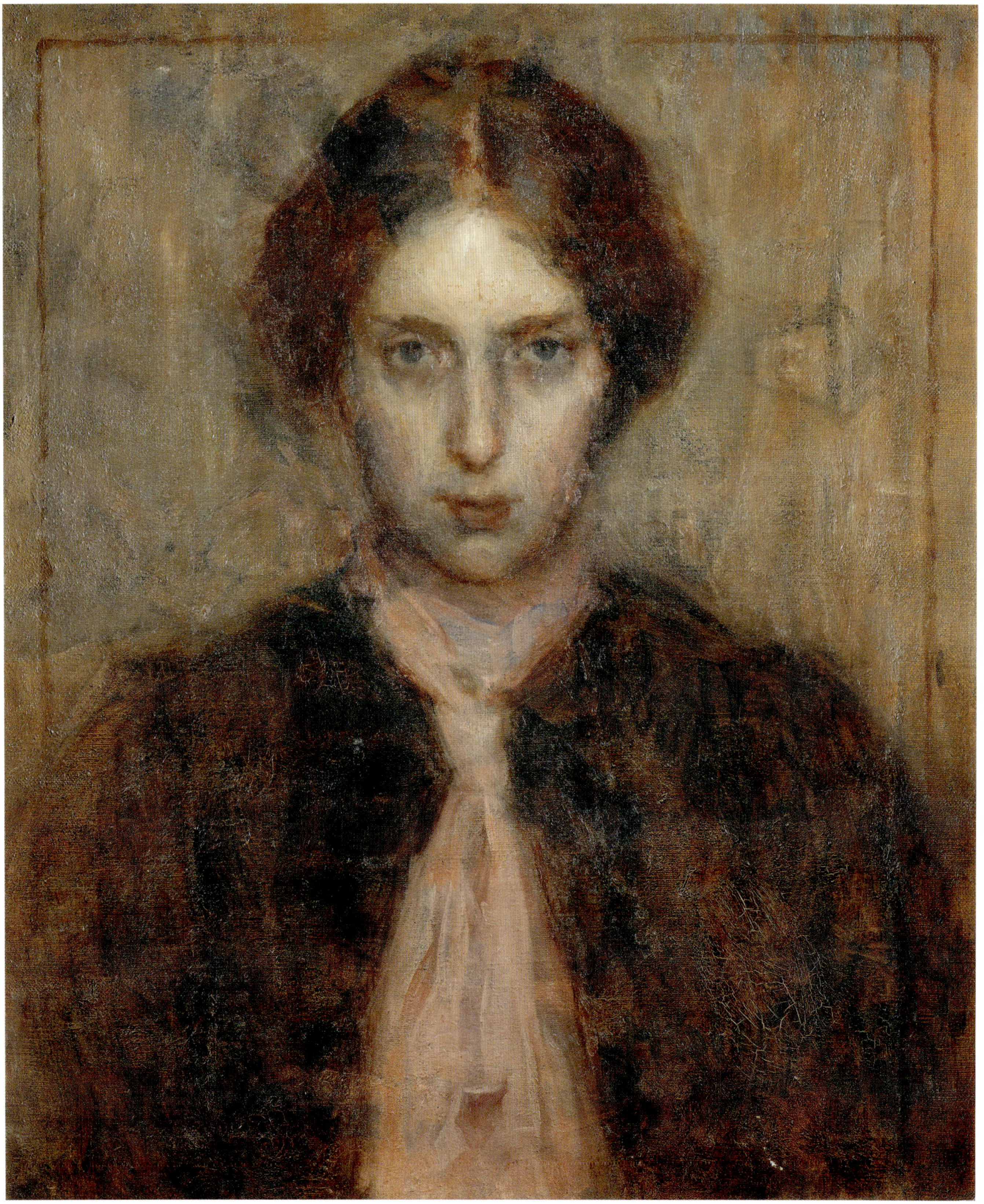

Opposite: 110. Few portraits or self-portraits by Staithes artists are widely known; there appears to have been no concerted effort to form an artistic identity, unlike in some other colonies. This portrait of Laura Johnson by Harold Knight (c. 1900) was bought by their great friends the Sheppards, and taken by them to Dublin after their marriage in 1901.

Below: 111. This 1895 work is unusual among the pictures painted by Fred W. Jackson and its current title, *Faraway Thoughts*, is probably not original. It has a romantic, even slightly symbolist air, enhanced by the crepuscular light, the wild flowers and lack of specific, recognisable geographic features.

Harold Knight did paint Laura Johnson several times, of course, from their meeting at Nottingham School of Art (**65**) to their departure as husband and wife for Cornwall. However, supposition that she modelled for him for *Grief*, among other works. is surely just that. Fred Jackson's painting, presently entitled *Faraway Thoughts...*, seems somewhat singular in his work. The lone woman, whose identity is unknown, lacks a bonnet, though she is painted in the lavender tones of traditional half-mourning. The work bears close similarity to a painting by Skagen's principal proponent, P. S. Kroyer. In his *Summer evening on south beach at Skagen,* Kroyer pictures his new wife and Anna Ancher strolling into the distance. A similar high horizon, evening light and slightly symbolist feel pervades both works, though this was long before Jackson's own marriage. Mark Senior painted both of his pupils, Gertrude Hudson and Florence Hess, at Runswick in a variety of pictures, including a commission of the latter for her parents.[142] However, there is no sense that this reflected any encouragement to promotion of the group.

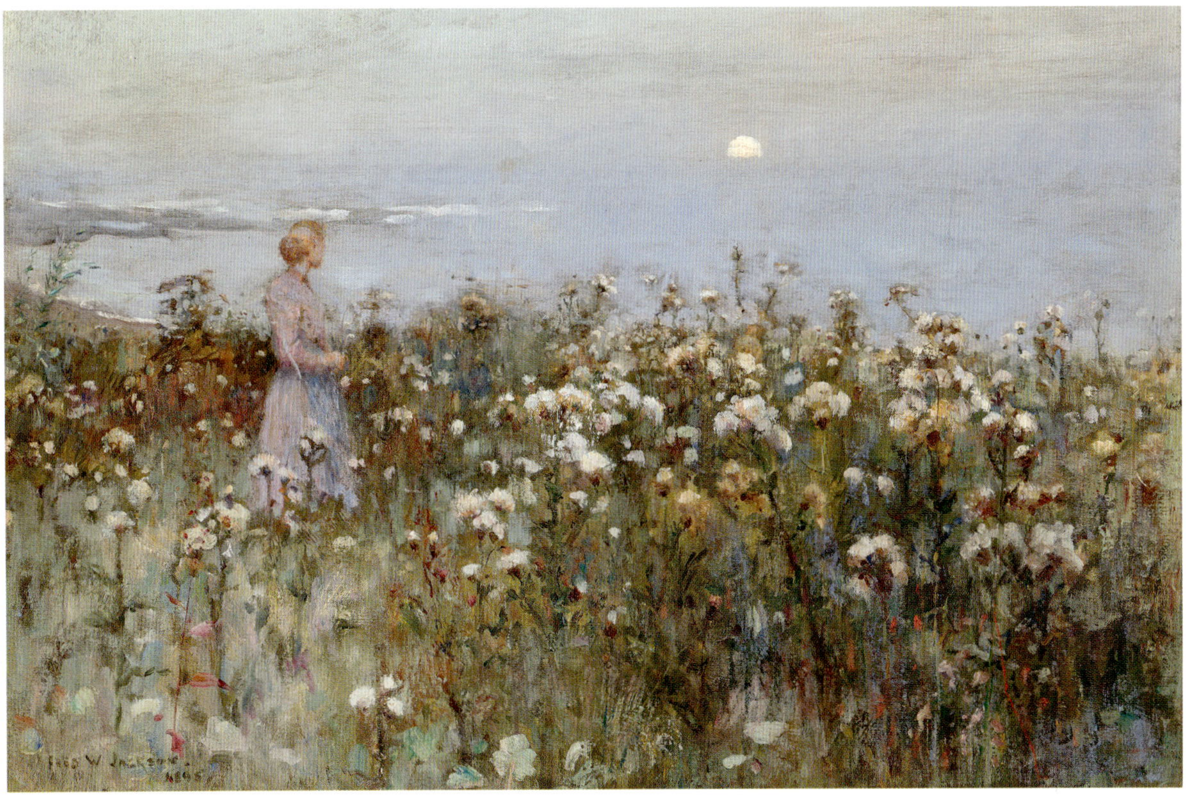

An early self-portrait in oil by Ernest Rigg, recently rediscovered, is an intriguing addition to the few other such works by the artists. These include a portrait of Rosie Good by Harold Knight, described in the making by Rosie herself. Apart from these, likenesses seem to be limited to sketches,[143] such as those by Knight, Johnson, Good and Sheppard, or the caricatures of Pease Robinson (**11** and **27**). It is therefore left to the literary sources to provide the evidence for the artists' relationships with villagers, and to give accounts of their own lifestyles. Whether in Robinson's diary, Knight's memoir, Good's letters or Turnbull's journal, the narration of events contains a uniformly warm tone that some would argue fails to reflect the attitudes, differences of age and perceptions that must have been present among artists of such a varied span of age and background.

One must, of course, bear in mind the similar nature of the sources, all female and of a certain age. These may be offset against the reminiscences, written and intended for publication, in the 1930s by Rowland Hill and Laura Knight, complemented by the anecdotal, oral accounts of friends and relations recounted to Dr Phillips, Michael Parkin and others in the 1970s. However,

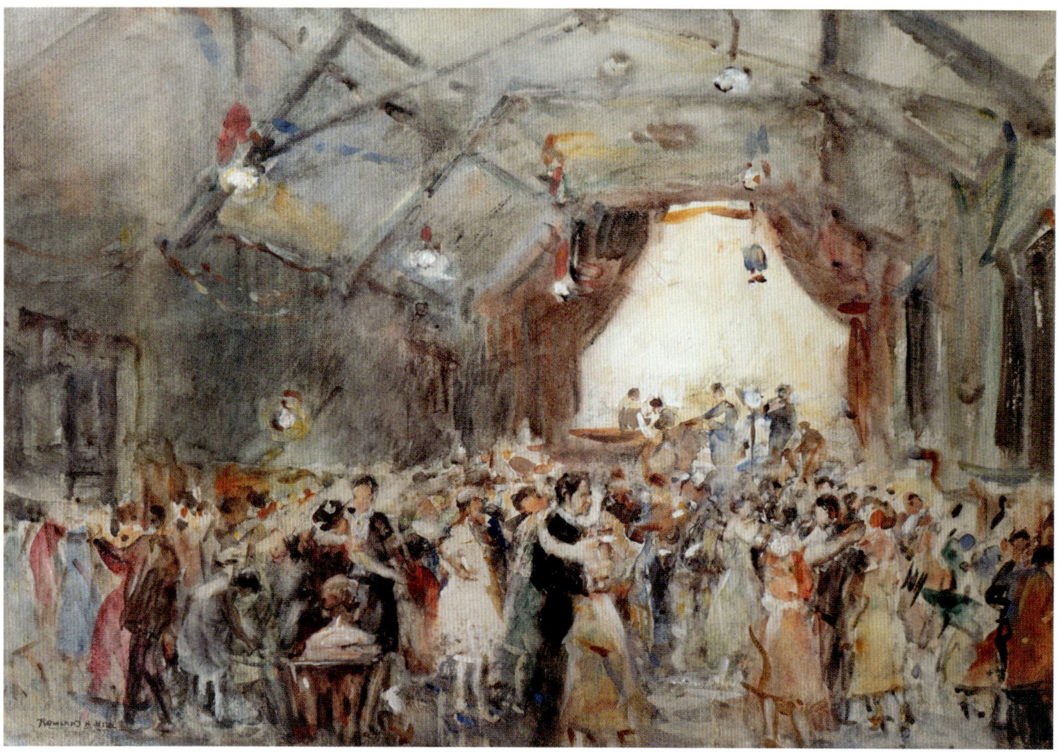

112. Rowland Hill entitled this watercolour *The First Hunt Ball, Hinderwell*, though it is not dated. One may draw immediate parallels with the newspaper reports of the *bal costumé* of 1909 (Chapter 4), rather contradicting assumptions that artists of the area lacked the bohemian nature of fellow colonies.

these are in turn open to the suggestion that a significant lapse of time, that included years of conflict and austerity, had coloured the retelling.

It is frustrating to read of a potential account of the artists' lives by Harold Knight, mentioned in a letter from Rosie Good to her fiancé:

> Harold had a letter from Conway the other day who wants him to send an account of his life for the 'Artist'. Harold has just sent the account off to him, which is an amusing medley of facts strung together. I shall be anxious to see what Conway makes out of it for the interview.[144]

In the event this does not appear to have been published; it might well have shed further light on the group for Knight, though often taken as a rather diffident figure, had a mischievous sense of humour. It might too have shed more light on their social activities, which have been consistently downplayed by commentators seeking to explain away the Knights' move to Cornwall.

Those same caricatures penned by Pease Robinson picture Jobling family members singing and playing at concerts. The 20-year-old diarist also mentions artists heading off together for either golf or cricket, returning on a conveyance in the evening. Mildred Turnbull's diary describes bicycle trips, often over 20 miles, out to local beauty spots such as Ellerbeck and Falling Foss on the Goathland moors with friends, including Bagshawe and Walker.

Knight's memoir recalls Harold ushering her away from a rowdy village parade when language turned rough; she also details performances in the Fishermen's Institute with artists, as at Newlyn, dressing up as minstrels. Frank Mason's performances are picked out in particular. Rosie Good's letters recall not only Laura practising a song for just such an occasion, but the two of them visiting the Verrill house, music-making until after midnight. Her future mother-in-law writes to her at the time, urging them together to look to Oliver Sheppard's best interests given he was such a 'bohemian'.

These glimpses from personal memoirs are tantalising, their visual equivalent captured in the photos of Foster and companions acting and music-making. Together with Hill's retrospective summary, they suggest not only a vibrant group of friends, but also a lively interaction with the villagers:

> the Staithes School – we use the term not in the meaning of a distinct style of painting, but as a colony of artists who 'Bohemianise' annually...[145]

I'm afraid we were a somewhat hilarious and sociable crowd, prone to fits of exuberance. But there was never any hooliganism ... They were great days – when we said jump and everybody jumped. We were always organising concerts and tableaux, and we always had extremely picturesque settings for them, although the dresses and scenery would be made from all sorts of bits of odd material ... We organised the first sports ever held at Runswick, and we had some great fun racing on the sands.[146]

Whether this bears comparison or contrast with other colonies depends perhaps on further first-hand accounts coming to light.

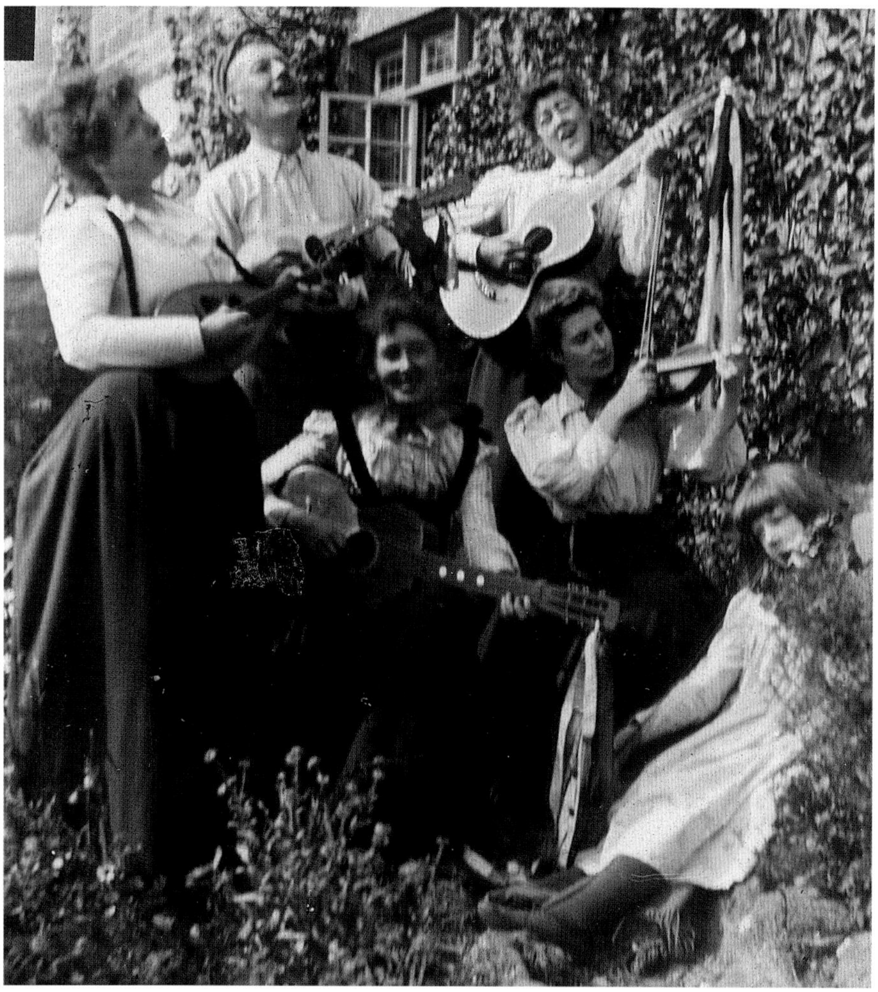

113 and 114. These two images of musicians and actors at Runswick Bay, part of a recently discovered cache of magic lantern slides, may in all probability be attributed to W. G. Foster and dated to around 1900. They include images to be found in paintings by Foster in similar fashion to the photographs taken and used by P. S. Kroyer at the artists' colony at Skagen in Denmark.

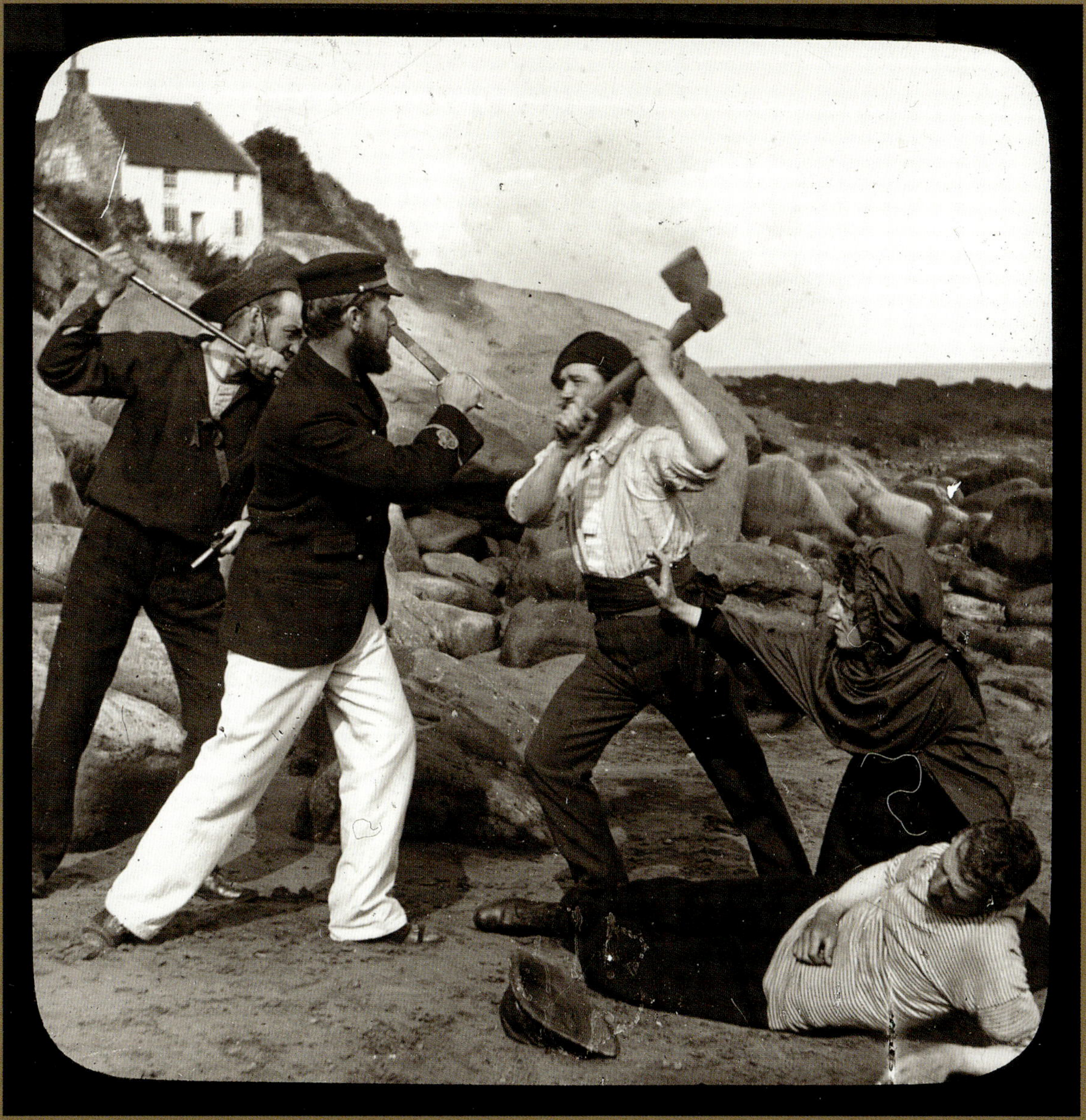

ENDNOTES

77 *Harper's Magazine*, 1884, 529.
78 *The Magazine of Art*, 1879: T. McQuoid, 'Costume of South Brittany', 89–93.
79 *The Magazine of Art*, 1879, ibid.
80 For Forbes's comments, see Chapter 1, p. 90. Garstin, *The Studio*, 1901, vol. 23: Garstin, *The work of Stanhope A. Forbes ARA*, 88.
81 *The Artist*, 1880, W. W. Fenn, 'Clovelly as a sketching ground'. 91.
82 *Scribner's Magazine*, 1880, 527.
83 *Scribner's Magazine*, 1880, 518.
84 See excerpt from the foreword to the 5th Staithes Art Club exhibition, quoted in Chapter 1, p. 69.
85 A painting by Raph Hedley exists in which one of the figures purports to be a portrait of Robert Jobling, depicted in a gathering of fisherfolk.
86 *Horne's Guide to Whitby*, 1926.
87 *Horne's Guide to Whitby*, 1926, 127. The work highlights the stretch of coast from Staithes in the north to a point half-way between Whitby and Scarborough.
88 Isa Jobling exhibited a picture entitled *Whitby Abbey from Sandsend*, but in painting the coast many of the artists included the Abbey ruins or other notable features. Joseph Bagshawe also sketched the Abbey ruins from the perspective of a navigator, picturing them at certain crucial points on the way to the harbour.
89 For a typical description see Frank, P., *Yorkshire Fisherfolk*, 2002, 33, caption to pl. 14, quoting George Roberts, *Topography and Natural History of Lofthouse*, 1882.
90 Knight, L., *Oil Paint and Grease Paint*, 1936, 86.
91 *Mark Senior 1862–1927*, Manwaring and Miller, 1983, exh. cat., Wakefield City Art Gallery; *Reminiscences of Mark Senior* by Mary Oddie; Phillips, *The Staithes Group*, 1993, 49.
92 Captain James Cook RN, who led three famed expeditions to the Pacific. His apprenticeship took place in both Staithes and Whitby.
93 This picture was once listed in the Danum Gallery, Library & Museum Collection catalogue, but whether as part of the permanent collection or a loan is not recorded. However, it is no longer a part of the collection there.
94 See Frank, P., *Sea Painter: The Life of J. R. Bagshawe*, 2010, 59, pl. 44 for a watercolour of the yacht *Beatrice*.
95 For similar experiences of a yacht-owning artist see 'The Work of C. Napier Hemy' in *The Magazine of Art*, 1900, 1–9.
96 Bullamore, C., *The Staithes Group of Artists*, 2014, 63. Dade assumed the role again in 1904.
97 In addition to Mason's time in the Royal Navy, Dade had crewed on a yacht *Dauntless* to the Americas, Hopwood had 'signed on as a deckhand' to Australia and Mayor had become renowned for building accurate model boats.
98 The adaptation of Whitby's old bridge, designed to enable larger boats to pass through to the upper harbours, is the obvious example.
99 *The Artist*, 1895, 160, 'Mr Frank Sutcliffe of Whitby'. In commenting on the depressing nature of seeing a once prosperous town now deserted, Sutcliffe notes that 'iron ships have ruined the place'.
100 Hiley, *Frank Sutcliffe*, 1974, 86. *Yorkshire Evening Post*, 16 December 1911.
101 *The Magazine of Art*, 1882, 405. The author is actually describing the Scottish fishing fleet, but all were bound for the same grounds.
102 These articles were collated by his son in a volume, *The Wooden Ships of Whitby*, published in 1933. See illustration, Chapter 1, p. 80. He journeyed to several Baltic countries and Ireland shortly before he died.
103 At that time the first herrings were fished in May, with the main shoals arriving from June to September. A visit to Staithes at the time of writing encountered the same complaints as were made towards the end of the nineteenth century, though no Scottish boats were seemingly involved.
104 Frank, P., *Yorkshire Fisherfolk*, 2002, 141.
105 In their book on Staithes, Jean and Peter Eccleston recount his providing an introduction for the Knights to various fishermen. See Eccleston, J. and P., *A History and Geology of Staithes*, 1998, 165. There was a further fish salesman in Staithes who is also supposed to have hailed from Newlyn: Benjamin Ridge. See Jewell, *Between Two Nabs*, 2013, 51.
106 National Visual Arts Library of Ireland (NIVAL): Special Collections: The Oliver Sheppard Papers. Letter from Rosie Good to Oliver Sheppard, May 1900, which details visits to exhibitions. The artist F. S. Richardson exhibited at least one image of Looe Bay in the 4th Staithes Art Club exhibition in 1904. He also later met his future wife in Cornwall.
107 The foreword to Dade's book, *Sail and Oar*, 1933, is written 'by a Filey Fisherman'.
108 Pen & Palette Club Papers, December 1901, 81. 'Word Pictures', quoted in Millard, J., *A Romance with the Northeast: Robert & Isa Jobling*, 1992, exh. cat., Chapter 7, n. 8.
109 Knight, L., *Oil Paint and Grease Paint*, 1936, 84. Knight, L., *Magic of a Line*, 1965, 113.
110 It may have helped that the innkeeper's daughter Anne joined the ranks of the artists, eventually marrying one of them.
111 Examples of pictures include Ernest Dade's *Ashore* (RA exhibit in 1888) and untitled watercolours by Harold and Laura Knight and James Booth.
112 National Visual Arts Library of Ireland (NIVAL): Special Collections: The Oliver Sheppard Papers. Letter from Rosie Good to Oliver Sheppard, 1898.
113 The farms were run by Mrs Redman and Mrs Bowman.
114 *The Magazine of Art*, 1882, 411. Pronounced differently north and south of the Tyne.
115 For the introduction date of coloured cobles see Howard, J., *Staithes: Chapters from the History of a Seafaring Town*, 2000. Laura Knight recalls one coble remaining black, see Knight, L., *Oil Paint and Grease Paint*, 1936, 117. See Introduction for the naming of boats after the visit by William Gladstone, then Prime Minister (p. 28). See McGee, G., *Staithes: A Life Story*, 2023, for the naming of a coble after Sir Charles Palmer.

116 Staithes's fleet had contained as many as 70 cobles, in comparison to 35 each at Runswick or Robin Hoods Bay. Two cobles, nicknamed 'caufs' (calves), were loaded onto the larger yawls for off-shore fishing.

117 Because of the nature of the coast, the boats had to be landed stern first, which necessitated both skill and experience.

118 National Visual Arts Library of Ireland (NIVAL): Special Collections: The Oliver Sheppard Papers. Letter from Rosie Good to Oliver Sheppard, 28 May 1899, Knight, L., *Oil Paint and Grease Paint*, 1936. 109.

119 Though the current title of this watercolour presently locates the scene at Staithes, similar watercolours by Jackson and the depiction of the wheeled carriage used by the Lifeboatmen suggest this is Runswick.

120 Stanhope Forbes in Newlyn, for example, painted three major pictures between 1888 and 1890:*The Village Philharmonic*, *The Health of the Bride* and *By Order of the Court.* Few equivalent Staithes pictures are seemingly extant.

121 *Yorkshire Evening Post*, 31 August 1939, 'A Seaside Colony of Artists'. Hill also recalls the tradition of not painting on the Sabbath and Rigg is identified as the painter who suffered (Phillips, *The Staithes Group*, 1993, 92, conversation between Dr Phillips and Lt Col Peter Hill).

122 Originally known as Seaton Garth, it denoted the settled area of the ancient manor of Seaton which lay beside the sea. In the artists' time the fair moved to the top of the village to take advantage of the greater open space of the fields above.

123 This well, the only source of fresh water on the southern side of the village, was situated at the foot of Penny Nab. It is included in Laura Johnson's painting *Staithes* (**75**) and Harold Knight's *The Last Coble* (**47**). It was later covered by a landslide.

124 *The Artist*, 1900, vol. 29, 195. This was issued under the auspices of the Royal College of Art.

125 This had the effect of loosening this structure, eventually causing its collapse around 1905. The bridge was subsequently replaced with a metal and stone structure.

126 Knight, L., *Oil Paint and Grease Paint*, 1936, 107. Images of the modern bridge with its viaduct were captured by photographers. One notable image apparently pictures Fred Jackson (and Laura Knight?) *plein air* painting at the beck. Jewell, *Between Two Nabs*, 2013, 2.

127 Crawshaw painted two versions of this scene. The smaller version, cooler in tone and with a variation in the figural composition, features the cottage. This was omitted in the larger version.

128 In 1907, at the Leicester Galleries Exhibition, Harold exhibited *Roses; Blossom; Roses and Poppies; The Yellow Rose* and *Pansies*. Laura exhibited *Canterbury Bells; White Lilies; The White Cottage; A Rose Garden; A Bowl of Pansies; The Potato Patch; Pink and White Roses; Poppies; A Bowl of Roses* and *Hollyhocks*.

129 The fishermen's year was as seasonal as that of the tourists. Spring fishing commenced in May, as the first of the herring arrived; these were caught most often as bait, alongside potting for crab and lobster. In June all eyes turned to drift-netting for herring as the shoals migrated south. As the tourists disappeared in October, the fishermen overhauled boats and turned to long-lining. They headed out in the bigger boats to deeper waters and were away for weeks at a time until February.

130 Knight, L., *Oil Paint and Grease Paint*, 1936, 145.

131 *Mark Senior 1862–1927*, Manwaring and Miller, 1983, exh. cat., Wakefield City Art Gallery: exh. nos 14 and 15: *Runswick Fisherwoman Knitting*, *Fisherman Mending a Crab Pot*; H. S. Hopwood, *Industry*, Tate Gallery Collection, Chantrey Bequest.

132 Phillips, *Florence Hess & Mark Senior*, exh. cat., 1981, introduction.

133 Parkin, *Mark Senior*, 1974, exh. no. 7. Parkin attributes the sitter as Lizzie Toes [*sic*]. Phillips, *Florence Hess & Mark Senior*, 1981, exh. no. 7. (illus. colour, back cover).

134 Knight, L., *The Magic of a Line*, 1965, 117.

135 Knight, L., *Oil Paint and Grease Paint*, 1936, 103.

136 Phillips, *The Staithes Group*, 1993, 46. Letter from Mrs Wynne Hoyland to Phillips, 1 November 1976.

137 Hart, J. (ed.), *The Secret Staithes Diary of Enid Lucy Pease Robinson*, 2010, 85.

138 *Yorkshire Evening Post*, 30 August 1939, 'A Seaside Colony of Painters'.

139 Papers of Stanhope Forbes. In the collection of Ms Monica Anthony, Newlyn Orion Galleries, Newlyn. Reproduced in Phillips, *The Staithes Group*, 1993, 20.

140 The phrase 'myth-making' describes the Danish artists' attempts to create an idealised image of their bohemian lifestyle at the Skagen colony as an inducement to other (international) artists to join them.

141 All groups lack images of artists mingling with the local fishing communities. This may be the result of their commitment to realism, a desire to maximise the commerciality of their pictures or a conscious decision to maintain social differences.

142 Parkin, *Mark Senior*, 1974, exh. nos 10, 32. Phillips, *Florence Hess and Mark Senior*, 1981, exh. no. 1.

143 Laura is responsible for several watercolours of herself, Harold and her friend Rosie Good. Likenesses of Harold, Rosie and Laura are to be found in Oliver Sheppard's sketchbook.

144 National Visual Arts Library of Ireland (NIVAL): Special Collections: The Oliver Sheppard Papers. 28 May 1899.

145 *Whitby Gazette*, 7 August 1903, 2, Reproduced in Slater, 2010, Introduction, 5.

146 *Yorkshire Evening Post*, 30 August 1939, 'A Seaside Colony of Painters'.

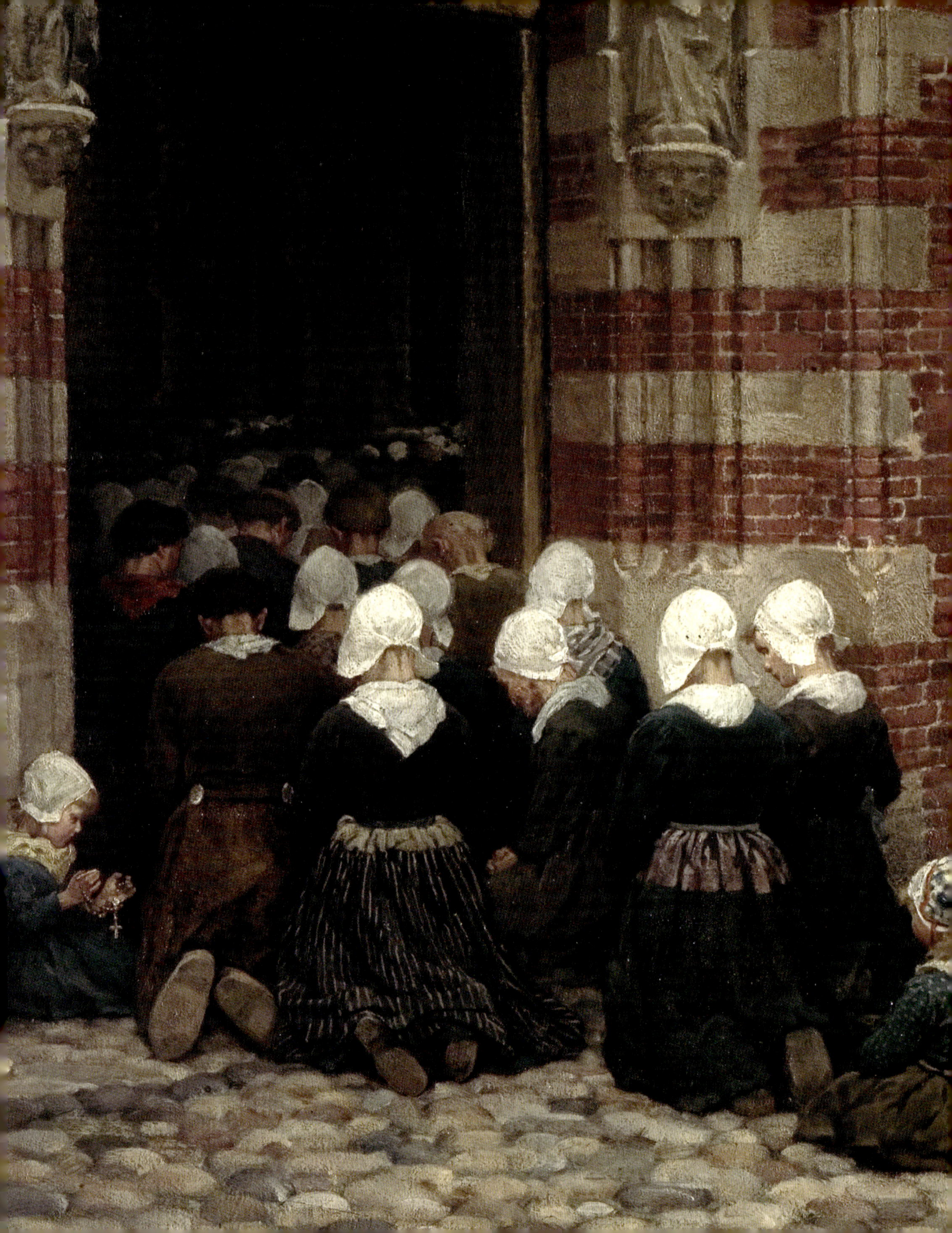

CHAPTER 3
LIGHT

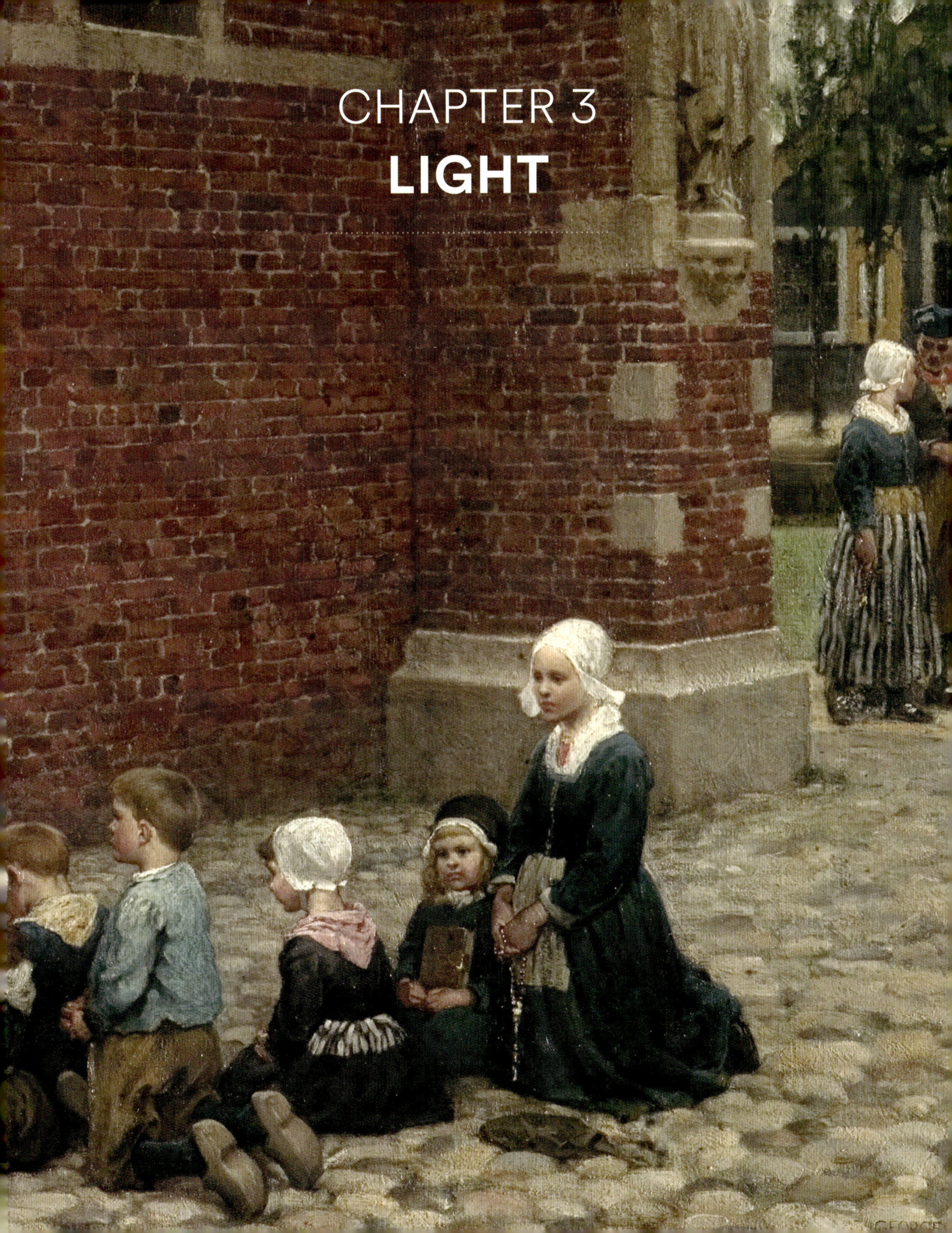

Previous spread: 115. George Clausen was a committed supporter of Staithes artists, both in his written articles for the press and in his agency for acquisition of their works. His first Academy exhibit, *High Mass at a Fishing Village on the Zuyder Zee, Holland*, of 1876, was the result of studies painted at different locations in Holland. His visit acted as a prelude to its later international popularity with travelling artists, and the work was actually mistaken for a Hague school picture.

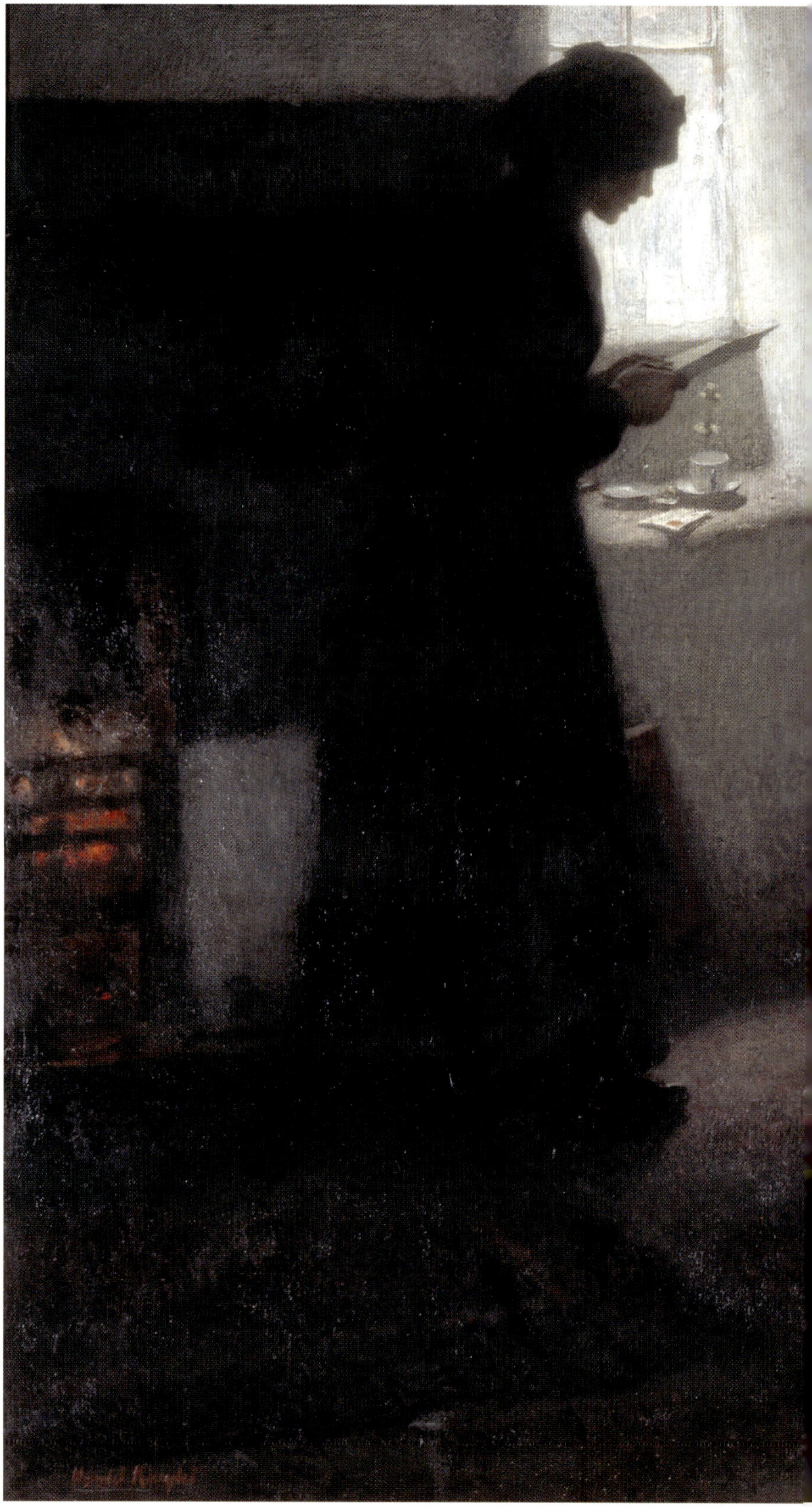

116. Completed during a period when the Knights visited Holland three times (1904–7), Harold Knight's *The Girl and the Letter* of 1906 shows the suppressed colour, close interior scene and subtle narrative, underpinned by dramatic lighting, typical of his best work.

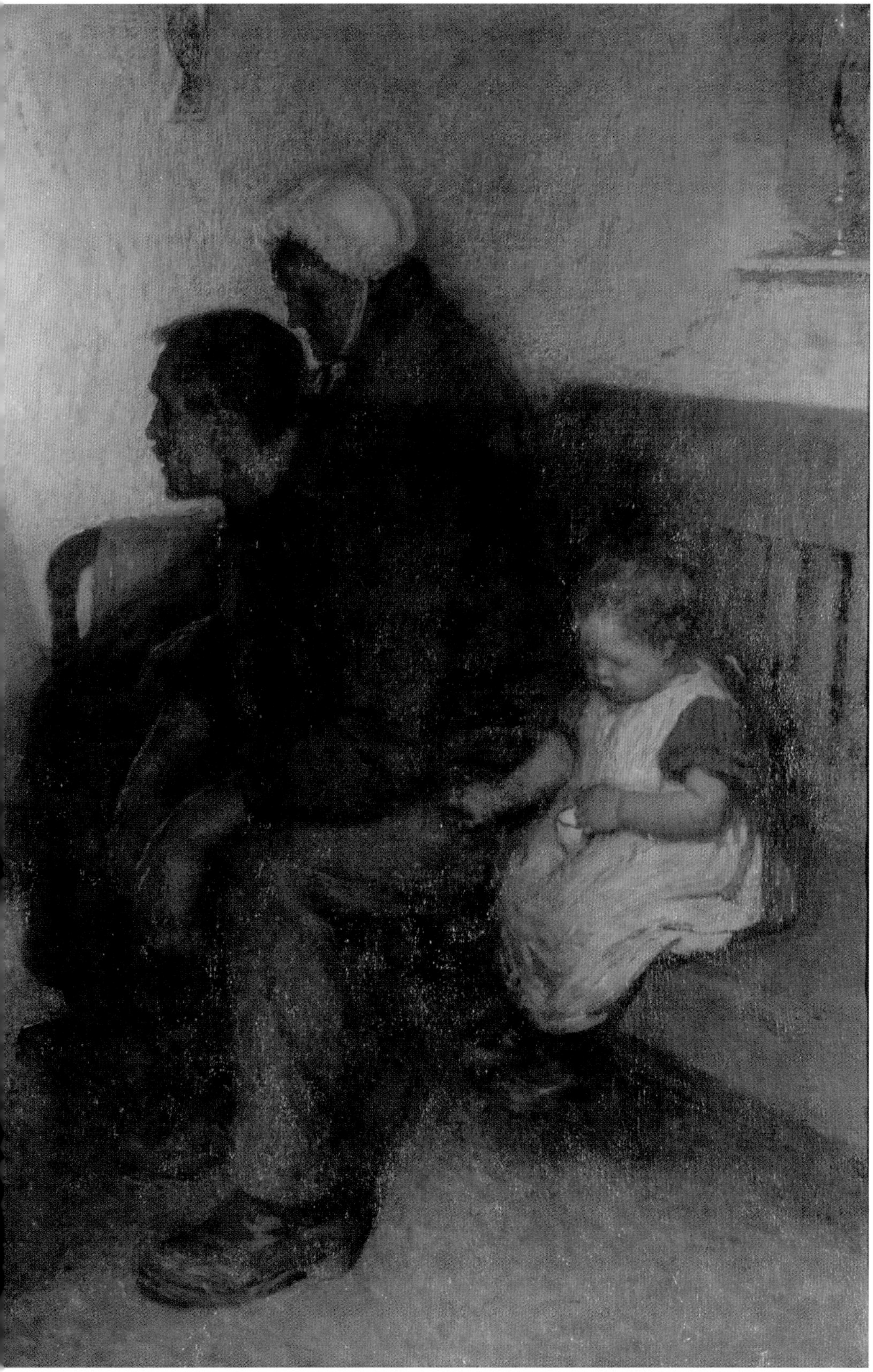

CHAPTER 3
LIGHT

> I have repeatedly said during the last 15 years that I think the time is coming … when Staithes and Runswick – especially Staithes – will be very formidable rivals as painting grounds to Newlyn and Clovelly.[147]

> There appears to be no particular leader or style such as was to be found in the Newlyn or even the Glasgow school. The exhibition, in consequence, possesses a most varied and agreeable interest.[148]

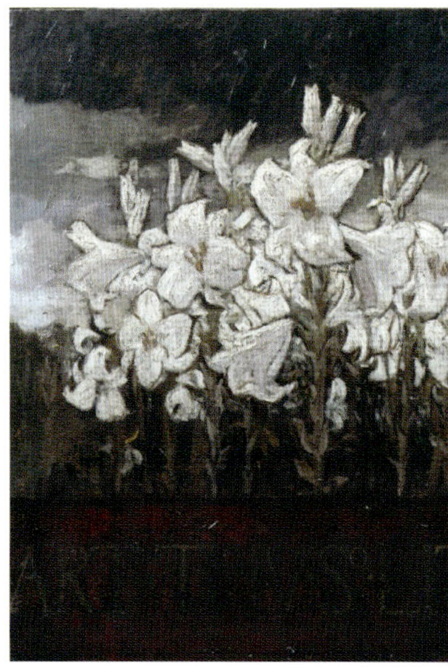

117. Laura Johnson's panels illustrating Tennyson's *Idylls of the King* were not strictly mural paintings but did form a decorative frieze, of which this example part-illustrates the story of brothers Balin and Balan. Other Staithes artists such as Harrington Mann, Charles Mackie and Fred Jackson had all completed mural commissions in the 1880s and 1890s, several on Celtic revival themes.

Having considered the group's social and historical context and introduced the lives of its members and their models, it is now time to consider their artistic approach more fully. What is suggested by both primary and secondary sources is the fact that the artists adopted a plethora of techniques and media. They arrived at the coast open to the influence of others, many in the early stages of a career. Imbued with a zest and appetite for new thinking, whether through training abroad or agitation within the British art establishment, they increasingly pursued a bold and direct approach to their craft with nature as its guiding light.

BRITISH IMPRESSIONISTS

This attempt to chart a new artistic course is exemplified by Fred Jackson's flirtation with membership of the New English Art Club. Like the Staithes Art Club, it was still to be formally constituted before the initial display in 1886, but enthusiastic discussions garnered over 80 works by around 30 artists.

118. This photograph of around 1905 portrays the panels (**117**) in situ. They were gifted to her great friend Rosie Good and husband Oliver Sheppard for their wedding. Here the works are pictured in the Sheppards' house in Dublin, to where the couple moved from Nottingham in 1902. They hang above a portrait of Laura, painted by Harold, which they also acquired (**110**).

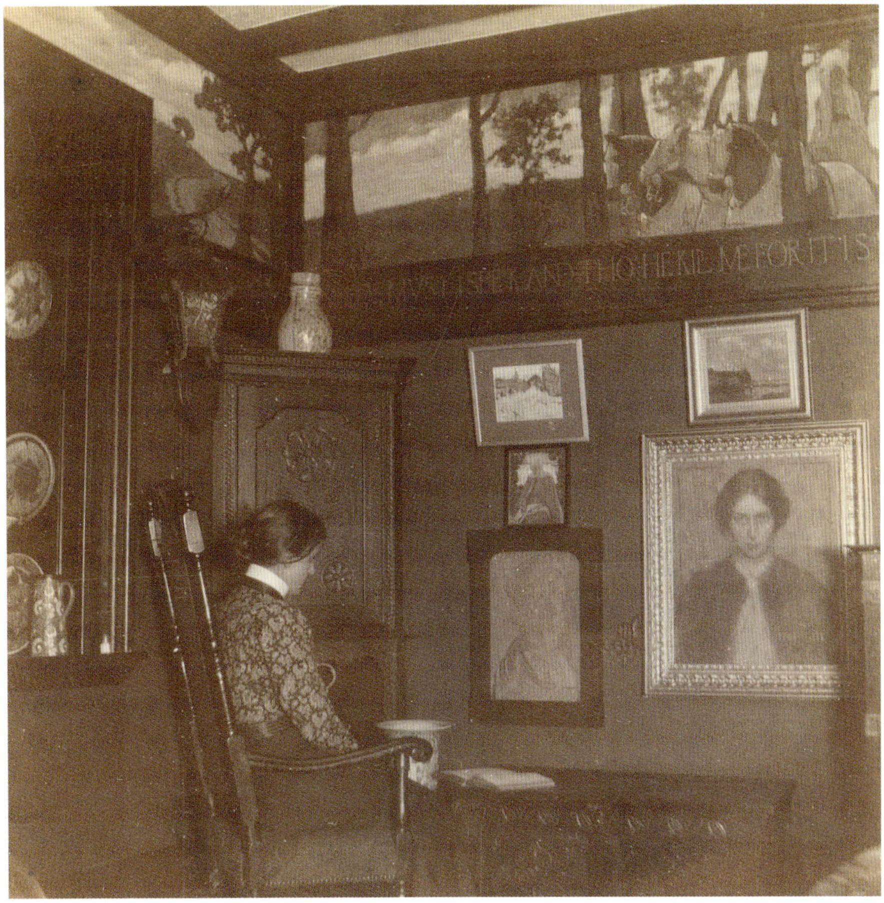

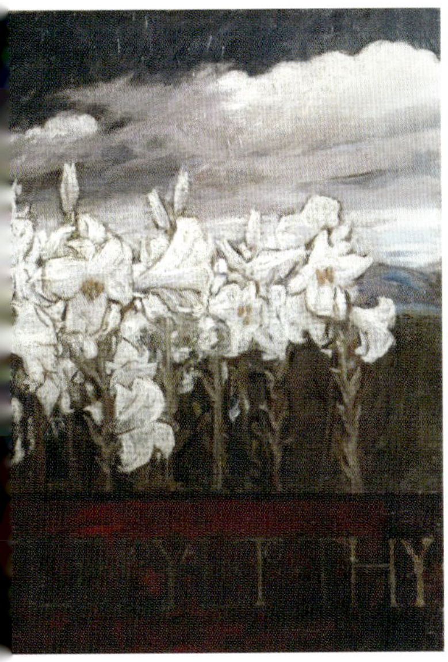

Exhibitors were required to send examples of their best work and Jackson submitted a single entry with the surprising title:

> *Soon as the Shades of Eve Prevail, The Moon takes up the wondrous tale, and Nightly to the Listening Earth proclaims the story of her birth.*[149]

Its literary and religious connotations are a stark contrast to his following seven exhibits, which appeared in consecutive years to 1891.[150] However, its adoption does bear comparison with other early works by Staithes artists, which took quotations from august poets such as Alfred Tennyson, Henry Wadsworth Longfellow and Charles Kingsley.[151] These initial works continued to reflect, at least in part, the narrative quality and social 'mission' of high Victorian painting even as it was ebbing away.

The then President of the Royal Academy, Scarborough-born Sir Frederick Leighton, on viewing the show nevertheless described the New English group as 'those Impressionists'. He predicted its demise within three years, perhaps also aware that the original backer had pulled out, challenged by the nature of the pictures he had seen in studios in the lead-up to the show.

Naturally sympathetic to the spirit of what was almost christened the Society of Anglo-French Painters, it is no surprise that Jackson was among the founding members of the Club. However, he is not reported as having attended the initial meeting, nor is it clear which of the members he might have been close to. Fred Brown had trained in Paris at the same time and painted in Runswick Bay and Edward Stott shared his Lancashire roots; George Clausen, who wrote to praise Jackson at the time of his memorial exhibition in 1918, was a founder member and Ernest Dade exhibited with the Club from 1887.[152]

When the more 'progressive' members attempted to test aesthetic opinion further, it must be supposed that Jackson did not sympathise. He was either not invited or declined to show with the more avant-garde artists, who went on to style themselves specifically as the 'London Impressionists'.

Jackson was not alone in cooling towards the aims of this faction, led by Walter Sickert. Although those who came to be known as the Glasgow Boys had initially signed up to exhibit side by side, within five years they had left to forge their own, arguably more progressive, path. The group went on to make their mark on the London art scene with the Grosvenor Gallery exhibition of 1890, attended by Harrington Mann in the company of James Guthrie and John Lavery. In it, exhibitors proposed a 'robust, richly textured alternative' artistic vision. The freshness this conveyed was in clear opposition to both the New English Art Club and the tonalities of the Newlyn school.[153]

Jackson's attitude may at face value appear confusing, given not only contemporary reviews of his work and those of other Staithes artists, but also the styling of the group in catalogues from the 1970s onwards. In the former, terms such as 'impression' or 'impressionism' are frequently applied to their work:

> Their aims are similar, but their methods are very dissimilar. They each try to give the broad truths of nature, ignoring almost entirely anything which would detract from the first impression.[154]

> He seeks the poetical effects of atmosphere and movement in atmosphere … in these rapid sketches, impressions rather we may call them, he seeks to give with a few strokes what in nature is of momentary duration.[155]

Opposite: 119. While travelling through Europe during his period of study in Paris, Fred Jackson visited the islands of Chioggia and Capri near Venice and Naples respectively. This provided inspiration for *Scene in Capri*, an oil of c. 1882. The locations must have presented a dazzling contrast to the cool, grey tones of the Yorkshire coast, to which Jackson returned only a year later.

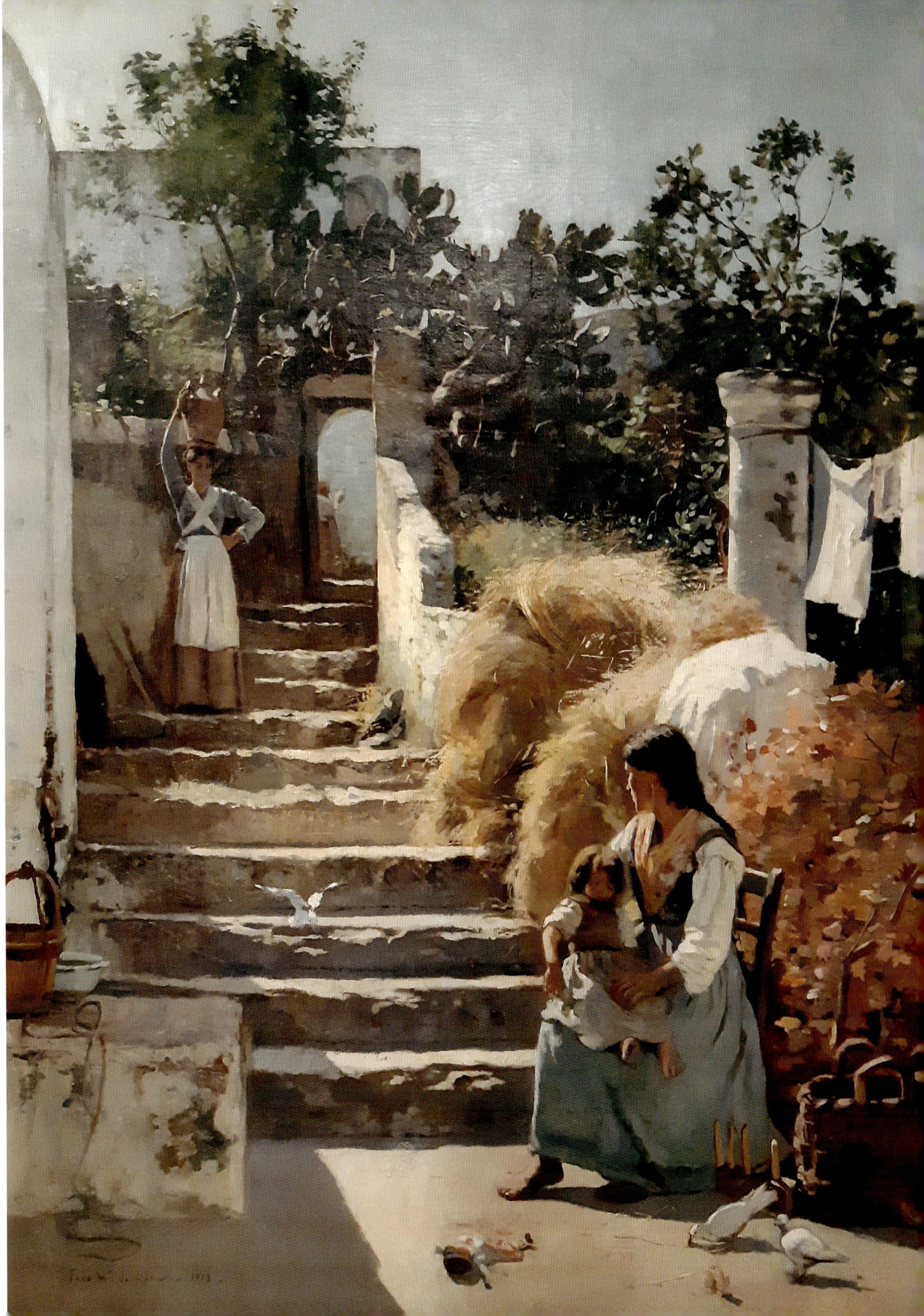

This phraseology was however widespread when referring to contemporary art, used to denote a painting style that was free, sketchy, lacking in high finish or simply modern.

As discussion of impressionism has come to dominate subsequent art criticism, with detailed academic debate of its nuances, the term has become less relevant to these artists. Rather than forging an alternative, progressive new path, Jackson and others such as Garrido, as laid out in his biography of 1912, resisted this approach. They were wedded to traditions of modelling and too reluctant to dismiss the importance of form within their work to be classified as 'impressionist' in the strictest terms. However, continued association for reasons of popular appeal and, latterly, for commercial purposes has persisted to the present day.[156]

REALISTS AND NATURALISTS

Stanhope Forbes and several 'Newlyners' were among the foremost exhibitors of the inaugural New English shows. Infused by 'a fresh wave of foreign influence', in the words of the Club's biographer, the third year's exhibition received the following review:

> But that they are most of them imbued with the French spirit, or at any events the French style of workmanship, and with a preference for tone rather than for colour, is a fact that the Royal Academy cannot afford to overlook.[157]

Their work continued to reflect much that had been current in the Paris ateliers of Bonnat, Gerome and Laurens during their student years. A contemporary review in *The Magazine of Art*, for example, sets out the ethos of Bonnat:

> The Atelier Bonnat was started in 1865 with the wholesome purpose of studying nature as closely as possible, avoiding the vagueness of the impressionists, and, on the other, the conventionalism of the academical style of work upon which the flowers of Bonnat look with contempt.[158]

His studio of the 1870s and 1880s had a strong tradition of attracting Scandinavian students such as Anna Ancher of the Skagen colony (p. 132). She may well have been a contemporary of Isa Thompson who, alongside Jackson and Fred Richardson, was arguably the earliest of the Staithes group to study in Paris. Thompson was sent 'to finish her studies' and, though private ateliers accepted female pupils, these were usually wealthy society figures; the Académie run by Rodolphe Julian was likely her only option.[159]

Founded just after the Atelier Bonnat, one of the Académie's signal aims was to provide training to women alongside men, with a view to their having a professional career. This was not permitted in the official schools until the late 1890s. Although social pressure subsequently forced Julian to provide separate ateliers, the women still had access to all the facilities that male students enjoyed and competed for the same prizes.

The main advantage over an English schooling was the concentration on figure painting and the ability to study both the male and female figure from life. Sources all stress the international nature of classes, as well as the relative independence of lifestyle and individuality that female students enjoyed. They also emphasise the rigour and discipline of working in a wide variety of styles and media.

The resulting scene is described by an English student of the early 1880s:

> We English girls, among those of many other nationalities in Paris for the purpose of study, worked the hardest, in the deepest earnest. We rose before it was light, and dressed ourselves with freezing fingers. We were out at 'first breakfast' in a humble crémerie, drinking our hot chocolate, in thick white bowls like mortars; crunching our crisp rolls with the worthy working folk of Paris in their blue blouses at the marble tables; then trudging bravely for an hour, through the snowy streets and leafless Elysian Fields and boulevards … long before the majority of the Paris students had left their warm nests.[160]

Marie Bashkirtseff, a wealthy aristocrat, was an atypical student of the Académie. Nevertheless, she provides a colourful description of life there, both through her own journal and paintings and as a feature of correspondence and caricatures by her fellow students. In the last pages of her journal she details visits to Jules Bastien-Lepage, a crucial figure and formative influence on so many English painters of the period. As early as the 1880s exhibitions of his work took place in London, where he himself painted the Prince of Wales, Sarah Bernhardt and Henry Irving. A significant group of admirers developed, including George Clausen and Henry La Thangue, who continued to paint in the same style throughout the 1890s.

Lepage's influence is likely to have reached Staithes artists via these latter painters, either through shared membership of Clubs such as the New English or through activities such as those undertaken by Mark Senior, who acted as advisor to Leeds Art Gallery (with George Clausen) around the bequest of the philanthropist Sam Wilson.[161] It is perfectly possible too, of course, that early Staithes painters saw Lepage's work in Paris or London – or indeed Glasgow. Certainly there were collectors and exhibitions in the north of England, such as that of Councillor John Maddocks at Bradford, which displayed a wealth of painting by his followers. The Bradford show of 1890 featured works by Clausen, La Thangue, Forbes, Dagnan-Bouveret and L'Hermitte; it also included works by Jackson and James Charles.[162]

Devotees were drawn to what they perceived as the literal truth of Bastien-Lepage's work – seriousness, scale, rich detail in finish, breadth of handling, tone rather than colour, and a balance between summary treatment and smoothness. From foreground to horizon, depth was implied by alteration in handling.[163]

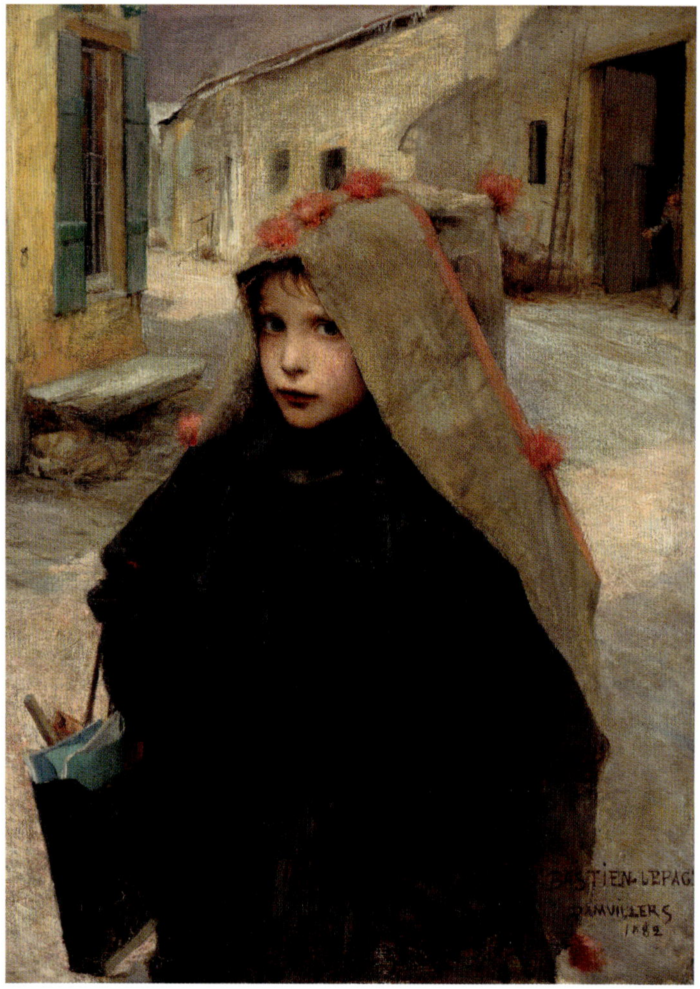

120. Jules Bastien Lepage's *Going to School* (1882) was owned by the railway entrepreneur James Staats Forbes. His vast collection included other works by artists such as Millet, Corot, Israels, Maris, Mauve and Whistler. Admired by several of the Staithes artists when prominently exhibited, works from the collection were sold in 1905 and 1908.

'JUSTE MILIEU': A HAPPY MEDIUM

This term, applied to Lepage's path between the avant-garde and the traditional academic approach, is useful to bear in mind when examining early 'Staithes' exhibition pieces – particularly those that feature significant figural compositions in his style. Isabella Thompson's first significant exhibits finally made the Royal Academy hang in 1892 and 1893, almost a decade after she started showing in the northeast. The painting hung in the latter exhibition, *Fisherfolk* (**44**), features statuesque female figures on a four-foot canvas. The individuality of the figures may arguably derive from a confidence in figural modelling and composition emphasised by her French training.

Though the bonnet and manner in which the older woman carries her basket implicitly tie the imagery to Staithes, the work does not possess the narrative feel revealed in some of her other earlier paintings.[164] The picture does display the sombre earthy palette of Thompson's Cullercoats period, but she lends texture and density, enhanced by touches of orange, green, red, blue and pink with long brush strokes. The square brush technique so associated with the followers of Lepage she reserves for smaller pictures in a brighter palette – notably her 1892 exhibition piece *Blossom* and the later picture (signed with her married name) *Haymaking* (**122**). In these works, the changes to the handling of paint more obviously provide depth, while the figures are positioned far closer to the picture plane.

121. An undated picture, *Fishergirl* falls some way between the statements of Isa Jobling's 1893 *Fisherfolk* and her later *Haymaking* of 1903. The colour palette is fresher and the figure more assertively defined than in the former work, yet it lacks the movement and dynamic brushwork of the latter (**122**).

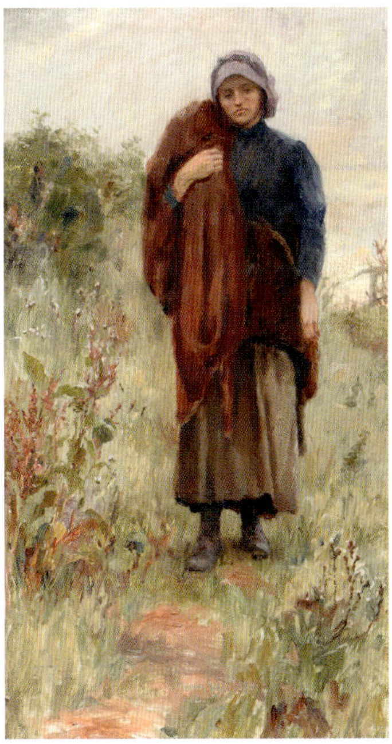

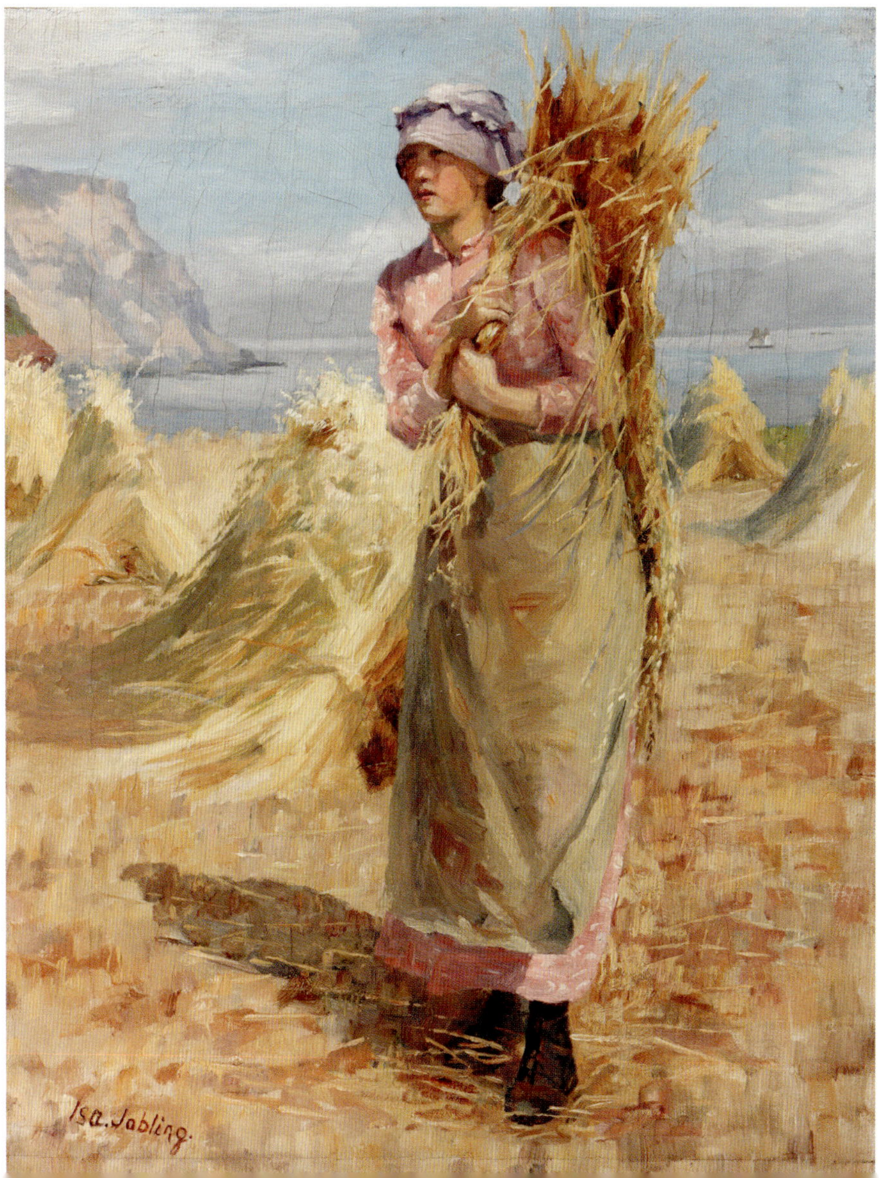

Right: 122. Isabella Jobling's 1903 picture *Haymaking* exemplifies not only the palette of her time in Staithes, but also the square brush and perspective techniques of earlier French painting and the work of Lepage. It is interesting to compare this with her RA exhibit *Blossom* of 1892 and *A Runswick Window* by her husband Robert (**126**).

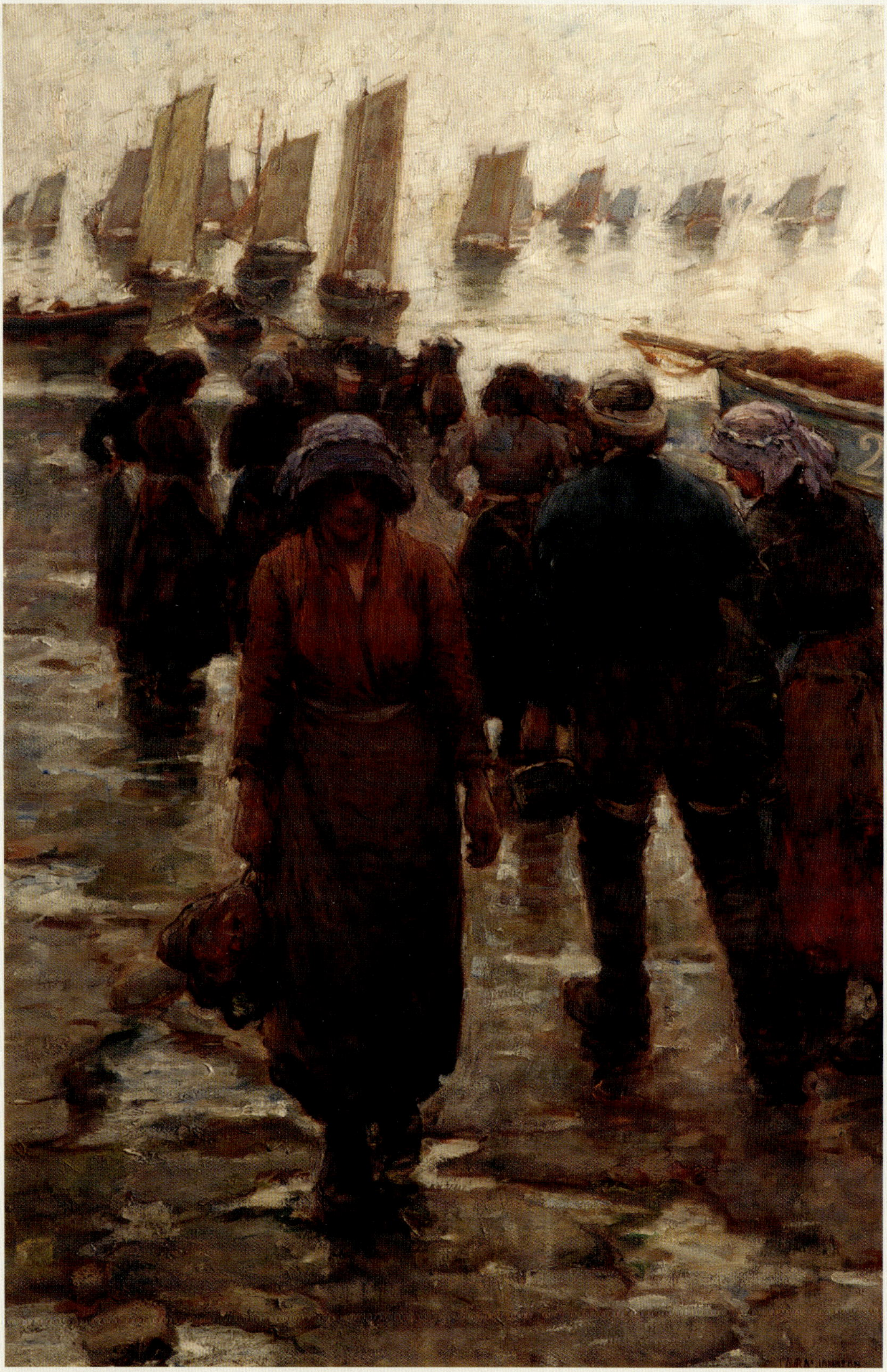

Of equivalent size and an Academy exhibit from 1901, *Toil* by Mark Senior draws natural comparison (**86**). Its title is slightly more suggestive than Thompson's, though both eschew direct female associations, and it features a similar pairing of old and young women. In this later work, though the horizon is higher, one figure advances towards the viewer and her driftwood bundle turns to an eye-catching basket of fish. Laura Johnson's two contrasting compositions (of the same dimensions), *The Fishing Fleet* and *Packing Fish on the Quay*, were the closest she came to such specific female figural works. Although both have far busier backgrounds, the former displays, like Thompson's painting, a monotone palette heightened with dashes of colour to the foreground, in this case orange.

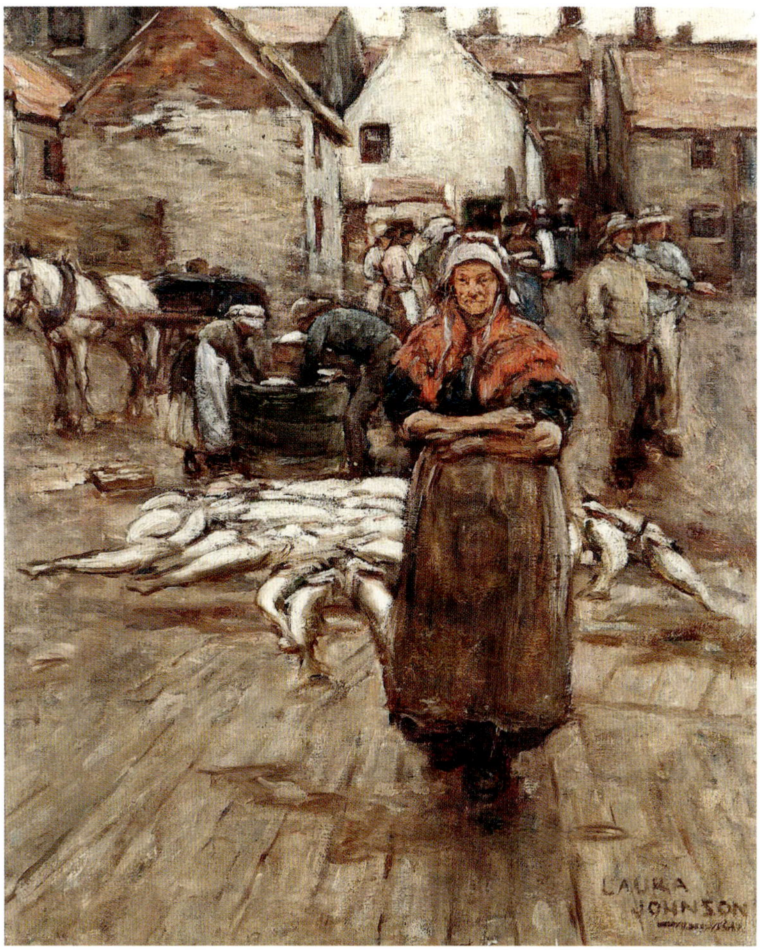

Opposite: 123. As large a picture as Laura Johnson painted in Staithes, *The Fishing Fleet* bears an unusual, stylised signature (**127** and **151**). Though undated, it also bears comparison with the description in her memoir of 'her first really big picture', *Off to the Herring Fishing*, which she reworked two or three times over four years before apparently destroying it.

Right: 124. *Packing Fish on the Quay, Staithes* and *The Fishing Fleet* by Laura Johnson complement one another in content and theme, bearing comparison to Harold Knight's *Herring Boats* and its pendant (described in her memoir). The elements of each composition mirror those of the other: heading to and returning from sea, youth and age, village and fleet, staith and scaur.

Hopwood's *Messmates* of 1892 (**14**), exhibited in Manchester that year, is on the same scale again. However, it is a fine large watercolour rather than oil and landscape in format, with male deckhands of contrasting ages and (probably) nationalities featuring as a central pair. Harold Knight's RA exhibit of 1900, *The Last Coble*, another landscape work (**47**), finds the main figure pairing amplified as a family group; its make-up is echoed into the diminishing beachscape. Likewise his fascinatingly foreshortened *Fishermen Coming Ashore* (**127**) sees a single imposing figure striding out of the picture. Although not quite on the same scale, Fred Mayor's watercolours contain several portraits of fisherfolk tight to the picture plane, either half or three-quarter length.[165]

This selection of works is the closest that Staithes artists come to the influence of Lepage's work and to that of his admirers in Newlyn and Skagen. Their developing styles would seem otherwise to owe much to their own varied backgrounds and contacts, given the significant number of painters that can be associated with the Club members (see Chapter 1). Artistic paths, however, were surely most affected by a number of significant and close relationships cemented over this period, not least those that led to marriage. Of these the best-known is perhaps that of Laura Johnson and Harold Knight (1903), but there were also weddings for their close friends Oliver Sheppard

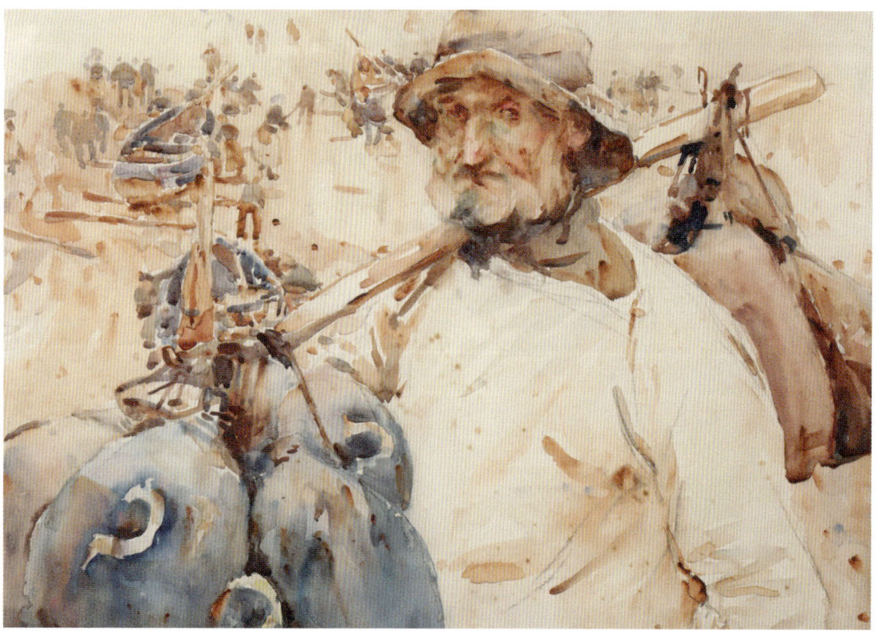

125. In Fred Mayor's watercolour painting of *A Staithes Fisherman* (*c.* 1898–9), the subject is (as with **127**) situated in the forefront of the picture. Here, however, he dominates still more, with an unflinching, direct gaze and the scene of boats separated from him by the strong diagonal rod on which he carries the net bladders.

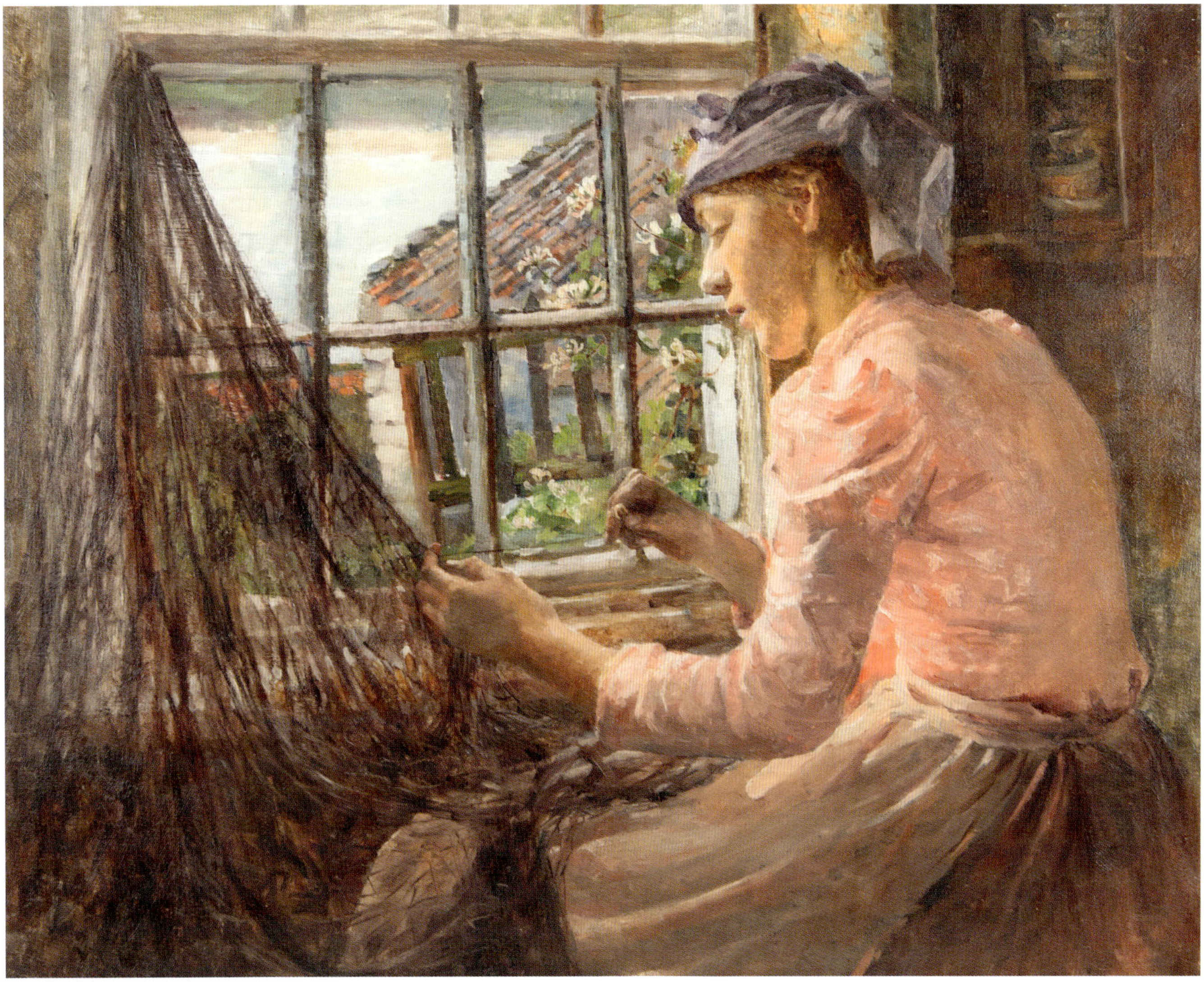

126. Contemporary critics noted the change in Robert Jobling's palette from his regular visits to Staithes after 1897. *A Runswick Window* is one of the most obvious examples, using a model that surely was shared with his wife, although set somewhat unusually outside Staithes.

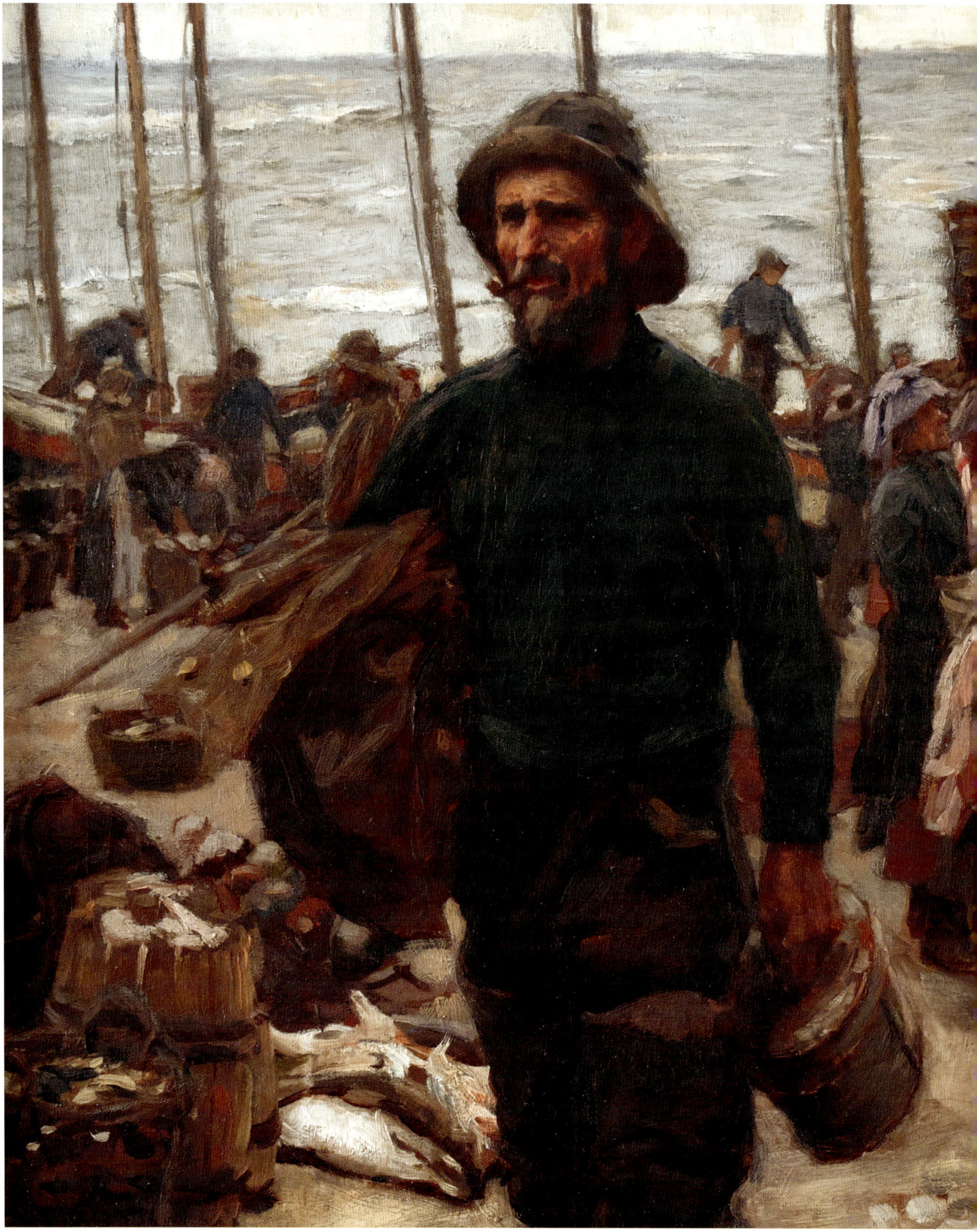

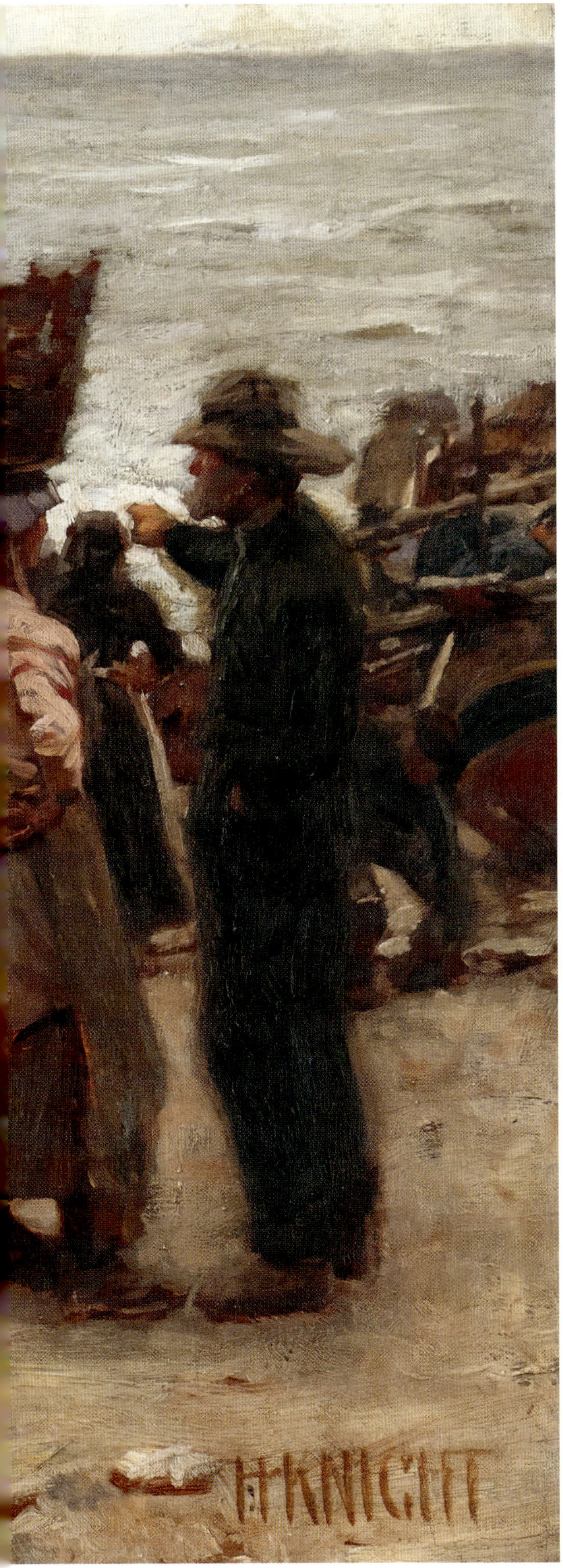

and Rosie Good (1901), Fred Mayor and Hannah Hoyland (1902) and Robert Jobling and Isbella Thompson (1893).[166]

Isabella Thompson's work is sometimes contrasted with the 'poeticism' of Robert Jobling. She married him in the same year that *Fisherfolk* appeared at the Academy, and it is suggested that her subsequent work evidences a compromise in her ambitions from this point. She gave up her studio, with the freedom it offered to accommodate larger pictures, and her subject matter moved away from that of her earlier works, though several free-flowing oil sketches of fishergirls are attributed to her.[167] He in turn spent far more time in Staithes than previously and either its surroundings or her influence is considered to have lightened his palette significantly, with one notable painting by him attaining the same colour pitch as Isa's brightest works.[168]

Developments in his technique at this point also enabled him to disguise earlier issues that he had with figural composition. Some writers have even speculated on the possibility of Isa collaborating on pictures, given how many works with the Jobling imprimatur have children as their subject.[169]

127. The visual description of Harold Knight's *Fishermen Coming Ashore* is yet another picture that corresponds to Laura Knight's specific scene-setting in her memoirs, this time *Magic of a Line*. Here the fisherman strides towards the picture plane but, rather than confronting the viewer, his gaze leads away and his figure acts as an aid to perspective, lending the picture depth.

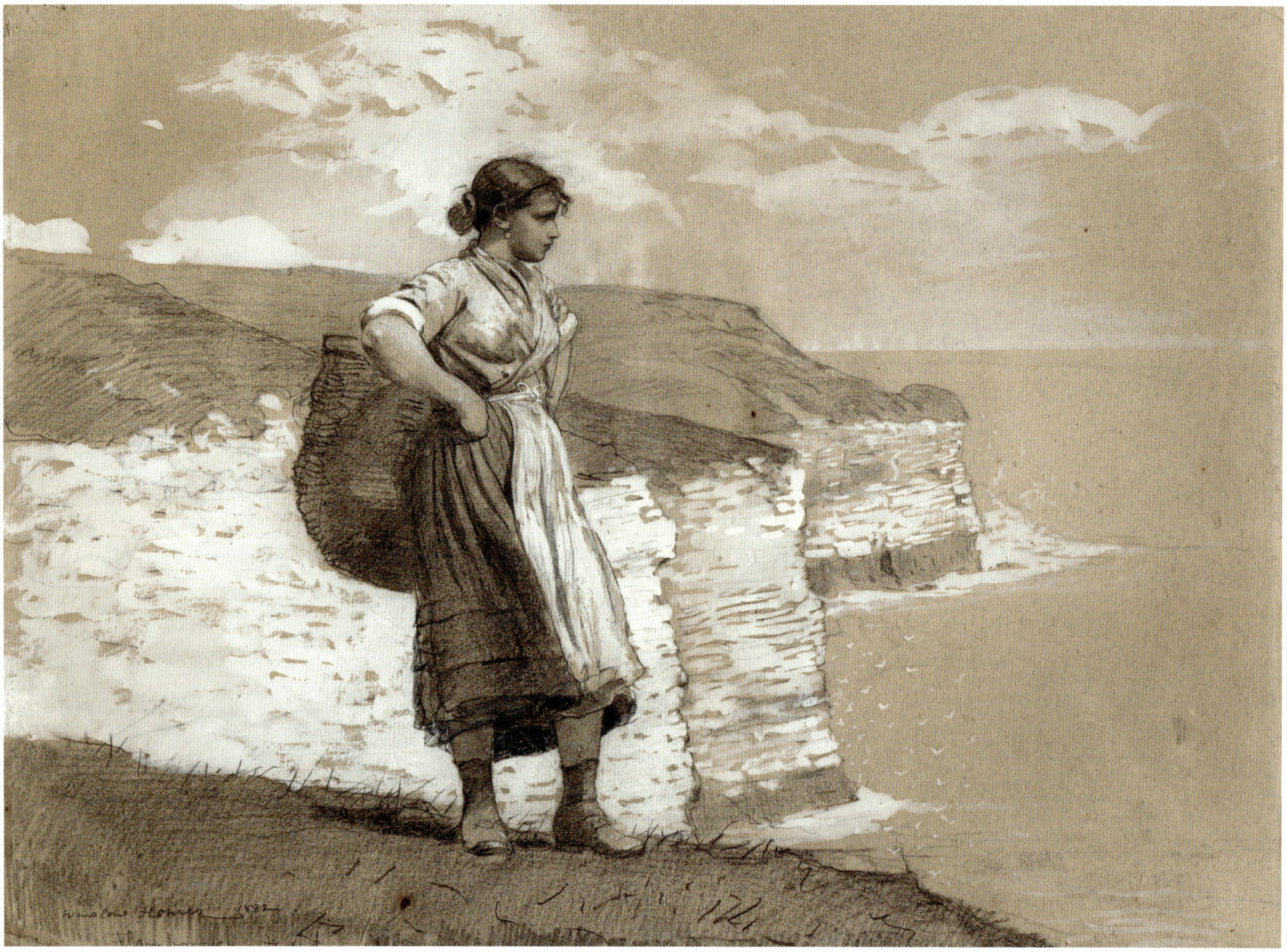

128. Although Winslow Homer centred the work of his 18-month period in England at the Cullercoats colony, he painted as far south as the chalk headland of Flamborough. In this interpretation of *Flamborough Head* (1882) his use of white bodycolour for both cliffs and costume invests the lone fisherwoman with a sense of timelessness.

Notwithstanding this conjecture, the figures in Jobling's works rarely dominate their context. In this respect, perhaps, his paintings align more closely in style to those of the famous American artist Winslow Homer (1836–1910), who worked 'alongside' him at Cullercoats. Homer's fisherfolk – particularly women – are often pictured at rest and always on a smaller scale, as part of their surroundings. Yet there remains a monumentality to them, perhaps the result of fishwives pictured apart from their menfolk and so very much the subject of his work, rather than ciphers in the telling of the fishermen's story.

HAROLD KNIGHT AND LAURA JOHNSON

The evenness of tone and suppression of colour, set alongside a specificity of costume, craft and place, is an admired part of Homer's work. However, this same quality has been somewhat dismissed in the examination of early work by the Staithes group – particularly that of Johnson and Knight. Knowing their later work, it is hard not to compare its bright, gem-like hues with some of their early opalescent tones. Yet it is a trifle glib to suggest that the south-west coast, so beloved of the Newlyners of the 1880s for its grey, silvered tone, was so very different from the north-east coast.

> It is the general absence, or the extreme gentleness, of colour that enables the Newlyners to achieve so much light. A grey or white sky can be valued in a picture as – what a sky always is – the brightest passage of it…[170]

Johnson is clear about her struggles to establish an overall artistic style, let alone a personal approach to colouring, in response to what she saw as a bewildering array of subject matter at Staithes. Though schooled in Nottingham by Wilson Foster, himself trained in Paris and Antwerp, she had not had the opportunity to train abroad.[171] She subsequently cursed the lack of drawing from life and the separate studios for men and women, believing herself the only woman to be serious (and by implication professional) about her work. It left her unprepared, so she thought, for the independence of colony life.

The one constant companion was her friend Harold Knight, whose style she confesses she initially tried to copy at school, but whose independent attitude and reluctance to be didactic proved both an advantage and disadvantage to her. She attests to his return from an apparently disappointing time in Paris, only to enjoy a wonderfully productive six-month period in Staithes immediately after their initial time there together.[172]

She remembers thrilling to the resulting advances in his technique while downplaying her own progress. She was consistently self-critical, destroying much of her early work, and deploring her lack of successful exhibition submissions.

This early period is recorded in Johnson's letters to her friend and one-time pupil Rosie Good – and in turn Rosie's to the artist Oliver Sheppard, who seems to have spent much of 1898–9 visiting them in Staithes or Nottingham. All three produced sketchbooks full of work illustrating the village and its life at the coast.

129. Oliver Sheppard joined Rosie Good intermittently in Staithes from Nottingham throughout 1899. His biographer describes his technique as being 'at variance with standard academic life drawing ... [with rendering] ... similar to his approach as a clay modeller'. The sympathetic portrayal of character shown in his sketchbooks enabled the figures to serve as valuable exercises in portraiture.

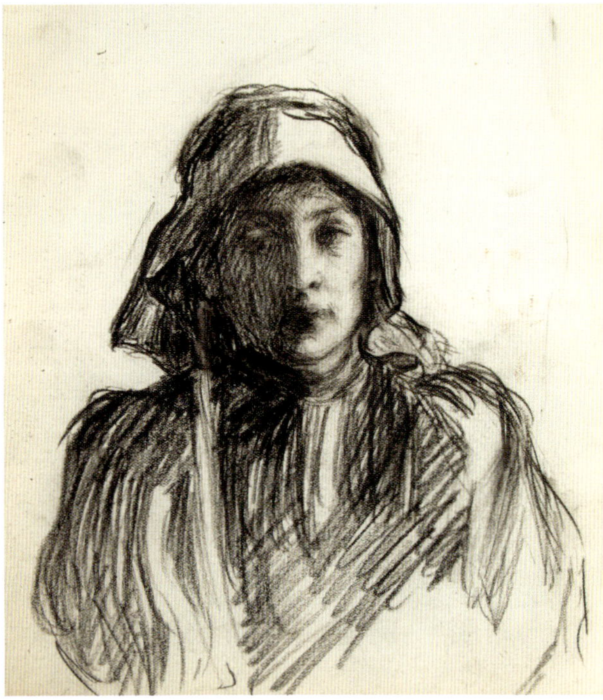

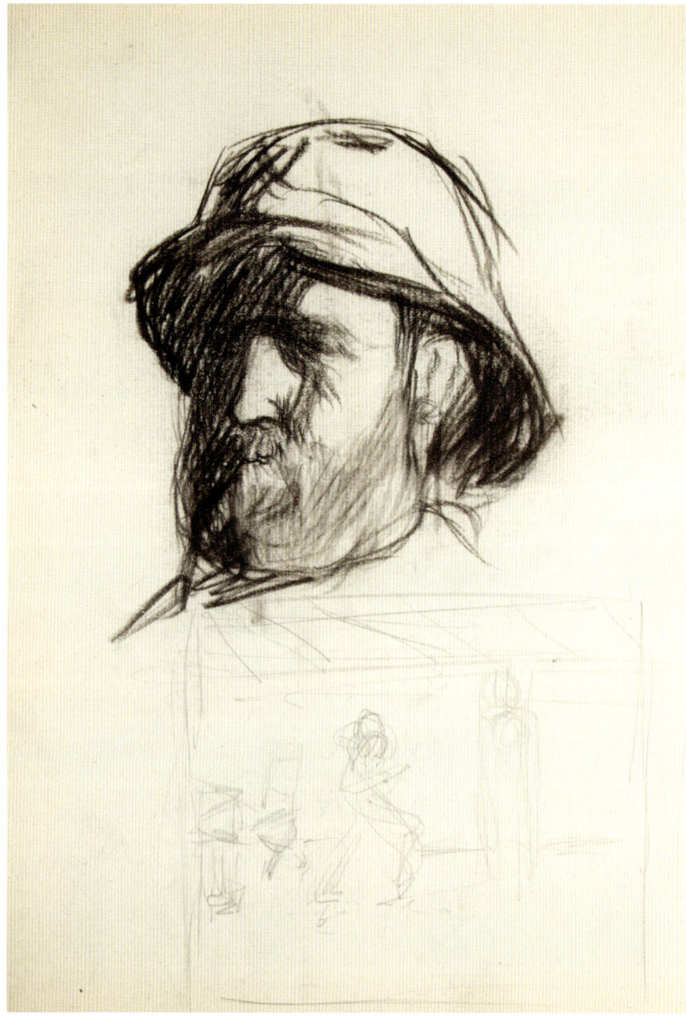

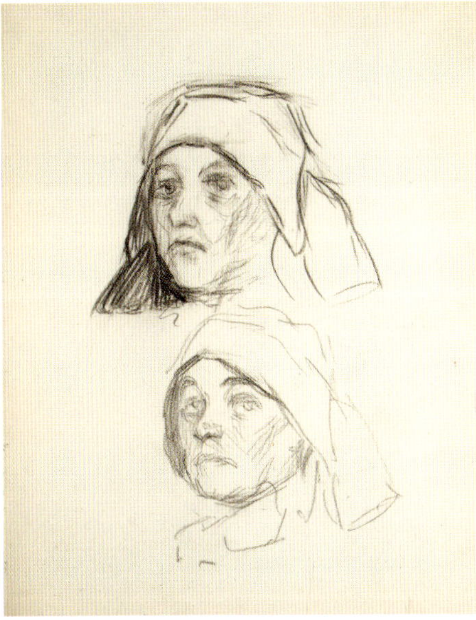
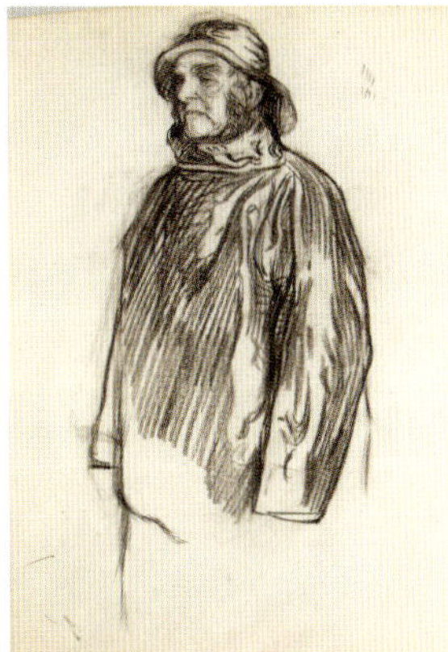
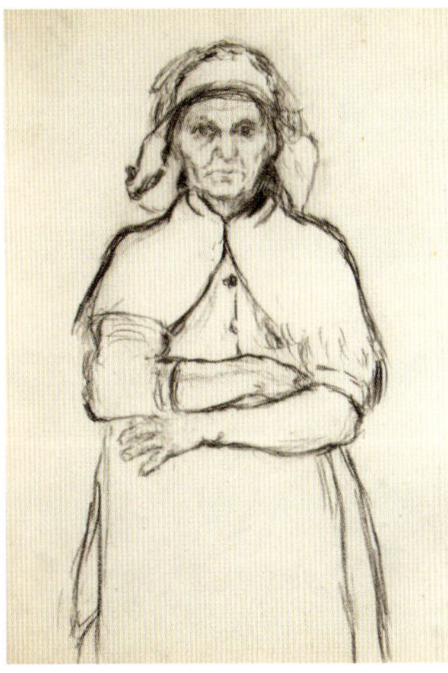
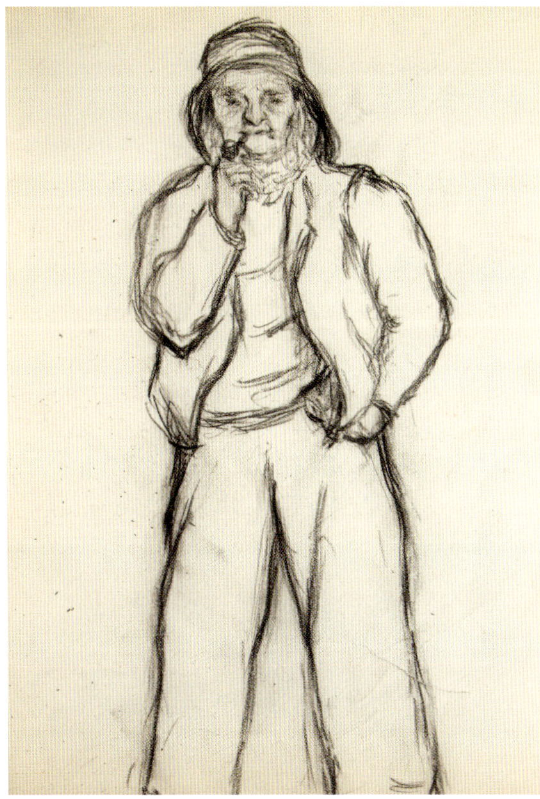
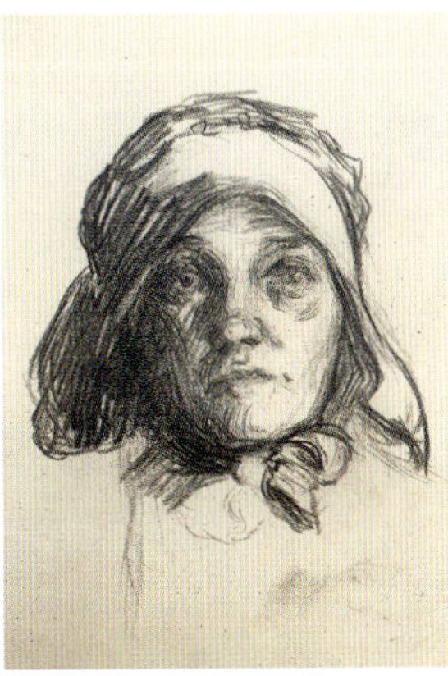

SKETCHING

Johnson's ambitions are later recalled in her memoir:

> Through Harold I heard of the great Brangwyn's draughtsmanship, and although I had never seen any of his work … I tried to imitate his simple line.[173]

In it she acknowledges her hard work, although implicitly disparaging her concurrent modest achievement:

> Many days I was out drawing from morning until night. The training I went through in doing notes of moving figures has proved an invaluable asset to later work.[174]

She is clear that the expense of hiring adult models was too great at that time. As a result, drawings made outside were used as notation for paintings to be worked up in the studio. This was in opposition to other views – exemplified by those such as Homer, Hopwood and possibly even Knight:

> I prefer every time a picture composed and painted outdoors... It is impossible to paint an outdoor figure in studio light with any degree of certainty... These making studies and then taking them home to use them is only half right. You get the composition, but you lose freshness; you miss the subtle and, to the artist, the finer characteristics of the scene itself.[175]

A reminiscence of Hopwood's technique outlined:

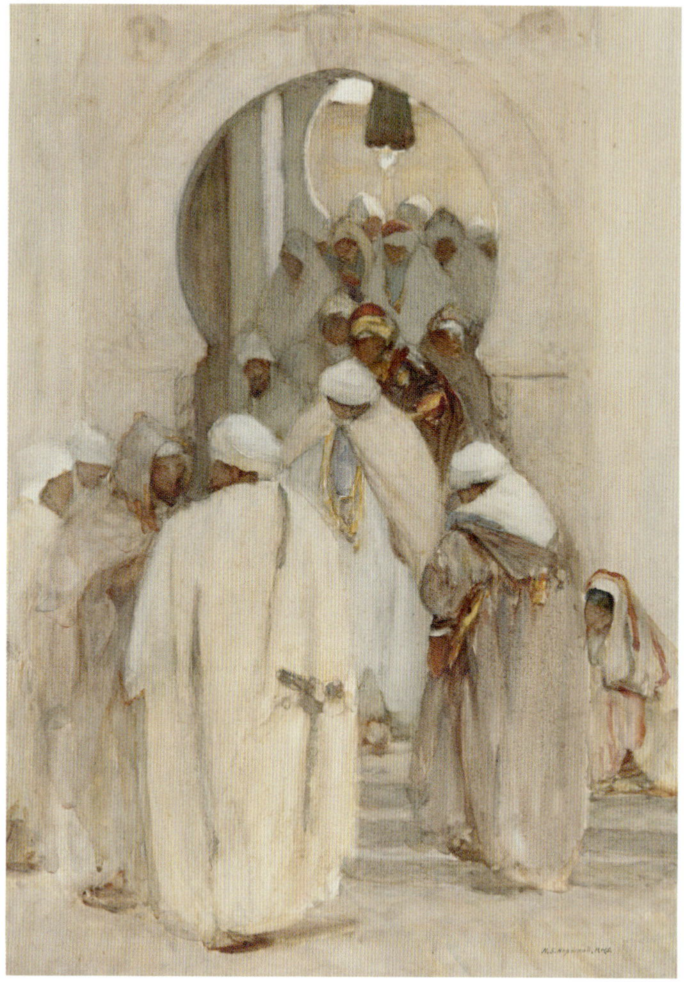

130. From 1905 onwards Henry Hopwood spent winters in Tunis or Algeria, returning every summer to Montreuil. *Archway, Biskra*, a watercolour painted on the edge of the Sahara, was produced and submitted for his diploma at the Royal Watercolour Society in 1908.

Opposite: 132. Laura Johnson lends this untitled sketch of c. 1900 a somewhat symbolist air. Its cartouche outline, quick, strong hatching, wistful portrait and rising moon all combine to this end.

131. Oliver Sheppard's Staithes work mostly focuses on portraits of fisherfolk, with a sculptor's focus on drapery. However, this sketch of 1898–9 gives a glimpse of the symbolism that emerged in his work from the mid-1890s – a feature that was to mark him as the leading sculptor of the Celtic revival in Ireland.

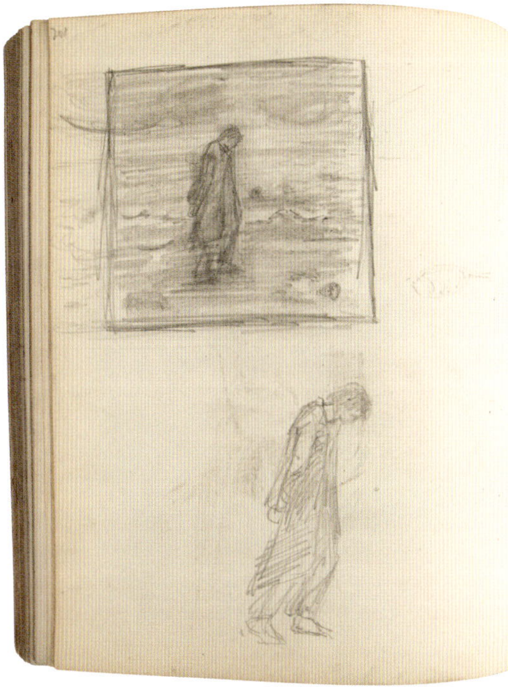

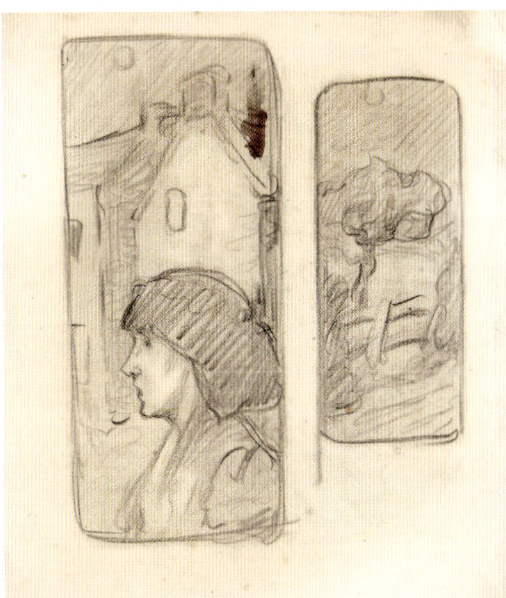

> He was not in the habit of elaborating his work in the studio from smaller sketches; he would begin work straight on the picture itself in the open air … plunging finished detail into a picture that in every other respect was still in the earliest stages.[176]

Johnson and Sheppard, who stayed in Staithes in 1899, filled books with snatches of the life of the fisherfolk, practising the advice he had written to Good:

> Keep looking out for little bits for your pictures; there is always so much to be seen when one looks for it in nature.[177]

One example of a woman encumbered by nets and floats Sheppard subsequently modelled in plaster (**19**).[178] His more detailed portraits of fishermen and women exemplify his interest in the sculptural aspects of costume; of particular note were the shadows cast by the Staithes bonnet across the features of fisherwomen.

These bonnets were a distinctive totem of the villages and had a practical design, the brim stiffened with piping but the whole folding flat to be ironed. They could be tied under the chin or behind the ears and the colours were specific to times and uses, with black and lilac denoting periods of mourning.[179]

There is also something of a poetic or dreamlike feel to some of Johnson's (and Knight's) sketches and watercolours. It is interesting to ponder whether Sheppard, and in particular his burgeoning symbolism and modelling techniques (shown through his unusual drawing style), may have had an influence on either or both of their approaches.

Bagshawe was another inveterate sketcher who also often stayed in Staithes in 1898–9. While he constantly noted light and colour, and used these in his larger works, these paintings are nevertheless distinguished by a low tone, often giving the impression that they were painted at dawn or dusk, rather as described by Good:

> I feel very keen on work just now. Last night the cobles went off late and it was fine to see them with their bogey fires lighted.[180]

Bagshawe sketched just such a scene of a coble leaving Staithes which Knight in turn painted in an oil, turning the surface of the sea to a silvery sheen and picking out the shadows with small streaks of colour.

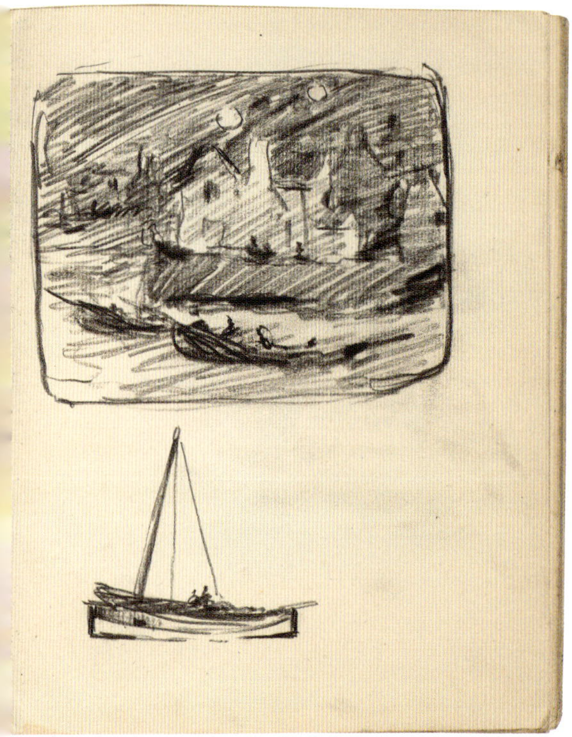

133 and 134. Harold Knight and Joseph Bagshawe were in Staithes together in the winter of 1898. In her memoir Laura Knight describes the two men being the last to leave the beach, having helped to haul cobles up to safety. In these two images, *Leaving Harbour, Evening* and an untitled sketch, they picture cobles departing Staithes with 'bogie' lights lit as the moon comes out.

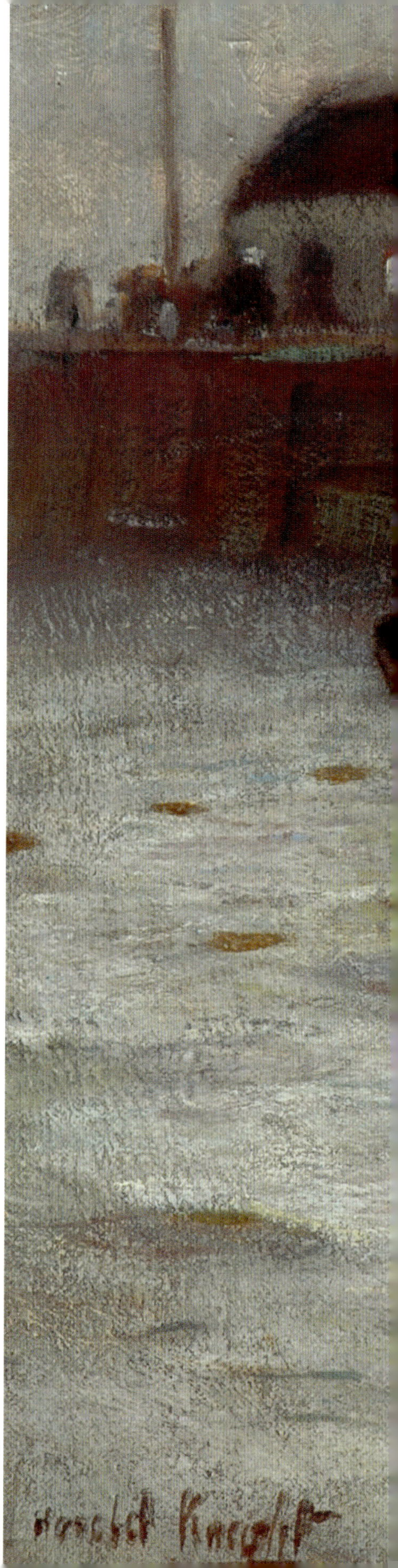

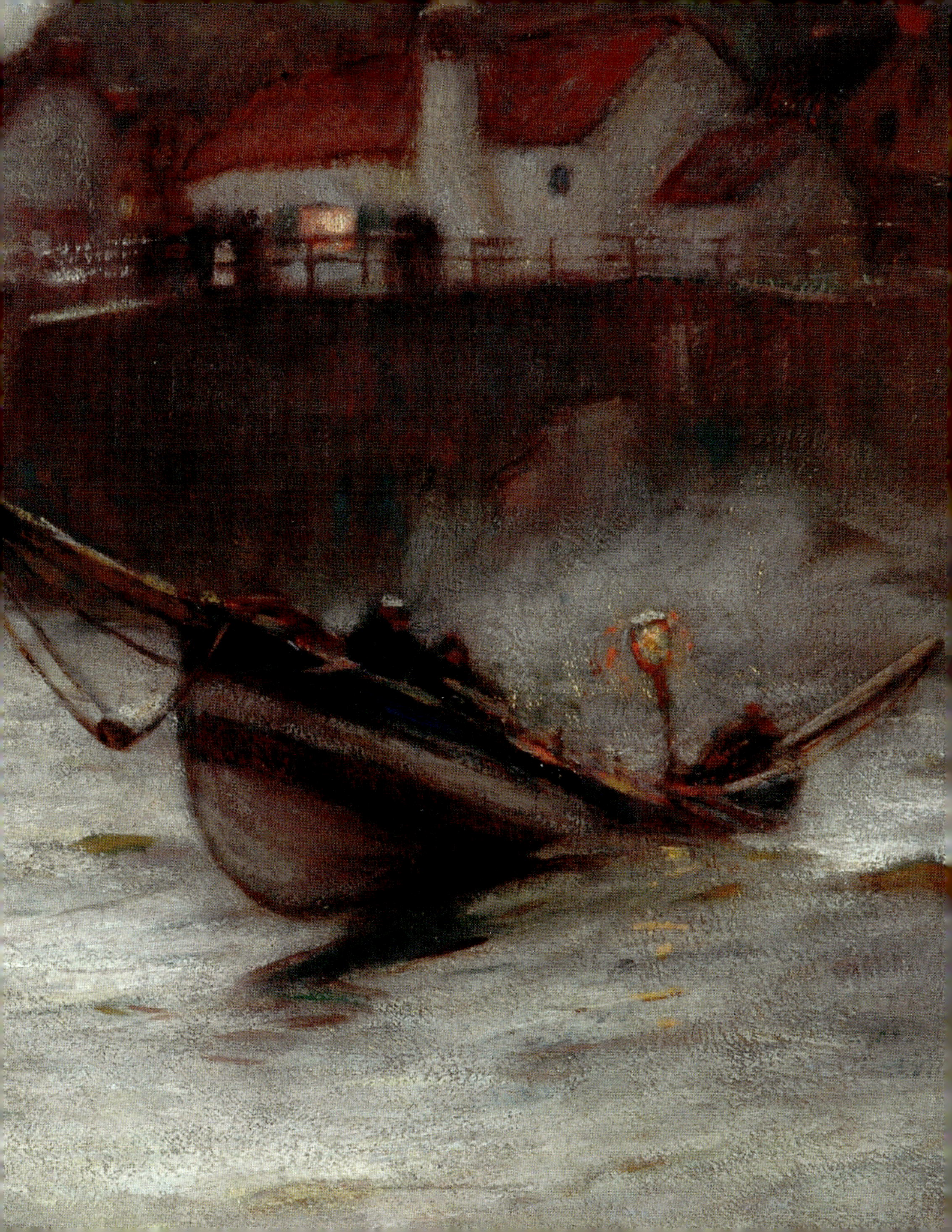

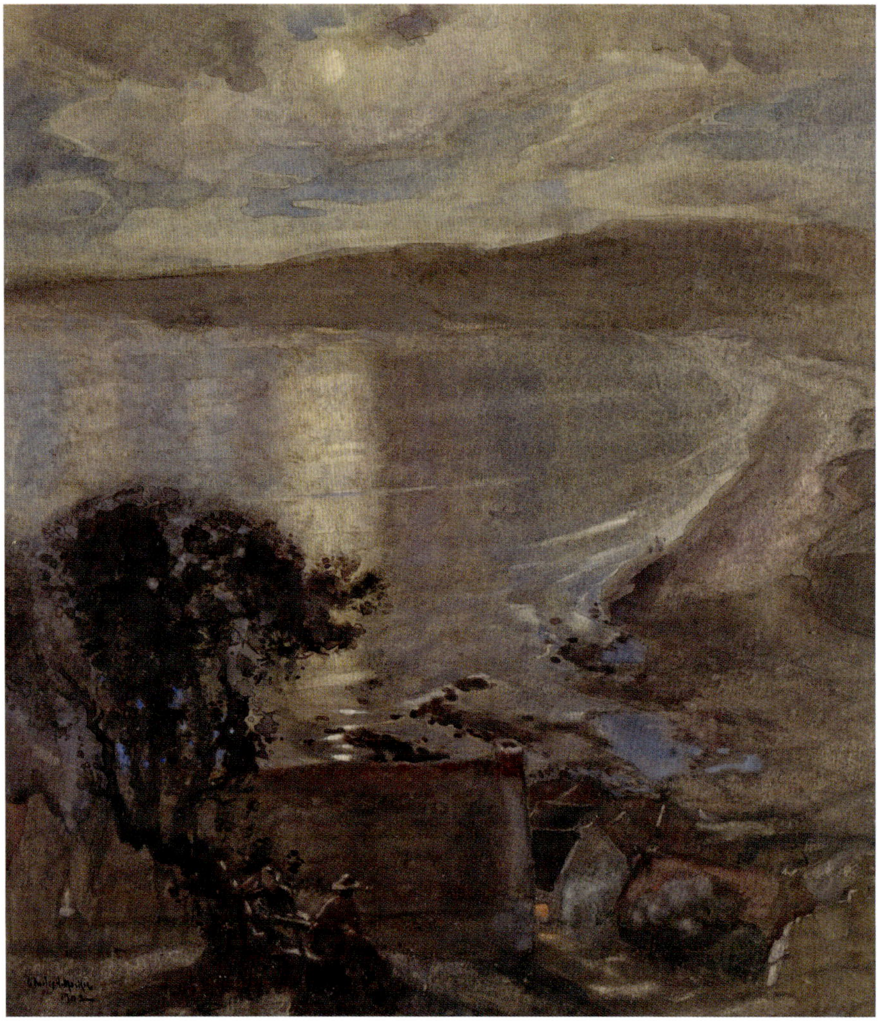

135. Listed as no. 13 at the 2nd Art Club exhibition in 1902, *Moonlight on the Bay* by Charles Hodge Mackie was the most expensive item for sale at £60. Typical of his tonal work, the watercolour reflects Laura Knight's recall of the method with which he helped her to address a system for employing colour.

Other artists, including Joseph Terry, Hirst Walker, Fred Mayor, Arthur Friedenson and Edward Anderson, also explored the crepuscular effects of dusk and indeed the effects of moonlight. The most expensive painting in the second Staithes Art Club exhibition was *Moonlight on the Bay* by Charles Mackie.[181]

Although not one for preliminary studies, Hopwood was a skilled draughtsman in charcoal. In 1902 he held an exhibition of just such works in London, featuring scenes of Staithes, Runswick and Whitby.[182] His work was remembered thus:

> Next to water-colour the method he favoured most was drawing in charcoal, sometimes with a suggestion of tinting. These drawings were exceptionally bold and vigorous, and Hopwood did not here disdain to gain his effects by acute contrasts between light and shadow.[183]

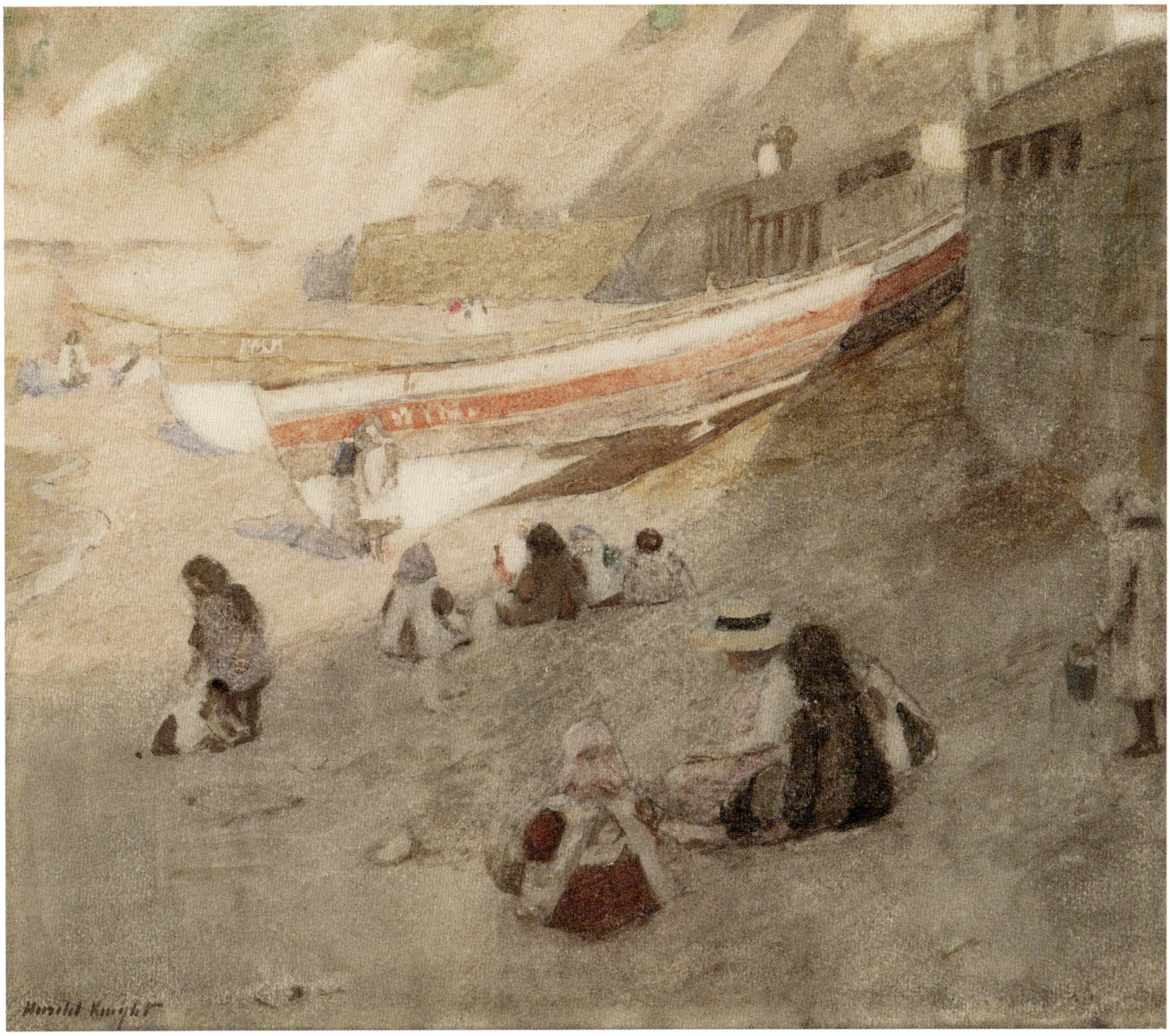

136. In contrast to so much of Harold Knight's work, this watercolour pictures the calm in Staithes on a fine day. Variously titled over the years, in *Light and Shade, Staithes Beach* knots of children lead the eye into the distance, where the red band of the beached coble provides a strong horizontal axis.

To OS. Castle Rooms Lenton Rd. N'gham
Palm – Staithes · 15 Sept 1899.
(enclosing Lizard sketch + RHA [illegible] 1901 [illegible])

Oliver my dearest, Poor lonely lad I do feel as if I should like to fly to you, you must feel miserable ~~desolate~~ all by yourself. Tonight the wind is howling & we have been reduced to a fire which makes things look cheerful. It takes to raining in the afternoons though we have had lovely morning & I have taken to rising at 7 oclock & going for a walk on the cliffs with Laura after her bathe I dare not go bathing as the weather is too fearfully cold & they come back in their wet things. I feel very keen on work just now, Last night the cobles went off late & it was fine to see them with their cozy fires lighted Perhaps I will come home ~~with~~ Catherine you know dearest how much I would like to be near you I cannot bear to think of your lone liness shall I come, work of course is the only attraction & I am working hard, only dont seem to do anything. We have long evenings indoors I think I shall do a little drawing I must get on with this letter is shocking blots & scraps but I couldnt bear to think of your being disapp-ointed tomorrow.

Laura is singing the most dismal song she can find it is called "Parting" ~~though~~ I happened to suggest it was rather dole ful it is approved of by the rest of the company & we are having it through again, It runs like this – "This firmly fixed in Gods decree That though we on earth shall certain be Sadly parting" etc nice & lively on a wet windy night when you are parted from the one you love best on earth.

It is coming again she has decided to learn it for a concert a week tomorrow

Opposite: 137. Rosie Good stayed in Staithes with Laura Johnson several times, but the most consistent series of letters is from 1899. Dated 15 September, this letter to Oliver Sheppard provides a revealing glimpse into the lives of Laura, her sister Sissy, Harold Knight and Oliver Sheppard himself.

Below: 138. Currently titled *By the Village Brook*, this painting of 1897 is arguably Arthur Friedenson's signature work from his time in Yorkshire and sits alongside his landscapes of Runswick Bay. While those are golden in tone, here the light silvery sea mist and haze of chimney smoke link to reflections of light in the beck and the scales of fish in the women's baskets.

W. Gilbert Foster's works of Runswick Bay were published with titles *Lingering Light* and *The Silver Strand*, the latter complimented as 'an admirable example of memory-painting *a la japonaise*'. His experimentation in layering of charcoal and watercolour was also illustrated in *The Studio*. The article discussed his use of a paper with particular tone and roughness, supplying a pleasing effect that evoked the 'mellowness of an old drawing'.[184]

Mayor was inventive not only in terms of his style, but also in his approach to technique. He is said to have patented a design for an integrated sketching easel and stool, and Laura Knight recalls his 'Bloody Rotters' (blotters) innovation. This, she writes, started a fashion for small water-colour studies.[185]

Pease Robinson's diary gives a colourful narrative of the sketching sorties of Mayor and Friedenson, seemingly teaching two amateur female artists from Manchester during the weeks before the first Art Club exhibition. Other sources portray friendly rivalries, both romantic and otherwise, within the group.[186]

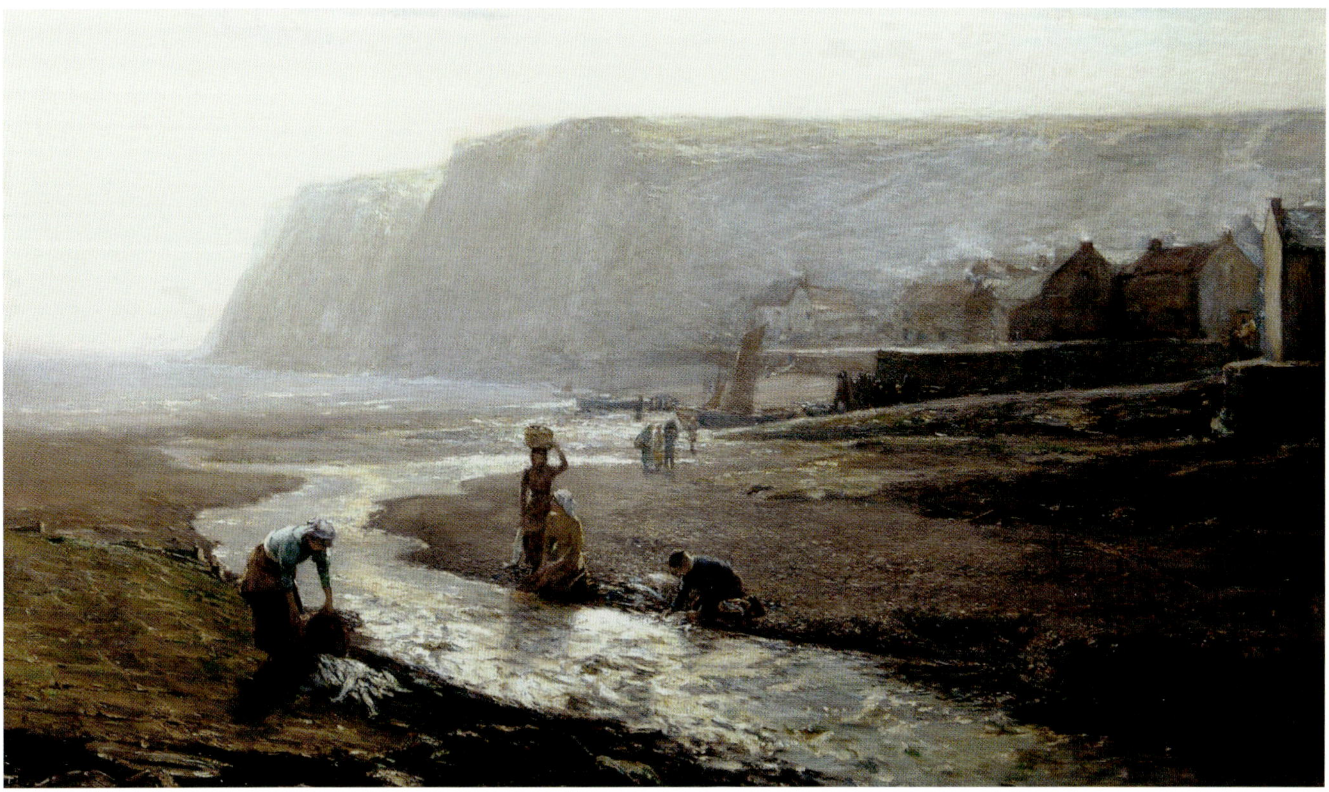

Already secretly engaged, Good wrote to her fiancé Sheppard assuring him that she would not be jealous of his granting private sketching lessons to Cissy Johnson, Laura's sister.[187]

In the same letter, in an amusing reversal of Laura's earlier deference to his technique, Good described her attempts to improve Knight's work:

> Harold is trying to draw you; Laura wants to improve on his drawing, but is not allowed. Love, if only you were sitting on this sofa beside me... Cissy is drawing what she calls my imagination – which is you with a halo round you. They are going to all spend the rest of the evening drawing you. Harold's 1st sketch is really very good. He is now drawing you in your old straw hat and knickerbockers, with Pat at one side and I in my jersey on the other.

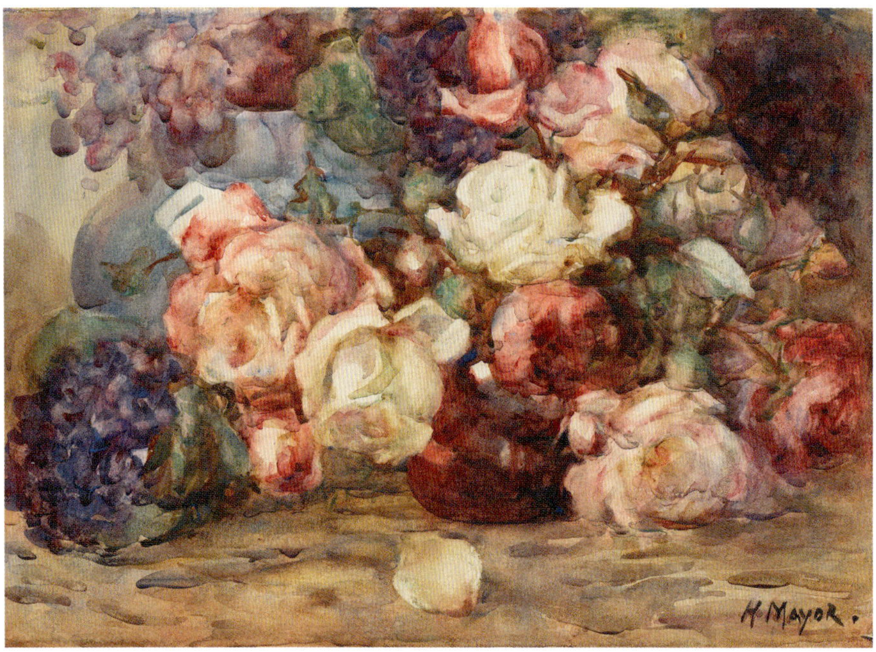

139. Still lives such as this untitled work of roses were a staple of Hannah Mayor's painting from her student days, when Queen Victoria bought a flower piece on a visit to Westminster School of Art. A few extant landscapes and figure studies in watercolour survive, but it was to flower pieces that she returned to support herself after Fred's untimely death in 1916.

WATERCOLOUR, PRINTS AND PASTEL

Mayor's wife Hannah produced some notable still-life flower pieces. Her extant work is frustratingly sparse, however – even more so than Isabella Thompson's. This makes it difficult to mark a consistent comparison with the work of her husband, or to define a particular individual style.

140. This illustration of *The Storm*, Fred Mayor's watercolour of 1898–9 reproduced in *The Artist* magazine, suggests the artist painting the same scene as Harold Knight, which the latter included in *The Last Coble*. Other similar 'shared' storm scenes also exist, and it is probably significant that the two men lodged with the Porritt family in Gun Gutter in 1899.

It is clear though that Laura Knight took up Fred's 'blotter' technique and, from a distance of some years, recalled his work for its technical association with Edward Stott and Arthur Melville, while intimating the lack of a personal style. However, a contemporary review of four of his pictures in *The Artist* states:

> It may be because no one knows he has worked with Brangwyn and Stott that one seems now and then to see their respective manners in his work; be that as it may, it is individual enough easily to stand alone.[188]

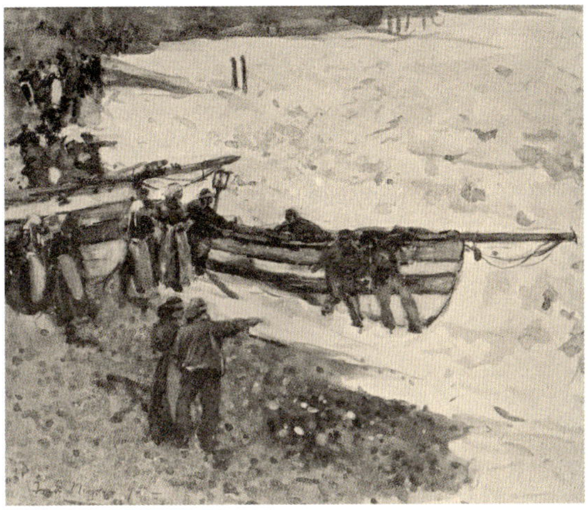

Mayor's increasingly loose handling of wet-on-wet watercolour technique is notable and does follow the innovative style of Melville. Having pre-prepared his paper with a specific white ground, Melville's technique found expression as follows:

> Then he applied his colour very wet with vigorous brush strokes sponging out any superfluous detail ... often he would put in his background on damp paper, sometimes very wet ... and when this was nearly dry, he would add the full bright patches of colour so characteristic of his painting.[189]

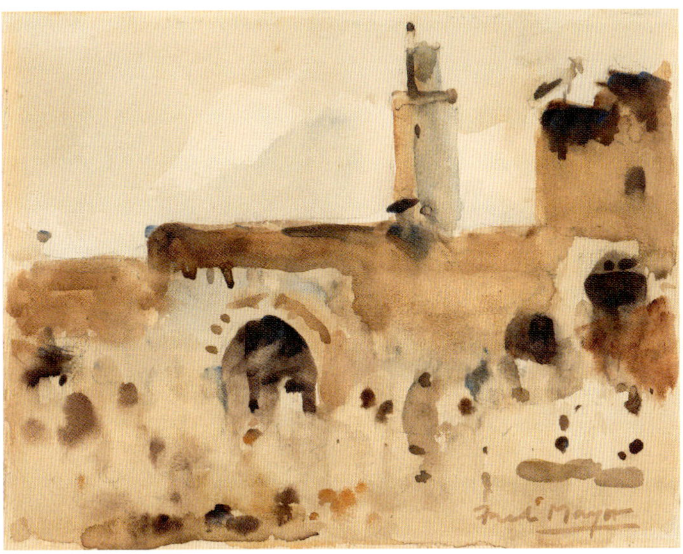

A classic example, similar to that illustrated, is the work bought by Oliver Sheppard, mentioned in a letter to his fiancée and now in the Hugh Lane Gallery.[190]

141. Mayor travelled through Morocco as far as Fez between March and May 1899, and it is probable that *A Mosque in Tangiers* was painted during his trip. Another watercolour scene from this tour, mentioned by Oliver Sheppard in a letter to Rosie Good, is likely that bequeathed to the Hugh Lane Gallery, Dublin by Sheppard's daughter.

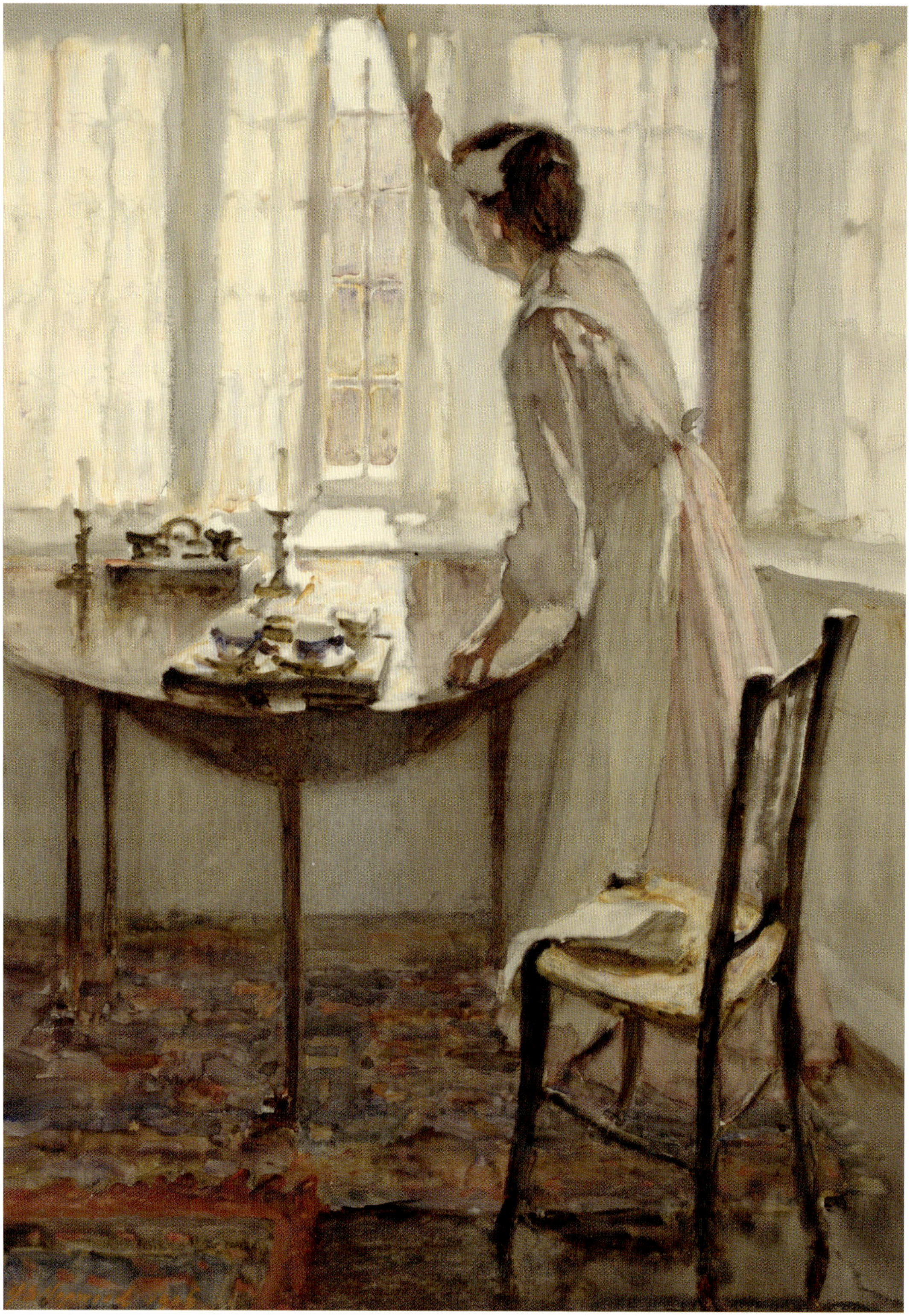

Opposite: 142. A retrospective of Henry Hopwood's career in 1924 recalled, 'On arriving in Montreuil, [he] was so delighted by the effect of sunlight streaming ... on to the table, all spread with gleaming china, that he immediately set out to capture it in *The Breakfast Table* (1908). Not only did he refuse to allow anything ...to be removed, but he forbade anyone to even enter the room'.

A review article in *The Artist* states his watercolours illustrated there were done on 'a very large scale'. Certainly Mayor did produce other sizeable works, such as *Waiting for the Cobles*, on the theme of a storm at Staithes, painted similarly by Knight in both watercolour and oil format.[191] However, for larger works he generally turned to oil.

Henry Hopwood's watercolour credentials were first forged in Australia, where commentators followed his activity long after he left. His later work was generally acknowledged to be in a silvery and quiet key of colour, with one of his better-known works described thus:

> The Breakfast table – the cool tones having, within a limited range, a remarkable gradation... The textures and silvery tones ... are admirably rendered.[192]

Watercolour was, of course, used by almost all members of the group. Other artists such as John Spence Ingall worked almost exclusively in this medium.

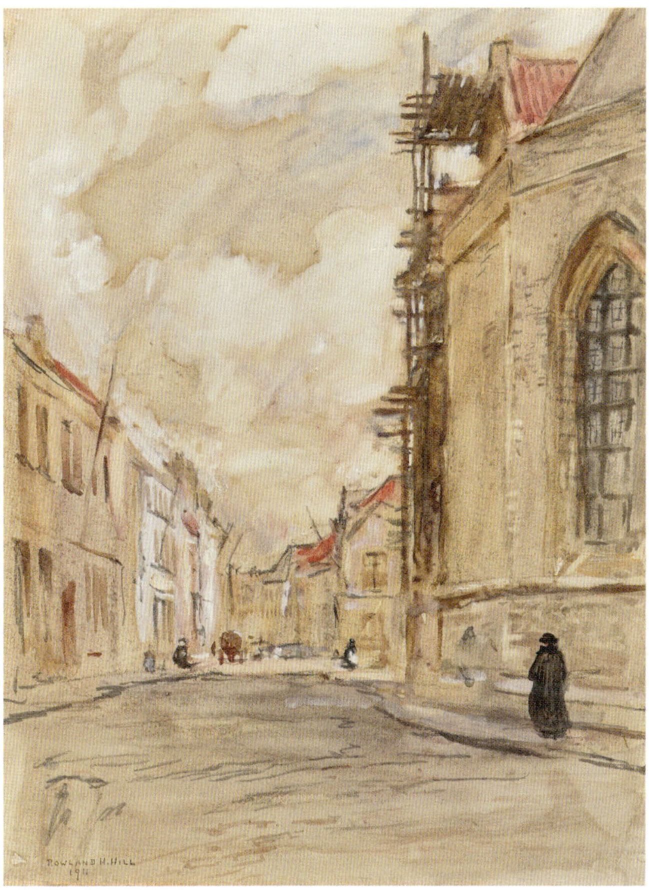

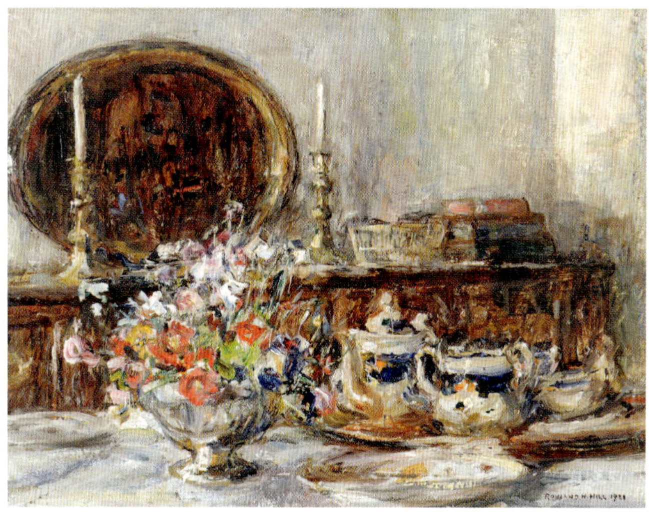

Left: 143. Rowland Hill exhibited European scenes from his first exhibition with the Art Club. *Street in Bruges*, a watercolour of 1911, is painted on brown paper, which invests the work with a wonderful tonal quality in what is a very spare street scene. Hill's use of colour in the work is very subtle and contrasts with his later work from the 1920s and 30s, which is looser but more effervescent.

Above: 144. This undated still life by Rowland Hill is set in Florence Hess's family home; her association with Mark Senior, and consequent time spent in Runswick Bay, must have brought the pair into contact. Although painted in oil, the work feels very typical of Hill's approach to watercolour.

He and Freds Richardson and Jackson are notable for their range – to be discussed in Chapter 4 – with all three travelling widely.

Rowland Hill recounted how his constant sketching in the books of the family firm finally persuaded his father to accede to the encouragement of Ralph Hedley and send him to the Bushey Academy in Hertfordshire. He also married a fellow artist and settled in Ellerby, having travelled and exhibited widely throughout the 1890s. Perhaps because of this, a large amount of Hill's work is also in watercolour. Oil tends to be reserved for his portraits, larger figure studies (such as children collecting primroses) and still lives or interior scenes.

In Hill's early dated work (*c.* 1910) deftness of touch is allied to a confidence in leaving much of the ground evident; in the 1920s his colour becomes brighter and his exploration of shades of a particular colour within a single work holds subjects of a busy nature together. There is a looseness to Hill's later work which is not altogether convincing, but it may be well to consider how the paintings of Mark Senior and J. W. Howey, two of Hill's great friends, may have affected his work.

145. Frederick Richardson travelled throughout Holland from Walcheren in the south all the way to the Zuiderzee over a number of years. His mastery of pastel is clear from this untitled work of *c.* 1905, which clearly speaks of his time on the continent, given the coastline and costume depicted.

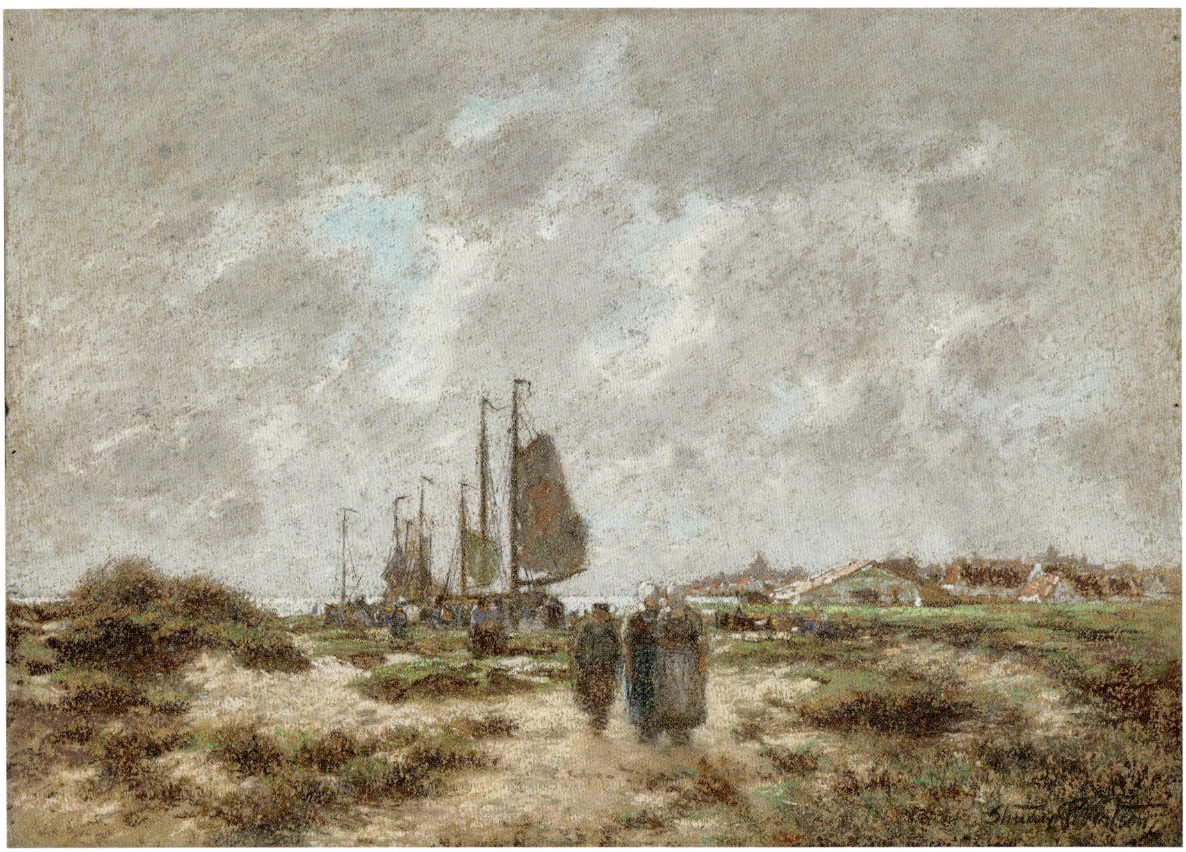

146. The mezzotint technique employed by Thomas Barrett in this print, entitled *On the Quay*, lends a velvety texture to the image. It results in a richness of tone, binding all the picture elements together, in contrast to the purposefully sketchier feel of his etchings.

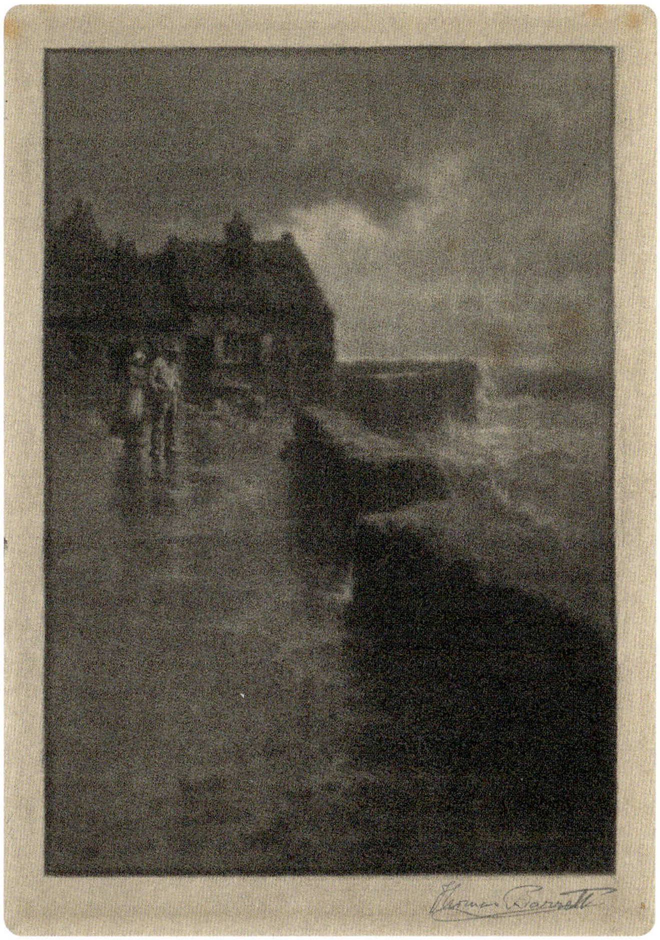

Thomas Barrett was listed in the 2nd Art Club exhibition as a member of the Royal Society of Painter-Printmakers (RE). He produced a string of small etchings to some acclaim, as well as mezzotints, with agricultural and coastal themes. Frank Mason was another artist from the group who etched and went on to work in a whole host of media during his long career. His work as illustrator and graphic artist lent itself more to pen and ink and washes than to pencil, but he used watercolour and etching throughout his work as an official war artist.[193]

Alongside watercolour, pastel was an increasingly popular medium among contemporary painters such as the noted Glasgow 'Boy' James Guthrie – not only for sketching but also for exhibiting, as the shows put on at the Grosvenor Gallery in 1888–9 reveal. Like Guthrie's second series of works, Fred Mayor's regular exhibits at the Art Club shows in this medium were often simply entitled 'Pastel'.[194] His association with Edward Stott, including suggestions that he spent time at Amberley, would only have served to encourage him in this medium.[195] Contemporary criticism perceived Stott's strength to lie in his originality of vision and noted colour sensibility rather than in his ability to record a scene accurately; he might then have acted as a natural model for Mayor's developing style.[196]

While no sketchbooks are seemingly available to illustrate Ernest Rigg's working, he did produce pastels. So too did Fred Richardson, particularly on his trip(s) to the continent with Joseph Bagshawe (**145**). Pastel also suited Mark Senior's penchant for colour, as well as his loose technique, resulting in an increasing emphasis on movement allied to colour (**178**).

PHOTOGRAPHY

The use of photography as an aide to artists is much discussed during this period. P. S. Kroyer, the most celebrated member of the painters at Skagen, has recently been recognised as the photographer behind a group of over 250 images of his life and that of the colony. He was candid about the use of photos as inspiration even for some of his most famous works. Kroyer used them as the equivalent of sketches for works that, although purporting to be created *en plein air*, were often the product of careful studio work. Michael Ancher, the creator of a body of monumental pictures of Danish fishermen, also employed photography in a deliberate and systematic way. He maintained its method as being real, working in front of the subject out of doors, and therefore their use in studio compositions entirely in accordance with their principles.

Scrapbooks with snapshots of Florence Hess and Mark Senior in Runswick Bay have survived, but perhaps more apposite are a quantity of lantern slides recently discovered, which show a variety of painters at work in the area. These are thought to have been taken or arranged by W. Gilbert Foster who, alongside his family, is featured in several of them.[197] Evidence will be provided in a forthcoming book for the use of photography in Foster's work. In light of this, it might be fruitful – though space does not allow here – to

147. The pastels of Mark Senior, many dated to the Art Club years, are often extremely vivid in colouring; this undated view of a Runswick yard, entitled *Courtyard Gossip*, weaves this colour into the shadows, holding them in check. The figures in turn are only half-revealed, lending all focus to the medium itself.

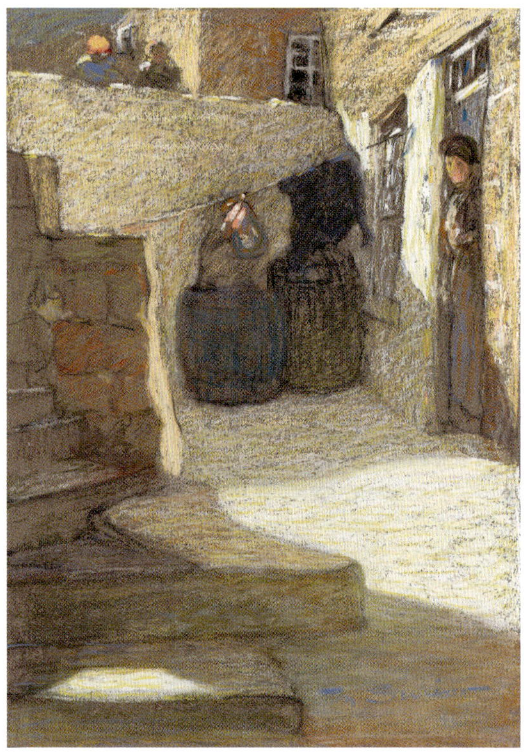

examine the images of Staithes photographer H. C. Morley, whose work runs entirely in parallel with the views depicted by the artists.[198]

Further comparisons though can be made between artwork and the photographs of Frank Sutcliffe, as he himself was wont to point out.[199]

Sutcliffe's father was a watercolourist, and for much of the time that Sutcliffe could spend away from the studio – limited to early mornings and evenings during the tourist season – he espoused the *en plein air* approach. He much preferred allowing nature itself to affect a picture rather than his own artificial intervention, using 'rough paper or sheets of celluloid' and revelling in atmospheric effects. Sutcliffe felt that he had to *imagine colour away* to frame a scene in his mind, but sometimes the haze of either smoke from Whitby's chimneys or the rolling fogs off the North Sea did this for him.

> They are but dark grey silhouettes against a lighter grey background, but their beauty and infinite variety are wonderful… Millet might have designed [these] groups.[200]

148. Frank Sutcliffe recognised many of the artists' techniques in composing and simplifying pictures; he constantly challenged himself and experimented with his photographs *en plein air*. In *Trees in Mist* his use of the natural sea fret turned a mundane subject into a prize-winning exhibit at a Tokyo show in 1893.

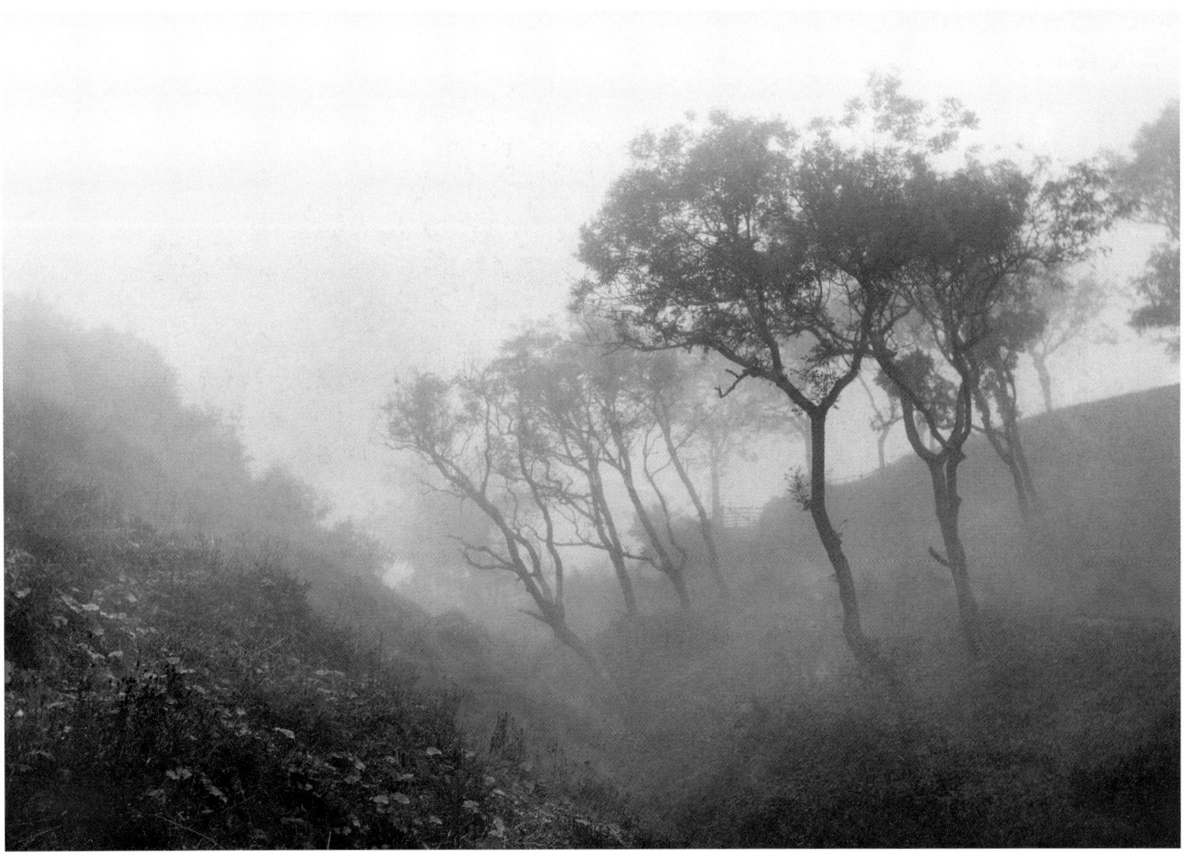

Rather as the critic of *The Magazine of Art* referred to Stott's technical limitations as the key to developing his own style, so through long experience Sutcliffe's struggles with equipment resulted in his individual 'look'. This distinctive style attempted to combine publicly-admired sharpness with subtle differentiation of focus. When he revelled too greatly in nature, however, admiration fell flat:

> One bright July day … it suddenly became dark… There was not a sound to be heard, and it got darker and darker. Then all at once instead of fire and brimstone coming out of the black inky night above came rain. Such rain … seen against the brighter sky in the west… As it fell, it looked like long black hair falling from some invisible black beast… The plate which saw [it] might as well have never seen the light at all for any use it has been.[201]

His chagrin can only have been enhanced by the fact that popular paintings of Whitby harbour by another renowned Yorkshire artist, John Atkinson Grimshaw, were almost exact equivalents of many of Sutcliffe's *contre jour* or moonlight scenes. However, Sutcliffe never allowed his experimentation to be discouraged and relished the constant challenge:

> This battle of daylight and lamplight has many times bewitched me. Often have I watched the sun take shine out of the lamp. To paint this would be easy; how to photograph it is what bothers me… How can I express in chemicals the glorious contrast between the yellow lamplight and the blue daylight?

Changes to the equipment which initially prevented Sutcliffe solving this conundrum gradually appeared during the course of his career. However, he was nevertheless continuously prompted as to how colour would register on the photographic plate. Naturally, he compared this process with that of painters who:

> often use a set of various coloured glasses, hinged together at one end like a pocket lens, when studying their landscape subjects. If the colours appear scattered all over, an examination of the scene through the different glasses will often suggest the best way of bringing them – the colours – together.[202]

OIL PAINTING

With this review in mind, one turns again to the struggles with colour that Laura Johnson experienced at Staithes. Her memoir paints a glowing literary description of the village:

> The sun gilds the brightly painted cobles in the Wyke. One boat disappears round the Penny Nab, her red-tanned mainsail, mizzen and jibs all set. In another boat a man hauls the sails, Venetian red drapery unfolds. A big main sail goes up, a patch of shining white that has not yet seen the barking copper. The women's knitting needles click as they stand gossiping on the quay, their figures in sombre black and lavender silhouette.[203]

149. 'On the shadowed Staithe old men crouch on their hunkers .... wives pull their knitting needles from holders at the waist. Click, click, click, they sound ... All eyes watch the cobles vanish.' The memoir of Laura Knight (née Johnson) beautifully evokes her unusual pastel *Knitting*, signed with her maiden name and so created prior to 1903.

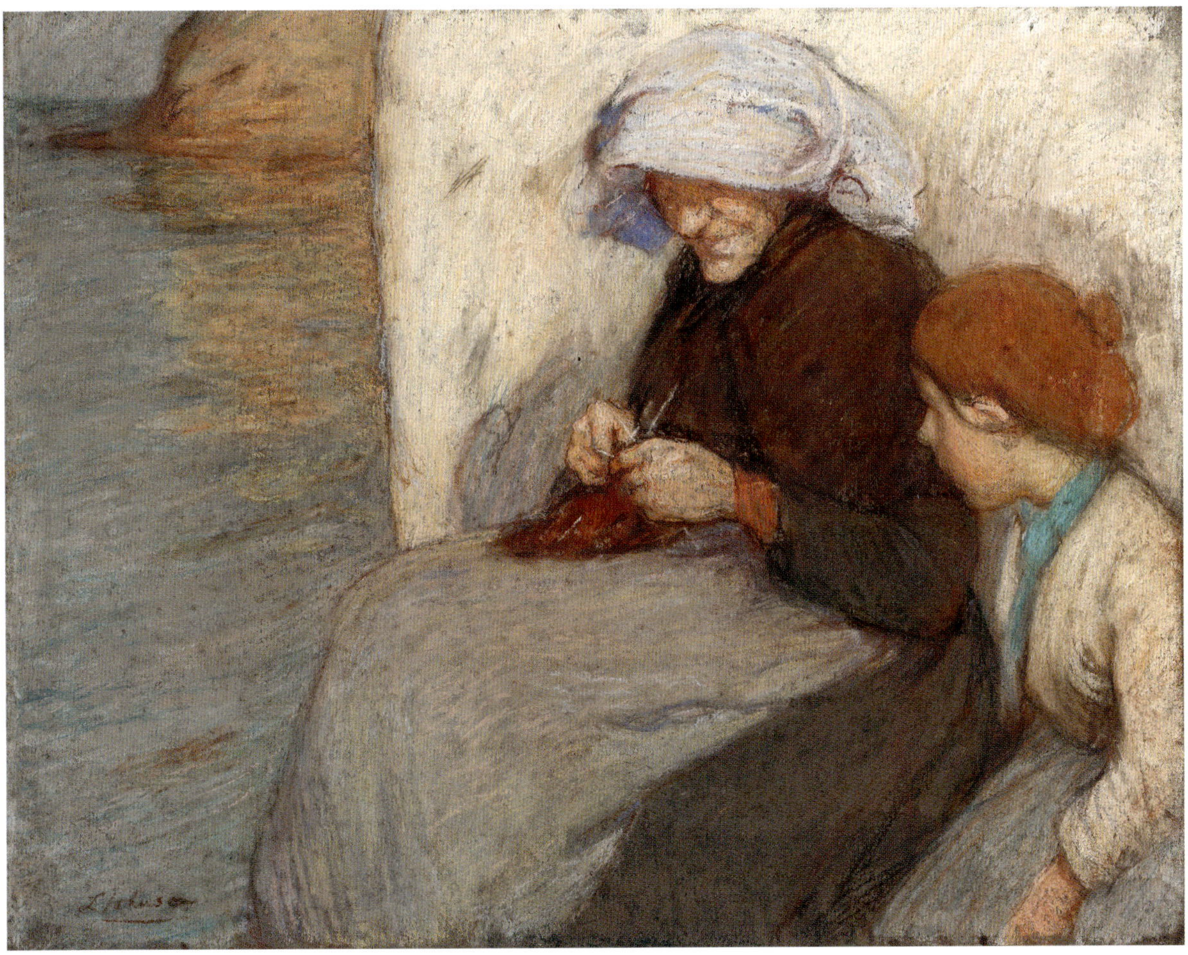

The intervening experience of Cornwall and the development of her style may well have influenced this passage, but Pease Robinson's diary entry for 23 August 1901 describes her positive attempts to develop the use of colour:

> She paints in the strong 'blob-and-dash-I-know-what-I- am-doing' style. I don't care for her pictures much but liked the sketch of a boy with some small green floats (bladders) very much and almost thought of buying it as it was only £4-4-0.[204]

Knight's own reflections on her colour experimentation chime with the diarist's entries:

> I started painting in pure spots of colour, the impressionists' method of giving light and atmosphere...[205]

While she believed no such painting had survived, *Baiting Lines* suggests otherwise. This composition allows us to judge for ourselves whether to side

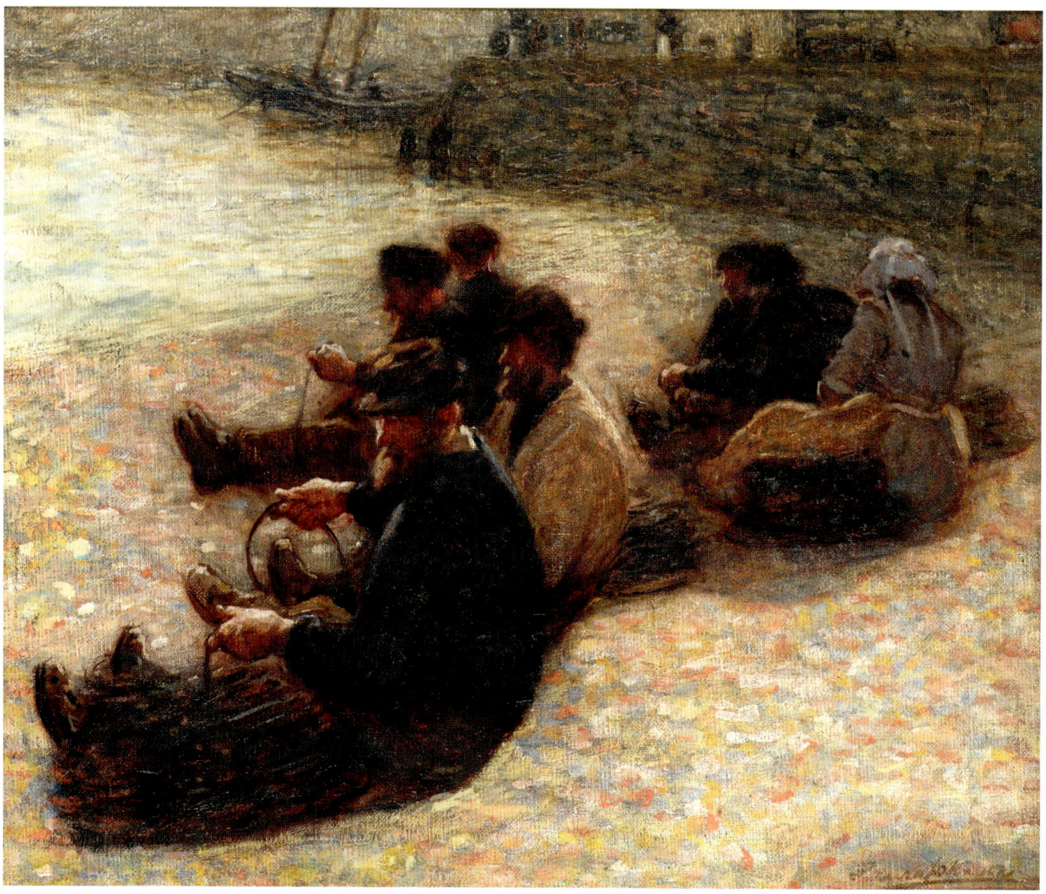

150. *Baiting Lines*, the current title of this undated oil painting by Laura Johnson, was a popular subject for the Staithes artists, incorporating both male and female models. The artist's technique was described in 1901 by Enid Pease Robinson as 'blob-and-dash-I-know-what-I-am-doing'; she herself remembered working in 'pure spots of colour, the impressionists' method of giving light and atmosphere', but was never entirely satisfied with the results.

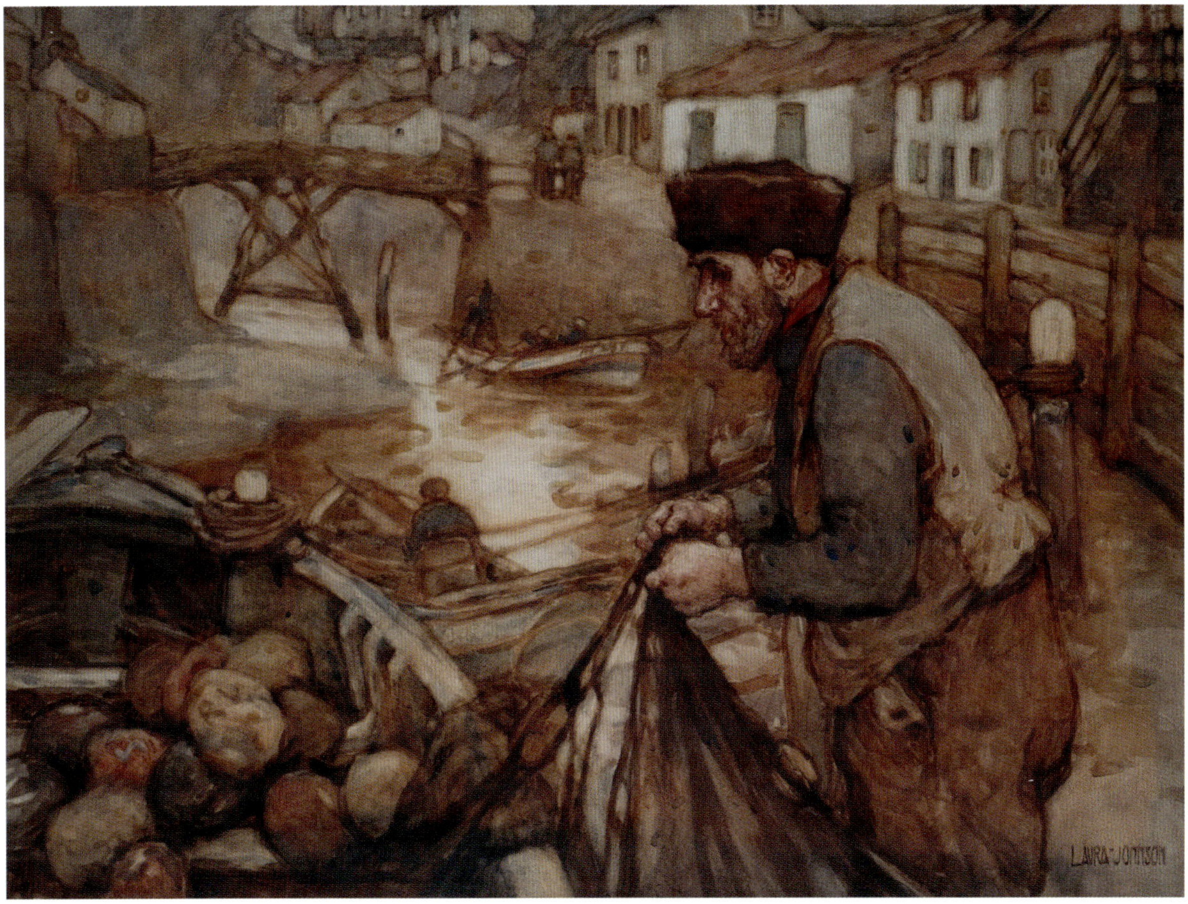

151 and 152. This finished watercolour by Laura Johnson features the same stylised signature as her large oil, *The Fishing Fleet* (**123**). Entitled *Staithes Fisherman*, this work develops the accompanying sketch (right) with far more detail that includes the cargo of bladders, cobles on the beck, figures on the bridge and the fisherman's waistcoat over his smock jacket.

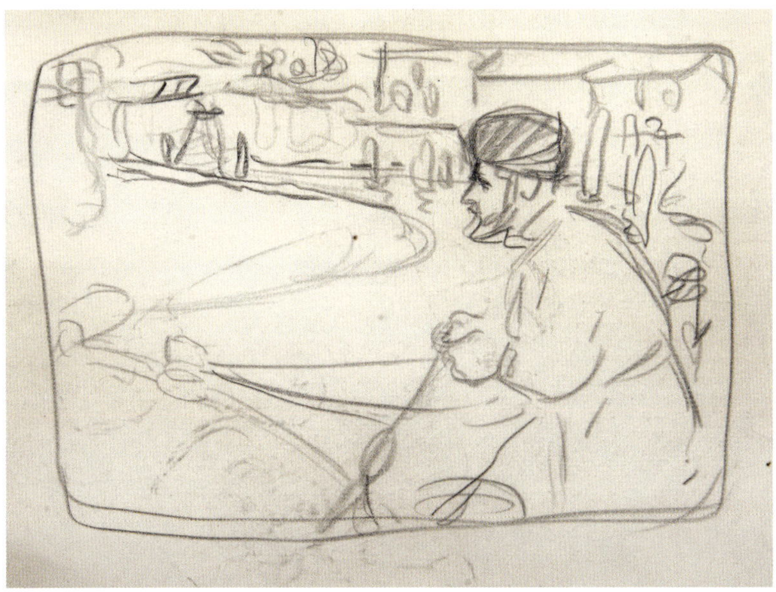

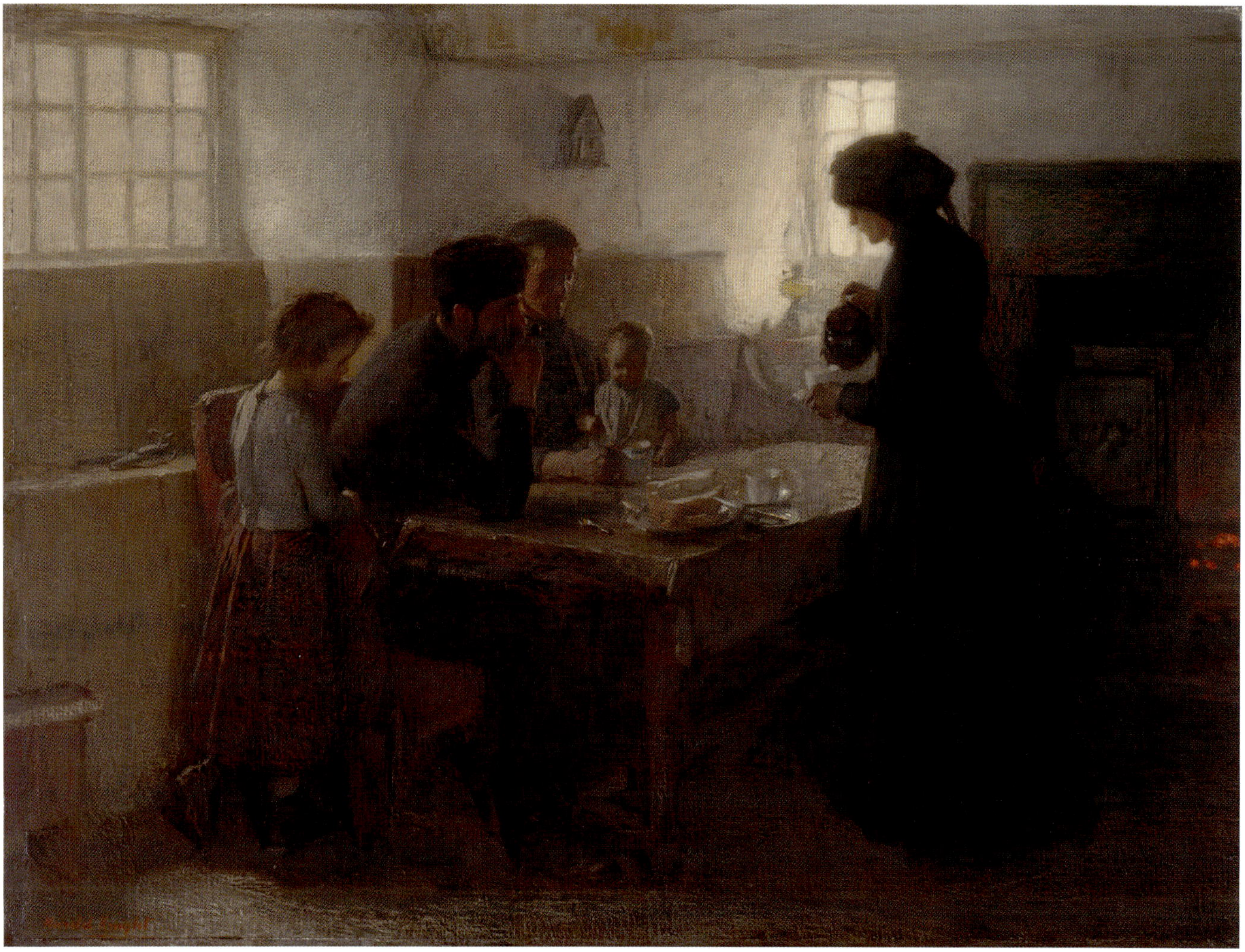

with the contemporary critic of *The Artist*, who describes her 1900 exhibits in Nottingham as follows:

153. *A Cup of Tea* by Harold Knight was bought from the Royal Academy show of 1905 by the Queensland Art Gallery. At this time Dutch influence was evident in many of the Staithes artists' work – not only because of exhibitions in Britain, but also the result of artists travelling to Holland.

> The works of Miss Laura Johnson at once impress by their dignity and subdued richness of colouring. Her groups of fisherfolks are happily and dramatically portrayed; every face is full of character and tells its story well. No less masterly is her rendering of the sea in its varying moods, and her grasp of atmospheric effect is indeed praiseworthy.[206]

In a later review of the work of both Laura and Harold Knight in *The Studio* 1913, Norman Garstin, the Irish artist, 'Newlyner' and journalist, imagines the stimulating atmosphere provided to them at a key moment in their development by artists such as Jackson, Mayor, Hopwood and Mackie. It is to the last that

Laura famously gives credit for the ordering of her palette and directing a more disciplined approach to colour, in particular.[207]

Garstin goes on to note a lowness in tone and sentiment that entered the Knights' work only after their first visit to Holland in 1904. Equally, he judges that the opulent colour and sensuous gaiety of their work in Cornwall is not a direct result of their surroundings, but rather a reaction to experiments in the Dutch influence.

Neil Walker, then curator of Nottingham Museum, writing in the 1993 exhibition catalogue on the Staithes Group,[208] agrees and recognises how the brightness of the colour, even in some of her works of this date, anticipates the Newlyn paintings. He conjectures whether this was part of the reason for Laura's growing dissatisfaction with the theorising and sombre palette of Wilder Darling, their unappointed guide and advisor in the Laren colony.[209]

This colony had been founded by Albert Neuhuys and Anton Mauve around the same time Jackson and others started visiting Runswick Bay. Their success was such that Americans like Darling flocked to the hamlet – which was, as a consequence of its increasing popularity, linked to Amsterdam by the railway.

The harmonies and unity of Josef Israels, another standard bearer of the contemporary Dutch school, chimed closely with the principles that Mackie espoused. While Laura recognised the improvement that both brought to her awareness of technique, she was not prepared to sacrifice her individual style and instinct.[210]

154. Frank Mason was one of the most enthusiastic Staithes visitors to Holland. His visits, which peaked around 1907, included trips to the museums of major cities and artists' colonies such as Laren. He also travelled to coastal locations such as Scheveningen and Katwijk, where this undated watercolour of a Dutch beach scene may have been painted.

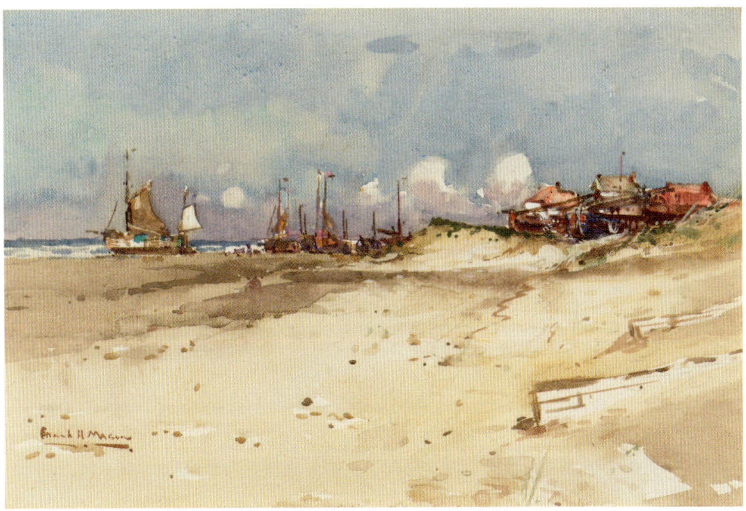

THE DUTCH SCHOOL

The first Dutch trip occurred in 1904, a year after Harold and Laura's marriage and honeymoon that included a visit to London and an exhibition of Dutch pictures at the Guildhall. This contained six pictures each by Hals and Rembrandt, a Vermeer and over 20 each by Jacob and Matthew Maris and Anton Mauve, as well as nearly 30 paintings by Jozef [*sic*] Israels. This reflected the balance of other recent if smaller shows in the UK. It also contained pictures from the Drucker

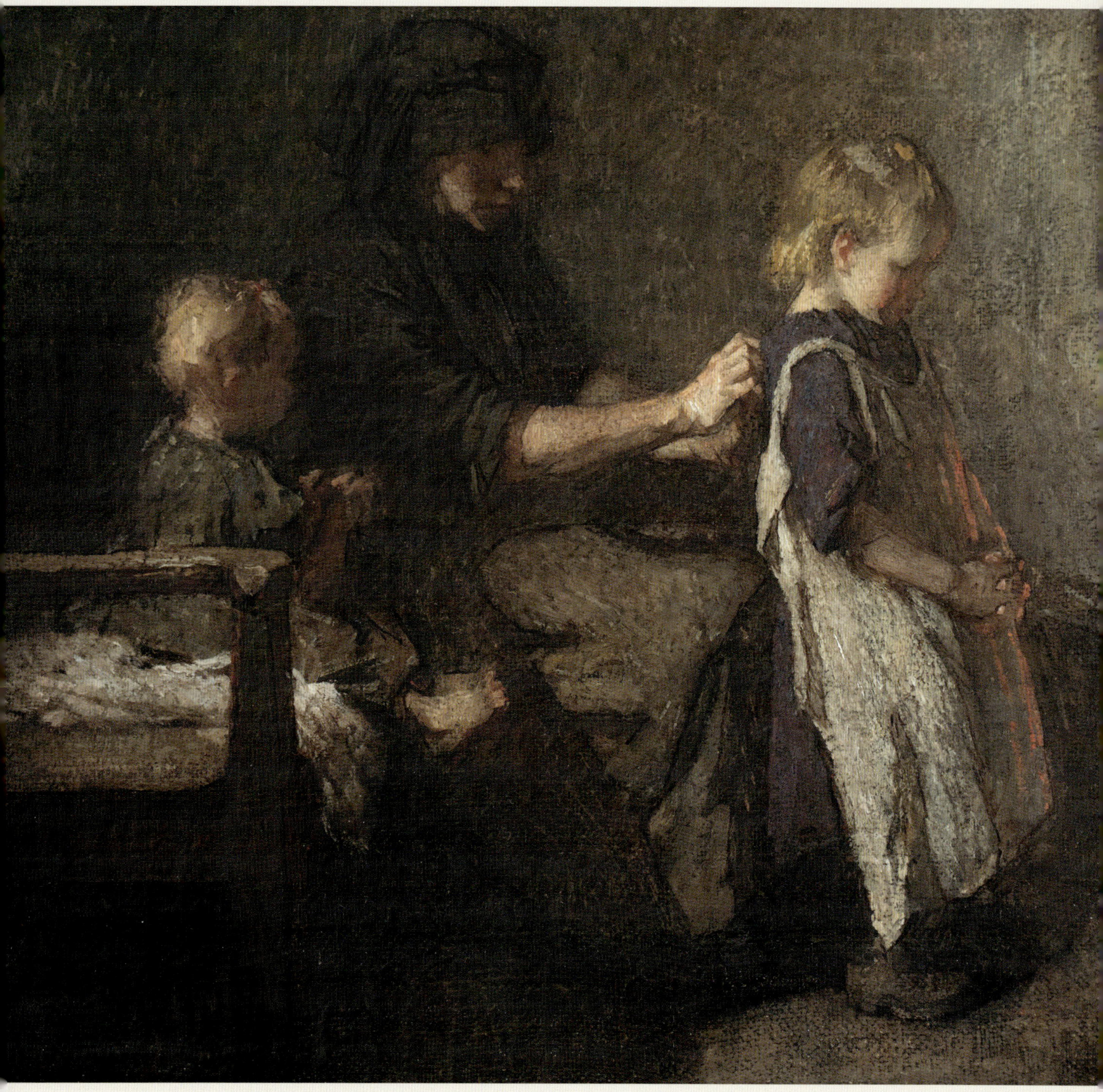

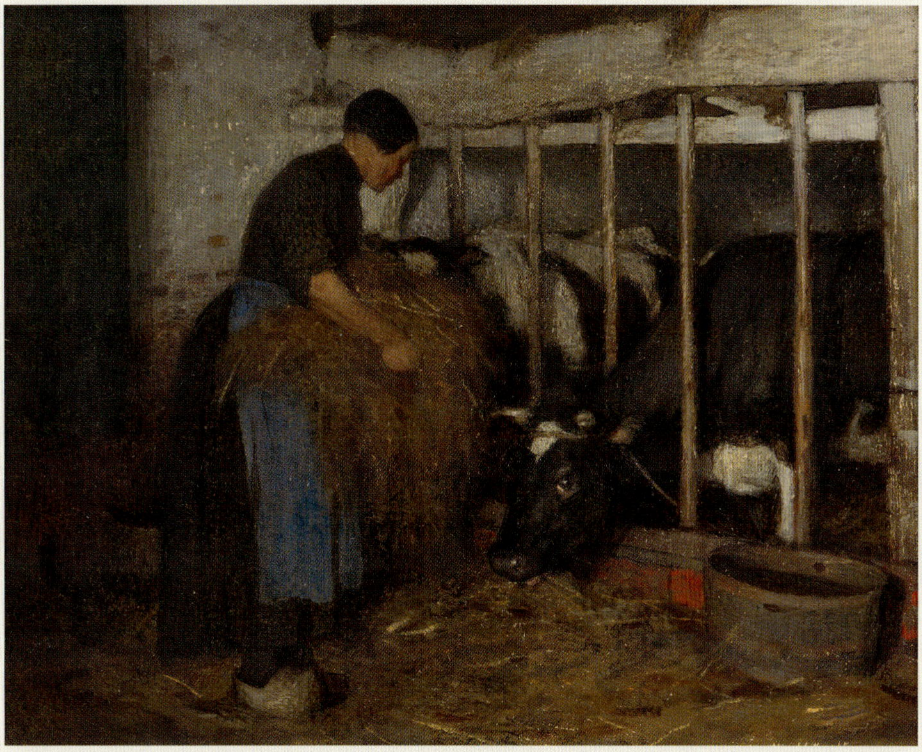

156. Harold Knight's Dutch Interior is likely to date from one of his three trips to Holland between 1904 and 1907. It exemplifies the interior scenes he produced in the artists' colony of Laren but, rather than his manipulation of light to suggest a narrative, he presents a timeless image in low, even light.

155. After their first trip to Holland in 1904, the Knights returned to live on the moors above Staithes. Laura worked at a miner's cottage on Cowbar Nab, painting a series of canvases of the family who lived there, including *Dressing the Children*, which derived much from her extended time working on indoor scenes in Holland.

collection, which was subsequently donated to the Rijksmuseum and about which they were so excited upon arriving.[211]

The Knights were not alone in their attraction to Dutch painting, whether the old masters or the modern school. Their fellow Staithes artist Henry Hopwood instigated their initial trip and many others also spent time either visiting collections in the larger cities or else visiting the colonies, on what was by this time a well-trodden 'sketching tour' of the Low Countries.

In 1898 Friedenson and Mayor had spent time at the famous Hotel Spaander in Volendam. So had Mason, who then toured for much of 1899 to Rotterdam, then Katwijk, Scheveningen and Volendam on honeymoon. Garrido, who had studied with Crawshaw in Paris and who came to Whitby in 1906, invited him to visit the Amsterdam museums in 1905.[212] Jobling visited with Hodgson Campbell, and possibly Atkinson, in 1907, the year of the Knights' last visit. However, he had already shown pictures on Dutch subjects at the Staithes Art Club exhibition in 1904.[213]

Bagshawe was at Katwijk too, travelling with Richardson after the two men visited the coast of France together.[214] Richardson visited regularly between 1894 and 1913; like Mason, he spent his honeymoon there in 1912. His regular exhibiting through the 1890s in oils to pastels indicates that he ranged from Walcheren all the way to Monnichendam, Volendam and the Zuyder See.[215]

What is very clear is the effect that Holland had upon the work of the Knights; it inspired them to return several times, enabled finally by commercial success at the Royal Academy. Harold's sale of *A Cup of Tea*, his 1905 Academy exhibit (**153**), to the Queensland Art Gallery through Sir Frank Dicksee sparked ongoing sales and prompted them to generate a series of 'Dutch' interiors. These were exhibited at the Knights' successful combined shows in London, which in turn prompted further sales to major foreign galleries, including the National Gallery of South Africa through George Clausen.

Exchanging *en plein air* work for the close interiors of Laren brought success, but also a working proximity that perhaps even the cramped conditions at Staithes had not provided. The artists stayed at a pension with other (English-speaking) artists and rented 'a location' for a fixed weekly rate. This meant sharing models and subjects and resulted in only four landscapes out of their initial show of over 60 paintings. In writing of their resulting ill-health, Laura regrets the overwhelming time spent indoors. It is thus perhaps no surprise that on their return to Staithes they chose to lodge at farms and walk down from

Opposite: 157. Time in Holland allowed the Knights to work through the possibilities provided by the warm tonality and muted colour, of the Dutch school tradition. However, there are bursts of colour, such as this image *Interior with Children reading* (c. 1906–7), which prefigure its much broader use in their later Cornish works.

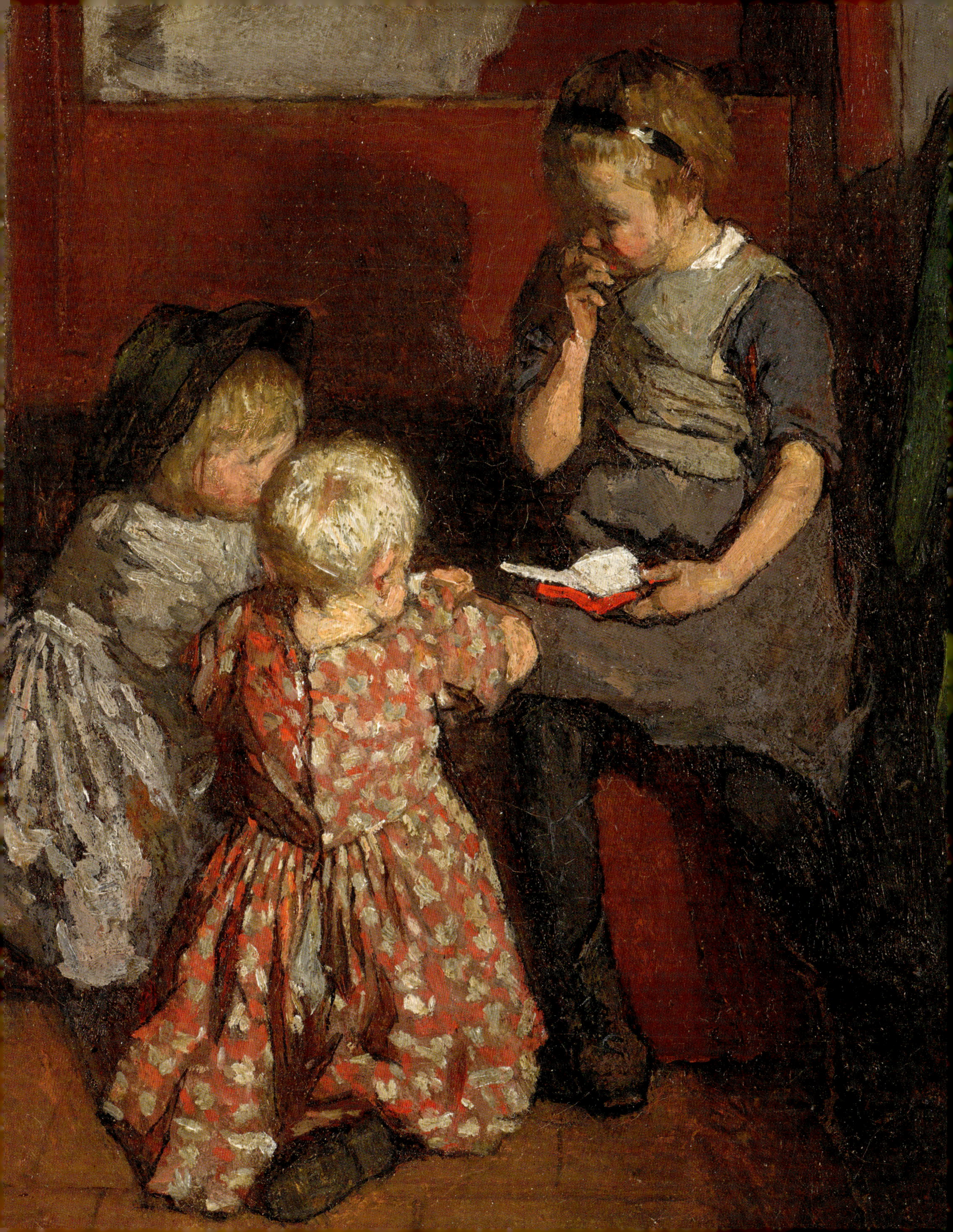

the moors, no matter the weather, rather than live and work in the village. It is perhaps also understandable that Laura's 'studio' was out of the village on the top of Cowbar, where she hired a miner's family as models and in whose cottage she left her materials overnight. It intimates the loosening of bonds which, after further visits to Holland and the increased financial freedom provided by gradual success of sales, resulted in the Knights eventually leaving the area.

MARK SENIOR

It is perhaps curious that the one artist so well known for his colouring, so consistent in his return to the coast and with his own connections to the continent is not mentioned as an influence by Knight. Mark Senior, who had been painting in Runswick Bay throughout the 1890s and was established both through his RA exhibits and his local social and patronage connections, might have been an obvious figure to whom to turn. However, Senior exhibited rarely beyond Burlington House – featuring only once (1901, it is presumed) in the

158. Laura Knight continued to work with children as models in Holland, but in these pictures the figure groups are more closely combined and the effect increasingly patternistic. *The Rocking Horse* (c. 1906) illustrates their location in subtly incorporated details of costume, flooring and painted furniture.

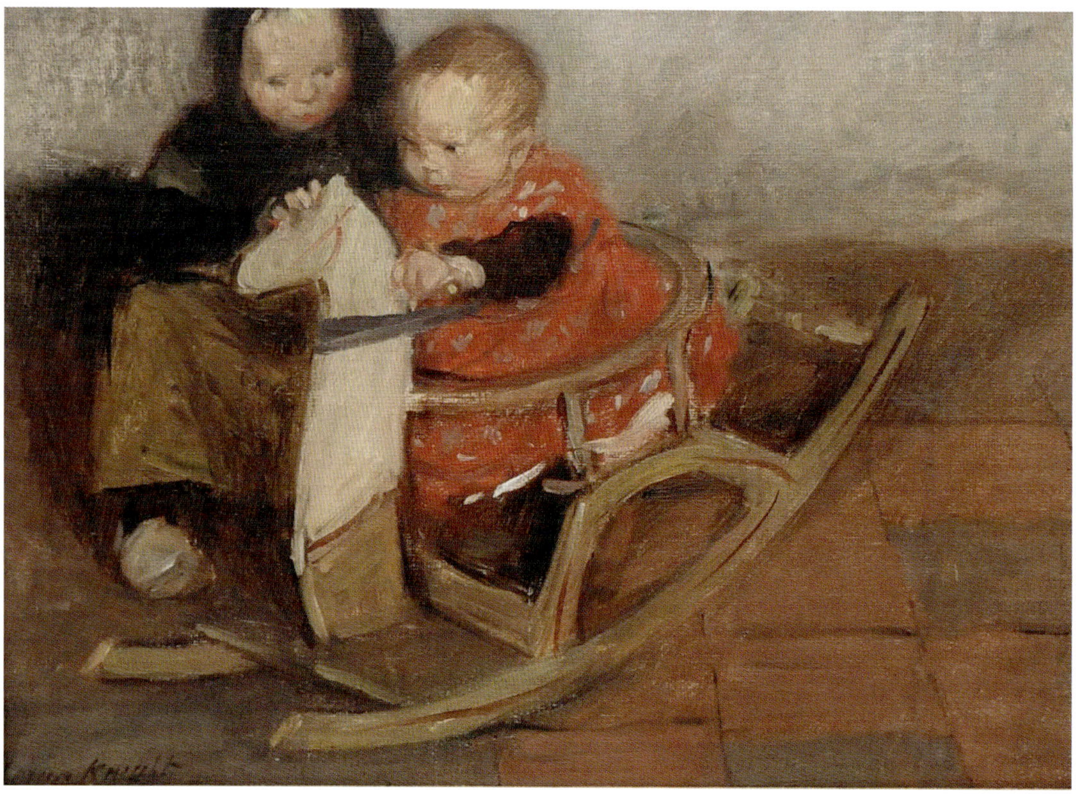

Art Club exhibitions – and it seems hardly ventured to Staithes (if at all).[216] In addition, he was developing his own private pupils in the early 1900s, just at the time the Knights started to spread their wings.

As previously mentioned, Senior came early to Runswick, possibly encouraged by Gilbert Foster. His old studio survives still, identified by the paint smears on the wall, much in the fashion of students in Paris in 1882.

> The walls of the studio are painted a reddish brown… but in many places the monotony of the wall surface is broken by dabs and smears of paint, showing what a convenient receptacle a wall is for the scrapings of one's palette.[217]

He was not one of those who studied abroad, but took regular trips to the continent from 1907– 10 and again in 1919. The work he produced following these, such as his exhibit at the Venice Biennale of 1910, 'affiliated him to the best colourists of the Flemish school', according to a critic writing for *The Studio* in 1916. Another was later to look back on his career and observe:

> He was certainly entitled to the comparatively rare description of a colourist, for there was never a false note in his colour schemes which to the end of his career grew in richness and the prismatic quality sunlight can give.[218]

They also connected him with Frank Brangwyn, George Clausen and Alfred Gilbert, the eminent sculptor. As a consequence Brangywn was responsible for the purchase of two of Senior's works for the collection of Konjo Matsukata, whose plan was to establish a Museum of Western Art in Japan.[219] Senior's connections to other leading painters of the day are mentioned in various sources – among them the oral testimony of his granddaughter, who cites a trip to Walberswick in 1906 with Philip Wilson Steer. The personal gift of a painting as early as 1892 supports the idea of a lengthy friendship between the two men.[220] The pointillism associated with Steer – note the example of Laura Johnson above (**150**) – never presents itself in the work of Senior. Instead, Steer's influence has been described as follows:

> [From Steer] Senior derived the liquid paint stroke found in his small panel sketches which gives the paint surface its own vitality independent of colour.[221]

His generosity of spirit, gregarious nature and boldness of technique seems to have encouraged private pupils. Senior is now well known for his guidance of Gertrude Hudson, whose brother later married one of Senior's daughters, and of Florence Hess. Patrons of Senior, Hess's family came from Leeds, and numerous examples exist of small gifts, purchases and commissions to Florence, her brother and her parents, including the portrait featured in Chapter 4 (**163**).[222]

The two are described as developing a particularly close friendship, which graduated from that of pupil and teacher to assistant, artist, model and companion. She accompanied him on numerous travels, exhibiting prolifically, in contrast to her teacher, and developing a confident, painterly style with obvious similarities to Senior's work.

Her example therefore stands in contrast to that of Laura Knight whose works underpin this chapter. Juxtaposed with those who had the opportunity to influence her work, they illustrate an ongoing search for a personal style which seems to have been as yet unresolved at the time of her departure for Cornwall in 1907.

An exploration rather than a formal assessment, this chapter does, I hope, respond to the circumstances of artists who arrived at different stages of their careers and were subject to ongoing and formative personal and professional relationships throughout their time together. Innovation in this relaxed and spectacular environment was cultivated in different ways, as is clear from the sources. At times it was sparked by conversations, such as those recalled between the Hopwoods, Jacksons and Knights, at others communicated through written description in journals and letters, such as those between Garrido and Crawshaw or Sheppard and Good. Finally there were the social occasions, formal and informal, not previously considered significant enough to have lent identity to the 'colony'. Of these the exhibitions of the Art Club, though relatively short-lived, may have lent a vital focus for as diverse a group as they appear to have been – in an age when there was less public consensus about style than at any point in the previous 100 years.

Opposite: 159. This picture by Laura Knight, currently titled *Friends*, is dated to 1905, like *Dressing the Children* (**155**). It is tempting, however, to link it to the painting *Birdcage*, listed among the exhibits of the 5th Art Club exhibition of the same year. Interestingly, too, it may be pictured in the background of an undated portrait of Laura by Harold Knight in the Nottingham Museums collection.

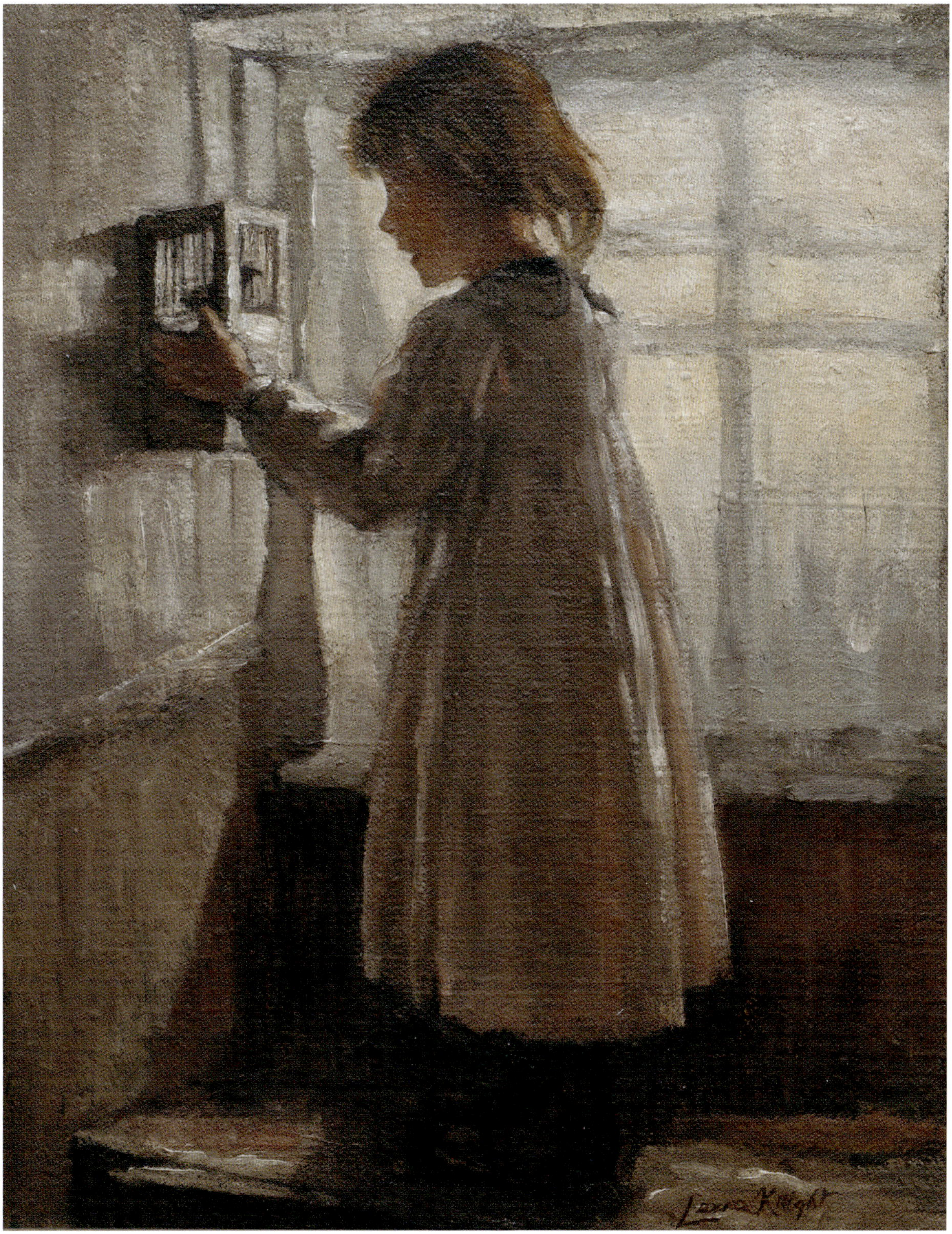

ENDNOTES

147 *Whitby Gazette*, 13 September 1901, 'The Picture Exhibition at Staithes'.
148 *Whitby Gazette*, 18 August 1905, 5th Staithes Art Club Exhiibtion review.
149 From 'The Spacious Firmament' by Joseph Addison (founder of *The Spectator*).
150 These are (in date order): *May*; *A Stormy Day*; *In Summer Time*; *Sunshine and Shade*; *Bad Weather*; *Gathering Potatoes*; *Geese-Study*.
151 Robert Jobling and Isa Thompson, for example, used quotes from Longfellow and Kingsley respectively as titles to two of their works: *The Day is Done and the Darkness falls from the wings of Night* and *Storms be Sudden and Waters Deep*. Laura Johnson painted a series of panels on Tennyson's *Idylls of the King* and Gilbert Foster used a sixteenth-century text for *Be the day weary or be the day long, at last it ringeth to evensong*.
152 Following Jackson's early lead, a group comprising Atkinson, the Joblings, Watson and Hedley all exhibited at the NEAC's Newcastle show in 1893.
153 McConkey in *Pioneering Painters: The Glasgow Boys*, 2010, exh. cat., 102–3.
154 *Whitby Gazette*, 18 August 1905, 5th Staithes Art Club Exhibition review.
155 Leicester Galleries: *In Sunny Places*, 1902, exh. cat., 9, with reference to Fred Mayor.
156 *Pioneering Painters: The Glasgow Boys*, 2010, exh. cat., 103. In his description of the progress of the Glasgow 'school', McConkey describes how the term 'impressionism' came back to haunt the entire group.
157 Thornton, *50 Years of the New English Art Club*, 1935, 3.
158 *The Magazine of Art*, 1882, 'L'atelier Bonnat', 138.
159 The reference to Isa Thompson's time in Paris was included as the briefest of notes in an obituary of 1926, the details of which are reproduced in Millard, J., *A Romance with the North-East: Robert and Isa Jobling*, 1992, 13, n. 3.
160 Becker, R. J. and Weisberg, G. P., *Overcoming All Obstacles: The Women of the Académie Julian,* 1999, exh. cat., 76.
161 Senior was referred to as Clausen's disciple by the critic of the *Yorkshire Post*. In his role of agent Clausen was responsible for placing works by Harold and Laura Knight at Galleries in Cape Town, among others. See Spencer, Gillian, *Mark Senior 1862–1927,* 1983, exh. cat., introduction, 4, n. 1.
162 *The Magazine of Art*, 1891, 'Butler Wood: The Maddocks Collection at Bradford', Parts I and II, 298–306; 337–44. The two works listed by Jackson were *Hayfield* and *Low Tide, Bosham*.
163 *Art History*, vol. 1, no. 3, September 1978: McConkey, *The Bouguereau of the Naturalists: Bastien Lepage and British Art,* 375.
164 Newton, *Cullercoats: A North-East Colony of Artists*, 2003, 104. For detail on bonnets see Doris A. Cleverley in *The Dalesman,* 1950–1, vol. XII, 401–2.
165 Examples include a watercolour of a *Fisherman* hanging at the Pannett Gallery (incorrectly attributed to Mayor's wife Hannah in the museum guide).
166 This excludes the marriage of Joseph Bagshawe to Mildred Turnbull in 1901, as well as the romantic relationships cultivated between Enid Pease Robinson and Ernest Rigg (which resulted in an unsuccessful proposal) and Ernest Dade (who has been confirmed as the object of the diarist's affection known as 'D'). Friedenson married an artist whom he met in Runswick Bay in 1906 and Hopwood, Hill and Garrido all had artist wives.
167 Another notable example of artistic compromise after marriage might be that of Stanhope Forbes's wife Elizabeth.
168 The latter's works *Haymaking* (**122**) and *Blossom* feature a girl in the same pink costume as the child portrayed mending nets in *A Runswick Window*.
169 Far fuller analysis of their work would be needed, but it is interesting to note the letter from Rosie Good which suggests that Laura Johnson tried to work on a portrait of Harold Knight (**137**).
170 *The Art Journal*, 1898, W. Meynell, ' Newlyn', 138.
171 She had spent time with her family in Saint Quentin where she took lessons, but by her own admission was set only to copy prints and newspaper illustrations. Wilson Foster is mentioned in Garstin's article on Harold and Laura Knight, *The Studio*, 1912, vol. 57, 192.
172 He won a two-year scholarship of which he spent 'a year' in Paris until June 1897.
173 Knight, L., *The Magic of a Line*, 1965, 117.
174 Knight, L., *Oil Paint and Grease Paint*, 1936, 80.
175 The *Art Journal,* 1880, 'G. Sheldon: Sketches & Studies II', 105.
176 Davies, Randall (ed.), *Old Watercolour Society's Club*, vol. 2, 53, Cyril Hughes Hartmann: H. S. Hopwood.
177 National Visual Arts Library of Ireland (NIVAL): Special Collections: The Oliver Sheppard Papers. Letter to Rosie Good, 1900.
178 National Gallery of Ireland: Coll. No. 8318. Previously catalogued as *Peasant Girl with Gourds*, the figure is unmistakeably wearing a Staithes bonnet and carrying nets and floats. There are also similarities with some of his sketches.
179 Doris Cleverly in *The Dalesman*, 1950, vol. 12, 401–2. The author recounts that 'Laura Knight, among the many artists who lived in Staithes, always wore a bonnet'.
180 National Visual Arts Library of Ireland (NIVAL): Special Collections: The Oliver Sheppard Papers. Letter to Oliver Sheppard from Rosie Good, 15 September 1899.
181 *Autumn Sunset and October Moonrise* by H. Walker; *Eventide* and *A Summer Evening* by F. Mayor; *Sundown at Runswick Bay* by C. Mackie. *Twilight* was submitted by A. Friedenson to the South Kensington Summer Holiday Competition, 1900.
182 *The Studio*, 1910, vol. 49, 27–33.
183 Davies, Randall (ed.), *Old Watercolour Society's Club*, vol. 2, 55–6, Cyril Hughes Hartmann: H. S. Hopwood.
184 *Lingering Light* was exhibited at the Yorkshire Union of Artists

Show in Hull in 1904; *The Magazine of Art*, 1891, 51–2; *The Studio*, vol. 30, 1904, 155–6.

185 Phillips, *The Staithes Group*, 1993, 87; Knight, L., *The Magic of a Line*, 1965, 117. This was a small, watercolour 'blotter' used for making multiple sketches.

186 Rowland Hill's reminiscences in 1939 do refer to artists' quarrels and differences, though he is definitive that they were 'never washed in public'.

187 National Visual Arts Library of Ireland (NIVAL): Special Collections: The Oliver Sheppard Papers. Letter from Rosie Good to Oliver Sheppard, 18 September 1899. The mutual amusement is extended by the fact that the couple had become engaged, though in secret, and Rosie's mother continued to try and attach Oliver to Cissy.

188 *The Artist*, 1899, vol. 26, 92–5.

189 Mackay, A. E., *Arthur Melville Scottish Impressionist 1855–1904*, 1951, 26. In *Pioneering Painters: The Glasgow Boys*, 2010, 96.

190 This was likely the picture bequeathed to the Hugh Lane Gallery in Dublin (Coll. No. 1750) by their daughter Cathleen Sheppard. Presently it is misattributed to Frank Mayor and bears no title or date, though clearly a North African Market scene and likely to date from 1899.

191 Tom and Rosamund Jordan, *Big Picture Show*, exhib. list, May 2009, no. 149. Phillips: *The Staithes Group*, 1993, 68 (and cover), cat. no. 36.

192 *Art & Architecture (Australia)*, 1908, 77. Report of the Leeds Art Gallery Spring Exhibition.

193 John Atkinson is also mentioned as an etcher, though this was later on his career and perhaps prompted by economic necessity rather than by artistic choice. See Moss, Brian and Rachel, *John Atkinson 1863–1924*, 1981, exh. nos. 67–9. Fred Jackson is also mentioned in a letter of William Brymner, dated November 1884, as buying copper plates and being taught to etch by a Mr Morton, a professional engraver.

194 Guthrie's works were exhibited at the Dowdeswell Galleries in London in 1890.

195 There are works with Amberley as subject matter, but no literary references to a stay there. To date, I have only been able to locate a single example of one of his pastels.

196 *The Magazine of Art*, 1900, 529–36. Laurence Housman, *Edward Stott, Painter of Field and of Twilight.*

197 Jewell, R., *Staithes (Boulby and Dalehouse) Between Two Nabs*, 2013, 188.

198 Views such as that used by Sydney Lee of the bridge or the view of cobles in the beck by Lough Thompson or Robert Jobling; views of fish auctions or fish packing, such as those by Booth or Harold Knight on the staith etc.

199 Sutcliffe's photo entitled *Dorothy Taylor Baiting Lines, Runswick Bay* is a close comparator to Senior's pastel (**147**).

200 Hiley, *Frank Sutcliffe: Photographer of Whitby*, 1974, 68.
Hiley also provides an unattributed quotation to Sutcliffe from 1904: 'I believe that J. F. Millet has shown me more than any others'. *Frank Sutcliffe*, 1974, 81.

201 Hiley, *Frank Sutcliffe*, 1974, 67, n. 4.

202 Hiley, Frank Sutcliffe, 1974, 73, n. 16; *Yorkshire Weekly Post*, 23 March 1912.

203 Knight, L., *Oil Paint and Grease Paint*, 1936, 81. See also Knight, *Magic of a Line*, 1965, 110–11.

204 Hart, J. (ed.), *The Secret Staithes Diary of Enid Lucy Pease Robinson*, 2010, 64 (entry for 23 August 1901).

205 Knight, L., *Oil Paint and Grease Paint*, 1936. 87.

206 *The Artist*, 1900, vol. 28, 193, Reviews of the Art Centres.

207 Knight, L., *Oil Paint and Grease Paint*, 1936, 87–9.

208 Phillips, *The Staithes Group*, 1993. 25.

209 Darling was the senior figure in the colony at Laren to which the Knights migrated. His knowledge of Dutch masters was profound, but his painting uninspiring.

210 It is interesting to read correspondingly of Mackie's own development in this respect, as he increasingly assumed 'a disposition to express his personal and immediate impressions of reality', rather than remain wedded to the system he had espoused to her. See James Caw in Newton, *Painting at the Edge: British Coastal Art Colonies 1880–1930*, 2005, 107.

211 Jean Drucker was Dutch by birth, but became a naturalised British citizen. He lived in London and was married to an English woman. Works from Drucker'ss collection were loaned to the Rijksmuseum from 1903. They were installed in a specially decorated room from 1904 and then in a purpose built extension from 1909. He subsequently donated works to the Rijksmuseum and to the National Gallery, London.

212 Qiugley, J., *L. R. Garrido: His Life and Art*, 1913, 35–6. Crawshaw subsequently credited this, Garrido's first visit to Holland, as the turning point in his use of a much fuller colour palette.

213 Newton, *Cullercoats: A North-East Colony of Artists*, 2003, 20.

214 Walker Galleries: *J. R. Bagshawe*, Harrogate 1983, exh. nos. 47 and 49, with Dutch subjects. Private collection: a notebook belonging to Bagshawe has coastal sketches, administration lists and the names of both artists. See also Frank: *Sea Painter: The Life and Work of J. R. Bagshawe*, 2010, 69 (caption to pl. 49) and 71.

215 Phillips, *The Staithes Group*, 1993, 24. Letter from family of F. S. Richardson to Dr P. Phillips, April 1988.

216 Senior is listed as a proposed member in the original MS notes surrounding the Club's establishment. He figures in none of the exhibitions from 1902 onwards and, without an exhibit list for 1901, we must assume that this is the only time he may have exhibited.

217 *The Magazine of Art*, 1882, Barclay Day, *L'Atelier Bonnat*, 139.

218 *Batley Reporter*, 8 January 1927. Quoted in the Introduction to Spencer, *Mark Senior 1862–1927*, exh. cat., 1983.

219 Matsukata's huge collections now form a part of the collections of the Tokyo National Museum (Japanese prints) and the National Museum of Western Art (also in Tokyo).

220 Parkin, *Mark Senior*, 1974, exh. no. 69.

221 See introduction to Spencer, *Mark Senior 1862–1927*, exh. cat., 1983.

222 At time of writing, a group of pictures with just such inscriptions has come to auction. The group belonged to the Hess's housekeeper, Doris Bilbrough (née Sykes), and was sold at Tennant's Auctioneers, 12 July 2025.

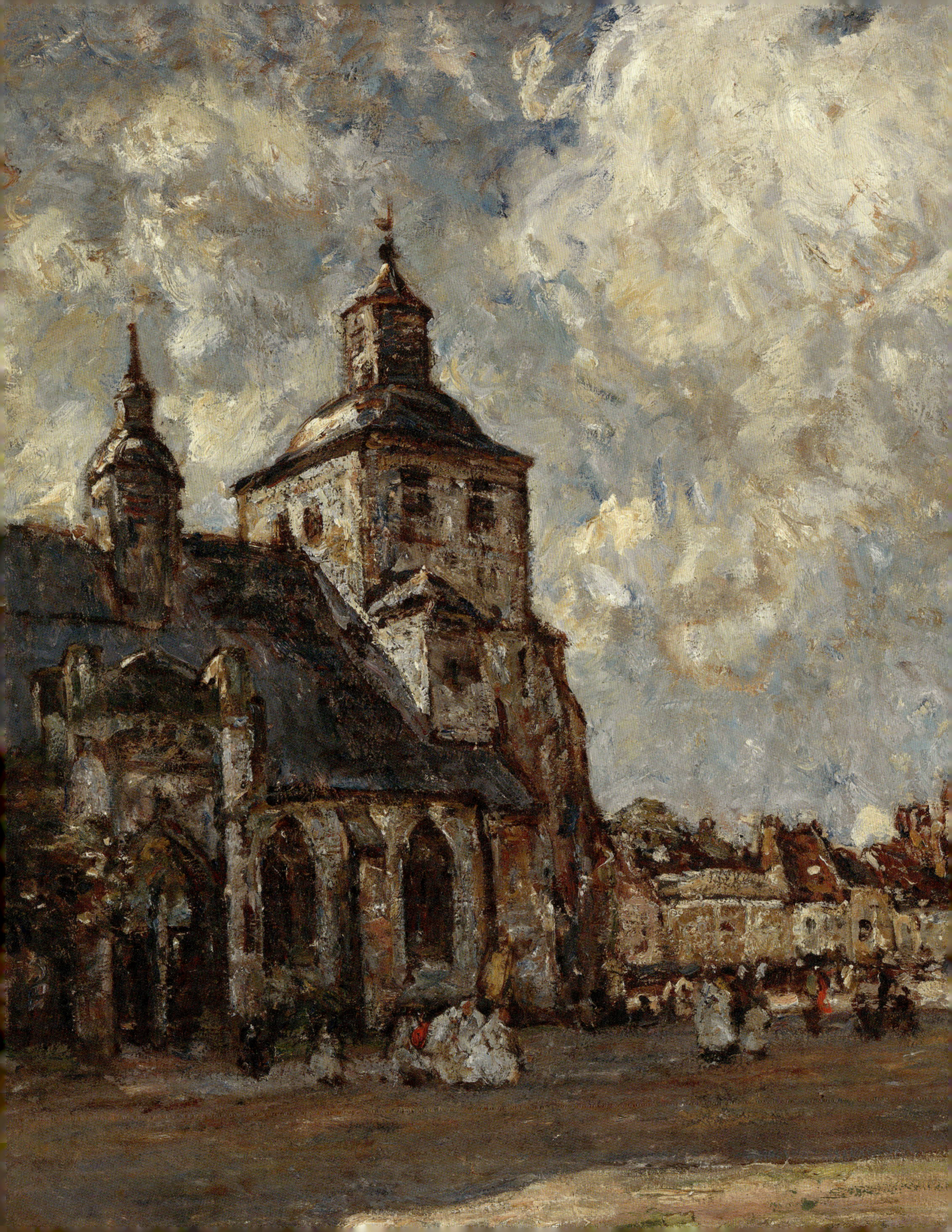

CHAPTER 4
LANDSCAPE

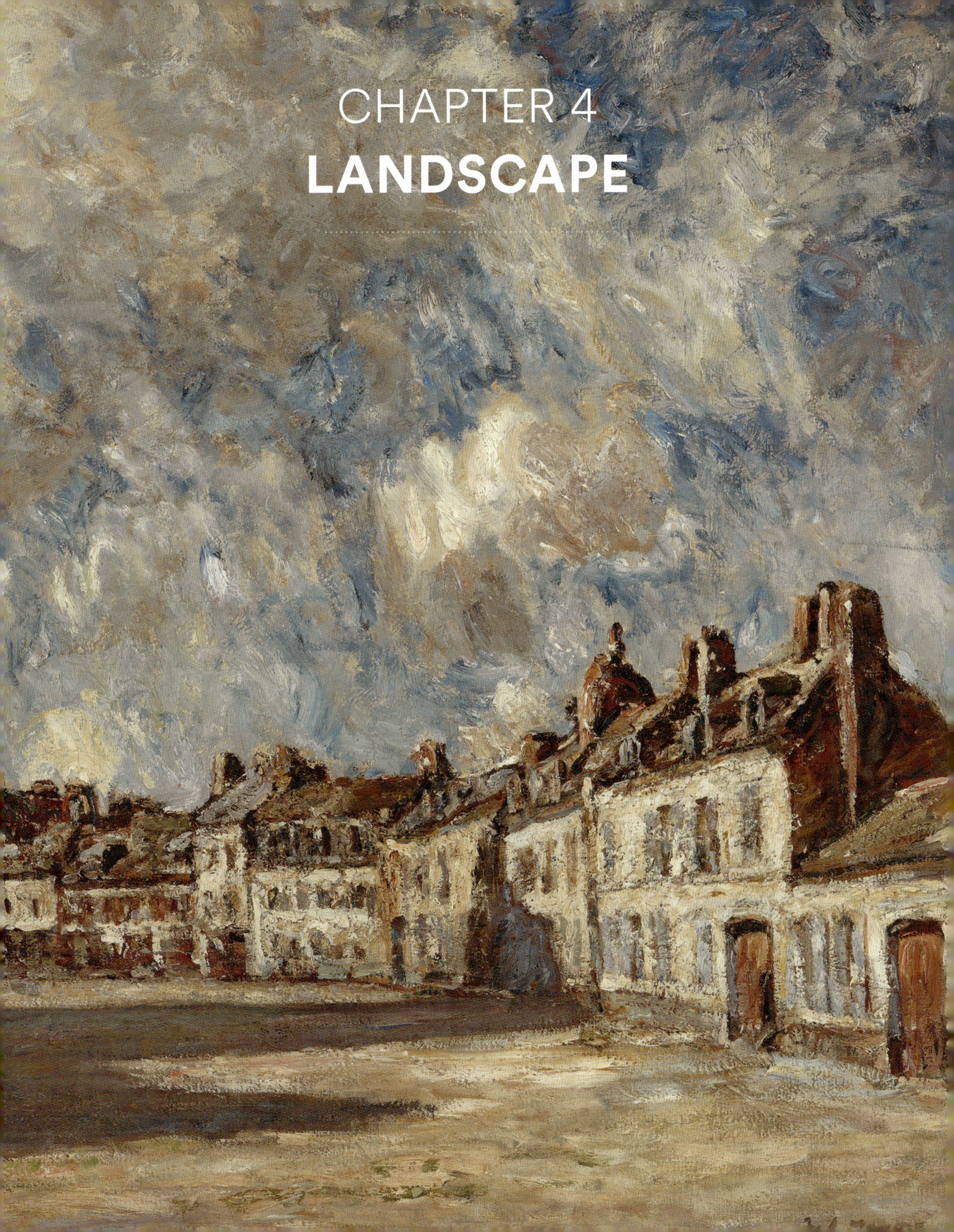

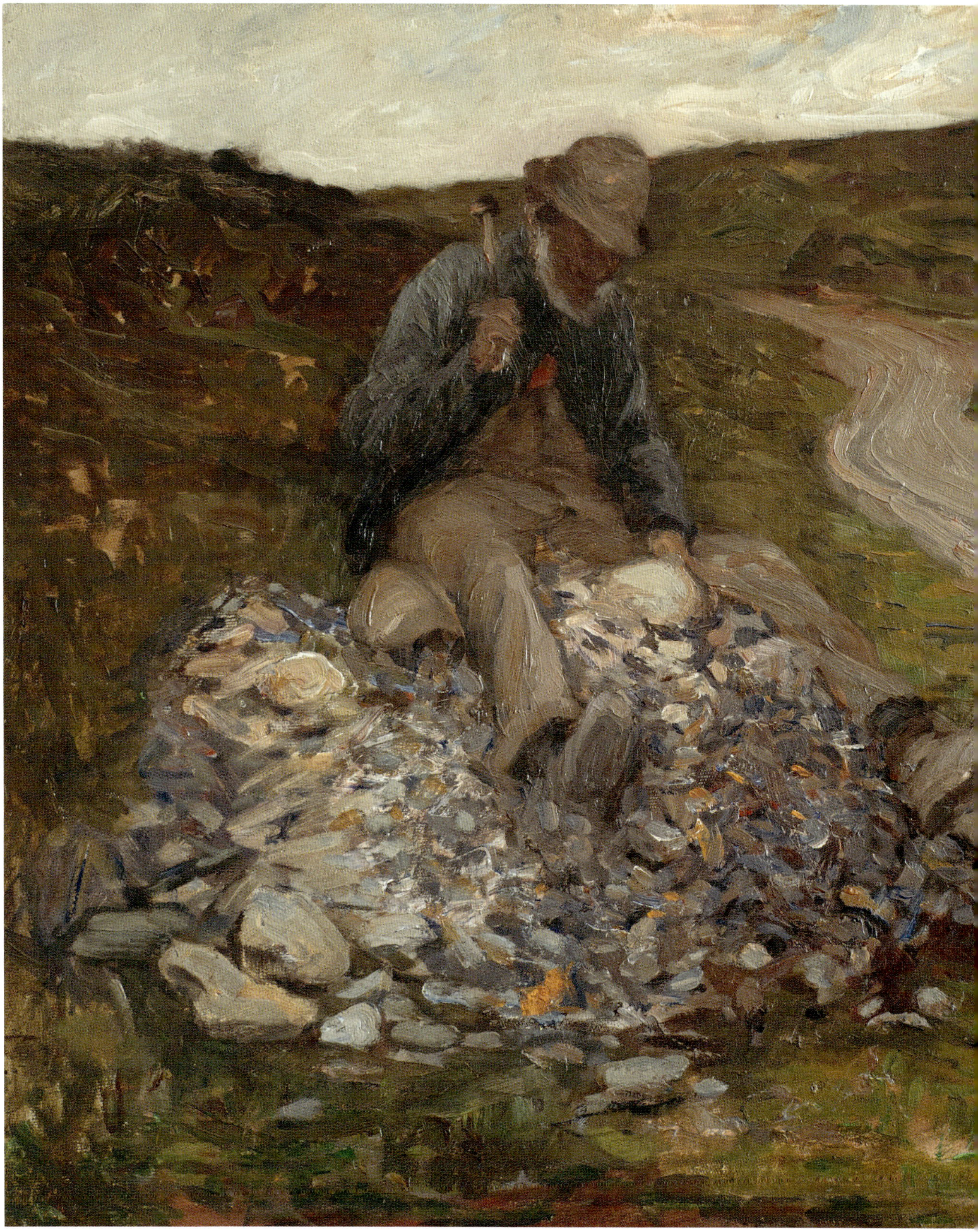

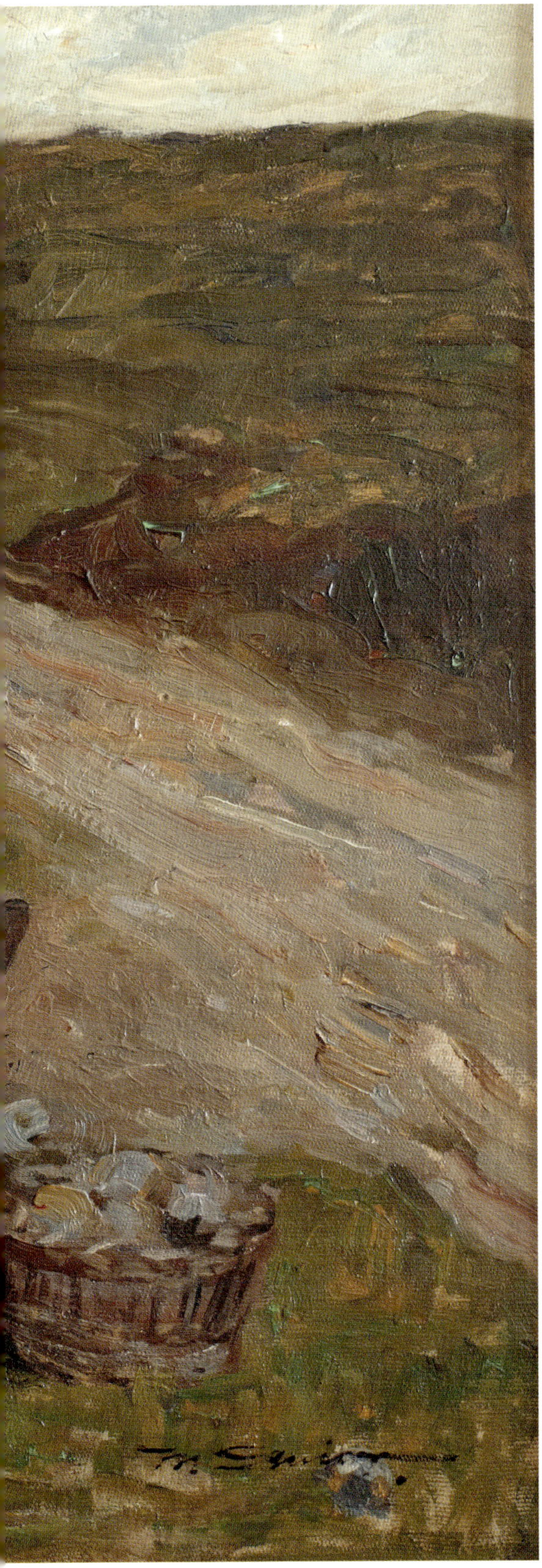

Previous spread: 160. After their elopement in 1902 Fred and Hannah Mayor made the fortified town of Montreuil in the Pas-de-Calais home; their house was close to the *Place de L'Église Sainte-Saulve*, illustrated here (c. 1905). The town surveyed the surrounding countryside all the way to the coast at Étaples and Le Touquet. Artists' colonies in both towns welcomed several of the Staithes artists during their time there.

161. Mark Senior's undated oil *The Stonebreaker,* like *Homecoming* (Lotherton Hall, Leeds), is an example of his connection to the work of George Clausen and the renewal of the landscape tradition in England at the turn of the century. Here the figure dominates the composition rather than, as so often, acting as just one element of the whole.

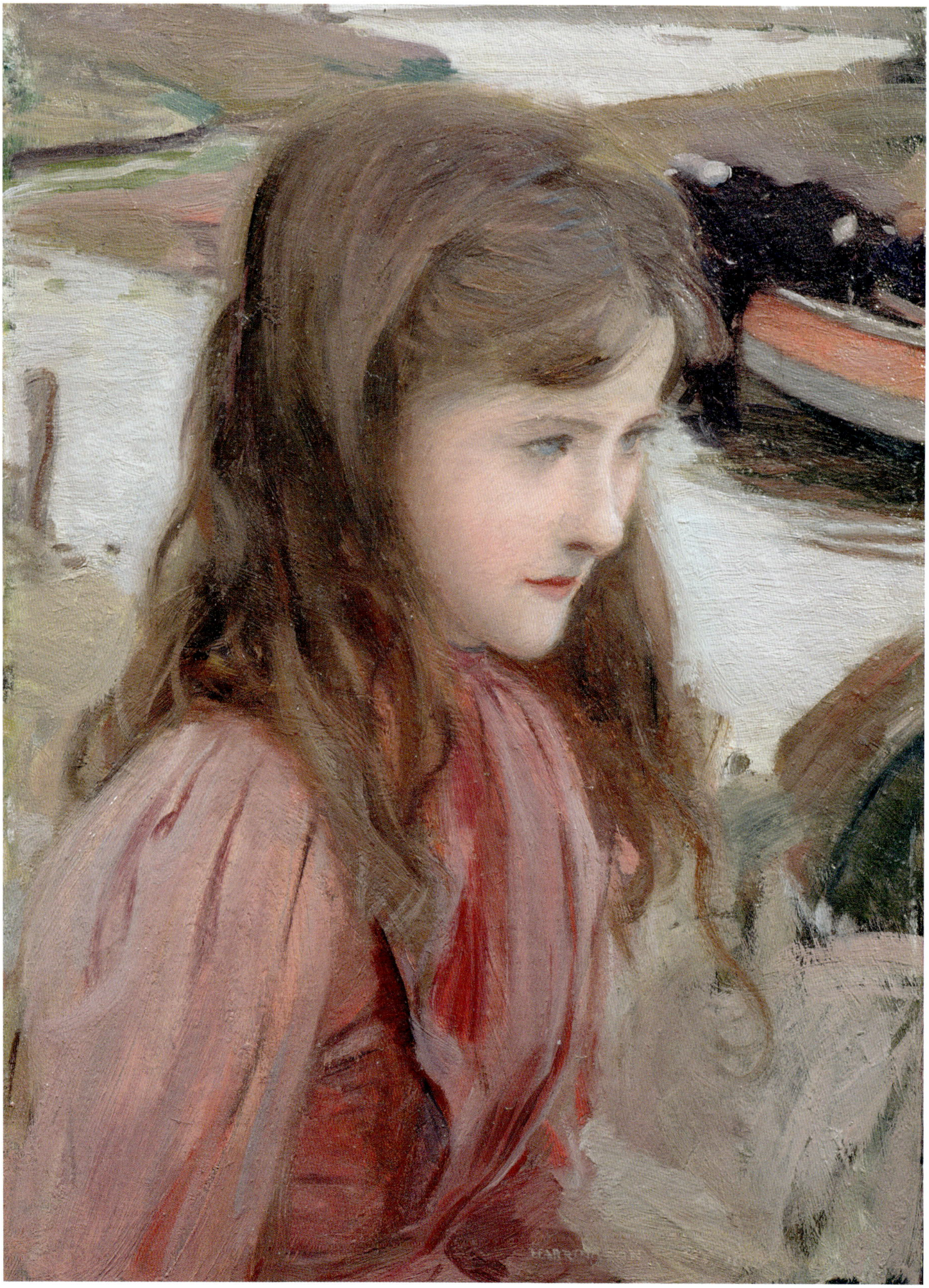

CHAPTER 4
LANDSCAPE

> Portrait painting may bring the dollars, but this – notwithstanding the temptations – does not succeed in alluring him from his true and only line – land and seascapes … and he flies away from his Manchester friends … to gain hope and inspiration on the shores of the Adriatic or at his cottage by the North Sea.[223]

The Society of Portrait Painters, founded in 1891, reflected the new priorities of the art market at the end of the nineteenth century. The increased status of the portrait genre affected the whole range of artists, from the most fashionable painters such as John Singer Sargent – who seemingly had not time even to dine, so great was his weekly waiting list – to many of the Staithes artists. This excerpt, from a review of the 3rd Staithes Art Club exhibition, reiterates the significant money to be made in portraiture. It is supported by ample evidence that the painters of the north-east coast responded to the demand.

Laura Knight recalls that her marriage to Harold took place near Nottingham after he had left Staithes to answer a commission in the city. The letters of Rosie Good recount the news that admiration for a recently completed example of his work (on view at her family home there) promptly resulted in another. Fred Jackson, about whom the excerpt above was written, regularly painted the aldermen of Oldham and the surrounding area, as the collections of the Art Gallery there still testify. Mark Senior, whose early training was based in the studio of a portraitist, painted friends such as Edward Caldwell Spruce, as well as patrons such as Sam Wilson and his wife. From the 1890s Harrington Mann is said to have only exhibited portraits at major exhibitions, signalling a

Opposite: 162. *Study of a Young Girl*, painted by Harrington Mann in 1898, hints at Staithes as its location with the beck and coble as context. The year before producing this work Mann was commended in *The Artist*, vol. XX, 368 for achieving a 'distinct and original success mainly by reason of a spirit of absolute naivete in harmony with the subject'.

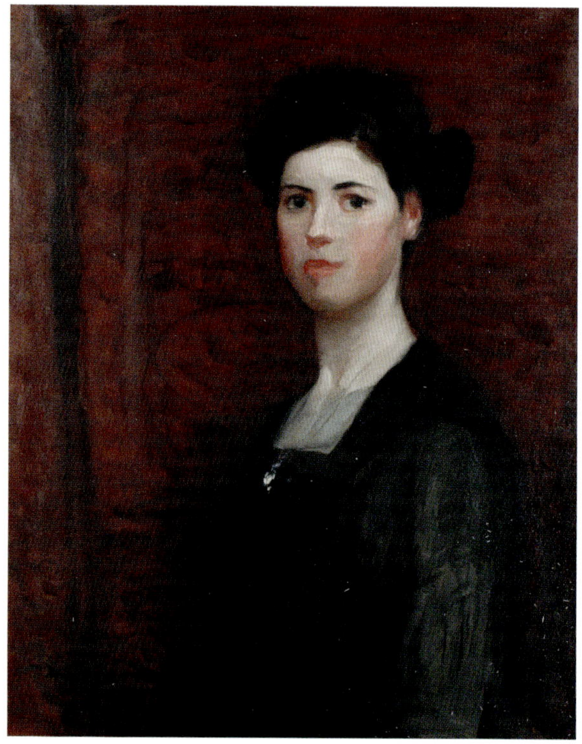

163. Florence Hess began lessons with Mark Senior in 1905 and a similar portrait to this was commissioned by her parents in 1911. This image, of unknown date, proves a contrast, with a richly coloured backdrop and the sitter in black, her hair more tightly coiffed.

burgeoning transatlantic career which developed to capitalise on the demands of his sitters. Even the few pictures recognisably painted at Staithes often include portrait studies. Leandro Garrido discusses the demands that his clients made on his time in correspondence with both Joseph Terry and Lionel Crawshaw – citing these as the reason for his lack of available work to submit for exhibition.[224]

Such portraiture, it appears, was not for the most part the result of time spent in Staithes and Runswick Bay. On the contrary, working in these quieter settings rather provided a break from the steady stream of commissions, putting a welcome distance between artist and client.

The Whitby photographer Frank Sutcliffe was similarly hard-pressed by the demand for likenesses. However, the seasonal demand at the coast did not allow him to quit the area, and so he sought the necessary respite early in the morning or late in the day:

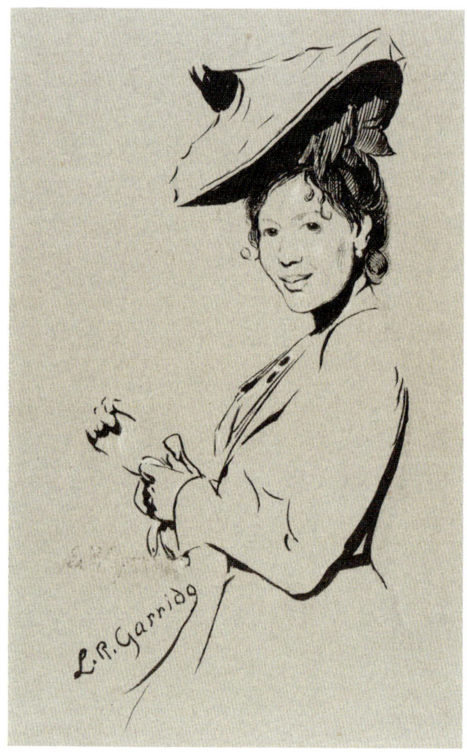

164. Mme Palezna, a pupil in Montreuil in 1901, was forced by the limited studio lighting to stand close to Leandro Garrido, who was unable to retreat for lack of space. This immediacy, exaggerated by very few sittings, prompted a very striking portrait now in the Glasgow Museums. *La Dame aux Gants* is a preparatory sketch.

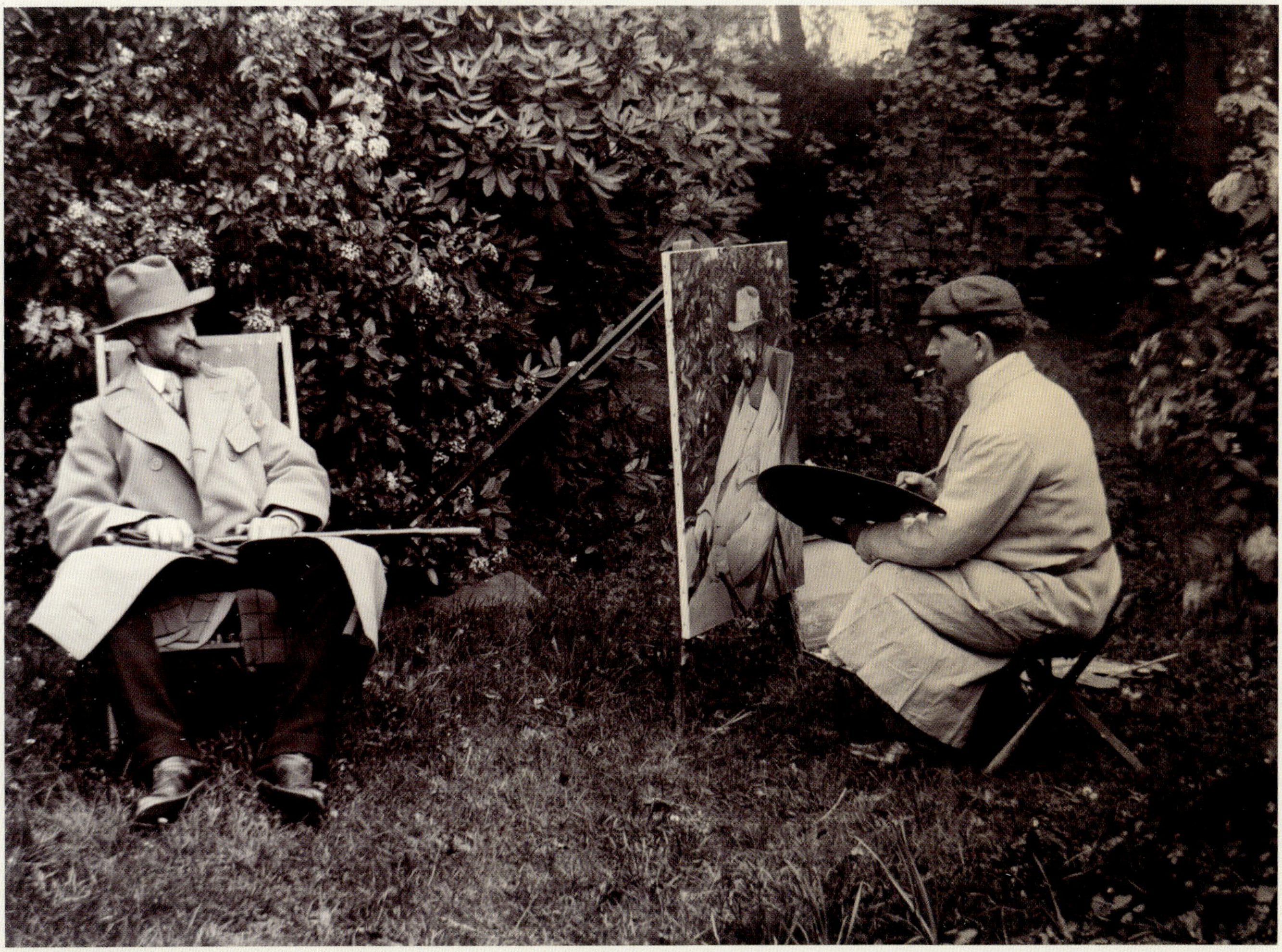

165. This previously unseen image of Ernest Rigg painting lends much authenticity to Enid Pease Robinson's sketch of him, reproduced in her *Secret Staithes Diary*. This photograph, dating from around 1920, possesses an additional sense of humour, given the sitter's fierce expression and the proximity of the artist.

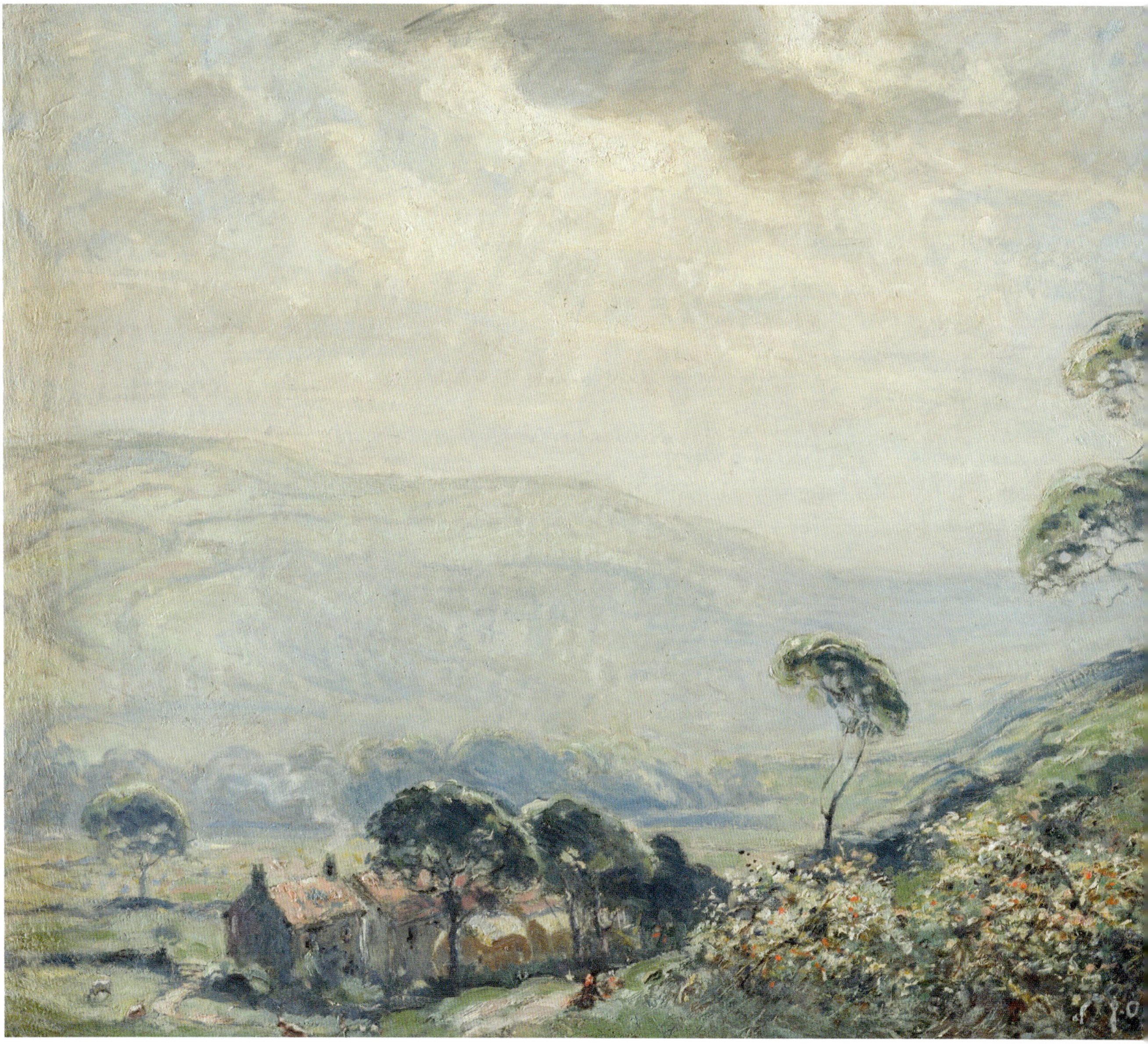

166. Joseph Terry lived in Sleights, a beautifully situated village right under the moors, and the inspiration for *Underhill Farm, Sleights*, painted around 1920. Garrido joined him there in 1906 for 18 months, having been persuaded by Crawshaw. The men became such firm friends that on leaving Garrido wrote: 'had all else been unpleasant, making such a good friend as yourself would in itself be enough to have made it … memorable'.

> Nature demands an open mind, one free from the cares and worries of this restless world.[225]

Jackson too, whether writing for an audience or in private conversation, always maintained that Nature was his greatest teacher, reaffirming the ethos of his student days.

The traditions of landscape had been open to all the Staithes painters as part of their training. Arthur Friedenson, for instance, had the option of attending specific landscape classes as well as 'Natuur' and 'Antiek' in Antwerp. However, the grandeur and drama of earlier landscape vistas was increasingly replaced by more intimate local views. The Staithes artists responded to the zeitgeist, focusing on the simplicity of everyday rural scenes and the unadorned lives of their inhabitants.

The French influence, so prevalent for many of the earlier Art Club members, continued to be emphasised by those such as George Clausen. He urged his fellow artists to resist following convention in regard to landscape. A willingness to forsake romantic ruins, such as those of Mulgrave Castle, or picturesque historic buildings followed the example of other colonies, such as that at Cockburnspath in the Scottish Borders. There artists for the most part ignored the village's ancient church and historic aspect.[226]

Romanticism or spirituality might be exemplified in other ways, drawing upon other influences. Edward Stott infused just such a spirit into his pictures of the Sussex village Amberley, surrounded by the rolling South Downs and the Weald, echoing the semi-religious tradition of Samuel Palmer's work.

Fred Mayor was a one-time resident there and Jackson owned examples of Stott's paintings. He was acquainted with the artist's work through his Sussex-based travel companion James Charles, who knew Stott well. However, the closest examples to Stott's work are probably Harold Knight's images of Holland. In these, though interiors rather than landscapes, light is used to convey suspense, rendering timeless moments (**156**). Neil Walker describes his tableaux as verging on the religious: spiritual icons of peasant life.

Despite exhibiting almost the complete opposite to Stott's golden hues and soft colours, the Scottish artists who retreated from the busy industrial life of cities such as Glasgow conjured an equivalent presence from the bleak landscape of Scotland's east coast. The mainstay of this group, James Guthrie, stayed in Cockburnspath throughout the year, with many of his finest paintings depicting scenes from the autumn and winter months.

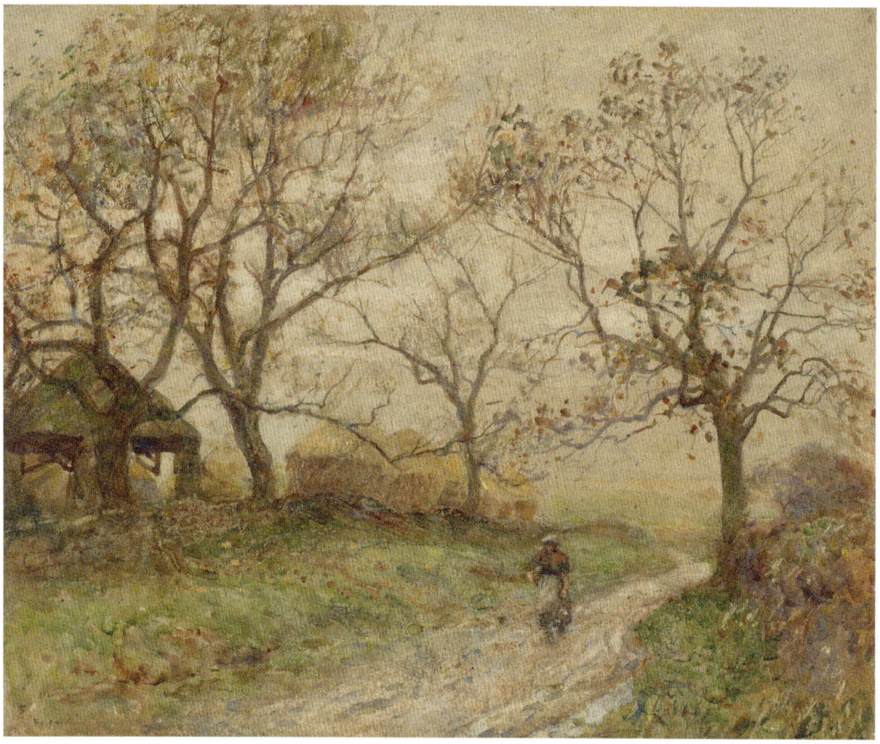

167. *The Wheelhouse, Ellerby*, an undated watercolour by Fred W. Jackson, pictures the lane going past farm buildings at the top of Ellerby Bank. Described at least in one source as 'The Wheelhouse', the particular form of this building features in many of the Staithes artists' work.

THE CHALLENGES OF WINTER

The Yorkshire countryside inland from Staithes and Runswick bore a similar, rather stereotypical reputation for bleakness. Artists who remained in the area, bucking the seasonal trend of retreating to urban bases, sought inspiration from a landscape punctuated only by isolated farmsteads or tiny hamlets such as Roxby, Borrowby and Mickleby on the gentle incline from coast to moorland plateau. For the artists, the seasonal changes were consequently wild and unspoiled. Fogs and sea-frets, with their low-tones, provided atmospheric opportunities which might be accentuated by the few – often distinct – architectural forms such as the mill in Hopwood's *January* or the curiously named 'Wheel-house' depicted in Jackson's *The Wheelhouse, Ellerby*.

A fair degree of stoicism was required by the artists who remained in the area 'out of season'. Their contemporary Norman Garstin observed ruefully that no work could be considered good 'until you have caught a cold doing it', and the painters' many recollections, or evocative titles such as Paul Paul's *Cold and Grey, a Beastly Day*, stand testament to the hardship of their task.

Florence Hess insisted on the intensity of Senior's focus on his work no matter his surroundings in her conversations with Michael Parkin, while Laura Knight's well-worn literary description of Jackson bears out his commitment:

> He painted out of doors in any weather. Under the mittens he wore, his hands were swollen, stiff and chapped, as were the edges of his ears and the wings of his nostrils.[227]

Knight's own lifestyle was relatively spartan, according to her friend Rosie Good. She observed how:

> It takes to raining in the afternoons though we have lovely mornings, and I have taken to rising at seven o'clock and going for a walk on the cliffs with Laura after her bathe. I dare not go bathing as the weather is too fearfully cold.[228]

A winter walk to the station in the bitter cold is retold by Laura's sister Cissie in a letter to Rosie:

> A very stormy walk to the station from Roxby in the snow. Across the pasture, Laura said, the snow made one side of Harold's face bleed, the wind blew with such force.[229]

The artist Owen Bowen installed a stove in the caravan he had adapted, to keep warm in the winter.[230] Rowland Hill remembered Charles Mackie similarly owning 'something like a chestnut seller's stove'. Mackie took it to the beach where he painted, using it to keep his hands warm in the freezing weather and 'for drying his watercolours when there was a lot of moisture about'.[231] Hill himself painted Ellerby in all seasons. Several of his cheerily colourful winter works belie the challenges that the artist faced:

> Our 6ft canvases would be tethered by large stones and we would sit painting away in a cold wind, with as many clothes on as it was possible to wear.

John Atkinson's daughter recollects her father's ability and energy to paint all day, 'even up to his knees in snow'. [232] Frank Sutcliffe noted that his moustache and eyebrows sometimes froze to his focusing screen when he was taking pictures in harsh winter weather.

Although unrelenting in their commitment to working *en plein air*, the cold drove even the hardiest indoors at certain points. As Laura Knight wrote in November 1903:

> I gave up working up here [Mrs Bowman's farm] a month ago; it was so wet and windy I got chilblains all over my feet. Since then, I have worked down in Staithes...[233]

Not all the Staithes artists endured such conditions, or at least not every winter. By the time Knight wrote her letter to Good, Senior had already retreated from Runswick Bay to Leeds, to improve and work up the plentiful summer and autumn sketches by memory.[234]

Charles Mackie admitted as much to the Gallery at Leeds after it purchased a work from him. In responding to questions on the exact location of the windmill pictured, he confessed that he had not painted one particular windmill, but rather created a scene from memory.[235]

It seems too that local studios did not always protect their inhabitants from the winter weather. Leandro Garrido's biographer recounted a fortunate escape for the artist and his friends:

> Mr Terry speaks of a night of a terrible storm at Whitby. Rain fell heavily and came through the roof into the room where they were at work, while a raging wind howled outside and threatened to carry away the building.[236]

Such winter storms could sometimes pose rather more direct threats than ongoing damp and cold. In the May 1903 edition of *Amateur Photographer* magazine, Frank Sutcliffe vividly described his experience of trying to capture such a storm's effects:

> In a gale of wind one man can do nothing with a camera; even in a sheltered corner one [extra] man is wanted to hold onto the legs.

Sutcliffe went on to give an example of just such an occasion, when he was forced to crawl on all fours and enlist a passer-by to secure the tripod.[237] He continues:

> But worse than the force of the wind is its keenness. On our coast we only get rough seas when the wind is north-easterly. I have felt the wind go through my coat and cut my arm like a knife ... Sometimes, after waiting for a gleam of light for half an hour, the photographer finds his hands so benumbed that he has lost the power of using them....[238]

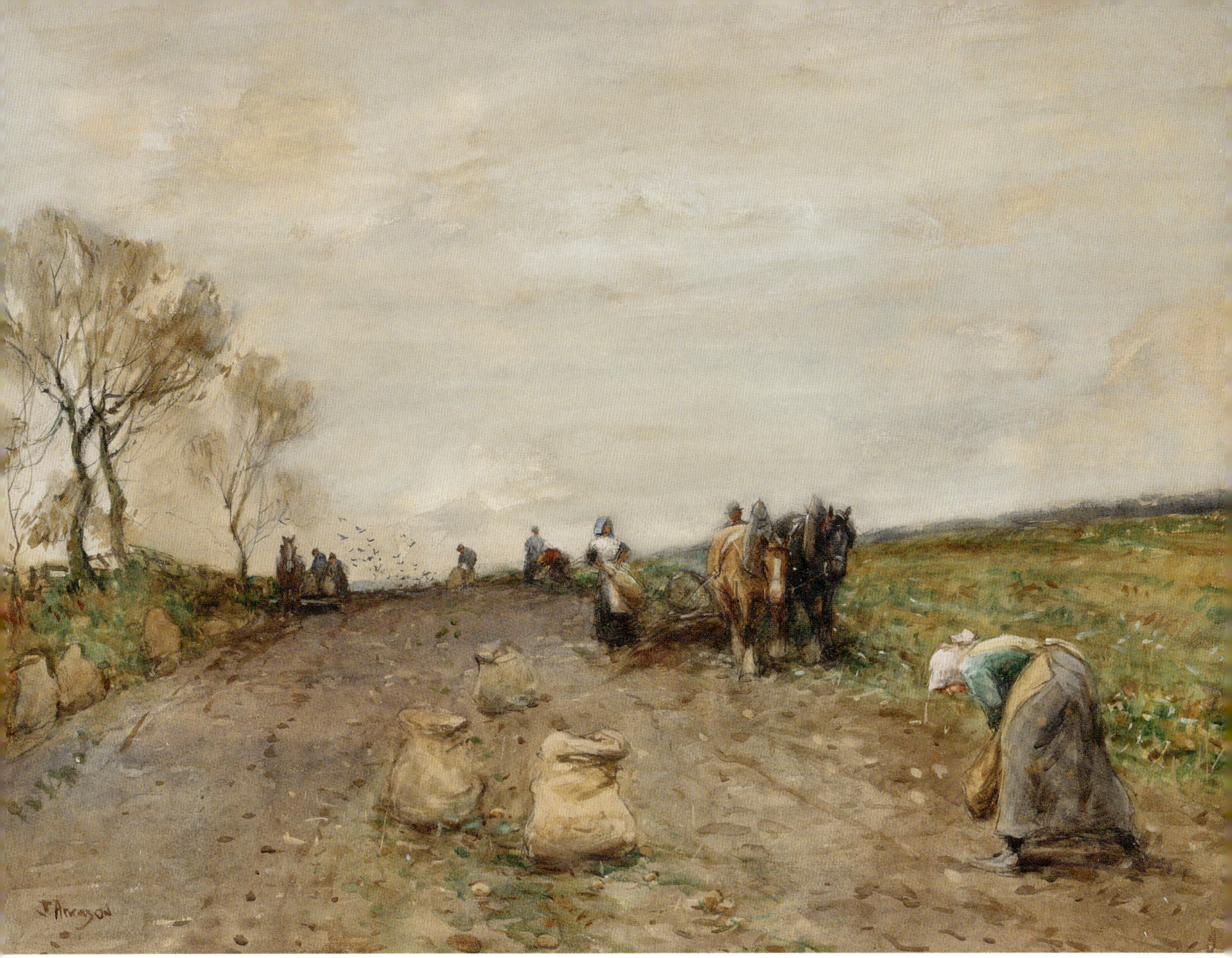

168. John Atkinson's watercolours, such as his undated *Potato Pickers*, were painted in and around Glaisdale for almost a decade at the turn of the century. He captured all aspects of rural life in villages inland from the coast, no matter the weather, and insisted on a special pocket in his suit to protect his sketchbook.

Indeed, he actually decries the relative ease with which he thought the painter might effect a storm scene, conjuring figures in the forefront of his design when in reality 'the black mass of humanity [is] sheltering as much as possible out of the wind' and portraying towering waves, even though '[when] ... the wind is at its worst, the sea is flattened and lacking in drama'.[239]

Indeed, relatively few pictures by the Staithes artists do seem to focus on winter storms, or even on the sort of spectacular summer weather described by Enid Pease Robinson:

> A gloriously fine day with tremendously strong wind, and a splendid sea, – the waves dashing quite over the houses in the coast-guards yard, – about 30 ft high.[240]

Anticipation of brooding weather was a popular feature, however. Jackson, as an example, was prone to titles such as *The Coming Storm*, while a work such as *Rough Sea at Staithes* is a rare view.[241] Storm scenes such as those by Harold Knight, Mayor or Frank Mason focus on the human activity of the staith, beach or pier without introducing the seascape beyond. Exhibitions do, of course, list other works by Art Club members bearing titles such as *In the roar of the sea*, *Wild weather* and *Noreaster;* suggestive as they are, a survey of extant works – yet to be undertaken – would perhaps provide further evidence in this regard.[242]

Notwithstanding the challenges, the winter atmosphere was clearly tantalising to artists and photographers. Sutcliffe was clear that when snow or frost transformed the landscape, he was eager to be out and about:

> How many pairs of new boots have we spoiled, how many weeks have we spent in bed, how many plates have we spoiled over snow scenes.

Below left: 169. An unusual picture format for Arthur Friedenson, *End of Day* projects horse and man as more dominant features of the landscape than is the hallmark of his work. In this undated work the pale sky of dusk is echoed in the light cast on to the man's face by the burning tobacco of his pipe or cigarette.

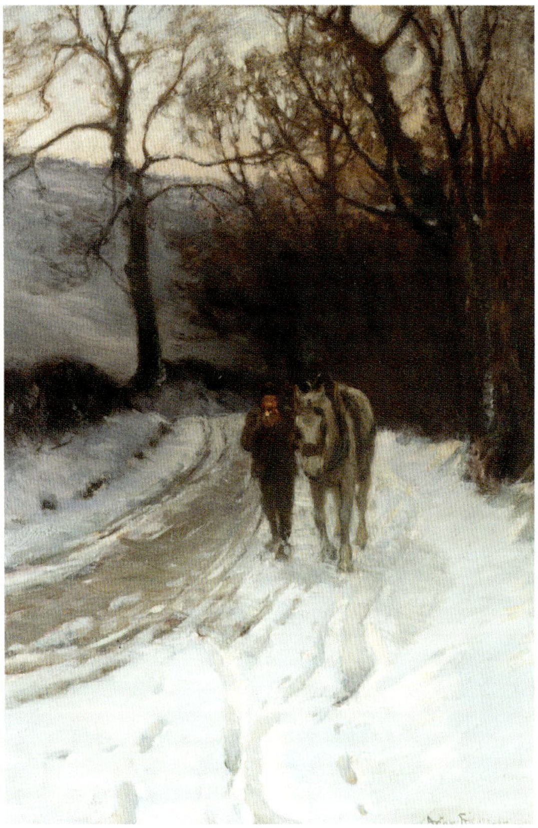

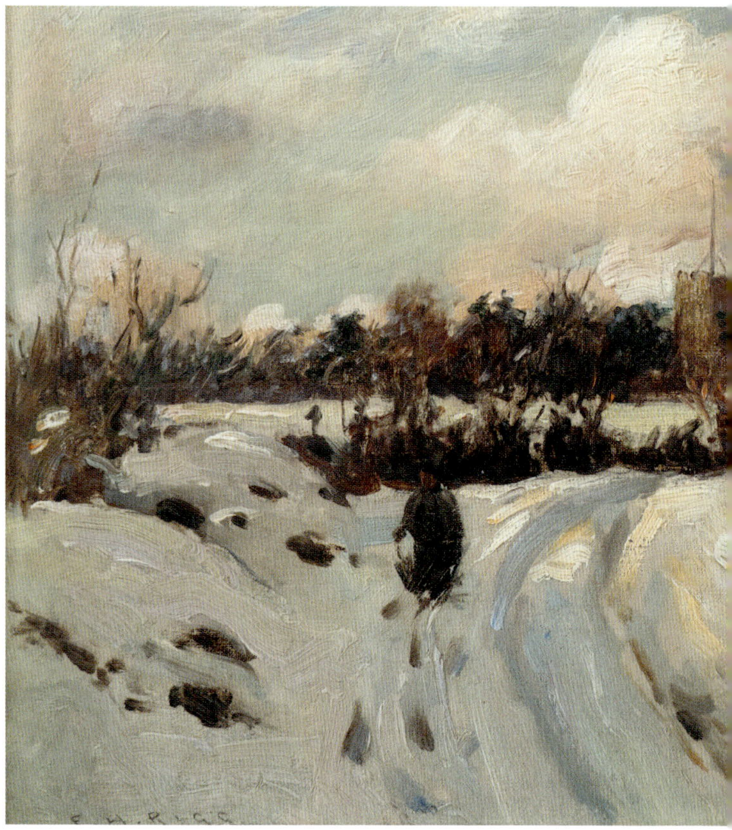

Right: 170. In *Stormy Weather, Staithes*, Richardson's subtle watercolour technique conveys the bleakness of a winter storm. Penny Nab appears faint in the mist, complemented by the sweep of smoke from the chimney, wheeling seagulls, creamy water on the beck and the wind whipping the clothes of those crossing on the bridge. He did exhibit a work entitled *Signs of Storm, Staithes* at the 6th Annual Art Club exhibition.

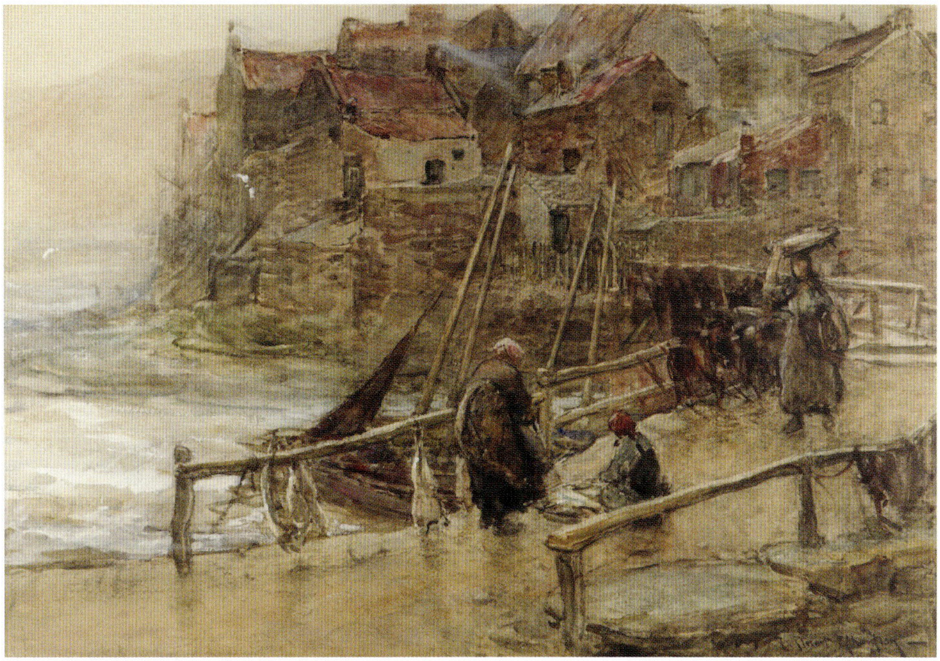

Below: 171. The artist Ernest Rigg experienced plenty of winter weather in Swaledale, one of the most northerly of the Yorkshire dales, to which he moved from Runswick Bay. His winter paintings there are matched in quality by *Snow in Hinderwell*; Rigg's use of colour introduces a wonderful luminescence to the winter landscape.

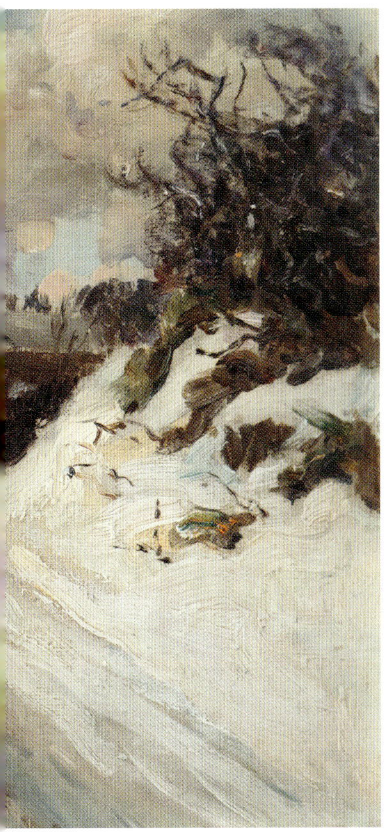

Although this apparently came at a cost; he wrote caustically under one negative: 'Don't do any more snow scenes: nobody buys them!'[243]

The most prominent painter of snow scenes of the Art Club members may perhaps have been Ernest Rigg. The preponderance of his extant work features the surroundings of Swaledale, west of Richmond, where he settled after the First World War.

As with the changing effects of dawn, dusk and moonlight, Rigg draws out subtleties of colouring and a refined rendering of tone that surpass some of his work from other seasons. So too Arthur Friedenson. In *End of Day*, a work of atypically portrait format, he combines the contrasting natural light of dusk with the artificial light of a cigarette or pipe, all within the black and white tones of the snowy landscape.

Mayor, who painted various village street and countryside scenes around Hinderwell, was another Staithes artist who exploited these effects. Examples of further works to do this include Bagshawe's *Back from the Hunt*, Senior's *Winter in Runswick* and Paul's low-toned, untitled scene of rough seas below Lady Palmer's cottage, *Runswick Bay*. John Atkinson completed a seasonal cycle of ploughing and market day pictures, with specifically titled winter scenes.[244]

As if the Yorkshire cold were not enough, in 1913–14 Fred Jackson set out for Russia. There he painted *en plein air* in springtime temperatures that must have been well below those of winter in Britain. Jackson's trip is well

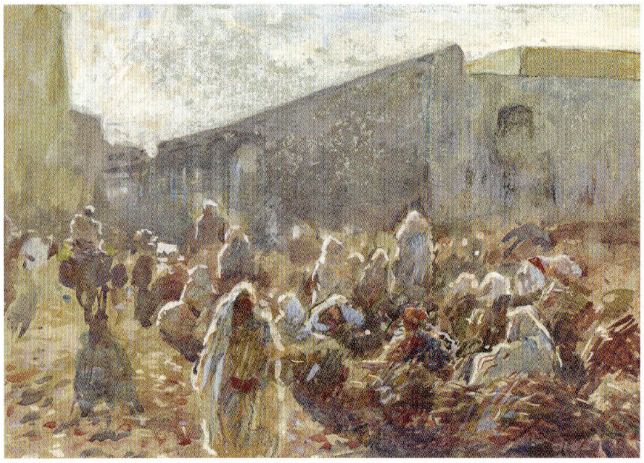

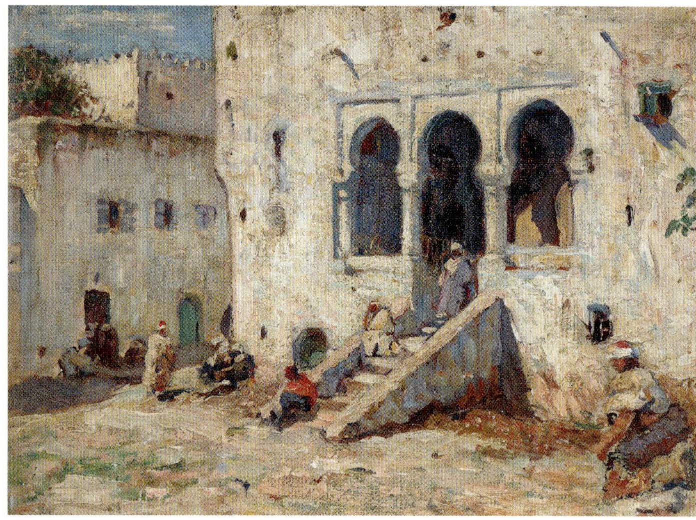

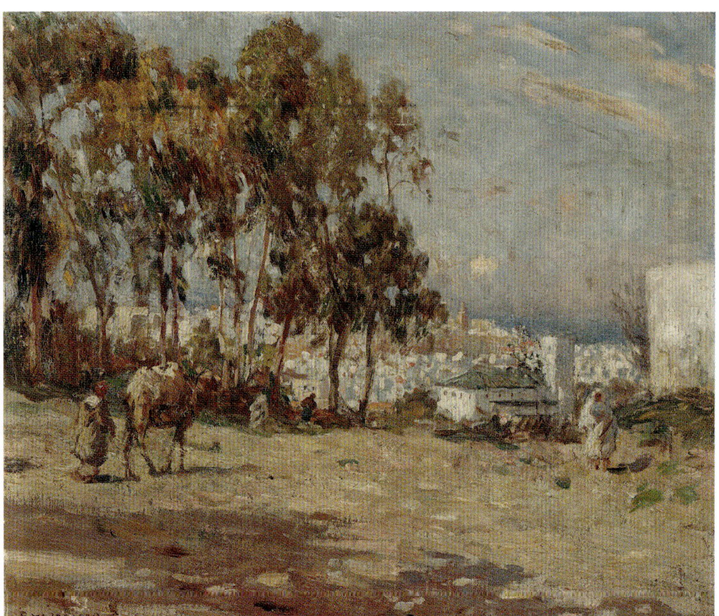

172. Jackson's oil sketches and watercolours are here taken from his trips to North Africa and Russia. He spent time in and around both Moscow and Tangier, evidently exploring the dramatic light effects of the contrasting climates.

Specific details and/or titles are difficult to link to titled works that he exhibited, but the two works above likely portray the charcoal stick market and treasury in the Kasbah of Tangier. *Spring in Russia* is opposite, bottom left.

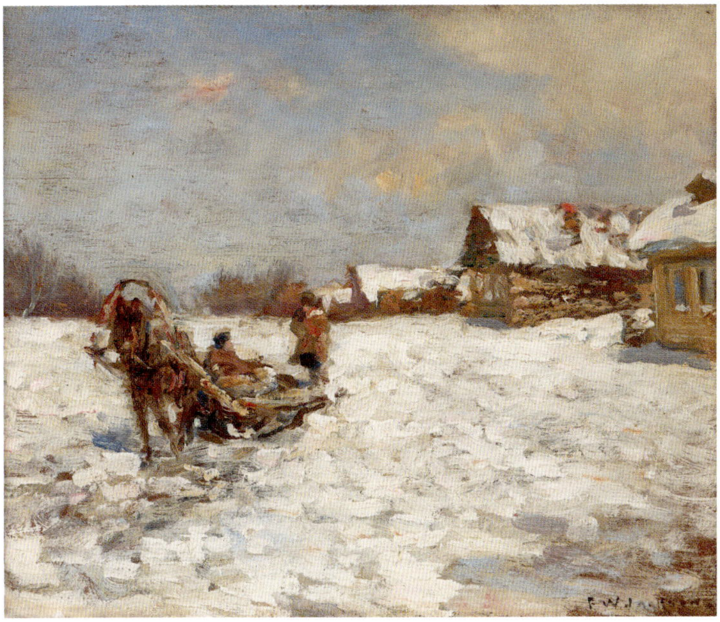

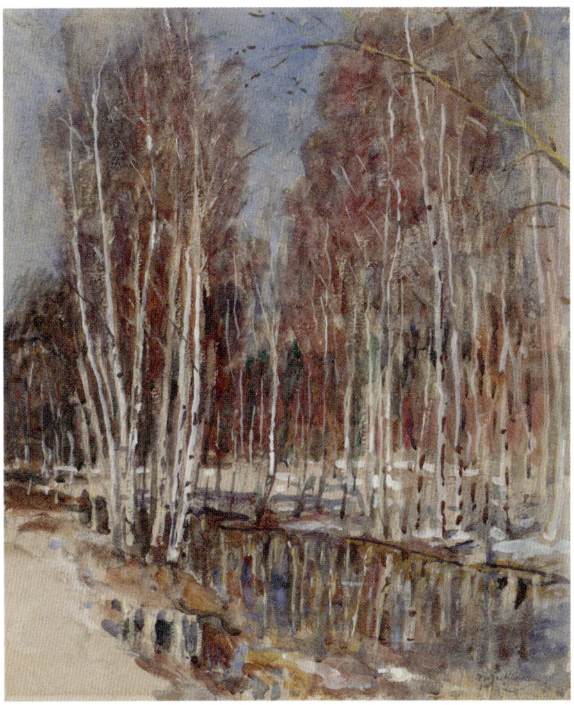

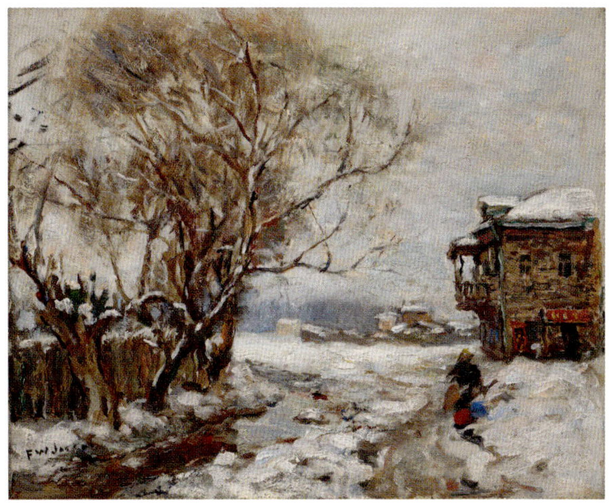

documented by around a dozen scenes in both oil and watercolour; his travelling companion, Walter Butterworth, enthused about the 'vigour and dash' lent to the variety of sky and cityscapes, as well as the deep snow of the countryside scenes. The Press reviewed them similarly, though sadly this took place at the memorial exhibition for Jackson in Manchester (organised by Butterworth) in 1918. It was widely conjectured that his death was a result of continuing ill-health brought on by the conditions of their Russian journey.[245]

WINTER IN THE SOUTH

All of these works reflect the commitment of artists to the north-east coast, even in winter. Despite this, many increasingly took the opportunity to travel, following the well-established 'artistic trails' laid by their peers. The perfect time to leave England, those with means could head down from the south coast by train or steamer to southern Spain, and then on to the North African coast.

The trip to Toledo by Mackie and Crawshaw has already been mentioned (p. 97, note 36). Jackson too was in Seville in 1908, after crossing the Bay of Biscay where he painted on board ship – destined, it would appear, for North Africa and Tangier. Hess painted in Portugal and Mayor stopped off at Gibraltar on his way to North Africa in March 1899; he then travelled on from Tangier, reaching Fez.[246] It is suggested that during his time living in Montreuil Mayor also visited Algiers. So did Hopwood, who on trips to Algeria, Tunisia and Morocco continued into the interior of each. He managed to reach the Sahara Desert, as well as to visit the capital cities.

John Spence Ingall's initial spur for travelling was apparently brought on by suffering illness during a severe Yorkshire winter. Whether or not that was because he was painting through inclement weather, as Jackson did in Russia, it appears to have resulted in his making regular journeys to and from Morocco. Ingall's obituary describes how he spent a good deal of time in the country, wintering there regularly after the First World War until he died, in 'his own little house outside Tangier'. In April 1905 Yorkshire newspaper reports were quick to take up the news from the *Daily Mail* when, on the visit of the German Kaiser to Morocco, its German colony presented him with four drawings of Moorish scenes by:

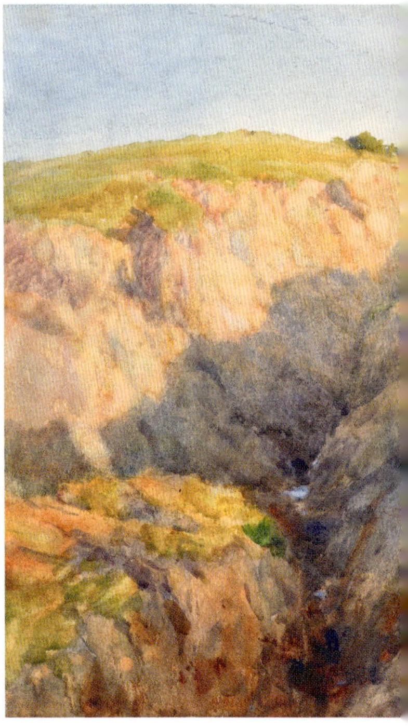

> Mr. Spence Ingall, a Yorkshire artist resident here. The Emperor admired the pictures and shook hands and conversed for some time with the artist.[247]

Dr Peter Phillip's conversations with Rowland Hill's son Peter in the 1970s recalled his vivid memories of Ingall from their time as neighbours at Bank Top above Runswick. It appears that Ingall brought back mementoes and habits of his life living in Africa, much as the Staithes fishermen had, over the years, from far-flung ports at which they docked.[248]

A hint of this is represented in the *bal costumé* put on in the Commercial Hotel, Hinderwell in August 1909, when the

> walls of the ballroom were hung with fine oriental rugs and carpets, portières of Egyptian embroidery and two magnificent leopard skins.

The contributor could not restrain himself from picking out certain costumes for comment. These included Mrs Fred Jackson's 'beautiful and demure gown, inherited from her grandmother' and other characters, among them the Reverend Alfred Crompton as an Arab sheikh.

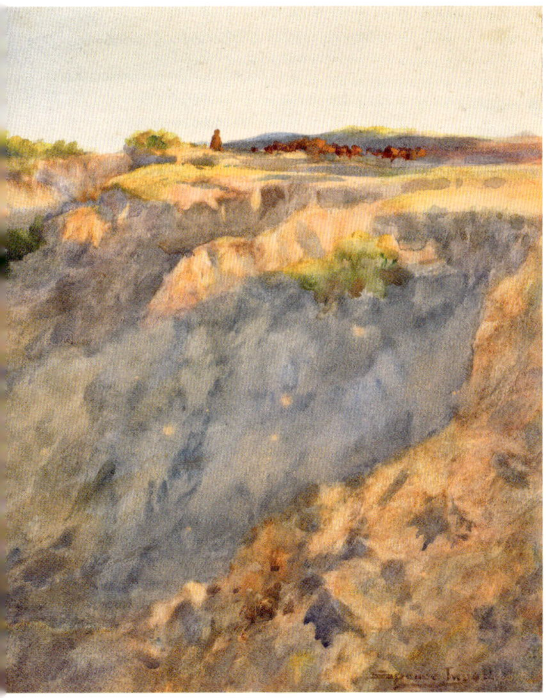

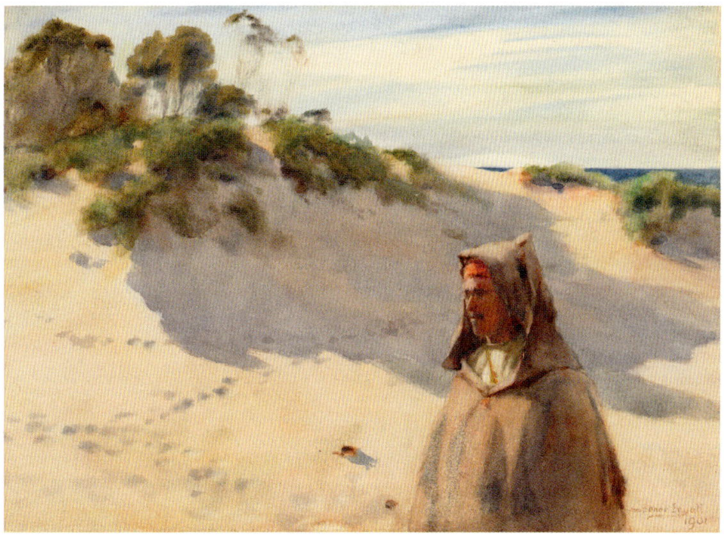

Left: 173. Many of John Spence Ingall's works feature mountains or, in the case of Yorkshire, moors and dales. He travelled in Switzerland and made an extended trip, during the First World War, to Assam. This work, Moroccan Landscape with Shepherd, reflects his long association with a country in which he spent consecutive winters for many years.

Above: 174. John Spence Ingall's obituary recounts his connection to Tangier, the port city on the north coast of Morocco, over 20 to 30 years. It states that he had 'his own little home and his wants were attended to by a Moorish manservant'. Here he paints an undated, unidentified portrait in the context of massive dunes and a distant view of the sea.

> Mr Spence Ingall and Mr J. Hodgson appeared to endure the fatigues of the evening lightly in their cool white linen suits – Mr Ingall as a French 'chef de cuisine' and Mr Hodgson in a European's tropical attire … Mr Ernest Rigg, too, had left his brushes and palette for the nonce [*sic*], and appeared in the fine costume of a Turkish bey.[249]

It is further suggested in several sources that Staithes artists visited Ingall at his house in Tangier. Work by Hopwood, Mayor and Jackson would support this, but there is little further specific literary evidence.

It is interesting to compare works produced by the artists in these very different surroundings. Hopwood's oils rather than watercolours stand out with a brightness of colour and swift, fluid brushstrokes, belying his reputation as a fastidious and painstaking master of tone. Ingall's usually feathery watercolours, which rarely suggest anything other than movement, are stilled; the intensity of the light produces a tension between the muted, matt earthy ochre tones and the glow of the white highlights. Mayor's looser technique describes a haziness that only enhances his characteristic powers of suggestion; his colour sense and feeling for space are emphasised rather than dulled.

175. Hirst Walker continued to exhibit with former members of the Art Club such as Crawshaw, Terry, Hill and Senior long after its conclusion. He too travelled widely, both to Northern Europe and also to the desert. This watercolour, *Towards the Western Isles* (c. 1930) is typical of his stylised depictions.

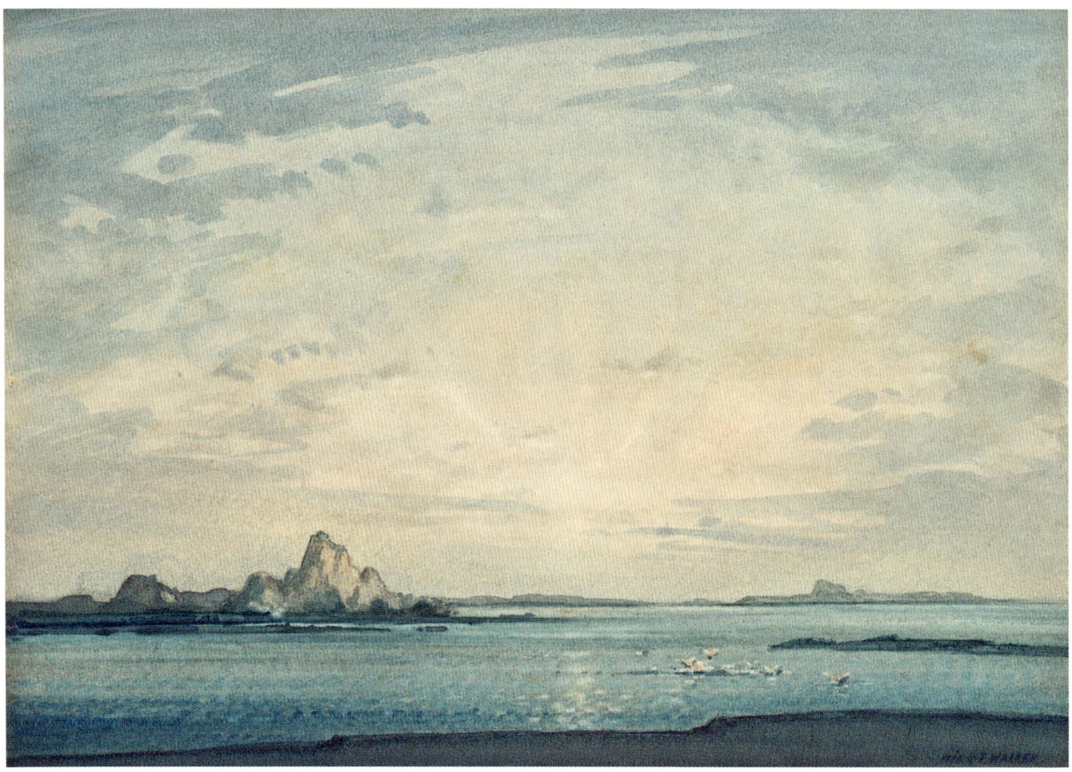

Another who painted scenes in the desert was Hirst Walker. He has been mentioned as the only amateur who regularly showed at the Club's exhibitions, and as Treasurer who assumed the role after Thomas Barrett stepped down. A close friend of the Bagshawes and then Joseph Terry, acting as best man at his wedding, Walker may well have mixed with Crawshaw and Garrido during the latter years of the Staithes Art Club. His landscapes show not only that he went south to Italy, but also that he exhibited scenes from the Lake District, Scotland (including the Hebrides) and even Iceland.

Walker's pure, stylised landscapes often focus on the contrast between mountainous crags and low, flat areas of plain or sea; they are generally in watercolour, many without specific locations, and on occasions bear close comparison to Terry's Italianate vistas. The latter's work was heavily influenced by time spent in Corsica (where Crawshaw also painted), Greece and Italy. However, his scenes are often an amalgamation of influences striving for dreamlike, almost roccoco landscapes. Terry more often than not interjects figures dancing and relaxing, in contrast to Walker. In so doing he adds further invitation to the viewer to take in the vista, although the figures remain very much part of the decorative pattern-making of the overall scheme.

176. A review of Joseph Terry's work in 1913 referred to his ability to move with grace from Wales to Normandy, then from Normandy to Florence. The Italianate aspect of his stylised landscapes is most in evidence in the undated *A Fantasy Landscape*, though his work seems usually to be an amalgam of influences.

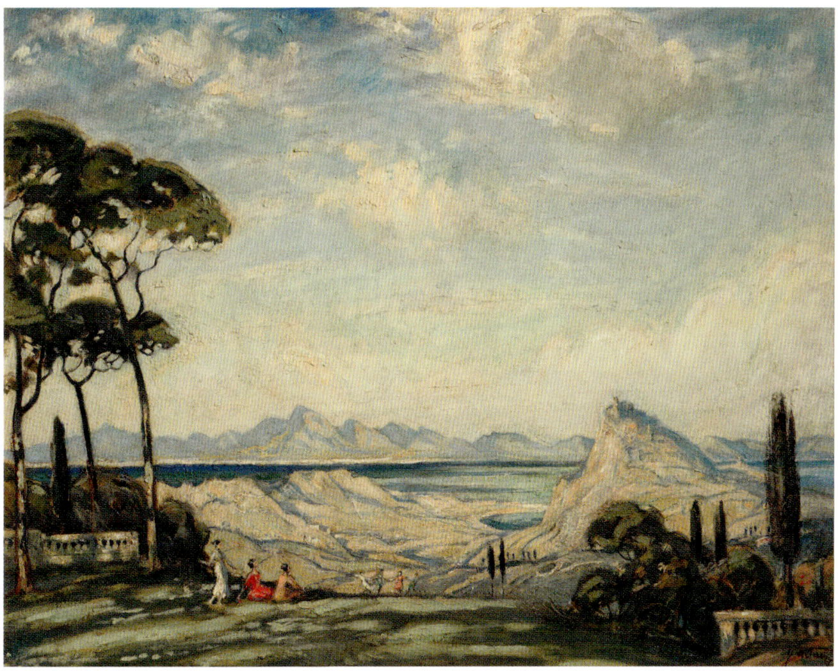

CAPTURING THE SPRING

> From my window I see a big luminous sky, a ploughed field with patches of snow. In the distance a man is ploughing. A Herald of Spring. What thoughts spring. It makes me feel how glorious it is to be alive.[250]

Mark Senior's return to Runswick Bay around Easter each year marked the start of his seasonal six to eight months stay. He was one of the first to have responded to recommendations to visit, on account of the magnificent scenery and the kaleidoscope of atmospheric vistas in the area.

The directness of Senior's oil sketches matches the immmediacy of the best works in charcoal and pencil by other artists, with the added vitality brought by his liberal use of colour. Painting over such an extended period in Runswick, it is fascinating to chart the variation in his attempts to picture not only the rocky point and headland on which the village itself is situated, but also the sweeping arc of the bay. The more rapid the sketch, often the stronger the use of colour and the more natural and instinctive the brushwork.

Senior responds to the cloudscapes and changes in weather patterns in ways that reflect, according to the more experienced eye, the time of day as well as the season. Figures diminish to tiny pinpricks in more panoramic views or else, as the product of a mere two or three strokes, merge almost indecipherably into the breaking waves, flowery meadows, gardens or surrounding trees.

This looseness of technique in Senior's beach scenes comes close to abstraction in the period from 1910–20. The artist's preoccupation is illustrated by studies titled on a theme of individual colours such as blue, orange and brown. This patternistic sense of picture-making develops after the First World War to offer, on the one hand, a stillness and attention to colour tone, as in works such as *June* and *Girls on Headland*, and on the other an emphasis on vibrant, natural movement, such as that generated in *Away to the sea, By the sea or Dancing at Runswick*. Figural features are pared down and location veiled to enhance the symbolism and spirit of the pictures.

Works from Senior's regular trips in the UK or abroad, such as to Ludlow, provide similar indications of this increasing change. The anecdotal references of a 1906 visit to Walberswick in Suffolk lend grist to the mill of those who see in his work a closeness to the style of Philip Wilson Steer.

Opposite: 177. *Spring*, an oil painting of 1906, not only captures the colour for which Senior is renowned but also the movement that became a hallmark of his work. This is particularly evident when he describes cliff-top scenes with a combination of wildflowers, woodland, dappled light and breeze.

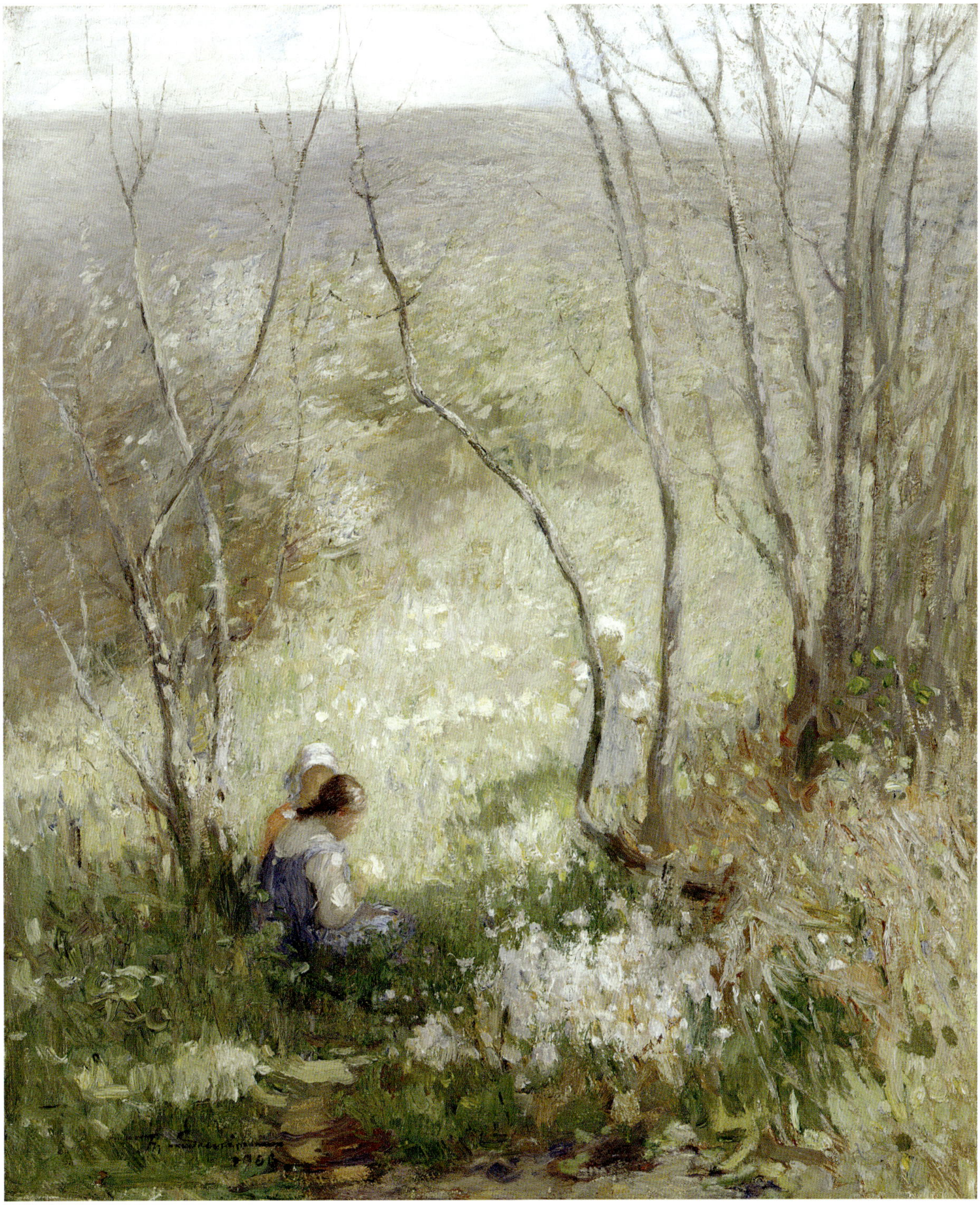

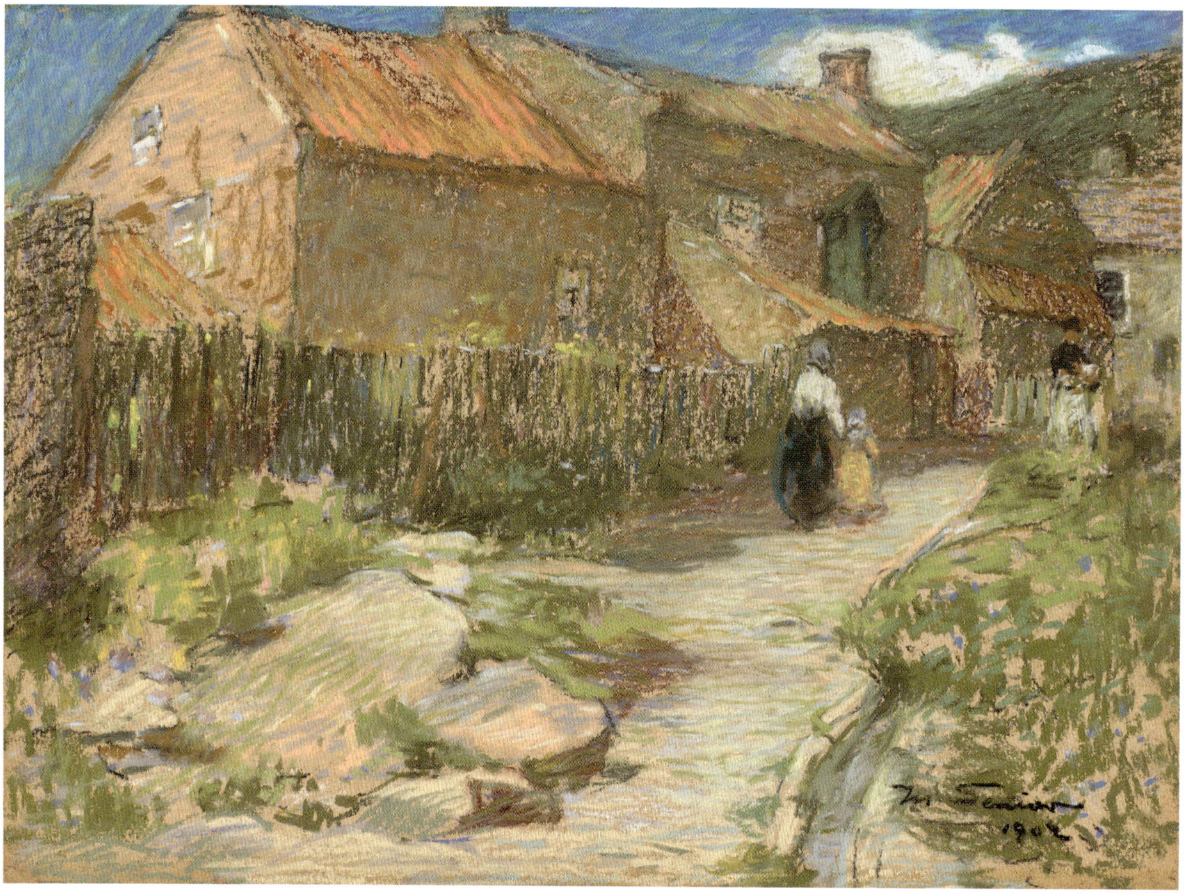

178. Mark Senior's association with Runswick Bay lasted for around 40 years. This pastel of 1902 is entirely evocative of the red tiles, green paintwork and atmosphere of plants and gardens that pervade the village.

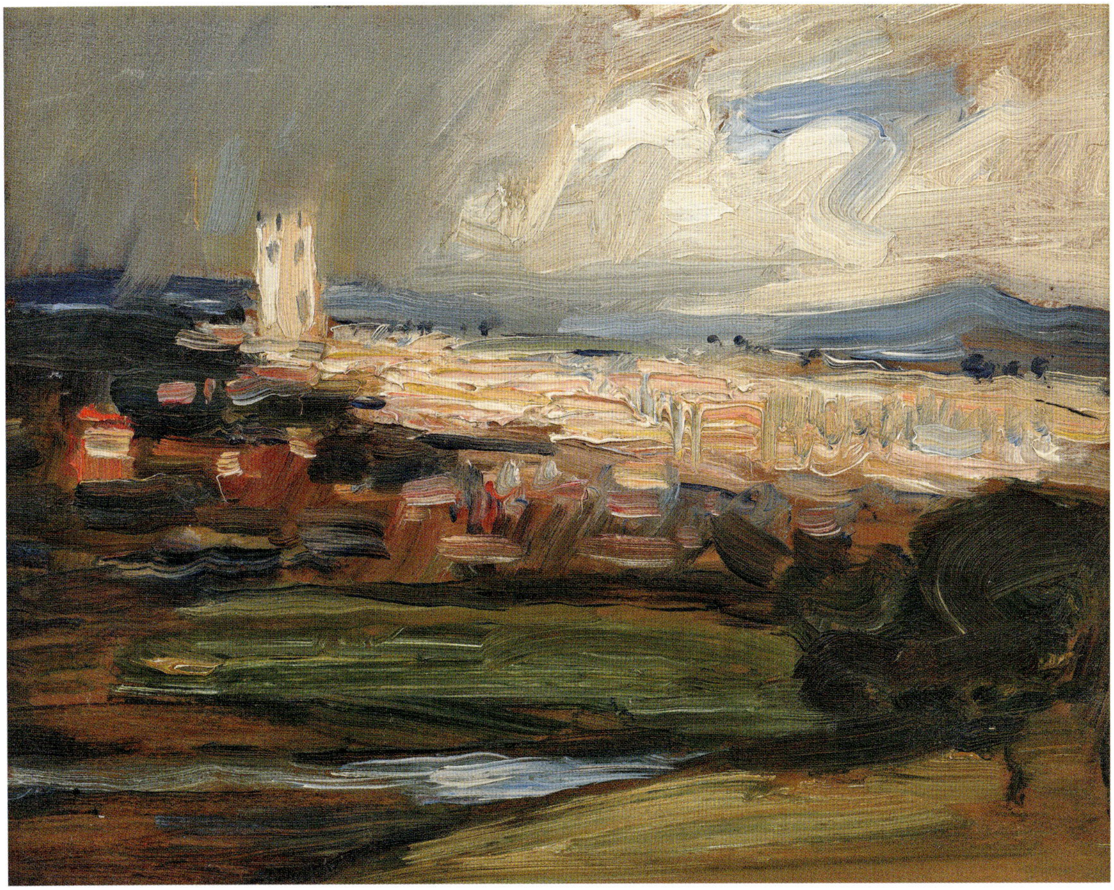

179. Ludlow in Shropshire was the focus for at least one of Mark Senior's sketching trips with Florence Hess. In this panel, so typical of his oil sketches, the vibrancy of colour is matched by the flourish of his brushwork.

The retrospective exhibition of Senior's work at Wakefield in 1983 picked out traits such as allowing a pre-varnished panel to appear through his paintwork, the type of agitated brushwork characteristic of Steer's beach scenes and the tension produced to 'freeze' figures within the constraints of a picture.

Senior's commitment, witnessed in his oil sketching by Hess, matched that of others such as Jackson or Mayor. One can picture the artist outdoors with his customary set of small oil boards, just like Mayor with his watercolour blotter or Sutcliffe with his set of 8½ by 6½ inch photo plates.

Sutcliffe urged his fellow photographers to come to Yorkshire in the spring, the season when variations in the weather created the most fantastic effects and, as he claimed, 'the country smiles the most'. He describes the views looking up from locations such as his particular favourite, the Esk valley:

> What charming colours the fields take when sprinkled with hail. The ploughed fields have turned a delicate pink, while the grass fields are the palest pea-green imaginable, the trees are like ghosts as they appear and disappear as the shower passes over them.[251]

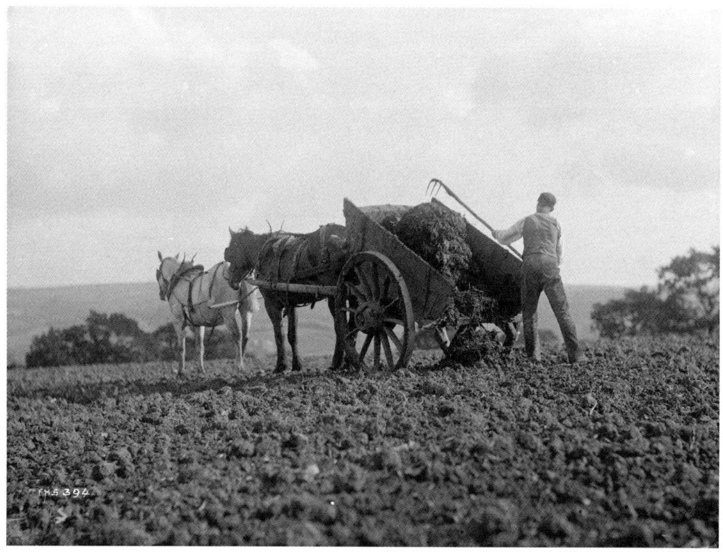

180. This photograph of a farmer unloading manure from his cart is unusual for its very limited depth of field, which renders both background and foreground out of focus. In *Farmer and Cart* (c. 1890), Sutcliffe uses this method to ensure an 'action' photograph without overly posing his subject.

In most circumstances he knew the photograph he was after and employed someone – sometimes a Whitby fisherman – to carry his gear. In the odd instance, though, he might set off on a commission but, captivated by a scene in front of him, use up the plates he had brought. He specifically recalled an occasion when he had been able to rely on the local station master, an amateur photographer, who lent him spares.[252]

The other artists fanned out in the wooded valleys between the coast and moors. Many took advantage of the spring blossoms both in the villages and beyond, along the cliffs or the various watercourses. Laura Knight describes how foraging trips for wildflowers to Pearly or Parly Bottoms inspired her to paint landscape:

No-one could take a step there without crushing the virginal green and yellow that was springing from the black earth.

With enthusiasm she planned a 'great work' entitled *Spring* to include all of her experience; this was to materialise years later in a picture completed in Cornwall.

The combination of floral effects with landscapes, woodscapes etc. is his one particular speciality ... banks and ditch-sides of meadow-sweet and wild thyme, blue wood jacinths [*sic*] and nodding yellow daffodils, thistledown and mist.[253]

181. Although painted in Cornwall like *On the Beach* (**108**), Laura Knight attributes this work, *Spring* of 1916, to specific ambitions and outings to sketch in and around Staithes. Pearly Bottoms was one of the small, wooded dales inland from the village where wild flowers flourished.

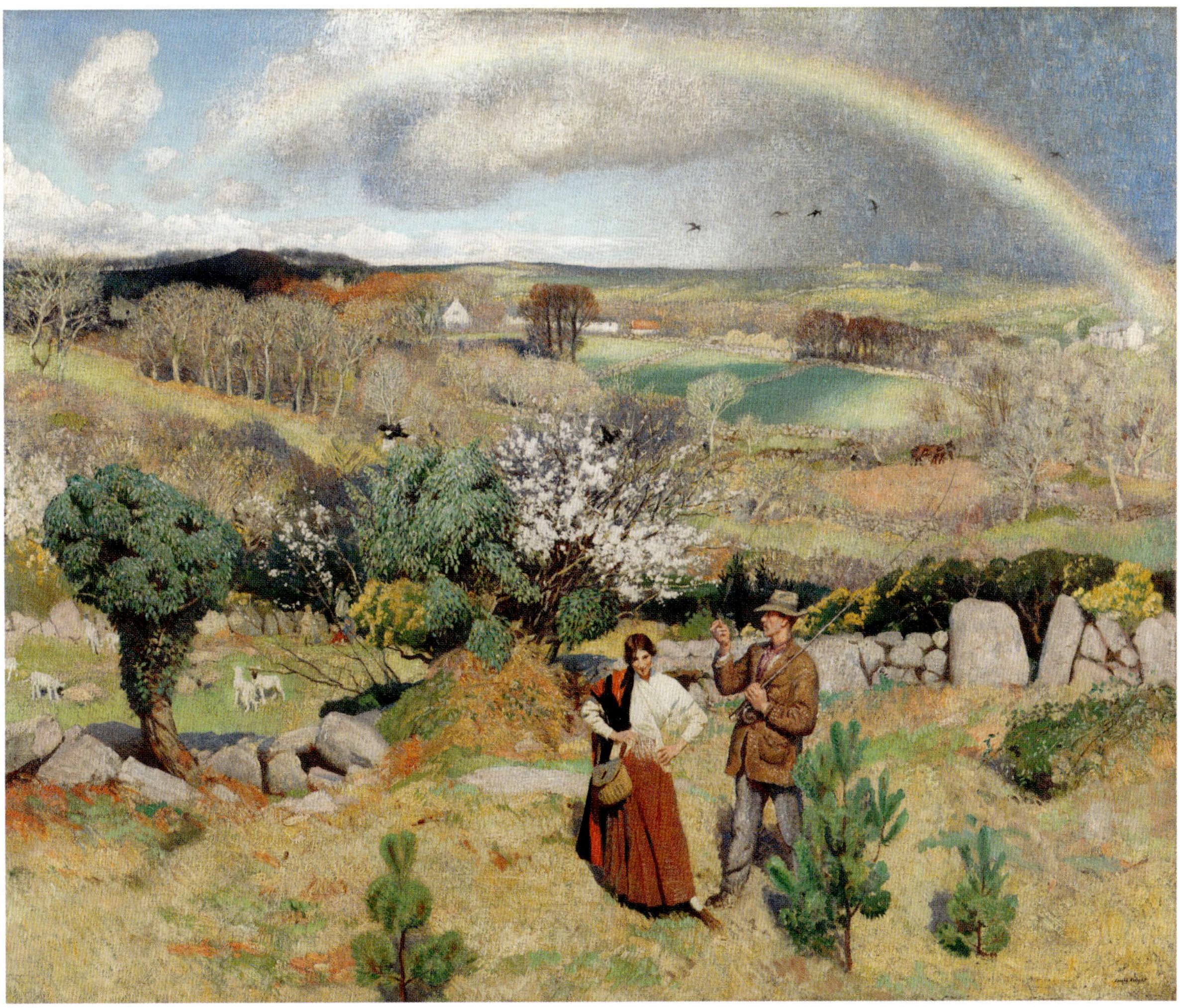

Encompassing all the seasons in his eulogy, the correspondent of the *Leeds Mercury* pictures Gilbert Foster overlooking Runswick Bay towards Kettleness, clad in a white linen hat and jersey:

> Half-way under a huge sketching umbrella, covered with drab cotton and tethered to the ground by its bamboo handle … His rickety bamboo easel was weighted down among the knapweed plants with a fishing line and a glass honey-jar full of water.

Arthur Friedenson repeatedly painted the wooded cliffs and slopes of the coast around Runswick. A typical view of low, hazy morning light was chosen for the National Collection as part of the Chantrey Bequest of 1910 (**54**). His landscapes feature small figure groups of women and children, with titles sometimes the only way of picking seasonal images one from another.

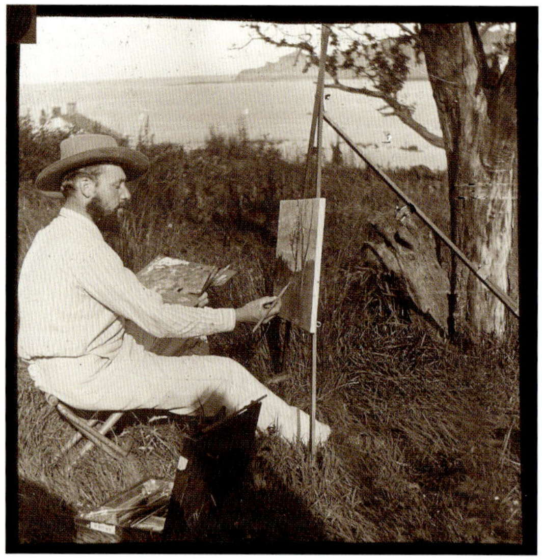

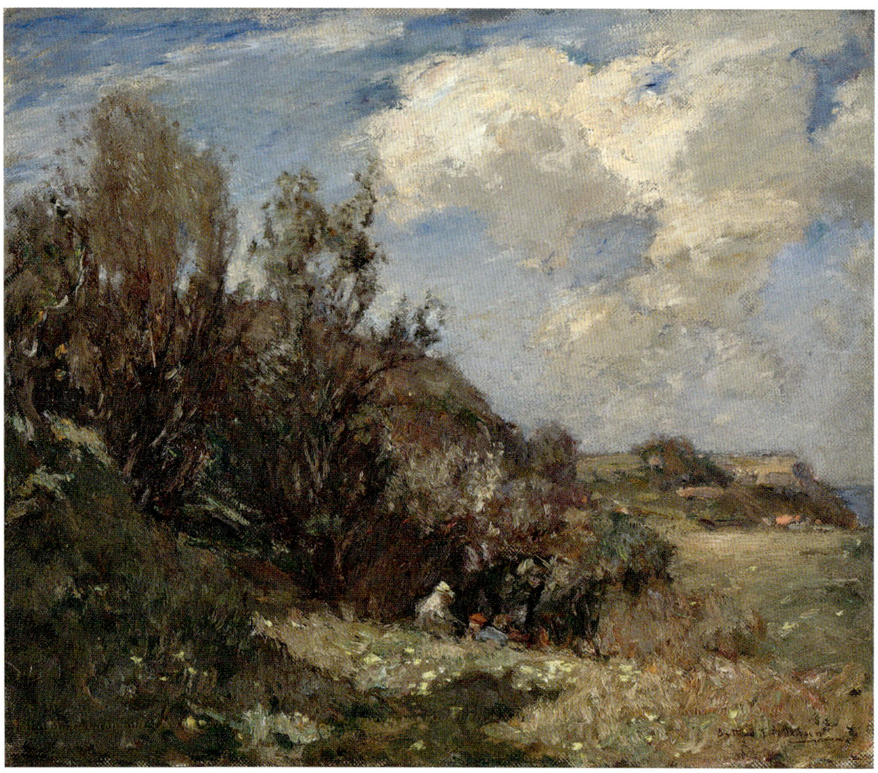

Above: 182. This image is another of the magic lantern slides from the recently discovered group of W. G. Foster, his family, friends and fellow artists, likely dating to the mid-1890s. It reinforces the image of *en plein air* painting at a time when he may have been using photography to assist with his picture-making.

Left: 183. Arthur Friedenson often painted on the wooded hillsides overlooking the sea. In the undated *Picking Primroses, Runswick Bay* he focuses on the folds in the landscape sprinkled with flowers, and the dappled shade balanced by shifting clouds.

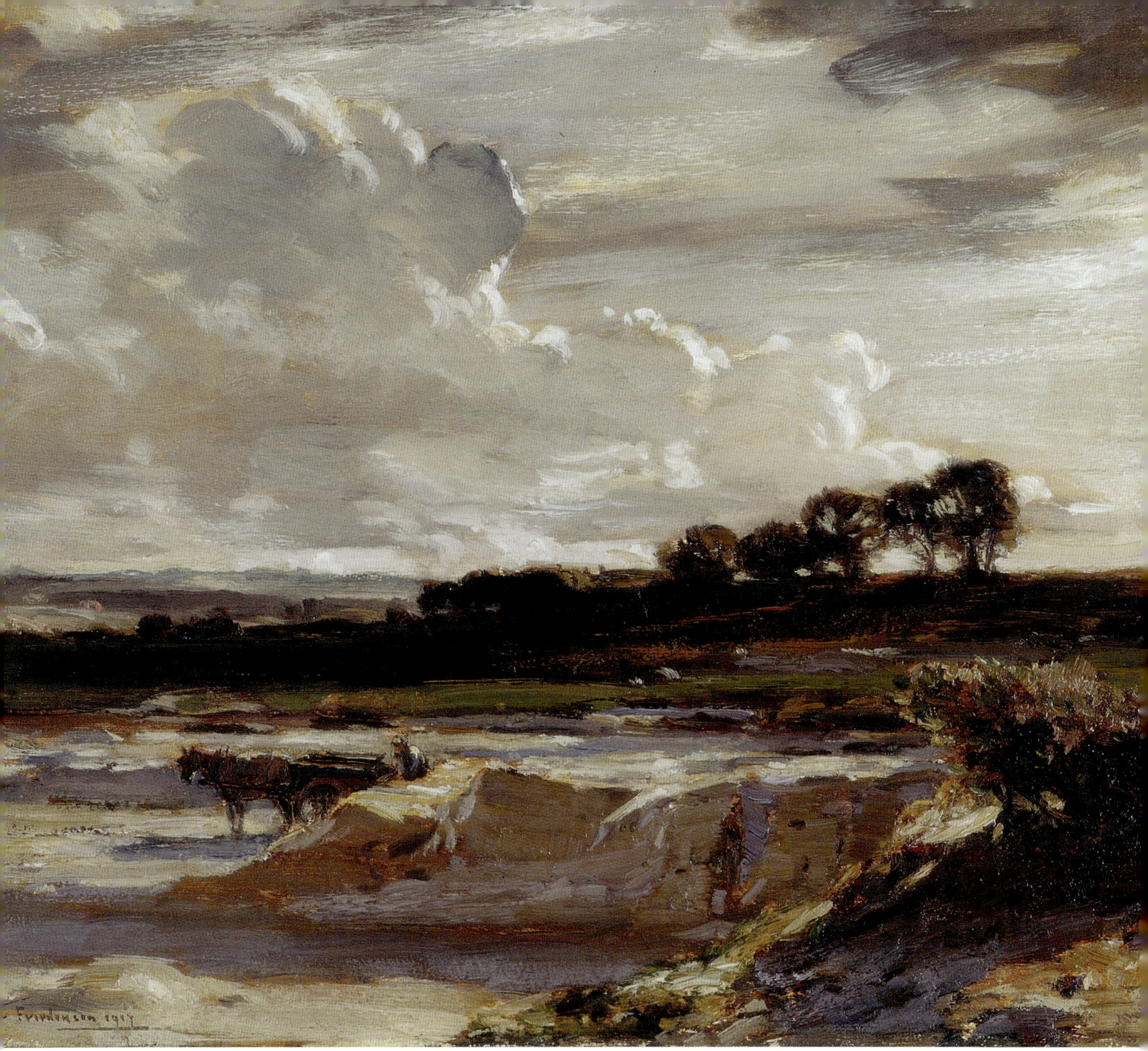

184. Arthur Friedenson's move away from Yorkshire in 1909/10 took him to the southwest. He painted around Wareham and Corfe Castle in Dorset; this oil painting on panel, *A Sand Pit*, was created in 1917. Little has been written about Friedenson, but he is remembered in the memoir of the painter John Everett, who exhibited locally with him.

Around the time of the Chantrey purchase, Friedenson moved south and settled in Dorset, painting scenes around Wareham, Lulworth Cove and Corfe Castle. In these surroundings he indulged something of an obsession with the sky, work which prompted the admiration of none other than Winston Churchill. Peter Phillips's research prompted a wonderful personal memory of Friedenson out sketching in a Lovat tweed cap and knickerbocker suit:

185. John Wright painted in Robin Hood's Bay, but in this watercolour landscape he turns his gaze inland. This unknown beck or river is typical of the streams that tumbled down off the moors through the wooded dales or valleys before reaching the coast.

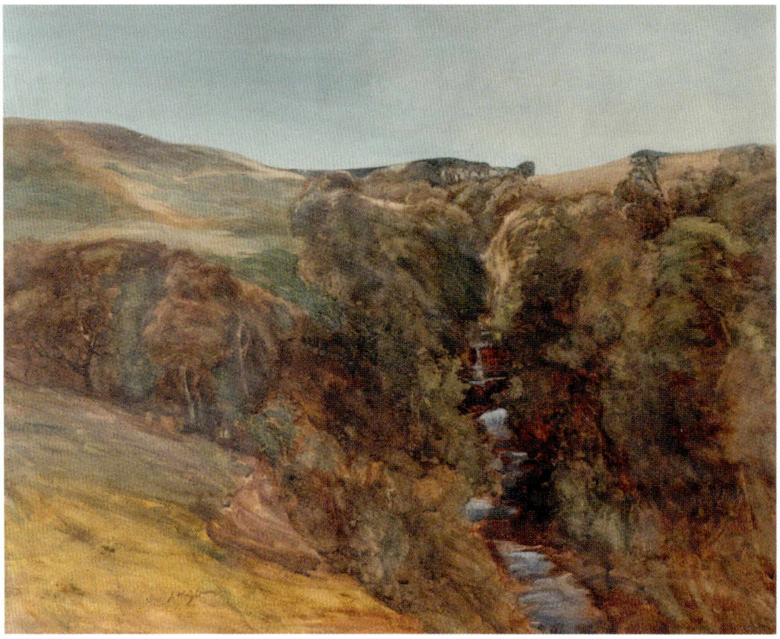

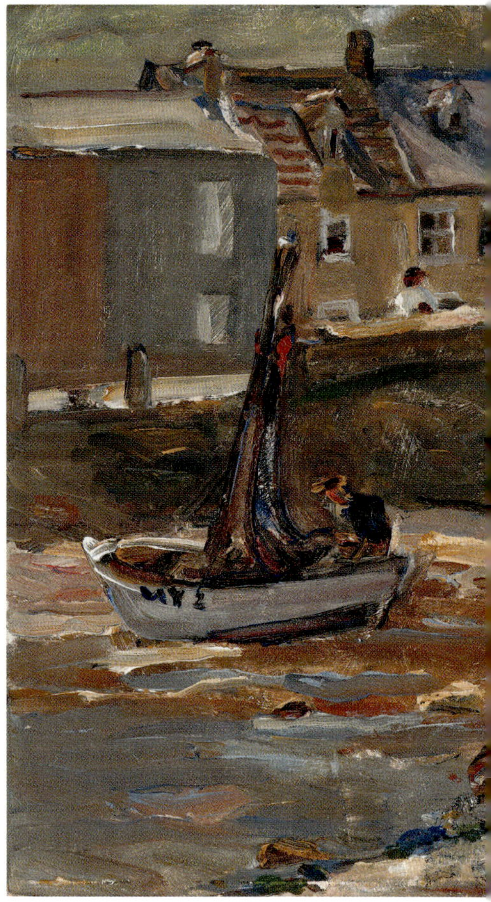

> The day had been wet, but, in the evening, the sun broke through and the sky contained massive cumulus clouds. The lighting effect was brilliant and dramatic – this was what had brought Friedenson out. He was facing the sunset sky where a large cloud covered the sun. ... [He] took his brush and, without any fluster, put stroke after stroke on that board until the complexity and subtlety and brilliance of the scene was recorded.[254]

Hopwood, Hill and others also depicted the spring landscape. Their work reveals specific features that acted as foils to the changing seasons. These might be buildings, such as the 'wheelhouse', a structure at the top of Ellerby Bank painted by Fred Jackson in the winter (**167**), which was painted by Senior and Hill among others in the spring. The pathway from Ellerby to Hinderwell was another setting often described both in literary sources and in works exhibited under a wide array of titles that reflect the ebb and flow of the seasons (**25**).

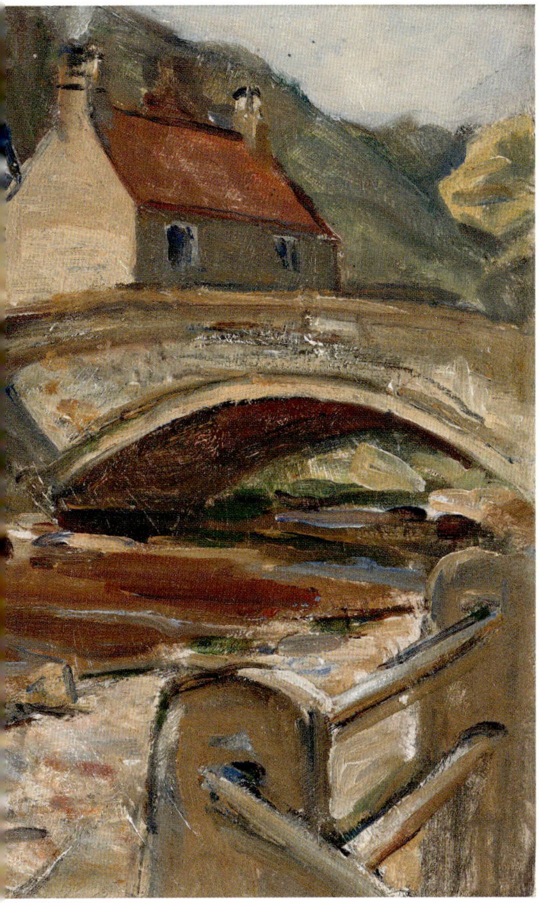

FEATURES OF THE LANDSCAPE

Significant natural features, such as local streams – becks – and rivers were obviously attractive to the artists. These included Roxby Beck, falling downhill from the Grinkle estate (of Sir Charles Palmer) and moors to Dale House and thence into Staithes, those that emptied into Sandsend through Mulgrave Woods and, of course, the River Esk, running down past Sleights through Ruswarp and into Whitby harbours. Knight's memoir recalls:

> I painted a lot at Roxby ... that inspiring landscape had considerable effect upon my development.

Newly married, Laura and Harold Knight walked down to Staithes from Roxby when they stayed with Mrs Bowman, while the Joblings sketched up and down the beck from the nearby village of Dalehouse. John Spence Ingall sought out the farms and hilltops, as well as following the beck upstream to the moors. His watercolours match the skittish, windy weather of the higher ground, making play of the meeting of earth and sky. His image of Ellerby Moor, for instance, includes the diminutive figures of peat cutters (**188**) and a distant windmill, but the real drama is provided by the rainclouds above.

Above: 186. Florence Hess's undated painting *Sandsend Beck* depicts a coble about to pass the White Hart Inn as it heads out to sea. The beck flowed through Mulgrave Woods to the village at the foot of Lythe Bank where John Bowman lived for eight years from 1903. Joseph Bagshawe rented a house, Moss Brow, overlooking the beach there after his marriage in 1901.

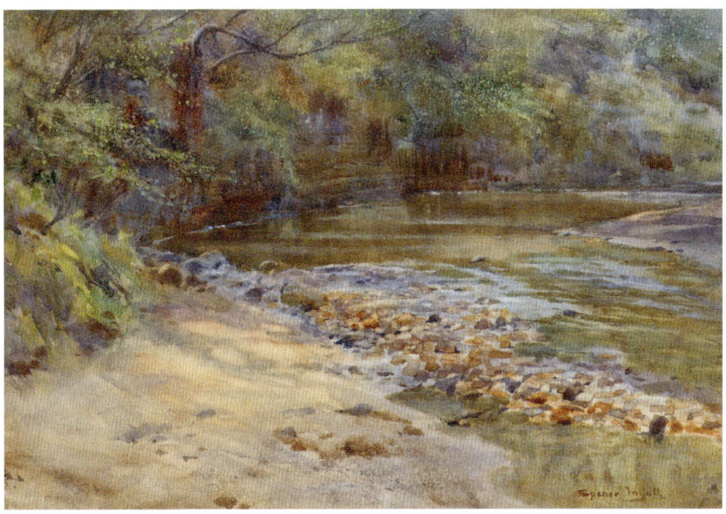

Right: 187. The stream portrayed in John Spence Ingall's undated *Roxby Beck* ran down from the moors and emptied into the sea at Staithes. In 1903 Laura Knight wrote to her friend Rosie Good that 'We had a frightful storm ... could scarcely get through at Dale House ... Great trees were coming down the beck; Staithes is stocked with firewood for months to come'.

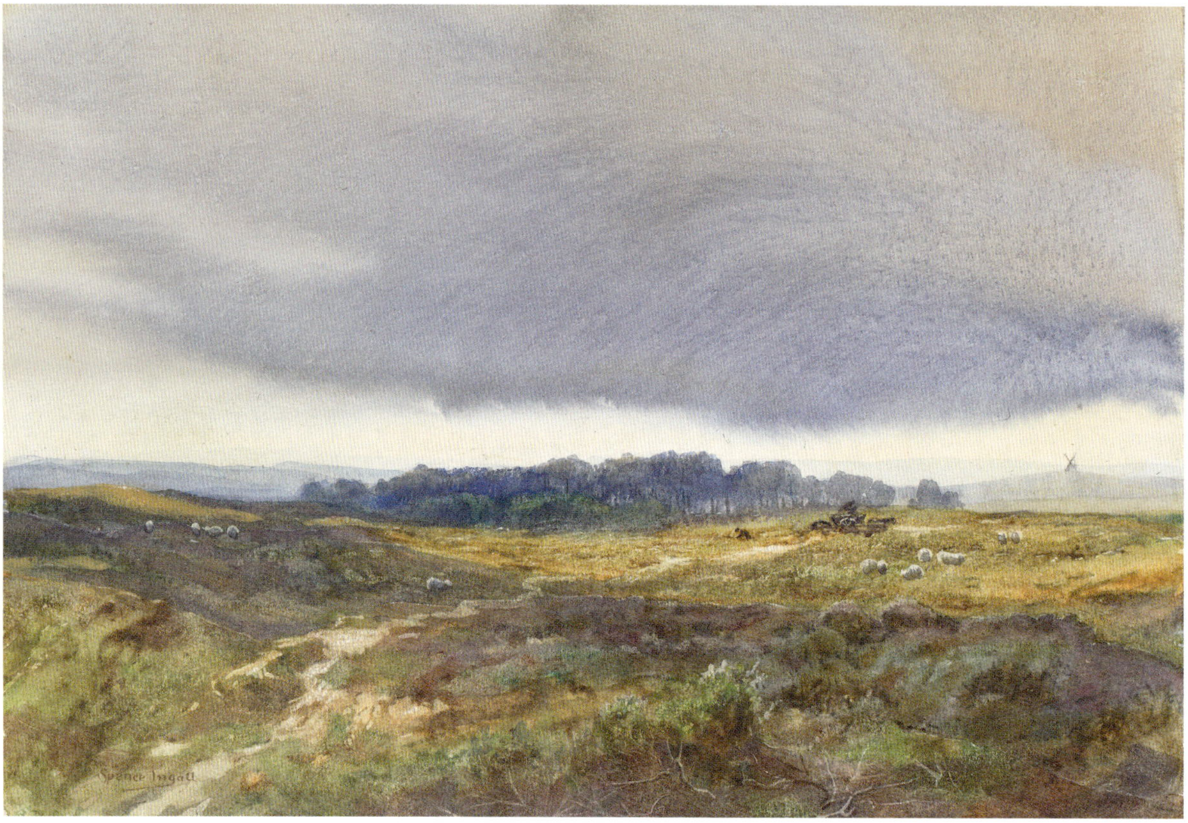

Windmills were rarely depicted as incidentally as this, and one in particular, at Ugthorpe, was painted repeatedly and prominently by the artists. It still stands today, freshly whitewashed though lacking its cap and sails, appearing by turns squat and huddled against the prevailing weather, as in John Bowman's image, or like the tip of a steeple, reaching for the sky, as in the works of Hill, Atkinson, Booth and others.

Mills are scattered throughout Owen Bowen's work, with that of High Hawsker in the Pannett Gallery collection being a notable example. They also often appear in the paintings of Mayor and naturally in an array of work by the artists in Holland, as journeys to the continent became increasingly popular.

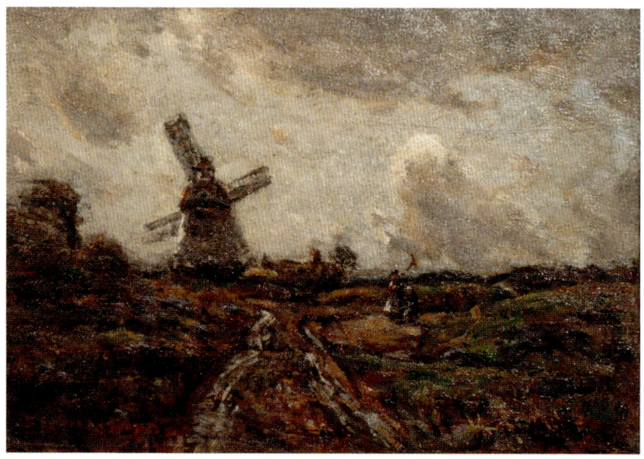

Top: 188. Following Roxby Beck from Staithes up past Grinkle Park, the house of Sir Charles Palmer, one reaches Roxby Moor that formed part of his estate. Ellerby Moors, here pictured, abut that of Roxby, and looking south Ugthorpe windmill may be pictured in the distance.

Above: 189. John Bowman's view of Ugthorpe's windmill embeds it in the moorland landscape. In this undated work the artist conjures up the moody atmosphere of the funeral procession described by Laura Knight: 'Above a ... cone of whitened stone, perched on a black-red cap of tiles, the grey sails flared high against the sky'.

CELEBRATING SUMMER

It was not weather that caused the Mayors to journey abroad in 1902, but the more abrupt matter of their elopement. Despite being well known to her parents, who holidayed regularly at the Yorkshire coast, Fred Mayor was not considered to be a suitable prospect for his fellow artist and Club member Hannah Hoyland. However, once settled in Montreuil-sur-mer, the couple seem to have acted as something of a magnet for Staithes Art Club painters, who travelled to join them in the flat lands of Picardy on a regular basis. It is not clear why they chose this particular location, although the time Fred spent in Paris (where he studied at the Académie Julian) may have established a familiarity with the area. The old walled town, a historic stop *en route* from Calais to Paris, was well known to both French and American artists. Harry van der Weyden, born in Boston, Massachusetts, was the latter's key representative, while the varied series of 'Anglo-Saxon' artists who spent time there included Steer, Fred Brown and in later years Dermod O'Brien (**61**).

Though not picturesque in the classical sense, the region's winding rivers, meadowlands, sand dunes, wide estuaries and open market towns presented intriguingly different contours to the moorland, dales, clifftops and huddled streets of the Yorkshire coast. Cissy Johnson's letter to Rosie Good in 1903, written from Haut-de-France where her uncle ran his factory, gives a flavour of the countryside's appeal for the artists:

> … in many places marshy. There would often be little woods of poplar and birch trees and gleaming streaks of water on the low-lying parts shone out among the reeds.

She goes on to describe the thatched mud cottages and other elements of rural life:

> It would be ripping if a party of us spent a summer there, or rather near there at village called Vendeuil, which is perfectly wonderful. Quaint cottages and country life, old agricultural implements, hills and long flat planes [*sic*] of country with … droves of oxen, winding streams and unexpected woods.[255]

By November of 1902 (the year in which the couple left), Fred Mayor's solo show, while incorporating work from Yorkshire and scenes from their route to

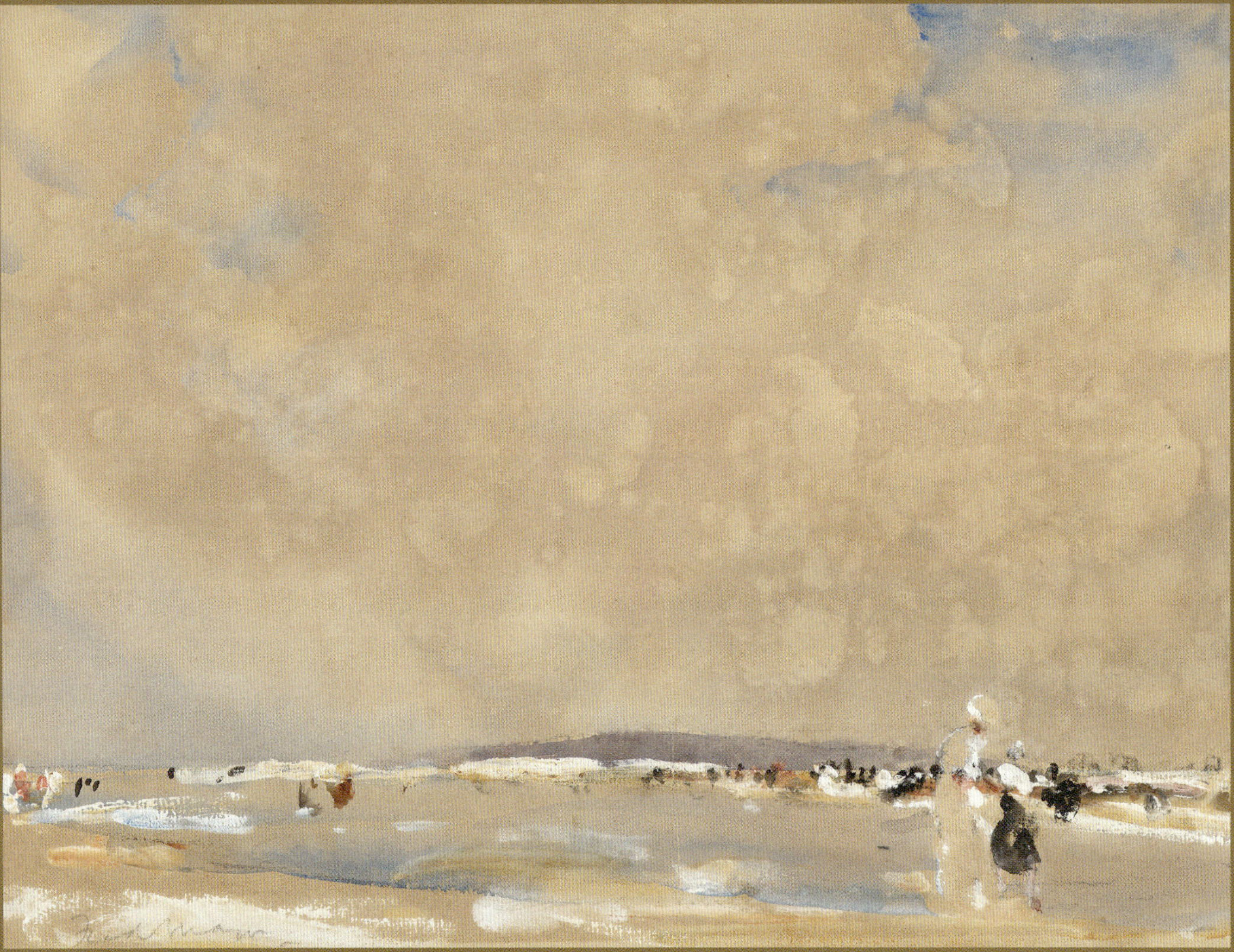

190. *Le Touquet, Paris Plage*, the title of this painting of *c.* 1905, was the highly fashionable setting of many of Fred Mayor's French watercolours. On occasion his works have specific family subjects, but more often they take advantage of the possibilities for abstraction and suggestion offered by the region's sweeping beaches, huge skies and bright summer light.

Portsmouth and the Channel, also included pictures from across the Pas-de-Calais. From Boulogne to Étaples, Montreuil and Chartreuse, they focused on the life of the coast, but also encompassed a full range of subjects, among them several beach scenes which became the hallmark of Mayor's work. The catalogue introduction pointed out:

> He seeks the poetical effects of atmosphere and movement in atmosphere … in these rapid sketches, impressions rather we may call them, he seeks to give with a few strokes what in nature is of momentary duration.[256]

191. Probably painted around 1908, this small oil *A Picardy Farm* is typical of Henry Hopwood's seemingly spontaneous sketches from Europe and Africa. He submitted pictures for exhibition from regular visits to France, especially Picardy, until the beginning of the First World War.

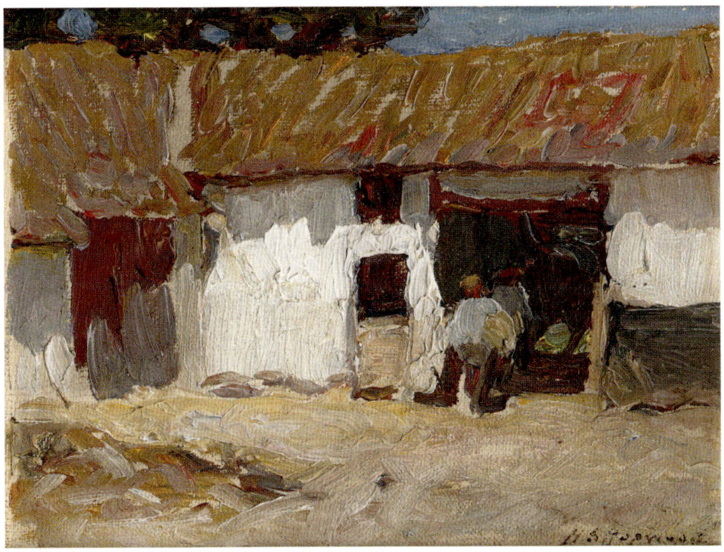

Several of the artists from the Club went on to create work in the area, whether or not they were introduced by the Mayors. Garrido, of course, had lived in Étaples for some time and was witness at the birth of the Mayors' son Charles and van der Weyden's daughter Helen, before removing to Whitby. Hopwood, a previous visitor to Normandy in 1897, sent in exhibits including *A Picardy Farm* and *The Buttermarket* from an address in Montreuil around 1908; he was still showing pictures from the area at his Fine Art Society show in 1913. Mackie too had a studio near Étaples between 1904 and 1908, and it is likely that Fred Richardson and Joseph Bagshawe travelled along the coast together through Berck to Normandy. Fred Jackson also seems to have visited there with James Charles, with whom he had previously exhibited and travelled.[257]

The Mayors themselves developed a seasonal pattern of migration, similar to that of Senior, it seems. However, theirs also involved a significant journey down to the south coast of France. In winter Mayor painted from Cassis to Villefranche, travelling on as far as San Remo in Italy; he had tried Algiers too, apparently, but settled for the most part on France's Mediterranean ports, in particular Cassis. Only after six years away did the couple return to England. They settled first in Buckinghamshire and then, with war on the horizon, moved to London.

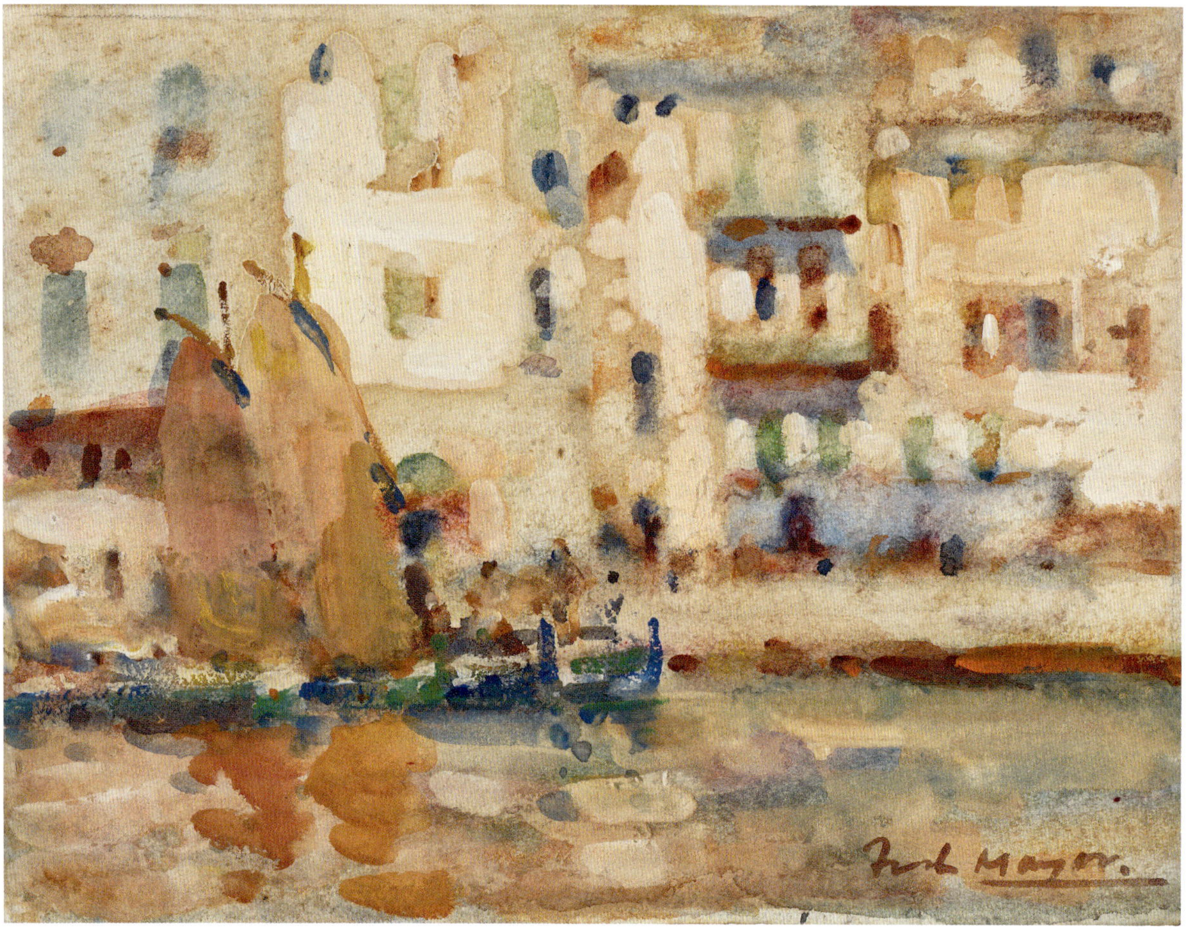

192. Fred and Hannah Mayor, once settled in Montreuil in 1902, developed a habit of travelling to the South of France each year, painting along the coast. This undated watercolour, previously thought to picture Cassis, is inscribed *The Quay, Villefranche [sur mer]* to the reverse.

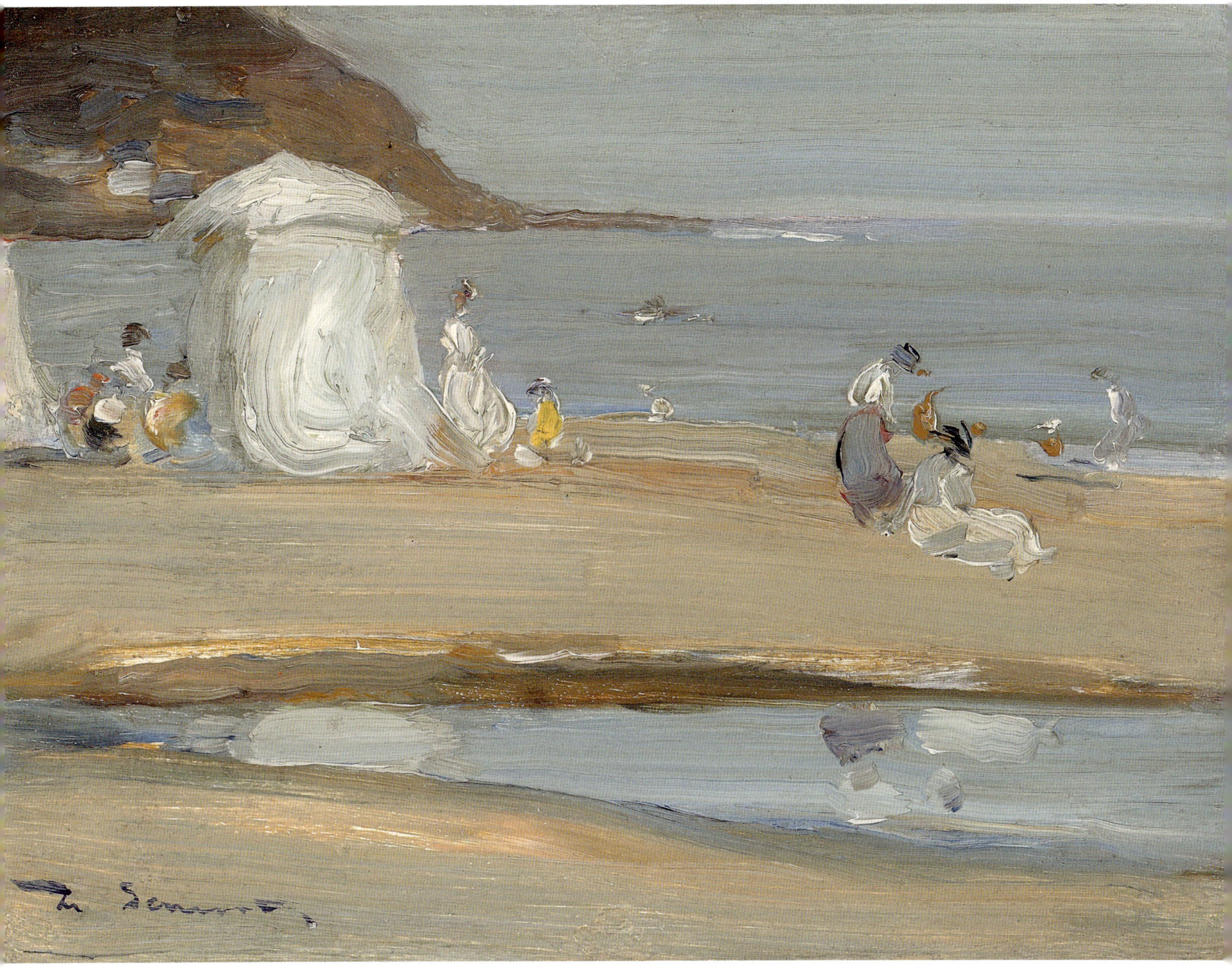

193. Familiarity of location surely played a part in the move towards abstraction in in Mark Senior's work. The repetition of painting scenes such as *On the Beach, Runswick Bay* (1905) allowed the artist room for creativity, particularly with the bright colours and spectacle of holidaymakers.

THE FRUITS OF AUTUMN

While the Mayors may have hosted friends in Montreuil variously from June to September, the holiday season at the coast in Yorkshire was coming to its peak. The herring fleets also congregated off the coast during these months to take maximum advantage of the passing shoals. The majority of Club artists were therefore regularly stationed 'at home'. As late summer drew on, the industry of the towns, villages and ports was matched by that in the fields and on the farms above the coast as preparations for harvest intensified.

In later life Sutcliffe recalled the multitude and variety of characters to be found on the highways and byways at this time. He gathered them all, in his literary description, into a single striking cavalcade.

> Haymakers, horse dealers, travelling musicians, scissor grinders, gypsies by the score, sailors tramping home … having spent all their money, fishermen with a cartload of nets, to say nothing of the professional tramp and his followers. The people on the road today are quite as interesting as they were in Chaucer's time … the old rat-catcher with his troupe of mongrel dogs, the hedger and ditcher, clothed from head to foot in leather, the old thatchers, the Irish harvest men with knee breeches, blue stockings, red bundle and sickle.[258]

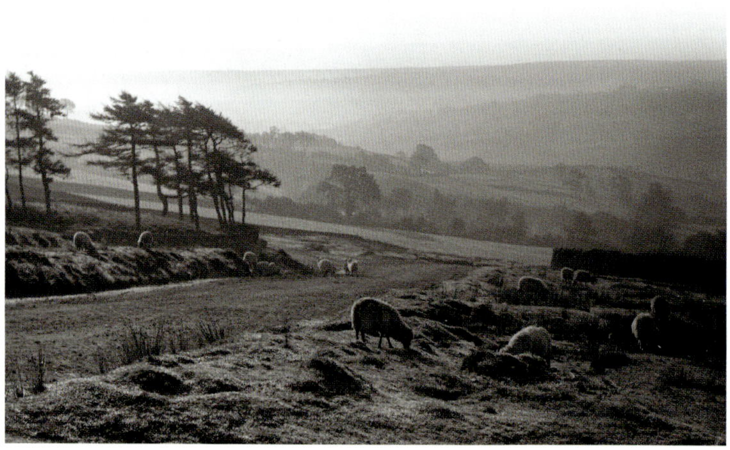

194. Sutcliffe's experience of photographing rural workers could be difficult, as superstitions about having their likeness taken persisted. *Lealholm Bank Top* is an example of his choice to set such figures aside and use sunlight and mist to produce 'pure' landscape.

This happy portrait was tinged with wistfulness. The practical challenges faced by Sutcliffe in capturing their portraits were offset by a realisation that many of these familiar sights would soon pass from view, never to be seen again.

When describing these challenges in the 1920s, Sutcliffe recalled how a ploughman had run off, leaving his horses in the field, when he caught sight of Sutcliffe's camera; young girls also usually disappeared at the first opportunity if asked to pose; when persuaded, it was all he could do to stop them from staring at the camera and ruining the 'natural' look of the image. Agricultural workers too had to be talked into working poses, or offered tobacco or similar item to distract them. In artists' attempts to attain the 'perfect' viewpoint, the reverse often occurred; situating themselves in the middle of a field greatly annoyed local farmers.

Activities such as sowing and scything presented pictorial challenges; the regular movement was too quick for the slow-exposure plates or the methodical strokes of the brush. Even the turning of the hay to dry was a relatively swift activity, with many hands pressed into action. However, the real opportunities came with the slow loading of hay from the haycock to the wagon. The carts gradually inched up the field, giving the onlooker time to select a position, the sun at his or her back.

Jackson, Rigg, Senior, Friedenson, Isa Jobling, Barrett, Booth, Bowen, Atkinson, Paul and Hill all pictured scenes that encompassed everything from the bound stooks and hay wagons to rival flocks of geese fighting in the stubble and harvesters' children picking blackberries in the hedgerows.

Sutcliffe often rented a summer house in Glaisdale and photographed on neighbouring Lealholm Hall Farm. Atkinson, a frequent exhibitor with the Staithes Art Club, also lived in the village where he hosted Jackson, Hill, Rigg and Albert Stevens. Though not a rider himself, Atkinson clearly enjoyed the challenge of painting horses as part of the rural life around him – he not only portrayed equine teams at rest while loading, but also their coming together at market, fair and hunt. He did paint some action scenes at the races, but usually his horses are shown at rest, gathered oustide an inn as the 'stirrup' cup was served, stabled at day's end, tethered for sale or in the open among gypsy

Below: 195. The daughter of a local farmer remembers her father labelling the painters with the affix 'artist' instead of Mister (Artist Paul) and being told not to bother them. However, he would sometimes return to the house affronted that one had trampled the corn trying to improve their view for a sketch, such as this by Paul Paul.

Below right: 196. As with peers such as Senior and Hopwood, Fred Jackson's small landscape oils display an increasing freshness and spontaneity. This picture, *Hayfield*, was exhibited at the Yorkshire Union of Artists in 1902.

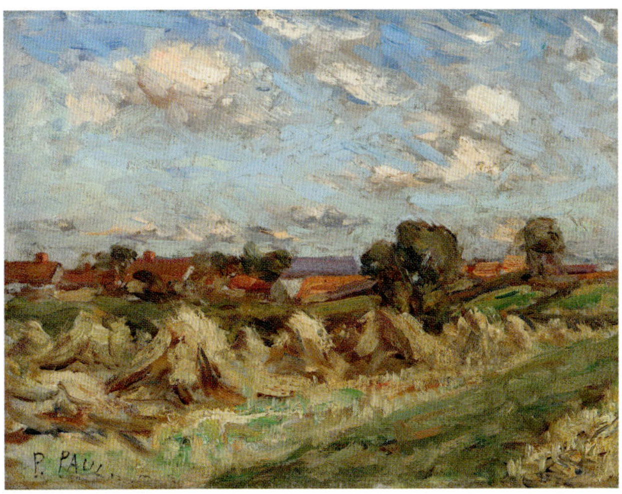

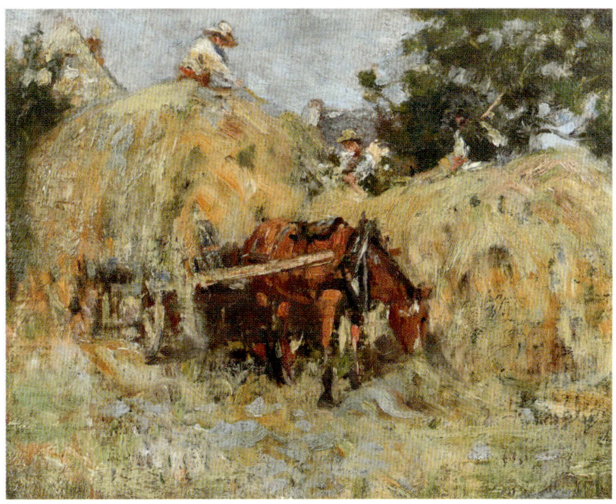

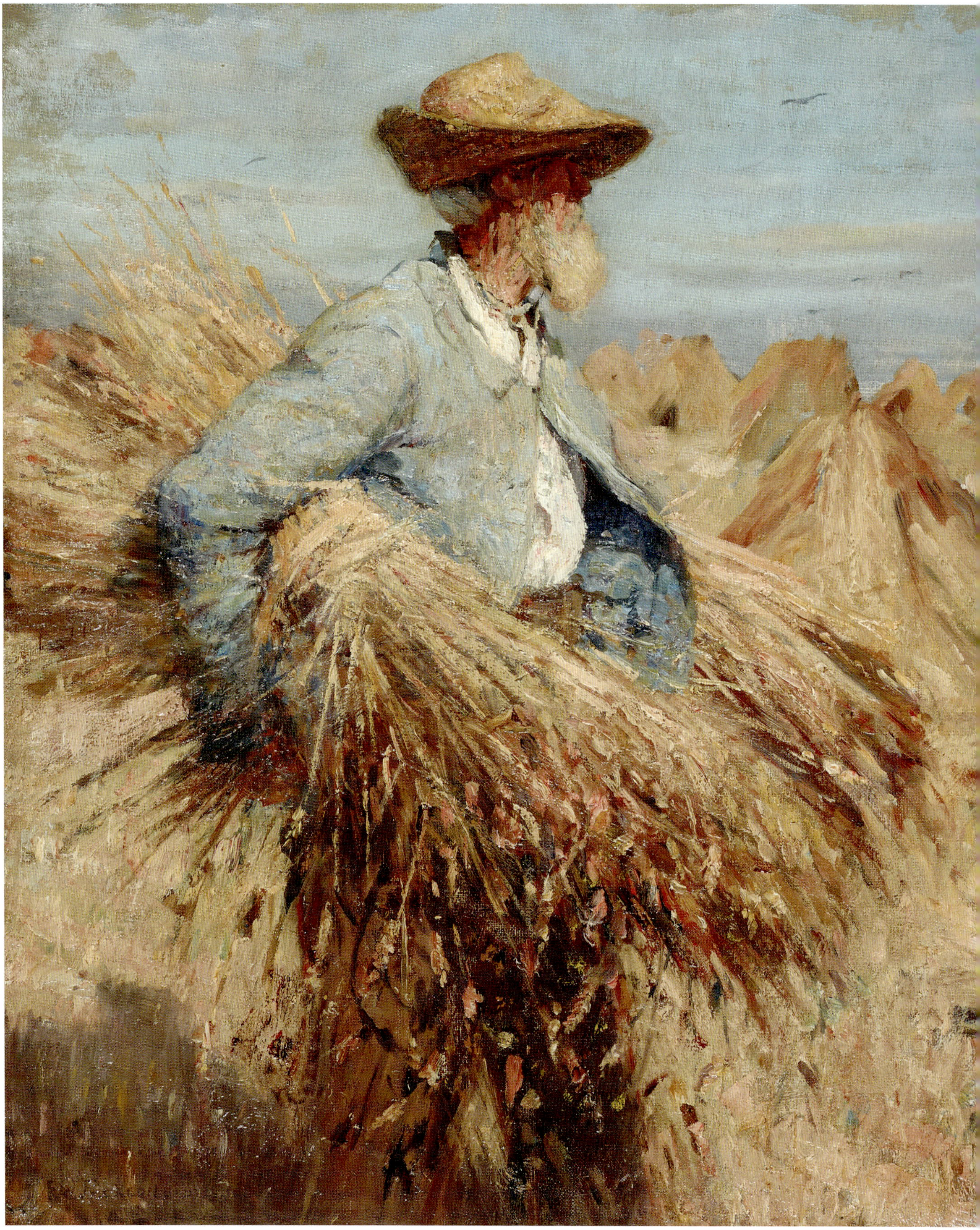

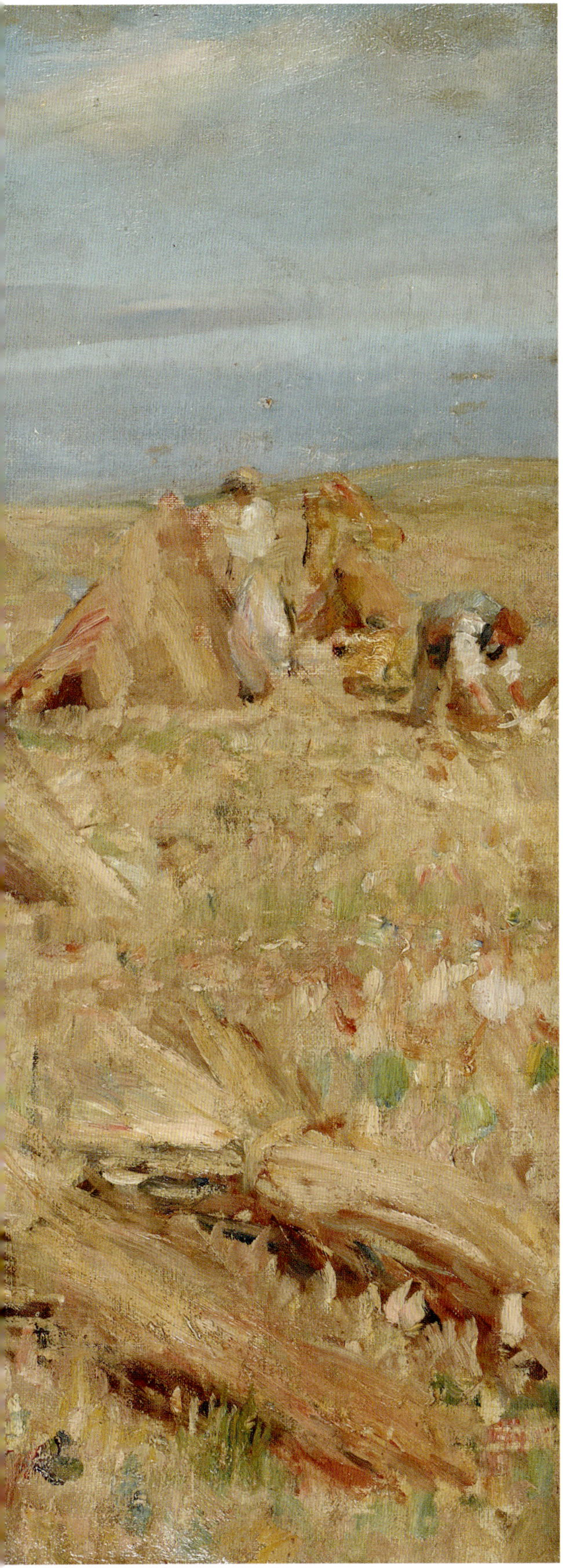

197. Fred Jackson's undated painting *Harvest Time* has a fascinating parallel in the work of Paul Paul; both picture the same model, in identical costume and pose. Paul includes only one sheaf under his near arm and, in portrait rather than landscape format, features pigs and cattle instead of fellow harvesters.

caravans or holidaymakers on the beach. He painted equine portraits too, including the local doctor, Thomas Harks English, from Sleights, with his horse, gig and groom which were well-known fixtures of the local community.

James Booth was the other artist noted for his fascination with horses. He was reputed to visit the abattoirs, in the manner of the great George Stubbs, to improve his grasp of their anatomy. He too portrayed horses mostly at rest – while wagons were loaded up in quarries, on their delivery rounds through the villages, collecting fish at the quayside or in the moments before pulling up the cobles on the beaches at Filey, Robin Hood's Bay or Runswick.

Other sports also caught the attention of artists, reflecting the season portrayed in the work. Atkinson was reputed to be a keen angler and, with his focus more on rural rather than coastal life, it is no surprise that he pictured fishing on the Esk. Garrido's self-confessed love of fishing must surely have brought the two men together, given their mutual acquaintances and the fact that they were almost neighbours. On his travels to Scotland and Ireland Bowen pictured rivers accented by lone fishermen. Shooting also features in several works by artists who painted on the Yorkshire moors or heathlands further afield.

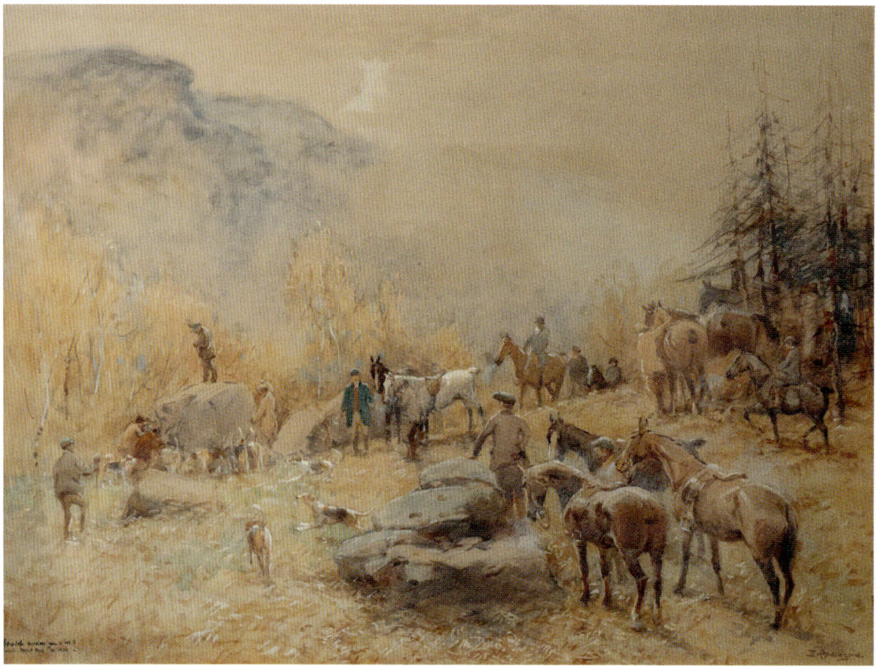

Left: 198. As with Rowland Hill, John Atkinson painted many pictures on the theme of local hunts and huntsmen. Perhaps because he was not a horseman himself, these tend to focus on pre-hunt gatherings or, as *Glaisdale Harriers Run a Fox to Ground, Fryup Head* (1909), shown here, the moment when riders reined in their charges.

Below: 199. James Booth was a firm friend of Fred Jackson, also hailing from Middleton. He followed the latter's path to Runswick Bay and shared a studio with the Knights in Staithes. This undated work, *Unloading the Cart*, is typical of both his style and subject matter, with the horse as the focus of daily life.

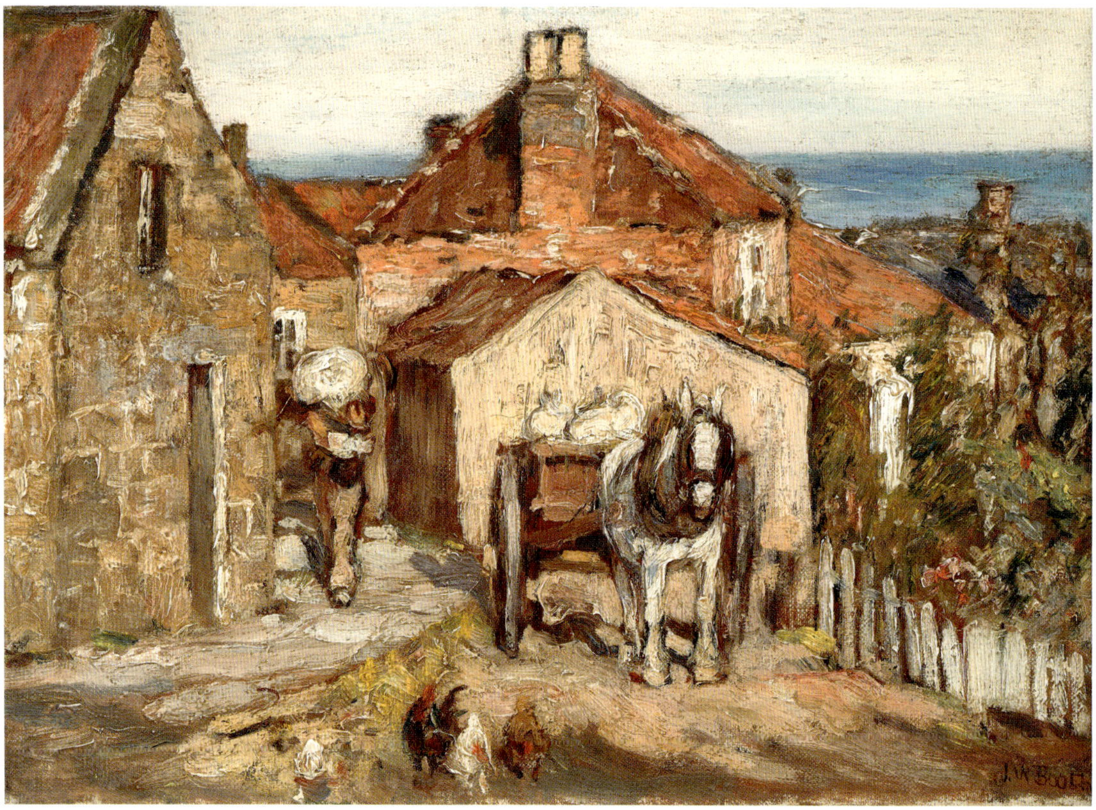

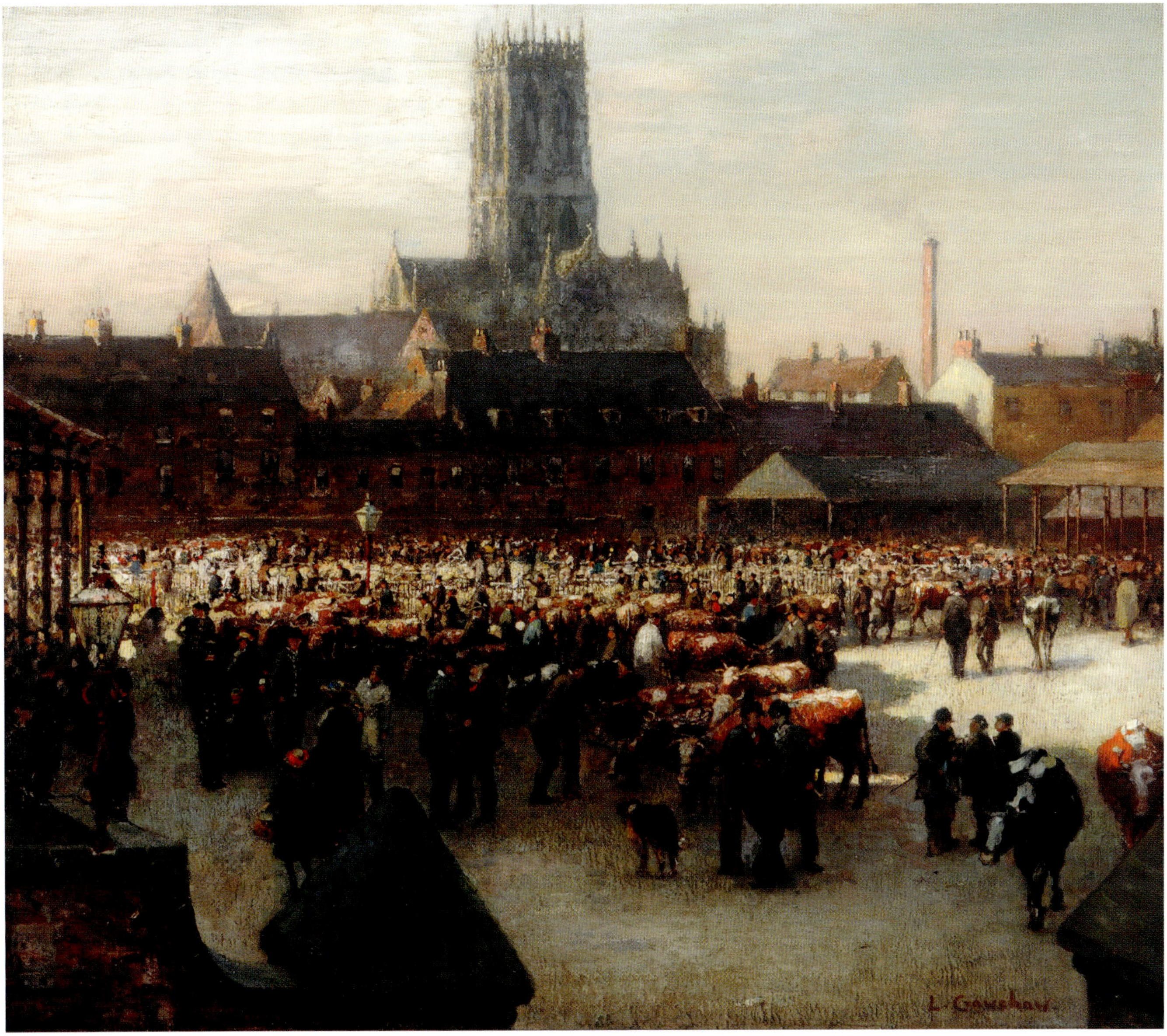

200. Lionel Crawshaw maintained a studio in Whitby, but always retained strong ties to his home town. *Cattle Market, Doncaster*, exhibited at the Royal Academy in 1915, was donated to the Doncaster Museum the following year by 'C. H. Mackie'; it is unclear whether this was Charles Hodge Mackie, his fellow Staithes painter.

A TIME OF CHANGE

The rural traditions captured by these artists were, of course, to be upended not once but twice between 1914 and 1945. This period covered the same amount of time that elapsed between the arrival of the first of the Staithes Art Club artists at the coast and the outbreak of the First World War. The brief activity of the Club must have seemed insignificant compared to the challenges of these years. Yet the formative experiences and friendship were a valuable source of solace, as confirmed by those writing in the 1930s.

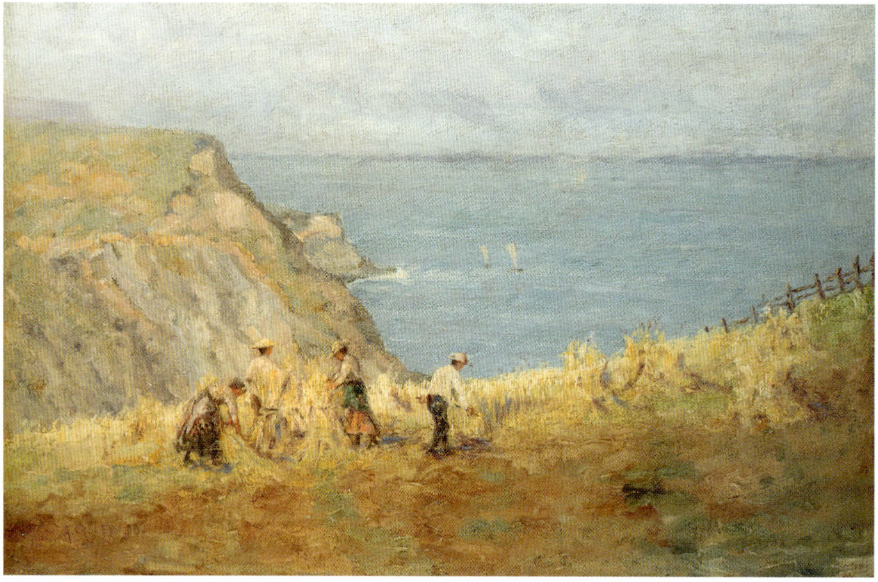

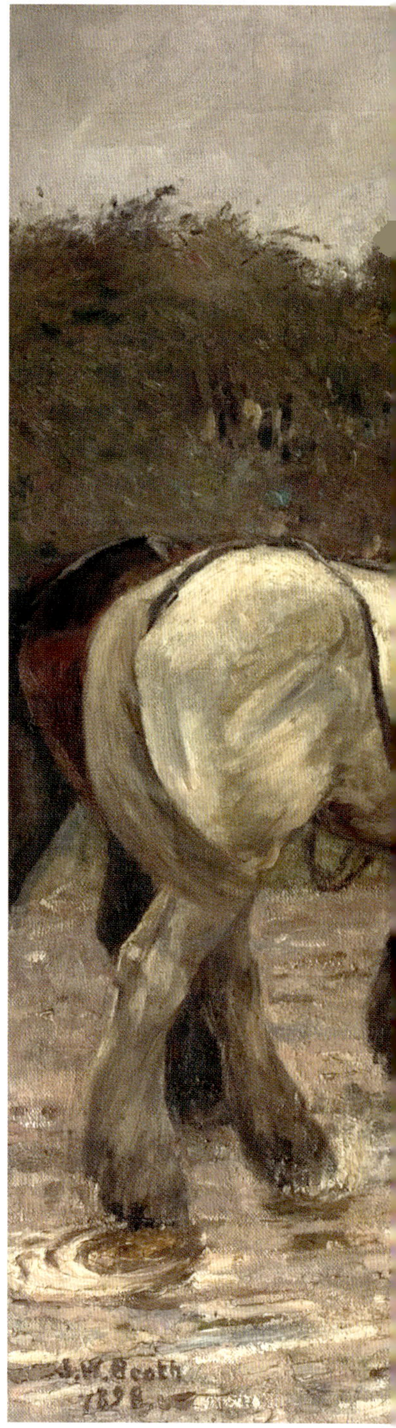

Above: 201. Andrew Colley's extant works seem to be few and far between. Though not a member of the Art Club, he is often mentioned in the context of its artists. Works ascribed to him stretch as far afield as Italy, but here he pictures the harvest on *Old Nab from Quarry Bank* (date unknown).

Right: 202. A Royal Academy exhibition piece from 1898, J. W. Booth's *Homeward Bound* was bought by the Shipston family. It was later donated to Nottingham Museums, along with another large oil by the artist from 1904. Just one year after painting it, he was elected an Associate Member of the Royal Cambrian Academy.

The seasonal rhythm of work was disrupted and the ability to travel to the continent cut short. Whatever the location in which the artists found themselves, they witnessed changes which forced themselves into their pictures. The Joblings painted troops patrolling the coast in Yorkshire, Ernest Rigg painted horses that had experienced the conflict of the First World War on the estate in Hertfordshire to which they were 'retired' and Hill travelled to France to paint the aftermath of the conflict. Frank Henry Mason, appointed a war artist, travelled widely, painting naval activity wherever he was assigned.

However, the artists' commitment to outdoor painting and the importance of nature as the axis of their work remained. It does take on a different feel in its new, more troubled context; it translates rather to a pastorale in which the fierce freshness and realism of the pre-war paintings are tempered. The painterly or patternistic quality of these works helps to distract rather than focus the viewer on the persistent, troubled undercurrents of the times.

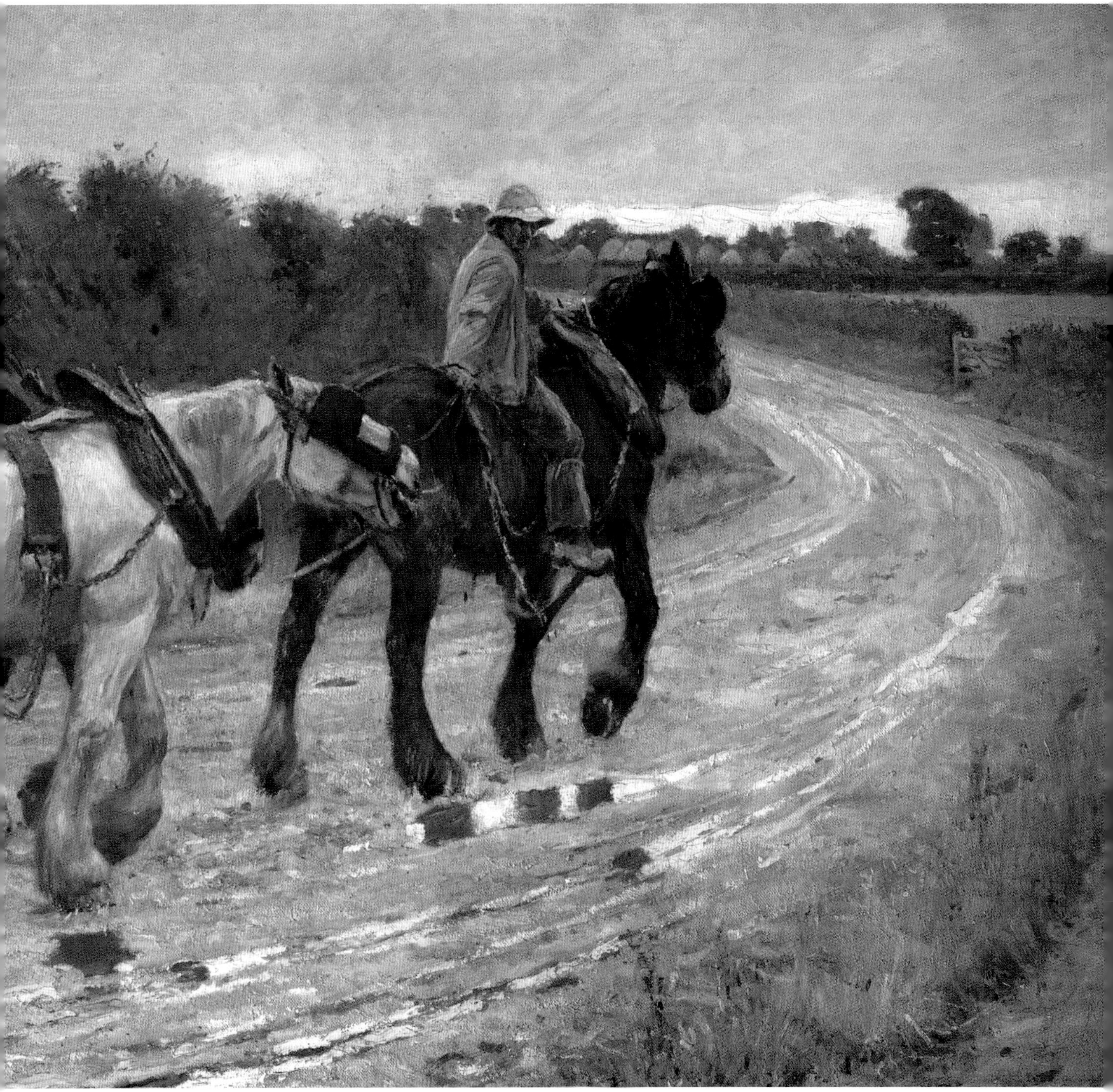

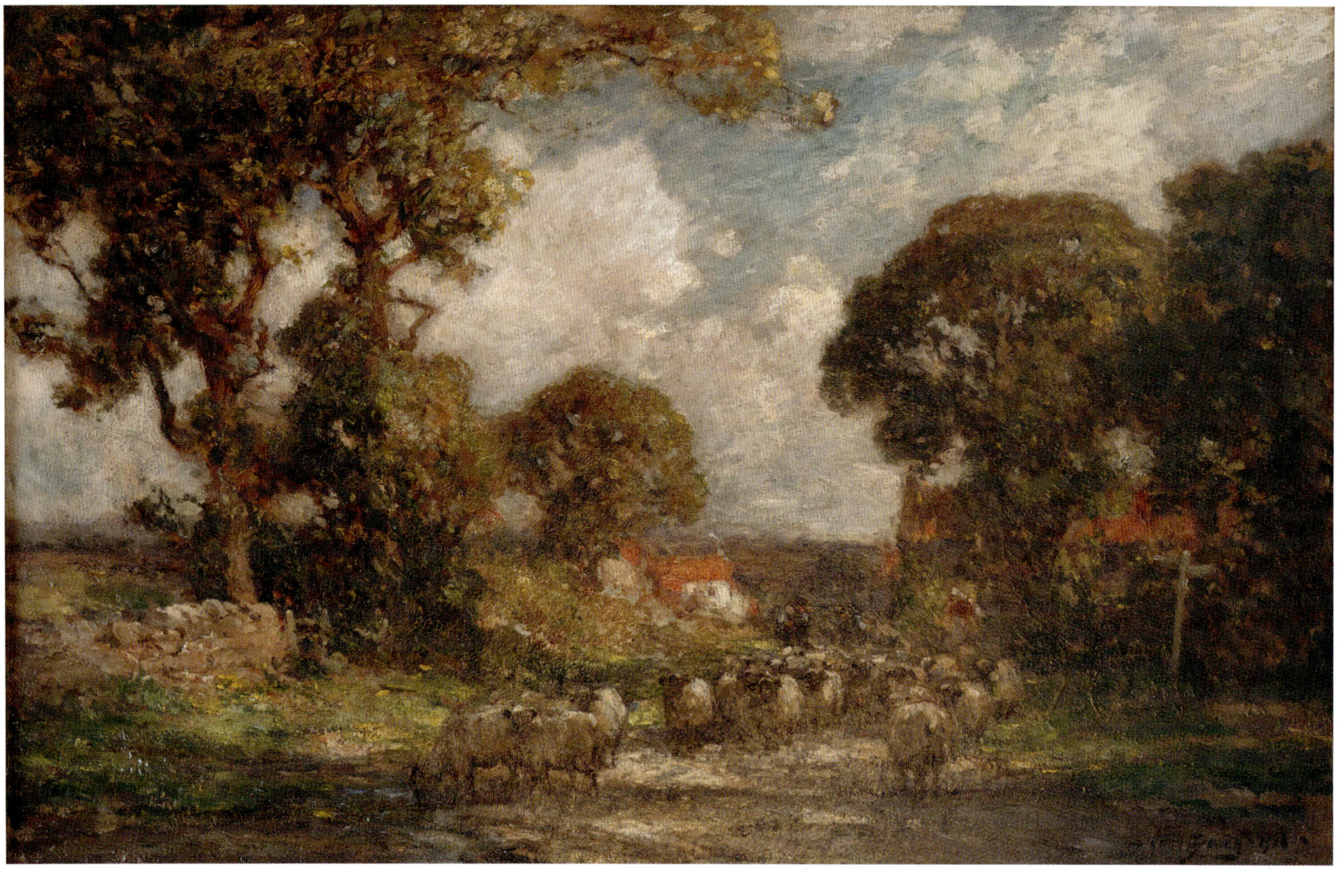

203. Owen Bowen's beautiful image of Kelling Village, Norfolk (1910) pictures shepherd and flocks on The Street that runs up through the village. Its situation, between the coast and the uplands of the heath, recalls the geography of the area around Robin Hood's Bay.

What cohesive practice the fellow artists may have been able at one time to generate dissipated; their individual paths diverged rather than crossed. Despite this, members of the Art Club continued to exhibit together; the Knights in Cornwall and London, Crawshaw, Terry and Rigg in Yorkshire, for example. They also maintained friendships prompted by it, such as that of Hill and John William Howey.

It is hoped that this book marks an impression, albeit on shifting sands, of the members of the Staithes Art Club and their relationships that endured over turbulent years. Through exploring their diverse characters, skills and achievements, it seeks to provide impetus and enthusiasm for further study and lasting appreciation of their work.

ENDNOTES

223 *Whitby Gazette*, 21 August 1903; review of 3rd Staithes Art Club Exhibition.

224 Quigley, J., *Leandro Ramon Garrido, His Life and Art*, 1913, 122.

225 Hiley, M., *Frank Sutcliffe: Photographer of Whitby* 1974, 47, n. 3.

226 While the castle is rarely, if ever, pictured, its woods are included in several pictures. Whitby Abbey, of course, is pictured many times, but is rarely – as in the example from the list of Art Club exhibits by Isabella Jobling, *Whitby Abbey from Sandsend* – the focus of the title.

227 Knight, L., *Oil Paint and Grease Paint*, 1936, 133.

228 National Visual Arts Library of Ireland (NIVAL): Special Collections: The Oliver Sheppard Papers. Letter from Rosie Good to Oliver Sheppard, 15 September 1899.

229 National Visual Arts Library of Ireland (NIVAL): Special Collections: The Oliver Sheppard Papers. Letter from Cissy Johnson to Rosie Good, *c.* 1903.

230 *The Dalesman*, 'O. Bowen: 60 years of painting', vol. 29, August 1967, 370–4; September 1967, 464–8; October 1967, 539–44.

231 *Yorkshire Evening Post*, 31 August 1939, Rowland Henry Hill, 'A Seaside Colony of Artists'.

232 Moss, Brian and Rachel, *John Atkinson 1863–1924*, 1981, 6.

233 National Visual Arts Library of Ireland (NIVAL): Special Collections: The Oliver Sheppard Papers. Letter from Laura Knight to Rosie Good, 3 November 1903.

234 *Leeds Mercury Weekly Supplement*, 24 December 1904, Harwood Brierley: 'A Yorkshire Itinerary: Runswick to Staithes'. Rowland Hill also maintained that Mark Senior often visited or even stayed for periods during the winter months, see *Yorkshire Evening Post*, 1939.

235 Clark, *People, Places, Piazzas: The Life and Art of Charles H. Mackie*, 2016, 87.

236 Quigley, *Leandro Ramon Garrido: His Life and Art*, 1913, 130.

237 *Amateur Photographer* magazine, 14 May 1903. This was in relation to his image *The Flag of Distress* (**76**).

238 Hiley, *Frank Sutcliffe: Photographer of Whitby*, 1974, 76.

239 Hiley, *Frank Sutcliffe: Photographer of Whitby*, 1974, 76.

240 Hart, J. (ed.), *The Secret Staithes Diary of Enid Lucy Pease Robinson*, 2010, 78 (entry for 27 August 1901).

241 Both pictures are now in the collections of Manchester Museums. There is also a further sketch which, though its visual connection appears tenuous, bears an artist's inscription stipulating that it was a preparatory study for *The Coming Storm*.

242 Fred Richardson, 1904; Joseph Bagshawe, 1902; Bagshawe and Mackie, 1903 and 1904.

243 Hiley, *Frank Sutcliffe: Photographer of Whitby,* 1974, 48, n. 4.

244 Moss, Brian and Rachel, *John Atkinson 1863–1924*, 1981, cat. no. 11, *Winter at Egton near Whitby*; cat. no. 17, *Ploughing in Winter*.

245 Butterworth was actually interned in 1914 while on a trip to Germany. He was only released in 1918, the year of Jackson's death. Press reviews of the exhibition are held in Jackson's artist's file at Manchester City Art Gallery.

246 Mayor, Fred, 'Diary, From Tangier to Fez with a trader', 1899 (unpublished).

247 *Barnsley Chronicle*, 8 April 1905.

248 Phillips, *The Staithes Group*, 1993, exh. cat., 52. Knight, L., *Oil Paint and Grease Paint*, 1936, 93 contains an anecdote about an exotic embroidered coat brought back by a sailor from an unremembered country.

249 *Whitby Gazette*, 27 August 1909. It was also reported that Fred Jackson did not dance, but otherwise seemed to enjoy himself greatly as a 'Shropshire lad' in his bucolic smock-frock and hosen grey, puffing at his long clay pipe and meditating, possibly, over new and charming pastoral pictures.

250 Parkin, M., *Mark Senior*, 1974, 3.

251 Sutcliffe often took a house in the village of Glaisdale, 'commuting' into Whitby to his studio.
Sutcliffe in the *Yorkshire Weekly Post*, 2 May 1908.

252 Hiley, *Frank Sutcliffe: Photographer of Whitby* 1974, 77.

253 *Leeds Mercury*, 24 December 1904; Harwood Brierley, 'A Yorkshire Itinerary', Part 1.

254 Phillips, *The Staithes Group*, 1993, exh. cat., 47; correspondence with Mr H. J. S. Clark, 1975–8.

255 Though not in the Pas-de-Calais, the countryside of the two regions is very similar. National Visual Arts Library of Ireland (NIVAL): Special Collections: The Oliver Sheppard Papers. Undated letter from Cissy Johnson to Rosie Good.

256 Leicester Galleries, *In Sunny Places*, 1902, exh. cat., 9.

257 McConkey, K., *Impressionism in Britain*, 1995, exh. cat., 445, no. 101.

258 Hiley, *Frank Sutcliffe: Photographer of Whitby*, 1974, 54, n. 24.

APPENDIX: STAITHES ART CLUB, 1902–4

STAITHES ART CLUB.

CATALOGUE.

		PRICE.		
1.	"Haytime," J. Bowman	£4	4	0
2.	"The Valley," J. Bowman ...	4	4	0
3.	"Summer," J. Bowman	4	4	0
4.	"Roses," Isa Jobling	4	4	0
5.	"Uplands," A. A. Friedenson	5	5	0
6.	"The Orchard," Robert Jobling ...	10	0	0
7.	"The Ropery," T. Barrett, R.E. ...	10	0	0
8.	"A Bit of Staithes," ,, ,, ...	7	7	0
9.	"Hyacinths," A. A. Friedenson ...	5	5	0
10.	"Haytime," J. Booth	5	0	0
11.	"In Grinkle Wood," A. A. Friedenson ...	6	0	0
12.	"The Pool Below the Bridge," C. H. Mackie, A.R.S.A.	10	10	0
13.	"Moonlight on the Bay," Chas. H. Mackie, A.R.S.A.	60	0	0
14.	"The Hill, Runswick," ,, ,, ,,	12	12	0
15.	"Winter Quarters," H. S. Hopwood, A.R.W.S.	10	10	0
16.	"A Brother Brush," ,, ,, ,,	8	8	0
17.	"Evening," ,, ,, ,,	15	15	0
18.	"A Breezy Upland," ,, ,, ,,	8	8	0
19.	"Loading Hay," Harold Knight ...	5	5	0
20.	"Launching Cobles,"	8	0	0
21.	"Haying," ,, ,, ...	5	5	0
22.	"On the Staith," ,, ,, ...	3	3	0
23.	"Mezzotint," T. Barrett, R.E.	2	2	0
24.	"The White Gate," F. W. Jackson ...	10	10	0
25.	"A Bit of Runswick," F. W. Jackson ...	8	8	0
26.	"La Fête Dieu Coucarneau," F. W. Jackson	10	10	0
27.	"Mezzotint," T. Barrett, R.E. ...	2	2	0
28.	"The Mother Child," Laura Johnson ...	5	5	0
29.	"And Women Must Weep," Laura Johnson	18	18	0
30.	"The Knitting Lesson," ,, ,,	10	10	0
31.	"Staithes Beach," J. Richard Bagshawe	6	6	0
32.	"On the Coast," ,, ,, ...	6	6	0
33.	"Northerly Breeze," ,, ,, ...	5	0	0
34.	"A Timber Ship," ,, ,, ...	5	0	0
35.	"A Breezy Day," Hirst Walker ...			
36.	"An Autumn Sunset," ,, ,, ...			
37.	"Pastel," Fred Mayor	2	2	0
38.	,, ,, ,, ...	2	2	0
39.	"Pets," J. Bowman	15	15	0
40.	"Pastel," Fred Mayor	2	2	0
41.	,, ,, ...	2	2	0

The Unframed Drawings in the Portfolio are marked on the back with the price.

STAITHES ART CLUB

CATALOGUE.

		PRICE.		
1.	"A Sketch on the Cliff," J. Bowman ..	£8	8	0
2.	"A Hillside," J. Bowman ..	5	5	0
3.	"Harvesting," J. Booth	8	8	0
4.	"A Hinderwell Hayfield," F. W. Jackson ..	10	10	0
5.	"A Showery Haytime," A. A. Friedenson ..	10	10	0
6.	"An April Day," A. A. Friedenson ..	5	5	0
7.	"The Bridge," J. Bowman	6	6	0
8.	"Ailing," H. S. Hopwood, A.R.W.S. ..	15	0	0
9.	"The Highfields," T. Barrett, A.R.E. ..	7	10	0
10.	"The Harvest Cart," A. A. Friedenson ..	6	6	0
11.	"Staithes Beach," A. A. Friedenson ..	5	0	0
12.	"A Portrait," F. W. Jackson ..			
13.	"Off to the Rescue," F. W. Jackson ..	25	0	0
14.	"A Sunny Hour," F. W. Jackson ..	12	0	0
15.	"Wild Weather," J. Richard Bagshawe ..	4	4	0
16.	"A Study of a Calf," H. S. Hopwood, A.R.W.S.	10	10	0
17.	"At Rye," Harold Knight	7	7	0
18.	"Morning," T. Barrett, A.R.E.	3	3	0 X
19.	"A Rough Landing, Runswick," Rowland H. Hill	3	3	0
20.	"In the Dawn," J. Richard Bagshawe ..	12	12	0
21.	"The Carpenter's Shop," H. S. Hopwood, A.R.W.S.	40	0	0
22.	"The White House," Harold Knight ..	8	8	0
23.	"On the Beach," Laura Knight ..	8	8	0
24.	"Filey Fishing," J. Booth	3	3	0 X
25.	"North-Easter," J. Richard Bagshawe ..	4	4	0
26.	"Off Whitby Rock," J. Richard Bagshawe ..	15	15	0
27.	"The Farm Pond," Laura Knight ..	10	10	0
28.	"A Bavarian Shrine," Rowland H. Hill ..	3	3	0
29.	"A Timber Yard," Harold Knight ..	6	6	0
30.	"Hinderwell Beck in June," S. Gardner ..	4	4	0
31.	"The Road to the Farm," Laura Knight ..	25	0	0
32.	"The Mower," J. Bowman	7	7	0
33.	"Hill-side near Harrogate," Hirst Walker			
34.	"Moorland," T. Barrett, A.R.E.	3	3	0
35.	"The Mill on the Hill," Laura Knight ..	5	5	0
36.	"A Corner in Runswick," H. S. Hopwood, A.R.W.S.	10	10	0
37.	"A Moorland Road," T. Barrett. A.R.E. ..	3	3	0
38.	"A Farm Pond at Hinderwell," S. Gardner ..	4	4	0
39.	"A Bavarian Landscape," Rowland H. Hill ..	3	3	0 X
40.	"Low Water," Rowland H. Hill ..	3	3	0
41.	"A Morning Chat," James Watson ..	7	10	0
42.	"Whitby Abbey from Sandsend," Isa Jobling ..	3	3	0
43.	"Runswick," Isa Jobling	3	3	0
44.	"Pastel," Fred Mayor	2	2	0

The Sketches in the Portfolio are marked on the back with the price.

STAITHES ART CLUB.

FOURTH ANNUAL EXHIBITION

AT

Anderson's West Cliff Art Gallery, Well Close Square.

CATALOGUE.

NO.		PRICE. £	S.	D.
1.	Evening Calm—Hirst Walker			
1A.	A Study—Fred Mayor	4	4	0
1B.	In Algiers—Fred Mayor	7	7	0
1C.	Eventide—Fred Mayor	5	5	0
2.	Katwyk Sands—Frank Mason, R.B.A.	10	10	0
3.	A Study—Rowland H. Hill	5	5	0
4.	September—John Bowman	7	7	0
5.	The Farmstead—Isa Jobling	7	0	0
6.	Landing Herrings at Scarborough—Harold Knight	25	0	0
7.	Harvesting—James Booth	6	6	0
8.	Ploughing—James Booth	6	6	0
9.	Mother and Children—Mrs. Harold Knight	25	0	0
10.	Whitby Roads—J. Richard Bagshawe, R.B.A.	7	7	0
11.	The Wreck of the Carrulla at Runswick—F. W. Jackson	200	0	0
12.	The Jap Album—Chas. H. Mackie, A.R.S.A.	35	0	0
13.	Off Godrevy: Freshening Breeze—J. Richard Bagshawe, R.B.A.	25	0	0
14.	A Breton Heath—Rowland H. Hill	22	0	0
15.	On the East Coast—F. W. Jackson	50	0	0
16.	Carrying Baits—P. Morton Teasdale	8	8	0
17.	A Runswick Home—J. Bowman	7	7	0
18.	Early Morning: Runswick Bay—A. A. Friedenson	40	0	0
19.	Brocketts, Robin Hood's Bay—Owen Bowen, A.R.C.A.	8	8	0
20.	A Stockinger—Mrs. Harold Knight	8	8	0
21.	Potato Gatherer—Isa Jobling	15	0	0
22.	Seed Time—Rowland H. Hill	40	0	0
23.	Brambles—Isa Jobling	5	0	0
24.	Staithes Wyke—J. Richard Bagshawe, R.B.A.	15	0	0
25.	In the Roar of the Sea—F. Stuart Richardson, R.I.	47	5	0
26.	End of the Day—James Booth	52	10	0
27.	Toilers of the Deep—Harold Knight	150	0	0
28.	Making the Stack—J. Bowman	5	5	0
29.	Staithes—A. A. Friedenson	7	7	0
30.	Newton Mulgrave—John Bowman	5	5	0
31.	A Breton Cider Orchard—Rowland H. Hill	30	6	0
32.	June Weather—J. Richard Bagshawe, R.B.A.	30	0	0
33.	Portrait of Miss Watson—P. M. Teasdale			
34.	The Children's Hour—Robert Jobling	8	0	0
35.	Study in Toledo—Lionel T. Crawshaw	4	0	0
36.	"	4	4	0
37.	"	4	0	0
38.	Whitby—Lionel T. Crawshaw	3	0	0
39.	Runswick—Lionel T. Crawshaw	3	0	0
40.	A Dutch Maiden—Robert Jobling	10	0	0
41.	The Laurel Inn—Robin Hood's Bay—Owen Bowen, A.R.C.A.	8	8	0
42.	Evening: Whitby Harbour—E. E. Anderson, R.B.A.	8	0	0
43.	Near Robin Hood's Bay—T. Wright, A.R.E.	20	0	0
44.	At Runswick—F. W. Jackson	20	0	0
45.	October Moonrise—Hirst Walker			
46.	On Green Howe Hill—Hirst Walker			
47.	Low Tide: Whitby Harbour—E. E. Anderson, R.B.A.	20	0	0
48.	Port after Storm: Rest after Toil—F. W. Jackson	35	0	0
49.	In Shoal Water—J. Richard Bagshawe; R.B.A.	10	10	0
49A.	Whitby: Grey Day—J. R. Bagshawe, R.B.A.	4	4	0
50.	A Summer Eve—Fred Mayor	70	0	0
51.	A Little Mother—Mrs Harold Knight	15	0	0
52.	The Widower—F. W. Jackson	20	0	0
53.	From the Baltic—J. Richard Bagshawe, R.B.A.	6	6	0
54.	Wind against Tide: Whitby Rock—J. Richard Bagshawe, R.BA.	12	12	0
55.	A Yorkshire Farmstead—James Booth	10	10	0
56.	High Tide: Whitby Harbour—E. E Anderson. R.B.A	12	0	0
57.	Hay Time—F. W. Jackson	35	0	0
57a.	Outward Bound—J. R. Bagshawe, R.B.A.	4	4	0
58.	Near Boulogne—Hirst Walker			
59.	A Runswick Corner—Rowland H. Hill	7	7	0
60.	In Dalehouse Woods—Spence Ingall	6	6	0
61.	A Breton Sunday—Rowland H. Hill	6	6	0
62.	The Fisherman's Family—F. W. Jackson	15	0	0
63.	A Whitby Wharf—E. E. Anderson, R.B.A.	3	3	0
64.	A Study of Fighting Cocks (in monotype)—Lionel T. Crawshaw	5	0	0
65.	Ditto ditto	5	0	0
66.	Ditto ditto	5	0	0
67.	A Roadside Study—Chas. H. Mackie. A.R.S.A.	6	0	0
67a.	In the Spring Time—F. W. Jackson	5	5	0
67b.	The End of the Fishing Season—F. W. Jackson	5	5	0
68.	On the Tagus at Toledo—Chas. H. Mackie, A.R.S.A.	12	0	0
69.	A Nor'-Easter—Chas. H. Mackie, A.R.S.A.	8	0	0
70.	Sundown at Runswick Bay—Chas. H. Mackie, A.R.S.A.	8	0	0
71.	Leisure Hours—F. Stuart Richardson, R.I.	3	3	0
72.	Whitby—E. E. Anderson, R.B.A.	3	3	0
73.	A Landscape—Hirst Walker			
74.	Treacherous Waters—F. Stuart Richardson, R.I.	10	10	0
75.	Looe Bay—F. Stuart Richardson	9	9	0
76.	Study of Cattle—Jas. Booth	4	0	0
77.	The Sea Wall—F. Stuart Richardson, R.I.	6	6	0
78.	Whitby Harbour—Robert Jobling	4	0	0
79.	The Way Foot Robin Hood's Bay (aquatint) J. Wright, A.R.E.	1	5	0
80.	Canal des Baudets, Bruges—J. Wright, A.R.E.	1	5	0
81.	Canal at Sluys—J. Wright, A.R.E.	1	5	0
82.	The Watchman at Knole (aquatint)—J. Wright, A.R.E.	1	10	0
83.	Robin Hood's Bay—J. Wright, A.R.E.	1	5	0
84.	Grasse (drypoint)—J. Wright	1	10	0
85.	Volendam Harbour—R. Jobling	8	0	0
86.	Summer Calm—Hirst Walker			
87.	Staithes—G. Harold Knight	8	8	0
88.	Ditto Ditto.	8	8	0

A number of Sketches in the Portfolio are marked on the back with the price.

"TIMES" PRINTING WORKS

LIST OF ILLUSTRATIONS

AUTHOR'S ACKNOWLEDGEMENTS

INTRODUCTION

CHAPTER 1: THE STAITHES ART CLUB

Divider 1:

30. **James Guthrie**
Hard At It
Oil on canvas, 1883
© Glasgow Life Museums / Bridgeman Images

Divider 2:

31. **Joseph Bagshawe**
Untitled Sketch for *A Week in a Long Liner*
Charcoal, c. 1909
Private collection, courtesy A&A Arts

32. **Enid Pease Robinson**
Staithes Diary
Pen and ink, 1901
Courtesy James Hart

33. **Joseph Bagshawe**
Design Sketches for Art Club posters
Charcoal, c. 1901
Private collection, courtesy A&A Arts

34. **Laura Johnson**
Untitled Leaves from her Staithes Sketchbook
Pencil, charcoal, coloured crayon on paper, c. 1898–1903
Courtesy Chris Beetles Gallery, St. James's, London
© Reproduced with permission of The Estate of Dame Laura Knight DBE RA 2025

35. **Ernest H. Rigg**
A Fireside Read
Oil on canvas, c. 1895
© Pannett Art Gallery, Whitby

36. **Owen Bowen**
Showery Haytime at Robin Hood's Bay
Oil on canvas, 1903
Private collection, courtesy A&A Arts

37. **William G. Foster**
The Azure Mead
Oil on canvas, 1894
Private Collection, Courtesy Bonhams Auctioneers

38. **George Weatherill**
Steam Tug, Whitby Bridge
Watercolour, 1888
Pannett Art Gallery, Whitby

39. **Frank Meadow Sutcliffe**
Whitby
Photograph, c. 1890
Whitby Museum

40. **The Honorable Duff Tollemache**
After the Catch
Oil on canvas, 1885
Purchased 1928 with the aid of the Felix Cobbold Bequest Fund
© Colchester and Ipswich Museums Service: Ipswich Borough Council Collection

41. **Fred W. Jackson**
Runswick Bay
Oil on canvas, undated
Private collection, courtesy McTague of Harrogate

42. **Ernest Dade**
The Amity *Going to Sea*
Oil on canvas, 1893
© Scarborough Museums & Galleries / Bridgeman Images

43. **William Brymner**
The Lonely Orphans Taken to Her Heart
Oil on canvas, 1884
Collection of the Montreal Museum of Fine Arts, purchase, F. Cleveland Morgan Fund (2015.224)
© MMFA, Christine Guest

44. **Isabella Jobling (née Thompson)**
Fisherfolk
Oil on canvas, 1893
Laing Art Gallery, purchased with assistance of the Victoria & Albert Museum Purchase Grant Fund and The National Art Collections Fund
© Laing Art Gallery / Bridgeman Images

45. **Harrington Mann**
Low Tide on the Beck
Oil on panel, 1898
Gift of George Bednar, 2005
© Pannett Art Gallery / Bridgeman Images

46. **Charles H. Mackie**
The Jap(anese) Album
Oil on canvas, 1904
Art Gallery New South Wales, purchased 1912
© AGNSW

47. **Harold Knight**
The Last Coble
Oil on canvas, 1900
Nottingham City Museums & Galleries, gift from the Holbrook Trust, Trustees of the William S. Holbrook Bequest, 1902
© Estate of Dame Laura Knight. All rights reserved 2025 / Bridgeman Images

48. **Sydney Lee**
The Bridge, Staithes
Woodcut, 1904
British Museum, Campbell Dodgson Bequest
© The Trustees of the British Museum

49. **John Wright**
Canal at Sluys
Etching, c. 1904
Pannett Art Gallery, Whitby

50. **Hirst Walker**
Letters to Robert and Isa Jobling, 1907
Private collection, courtesy A&A Arts

51. **Robert Jobling**
Cowbar Nab, Staithes
Oil on canvas, 1914
Courtesy McTague of Harrogate

52. **Mark Senior**
Eventide
Oil on board, 1892
© The Hepworth, Wakefield / Bridgeman Images

53. **Laura Johnson**
Under the Bridge, Staithes
Oil on canvas, 1901
Private collection, courtesy
Christie's Images / Bridgeman Images
© Reproduced with permission of The Estate of
Dame Laura Knight DBE RA 2025

54. **Arthur Friedenson**
Runswick Bay
Oil on canvas, c. 1908
Private collection, courtesy A&A Arts

55. **James William Booth**
A Country Horse Fair at Hinderwell
Oil on canvas, 1897
© Rochdale Arts & Heritage Service / Bridgeman
Images

56. **Thomas Barrett**
Pilchard Boats
Etching, c. 1890
Gift from the artist to his pupil Mabel Annie Levy
Courtesy A&A Arts

57. **Joseph Bagshawe**
Untitled Sketch of the yawl *True Love*
Charcoal, c. 1909
Private collection, courtesy A&A Arts

58. **Joseph Bagshawe**
The Old Skipper in a Squall
Watercolour, c. 1898–9
Pannett Art Gallery, Whitby

59. **Henry S. Hopwood**
Hauling the Sheets
Watercolour, c. 1890
Courtesy Charles Miller Auctioneers

60. **Henry S. Hopwood**
Dinner in the Foc'sle
Watercolour, 1889
Art Gallery New South Wales, purchased 1889
© AGNSW

61. **Dermod O'Brien**
The Fine Art Academy, Antwerp
Oil on canvas, 1890
© National Museums NI

62a. **Ernest Higgins Rigg**
Sitting Nude
Oil on canvas, c. 1892
Private collection, courtesy A&A Arts

62b. **Ernest H. Rigg**
Standing Nude
Oil on canvas, c. 1892
Private collection, courtesy A&A Arts

63. **Fred W. Jackson**
Sardine Boats at Concarneau
Watercolour, c. 1885
© Manchester Art Gallery / Bridgeman Images

64. **Fred W. Jackson**
Venice
Oil on panel, c. 1890
Gift of L. M. Angus-Butterworth in
memory of his father Walter
© York Museums Trust

65. **Harold Knight**
Portrait of Laura Johnson
Oil on canvas, c. 1900
Royal Academy of Arts, bequest of
Dame Laura Knight 1970
© RAA / Bridgeman Images

66. **Hannah Hoyland**
Still Life
Watercolour, c. 1890
Courtesy A&A Arts

67. **W. Fred Mayor**
Fishermen
Oil on board, c. 1898
Middlesborough Institute of Modern Art, purchased with the assistance of the Victoria and Albert Museum Purchase Grant Fund, 1980–1
© MIMA / Bridgeman Images

CHAPTER 2: LIFE

Divider 1:
68. **Fred W. Jackson**
The Harvest of the Sea
Oil on canvas, 1885
© Gallery Oldham / Bridgeman Images

Divider 2:
69. **Walter Langley**
In a Cornish Fishing Village – Departure of the Fleet for the North
Watercolour, 1886
Penlee House Gallery & Museum, Penzance

70. **Joseph Bagshawe**
Untitled Sketch
Charcoal, c. 1900
Private collection, courtesy A&A Arts

71. **Charles H. Mackie**
La Ducasse / La Danse du Village
Oil on canvas, c. 1908
Work submitted for the RSA Diploma, 1918
Royal Scottish Academy of Art & Architecture

72. **William Brymner**
A Wreath of Flowers
Oil on canvas, 1884
Collection of the National Gallery of Canada, Ottawa, Royal Canadian Academy of Arts diploma work, deposited by the artist, Ottawa, 1886 (19) ©NGC

73. **Winslow Homer**
Tynemouth
Watercolour, 1881
The Art Institute of Chicago, Mr & Mrs A. Ryerson Collection, 1933.1254
© The Art Institute of Chicago / Scala, Florence

74. **Joseph Terry**
Yorkshire Cliffs at Sunset
Oil on canvas, c. 1920
York Art Gallery, Gift of the Artist 1924
© York Museums Trust

75. **Laura Johnson**
Staithes
Oil on canvas, 1900
Private collection, courtesy Christie's Images / Bridgeman Images
© Estate of Dame Laura Knight.
All rights reserved 2025 / Bridgeman Images

76. **Frank M. Sutcliffe**
The Flag of Distress
Photograph, 1885
Whitby Museum

77. **Ernest Dade**
Scarborough Harbour at Sunset
Watercolour, undated
Courtesy A&A Arts

78. **Frank Henry Mason**
After Trafalgar
Oil on canvas, 1907
Laing Art Gallery, gift from Waite Sanderson, 1944
© Laing Art Gallery / Bridgeman Images

79. **Harold Knight**
Rough Sea at Whitby
Oil on canvas, c. 1900
Private collection, courtesy Tennant's Auctioneers
© Reproduced with permission of The Estate of Dame Laura Knight DBE RA 2025

80. **Frank H. Mason**
St Ives Lugger Coming to Shore in a Storm
Watercolour, 1900
Pannett Art Gallery, Whitby

81. **Lionel T. Crawshaw**
Dancing on the Pier at Whitby
Oil on canvas, c. 1920
York Art Gallery, gift of of Colonel H. G. Crawshaw on behalf of the artist's widow, 1949
© York Museums Trust

82. **John Atkinson**
The Fish Quay, North Shields
Watercolour, undated
Courtesy A&A Arts

83. **Arthur Friedenson**
Harbourside, St Monan's
Oil on board, 1907
Courtesy A&A Arts

84. **Owen Bowen**
Barges at the Riverside
Oil on canvas, 1909
Courtesy A&A Arts

85. **Percy Morton Teasdale**
His First Ship
Oil on canvas, c. 1904
Courtesy Messum's, London

86. **Mark Senior**
Toil
Oil on canvas, 1900
Leeds Art Gallery, purchased 1901
© Leeds Museum & Galleries / Bridgeman Images

87. **Ernest H. Rigg**
Mending Nets, Runswick Bay
Oil on canvas, undated
Courtesy Messum's, London

88. **Owen Bowen**
Beached Fishing Coble, South Landing, Flamborough
Oil on canvas, 1906
Private collection, courtesy Tennant's Auctioneers

89. **Joseph Bagshawe**
Untitled Sketches
Pencil on paper, c. 1898
Courtesy Chris Beetles Gallery, St James's, London
© Reproduced with permission of The Estate of
Dame Laura Knight DBE RA 2025

90. **Laura Johnson**
Cobles at Runswick
Oil on board, c. 1900
Private collection, courtesy A&A Arts
© Reproduced with permission of The Estate of
Dame Laura Knight DBE RA 2025

91. **Joseph Bagshawe**
Untitled Leaves from a Staithes Sketchbook (see **58**)
Charcoal, c. 1898–9
Private collection, courtesy A&A Arts

92. **Fred W. Jackson**
Fisherfolk Watching the Lifeboat Rescue
Watercolour, undated
Private collection, courtesy A&A Arts

93. **Harold Knight**
Hauling Cobles
Watercolour, c. 1900
Private collection, courtesy A&A Arts
© Reproduced with permission of The Estate of
Dame Laura Knight DBE RA 2025

94. **Harold Knight**
Untitled
Watercolour, c. 1900
Private collection, courtesy A&A Arts
© Reproduced with permission of The Estate of
Dame Laura Knight DBE RA 2025

95. **James W. Booth**
Fishmarket on the Staith
Watercolour, c. 1900
Private collection, courtesy A&A Arts

96. **Sidney Lough Thompson**
Coble on the Beck
Oil on canvas, 1901
Gift of Mrs H. M. Thompson 1909
Aigantighe Art Gallery, Timaru, New Zealand
© AAG

97. **Sidney Lough Thompson**
Entrance to o'er t'Beck, Staithes
Oil on canvas, 1901
Gift of Mrs H. M. Thompson 1909
Aigantighe Art Gallery, Timaru, New Zealand
© AAG

98. **John Bowman**
The Bridge at Staithes
Oil on canvas, undated
Pannett Art Gallery, Whitby

99. **Harold Knight**
Herring Boats
Oil on canvas, c. 1900
Private collection
© Reproduced with permission of The Estate of
Dame Laura Knight DBE RA 2025

100. **Laura Johnson**
Untitled Sketch of the Bridge at Staithes
Pencil, c. 1898–9
Private collection, courtesy Chris Beetles Gallery,
St. James's, London
© Reproduced with permission of The Estate of
Dame Laura Knight DBE RA 2025

101. **W. Fred Mayor**
Untitled Sketch of the Bridge at Staithes
Watercolour, c. 1898–9
Courtesy A&A Arts

102. **Robert Jobling**
Girl on the Bridge
Oil on canvas, c. 1905
Private collection, courtesy A&A Arts

103. **Fred W. Jackson**
A Welcome Visitor
Oil on canvas, 1893
Gift of Mr W. H. Wood 1923
© Touchstones Rochdale / Bridgeman Images

104. **Lionel T. Crawshaw**
Hauling Cobles, Runswick Bay
Oil on canvas, c. 1930
Private collection, courtesy A&A Arts

105. **James Watson**
A Runswick Garden
Oil on canvas, c. 1900
Courtesy A&A Arts

106. **William G. Foster**
The Village Fleet
Oil on canvas, 1892
Private collection, courtesy A&A Arts

107. **Mark Senior**
The Cockpit
Oil on canvas, undated
Private collection, courtesy A&A Arts

108. **Laura Knight (née Johnson)**
On the Beach
Oil on canvas, c. 1909
Laing Art Gallery, purchased from H. W. Brooks, 1919
© Estate of Dame Laura Knight. All rights reserved 2025 / Bridgeman Images

109. **Mabel Annie Levy**
Joseph Verrill, 1st Coxswain Staithes Lifeboat
Etching, undated
Courtesy A&A Arts

110. **Harold Knight**
Portrait of Laura Johnson
Oil on canvas, c. 1900
Pannett Art Gallery, Whitby
© Reproduced with permission of The Estate of Dame Laura Knight DBE RA 2025

111. **Fred W. Jackson**
Faraway Thoughts
Oil on canvas, 1895
Private collection, courtesy A&A Arts

112. **Rowland Henry Hill**
The First Hunt Ball, Hinderwelll
Watercolour, undated
Private collection, courtesy A&A Arts

113. **William G. Foster**
Musicians at Runswick Bay
Magic lantern slide, c. 1900
Rod Jewell Collection

114. **William G. Foster**
Actors at Runswick Bay
Magic lantern slide, c. 1900
Rod Jewell Collection

CHAPTER 3: LIGHT

Divider 1:

115. **George Clausen**
High Mass at a Fishing Village on the Zuyder Zee, Holland
Oil on canvas, 1876
© Nottingham City Museums & Galleries / Bridgeman Images

Divider 2:

116. **Harold Knight**
The Girl and the Letter
Oil on canvas, 1906
Harris Museum, Art Gallery and Library, Preston
© Estate of Dame Laura Knight. All rights reserved 2025 / Bridgeman Images

117. **Laura Johnson**
Idylls of the King, Balin and Balan
Oil on canvas, c. 1901
Nottingham City Museums & Galleries / Nottingham Trent University, purchased with the assistance of the Heritage Lottery Fund and the Museums, Libraries and Archives Council/Victoria and Albert Museum Purchase Grant Fund, 2008
© Reproduced with permission of The Estate of Dame Laura Knight DBE RA 2025

118. **Photographer unknown**
Drawing room of Oliver and Rosie Sheppard, 30 Pembroke Road, Dublin
Photograph, c. 1905
Oliver Sheppard Collection, National Irish Visual Arts Library (NIVAL), NCAD, Dublin

119. **Fred W. Jackson**
Scene in Capri
Oil on canvas, c. 1882
Gallery Oldham, unknown acquisition method
© Gallery Oldham / Bridgeman Images

120. **Jules Bastien Lepage**
Going to School
Oil on canvas, 1882
Purchased 1927
© Aberdeen Art Gallery & Museums

121. **Isabella Jobling (née Thompson)**
Fishergirl
Oil on canvas, c. 1895
Private collection, courtesy Tennant's Auctioneers

122. **Isabella Jobling (née Thompson)**
Haymaking
Oil on canvas, 1903
Gift of Thomas Reed, 1920
© Shipley Art Gallery / Bridgeman Images

123. **Laura Johnson**
The Fishing Fleet
Oil on canvas, c. 1900
Bolton Museum & Art Gallery, purchased from Dyson Lister & Sons, 1926
© Estate of Dame Laura Knight. All rights reserved 2025 / Bridgeman Images

124. **Laura Johnson**
Packing Fish on the Quay, Staithes
Oil on canvas, c. 1899
Private collection, courtesy Christie's Images
© Estate of Dame Laura Knight. All rights reserved 2025 / Bridgeman Images

125. **W. Fred Mayor**
A Staithes Fisherman
Watercolour, c. 1898–9
Courtesy Rafael Osona Auctioneers

126. **Robert Jobling**
A Runswick Window
Oil on canvas, c. 1903
Private collection, courtesy David Duggleby Auctioneers

127. **Harold Knight**
Fishermen Coming Ashore
Oil on canvas, c. 1900
Private collection, courtesy A&A Arts
© Reproduced with permission of The Estate of Dame Laura Knight DBE RA 2025

128. **Winslow Homer**
Flamborough Head
Watercolour, 1882
The Art Institute of Chicago,
Mr & Mrs Martin A. Ryerson Collection, 1933.1240
© The Art Institute of Chicago / Scala Florence

129. **Oliver Sheppard**
Untitled Leaves from his Staithes Sketchbooks
Charcoal and pencil, c. 1898–9
Oliver Sheppard Collection, National Irish Visual Arts Library (NIVAL), NCAD, Dublin

130. **Henry S. Hopwood**
Archway, Biskra
Watercolour, c. 1908
Royal Watercolour Society, submitted for diploma 1908
© Royal Watercolour Society / Bridgeman Images

131. **Oliver Sheppard**
Untitled Sketch
Pencil, c. 1898–9
Oliver Sheppard Collection, National Irish Visual Arts Library (NIVAL), NCAD, Dublin

132. **Laura Johnson**
Untitled Sketch
Pencil, c. 1900
Courtesy Chris Beetles Gallery, St. James's, London
© Reproduced with permission of The Estate of Dame Laura Knight DBE RA 2025

133. **Joseph Bagshawe**
Untitled Sketch
Charcoal, c. 1898–9
Private collection, courtesy A&A Arts

134. **Harold Knight**
Leaving Harbour, Evening
Oil on canvas, undated
Pannett Art Gallery, gift of George Bednar in honour of Dr Peter Phillips
© Reproduced with permission of The Estate of Dame Laura Knight DBE RA 2025

135. **Charles H. Mackie**
Moonlight on the Bay
Watercolour, 1902
Courtesy The Fine Art Society Ltd.

136. **Harold Knight**
Light and Shade, Staithes Beach
Watercolour, undated
Private collection, courtesy A&A Arts
© Reproduced with permission of The Estate of Dame Laura Knight DBE RA 2025

137. **Rosie Good**
Letter to Oliver Sheppard, 1899
Oliver Sheppard Collection, National Irish Visual Arts Library (NIVAL), NCAD, Dublin

138. **Arthur Friedenson**
By the Village Brook
Oil on canvas, 1897
Private collection

139. **Hannah Mayor (née Hoyland)**
Still Life of Roses
Watercolour, after 1902
Private collection, courtesy A&A Arts

140. **W. Fred Mayor**
The Storm (47)
Watercolour, 1898–9
Reproduced in *The Artist* 1899, vol. 26, 92

141. **W. Fred Mayor**
A Mosque in Tangiers
Watercolour, c. 1899
Courtesy A&A Arts

142. **Henry S. Hopwood**
The Breakfast Table
Watercolour, 1908
Courtesy Tennant's Auctioneers

143. **Rowland H. Hill**
Street in Bruges
Watercolour, 1911
Courtesy A&A Arts

144. **Rowland H. Hill**
Still Life
Oil on canvas, undated
Private collection, courtesy Tennant's Auctioneers

145. **Frederick Stuart Richardson**
Untitled
Pastel, c. 1905
Courtesy A&A Arts

146. **Thomas Barrett**
On the Quay
Mezzotint, c. 1895
Courtesy A&A Arts

147. **Mark Senior**
Courtyard Gossip
Pastel, undated
Courtesy A&A Arts

148. **Frank M. Sutcliffe**
Trees in Mist
Photograph, c. 1893
Whitby Museum

149. **Laura Johnson**
Knitting
Pastel, before 1903
Courtesy Bonhams Auctioneers
© Reproduced with permission of The Estate of Dame Laura Knight DBE RA 2025

150. **Laura Johnson**
Baiting Lines
Oil on canvas, before 1903
Courtesy Bonhams Auctioneers
© Reproduced with permission of The Estate of Dame Laura Knight DBE RA 2025

151. **Laura Johnson**
Staithes Fisherman
Watercolour, before 1903
Pannett Art Gallery, Whitby
© Reproduced with permission of The Estate of Dame Laura Knight DBE RA 2025

152. **Laura Johnson**
Untitled Sketch
Pencil, before 1903
Courtesy Chris Beetles Gallery, St. James's, London
© Reproduced with permission of The Estate of Dame Laura Knight DBE RA 2025

153. **Harold Knight**
A Cup of Tea
Oil on canvas, c. 1905
Queensland Art Gallery, purchased 1905
© Reproduced with permission of The Estate of Dame Laura Knight DBE RA 2025

154. **Frank H. Mason**
Dutch Beach Scene
Watercolour, undated
Courtesy A&A Arts

155. **Laura Knight (née) Johnson**
Dressing the Children
Oil on canvas, c. 1905
Private collection, courtesy A&A Arts
© Reproduced with permission of The Estate of Dame Laura Knight DBE RA 2025

156. **Harold Knight**
Untitled Dutch Interior
Oil on canvas, c. 1906
Courtesy A&A Arts
© Reproduced with permission of The Estate of Dame Laura Knight DBE RA 20255

157. **Laura Knight (née Johnson)**
Interior with Children reading
Watercolour, *c.* 1906–7
Courtesy Sotheby's Auctioneers
© Reproduced with permission of The Estate of Dame Laura Knight DBE RA 2025

158. **Laura Knight (née Johnson)**
The Rocking Horse
Oil on canvas, *c.* 1906
Courtesy Woolley & Wallis Auctioneers
© Reproduced with permission of The Estate of Dame Laura Knight DBE RA 2025

159. **Laura Knight (née Johnson)**
Friends
Oil on canvas, *c.* 1905
Staithes Museum
© Reproduced with permission of The Estate of Dame Laura Knight DBE RA 2025

CHAPTER 4: LANDSCAPE

Divider 1:

160. **W. Fred Mayor**
Place de L'Église Sainte-Saulve, Montreuil
Oil on canvas, c. 1905
© (IWM) Imperial War Museum

Divider 2:

161. **Mark Senior**
The Stonebreaker
Oil on canvas, undated
Private collection, courtesy A&A Arts
© Reproduced with permission of The Estate of Dame Laura Knight DBE RA 2025

162. **Harrington Mann**
Study of a Young Girl
Oil on board, 1898
Private collection
© The Maas Gallery, London / Bridgeman Images

163. **Mark Senior**
Portrait of Florence Hess
Oil on canvas, undated
Courtesy Bonhams Auctioneers

164. **Leandro Ramon Garrido**
La Dame aux Gants
Chalk on brown paper, 1901
Purchased 1912
Victoria and Albert Museum, London

165. **Unknown photographer**
Ernest Rigg portrait painting
Photograph, *c.* 1920
Private collection, courtesy A&A Arts

166. **Joseph Terry**
Underhill Farm, Sleights
Oil on canvas, *c.* 1920
York Art Gallery, purchased from the artist, 1924
© York Museums Trust

167. **Fred W. Jackson**
The Wheelhouse, Ellerby
Watercolour, undated
Private collection, courtesy A&A Arts

168. **John Atkinson**
Potato Pickers
Watercolour, undated
Courtesy A&A Arts

169. **Arthur Friedenson**
End of Day
Oil on canvas, undated
Private collection, courtesy A&A Arts

170. **Frederick S. Richardson**
Stormy Weather, Staithes
Watercolour, undated
Gift of George Bednar
Pannett Art Gallery, Whitby

171. **Ernest H. Rigg**
Snow in Hinderwell
Oil on canvas, undated
Private collection, courtesy A&A Arts

172. **Fred W. Jackson**
Scenes from Russia and North Africa
Mixed media, c. 1905–13
Spring in Russia © Manchester Art Gallery/Bridgeman Images
All others Courtesy A&A Arts

173. **John Spence Ingall**
Moroccan Landscape with Shepherd
Watercolour, undated
Courtesy A&A Arts

174. **John Spence Ingall**
Arab Man in a Landscape
Watercolour, undated
Courtesy A&A Arts

175. **Hirst Walker**
Towards the Western Isles
Watercolour, *c.* 1930
Courtesy A&A Arts

176. **Joseph Terry**
A Fantasy Landscape
Oil on canvas, undated
Courtesy A&A Arts

177. **Mark Senior**
Spring
Oil on canvas, 1906
Lotherton Hall, bequest of Sam Wilson, 1925
©Leeds Museums & Galleries / Bridgeman Images

178. **Mark Senior**
Runswick Bay
Pastel, 1902
Private collection, courtesy A&A Arts

179. **Mark Senior**
Ludlow
Oil on board, undated
Courtesy A&A Arts

180. **Frank M. Sutcliffe**
Farmer and Cart
Photograph, *c.* 1890
Whitby Museum

181. **Laura Knight (née Johnson)**
Spring
Oil on canvas, 1916
Presented by the Trustees of the Chantrey Bequest 1935
© Tate
© Reproduced with permission of The Estate of Dame Laura Knight DBE RA 2025

182. **Photographer unknown**
W. G. Foster Painting
Magic lantern slide, *c.* 1895
Rod Jewell Collection

183. **Arthur Friedenson**
Picking Primroses, Runswick Bay
Oil on canvas, undated
Private collection, courtesy A&A Arts

184. **Arthur Friedenson**
A Sand Pit
Oil on panel, 1917
Laing Art Gallery, gift of Samuel Smith, JP, 1930
© Laing Art Gallery / Bridgeman Images

185. **John Wright**
Landscape
Watercolour, undated
Pannett Art Gallery, Whitby

186. **Florence Hess**
Sandsend Beck
Oil on board, undated
Courtesy A&A Arts

187. **John Spence Ingall**
Roxby Beck
Watercolour, undated
Private collection, courtesy A&A Arts

188. **John Spence Ingall**
Ellerby Moor
Watercolour, undated
Private collection, courtesy A&A Arts

189. **John Bowman**
Ugthorpe Mill
Oil on canvas, undated
Pannett Art Gallery, Whitby

190. **W. Fred Mayor**
Le Touquet, Paris-Plage
Watercolour, *c.* 1905
Courtesy A&A Arts

191. **Henry S. Hopwood**
A Picardy Farm
Oil on canvas, *c.* 1908
Courtesy A&A Arts

192. **W. Fred Mayor**
The Quay, Villefranche-sur-Mer
Watercolour, *c.* 1905
Courtesy A&A Arts

193. **Mark Senior**
On the Beach, Runswick Bay
Oil on panel, 1905
Private collection
© Christie's Images / Bridgeman Images

194. **Frank M. Sutcliffe**
Lealholm Bank Top
Photograph, *c.* 1890
Whitby Museum

195. **Paul Paul (né Politachi)**
Untitled Sketch
Oil on board, undated
Courtesy A&A Arts

196. **Fred W. Jackson**
Hayfield
Oil on board, c. 1902
Courtesy John Nicholson Auctioneers

197. **Fred W. Jackson**
Harvest Time
Oil on canvas, undated
Private collection
© Lyon & Turnbull / Bridgeman Images

198. **John Atkinson**
Glaisdale Harriers Run a Fox to Ground, Fryup Head
Watercolour, 1909
Presented by Mr T. Warters
Pannett Art Gallery, Whitby

199. **James W. Booth**
Unloading the Cart
Oil on canvas, undated
Private collection, courtesy A&A Arts

200. **Lionel T. Crawshaw**
Cattle Market, Doncaster
Oil on canvas, c. 1915
Danum Gallery, Library and Museum,
gift of C. H. Mackie, 1916
© Heritage Doncaster

201. **Andrew Colley**
Old Nab from Quarry Bank
Oil on canvas, undated
Courtesy McTague of Harrogate

202. **James W. Booth**
Homeward Bound
Oil on canvas, 1898
© Nottingham City Museums & Galleries /
Bridgeman Images

203. **Owen Bowen**
Kelling Village, Norfolk
Oil on canvas, 1910
Private collection, courtesy A&A Arts

ENDMATTER

204. **Laura Johnson**
Untitled Sketch of a Coble
Pencil on paper, c. 1900
Courtesy Chris Beetles Gallery, St James's, London
© Reproduced with permission of The Estate of
Dame Laura Knight DBE RA 2025

Endpaper (back):
Laura Johnson
The Trestle Bridge at Staithes
Pencil on paper, c. 1900
Private collection, courtesy Bonhams Auctioneers
© Reproduced with permission of The Estate of
Dame Laura Knight DBE RA 2025

SELECT BIBLIOGRAPHY

JOURNALS

Art & Antiques

Art History

The Artist (1895–1902)

Century Magazine

Harper's Magazine

Scribner's Magazine

The Art Journal (1849–1912)

The Centennial Magazine

The Dalesman

The Magazine of Art (1878–1904)

The Studio (1893–1964)

NEWSPAPERS

The Times

The Leeds Mercury

The Newcastle Weekly Chronicle

The Whitby Gazette

The Yorkshire Evening Post

COMMERCIAL GALLERY CATALOGUES

Annexe Gallery

Bourne Fine Art

Chris Beetles Gallery

Christine Pybus Fine Arts

Christopher Wood Gallery

Dean Gallery

Dowdeswell Gallery

Fine Art Society

Goupil Gallery

Grafton Galleries

Grosvenor Gallery

Lefevre Gallery

Leicester Galleries

Mayor Gallery

Messums

Moss Galleries Parkin Gallery

Phillips & Sons

Pyms Gallery

Walker Galleries

BOOKS

Angus-Butterworth, L. M. 1975. *Walter Butterworth 1862–1935: a Patron of art.* Memoir of Walter Butterworth, and details of gifts made in his memory to art galleries, museums and libraries in England, Scotland and Wales. London: Faith Press.

Arken Museum of Modern Art. 2007. *The Skagen Painters: In a New Light.* Copenhagen: Arken Museum of Modern Art.

Athens, Elizabeth, Brandon K. Ruud and Martha Tedeschi. 2018. *Coming Away: Winslow Homer and England*. London; New Haven, CT: Yale University Press.

Bagshawe, Joseph. 1933. *The Wooden Ships of Whitby*. Whitby: Horne & Son.

Baile de Laperriere, Charles. 1991. *Royal Scottish Academy Exhibitors 1826–1990*, 4 vols. Calne, Wiltshire: Hilmarton Manor Press.

Baile de Laperriere, Charles. 1996. *Society of Women Artists Exhibitors 1855–1996*. Calne, Wiltshire: Hillmarton Manor Press.

Baile de Laperriere, Charles. 2002. *Dictionary of NEAC Exhibitors*. Calne, Wiltshire: Hillmarton Manor Press.

Becker, R. J. and G. P. Weisberg. 1999. *Overcoming all Obstacles: The Women of the Academie Julian*. New York, NY: Dahesh Museum; New Brunswick, NJ: Rutgers University Press.

Billcliffe, Roger. 1985. *The Glasgow Boys: The Glasgow School of Painting, 1875–1895*. London: John Murray.

Birch, Lionel (Mrs). 1906. *Mr Stanhope A. Forbes ARA and Mrs Elizabeth Stanhope Forbes ARWS*. London: Cassell & Co.

Blanc, Benoit. 2015. *Des Américains à Montreuil*. Montreuil-sur-Mer: Association des Amis des Musées et du Patrimoine du Montreuillois.

Bradshaw, Maurice (ed.). 1973. *Royal Society of British Artists, Members Exhibiting 1824–1892*. Leigh-on-Sea: F. Lewis.

Bradshaw, Maurice (ed.). 1975. *Royal Society of British Artists, Members Exhibiting 1893–1910*. Leigh-on-Sea: F. Lewis.

Brierley, Ben. 1896. Edited by James Dronfield. *Ab-o th'-Yates: Sketches by Ben Brierley*. Oldham: W. E. Clegg.

Broude, Norma. 1990. *World Impressionism 1880–1920*. New York: Harry N. Abrams.

Buchanan, William. 1992. *The Art of the Photographer: J. Craig Annan 1864–1946*. Edinburgh: National Galleries of Scotland.

Buckland, Gail. 1974. *Reality Recorded: Early Documentary Photography*. Newton Abbot: David & Charles.

Bullamore, Colin. 2014. *The Staithes Group of Artists 1894–1909*. Nottingham: published by the author.

Buzard, James. 1993. *The Beaten Track: European Tourism, Literature, and the Ways to Culture 1800–1918*. Oxford: Clarendon Press.

Campbell, Julian. 1984. *Irish Impressionists: Irish Artists in France and Belgium 1850–1914*. Dublin: National Gallery of Ireland.

Carr, Frank. 1934. *Vanishing Craft: British Coastal Types in the Last Days of Sail*. London: *Country Life* Ltd.

Child, Dennis. 2001. *The Yorkshire Union of Artists 1880–1922*. Leeds: Leeds Philosophical and Literary Society.

Child, Dennis. 2002. *Painters in the Northern Counties of England & Wales*. Leeds: published by the author.

Clark, David. 1982. *Between Pulpit and Pew: Folk religion in a North Yorkshire fishing village*. Cambridge: Cambridge University Press.

Clark, Pat. 2016. *People, Places & Piazzas: The Life & Art of Charles Hodge Mackie*. Bristol: Sansom & Co.

Cross, Michael. 1978–9. *F. W. Jackson 1859–1918*. Rochdale Art Gallery & Chapel Bank Gallery, Cleveland.

Cross, Tom. 1994. *Shining Sands: Artists in Newlyn and St Ives 1880–1930*. Tiverton, Devon: Halsgrove.

Dade, Ernest. 1988 [1933]. *Sail and Oar: A hundred pictures by Ernest Dade. A North Sea Sketchbook*. Woodbridge: Robertsons. First published London: Dent & Sons.

Dunbar, Janet. 1975. *Laura Knight*. London: Collins.

Ecclestone, Jean and Peter. 1998. *A History and Geology of Staithes*. Staithes: published by the authors.

Eglon Shaw, Bill (ed.). 1974. *Frank Meadow Sutcliffe: Whitby and its people as seen by one of the founders of the naturalistic movement in photography*. Sutcliffe Gallery, Whitby.

Fabritius, Elisabeth (ed.). 2007. *Danish Artists Colonies*. Skagen: Skagen Museum.

Fenwick, Simon and Greg Smith. 1997. *The Business of Watercolour: A guide to the archives of the Royal Watercolour Society*. Aldershot: Ashgate.

Fenwick, Simon. 2004. *The Enchanted River: 200 Years of the Royal Watercolour Society*. Bristol: Sansom & Co.

Fine Art Society. 1976. *Centenary Exhibition: William Stott of Oldham / Edward Stott RA*. Uxbridge, Middx.: Hillingdon Press.

Fox, Caroline. 1979. *Artists of the Newlyn School 1880–1900*. Newlyn: Newlyn Orion Galleries.

Fox, Caroline. 1985. *Painting in Newlyn, 1880–1930*. London: Barbican Art Gallery.

Fox, Caroline. 1988. *Dame Laura Knight*. Oxford: Phaidon Press.

Fox, Caroline. 1993. *Stanhope Forbes and the Newlyn School*. Newton Abbot: David & Charles.

Frank, Peter. 2002. *Yorkshire Fisherfolk: A social history of the Yorkshire inshore fishing community*. Chichester: Phillimore & Co.

Frank, Peter. 2010. *Sea Painter: The Life and Work of J. R. Bagshawe*. Chichester: Phillimore & Co.

Freethy, Ron. 2012. *Memories of the Yorkshire Fishing Industry*. Newbury: Countryside Books.

Garratt, Morris and Colin Gilbert. 2001. *Frederick William Jackson (1859–1918): Middleton Artist*. In *Middleton Matters*, vol. 2. Middleton near Oldham: Middleton Civic Association.

Gillett, Paula. 1990. *The Victorian Painter's World*. Gloucester: Alan Sutton.

Good, Rosie. Oliver Sheppard Papers, National Irish Visual Art Library, National College of Art and Design, Dublin. Unpublished.

Gordon, Catherine and Mary Peskett-Smith. 2006. *British and Irish Paintings in Public Collections: An Index of British and Irish oil paintings by artists born before 1870…* New Haven, CT: Yale University Press.

Graces Guide to British Industrial History. www.gracesguide.co.uk

Graves, Algernon. 1901. *A dictionary of artists who have exhibited works in the principal London exhibitions from 1760–1893*. Third edition. London: H. Graves & Co.

Graves, Algernon. 1905. *The Royal Academy of Arts: A complete dictionary of contributors and their work from foundation in 1769 to 1904*. London: H. Graves & Co.

Gray Museum & Art Gallery. 1925. *The Art of J. W. Howey of West Hartlepool* (exh. cat.). Hartlepool: Gray Museum & Art Gallery.

Hall, Marshall. 1982. *The Artists of Northumbria: An Illustrated Dictionary of Northumberland, Durham and North Yorkshire Painters, Sculptors, Draughtsmen and Engravers Born Between 1625 and 1900*. Second edition. Kendal: Titus Wilson & Son.

Hall, Marshall. 1995. 'John Atkinson and The Staithes Group', *Antique Collecting*, February 1995.

Harker, Margaret. 1979. *The Linked Ring. The Secession Movement in Photography in Britain 1892–1910*. London: Willian Heinemann.

Harrison, Tony. 1995. *Winslow Homer in England*. Port Seton: Station Press.

Hart, James (ed.). 2010. *The Secret Staithes Diary of Enid Lucy Pease Robinson*. York: Historical Publishing.

Haworth, Peter. 2002. *Paintings by Members of the Staithes Group* (exh. cat.). Milnthorpe, Cumbria: published by the author.

Haworth, Peter. 2005. *From Runswick to Russia: Paintings by Members of the Staithes Group*. Milnthorpe, Cumbria: published by the author.

Hemming, Charles. 1988. *British Painters of the Coast and Sea: A history and Gazetteer*. London: Gollancz.

Hiley, Michael. 1974. *Frank Sutcliffe: Photographer of Whitby*. London: Gordon Fraser.

Holroyd, Michael. 2010. *A Book of Secrets: E. W. Beckett*. London: Chatto & Windus.

Holt, Ysanne. 1998. *The English Landscape. Modernity and the rural scene 1890–1914*. Unpublished PhD thesis, University of Northumbria.

Holt, Ysanne, Fiona Russell and David Peters Corbett. 2002. *The Geographies of Englishness: Landscape and the National Past 1880–1940*. Studies in British Art series. London: New Haven, CT: Yale University Press.

Horn, Pamela. 1987 [1976]. *Labouring Life in the Victorian Countryside*. Gloucester: Alan Sutton.

Horn, Pamela. 1984. *The Changing Countryside in Victorian and Edwardian England and Wales*. London: Athlone Press.

Horne & Son. 1895. *Horne's Guide to Whitby. Profusely Illustrated: Giving a Detailed Description of Places of Interest, Streets, Roads and Footpaths in and Around Whitby*. Whitby: Horne & Son Gazette Office.

Howard, John. 2000. *Staithes: Chapters from the History of a Seafaring town*. Scalby, N. Yorks.: published by the author.

Huneault, Kristina. 2002. *Difficult Subjects: Working Women and Visual Culture, Britain 1880–1914*. Abingdon, Oxon.: Routlege, Taylor and Francis Group.

Jacobs, Michael. 1985. *The Good and Simple Life: Artists' Colonies in Europe and America*. Oxford: Phaidon.

Jeffrey, Ian and David Mellor. 1975. *The Real Thing: An Anthology of British Photography 1840–1950*. London: The Arts Council of Great Britain.

Jenkins, Adrian. 2000. *Painters and Peasants: Henry La Thangue and British Rural Naturalism 1880–1905*. Bolton: Bolton Museum, Art Gallery and Aquarium.

Jewell, Rod. 2013. *Staithes (Boulby and Dalehouse) Between Two Nabs*. Sheffield: J. W. Northend.

Johnson, Jane. 1975. *Works Exhibited at the Royal Society of British Artists 1824–1893 and the New English Art Club 1888–1917*. Woodbridge: Antique Collectors' Club.

Johnson, Jane and A. Greutzner (eds). 1976. *The Dictionary of British Artists 1880–1940*. Woodbridge: Antique Collectors' Club.

Jordan, Rosamund. 2003. *Staithes Group Centenary Exhibition*. York: Staithes Group Publication.

Jordan, Rosamund. 2015. *William Frederick and Hannah Mayor* (exh. cat.). Stockton-on-Tees: T. B. and R. Jordan.

King, Julie. 1990. *Sydney Lough Thompson: At Home and Abroad* (exh. cat.). Christchurch, New Zealand: Robert McDougall Art Gallery.

Knight, Laura. 1936. *Oil Paint and Grease Paint*. London: Nicolson and Watson Ltd.

Knight, Laura. 1965. *The Magic of a Line: The Autobiography of Laura Knight*. London: William Kimber.

Knight, Vivien. 1999. *Landscapes and Sea Views*. London: Guildhall Library Publications.

Knipe, Tony (ed.). 1988. *Winslow Homer: All the Cullercoats Pictures.* Northern Centre for Contemporary Art, Sunderland.

Knowles, Elizabeth. 2012. *Laura Knight in the Open Air.* Bristol: Sansom & Co.

Koja, Stephan (ed.). 2005. *Nordic Dawn. Modernism's Awakening in Finland 1890–1920.* London: Prestel.

Kroyer, Peder S. 1998–9. *P. S. Kroyer and the artists' colony at Skagen.* Dublin: National Gallery of Ireland.

Laidlay, William James. 1907. *The Origin and First Two Years of the New English Art Club.* London: published by the author.

Laidlay, William James. 1911. *Art, Artists and Landscape Painting*. London: Longmans, Green & Co.

Lemoine, Serge. 2007. *Jules Bastien-Lepage* (exh. cat.). *Paris*: Musée d'Orsay.

Levy, Sophie. 2006. *Winslow Homer: Poet of the Sea* (exh. cat.). Chicago, IL: University of Chicago Press.

Long, Basil S. 1930. 'Henry Silkstone Hopwood' in *The Old Water-Colour Society's Club*, vol. II, edited by Randall Davies. London: Charles Whittingham.

Lubbren, N. 1996. 'Rural Artists' colonies in 19th-century Europe'. Unpublished PhD thesis, University of Leeds.

Mackie, Anne. 1922. 'Charles Mackie and Paris visit 1892–93', unpublished. National Libraries of Scotland.

McConkey, Kenneth. 1981. *Peasantries & Paysanneries: 19th-century French and British Pictures of Peasants and Field Workers.* Newcastle upon Tyne Polytechnic Art Gallery: Newcastle Festival Exhibition.

McConkey, Kenneth. 1989. *British Impressionism*. Oxford: Phaidon Press.

McConkey, Kenneth. 1995. *Impressionism in Britain*. London; New Haven, CT: Yale University Press in association with Barbican Art Gallery.

McConkey, Kenneth. 2006. *The New English: A History of the New English Art Club.* London: Royal Academy of Arts.

McConkey, Kenneth. 2021. *Towards the Sun: The Artist Traveller at the Turn of the Twentieth Century*. London: Paul Holberton.

McKee, Grant. 2023. *Staithes: A Life Story*. Stockport: 2QT Publishing.

McInness, Robin. 2014. *British Coastal Art 1770–1930*. Chale, Isle of Wight: CP Cross Publishing.

McWilliam, Neil and Veronica Sekules. 1986. *Life and Landscape: P. H. Emerson, Art and Photography in East Anglia 1885–1900.* Norwich: Sainsbury Centre for Visual Art.

Meyrick, Robert. 2013. *Sydney Lee: Prints, a Catalogue Raisonné.* London: Royal Academy of Arts.

Millard, John. 1990. *Ralph Hedley, Tyneside painter*. Newcastle: Tyne and Wear Museums.

Millard, John. 1992. *A Romance with the Northeast: Robert and Isa Jobling*. Newcastle: Tyne and Wear Museums.

Moore, William. 1934. *The Story of Australian Art: From the Earliest Known Art of the Continent to the Art of Today*. Sydney: Angus & Robertson.

Morden, Barbara. 2014. *Laura Knight, A Life*. Carmarthen, Carmarthenshire: McNidder & Grace.

Moss, Brian and Rachel. 1981. *John Atkinson 1863–1924*. Hexham, Northumberland: Moss Galleries.

Munn, Geoffrey C. 2006. *Southwold: An Earthly Paradise.* Woodbridge: Antique Collectors' Club.

Newton, Laura. 2023. *Cullercoats: A North-East Colony of Artists.* Bristol: Sansom & Co.

Newton, Laura. 2001. 'The Cullercoats Artists' Colony c. 1870–1914'. Unpublished PhD thesis, University of Northumbria.

Newton, Laura. 2005. *Painting at the Edge: British Coastal Art Colonies 1880–1930*. Bristol: Sansom & Co.

Nunn, Pamela Gerrish. 2006. *From Victorian to Modern: Innovation and Tradition in the Work of Vanessa Bell, Gwen John and Laura Knight*. Djanogly Art Gallery, Nottingham and London: Philip Wilson Publishers Ltd.

Parkin, Michael. 1974. *Mark Senior*. London: Parkin Gallery.

Payne, Christiana. 1993. *Toil & Plenty: Images of the agricultural landscape in England 1780–1890*. Yale Agrarian Studies series. London; New Haven, CT: Yale University Press.

Phillips, Peter. 1980. *Mark Senior and Florence Hess.* Marlow: Phillips & Sons.

Phillips, Peter, 1981. *Florence Hess and Mark Senior.* Marlow: Phillips & Sons.

Phillips, Peter. 1993. *The Staithes Group.* Marlow: Phillips & Sons.

Price, Jacqueline. n.d. *The Staithes Group of Artists 1894–1909.* Whitby: Pannett Gallery, Whitby (museum guide).

Puget, Catherine and Julian Campbell. 2004. *Peintres Britanniques en Bretagne*. Pont Aven: Musée de Pont-Aven.

Pybus, Christine. 2012. *George Weatherill: His Family and their Art*. Whitby: published by the author.

Quigley, Jane. 1913. *Leandro Ramon Garrido: His Life and Art*. London: Duckworth & Co.

Richardson, Geoffrey. 1992. *T. Watson, Photographer of Lythe, Near Whitby.* Hull: Lampada Press.

Sayer, Karen. 1995. *Women of the Fields: Representations of Rural Women in the 19th Century*. Manchester: Manchester University Press.

Scott, Richard. 2002. *Artists at Walberswick: East Anglian Interludes 1880–2000*. Bristol: Art Dictionaries Limited.

Sellin, David. 1982. *Americans in Brittany and Normandy 1860–1910*. Phoenix, AZ: Phoenix Art Museum.

Slater, Robert. 2010. 'Artists' Colonies in Staithes and Runswick Bay'. Unpublished PhD thesis, University of Leicester.

Spalding, Frances and Ian Jeffrey. 1983. *Landscape in Britain 1850–1950. London:* Arts Council of Great Britain.

Spencer, Gillian. 1983. *Mark Senior 1862–1927* (exh. cat.). Wakefield, W. Yorks.: Wakefield Metropolitan District Council.

Spender, Michael. 1987. *The Glory of Watercolour: The RWS Diploma Collection.* Newton Abbot: David & Charles.

Stewart, Ann M. 1985–7. *Royal Hibernian Academy of Arts: Index of Exhibitors 1826–1976*. 3 vols. Dublin: Manton Publishing.

Taylor, John. 1978. *Pictorial Photography in Britain 1900–1920*. London: Arts Council of Great Britain in association with the Royal Photographic Society.

Tedeschi, Martha and Kristi Dahm. 2008. *Watercolours by Winslow Homer: The Color of Light*. Chicago, IL: Art Institute of Chicago.

Thomson, Susan. 2007. *Manchester's Victorian Art Scene and its Unrecognised Artists*. Manchester: Manchester Art Press Ltd.

Thornton, Alfred. 1935. *Fifty Years of the New English Art Club 1886–1935*. London: Curwen Press.

Treuherz, Julian. 1987. *Hard Times: Social Realism in Victorian Art* (exh. cat.). London: Lund Humphries Publishers.

Turner, Peter and Richard Wood. 1974. *P. H. Emerson: Photographer of Norfolk*. London: Gordon Fraser.

Wallace, Catherine. 2008. *Catching the Light: The Art and Life of Henry Scott Tuke, 1858–1929.* Los Angeles, CA: Atelier Books.

Walmsley Society. 2017. *Robin Hood's Bay to Staithes: The postcard paintings of J. Ulric Walmsley.* Robin Hood's Bay: published by the author.

Walton, John K. 1983. *The English Seaside Resort: A Social History of Britain 1750–1914.* Leicester: Leicester University Press.

Waters, Grant M. 1975. *Dictionary of British Artists Working 1900–1950*. Eastbourne: Eastbourne Fine Art Publications.

Webb, Valerie. 2018. *Edward Stott 1855–1918: A Master of Colour and Atmosphere*. Bristol: Sansom & Co.

Weisberg, Gabriel P. 1980. *The Realist Tradition: French Painting & Drawing 1830–1900.* Cleveland, OH: Cleveland Museum of Art.

Weisberg, Gabriel P. 1992. *Beyond Impressionism: The Naturalist Impulse in European Art 1860–1905*. New York; London: Thames & Hudson.

Wood, Christopher A. 1978. *Dictionary of Victorian Painters*. Woodbridge: Antique Collectors' Club.

Wortley, Laura. 1988. *British Impressionism: A Garden of Bright Images*. London: Studio Fine Art Publications.

Yardley, Edward. 1996. *The Life and Career of Frank Henry Mason RBA; RI; RSMA.* Hartlepool, County Durham: Hartlepool Art Gallery.

Yardley, Edward. 2015. *Frank Henry Mason: Marine Painter and Poster Artist.* Stanton-in-Peak, Derbyshire: Colley Books.

INDEX

Page numbers in *italics* refer to illustrations and their captions.

First published in 2026 by
Kulturalis Ltd
14 Old Queen Street
London SW1H 9HP
United Kingdom
www.kulturalis.com

ISBN 978-1-83636-007-0 (hardback)
ISBN 978-1-83636-048-3 (paperback)

Project manager and copy-editor: Catherine Bradley
Designer: Matthew Wilson
Printed and bound in Czech Republic by PB Tisk, Příbram
Reproduction by Opero, Verona

10 9 8 7 6 5 4 3 2 1

British Library Cataloguing in Publication Data.
A catalogue record for this book is available from the British Library.

EU GPSR Authorised Representative:
EASY ACCESS SYSTEM EUROPE OÜ,
Mustamäe tee 50,
10621, TALLINN, Estonia
email: info@easproject.org

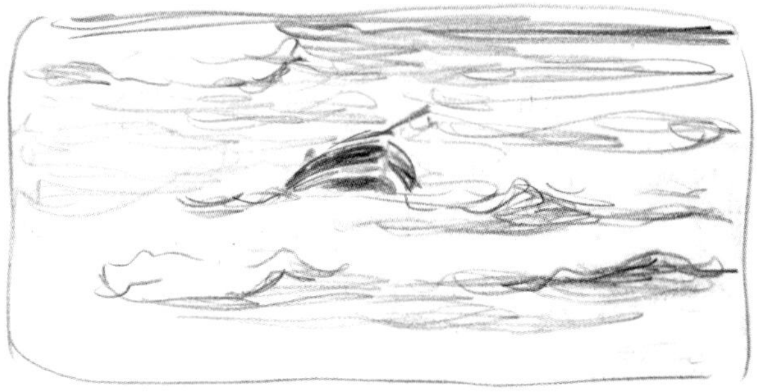

204. *Untitled Sketch of a Coble* by Laura Johnson.

Front endpaper: Laura Knight (née Johnson) recalls many aspects of her early work in Staithes with accuracy, though at times somewhat disparagingly. Her surviving sketchbook exemplifies her early enthusiasm for all aspects of the villagers' lives. In this work, inscribed *Time Changes All Things,* it is tempered with a certain wistfulness.

Back endpaper: *The Trestle Bridge at Staithes*, here sketched around 1900 in preparation for a finished watercolour, was one of the most distinctive features of the village. Used for mooring cobles and drying nets as well as providing passage over the beck, it was pictured by nearly all the artists who came to Staithes.

Frontispiece (pp. 2–3): 1. *A Stormy Day on the Slipway*, Fred Jackson's oil of Staithes from 1890, has many of the classic elements of life in the village: the unprotected harbour, precipitous face of Cowbar 'Nab', weathered cottages, a brightly coloured coble, distinctive bonnets and costume and a rough sea meeting the mouth of the beck.

Title page (p. 4): 2. Though undated and without a recognised model, it is tempting to associate Fred Mayor's *The Lookout* with Laura Knight's description of Captain Pinder, 'King of Steers' (Staithes). He lived in the cottage next door to her, high in the village, and regularly kept watch from the ledge outside his house using a large telescope.

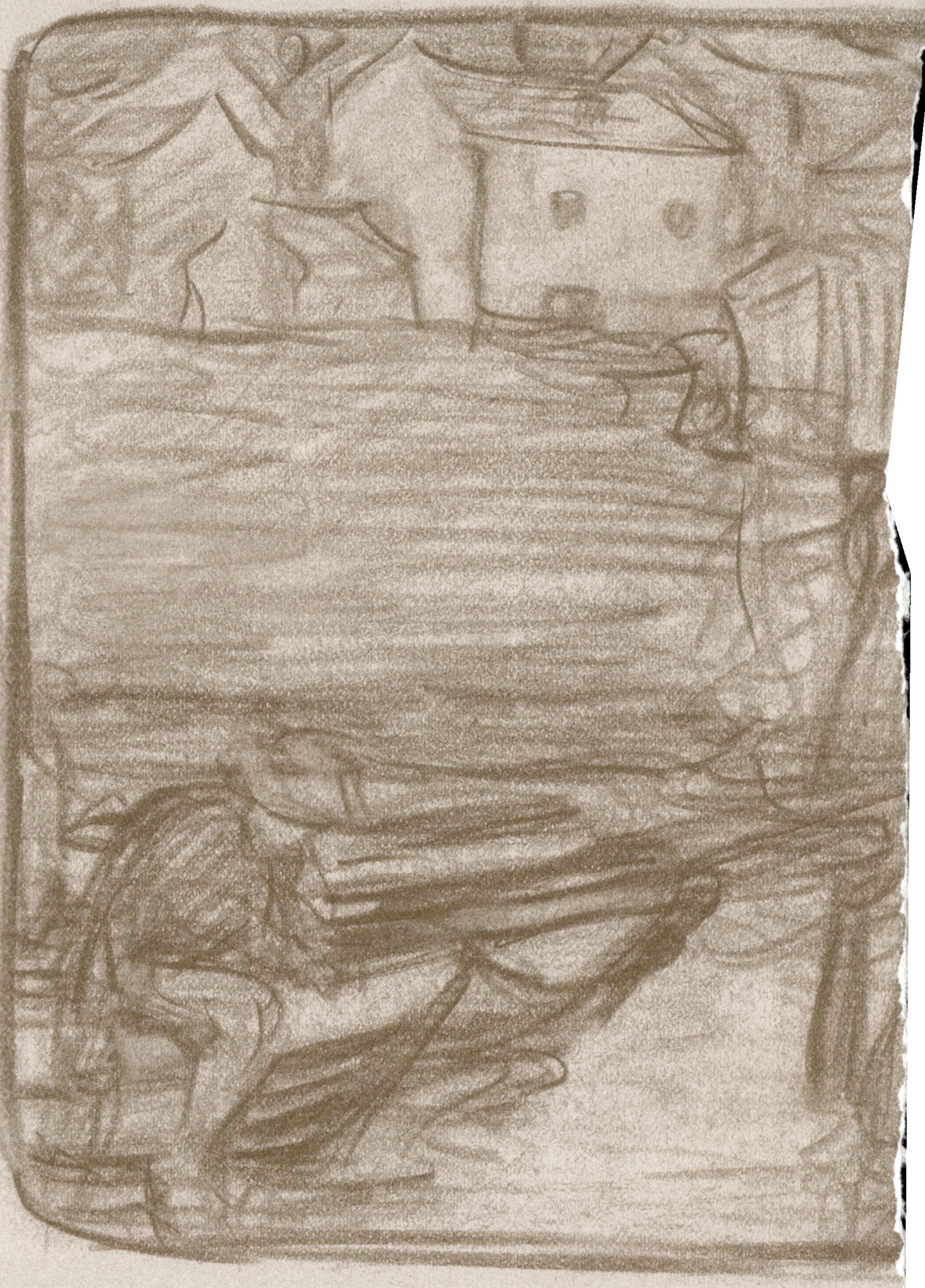